DATE DUE			
Jul 10'75			
Jul 18 '75			
Jul 24'75			
GAYLORD			PRINTED IN U.S.A.

JOHN RAE

POLITICAL ECONOMIST

JOHN RAE

Political Economist

AN ACCOUNT OF HIS LIFE
AND A COMPILATION OF HIS
MAIN WRITINGS

BY

R. Warren James

VOLUME I

Life and Miscellaneous Writings

UNIVERSITY OF TORONTO PRESS

© University of Toronto Press 1965

PRINTED IN ENGLAND BY
HAZELL WATSON AND VINEY LTD
AYLESBURY, BUCKS

PREFACE TO VOLUME I

Although the collective title of these two volumes is *John Rae, Political Economist*, this should not be taken to mean that they are exclusively concerned with economics. The appellation is, in part, meant to make it clear that the John Rae (1796–1872) who is concerned here should not be confused with three of his contemporaries with the same name. These other men are John Rae (1813–1893), the Arctic explorer; John Rae (1845–1915), journalist and economist; and John Rae (1813–1900), the Australian.[1] A brief account of their lives is included in the Biographical Appendix.

John Rae, the political economist, was a man of remarkable intellectual attainments who made an impressive contribution to the understanding of human societies. He remains a relatively obscure and little known figure, although he did leave at least one enduring monument, his brilliant book *Statement of Some New Principles on the Subject of Political Economy Exposing the Fallacies of the System of Free Trade, and of Some Other Doctrines Maintained in the "Wealth of Nations."*[2] It appeared in Canada in 1834 in a period of intellectual colonialism and political uproar. The book was initially a failure in the sense that its sales were small and it attracted little attention.

The main achievement of Rae's book was to outline a theory of economic development or more specifically to analyse the influences governing the accumulation of capital. The abstraction and generality of the work were such that its relevance to the economic problems of Upper and Lower Canada was not immediately evident. It did not bring Rae the prestige that he had hoped for and the book sank into comparative obscurity. Copies of it soon became scarce, which further hindered its influence on the development of economic ideas in the nineteenth century. However, around the end of the nineteenth century, there was a resurgence of interest in the theory of capital, arising partly out of the work of the Austrian school of economists, led by Eugen von Böhm-Bawerk, Carl Menger, and Friedrich von Wieser. A student at Harvard, Charles Whitney Mixter,

[1] The four John Raes are thoroughly mixed up, for example, in S. Austin Allibone, *A Critical Dictionary of English Literature and British and American Authors* (Philadelphia, 1874).

[2] Published in Boston by Hilliard, Gray and Co., in 1834. This book will be cited as *New Principles*.

then became interested in John Rae and in 1897 began to publish a number
of articles about him.[3] Mixter's interest persisted for a number of years,
and in 1905 he reissued Rae's book with the title *The Sociological Theory
of Capital*[4] and included a biographical sketch invaluable to anyone interested in Rae's career. Although Mixter deserves great credit for his
sympathetic account of Rae's life he was also guilty of an indiscretion
which is difficult to account for. In his reissue of Rae's *New Principles*, he
subjected it to a clumsy editorial rearrangement. Because of the scarcity of
copies of the original edition, Rae is known to several generations of
students of economics only through the 1905 edition and this has tended
to give a distorted image of Rae's book.

One of the principal justifications for the issuance of the present volumes
is to make available Rae's *New Principles* in its original form. This will
make it possible to convey to a wider group of people a better appreciation
of Rae's contribution to economics and its continuing relevance to the
economic problems of the mid-twentieth century. Apart from its remarkable
insights in certain technical areas of economic theory, the literary quality
of Rae's book is remarkable. From this point of view alone, the book is a
masterpiece, a real gem among the important writings of the classical
economists of the nineteenth century.

The first volume consists of three main parts. Part I is mainly devoted to
an account of Rae's life. Although Mixter dealt with the essential aspects
of Rae's career, his biographical sketch is incomplete in some respects
because of his unfamiliarity with the religious, political, and educational
conflicts in Canada in which Rae was intimately involved. It has also
seemed desirable from time to time to digress to try to explain something
about the nature of these conflicts.

Part II is primarily concerned with Rae as a social scientist and particularly with his *New Principles* and its genesis. The chapter dealing with the
background of the *New Principles* is in part, at least, an attempt to substantiate the view that the great contributions to economic theory are
historically a distillation or crystallization of real practical problems which
have generated emotional as well as intellectual conflict. However, no
serious attempt has been made to assess the influence of earlier writers on
economics on Rae's economic ideas. This is certainly a legitimate field of
inquiry but one which offers great difficulty because of the lack of detailed
information about Rae's academic training. Similarly no consistent effort

[3] A more detailed account of this episode is given in chap. 14 in Part II of this volume.
[4] John Rae, *The Sociological Theory of Capital being a Complete Reprint of the New
Principles of Political Economy*, 1834, ed. Charles Whitney Mixter (New York: Mac-
millan, 1905). This work will be cited as *Sociological Theory of Capital*.

has been made in Part II to assess the impact of Rae's *New Principles* on future generations of economists. Some instances of acknowledged indebtedness are referred to, but no pretence is made of presenting any complete or balanced assessment of economists who were influenced by Rae.

Part III consists of a collection of Rae's miscellaneous articles and essays and a few letters either written by Rae or directly concerning him. Some of this material was known to Mixter and was reproduced by him, but some of it has been found more recently and throws some new light on the broad range of his interests. The spelling and punctuation of the original documents have been retained, though obvious typographical errors have been corrected.

The preparation of the biographical material about Rae has been severely handicapped by the lack of personal information about Rae, particularly during his life in Canada. Mixter obtained the personal papers and manuscripts which Rae had with him when he died, but for the most part these have been destroyed or lost. The only part of these Rae papers which were preserved consist of the bulk of Rae's manuscripts on geology and some miscellaneous papers which were given by Mixter to the late Dr. T. A. Jaggar of the University of Hawaii about 1904.[5] Some years ago Dr. Jaggar and his secretary at that time, Miss Elizabeth B. Barrette, with the co-operation of Miss Janet Bell, Librarian in charge of Hawaiiana at the University of Hawaii, were kind enough to make copies of this invaluable material available to me.[6] I owe a special debt of gratitude to them for this kindness and particularly to Miss Bell for additional and unstinting help and guidance concerning Rae's life in Hawaii.

Extensive inquiries and a search of the papers left by Mixter, who died in 1936, have failed to unearth the remainder of Rae's papers. This will explain, in part, the attention which has been devoted to the biographical details of Rae's friends and associates. In some cases, the presumed associations cannot be documented but have had to be established in an indirect and sometimes tenuous way. For ease of presentation, a good deal of the biographical data is given in a Biographical Appendix which is alphabetically arranged.

In the preparation of this study, I have been helped, encouraged and

[5] Mixter wrote, "Among the manuscripts falling into my possession, by far the most extensive and orderly were those upon geology and kindred subjects, pertaining both to Canada and the Hawaiian Islands. These have been placed in proper hands, and may in part be printed." *Sociological Theory of Capital*, xxxiii. The material is described in chap. 9, of Part I of this volume.

[6] Microfilm copies of these Rae manuscripts have been deposited in the Public Archives of Canada, Ottawa.

guided by a large number of people. Librarians, archivists, relatives, civil
servants, friends, people in academic life and many others have assisted
me in major and minor ways. I will not enumerate them individually but I
hope nevertheless that they will be aware that I am greatly beholden to
them.

This work has been published with the help of a grant from the Social
Science Research Council, using funds provided by the Canada Council.

It has not seemed appropriate for me to offer any formal dedication of
my own contribution to these two volumes. I would simply hope that it
will be regarded as a partial expiation for the mean and shabby treatment
of Rae when he lived in Canada. He was, in the words of Juvenal, from
whom he sometimes quoted:

Rara avis in terris nigroque simillima cygno.

R. W. J.

CONTENTS

PART I RAE'S LIFE

PART II RAE AS A SOCIAL SCIENTIST

PART III   SELECTED PAPERS AND LETTERS

(A) Articles and Essays

(B) Miscellaneous Letters

PART I

RAE'S LIFE

1

Early Life and Education

(1796–1822)

John Rae, the political economist, was born on June 1, 1796, in Footdee, a suburb of Aberdeen, Scotland.[1] Rae's father, also named John, who is described as "an entirely self-made man, the son of a peasant or small farmer,"[2] became a merchant and possibly a shipbuilder. The exact nature of his business is uncertain but there is the following reference to a John Rae in a history of Aberdeen:

The "Daedalus" of Aberdeen, the sole property of John Rae, merchant and shipbuilder in the town, left the port in August, 1797, for Bergen, returning with tar and wood under the command of a Danish master and navigated by two Danish mariners. Doubt arose as to the legality of the importation owing to the fact that the build of the vessel was not that of the country from which the goods were imported.[3]

John Rae, the elder, married Margaret Cuthbert, the daughter of Peter Cuthbert, sometime in 1788. The date of the post-nuptial marriage con-

[1] The Register of Births and Baptisms for the Parish of Aberdeen preserved in The General Registry Office, Edinburgh, contains the following entry: "Aberdeen June first 1796, Mr. John Rae, Merchant, and Mrs. Margaret Cuthbert, his wife, had a son born named John; baptized by the Revd. Mr. Robert Doig, of Trinity Chapel in presence of William Rae, Druggist and William Littlejohn, at Pitmuxton." Pitmuxton was at that time outside the city of Aberdeen but is now included within its boundaries.

[2] *Sociological Theory of Capital*, xix. In the Parish Register of Old Machar there is recorded the birth of John Rae on September 13, 1766, in Gordonsmills, the son of Matthew Rae and his wife Jean Gill. Another son, William, presumably the druggist referred to in the footnote above, was born in 1769.

[3] Victoria Elizabeth Clark, *The Port of Aberdeen: A History of Its Shipping from the 12th Century, etc.* (Aberdeen, 1921), 105.

tract was April 16, 1788, and it is presumed that this was concluded shortly after the marriage. Mixter's information was that her family were "rather well-to-do 'large farmers, as farming went then.' "[4] Her father, in fact, was a wright, or a carpenter or joiner, in Aberdeen.

There were six children in the Rae family in addition to John. Ann Cuthbert (b. 1788),[5] Patrick (b. 1790), James (b. 1791), Jean (b. 1792), Arthur (b. 1794) and Alexander (b. 1797). Two of the children, Jean and Arthur, appear to have died in infancy. Both Patrick and James survived long enough to attend Marischal College without, however, completing their courses.[6] James was drowned at sea as a young man,[7] but the cause of Patrick's death is not known. Alexander studied at Marischal College in the period 1810–14 and received the degree of M.A. in 1814.[8]

Mixter was able to obtain some information about John Rae the elder and Margaret Cuthbert both from papers left by John Rae and from Rae's great-nephew, William Thurburn, who was living in Scotland around 1900. Mixter says that, according to John Rae the younger, Margaret Cuthbert was about fifteen years younger than her husband and markedly different "in character, disposition, habits, tastes and education."[9] Mixter quotes his informant in Scotland as saying, "He [Rae the elder] was considered a very upright man, kind, and a lover of peace. Mrs. Rae was an exceedingly kind woman and kept a comfortable home. She was a beauty; dignified in her manners, and paid great attention to the manners of her family."[10]

Whether from ignorance or from motives of delicacy, Mixter's informants conveyed a completely erroneous impression of the household. The fact is that life in the Rae family was characterized by bitter disagreement and quarrelling between the parents, culminating in separation. Since this marital discord seems to have had a profound effect on John Rae the son, it is worth recording the details which are still available in the public records.

---

[4] *Sociological Theory of Capital*, xx.

[5] The entry in the Register of Births and Baptisms is headed simply "Eleventh" and states that she was baptized on January 4, 1789.

[6] P. J. Anderson, ed., *Fasti Academiae Mariscallanae Aberdonensis: Selections from the Records of the Marischal College and University* (Aberdeen, 1898), II, 390, 393. Cited hereafter as *Fasti Academiae Mariscallanae*.

[7] *Sociological Theory of Capital*, xx.

[8] In the *Fasti Academiae Mariscallanae*, II, 408, Alexander is described in a footnote as a surgeon in Turriff, Aberdeenshire, but this appears to be an error. He had been confused with Dr. Alexander Rae (1791–1876), a surgeon of the Royal Navy who lived in Turriff after his retirement.

[9] *Sociological Theory of Capital*, xx. The statement that she was fifteen years younger than her husband is not consistent with the assumption that Rae the elder was born in 1766. It must be assumed that the age difference was overstated.

[10] *Ibid.*, n. 1.

The trouble must have begun soon after the marriage of John Rae and Margaret Cuthbert for, on October 29, 1791, the following inhibition was officially registered:

[It has been] shewn to us by our Lovite John Rae Merchant in Aberdeen That he was some time ago married to Margaret Cuthbert who having of late shaken off the natural affection which she owed her husband has not only embezzled given away and disposed, or threatens to embezzle give away and dispose of the Complrs goods & effects but has also contracted & taken on debts to a great extent, & purchased considerable quantities of goods apparel and furniture in which she was otherwise sufficiently provided by her husband & still seems disposed to persist in these practices to the Complrs great hurt & prejudice unless remedy be provided there against as is alleged. . . .

In consequence, the husband was no longer to be held responsible for her debts and she was prohibited from selling any of his possessions without his permission. The Messenger at Arms, Patrick Webster, was unable to serve the writ personally but explained that he had conveyed its intent:

This I did by leaving for the sd Margaret Cuthbert with a maid servant within her dwelling house at Justice Mills near Aberdeen as I could not find her personally a just Copy of Inhibition to the effect forsaid and the like just Copy of Inhibition I affixed and left for all and sundry his Majesty's leiges, and others whom it effects, on the Market Cross of Aberdeen.[11]

In 1797, Rae the elder bought a tenement with close and yard on the east side of the Correction Wynd in Aberdeen.[12] His business appears to have prospered for in 1812 he bought the property of Wester Auquharney in the Parish of Cruden and from then on was known as "Rae of Auquharney."[13] Then in 1813, together with his wife he purchased an interest in Slacks of Cairnbanno in the Parish of Auchredie.[14]

In 1816, Rae and Margaret Cuthbert finally separated and, in accordance with the terms of the marriage contract, he had to provide her with an income.[15] Later that year, it appears that Margaret Cuthbert recognized some deterioration in her husband's financial condition. To protect her own position she registered two inhibitions to enjoin him from selling Wester Auquharney, the source of her income.[16] These inhibitions were later revoked by warrant of the Court of Session on January 18, 1817. Possibly this was because Margaret Cuthbert had again been contracting

[11] Particular Register of Inhibitions for Aberdeenshire, vol. LXXVI, folio 464.
[12] Minute books, Burgh Register of Sasines, Aberdeen, vol. 3, folio 210.
[13] Particular Register of Sasines, Aberdeenshire, vol. 53, folio 69. The property was acquired from Colin Gillies, a merchant in Brechin on Nov. 2, 1812.
[14] Ibid., vol. 63, folio 205.
[15] Ibid., vol. 63, folio 83. The Deed of Separation was recorded in the Sheriff Court Books of Aberdeen, June 27, 1816.
[16] Particular Register of Inhibitions for Aberdeenshire, vol. LXXIX, folios 211 and 214.

debts in her husband's name. In any case, on June 26, 1817, there is another inhibition brought by John Rae against his wife for the same reasons as those given in the earlier injunctions of 1791.[17]

On September 15, 1818, Margaret Cuthbert died, probably in her late forties. Her earlier suspicion that her husband's financial affairs were shaky was evidently well founded. In December, 1819, Rae renounced his interest in Slacks of Cairnbanno. In early 1820 Wester Auquharney was heavily mortgaged and finally sold on May 2, 1820.[18] Then on December 8, 1820, Rae went bankrupt and, according to the General Register of Inhibitions for Aberdeenshire:

The Lords having considered this petition with the writs produced sequestrate the whole Estate & effects of the petitionery John Rae in terms of the statute and appoint the Creditors to hold two meetings at the times and place mentioned in the Petition for choosing an interim Factor and Trustee or Trustees as directed by the Statute Grant Commission as prayed for and Ordain the Petitioners to advertise the sequestration and times and place of the meetings in the Edinburgh and London Gazettes. . . .[19]

According to Mixter's informants in Scotland, "Mrs. Rae died a good many years previous to her husband—sometime between 1815 and 1820. Subsequent to her death Mr. Rae lost his money. Later, in his old age, he went a voyage with one of his sons and the ship was wrecked, and both father and son drowned."[20] The son who drowned was Alexander, but nothing more is known of this tragedy.

Despite the discord in the Rae family a good deal of attention was evidently paid to the early education of the children. Two of the brothers, Alexander and either James or Patrick, were tutored by Dr. Neil Arnott for a period prior to September, 1806, when Arnott left Aberdeen for London. Arnott (1788–1874) was a Scottish physician and inventor who gave his name to the "Arnott water bed," the "Arnott ventilator," and the "Arnott stove."[21] He became a prominent man and among other things actively encouraged the study of practical scientific problems in universities. Ann Cuthbert as a girl was under the tutelage of a Miss Eliza Farquharson Cruden. If John Rae had a private tutor, this has not come to

---

[17] *Ibid.*, vol. LXXIX, folio 27.

[18] Particular Register of Sasines, Aberdeenshire, vol. 78, folio 92.

[19] Vol. CCLXXX, folio 164.

[20] *Sociological Theory of Capital*, xx.

[21] Arnott was a student at Marischal College (M.A., 1805). His medical education (M.R.C.S., 1813, and L.R.C.P., 1817) was interrupted by a voyage to China. He published a work *Elements of Physics* in 1827 and was appointed Physician Extraordinary to the Queen in 1837. He was awarded an LL.D. by Aberdeen University in 1871. For a mention of Arnott by Rae and John Stuart Mill see the miscellaneous correspondence in Part III of this volume.

light. In any case, the employment of tutors in the Rae household suggests that the family was financially secure during Rae's boyhood.

Rae's early life was marred by some personal trouble, presumably related to the disagreement between his parents. In one of his letters, he writes:

Natural disposition, strange and very early misfortunes, had marked me for a student—not a barren book-worm—but a man eager for knowledge—knowledge as power—the power in my conception of being a lasting benefactor to men. Thoughts inspiring as these could alone have carried me over years of terrible suffering which I endured before reaching my majority.[22]

In another place he speaks of "cruel mental suffering in early youth,"[23] but if this was not caused by family troubles one can only speculate on its nature. Whatever it was, it evidently barred him from normal childhood activities and encouraged an obsessive interest in scientific and literary matters.

One minor episode in his boyhood described in one of his letters written in the 1850's illustrates his preoccupation with natural phenomena:

I lived for many years in an isolated brick home, and, my dormitory being situated in an upper chamber, in stormy nights I was sensible of a slight tremor, responding to every violent gust. The walls beginning to leak in several points, to remedy this the coat of lime and sand with which the . . . building was invested was stript completely off, when several chinks, running for yards through the body of the wall, became apparent. These were secured by iron clamps, and then a fresh coat of a compound of lime and coarse sand was thrown on. Being then a boy my curiosity was excited by this strife between the force of the wind and human resistance, and I watched carefully the result. In the course of a year or two, small chinks, into which I could put the point of a needle, again became visible in the plaster above the course of the old fissures. The house stood however for thirty years when it was destroyed by fire.[24]

Nothing is known of Rae's elementary schooling. However, it does appear that he entered Marischal College in 1809 or 1810, when he was thirteen or fourteen years old. This is a tender age by modern standards, but it was not unusual for boys to enter university while very young in the

[22] *Sociological Theory of Capital*, xxii.

[23] *Ibid.*, xli.

[24] Rae mss. The letter was written to Dr. Archibald Hall of Montreal. Hall (1812–1868) attended the Royal Grammar School in Montreal where he was a student of Alexander Skakel. After being apprenticed to a doctor in Montreal he completed his medical studies in Edinburgh and became a prominent physician in Montreal. He joined the medical faculty of McGill University and at various times was Professor of Chemistry, Professor of Materia Medica, and Professor of Midwifery and Therapeutics. He was co-editor of the *British American Journal of Medical and Physical Science*, published in Montreal from 1845 to 1852 and editor of the *British American Journal* from 1860 to 1862.

early nineteenth century. At that time, the curriculum laid down by the
Senatus academicus in 1753 was still in effect and prescribed that "the
students after being instructed in classical learning, should be made
acquainted with natural and civil history, geography, chronology, and
the elements of mathematics; and they should then proceed to natural
philosophy, and terminate their curriculum by studying moral philosophy."[25]

The records of Marischal College show two entries which almost certainly refer to John Rae:

1809–1813 Joan. Rae, f. Joannis, mercator., Abredonen. s.[emi] t.[ertian][26]
1811–1815 Joan. Rae, f. Joannis, mercatoris Abredonensis m.[agistrand] A.M.[27]

The terms opposite Rae's name, *semi, tertian* and *magistrand*, correspond
roughly to the North American terms sophomore, junior, and senior;
there is no record of his *bajan* or freshman year. It is abundantly clear from
these records that Rae received the degree of Master of Arts from
Marischal College in 1815.

Rae's instructors at Marischal College are not all definitely identifiable
but probably included the following: John Stuart (Greek), James Davidson
(civil and natural history), George Glennie (moral philosophy), Robert
Hamilton (mathematics), Patrick Copland (natural philosophy), and
George French (chemistry).[28] There can be no question that Rae was
strongly influenced by this talented group, but it is difficult to trace their
influence in detail.

Even as a very young man, Rae developed an absorbing interest in
scientific invention. This trait was shared by his brother James who,

[25] John Marius Wilson, ed., *The Imperial Gazetteer of Scotland; or Dictionary of
Scottish Topography, etc.* (London, Edinburgh and Dublin, n.d.), article "Aberdeen."
[26] *Fasti Academiae Mariscallanae*, II, 407.
[27] *Ibid.*, 412.
[28] John Stuart (d. 1827), author of *Life of Dr. Duncan Liddell* (Aberdeen, 1790),
"Marischal College" in *Statistical Account of Scotland*, XXI (Edinburgh, 1799), and
Essays Chiefly on Scottish Antiquities (Aberdeen, 1846). James Davidson (d. 1841)
graduated in medicine from the University of Edinburgh (M.D., 1792) and was a
physician at Dunfermline. George Glennie (d. 1845) was one of the ministers of the kirk
in Aberdeen from 1813. Robert Hamilton (1774–1829) was appointed to the chair of
natural philosophy in Marischal College in 1779 but switched to the teaching of mathematics. Hamilton was the author of *Introduction to Merchandise* (1777), *Peace and War*
(1790), *Heads of a Course of Mathematics* (1800), *Inquiry concerning the Rise and
Progress, the Reduction and Present State and the Management of the National Debt of
Great Britain and Ireland* (1813), and posthumously *Progress of Society* (1830). Patrick
Copland (1749–1822) was a pioneer in the collection of models and materials for a
natural history museum and the owner of a collection of scientific apparatus which was
purchased by Marischal College for 700 guineas. He also gave popular courses of
lectures on natural philosophy. George French (d. 1833) was a physician in Aberdeen
(M.D., 1786).

according to Mixter's informants in Scotland, displayed "remarkable inventive aptitudes."[29] It is possible that Dr. Arnott conveyed some of his interest in invention to the boys of the Rae household. When he was a student at Marischal College, Rae undertook to devise an apparatus for determining the rate and direction of a current at sea. According to Mixter, the mechanism depended on changes in water pressure on air in a cylinder. At different pressures, weights attached to bodies of different specific gravity would be released. Rae had endeavoured to interest one of his teachers at Marischal College, Dr. Robert Hamilton, in his project but, according to Rae, "he allowed it sound in theory and ingenious, but smiled it down as impracticable."[30] Hamilton's objection was that "it was very good on paper, but that in so boisterous an element as the ocean it was almost absurd to think it could be of any practical utility." Rae nevertheless remained convinced of the value of his apparatus and much later in his life he defended it vigorously.[31]

Another of Rae's projects was a device for feathering the paddle wheels on steamboats. His scheme was to feather the blades vertically so that they would move through the right angle made by a vertical plane parallel to the keel and the surface of the water. This was before the days when feathering was used and the idea was ingenious enough, although the device later adopted provided for feathering parallel to the axis of the wheel. Modern aircraft propellers embody the kind of feathering principle Rae apparently had in mind.

Shortly after his graduation from Marischal College, Rae enrolled in Edinburgh University as a medical student. Between the fall of 1815 and the spring of 1817 he attended, among others, classes in chemistry, clinical surgery, clinical medicine, and the practice of medicine.

At this time there were two sessions in the academic year, the winter beginning in October and the summer beginning in May. Rae's known instructors were Professor Thomas Charles Hope (chemistry), Professor James Russell (clinical surgery), and Professor James Gregory (practice of medicine). He may also have studied anatomy and surgery under Alexander Munro tertius and materia medica under James Home, but this is not known for certain.

The *Statuta Solennia* of the University of Edinburgh passed in 1767, as

[29] *Sociological Theory of Capital*, xx.
[30] *Ibid.*, xxviii.
[31] There is a description of the device and some very rough sketches among the Rae mss., but they are difficult to decipher. The mechanism, however, was apparently similar to something developed later by Lord Kelvin and adopted by the Royal Navy in 1878. Kelvin's apparatus is described in Singer, Holmyard, Hall, and Williams, eds., *A History of Technology* (New York and London, 1958), V, 453 and 461.

amended in 1777 and 1783, were in force in 1815–17 when Rae was a medical student. Candidates for a degree were required to complete a course of three years, covering the following fields: anatomy and surgery, chemistry, botany, materia medica and pharmacy, theory and practice of medicine, and clinical lectures at the Royal Infirmary. The regulations also required the following: (a) two professors were to examine the candidate in the presence of the faculty; (b) the candidate was to prepare written comments on two aphorisms of Hippocrates and to defend them before the faculty; (c) similarly two cases were to be commented on and defended; (d) candidates were required to submit copies of a printed thesis to each medical professor and to defend it at the time of graduation. All these written and oral exercises were to be in Latin. There is clear evidence that Rae did not fulfil all the requirements for a medical degree.

On March 15, 1816, at the age of nineteen, Rae was elected a Fellow of the Royal Medical Society of Edinburgh, an association of medical students, and some months later to the Committee on Domestic Economy which controlled the business aspects of the Society's affairs. Rae's participation in the Society seems to have been limited to business matters and there is no record of his having spoken on medical topics.

By 1817, Rae had already formulated a general philosophical conception of human society as well as some original views on natural science which he described in his thesis. Rae's ideas were apparently revolutionary and led to the interruption of his formal academic career. According to an unidentified quotation of Mixter's, presumably Rae's, Rae "had come to the conclusion that the physiological medical theories of the day were opposed to all true philosophy and therefore fundamentally false," and had arrived at "a conclusion concerning the origin of man very different from the orthodox one."[32] He explained the circumstances many years later in a letter to some friend:

I was preparing an inaugural dissertation, as was then the custom in Edinburgh, previous to taking my degree; its title was "De Vita," and I intended to propound in it my general views. I was prevented by leading men in Edinburgh who had taken an interest in me, among others Dr. Abercrombie, a physician in extensive practice, known to you perhaps as the author of some metaphysical works.[33] They represented to me that the course I was preparing to take was highly presumptious and imprudent. I should at once have yielded to them with thanks, had they shown me it was erroneous. But they would not listen to my reasons, they looked only at my conclusions. In this state of affairs I thought I

[32] *Sociological Theory of Capital*, xxi.

[33] Dr. John Abercrombie (1780–1844), at one time one of the chief consulting physicians in Scotland. Abercrombie was appointed first physician to His Majesty in Scotland on July 28, 1828. He was keenly interested in the training of medical students.

would advise with my father. He knew nothing of philosophy and physiology, but he knew the world. His opinion was that if I was to fight I had better defer for a year or two till I gathered more strength, and then if, as I had proposed, I wished to go to Paris, where physiology was then more advanced than in England, he would consent. It was perhaps good advice, as I was then only twenty years of age. I had thus to pass a few years in gaining knowledge and experience. I turned myself to a subject kindred to my previous studies and thus said to myself: If I am right, deep is the pit from which we men have opened to ourselves a passage. The deeper the pit the higher comparatively the height to which we have ascended, and therefore still greater the height we may hope to gain. Whence then are the forces which have so elevated us, and whence is it that humanity has been continually . . . from the great heights to the most profound depths, and that its real substantial progress is to the philosophical eye so uncertain?[34]

Some glimmering of what Rae had in mind may be found in a letter written in 1852, in which he says:

I have at this moment more particularly in eye the advance that has been made in the conjunct sciences of physiology and medicine. This has I take it been twofold more philosophical reasoning and experimenting having led to great and positive results & these results having in turn given fresh impetus to a spirit of sober rational and perservering inquiry. Thus the old senseless and irrational mode of speaking about things under the names of irritability debility &c. &c. &c. thus raising up phantasms which, under the name of vital powers all the old plastic nature of the ancients were supposed to move and mould all things, has been done away with or is in process of being so. This was a task which at one time, more than thirty years ago, I had proposed to myself & it is surprising to myself how moved by a better and juster spirit of inquiry I had anticipated so much of what has been done.[35]

France at this time, as Rae recognized, was in the forefront in the study of natural history. Lamarck (1744–1829) and Cuvier (1769–1832), among others, were dominant figures. Indeed, Cuvier's fundamental contribution to taxonomy appeared in 1817.

Rae's attention was thus diverted from his initial attack on the academic strongholds of Edinburgh to "a subject kindred to my previous studies." Evidently, this was the extraordinarily ambitious project which Rae described in the preface of his *New Principles*:

Many years ago, I became engaged in a series of inquiries into the circumstances which have governed the history of man, or, to vary the expression, into the causes which have made him what he is in various countries, or has been in various times. It seemed to me, that, by gathering together all that consciousness makes known to us of what is within, and all that observation informs us of what

[34] *Sociological Theory of Capital*, xxi.
[35] Letter, Rae to Archibald Hall, April 15, 1852. See Part III, item 14.

lies without, the real agents of the production of the great events by which the fortunes of our race have been diversified, might be at least partially discovered, the laws regulating their procedure traced, and that thus the materials for a true *Natural History* of man might be reached. The pursuits in which I was engaged led me to the subject on the side of physiology, and what is termed metaphysics, and imagining that I saw a ray of light struggling through the obscurity of the objects, amidst which these investigations placed me, I began to conceive hopes of being able to dispel some of the darkness, in which are involved causes that have produced and are producing, results of the highest importance to us. To this pursuit I determined to devote myself.[36]

It must be understood that Rae, in referring to physiology in this passage, meant primarily the systematic study of natural science and not human physiology, which is the most usual modern meaning of the term.

There was a remarkably widespread interest in natural history around the beginning of the nineteenth century particularly in England. The Linnaean Society had been founded in 1790 and the cultivation of the art of observing and classifying many types of natural objects and phenomena was pursued with great zeal. It was particularly the preserve of the leisured classes and it was to this type of activity that Rae anticipated being able to devote his life. He was, of course, not primarily concerned with fossil-collecting, bird-watching, or measuring rainfall or similar pursuits, which, however laudable, were hardly enough to satisfy his urge to deal with more fundamental problems.

Rae's plans as a young man were based in part on the expectation that he would be free from financial worry and would not have to concern himself with the mundane problems of earning a living. In one place Rae wrote of "a small estate to which I was then reckoned heir would, I thought, furnish me with sufficient means to enable me to give all my energies for all the years I might have to live to these pursuits . . . But I was mistaken."[37] Undoubtedly he was referring to Wester Auquharney.

There is a lamentable scarcity of information about Rae's life during the five years following his departure from Edinburgh University. Something is known of several episodes, but this period of his life remains very obscure.

It is known that during 1818 he made a tour through Norway. Rae referred to this trip in two places in his writings but its purpose was not made clear.[38] In one of his comments there is an incidental mention of the export of timber from Norway, a field of trade in which his father was

---

[36] *New Principles*, iv.

[37] *Sociological Theory of Capital*, xxii.

[38] *New Principles*, 317, and in *British American Journal of Medical and Physical Science*, Aug., 1845,

engaged. Possibly he was travelling on business. He may, on the other hand, have been interested in the geology of Norway.

Rae also referred in a letter to an episode which occurred in 1819:

At that time the propriety of greatly reducing the duties on ardent spirits was a question much agitated in Scotland, my native land; and while my position led me to listen to the discussion going on, my prospects were then such as to make that and all other questions connected with the well-being of the people a matter of considerable interest to me. The Highlands of Scotland were then, and had long been, famous for the manufacture of a sort of whiskey which, partly perhaps from its being made in small stills, was thought of superior flavour, and was greatly esteemed. The traffic was altogether illicit and there was a constant struggle between the smugglers and the revenue officers, the one striving to carry through their objects by stratagem or force, the other endeavouring to baffle them; so that the magistracy and the courts of justice had constantly cases coming before them which were generally settled by fine or imprisonment, and not infrequently by transportation. It was proposed to put an end to this state of things by greatly reducing the duty on legally manufactured whiskey, and by authorizing its manufacture in stills of a small size. Almost everyone thought that great good would result from such a change of system and laughed at the fears which some few entertained of its bad effects on the general morals of the people. The authority of Adam Smith was cited as decisive of the question, and the measure was carried through amid a general acclaim of approbation. I own that I was among the doubters, and that knowing the habits of my countrymen I feared that the immediate and obvious good resulting would be counter-balanced by more remote but greater evils. It was in vain for me, however, to open my mouth against the general voice, and when I attempted it my imper-tinence in opposing my elders and betters was only excused as one of the eccen-tricities of a strange youth. Time has now shown that I was not far wrong.[39]

Rae's comment in this letter that "my prospects were then such as to make that and all other questions connected with the well-being of the people a matter of considerable interest to me" is baffling. It throws no light on his activities at the time, but the letter does seem to make it clear that Rae was in Scotland in 1819.

There is considerable indirect evidence to indicate that Rae spent some time at this period of his life in Paris. It had been part of his plan when at Edinburgh University to continue his studies of physiology in Paris. There are indications however that by the time he actually arrived his interests were focused primarily on history and political economy.[40]

It is also clear that Rae married during this period. Very little is known of his wife, although some unidentified correspondent of Mixter stated that "his wife [was] in education far beneath him, she being the daughter

---

[39] Quoted in *Sociological Theory of Capital*, 475.
[40] The records of the University of Paris do not indicate that Rae was ever enrolled as a student.

of a Scotch shepherd."[41] Her name was Eliza, but her birthplace or maiden name have not been ascertained.[42]

The bankruptcy of his father occurred during this shadowy period in Rae's life. Rae's own explanation does not go into detail. He wrote that "a sudden and unexpected change took place in my circumstances, and I exchanged the literary leisure of Europe for the solitude and labors of the Canadian backwoods."[43] His anticipated inheritance did not materialize and he found himself unable to follow the kind of scholarly or academic pursuits he had intended. He determined to leave his native land and to leave behind him some intolerable situation which may have had both financial and social aspects.

On the basis of information obtained from an acquaintance of Rae, Mixter has suggested that Rae may have been induced to leave Scotland in part because of some stigma associated with his marriage. Mixter's correspondent said that Rae left Scotland "under a sort of bad luck, having married in haste."[44] It must be borne in mind, however, that Mixter's inquiries did not begin until eighty years after Rae's marriage and his informant may have conveyed an erroneous impression.

Whatever the precise reasons, in the spring of 1822, when he was twenty-five, Rae and his wife came to Canada.[45] The prospect of separation from the great libraries and the great thinkers of Europe must doubtless have saddened him. He could not have realized clearly at the time that new vistas were opening for him. He was to be exposed to the stimulation and challenge of new social and economic problems which forced him to reconsider what he had learned about political economy and, having done that, to launch a series of ideas which combined originality, brilliance, and felicity of expression.

[41] *Sociological Theory of Capital*, xxii.

[42] A search was undertaken in the parish records of Aberdeenshire in the Registrar-General's office in Edinburgh for the period 1817–1822 to try to ascertain some additional facts about Rae's marriage. There are eighty-four parishes and in the twenty-eighth search (Ellon) an entry was found describing the marriage of John Rae to Eliza Bruce on October 30, 1817. Subsequent investigations revealed, however, that this was another John Rae and at this point the project was abandoned.

[43] *New Principles*, iv.

[44] *Sociological Theory of Capital*, xxii.

[45] In a number of places Mixter says that Rae came to Canada in 1821, but this appears to be incorrect. Some material written by Rae dated July, 1840, contains a reference to "18 years that the author has lived in Canada," and again an article written in July, 1845, states "I arrived in this country twenty-three years ago."

2

A Decade in the Canadian Backwoods

(1822–1831)

Although all the circumstances underlying Rae's emigration to Canada are unclear, it was understandable that he should head for Montreal. There were at this time strong cultural ties between Aberdeen and Montreal. Many of the successful merchants of Montreal as well as other prominent residents were from Aberdeenshire, and Rae undoubtedly knew some of them personally. In 1821 the population of Montreal was about 19,000, and social conditions were primitive. One traveller reported:

If you enjoy good eating, card-playing, dancing, music, and gayety, you will find abundance of all. If literary society is your choice, you will discover I am afraid but little; and if religious, still less. I was particularly struck with the extent to which card-playing and the dice-box abound; they seem to be the only resource in an evening party, if it is not professedly a dancing one. . . . Of the British residents the greater part are eagerly intent upon the acquisition of wealth, and in general anticipate a return to their native country to spend it; and if in their hours of intermission from other pursuits, they can glance at a novel, or a fashionable poem, it is all that is in most cases attempted.[1]

It is very probable that Rae's decision to come to Canada was influenced by the fact that his sister Ann Cuthbert was living in Montreal.

This remarkable woman had married James Innes Knight, described as a merchant of Portsoy, Banffshire, Scotland, on July 3, 1810. In 1811, they emigrated to Montreal, in the company of a son of six weeks, Robert Knight, who had been born on April 27, 1811. They returned to Scotland

---

[1] John M. Duncan, *Travels through Part of the United States and Canada in 1818 and 1819* (New York and New Haven, 1823), 171–2.

after a short stay in Canada, and during this stay in Scotland, Mrs.
Knight had a daughter, Jessie. The Knight family came back again to
Montreal probably in early 1815,[2] with the exception of Jessie who remained in Scotland. Upon their return they lived in St. James Street, in a
house which was later the Post Office of Montreal, according to the recollections of the son, Robert. James Innes Knight died suddenly in Montreal
sometime in 1815. After this melancholy occurrence the young widow
turned to teaching school. In October, 1815, a newspaper advertisement
announced her intentions:

> Mrs. Knight informs her Friends and the Public, that she will on the first of
> November next, open school in The House in St. Vincent's Street opposite the
> Sheriff's Office for the tuition of young ladies, in plain and fancy needlework the
> English language writing arithmetic geography and drawing. For terms and any
> other information, application may be had to her at Mr. Skakel's, St. Jacques'
> Street. Montreal, October 9th, 1815.[3]

It was at about this time that Ann Cuthbert Knight published two
volumes of poetry. The first, entitled *Home: A Poem*, was written in Canada
about the time of the War of 1812 and published in Edinburgh in 1815.[4]
A second volume, *A Year in Canada, and Other Poems*, published in 1816,
also in Edinburgh, is an admirable little book consisting mainly of a long
descriptive poem in five parts. It is full of keen observations of Canadian
life and customs early in the nineteenth century.

On May 8, 1820, Ann Cuthbert Knight and James Fleming were married
at Chambly, Quebec.[5] Fleming was about forty-two at the time and it is
possible that this was a second marriage for him also. He was a dry goods
merchant in Montreal, but little is known about his personal life or qualities.[6]

The date of Rae's arrival in Montreal and the name of his ship are not
known. He was not idle long and busied himself writing notes on the

---

[2] The following item appeared in the *Quebec Gazette*, June 1, 1815: "Mr. and Mrs.
Knight passengers on board ship Brutus arrived from Portsmouth."

[3] *Montreal Gazette*, Oct. 9, 1815. An 1819 city directory for Montreal lists "Mrs.
Knight Boarding School 7 Vincent Street." Thomas Doige, *An Alphabetical List of
the Merchants, Traders, and Housekeepers Residing in Montreal, etc.* (Montreal, 1819).

[4] One of the few copies of this book known to exist in Canada is in the library of
McGill University and is inscribed, "Prize obtained by Jane Porteous for second best
written copy book at Mrs. Knight's School Montreal August 1819."

[5] *Montreal Herald*, May 20, 1820. They were married by the Rev. Edward Parkin,
an Anglican clergyman.

[6] There were at least two children by this marriage. A son, John Ramsay Fleming,
born in 1824 or 1825, later became a well-known Canadian lawyer. There is a note
about him in the Biographical Appendix. There was also a daughter, Ann, who died in
infancy in Montreal on August 23, 1832, at the height of the cholera epidemic. An
obituary notice is in the *Montreal Gazette*, Aug. 23, 1832.

geological characteristics of the Gulf of St. Lawrence. This work was entitled "An Essay on the Geology of Canada, containing a description of the Gulf of St. Lawrence, as observed by myself as a newcomer," but has since been lost.[7]

Rae cannot have spent long in Montreal after his arrival. In the spring of 1822, he left to become a village schoolmaster in Glengarry County. A newspaper advertisement dated April 26, 1822, announced his appointment:

John Rae, A.M. &C.[8] Begs leave to intimate, that he has been appointed Master to the School of Williamstown, Glengary, U.C. where the following branches will be taught, viz. Reading, Writing, Arithmetic, English Grammar, Book-keeping, Geography and Mathematics, including Surveying.

Mr. R. Also intends to give private lessons on the principles of the Greek and French languages, on Elocution, English Composition and on Drawing.

A few Boarders could be accommodated, to whom every attention would be paid. As to his qualifications and terms, Reference may be made to the Rev. Mr. Mackenzie, Williamstown to the Rev. Mr. Esson, Montreal, or to Mr. Skakel of the Royal Grammar School of Montreal.[9]

These three interesting men given as references by Rae throw some light on his early associations in Canada. The Rev. John Mackenzie was the minister of the Scottish Presbyterian Church in Williamstown; the Rev. Henry Esson, who had been a fellow student of Rae's at Marischal College, was co-pastor of the St. Gabriel Street Church in Montreal, and Alexander Skakel was headmaster of the Royal Grammar School, Montreal, a close friend of Rae's sister and godfather to her son Robert.[10]

Williamstown is a small village on the Raisin River about twelve miles from Cornwall and fifty miles from Montreal. It was the centre of strong United Empire Loyalist feeling, many of the settlers, including Sir John Johnson, the founder, having emigrated from New York State at the time of the American Revolution. In the 1820's Williamstown and its immediate vicinity was the home of a number of wealthy and distinguished men, several of them partners in the North West Company who had retired from the fur trade after the merger with the Hudson's Bay Company in 1821. This group included John McGillivray, David Thompson, Hugh McGillis, Alexander Fraser, and Duncan Cameron.[11] Rae was engaged to teach the children of these men and of their neighbours.

[7] This essay was among the papers given by Mixter to Dr. T. A. Jaggar; it was evidently sent to some unknown person for review and has disappeared.

[8] The "&C." presumably represents "F.R.M.S.E." (Fellow of the Royal Medical Society of Edinburgh).

[9] Montreal Herald, May 4, 1822.

[10] More detailed information about these men is given in the Biographical Appendix.

[11] J. A. Macdonell, Sketches Illustrating the Early Settlement and History of Glengarry in Canada (Montreal, 1893), 335.

Very little is known about Rae's school, but it appears to have been privately supported by the fees of the pupils. Since it was a private school, no official records of its operations were required. Only two of Rae's pupils are known definitely; Robert Knight, his nephew, who was sent to live with his uncle after he had completed his preliminary schooling at the Royal Grammar School in Montreal, and Roderick William Cameron, the son of Duncan Cameron.

Information about Rae's life in Williamstown is very scanty. In 1825, Rae's name appears among the list of contributors from the congregation of the kirk in Williamstown for the relief of those suffering from the disastrous Miramichi fire of that year. He gave ten shillings.[12] It is also known that in 1827 he applied for the vacant position of headmaster of the Gore District School in Hamilton.[13]

It is probable that teaching school was not Rae's only source of livelihood. One of Rae's letters written in 1856 suggests that he may have engaged in the practice of medicine in Williamstown in the 1820's: "They [my earlier friends in Canada] thought me foolish in burying the attainments and ability they were pleased to give me credit for in the subordinate position of a village surgeon, or still worse in that of a country schoolmaster."[14] Certainly Rae was almost universally referred to as "Dr. Rae." As early as June, 1826, there is some correspondence between the Rev. Edward Black and the Rev. John Mackenzie relating to a chest of tea to be purchased in Montreal for "Dr. Rae."[15]

There were certain legal requirements for medical practitioners in the early part of the nineteenth century in Canada. Licensing requirements were issued and repealed sporadically in Upper Canada between 1795 and 1818. In 1815, an Act had been passed laying down certain licensing requirements but exempting, among others, any person with a degree from "any university in His Majesty's Dominions."[16] Then, in 1818, an Act was passed establishing a Medical Board which was empowered to license all medical practitioners but continuing the exemption for university graduates.[17] The Medical Board was first convened early in 1819 and continued to operate during the period of Rae's residence in Williamstown. The

[12] Montreal *Herald*, Dec. 21, 1825.

[13] See below, Part I, chap. 4.

[14] Letter to H. B. Willson, Dec., 1856, *Sociological Theory of Capital*, xl, reprinted in item 19 of Part III of this volume.

[15] Public Archives of Canada, Ottawa (hereafter P.A.C.), McGillivray Papers, VII, 103–14; letter, Edward Black to John Mackenzie, June 1, 1826.

[16] William Canniff, *The Medical Profession in Upper Canada, 1783–1850* (Toronto, 1894), 32.

[17] 59 Geo. III, c. 13. See W. R. Riddell,"The Medical Profession in Ontario. A Legal and Historical Sketch," *Canadian Journal of Medicine and Surgery*, Sept., 1911.

minutes of the Medical Board of Upper Canada have been preserved but contain no reference to Rae. It must thus be presumed that he qualified under the exemption which was continued in legislation passed in 1827.[18]

The Lieutenant-Governor himself referred to "Dr. Rae," so that, although no record of Rae's accreditation now seems to exist, he was apparently officially recognized as a medical doctor.

Whatever his activities in the medical profession were, Rae was appointed one of the coroners of the Eastern District on February 24, 1830.[19] Although it was perhaps not essential, it was usual to appoint practising doctors to such positions.

What is believed to be Rae's first published contribution to economic literature appeared about three years after his arrival in Williamstown. During this period in Canada, the publication of literary periodicals was not only unusual but financially precarious. There were, however, two magazines or reviews in Montreal in the mid-1820's which reflected the views of the English-speaking *literati*. The first was the *Canadian Magazine and Literary Repository* which appeared for twenty-four issues between 1823 and 1825. For part of this time it was edited by David Chisholme,[20] but following some quarrel with the proprietor he initiated a rival periodical initially known as the *Canadian Review and Literary and Historical Journal* which lasted for only five issues between 1824 and 1826. Both these magazines were of extraordinarily good quality. Although it was not usual to identify the authors or reviewers, it is known that among the contributors were Rae's sister Mrs. Fleming, her brother-in-law John Fleming, Alex Skakel, and probably the Rev. Henry Esson. Rae's article appeared in the third issue in March, 1825, with the main title "Sketches of the origin and progress of manufactures and of the policy which has regulated their legislative encouragement in Great Britain and in other countries"; the title then continues, "to which will be added an enquiry into the expediency of establishing some new branches of industry in the Canadas, more particularly with a view to the employment of women and children in the cities of Quebec and Montreal." The full text of the essay is reproduced in Part III, but unfortunately the promised sequel never appeared, probably because Chisholme's review lasted for only two more issues.[21]

[18] 8 Geo. IV, c. 3.

[19] The Commission, initialled by Sir John Colborne, is in the files of the Department of the Secretary of State, Canada, lib. I, fol. 484. Rae's fellow coroners in the Eastern District were Dr. Alexander Wylie of Matilda (Iroquois) and Albert French of Cornwall, who was murdered in 1836.

[20] For a brief account of Chisholme's career see the Biographical Appendix.

[21] The article was not signed, but some of the ideas foreshadow so exactly those which were later to appear in Rae's *New Principles* that there can be little doubt that Rae was the writer.

This was a very sophisticated essay in which Rae concentrated attention
on the historical evolution of manufacturing skills, with special attention
being devoted in the introductory part to the factors influencing the transference of new techniques from the continent to England. He says in one
place:

It may be necessary to stimulate the efforts of private individuals by imposing
duties on the importation of foreign manufactures, and thus rendering taxation
not merely the means of raising a revenue but an ingenious device for the introduction of the useful and liberal arts of life.

Then he went on:

There is also a species of encouragement less authoritative, though perhaps not
less efficient, and which ought not to be neglected in facilitating to the native
manufacturer the exclusive supply of the home market: We mean the influence
of example held forth by the higher classes of a community. When the Court
and the people of fashion give a preference to home manufactures, public opinion
is gradually strengthened in their favor; and nothing but a very considerable
superiority in the quality of the foreign goods can long prevent their being
driven from the home market, leaving a wide field to the national ingenuity
which should be exerted in finding substitutes for imported luxuries.

He was to return to both these themes later and to formulate the germinal
ideas with both literary skill and increased precision.

It is significant that when Rae announced his appointment to the school
in Williamstown in 1822 he gave as references two ministers of the Presbyterian Church of Canada in connection with the Church of Scotland. A
number of additional ministers of the Church of Scotland came to Canada
in the 1820's and early 1830's, several of whom Rae had undoubtedly
known in Aberdeen and Edinburgh.[22] Williamstown, itself, had the largest
congregation of any of the Scottish churches in Canada at that time, and
many wealthy and influential members of the Kirk lived in Glengarry.
One nineteenth-century commentator attributed great importance to this
group:

Large numbers of Scotch Presbyterians also settled in the provinces, and exercised a powerful influence on the social, moral and political progress of the
country. These pioneers came from a country where parish schools existed long
before popular education was dreamed of across the border. Their clergy came
from colleges whose courses of study cultivated minds of rare analytical and
argumentative power. The sermon in the Presbyterian Church is the test of the
intellectual calibre of the preacher whose efforts are followed by his long-headed

---

[22] Included in this group were the Rev. Hugh Urquhart (King's College), the Rev.
Alexander Gale (Marischal College), the Rev. John Machar (King's College), the Rev.
George Sheed, and the Rev. William Rintoul (Edinburgh University).

congregation in a spirit of keenest criticism, ever ready to detect a want of logic. It is obvious then that the Presbyterian clergyman, from the earliest time he appeared in the history of this country, has always been a considerable force in the mental development of a large section of the people, which has given us . . . many eminent statesmen, journalists and *littérateurs*.[23]

Because of personal and family connections as well as his own religious leanings, Rae allied himself closely with the Presbyterians during his early life in Canada. In turn, they welcomed him as a useful spokesman and supporter in the educational and other conflicts with the Church of England.

One of the disputes in which Rae was involved arose out of the ambiguity of the provision of the Constitutional Act of 1791 which set aside one-seventh of the Crown lands granted in Upper Canada for "the support and maintenance of a Protestant Clergy."[24] Initially, despite a large acreage set aside as Clergy Reserves, the resultant revenue was small, and not much interest was shown in them. By about 1817 the potential value of the Clergy Reserves became more apparent and not long after a number of steps were taken by the Church of England to establish its exclusive rights to the Clergy Reserves. The Church of England claimed that the phrase "a Protestant Clergy" did not include either the Church of Scotland or the Dissenters, this view stemming in part from a further provision of the Constitutional Act of 1791 which permitted the provincial governments to use the proceeds of the sale of the Clergy Reserves to endow parsonages and rectories "according to the establishment of the Church of England."[25] This view was repeatedly challenged by the Church of Scotland which was, itself, an established church. In the 1820's the air was thick with petitions and counter-petitions and the stage was set for a bitter controversy which was to bedevil Canadian political and religious life for many years. Only one episode, which was to involve John Rae, can be dealt with here in any detail.

In 1827, John Strachan, then Archdeacon of York, travelled to England to obtain a royal charter for the University of King's College, which was to be under the control of the Church of England. During his stay in England, the House of Commons had under consideration legislation to authorize selling or transferring part of the Clergy Reserves, a proposal which excited considerable debate, much of it ill-informed. On May 16, 1827, Strachan, apparently seeking to clarify matters, addressed a notorious letter to R. J. Wilmot-Horton, then Under-Secretary of State for the

[23] Sir J. G. Bourinot, *The Intellectual Development of the Canadian People; An Historical Review* (Toronto, 1881), 18–19.
[24] 31 Geo. III, c. 31, sec. 36.
[25] *Ibid.*, sec. 38.

Colonies, and enclosed an ecclesiastical chart for Upper Canada which purported to show the number and denominations of all the non-Roman Catholic clergy in Upper Canada. When this material was made public, both the Church of Scotland and the Methodists felt that Strachan's data exhibited some sectarian bias and conveyed an erroneous impression.[26]

In response to the outcry, the Legislative Assembly of Upper Canada appointed a select committee with Marshall Spring Bidwell as chairman which heard altogether fifty-two witnesses. The report of the committee, dated March 15, 1828, did not, in general, support Strachan's claims and formed the basis for an address to the King asking that the proceeds of the Clergy Reserves be allocated by the province for general education and national improvement.

In the meantime, the Scottish Presbyterians were goaded into further action by Strachan's dubious logic and inaccurate statistics. In the beginning of November, 1827, a committee was appointed by the session of St. Gabriel Street Church, Montreal, to communicate with the other kirk sessions in Canada in order to advance their own interests. The committee consisted of the Rev. Henry Esson and the Rev. Edward Black with three lay members. Acting in concert with a corresponding committee of St. Andrew's Church, Montreal, this group drew up a brief but impressive petition to the King outlining the claims of the Kirk in Canada.[27] This petition, dated December 20, 1827, was to be circulated in Upper and Lower Canada for signature by the Presbyterians. It was also decided to send J. C. Grant, a Montreal lawyer, to London to advance the Presbyterian cause in appropriate quarters.

The transoceanic pressure on His Majesty's Government in London was thus building up, mainly because of the various delegates and agents of the different denominations who undertook to present their special pleas in London. In response, William Huskisson, on May 2, 1828, moved the establishment of a committee of the House of Commons to investigate the problems of civil government in the Canadas.[28] The committee heard

[26] There was some indignation over the fact that Strachan's chart listed as ministers of the Kirk in Upper Canada only "J. M'Kenzie" and "J. M'Laurin." On Sept. 26, 1827, William Morris replied to Strachan in a letter to R. J. Wilmot-Horton listing the following additional ministers: Urquhart (Cornwall), Connell (Martintown), Machar (Kingston), and Sheed (Ancaster). It is only fair to point out that Machar and Sheed did not take over their charges until after the date of Strachan's letter, while Urquhart had been inducted on Feb. 18, 1827, during Strachan's absence in England.

[27] Robert Christie, *A History of the Late Province of Lower Canada* . . . (Quebec, 1850), III, 152–3.

[28] *Report from the Select Committee on the Civil Government of the Canadas*, ordered by the House of Commons to be printed July 22, 1828. Reprinted by Order of the House of Assembly of Lower Canada, 1829. Appendix 16.

an impressive array of witnesses and included in its report the petition from the Presbyterians in the Canadas of December 20, 1827. Four members of the Canada Committee, the Hon. E. G. Stanley, the Hon. John Stuart Wortley, J. E. Denison, and Henry Labouchère, had visited Montreal in the course of a tour of North America in the fall of 1824 and had some personal knowledge of Canadian conditions.[29]

Some months before the creation of the Canada Committee, there was a gathering of the Kirk dignitaries, lay and ecclesiastical, from both Upper and Lower Canada in Cornwall. The meetings, which began on January 31, 1828, were under the chairmanship of the Dr. James Harkness,[30] minister of St. Andrew's Church, Quebec City. The aim of this assembly was to promote these objectives: first, the establishment of the Church of Scotland in Canada on an equal footing with the Church of England; second, the payment by the government of one-half the stipends of the ministers of the Kirk; third, the apportionment of the Clergy Reserves between the Church of England and the Church of Scotland proportionally to the number of communicants; fourth, financial assistance from the government for church construction and for the payment of school teachers.

It was at around the same period that plans were made for the publication of the *Canadian Miscellany, or the Religious, Literary and Statistical Intelligencer*, whose editor was to be Henry Esson. The prospectus, appearing early in January, 1828, outlined the scope of the ambitious project:

An association of Gentlemen, in Montreal, have formed a resolution of undertaking the conduct of a periodical work of which the object shall be to embody in its pages information with respect to the state of Religion, Education and Learning in Canada; together with the History and Statistics of the Colony. . . . They resolve to exclude controversy, and to make their work a repository of facts rather than of opinions. . . .[31]

The exclusion of controversy was perhaps too much to hope for.

The first number of the *Canadian Miscellany*, appearing in April, 1828, was devoted to a diocesan letter by the Bishop of Quebec dated December 6, 1827, in which he reviewed and reiterated the exclusive claims of the Church of England deriving from the Constitutional Act of 1791; and a pastoral letter signed by eleven ministers of the Church of Scotland. The

---

[29] *Montreal Gazette*, Sept. 15, 1824.

[30] James Harkness (1789–1835) was born in Sanquhar, Scotland, and ordained by the Presbytery of Ayr in 1820, before taking over St. Andrew's Church in Quebec City in the same year. He was a great friend of Lord Dalhousie, a fellow Presbyterian, when he was Governor General. Harkness was distinguished by his personal idiosyncrasies and his exertions on behalf of the Church of Scotland in Canada.

[31] *Montreal Gazette*, Jan. 7, 1828.

pastoral letter was bitter enough and commented acidly on John Strachan's important role in the quarrelling:

Some features of resemblance may perhaps be discerned between the policy recommended and pursued in the days of Archbishop Sharpe and that which has been publicly avowed by the leaders of the Church of England in Upper and Lower Canada, and of these none is more remarkable than that Scotsmen and proselytes from presbytery to episcopacy could in both instances be the chief instruments.[32]

In the second number of the magazine appearing in May, 1828, there appeared an interesting article with the title "On the State and Prospects of Education and Learning in the Canadas." It ended with the tantalizing note "to be continued," but it never was, and perhaps for this reason was unsigned. There is considerable internal evidence, however, to indicate that the author was John Rae. The complete text is given in Part III among Rae's miscellaneous essays and letters, so it is necessary here only to summarize the general argument.

After a vivid opening statement of the beneficial effects of education on any nation, attention is turned to "the superior excellence of the national system of education" in Scotland and to the pervasive and enlightening influence of Scotsmen not only in the British Empire but throughout the whole world. Despite what is referred to as the "unspeakable advantage of a liberal and effective system of education" in a "young and rising country" there were certain dangers to be observed if the control of education fell into the hands of designing and ambitious men. It becomes quickly evident that the essay is a devastating attack on John Strachan and his proposals to establish King's College as an exclusive domain of the Church of England. Rae's views are expressed with vigour and at one point he says, "a University or a College, erected wholly or even principally for the purpose of proselytising . . . would be an enormous evil, and intolerable nuisance; and we are struck with equal astonishment at the folly and the assurance of the man who avows and publishes broadly to the world, a project so monstrously ridiculous!" One of the arguments was the purely factual one that the members of the Church of England were

[32] This was a pointed reference to the fact that John Strachan had begun his distinguished ecclesiastical career in the Church of Scotland and later turned to the Church of England, an act of apostasy which provoked considerable scorn among the Presbyterians. Charles Durand records one anecdote about Strachan: "He was dining a long time ago with a friend whose coat looked very seedy. 'Ah! my friend,' says Jock, 'shall I say—your coat is very shabby; why do you not look better?' 'Weel, Jock, I must tell ye, I ha' no' turned it yet.'" *Reminiscences* (Toronto, 1897), 225. Strachan's antagonist was supposed to have been the Rev. William "Father" Jenkins (1779–1843), an early Scottish missionary in Upper Canada connected with the United Secession Church of Scotland.

greatly outnumbered by other denominations and even by the "members of the Scottish Church, notwithstanding all letters, charts, pamphlets and circulars to the contrary." To exclude members of the Church of Scotland from the academic staff of King's College would be "a cruel wrong on a most meritorious people" and something of an anomaly as well, in view of the dominant role which Scotsmen had played in education in Canada. There was added an unkind comment on Strachan's career as a school teacher in his early days in Canada.[33]

Again, in the fifth issue of the *Canadian Miscellany*, dated August, 1828, Rae again turned his attention to the "exorbitant pretensions" of the Church of England, this time more specifically in connection with the Clergy Reserves. His contribution was entitled "Letter to the Honourable Mr. Stanley, on the Relative Claims of the England and Scotch Churches in the Canadas." Mr. Stanley was Edward George Geoffrey Smith Stanley (1799–1869), later to become the fourteenth Earl of Derby and three times Prime Minister of England. Stanley had replaced Wilmot-Horton as Under-Secretary for the Colonies in 1827 under Canning and continued in that capacity under Viscount Goderich until January, 1828. The original date of Rae's letter is not known, but it is likely that it was addressed to Stanley because of his official position. Apart from this Stanley was known personally to a number of the influential Presbyterians whom he had met during his visit to Montreal in 1824. He had also made it clear in speeches in the House of Commons that he believed the provisions of the Constitutional Act of 1791 relating to the establishment of the Church of England in Canada were absurd.[34]

Rae's epistolary essay, containing thirty-one printed pages excluding notes, was a remarkably eloquent statement of the claims of the Kirk. Because of its high literary quality and considerable historical interest the complete text is reproduced in Part III and the gist of it only needs to be given here.

Again Rae dwelt with glowing pride on the intelligence, industry, morality, and happiness of the people of Scotland as well as on their religion and religious instructors. He declaimed upon the inequity and ignominy of forcing Scotsmen to "wear the badge of inferiority and sub-

---

[33] "To Scotsmen education in this colony owes every thing. Its very Patriarchs and Apostles in Canada, of whom the Doctor might have claimed to himself the well merited honour of being the first in point of time, if not in point of merit, have been almost exclusively Scotch." This was a reference to the fact that Strachan was Master of the Eastern District School in Cornwall in the period 1804–12 and in the Home District School in what is now Toronto from 1812 to 1823. The implication that Strachan was not a highly competent school teacher does not seem to be justified.

[34] One of Stanley's statements on the subject was made on Feb. 20, 1827, and was reported in the *Montreal Gazette*, April 16, 1827.

jection" in Canada because of the machinations of the Church of England. His comments on the community of interest between Britain and Canada and its economic basis deserve special attention since they outline briefly views which he was later to deal with in much more detail:[35]

Britain, a great manufacturing and commercial nation, abounding in capital, redundant with population, finds her own welfare connected with that of a people, who take from her the products of her manufacturing industry, who offer an asylum to her superfluous population, and who supply her with the raw materials, which she cannot so easily raise within her immediate territories— We, again, may esteem the prosperity of the mother country our own, while that prosperity sends us the finished productions of human labour far more cheaply than we could manufacture them while it gives us in return, a market for the produce of our fields and forests, and while it sends capital to the country to enable us to call forth its abundant resources. While these circumstances in the relations of the two countries continue, and it is impossible for us to assign a time, when they shall cease, so long will it be for the benefit of both to remain under a common government. Capital will then flow more plentifully from the one country to the other, because it will flow far more securely; the commercial relations of the two countries will run no risk of being interrupted, and thence destroyed; and, above all, that lamentable but unavoidable jealousy of separate states, which leads to mutual seclusion and privation because one will not embrace a good, least it should prove a greater benefit to its rival, can have no place while we form a common people.

In speaking of the form of worship best calculated to promote prosperity, Rae again anticipated some of the ideas he was later to describe in more systematic form, saying, "The excellency of any religious system, considered merely as a means of promoting the prosperity of society, is chiefly to be estimated by its tendency to restrain offences against the laws, against the state, against morality" and went on to suggest that crime rates in Scotland compared very favourably with those in England.

The episcopal form of religious organization was not, Rae claimed, suited to Canada. The Church of England appealed mainly to those "of the higher orders," while the dissenters were concentrated "in the lower walks of life." Moreover, to preserve the Canadian attachment to Britain, it was desirable that the clergy should be primarily British, but it was clear that the clergy of the Church of England were reluctant to forsake the comforts and perquisites of home "to come to so distant and inhospitable a colony." The result was the recruitment of native Canadians and proselytes from other churches by the Church of England. He claimed that the Church of Scotland would be better able to provide a Canadian clergy, both domestic and imported.

Rae then went on to give a penetrating account of his reasons for believing that the Church of England would not suit adequately the

[35] See, for example, page v of the Preface to his *New Principles*.

conditions of Canadian society. He emphasized the importance of the division of society in Britain into disparate classes, headed by "a proud and powerful aristocracy," and contrasted this with conditions in Canada where Jack is as good as his master. "There is not," he wrote, "in truth, a prouder man than the Canadian farmer. He has no superior; he is not dependent on the assistance, scarcely on the co-operation, of a single individual." As a result of this, Rae felt that the principles and spirit of the Church of England were not suited to Canada. He granted that their clergy were men of curious and elegant learning, of polished manners and fine feelings, accomplishments which suited well enough the clerical patronage system in England but not the simple and egalitarian folkways in Canada. He quoted with effect Adam Smith's discourse on systems of morality contrasting the strict or austere and the liberal or loose system. On this question the Church of England, Rae emphasized, was at the head of the liberal or loose system and could not therefore find favour with the people. "I am, then, utterly astonished, how it could possibly be thought, by any one acquainted with the spirit of that church, and the character of the population of British extraction in Canada, that she is calculated to take firm root in the soil of this country." On other grounds, the involvement of the clergy in political life and the episcopal system of appointment of ministers, the Church of England would not do. He mentioned Strachan's political activities saying, "It has been universally reprobated, and has exacted the most unequivocal marks of public disapprobation and dislike."

On the other hand, Rae had no reservations on the ability of the Church of Scotland to flourish under colonial conditions. "This form of Christianity, so much more simple and less costly than that of Episcopacy, shows, by the condition of the people among whom it prevails, how well it is adapted for the diffusion of genuine religion, and the promotion of general happiness and peace. There can be no question that it is well suited to the state of society in Canada." He made it amply clear that he favoured state support of the church. The absence of any connection between church and state in the United States, Rae felt to be a mistake and a "defect in the constitution." His principal objections were the insecurity of tenure and the low incomes of the clergy and the fact that because the burden of maintenance often fell on the poorer classes, many of the people were without pastors altogether. Then in a remarkably prescient comment, he said:

Our North American neighbours, have, I believe, a greater sprinkling of fanaticism, and are somewhat less moral and less religious than if the ministers of religion had been connected with the state, and supported by it. They may shortly feel other evils arising from this defect in their constitution. That rivalry of interest and feeling, which every day is increasing, between the sections of their extended empire, must be met by a spirit of mutual forbearance and concession, or must ultimately terminate in the dissolution of the confederacy, and the conversion of that fair portion of the globe into a scene of commotion and bloodshed.

Rae's ultimate plea was for state support of both the Church of England and the Church of Scotland in Canada. He felt that the Clergy Reserves, amounting at that time to about 2,200,000 acres, would yield adequate revenues for the support of the Protestant clergy, if they were properly managed. He argued that the practice of leasing land in the Clergy Reserves for periods of only twenty-one years was unsuited to Canada and proposed that the leases should be extended to seventy, eighty, or a hundred years. He claimed that this would be more likely to induce settlers to make the heavy capital investment required in turning wild land into farms. He went on to suggest that it would be necessary to have only two Protestant clergymen in each township, of which 240 had been surveyed. When the settlers in a township agreed to provide £125 currency per year to support a clergyman, a fund derived from rentals of the lands in the Clergy Reserves should provide an equal amount. The total of £250 currency would, he claimed, be adequate. A substantial part of the burden would fall on the rent of land and Rae argued, along familiar lines, that this would be most advantageous. Rae's arithmetical calculations of anticipated revenues and outlays seem at once conservative and convincing.[36]

Rae's letter to Stanley was a temperate and carefully reasoned piece of special pleading. It illustrates clearly his acute powers of observation and his admirable literary ability. It is clear, too, that he had his blind side. Whatever might have been his personal convictions and those of his fellow members of the Kirk, it is difficult to understand how he visualized the long-run settlement of the issue of denominational rivalry and the Clergy Reserves without provision for the large number of Methodists in Upper Canada. Perhaps Rae shared the attitude of the English country squire described by Sydney Smith whose immediate impulse on hearing of a dissenter was "to commit it to the county jail, to shave its head, to alter its customary food, and to have it privately whipped."

Years later in a note written about 1858 to some unknown correspondent in Hawaii, Rae commented on this controversy:

[36] Dr. Craufurd Goodwin has called to my attention the similarity of some of Rae's ideas on the disposition of the Clergy Reserves with those in Robert Gourlay's *Statistical Account of Upper Canada, Compiled with a View to a Grand System of Emigration* (London, 1822), and those expressed later by Edward Gibbon Wakefield. See Craufurd D. W. Goodwin, *Canadian Economic Thought: The Political Economy of a Developing Nation, 1814–1914* (Durham, N. C., and London, 1961), 6–30,

No paper formalities ever effectually resist the onward march of events. We had proof of that in Canada. One-eighth of the lands there were deeded with all the most binding formalities that the best lawyers could devise to the English Church. Yet all these lands have been taken from it. Thirty years since I ventured to predict to that Church that this and its other exorbitant pretensions would not stand. They were against the natural order of things, and they implied an injustice, viz., the putting Scotchmen in an inferior position to Englishmen. I was laughed at. Not a lawyer of any eminence but gave it hollow against us, insomuch that when we determined to make it a national question, and to lay a solemn protest against the whole thing before the British Parliament on constitutional grounds, I who am no lawyer was intrusted with the drawing up of that paper. It produced warm debates in both Houses, was on motion of the Duke of Wellington referred to the twelve English judges, who to their honor gave it in our favor.[37]

This comment would suggest that Rae also may have drafted the shorter and more formal petition from the Presbyterians in the Canadas dated December 20, 1827. The "solemn protest" which Rae refers to is not an accurate description of his letter to Stanley, especially since it was not laid "before the British Parliament," nor did it apparently go through official channels.

It is difficult to assess the impact of Rae's long letter, although it appeared to be pleasing to the Presbyterians. Dr. James Harkness, in writing to the Rev. John Mackenzie, the minister of the kirk in Williamstown, made the following comment: "I gave Sir James [Kempt][38] Mr. Rae's letter,—it is certainly an excellent one & has been much praised by our Quebec friends. I beg you will offer my best respect to him, & assure him that I was delighted with it & that I feel grateful for his attention in sending me a copy. I hope it may lead to something to his advantage."[39]

In November, 1831, Rae left Williamstown for Montreal, evidently feeling that the time was ripe for him to present to the world the results of his ten years of study and reflection. He wrote to Alexander Fraser,[40] the member for Glengarry in the Upper Canada House of Assembly, resigning his office of coroner and remarking, "You are I believe aware

[37] *Sociological Theory of Capital*, xxiv–xxv. In mentioning the deeding of land to the Church of England, Rae was probably referring to the Clergy Reserves Corporation, a "Corporation for superintending, managing and conducting the Clergy Reserves of Canada" which had been legally established on July 4, 1820, and empowered to grant leases on land in the Clergy Reserves for periods not to exceed twenty-one years. The head of this corporation was the Anglican Bishop of Quebec and its directors were dignitaries of the Church of England in Upper Canada.

[38] Lieutenant-General Sir James Kempt had been appointed Governor-in-Chief of Upper and Lower Canada on Aug. 14, 1828.

[39] P.A.C., McGillivray Papers, VII, 165; letter, James Harkness to John Mackenzie, Feb. 1, 1829.

[40] P.A.C., Upper Canada Sundries; letter, John Rae to Alexander Fraser, Nov. 24, 1831.

that I have engaged in an undertaking which will prevent me from continuing to reside for any length of time in the Eastern District." He went
on to ask Fraser to inform him "how long the present session is likely to
continue as I wish to visit York [Toronto] ere it closes."[41]

Rae had doubtless visited Montreal many times in the 1820's and had
acquired a circle of influential friends. He had identified himself clearly as
a spokesman for the Kirk in the disputes with the Church of England and
as a result of personal association and intellectual conviction had developed
strongly held views on the problems of economic development in Canada.
Certainly the bitter political and economic controversies which bedevilled
Montreal in this period could not help but be an important influence in
shaping Rae's ideas.

[41] Alexander Fraser (1776–1853) of Fraserfield had been Quartermaster of the Cana-
dian Fencibles during the War of 1812. He became Colonel of the First Regiment,
Glengarry Militia, in 1822 and was Lieutenant-Colonel in command of the Williams-
town Glengarry Highlanders serving under the command of Sir John Colborne in
Lower Canada during the Rebellion of 1837–38. He was elected to the 10th Parliament of
Upper Canada in the election of August, 1828, and continued to represent Glengarry
until 1834. He served as Legislative Councillor (1838–53), Warden of the United
Counties of Dundas, Stormont and Glengarry (1841–49), and Registrar of Glengarry
County (1841–53).

3

Rae's Examination of the State of Canada

(1831–1834)

In Rae's letter to Alex Fraser resigning his position as one of the coroners of the Eastern District he did not elaborate on his future plans, but the reason for his proposed visit to the capital of Upper Canada is clear. It was related to an ambitious study which Rae had undertaken of the resources of the province. The object was to provide prospective settlers with accurate and useful information about the different areas of Upper Canada. The purpose of Rae's visit to York (Toronto) was to collect certain official statistical data and to obtain assistance in financing his investigations of the geology and economic prospects of Upper Canada. The nature of his endeavours is revealed in the petition which Rae addressed to the Lieutenant-Governor of Upper Canada, Sir John Colborne, asking for a grant of money to finance additional travel and research. On January 18, 1832, the petition was sent to the House of Assembly by Colborne who recommended it "to the favorable consideration of the House." The text of Rae's request shows clearly his concern with the problems of resource development:

The Memorial of John Rae, A.M. Fellow of the Royal Medical Society, Edinburgh—

HUMBLY SHEWETH,
   That Your Memorialist has for a considerable time been engaged in collecting information for a work which is intended to give the public an accurate account of the present state and resources of this Province.—That from the great extent and recent settlement of Upper Canada, it is yet imperfectly known.—That

though many publications have issued from the Press on the subject, they have in general been the work of individuals but partially acquainted with the Country; and that there is not, at present, any work comprising an account of the Province which can be referred to with confidence, by one desirous of obtaining information concerning the whole or any part of it.—That from the want of such information, erroneous ideas concerning the Colony prevail—its resources are not known— Settlers of capital are deterred from emigrating to it, or having emigrated—are at much unnecessary expense and loss of time in searching for suitable situations, and often, place themselves in parts of the country not well adapted to their means and abilities.

That Your Excellency will be able partly to judge how far the work which your Memorialist meditates is calculated to supply this want from the following detail of what it is intended to comprehend.

That Your Memorialist means to describe the leading features in the Geological Structure of the Country, from whence the nature and peculiarities of the soil in the different sections of it may, with most certainty, be deduced. The peculiarities of the climate and their causes. The state of agriculture over the Province, and the effects which increased experience, and capital, applied to its pursuits may be expected to produce. The state of the Country as to health and disease, and the complaints most prevalent—Constitution and Institutions of the Colony—each District, its Rivers and Lakes, what is peculiar to its soil, and what interesting mineralogical productions it may possess—sorts of timber that prevail in it, peculiarities in its system of agriculture, when settled, and from whence the population chiefly derived—its Towns and Villages and Population of each—tabular view of the different Townships in it—quantity of land in each —what quantity cleared,—quantity uncleared—by persons residing in the Township—quantity uncleared, held by persons not residing in the Township— quantity, if any, ungranted—quantity of land and sort of timber—prices of wild land of first quality—population, produce, and various other statistical details.

Further, Your Memorialist begs leave to state, that he has already expended considerable time and money in his researches, that he has travelled over a great part of the Province collecting information on the subject, and that in prosecution of his designs he intends visiting many other parts of it, and will thus be put to still further cost and labor. That in particular he is desirous of exploring some parts of that region of country extending from the north-east part of Lake Huron to the rear of the Midland District. That he is led to believe that the mineralogical and geological details of this region are very interesting, and that there is a probability of valuable minerals being there to be found.—That there is another tract of country lying between Notawasaga Bay and the part of Lake Huron to the north of the Canada Company's Tract, which he is desirous also of exploring, from similar reasons.—That these parts not being settled, they cannot be traversed without considerable expense.

That as the success of the labors of Your Memorialist would have a tendency to develope the resources of the country, and still further to direct public attention towards it, he would presume to hope they are in some measure worthy of the support and countenance of Your Excellency.

Your Memorialist, therefore, prays that Your Excellency will be pleased to take the subject of his Memorial into favourable consideration, and submit the same to the Legislature, with a view to obtain public aid in furtherence of the important objects in which he has engaged.

And your memorialist, &c.[1]

Rae's request for government aid was referred to the Committee on Supply, but no grant was made. This was perhaps not unnatural in view of the preoccupation of the House of Assembly with more contentious matters. At this particular time, the legislature in Upper Canada was absorbed in internal disputes which were symptomatic of the general political unrest in both Upper and Lower Canada.

In the course of his study of the economic development of Canada, Rae had become convinced that the maintenance of close political and economic ties with Great Britain would be mutually beneficial, a view which had been called into question on somewhat abstract grounds in England and more violently by dissident elements in Canada. He had already described eloquently in his "Letter to the Honourable Mr. Stanley . . ." in 1828 the economic benefits of these ties, a theme which recurred many times in his writings. In 1832 and 1833 Rae became involved in a vigorous literary campaign, consisting of a series of letters to the editor of the *Montreal Gazette* in which he belaboured successively the anti-British campaign of the *Patriotes*, the opposition to immigration, and the educational policy of Lower Canada.

At this time Rae was living in Godmanchester, a village in the township of Godmanchester then bounded on the south by the Trout and the Chateauguay rivers and on the north by the St. Lawrence. Although it was not far from Montreal, he describes it as "this remote and unfrequented corner of the Province." What led him to this locality is not explained. Mixter says in one place that Rae was engaged "in the lumber trade" for a period and there is a possibility that he may have been employed there in some capacity.[2] Certainly Godmanchester was a busy lumbering area and enormous quantities of pine and oak were cut on the Chateauguay in this period.

It is of interest to note that the township of Godmanchester contains the Canadian part of the St. Regis Indian reserve. A band of Catholic Iroquois from Caughnawaga settled on the south bank of the St. Lawrence about 1755, unwittingly straddling the border between Canada and the United States. Many of Rae's comments on the life and customs of the North American Indians in his *New Principles* were based on his personal observations of the St. Regis settlement, to which he specifically refers.[3]

[1] Upper Canada, *Journals of the Legislative Assembly*, 2nd Session, 11th Parliament, 2 Wm. IV, 100.

[2] *Sociological Theory of Capital*, xxii.

[3] *New Principles*, 136.

Whatever Rae was doing in this backwoods, this was a remarkably productive period in his life and he apparently kept in close touch with the developing crisis in political affairs. The first of his letters to the *Montreal Gazette* which appeared in December, 1832, was entitled "Loyal Address to the King" and arose out of the proceedings of an anti-*Patriote* indignation meeting in Montreal. This meeting of about 500 persons, described as both "numerous and intelligent," took place at the British American Hotel on November 4, 1832, with Horatio Gates as chairman.[4] It was resolved to present an address to the King to counteract the dangerous and subversive designs of the "ill-intended and disaffected." In general terms, the meeting approved of the government, the constitution of the province, and the continued appointment of the legislative council, and was fearful that actions of the "factious and designing men" would engender a degree of political excitement which would seriously damage commercial relations with Great Britain and Canada's sister colonies. The penultimate resolution summarized these attitudes:

That the measures pursued by disaffected persons, now disturbing this community, tend to estrange the affections of the people of this country from his Majesty, to weaken their adherence to his government, and to excite animosity against their fellow subjects from the mother country and the sister colonies. This meeting considers the time to have arrived, when it is the bounden duty of every well disposed subject of his Majesty, in these provinces, to declare openly his unalterable attachment to the government, his unimpaired confidence in the administration of the laws, his full reliance on the protection of the mother country, and his determination to maintain her sovereignty over this portion of the empire.

Having seen the petition, Rae entered the controversy with a forceful letter to the editor of the *Montreal Gazette* which was printed on December 24, 1832.[5] His letter, which was headed "Loyal Address to the King," had a curiously violent quality and shows clearly that Rae had a passionate and deep-rooted aversion to the politicians and others who would impair or destroy the ties between Canada and Britain. He inveighed against the "gross misrepresentations, infamous falsehoods and horrid blasphemies" of the anti-British faction and made it explicitly clear that their revolutionary tendencies might have to be put down by force. The history of the French Revolution was fresh in his mind and he declaimed, "The banners of imperial justice must be displayed, else in a short time will the reign of terror be attempted in Canada, and red ruin ride triumphantly." It would be inaccurate to suggest that Rae's letter was scurrilous in view

[4] An excerpt from the *Montreal Gazette*, Nov. 6, 1832, describing the meeting is contained in Christie, *History of the Late Province of Lower Canada*, III, 416–17.
[5] The text is given in item 4 of Part III of this volume.

of its literary quality, but it did demonstrate his bitter revulsion against what he called "the headlong and destructive course pursued by the Canadian agitators."

Apart from the general lack of sympathy between the merchant class and the French-Canadian faction, there were of course specific issues and events which generated bitterness and scurrility. One of these was the question of immigration. Almost every aspect of immigration to Canada in the 1820's and 1830's provided grounds for rancorous disagreement. The most obvious source of grievance from the French point of view was the high level of immigration around 1830. These alien arrivals seemed to them to threaten their whole way of life and their birthright—the land. The accompanying table showing immigration to Canada in the period 1819–1833 gives a statistical basis for their concern.[6] A large but unknown

IMMIGRATION TO CANADA, 1819–33

1819	12,907	1827	16,862
1820	11,239	1828	11,697
1821	8,050	1829	13,357
1822	10,468	1830	24,391
1823	10,258	1831	49,259
1824	6,515	1832	51,422
1825	9,097	1833	22,062
1826	10,731		

number of these arrivals were destined for the United States but this could hardly alleviate the worries of the French. A clear statement of their alarm was contained in the following two resolutions arising out of a protest meeting in the village of Debartzch, parish of St. George, on July 30, 1832:

That whatever may be the views of Great Britain, in causing a considerable number of her excess population to be transported to her North American colonies, it is always certain that these excessive emigrations are dangerous and expensive, especially for the colonies where these emigrants disembark, who often bring there nothing but their ills, the extreme of indigence, and pestilential diseases, necessitating the support of the provincial treasury, and the commiseration of charitable persons; which becomes, as regards this country, an indirect tax imposed by Great Britain.

That England will, in any case, have to justify herself for having suffered so considerable an emigration, at a time when she was under the frightful influence of the cholera, which by this means has been introduced into this colony, the climate which is the most healthy in all America, and has covered it with mourning and desolation.[7]

This last resolution referred to the catastrophic outbreak of cholera in

[6] Christie, *History of the Late Province of Lower Canada*, III, 512.
[7] *Ibid.*, 413–14.

1832. In June, 1832, there was an outbreak in Montreal of the Asiatic cholera, sometimes called Indian, malignant, or spasmodic cholera, an extremely deadly human disease. Within two weeks, 3,300 inhabitants of Montreal had been stricken and 900 were dead. Medical treatment was inadequate or foolish and many of the people were in a state of panic. Barrels of tar were burned at street corners to purify the air and the sewers were opened to dissipate the dreaded miasma. By the fall of 1832 the disease had run its course, causing 1,900 fatalities in Montreal alone. In the meantime, it had quickly spread into the settlements along the St. Lawrence and into the back concessions of Upper and Lower Canada, leaving death and misery in its wake. The people did not understand the etiology of cholera but they were well aware of the undeniable fact that it had been brought to Canada in the immigrant ships. If proof of the wicked folly of unlimited immigration were needed, the continuous tolling of the death bells in Montreal would serve.

The fact that many immigrants arrived in a state of poverty and ill health was recognized by the Colonial Office which in February, 1832, instructed Lord Aylmer, the Governor-in-Chief, to recommend to the House of Assembly in Lower Canada a tax on immigrants.[8] The tax, recommended not to exceed one dollar per head, was to be collected from the captains of the ships bringing the immigrants from the United Kingdom and was to constitute a fund to provide for the medical care and travel costs of indigent immigrants. The merchants of Montreal and a large body of opinion in Upper Canada regarded such taxation as discriminatory and economically unsound. In general, the whole subject excited passion and bitterness on both sides.

It was natural that John Rae should be intimately concerned with the whole question of immigration and he undertook to enlighten its opponents in a polemical letter dated early in 1833 to the editor of the *Montreal Gazette* headed "The Opposition to Emigration."[9] Rae had two main targets in this letter, the anti-British faction and William Evans.[10] Evans, writing in the *New Montreal Gazette*,[11] had been injudicious enough to include

---

[8] *Ibid.*, 383.

[9] *Montreal Gazette*, Jan. 19, 1833. The text is given in item 5 of Part III of this volume.

[10] William Evans (1786–1857) was a native of Ireland who emigrated to Montreal in 1819 and was an early exponent of improved farming methods in Canada. He was the secretary of the first agricultural society in Montreal and in 1838 founded the *Canadian Quarterly Agricultural and Industrial Magazine* which ceased publication not long after. In 1843 he founded the *Canadian Agricultural Journal*, which he edited until his death. In 1853, he became secretary and treasurer of the Board of Agriculture for Lower Canada. He was also the author of a number of books on the theory and practice of farming.

[11] Founded in 1827, not to be confused with the *Montreal Gazette*.

some good physiocratic doctrine to the effect that the origin of wealth was in the earth. Rae commented on this unkindly and at length. On Evans' main point, Rae remarked "that labour, whether morally or physically considered, constitutes wealth is a principle which has been long established by the most irrefragable arguments."

His ridicule was not very gentle. He wrote:

If the land constituted wealth, then must Canada before the conquest have been the richest country upon earth when each *enfant du sol* owned his hundreds of acres of forest land, could sit in security and peace under his own butter-nut tree smoking his eternal calumet, when ignorance of the happier lot of others made him entirely satisfied with the comparative wretchedness of his own, and when no cares intervened to disturb the tranquility of his repose but the trouble of wheeling the produce of his stable and barnyard into the waters of the St. Lawrence.

Rae's general theme, which he illustrated by a number of historical examples, was that the prosperity of a country was increased in proportion to the growth of its industrious population. He indicated considerable contempt for the anti-British group and for the agricultural practices of the French-Canadian farmer, and some prejudice in favour of British immigrants, saying:

Even the pauper population of England must be a blessing to Canada, whatever Mr. Evans may advance to the contrary. Indeed, so thoroughly convinced am I, that the prosperity of Lower Canada depends upon continued emigration, that I have no hesitation in saying, I consider it would be for her interest to receive a yearly importation of 20,000 emigrants, did they even come with nothing to cover their nakedness but the clothes upon their backs. They bring with them the bone and muscle, the power of knowledge and the rectitude of principle which would render them a blessing to any state, but especially to so poor and thinly inhabited a country as this.

Evans was not content to let the matter rest and wrote a letter to the editor of the Montreal *Herald* sometime in January, 1833, defending his position. No copy of Evans' letter can be located, but in the *Montreal Gazette* of February 26, 1833, Rae wrote a rejoinder, in which he proceeded to demolish Evans' views *seriatim*.[12]

Altogether, Evans appears to have been beyond his depth. Rae's diatribe would perhaps not have been so severe, if Evans had not provided some support for the anti-British faction, perhaps unwittingly. The public controversy between Evans and Rae seems to have subsided and Rae turned his attention to other matters, particularly the question of elementary education in Lower Canada.

In order to explain Rae's involvement in the embittered educational

[12] The text of Rae's letter headed "Emigration—Mr. Evans' Letter," is given in item 6 of Part III of this volume.

controversies in Lower Canada of the 1820's and 1830's, it is essential to sketch briefly the outlines of the problem. An early and significant development was the statement made in 1800 by the Governor-in-Chief "that his Majesty, [George III] from his paternal regard for the welfare and prosperity of his subjects of this colony, has been graciously pleased to give directions for the establishing of a competent number of free schools, for the instruction of their children in the first rudiments of useful learning, and in the English tongue, and also, as occasion may require, for foundations of a more enlarged and comprehensive nature . . ."[13] Accordingly, in 1801, "An act for the establishment of free schools and the advancement of learning in the province" was passed.[14] This Act authorized the establishment of a corporation to be known as "The Royal Institution for the Advancement of Learning," the trustees of which were to be appointed by the Governor. This corporation was to be responsible for the management of educational institutions of royal foundation and of any property set aside to support them. Rules and regulations for the schools were to be drawn up by the trustees and were subject to review by the Governor. The Governor could establish one or more free schools in each parish when desired by the inhabitants and appoint and pay the teachers. The inhabitants were to share the cost of building school houses which were to be turned over to the corporation. However, no land was set aside and nothing of consequence happened until 1818 when letters patent were issued to the Royal Institution for the Advancement of Learning. The Anglican Bishop of Quebec was named principal and a number of additional trustees were appointed. The Royal Institution took over the supervision of all government-supported schools but its success in increasing the number of schools was negligible. In fact, its whole history was a dismal story of popular distrust and antipathy. This stemmed from its British and Protestant character which doomed it in a community predominantly French and Roman Catholic. The Royal Institution was boycotted by the people and vehemently attacked in the House of Assembly. Various legislative expedients were tried in the period 1818–29 to modify the educational system but nothing very effective was done until 1829 when a new bill was passed with the object of providing urgently needed educational opportunities to the French-Canadian population.[15] One report of a committee of the House of Assembly pointed out that in many parishes only five or six people could write at all, and that in the general population 75 per cent

[13] Sir C. P. Lucas, ed., *Lord Durham's Report on the Affairs of British North America* (Oxford, 1912), III, 245.
[14] 41 Geo. III, c. 17.
[15] 9 Geo. IV, c. 46.

could not read and 90 per cent could not write. The essential features of the Act of 1829 were: to assign the responsibility for the management of schools in the parishes and townships to boards of five trustees to be elected by the voting residents; to provide for government assistance to school construction with a maximum of £25 per school; and to fix the remuneration of the schoolmasters. Their annual salary was set at the princely sum of £20 so long as there were twenty pupils with an additional allowance of 10s each for poor children provided there were at least twenty of them. The trustees were to report annually to the House of Assembly and the legislation was to expire in May, 1832.

There were some minor modifications to the Act of 1829 in 1830 and 1831, including the establishment of a system of visitors, but the main legislative action was the creation of a standing committee on education in 1831. The committee sounded its first warning in 1831 by referring to "the abuses and corruption which uniformly attend the lavish expenditure of public money." It went on to say:

Education itself suffers in the estimation of the public; false ideas are spread abroad among the people, that education is rather an object which concerns the community than themselves individually, and it is undervalued, while in reality it is become nearly as needful in the present state of things in this province as religious instruction, or instruction in the means of gaining an honest livelihood, for which it is the bounden duty of every head of a family to provide to the utmost of his power. To draw the money from the people by taxes, to be restored to them for these purposes, after undergoing all the diminution of the expenses of collection, management and waste, would soon impoverish them without effecting the object in view.[16]

In 1832, the committee returned to this theme and emphasized the need for diminished reliance on government funds and increased local responsibility. It was on the basis of this report that the Act of 1832 was passed.[17] It provided for 1,321 school districts and an annual allowance of £20 for the teacher provided that a fee of not more than two shillings per month was required from each pupil. At least twenty scholars, between the ages of five and fifteen, had to be in attendance for 190 days in the school year. The teacher, to qualify for appointment, had to produce a certificate that he was "of good character" and was capable of teaching reading, writing, and arithmetic. The visitors for the schools were to be the legislative councillors living in the county and the county representative in the House of Assembly as well as other dignitaries. The schools operating under the aegis of the Royal Institution for the Advancement of Learning were also to be covered by the Act of 1832.

[16] Lucas, ed., *Lord Durham's Report*, III, 252–3.   [17] 2 Wm. IV, c. 26.

The passage of this Act provoked a vigorous attack on its main provisions by John Rae. This took the form of a letter dated February 25, 1833, to the editor of the *Montreal Gazette* headed "Remarks on the Education Bill."[18] Rae was scornful of the provision limiting the benefits of the Act to children between the ages of five and fifteen years. His feeling was that the receptivity of children to learning did not reach its maximum until after the age of fifteen and yet it was the "wicked intent" of the Act to deprive them of further educational opportunity. He went on to say:

in their rage for legislation, they might have taken a leaf out of the History of Iceland, a history which should cover every *enfan du sol* with shame and confusion, and have declared that the Clergy should have the power of preventing any marriage, where the woman was unable to read: they might have gone a step farther, and in place of voting away the public money, to reward one or two of their especial favourites for the silly books they have published, have imitated the same interesting people, when, about one hundred and thirty years ago, they ordered a man to be whipped for the errors he had committed in a translation of the book of Genesis.

He was particularly incensed by the section of the Act requiring a teacher to obtain a certificate that "he is known as a person of sober life and conversation, and has been examined and found qualified to teach reading, writing and arithmetic." Rae's comments, in part, are:

All . . . that is required of a teacher is that he be acquainted with reading, writing, and arithmetic, and that he do not drink or swear. It is not necessary that he should have had experience in the difficult art of teaching, that he be skilled in the workings of the human mind, that he be a man of patient and industrious habits, and above all, that his moral character stand fair and unspotted in the world. None of all these things is requisite, and hence it would be no difficult matter to fill up every school in Lower Canada, with teachers taken from the labourers employed on the canals, and other public works now in progress throughout the country. Who but a fool would engage a man to build him a house, without enquiring whether or not he was a good mechanic, and who but a scoundrel would engage a person, with the information of a ploughboy or a coalheaver, to conduct the education of his child, to form his character and habits, and to lead him, by example of his own life, and the beautiful precepts of morality with which he inclines his youthful mind to entertain an abhorrence of vice, and an admiration of virtue.

Rae's indignation was again stimulated by the meagre remuneration of schoolteachers proposed in the Act. He estimated that the average number of pupils attending the schools would be twenty and on this basis concluded that the annual earnings of a teacher would be three-fourths those of a common labourer and three-tenths those of an ordinary artisan such as

[18] *Montreal Gazette*, March 19, 1833. The complete text is given in item 7 of Part III of this volume.

a carpenter. But the picture he paints if the number of pupils falls below the quota and the parliamentary allowance denied is black indeed:

The bright visions of temporary wealth, which for many a long month had floated before his [the schoolmaster's] fancy, and cheered him amid the arduous duties of his thankless office, is suddenly withdrawn from before him, the debts he has been compelled to contract, now press heavily upon him, and the merciless creditors, whom he is unable to satisfy, either forcibly possess themselves of his meagre library and scanty wardrobe, or give him leisure ere long to reflect amid the darkness and gloom of a prison, upon the unprincipled laws by which he has been led to devote his time and talents to obtain a pallet of straw in jail, and to become a beacon to all others of the danger there is in attempting to counteract the ambitious projects of the dominant faction, by instructing or enlightening the inhabitants of Lower Canada. . . . Men generally expect to be rewarded for the exertion of their talents, and accordingly it happens, that as the profits arising from the cultivation of any branch of industry are great, the numbers of clever men who follow it is great also. When a nation is litigious there is no lack of lawyers; when it is bilious or hypochondriacal, there is no scarcity of physicians; when it is ignorant and superstitious, there is no dearth of ghostly advisers; and when it is determined to be enlightened and free, men of learning and worth will readily present themselves as candidates for the honors and rewards, which are to be obtained by the education of youth and the diffusion of knowledge.

Rae, of course, was not alone in his strictures on the educational system of Lower Canada, although every critic did not rise to his level of poetic prose. Arthur Buller, having been appointed a commissioner of inquiry into the state of education in Lower Canada in connection with Lord Durham's famous investigation of Canadian affairs, reported in 1838 and echoes some of Rae's earlier views as well as some of his vehemence:

The system patched up at different times by the Assembly, into what was called the elementary school system, was not merely a vicious and imperfect one, but of late years, especially, pernicious in the extreme. It is obvious that it was mainly recommended to that body by its vast utility as a political machine.[19]

Buller went on to say:

Can it excite wonder that this combination of imperfections and vices should have produced no good result?—that education should have languished under systems, where the masters were illiterate and needy; the supervision careless and dishonest; the school-houses unfit for occupation, and ill-supplied with fuel; the children unprovided with books; and parents utterly indifferent to an institution of which they could not appreciate the importance, and the trouble and cost of which, at all events, they deemed the province of the legislature?[20]

During this period of letter writing Rae was busy with the preparation of his book on political economy. A version of it was completed by July,

[19] Lucas, ed., *Lord Durham's Report*, III, 262.
[20] *Ibid.*, 265.

1833, by which time Rae had evidently moved from Godmanchester to Montreal.

Initially, Rae's intention had been to publish his book in England, but his plans changed for obscure reasons. He was then advised to investigate the possibility of publishing it in Boston and with this in mind spent the early part of 1834 in that place. His plans were discussed with "some gentlemen" in Boston and with their encouragement a somewhat revised version was issued, probably in the early summer of 1834. This whole episode is dealt with in more detail in chapter 10, Part II, and it is necessary only to make passing reference to it in this place.

Rae's book, far from bringing him the acclaim and financial rewards he must have hoped for, was in general not well received. He was deeply disappointed by its reception, and having failed to establish a literary reputation was faced with the necessity of earning a living in a more prosaic fashion. Thus it was that he again turned to teaching school in 1834, this time in Hamilton, a small village in what was then Upper Canada.

4

A Village Teacher in Hamilton

(1834–1848)

John Rae was the headmaster of a district or grammar school in Hamilton, Ontario, in the period from 1834 until 1848. In order to make clear the nature of this position and some of the difficulties which plagued the evolving educational system of Ontario, it is essential to review briefly the historical background.

The grammar school system in Upper Canada was conceived by John Graves Simcoe, whose views on education were influenced by his own experiences at Eton and Oxford. Simcoe was partly motivated by a desire to foster a native aristocracy which would be immune to the blandishments of republicanism and democracy. If the schools in Upper Canada were inadequate, the children of wealthy parents would be sent to the United States to be educated, something which might lead to the dilution of British traditions. Simcoe's appeals to the Colonial Secretary for approval of an educational grant were supplemented by a joint address to the King from the legislature of Upper Canada in 1797.[1] The petition was granted and late in 1797 authorization was given to set aside about 500,000 acres of waste lands of the Crown for the endowment of grammar schools and at some appropriate future time for "other seminaries of a larger and more comprehensive nature."[2] Initial progress was slow but educational

[1] J. George Hodgins, *Documentary History of Education in Upper Canada from the Passing of the Constitutional Act of 1791 to the Close of Rev. Dr. Ryerson's Administration of the Education Department in 1876* (Toronto, 1894), I, 16. Hereafter this work will be cited as Hodgins, *Documentary History*.
[2] *Ibid.*

prospects improved with the passage of the Grammar School Act in 1807.[3] This Act authorized the establishment of a district school in each of the eight districts of Upper Canada and provided £100 a year for the salary of each teacher. The Lieutenant-Governor was to appoint at least five trustees in each district who were to be responsible for the management of the schools and the appointment of a teacher, subject to the concurrence of the Lieutenant-Governor. The following paragraph of the Grammar School Act of 1807 shows that the powers of the trustees were broad and not subject to any significant decree of centralized control:

The Trustees appointed under and by virtue of this Act, in each and every District of this Province, or a majority of them, shall have full power and authority to make such Rules and Regulations for the good government and management of the said Public (Grammar) schools with respect to the Teacher, for the time being, and to the Scholars, as, in their discretion, shall seem meet.[4]

The grant of £100 a year to each school was not enough to pay the costs of the schools, and tuition fees were charged to supplement the teacher's salary and to pay other expenses. Any of the children who came from out of town to attend the district schools incurred additional expenses for their board, which was often provided by the schoolmaster. Under these circumstances, education in the district schools was usually available only to the sons of relatively prosperous families.

The district schools quickly assumed a sectarian character, a fact which can be partially attributed to the pervasive influence of John Strachan. Strachan opened a private school in Cornwall in 1803 which became the Eastern District School in 1807. He showed marked abilities as a teacher and his success at Cornwall was repeated when he went to York in 1812 to take over the Home District School. Even before he became an honorary member of the Executive Council in 1813, it appears that Strachan was an unofficial adviser to the Lieutenant-Governor on educational matters. Indeed, it is claimed by Alexander Neil Bethune that Strachan was mainly responsible for the Grammar School Act of 1807.[5] After he became a full member of the Executive Council in 1817 and a member of the Legislative Council in 1820, he exerted a very powerful influence over educational affairs and particularly over the district schools. Strachan conceived of these schools as a preserve of the Church of England, an idea which was consistent with his general views on religious establishment. In one of his letters Strachan wrote:

[3] 47 Geo. III, c. 6.
[4] *Ibid.*, para. 5.
[5] A. N. Bethune, *Memoir of the Right Reverend John Strachan* (Toronto, 1870), 105.

The true foundation of the prosperity of our Establishment must be laid in the Education of Youth, the Command and direction of which must as far as possible be concentrated in our Clergy. This has hitherto been the silent policy of all the measures taken for the Education of the Youth adopted in this Province . . .[6]

In England in the early nineteenth century appointments of grammar school masters were in most cases ecclesiastical preferments. In addition, the great English public schools which served as an inspiration for their aspiring colonial counterparts were dominated by the clergy. In Upper Canada, however, the prevalence of the clergy of the Church of England as headmasters of the district schools and the resultant quality of the religious instruction was the cause of frequent and partisan disputes over a long period.[7] Moreover, since the cost of sending children to district schools was prohibitive for most families, there was no broad base of popular support for the institution. The grammar schools were mainly intended for boys destined to enter the professions or the civil service.

The agitation against the exclusive character of the district schools and the clear need for improved facilities for elementary education led to the passage of the Common School Act of 1816.[8] Under its terms, any group of persons who would undertake to provide a schoolhouse, at least twenty pupils, and part of the teacher's salary were eligible for a share in a government grant for common school education, originally amounting to £6000. The participating householders were to select three trustees to be responsible for appointing a teacher and making annual reports to the boards of education which were to be set up in each district. While there were a relatively large number of common schools, their educational standards and facilities were often deplorably poor and very much inferior to the district schools, as a general rule.[9]

A further concession to the critics of the district schools was made in the Grammar School Amendment Act of 1819.[10] This Act required the

[6] G. W. Spragge, ed., *The John Strachan Letter Book, 1822–1834* (Toronto, 1946), 212.

[7] The Rev. S. J. Mountain, the minister of the Church of England in Cornwall, wrote two impassioned letters to the private secretary of the Lieutenant-Governor on December 21 and 28, 1826, protesting against the proposal of the other trustees of the Eastern District School to appoint a minister of the Church of Scotland (the Rev. Hugh Urquhart) as headmaster. Mountain wrote: "A great advantage has been lost, a great injury done to the interest of our Church in this place, by his appointment . . ." He went on to say: "These things I have represented to the Lord Bishop of Quebec, and I flatter myself with the hope that the School will be solicited for a member of our Church." The Bishop of Quebec was Mountain's uncle. P.A.C., Education Papers, Upper Canada, nos. 93 and 95.

[8] 56 Geo. III, c. 36.

[9] In 1829, there were 372 pupils enrolled at grammar schools in Upper Canada compared to 10,712 in the common schools, according to John Strachan. This ratio probably did not vary much during the 1820's. Hodgins, *Documentary History*, I, 265.

[10] 59 Geo. III, c. 4.

trustees in each district to hold an annual public examination and to submit periodic reports to the Lieutenant-Governor on the condition of their schools. In part, this was a recognition of the excessive local autonomy granted by the Grammar School Act of 1807 and was a step in the direction of limited centralized regulation. The Grammar School Amendment Act of 1819 also provided for the free education of ten children in each district who were to be selected by lot from promising pupils recommended by the trustees of the common schools. It appears, however, that this was merely a gesture in the direction of a more democratic educational system and that the scheme was never put into effect.

A further step towards centralized control was taken in 1823 when, after consultation with the Colonial Secretary,[11] the Lieutenant-Governor, Sir Peregrine Maitland, appointed a General Board for the Superintendence of Education. This Board was to exercise general supervision over common and grammar schools in Upper Canada and was to be responsible for the administration of school lands and funds. Strachan was appointed President of the General Board and in this capacity was able to exercise increased authority in educational affairs. The General Board was created without reference to the Legislative Assembly and because it appeared to be an autocratic instrument was an object of continual political attack.[12]

The power of the General Board for the Superintendence of Education was repeatedly challenged in the Legislative Assembly in the 1820's, mainly because it was a symbol of high-handed executive action. The fact that John Strachan was President of the Board and that the other members were drawn from the official clique did not diminish the hostile criticism.[13] Finally, in 1832, the Board was disbanded at the suggestion of the Colonial Secretary who recognized it as a bone of contention.[14]

Its dissolution did not significantly alter the control over grammar school education since some of the basic powers of the Board were absorbed by the Council of King's College. The Council, under Strachan's chairmanship, was given the responsibility for administering all endowed school lands and was thus in a strategic position to influence the management of the grammar schools. Strachan looked on the grammar schools as nurseries for the University which he was instrumental in founding.

[11] Hodgins, *Documentary History*, I, 196.

[12] Hodgins says that the General Board for the Superintendence of Education was appointed under authority of 4 Geo. IV, c. 8 (Jan. 19, 1824), after having been discussed in correspondence between Lord Bathurst and Sir Peregrine Maitland. *Ibid.* However, the Board first met on June 14, *1823*, as he points out in another place. See *ibid.*, III, 1.

[13] Apart from Strachan, the original members of the Board were Joseph Wells, George H. Markland, Robert Addison, J. B. Robinson, and Thomas Ridout.

[14] Hodgins, *Documentary History*, I, 196.

Thus, the control of preparatory education by the Council of King's College fitted in well with Strachan's vision of an established church which dominated educational training at every level.

Various protests were made by the other denominations against the preponderant role of the Church of England in grammar school education. For example, in 1829, the United Presbytery of Upper Canada presented a petition to the Legislative Assembly, claiming that "the appointment of Trustees from one communion alone has occasioned a jealousy in the minds of the people, and destroyed the confidence that should ever be placed in the Public Institutions." A Select Committee was appointed to investigate this and similar charges and in February, 1830, reported that the Presbyterian claims were without the slightest foundation.[15] Although the Presbyterian charge was obviously exaggerated, the data presented by the Select Committee showed that the headmasters of the grammar schools were predominantly members of the Church of England and noted a surprisingly large number of cases where headmasters had changed their allegiance to the Church of England after being appointed.

The Grammar School Amendment Act of 1819 authorized, among other things, the creation of two new district schools, one of which was to be in the village of Hamilton in the Gore District. The Gore District, comprising what are now the Counties of Halton, Wentworth, Brant, Waterloo, and part of Haldimand, had been formed in 1816, and the establishment of a district school recognized the growing wealth and population of this part of Upper Canada.

The first headmaster of the Gore District School was John Law who was appointed on June 1, 1821. Law (1798–1844) was a Presbyterian and evidently an able man. One confidential comment on him was: "Mr. Law is a highly educated man, and a gentleman much respected and esteemed here; but he is unfortunately of intemperate habits . . ."[16] The school flourished under Law and one of his pupils in the 1820's was Egerton Ryerson. In 1827, Law resigned to enter a legal firm and in later years became Clerk of the District Court. He was named as a member of the board of trustees of the Gore District School in 1830 and continued in this capacity until his death in 1844.[17]

Following Law's resignation, there were three aspirants to his position, Stephen Randal, John Rae, and a man named Alexander.[18] An examination

---

[15] *Ibid.*, I, 307.

[16] P.A.C., Provincial Secretary's Officer, Canada West, no. 1763; letter, Miles O'Reilly to Macaulay, Jan. 28, 1839.

[17] P.A.C., Education Papers, Upper Canada, no. 44.

[18] This was probably James Lynne Alexander (1801–1879), who taught for a period in the district school in Toronto, and later became an Anglican clergyman.

for Randal and Alexander was held on August 24, 1827, and September 24 was fixed for the examination of John Rae who did not, however, appear. A final examination for Stephen Randal took place on October 25, but the trustees disagreed on his appointment. Randal had been one of Alexander Skakel's students in the Royal Grammar School which he entered in 1819 with the sponsorship of Bishop C. J. Stewart. Three of the trustees who were for Randal's appointment directed an appeal for guidance to John Strachan as President of the General Board for the Superintendence of Education.[19] Strachan settled the difficulty by recommending Randal's appointment on the grounds that one of the dissenting trustees agreed that Randal was qualified. Although Strachan's decision may not have been influenced by the fact that Randal was "a protégé of the Bishop's," it was probably a source of satisfaction to him to have the Gore District School in charge of an adherent of the Church of England.[20]

In September, 1833, James Cahill, a young man of eighteen, was appointed as an assistant to Randal, but within a few months Randal resigned to become editor of the *Hamilton Free Press*.[21] The trustees appear to have attached some importance to the appointment of a successor to Randal since on December 20, 1833, John Strachan attended the examination of candidates at the special request of the other trustees. In their report to the Lieutenant-Governor, the trustees noted that five candidates had been interviewed but felt "compelled to express their regret that although much natural ability was manifested, not one of the candidates came up to the Standard of Scholarship they had contemplated."[22] They recommended that the school continue under Cahill's direction until a new headmaster could be found and this arrangement was sanctioned by the Lieutenant-Governor.[23] In June, 1834, the trustees held another examination of candidates for the position of headmaster. The outcome was

[19] Archives of Ontario, Strachan Papers, Letterbook 1827–41; 3. The letter, dated Oct. 25, 1827, gave as a reason for the delay in appointing a replacement that two candidates had been examined "but a further day of September, was named for the accommodation of Mr. Rae who did not at that time or since appear." Also P.A.C., Education Papers, Upper Canada, no. 117.

[20] Strachan visited the school on September 9, 1828, and recorded his satisfaction with Randal's supervision. He wrote: "the School is prospierous [*sic*] under his management. The Trustees are pleased with him, and just before the vacation, he had 48 pupils." "Journal of a Tour through Upper Canada, August 19–October 23, 1828," Archives of Ontario, Strachan Papers.

[21] Randal (1804–41) was later described by one of his pupils as "a very odd but gifted young man from Quebec." Charles Durand, *Reminiscences*, 59. Randal later returned to teaching and at the time of his death was a teacher in the Township of Shefford, Quebec.

[22] P.A.C., Education Papers, Upper Canada, no. 437, Dec. 20, 1833.

[23] *Western Mercury*, May 8, 1834. Cahill apparently continued as an assistant teacher until 1835 when he resigned to study law. He became a police magistrate in Hamilton in 1863.

that the Rev. Philip Mills Rolls, "a gentleman of the first literary acquire-ments," was appointed headmaster and was to begin his duties on July 1, 1834.[24] However, Rolls died suddenly of cholera a few days after he took over the school, and the trustees began again.[25] They issued a further pub-lic announcement dated October 15, 1834, stating that they would accept applications for the vacant position of headmaster which should be sent to the Rev. Alexander Gale at Hamilton.[26] Gale had been appointed a trus-tee of the Gore District School earlier in 1834.

Rae, who was living in Montreal at this time, answered the advertisement and the Board of Trustees recommended his appointment as headmaster of the Gore District School on December 13, 1834, although he actually started teaching on December 6, 1834.[27] One of Rae's letters of recommend-ation was written by the Rev. Hugh Urquhart, at that time headmaster of the Eastern District School and minister of the kirk in Cornwall.[28]

Rae was evidently in financial straits when he arrived in Hamilton and early in 1835 the trustees petitioned the Lieutenant-Governor to divide the unused part of the school grant for 1834 between the widow of the Rev. P. Rolls and John Rae who had "incurred considerable expense in travel-ling with his family from Montreal and in making the necessary prepara-tions for opening the school."[29] The petition was denied and Rae was paid only £56 14s 6d for the period December 6, 1834, to June 30, 1835. No relief was forthcoming for the poor widow.[30] Rae's income as a school-master was, in fact, never enough to raise him above a state of genteel poverty. He received a government salary normally of £100 a year as well as other revenue from the fees of the pupils, probably between £150 to

[24] *Montreal Gazette*, June 26, 1834.

[25] P.A.C., Education Papers, Upper Canada, no. 461; letter, Thomas Taylor to Colonel Rowan, private secretary to the Lieutenant-Governor, Aug. 25, 1834.

[26] *Montreal Gazette*, Oct. 28, 1834. For an account of Gale's career see the Biographical Appendix.

[27] P.A.C., Education Papers, Upper Canada, nos. 463 and 490.

[28] The letter from Urquhart dated November 6, 1834, is referred to by Mixter in *Sociological Theory of Capital*, xxiii. Urquhart (1793–1871), a native of Ross, graduated from King's College, Aberdeen (M.A., 1814), and may have known Rae in his student days. After teaching at the Inverness Academy he came to Montreal in 1822 and taught in the Montreal Academical Institution along with Rev. Henry Esson. In 1827, Ur-quhart was appointed headmaster of the Eastern District School in Cornwall where he continued to teach until 1840. At the same time he served as minister of St. John's Presbyterian Church in Cornwall and later (1847–57) he was Professor of Church History and Biblical Criticism at Queen's College in Kingston of which he was a trustee. There is a biographical note about Urquhart in William Gregg, *History of the Presby-terian Church in the Dominion of Canada* (Toronto, 1885), 389.

[29] P.A.C., Education Papers, Upper Canada, no. 472; petition of the Gore District School Trustees to the Lieutenant-Governor, Jan. 2, 1835.

[30] Appendix to *Journals of the House of Assembly of Upper Canada*, 2nd Session, 12th Parliament, 6 Wm. IV, vol. I.

£200 a year altogether.[31] The government payments recorded for the Gore District School are £100 annually for the period 1836–40, £50 in 1841 and £90 in 1842 and 1843 but the variations are not explained.[32]

A notice appearing in the *Hamilton Gazette* in 1837 showed that the fees ranged from 12s 6d to £1 10s a quarter.[33] The incomplete statistics available show that the number of pupils in Rae's school was as follows: 1835, seventeen; 1838, thirty-five; 1844, fifty-six; 1845, forty-nine; and 1847, sixty to seventy. Despite the growth in attendance and the corresponding increase in revenue from fees, Rae can never have been financially comfortable.

One brief letter dated 1837 suggests that Rae was unable to pay his bills. In a note to a Hamilton merchant named McIntyre, Rae wrote, in part: "I am sorry that, as I anticipated, it will be out of my power to meet the bill. I had thought till this morning that I should be able to do something towards it but find it will be out of my power."[34] He lived in a rented dwelling which also housed the schoolroom judging from a newspaper advertisement appearing on several occasions early in 1837 offering for rent "the large and convenient Dwelling House and Premises, at present occupied by Dr. Rae."[35] His failure to finance the publication of some of his writings also indicates that he was handicapped by lack of money.

At different times, assistants were appointed to help Rae in his teaching duties. James Cahill continued as an assistant master until 1835. In 1837, Henry Lawson was the assistant master. William Tassie, who had been the teacher of the common school in Oakville, became Rae's assistant in 1839 and continued during the rest of Rae's tenure.[36] Although it is not

[31] Replies to a questionnaire circulated to the teachers of district schools in 1827 show the following gross receipts: Gore District School, £190; Eastern District School, £170; Ottawa District School, £148. See P.A.C., Education Papers, Upper Canada, nos. 152 and 153.

[32] Hodgins, *Documentary History*, V, 256–7. However, on p. 261 of the same volume a table shows that £100 was paid to John Rae in 1843–44. Again, an official return submitted by the Provincial Secretary shows that John Rae received a salary of £90 in 1836. P.A.C., Colonial Office Records, Q. 391, 45.

[33] July 26, 1837.

[34] This letter was uncovered in a collection of old documents in Welland and published by the late Charles R. McCullough in the *Hamilton Spectator*, Nov. 16, 1946.

[35] The advertisement signed by A. N. MacNab and dated Dec. 21, 1836, appeared in the *Hamilton Gazette* on Jan. 4, 11, 18, 25 and Feb. 1, 1837. The advertisement further stated: "The very extensive accomodations contained in this House, and its centrical position, render it a very desirable situation for a private Boarding-House, or the residence of a large family."

[36] William Tassie (1815–1886) came to Canada from Ireland in 1834. In 1853, he became headmaster of the Galt Grammar School, an institution which became famous under him. A few years before his death he was appointed principal of the Peterborough Collegiate Institute. Tassie was one of the most renowned teachers in Canada in the nineteenth century.

known with certainty, it is probable that the assistant masters were paid out of the pupil's fees which means that Rae's income was correspondingly reduced.

Rae's pupils seem to have looked on him with affection and admiration. This is borne out by the following editorial note and letter which were printed in the *Hamilton Gazette* on May 27, 1839:

We have much pleasure in giving publicity to the following note which was recently presented to Dr. Rae, the able and efficient master of our District School by his more advanced pupils, together with the very appropriate present of a handsome Inkstand, Pen-knife and Silver Pencil-case. It is a most important and interesting relation that exists between the Master and the Scholar, and any circumstance that tends to show the duties incumbent on the one are faithfully performed, and that respect and attachment are cherished by the other, ought to be regarded with peculiar satisfaction by the community.

Hamilton, May 9, 1839.

(*Copy*)
Sir,—We the undersigned beg that you will accept of this as a small token of our respect and gratitude for your unwearied diligence and attention to us as our Tutor.

Henry Racey,	*Wm. S. Sheldon,*
Andrew Geddes,	*William Lister,*
Richard Baxter,	*James Durno,*
Robert I. Thorner,	*James S. Carey,*
Robert N. Law,	*Joseph Lister.*
Robert Wallace	

To *Mr. John Rae,*
 Master of the Gore District School,
 Hamilton.

Rae was not a strict disciplinarian and his relations with his pupils were rather friendly and casual. It must be remembered that discipline and corporal punishment were regarded in those days as essential features of pedagogy.[37] Many a schoolmaster was guided in his relations with his pupils by Solomon's injunction, "Thou shalt beat him with the rod, and shalt deliver his soul from hell."

One of the only surviving anecdotes about Rae as a schoolmaster, quoted below, throws some light on his qualities as a teacher.

[37] John Strachan, who set the teaching fashion in Upper Canada, was a stern teacher and there was ample precedent for harsh and sadistic punishments for errant pupils in the English public schools. For example, an advertisement for an assistant master in the Bathurst District School in 1834 stated that "none need apply but one who has already been accustomed to conduct a school, and who is a strict disciplinarian." *Montreal Gazette*, May 10, 1834.

School boys the world over delight in having some fun at the expense of their teachers, and those attending Dr. Rae's school were no exception to this rule. He had a habit of leaning back in his chair, resting his head against the wall, and looking over the school to see if all were engaged in preparing their lessons. At this time he wore a wig, and where his head rested against the wall it left a spot somewhat discolored. This spot suggested to some mischief-making boys the idea of having some fun at the teacher's expense. So one of them got a small quantity of shoemaker's wax and put a light coat of it on the spot. The next morning the Doctor as usual leaned against the wall, and the genial warmth of his head softened the wax, and when he leaned forward, lo! and behold the wig had been transfixed to the wall. To laugh or not to laugh was the question for the boys to solve, but it was soon solved by the Doctor, who taking in the situation at a glance, roared with laughter in which the boys most heartily joined. Mr. Tassie, who was teaching in an adjoining room entered the master's room to see what had happened. He made an attempt to find out who had done the mischief but he failed, for no one knew anything about it. This annoyed Mr. Tassie so much that he flogged every boy in the room, and when he reached the last one he said, in as urbane a manner as possible, "Now, my lad, if you will tell me honestly who waxed the wall I will not flog you." The boy, looking up in a doubtful manner, replied, "Please sir, I did it."[38]

Despite its apocryphal quality, this story does seem to show that Rae had a light-hearted regard for his own dignity, something which may have endeared him more to the pupils than to the school trustees.

There are references to Rae and his school in the unpublished memoirs of the Rev. Canon George A. Bull. In referring to the period 1841–42, he wrote:

It was about this time I was sent to the "Grammar School"—on James St. north. Kept by Dr. Rae (Scotch) and his assistant William Tassie, Irish.

The building had been a stable. Hay seed and dust from the old loft often betrayed the roughness, inconvenience and discomfort of the place—outside accommodation and playground—nothing! A narrow lane or alley led from the street to the school about half-way to Hughson St. (Lister's block).[39]

Information about Rae's personal habits and characteristics during the time he lived in Hamilton is surprisingly meagre. One brief description, written by the historian of Rae's school, has survived and may be based on first-hand information:

In appearance he was tall, rather slender, and dignified. People looked on him as one of the most graceful skaters in the city, and many of his pupils labored diligently to master the long graceful stroke of the teacher, even going so far as

[38] J. H. Smith, *The Central High School Jubilee Re-union, August, 1903* (Hamilton, 1905), 14–15.

[39] These memoirs are in the possession of Canon Bull's grand-daughter, Miss M. H. Farmer of Hamilton. Canon Bull transferred to the school run by the Rev. J. G. Geddes which he attended for three or four years.

to steal away from their homes on the Sabbath day to practise at their leisure on the bay.[40]

Mixter was able to obtain from Rae's friend Sir Roderick W. Cameron, before his death in 1900, various letters and papers which led to correspondence with a number of Rae's pupils who were still alive around 1900. The recollections of these men are impressive tributes to Rae's personality.

George Hamilton Mills (1827–1901), a prominent Hamilton lawyer, who became Mayor of Hamilton in 1858, wrote:

He was quite different from ordinary men, or I think my youthful imagination would not have been so impressed as it was. He was undoubtedly a man of deep learning and research, and made a powerful impression on all who knew him. He was amiable and thoughtful of others.[41]

In an obituary notice of Mills, there is also a reference to Rae:

One of his early instructors was Dr. Rae, a very learned man, with broad views and ideas in advance of his time, who conducted a school for boys in the then village of Hamilton. Of his ability and literary attainments, Mr. Mills entertained a very high opinion.[42]

Stephen J. Jones, a lawyer and for many years Judge of the County Court of Brant, said:

I have a very pleasant and grateful remembrance of dear Dr. Rae. He was very much respected and loved by all his pupils. . . . He was considered a fine scholar, well up in Latin, Greek and Mathematics, and specially qualified in Geology, and also understanding French. His mind was, in fact, a vast storehouse of knowledge, though he had not a happy faculty of dispensing it. But he had a very loving disposition that endeared him to us all.[43]

John Robert Martin (b. 1825) of Cayuga, Ontario, also a lawyer, wrote:

Dr. John Rae was a man of great learning, and too little appreciated in his lifetime, like many others. . . . He was a great writer, sometimes writing night after night, and had a lot of manuscript. . . . His conversations with the boys that made his house their home was even more to them than their school studies. He entered into all their sports and amusements, often bringing his chemical knowledge into play.[44]

Altogether, the names of nearly 150 of Rae's students in Hamilton have been compiled. Of those that can now be identified there were a number who became well-known lawyers, or business men or ministers, but not

[40] Smith, *Central High School Jubilee Re-Union, August, 1903*, 14.

[41] *Sociological Theory of Capital*, xxiii.

[42] *Journals and Transactions of the Wentworth Historical Society*, III, 102. Mills was articled as a law student to Hugh Bowlby Willson for a year.

[43] *Sociological Theory of Capital*, xxiii. For a biographical sketch of Jones, see H. J. Morgan, *The Canadian Men and Women of the Time: A Handbook of Canadian Biography* (Toronto, 1898), 515.

[44] *Ibid.*, xxiv.

J.R. I—5

many of them achieved any national importance. Particular mention should be made of the special relationship which existed between John Rae and Roderick William Cameron and Hugh Bowlby Willson.[45]

Cameron, who had been born in Williamstown in 1823, was a pupil of Rae's for a short period as a young child, but completed his education under the Rev. Hugh Urquhart in the Eastern District School at Cornwall. Cameron came to Hamilton in 1839 and was employed in business there until 1847. It was during this period that Rae and Cameron must have begun a friendship which continued to the end of Rae's life. Although Mixter must have obtained a good deal of information about Rae from Cameron, the only thing he directly attributes to him is the following comment: "Rae was a charming companion for young and old. He taught me rabbit, mink, and muskrat trapping and other sports attractive to youth. . . . He was young in thoughts and acts to the end."[46]

The ages of Rae and Hugh Bowlby Willson, who was born in 1813, were somewhat closer and there existed between these men a warm, intimate, and also a lifelong friendship. Willson was a man of considerable intellectual ability and one must assume that he found in Rae a stimulating mentor. In later life Willson became a prolific writer on a variety of engineering and other topics and developed a special interest in monetary theory.[47] There must have been a voluminous correspondence between Rae and Willson and fortunately, a good many of Rae's letters were preserved and turned over to Mixter, but Willson's letters have not survived. Willson was referred to by Rae in one place as "his particular friend," signifying a very deep attachment.

It might have been expected that Rae's life as a schoolmaster in Hamilton

---

[45] For details concerning the lives of these two men see the Biographical Appendix. In a conversation with the writer in 1956, Mrs. Cameron Tiffany, Sir Roderick's daughter, recalled hearing her father speak of Rae in affectionate terms. She remembered also a portrait of Rae which hung in their home, "Clifton Berley," on Staten Island for years. There were many references to Rae in Sir Roderick's diary, but it has unfortunately been lost.

[46] *Ibid*.

[47] Mixter, who may have obtained information first-hand from Willson's friends, has the following interesting comment. "He [Willson] was a barrister, engineer, promoter, general railway agent and commission merchant, author and editor, during 1849, of the short-lived *Canadian Independent*, established in the interests of annexation. Rae was willing to be associated in this last enterprise, but was too much broken up at the time to take an active part. Willson's published works are on engineering and monetary subjects. Apparently he was a man of exceptional range of ability, but always unfortunate and poor. There is abundant evidence in Rae's papers that Willson was his best friend. Like cleaves to like." *Sociological Theory of Capital*, xxvii. Mixter's comment that Rae was willing to be associated with the annexationist movement is dubious. There is also some doubt about the accuracy of Mixter's information that Willson was "always unfortunate and poor."

would have been placid and uneventful. His occupation, to a person of his intellectual capacity, would not have been exacting and he had the leisure for reflection and writing. Before long, however, it became clear that Rae was involved in a bitter struggle for the control of education which was part of a wider controversy over religious and civil rights which rocked Upper Canada during the 1830's and 1840's.

It will be recalled that Lord Durham's famous report was bitterly critical of the state of education in Lower Canada. Similarly, the report had some harsh things to say about the educational system of Upper Canada. In one place the report said: "Even in the most thickly peopled districts there are but few schools, and those of a very inferior character; while the more remote settlements are almost entirely without any."[48] Following the publication of Lord Durham's report, the Legislative Assembly in Upper Canada requested the Lieutenant-Governor, Sir George Arthur, to appoint a commission to investigate and report on various departments of the government. The Commission was appointed on October 21, 1839, and a special Education Committee was formed to look into the aggravated problems in this field. The members of this committee were the Rev. John McCaul, Principal of Upper Canada College, the Rev. Henry James Grasett, an Anglican clergyman, and Samuel Bealy Harrison, then private secretary to the Lieutenant-Governor. Harrison, as secretary, wrote to many of those prominent in educational matters in Upper Canada enclosing a questionnaire to elicit their views on the state of education.

This whole subject was naturally of the keenest interest to Rae, who wrote to Harrison offering his advice on the day the Education Committee was constituted. Rae's letter was reproduced in full in the "Reports of the Grammar and Common Schools in Upper Canada for the year 1839" submitted by the Lieutenant-Governor to the legislature.

Hamilton, 21st October, 1839.

Sir,

The return herewith sent ought to have been forwarded three months since, having been then put into my hands by the Trustees. The delay has been owing to an oversight of mine, having forwarded the other papers connected with the school at the time, but altogether forgotten this, till I was reminded of it by a communication from one of the Trustees on Saturday.

I shall be very sorry if the circumstance has put your office to any inconvenience, but the fact is as I state, and I am alone to blame.

Since this circumstance, awkward as it is, gives occasion to my writing you, I am induced to trespass for a moment farther on your attention, from what the Rev. Mr. Gale of this place told me not long since.

[48] Lucas, ed., *Lord Durham's Report*, II, 184–5.

He mentioned that a few weeks since he had had some conversation with you concerning education and contemplated measures for the improvement of the existing system, that he had mentioned my name as that of one able to give some information on the subject, and that you had stated you would be glad to hear from me.

I feel obliged by your politeness in thus expressing yourself. I have been now teacher in Canada, in one situation or another, about 16 years. My thoughts have naturally turned themselves very often to the great existing defects in the present system, and the modes of remedying these, and latterly I have had some idea of giving them to the public in hopes that any good any suggestions of mine might be fitted to bring about, might in this way be presented to individual Legislators. But it would certainly be much more agreeable to me to communicate my ideas immediately to you, that so whatever in them was judged serviceable might directly come to bear on Legislative measures. I only fear that in so doing I might be in a manner obtruding matters on you, on which probably by this time your information from other quarters may be conceived sufficient.

In case then you really wish to hear from me on the subject, may I request that you will intimate this to me when I will do myself the honor of freely and briefly stating what I know and think on the subject.[49]

Rae's offer was evidently accepted, but circumstances intervened and Rae was not able to prepare a brief for the Committee. He did reply to Harrison in a letter dated December 9, 1839, which throws some light on his personal life.

It has been a subject of sincere regret to me that I have been unable to avail myself of the invitation with which your letter of the 23rd Oct honoured me to communicate my notions on the subject of education in this Province. At the moment of its receipt I was engaged in a correspondence on a private matter of vexatious importance to me and which proved far more lengthened and annoying than I could have anticipated. I have very little doubt that the issue of it will come to be my departure from the Province at no distant date. This circumstance however would have made no difference in my desire to communicate to you what I thought of the existing system, and of that which it may be desirable to substitute in its place. It would rather have given me greater freedom in informing you of my real sentiments but just when I had commenced writing you I had an attack of ague which laid me up for some time and required the aid of medicine for two or three weeks to keep it at such a distance as to enable me to perform even the ordinary duties of my office. I had not recovered from this when an inmate of the house, a young man [Stephen Balmer] in whom we were much interested, took sick and after a fortnights illness during which he was now at deaths door and now escaping from it at length died ten days since. During the time my domicile and my thoughts were so confused that I could find neither leisure nor a settled mind to write on a subject of this importance. When all

---

[49] Upper Canada, *Appendix to Journals of the House of Assembly*, 5th session, 13th Parliament, 3 Vic. (1840), 418. Part of Rae's letter is quoted in Hodgins, *Documentary History*, III, 254.

was over the meeting of the Legislature was so close at hand that I felt I was altogether too late.

I repeat that I much regret the circumstances.[50]

What the "private matter of vexatious importance" was is by no means certain, but he may have been referring to the negotiations connected with the publication of his book "Outlines of the Natural History and Statistics of Canada" which is described in the following chapter.

Rae was deeply involved not only in practical educational problems but in the philosophy of education as well. Mixter says that Rae had privately printed in Hamilton in 1843 an *Essay on the Question of Education, in as far as it concerns Canada*. He found the title page and some detached pages but no complete copy has ever been found. The following excerpts from Rae's essay were reproduced by Mixter:[51]

The unsatisfactory results on human happiness which the progress of civilization has hitherto exhibited, as measured by the visible condition of any ten thousand taken at random from the ancient and modern population of Great Britain, has given rise there to a feeling of despondency and alarm among a numerous and not uninfluential class, as to the results that are to spring from its farther advance. They dread any further progress. They would wish to stop where we are—even, if possible, to bring things back to the condition of the good old days of our fathers. It is a vain attempt, we are hurried forward by an irresistible impulse. All in our power to do is to use every effort to direct our onward course aright. Art and science, and with them wealth, must increase and advance. The sphere of real philanthropic exertion is confined to elaborating the possible good they may produce, restraining and extirpating their possible evils.

Now, though the subject has given rise to many intricate and perhaps not very satisfactory discussions, there is one view that may be taken of this progress of science, art, and wealth, as affecting the condition of humanity, by no means difficult to seize, and which will sufficiently indicate one main cause of the evils that have overtaken, and those which yet threaten to overtake, our modern civilization.

It is in the nature of this progress to convert the original simple and rude tools, first, into instruments of greater cost and efficiency, and these again into complex and difficultly constructed machines, still more costly and still more efficient. The distaff becomes a spinning wheel; and that, changing its form, and wrought by other powers, is made part of a woollen factory. The rough edged blade of the original knife is first cut into a regular saw, wrought by one hand; it is then put into a frame, which two men operate; and this, in turn, by means of crank and pinions, is made to go by water, and becomes a saw-mill. Even a farm, in this manner, with all its appendages, may be said to become a great machine or

[50] P.A.C., Education Papers, Upper Canada, 1791–1841, no. 749. An obituary notice in the *Hamilton Gazette* of Dec. 2, 1839, records the death of Stephen Balmer, age 23, "one of the young men who have lately devoted themselves to a course of study, preparatory to their admission to the Ministry of the Church of Scotland, and a native of Roxburghshire, Scotland."

[51] *Sociological Theory of Capital*, 234–6, and note L, 462.

factory—a factory for the production of crops. What was before the work of the hands from year to year, is now, in such countries as England, brought about in a great degree by machinery and scientific processes, requiring a large surface to operate on, and many years for their completion.

And so it is with all our implements, they are passing on to great machines. This progress can be averted by no conceivable process that would not have the effect of fettering all the active powers of humanity. It is the inevitable consequence of man's asserting and employing the dominion over the realms of nature which his Creator has bestowed on him. Placing ourselves in the position of the philosophers of the age of Bacon, it will be difficult for us to assign a reason why we would not have hailed the discoveries of which they are the results as great inventions, conferring benefits on the whole human race, without being a means of occasioning wrong or sorrow to anyone. [Footnote: Etenim inventorum beneficia ad universum genus humanum pertinere possunt—inventa beant et beneficium deferent absque alicujus injuria aut tristitia.] And yet there was a question which might by possibility have occurred to the philosophic philanthropists of that day. "Who are to be the owners of these great machines? Will the mechanics and artisans who now wield the tools own the machines, or will they be the property of a distinct class?" We cannot ascertain how they might have *a priori* determined the question. It is most likely, perhaps, that they would have conceived that the owners of the tools, clubbing together to purchase machines, would have owned the machines. To us, experience has determined it. So constantly has it occurred that it may be said it has invariably happened, that the former artisans, in giving up their tools, have never become the owners of the machines that have succeeded them. These machines, manufactories, or whatever name may be given them, come to be owned by a distinct class. The operative has no property share in the industrial operation, he owns nothing but his hands and the art of using them fitly. For opportunity to use them, and for pay for their use, he depends on the owner of the machine. He suffers in consequence a degradation in the social scale. Formerly he was a small capitalist, now it is the characteristic of his condition to be a mere operative, destitute of capital. The difference may be seen by recalling the pictures left by Hogarth and Scott, when the change was just coming over them. Compare the industrious apprentice and the father of Bailie Nicol Jarvie, with the present factory boy, or look at the fate which, in our conception, awaits any of our handicrafts when the revolution . . .

The whole earth is strewn with the ruins of empires. Civilization seems, at distant intervals, to have assumed form, and gathered strength in various points, and from each of these in succession, to have spread itself and the races that were the possessors of it, over large regions of the globe. Now it is very clear that each of these civilizations must have had a period of advance, a period when they were collecting that amount of knowledge of science and arts, and of civil rights and laws, which they possessed at the acme of their progress, and which gave them their superiority over the other races of their times. Like us, each of them must have witnessed a period when the social condition was ameliorating from age to age; like us, they must have looked forward to still succeeding improvement. Yet each of these civilizations nursed within it some disease that, coming to activity, nipped the germ of prosperity and life, and brought on decay and death . . .

With the exception of Greece, whose contracted territory unfits it for a parallel, other antecedent civilizations are known to history only in their concluding stages when the hand of death was on them. We cannot tell, we can only conjecture, what their condition was in the previous and more vigorous periods of their existence. But with regard to all of them, so far as we can glean anything of them from history, or trace them in their monuments, the remarkable fact is brought before us that the stage of their being immediately preceding their decay, and of course the form of existence with which the ruins of them that remain are impressed, was that of fixity and immobility. A period of torpid repose preceded their decay and dissolution. There is also another remarkable fact which we gather by carefully scrutinizing the faint traces, that in several of them the ages anterior to the concluding period of repose and immobility have left behind them. Preceding this period, an era of great strife and contention between the principles of which the particular civilization was made up, comes pretty distinctly before us. The result of the contest seems to have been, the preponderance of one of those main elements, and its crushing, subduing, and altogether preventing any farther expansion of the others, and, by the cramped position in which it placed them, occasioning their decay and death . . .

It well then becomes all men, having power to exert effective action in this our era, to see if we can gather any lessons of instruction from bygone ages, if there be any circumstances of the times having a tendency to produce a similar conflict of the existing elements of our civilization, possibly resulting in the domination of some of them, with like fatal influence.

Mixter claims that Rae also wrote another paper "On Education" late in life, but he was unable to locate a copy of it.[52]

Partly to meet the criticisms voiced in Lord Durham's report and echoed by many others, the Upper Canada legislature undertook to overhaul the legislation governing district schools by the Grammar School Act of 1839.[53] This Act reconstituted the district schools as grammar schools and authorized the Lieutenant-Governor to appoint not less than five trustees in each district who were to be responsible for the "superintendence" of the schools. The Council of King's College was to lay down uniform rules governing their operation and management. The Act did not specifically repeal the Grammar School Act of 1807 or the Grammar School Amendment Act of 1819, and gave rise to some uncertainty concerning the responsibilities of the existing trustees. There was no uncertainty about the fact that the new Act considerably strengthened the position of the Church of England in educational matters.

On July 1, 1839, a number of the trustees of the Gore District School addressed a communication intended for the Lieutenant-Governor asking for a clarification of some of the conflicts between the Grammar School Act of 1839 and the earlier legislation. The letter is in John Rae's hand-

[52] *Sociological Theory of Capital*, xxxiii.   [53] 2 Vic., c. 10.

writing and perhaps he was chiefly responsible for its composition.[54] It pointed out in a most conciliatory tone, that it was not clear whether they were to regard themselves as the trustees who were to be constituted under the 1839 Act or not. If not, the question arose who was to prepare the certification necessary before the schoolteacher could be paid. If, on the other hand, they were to continue as trustees they faced a dilemma which they outlined as follows:

By the 47th George the III [Grammar School Act of 1807] it is enacted, that the Trustees appointed by virtue of it "or the majority of them shall have full power and authority to make such rules and regulations for the good government and management of the said public schools with respect to the teacher for the time being and to the scholars as in their discretion shall seem meet"—and again the recent act enacts: "that it shall and may be lawful for the Council of King's College to make such rules and regulations and by laws, for the conduct and good government of the schools established under this act as to such Council shall seem proper." We do not distinctly see how the homogeneous action of the two rules to which district schools would in this case be subjected to is to be effectuated. We are in doubt whether, as to any contemplated regulation, the initiative is to be taken by the College Council or by us, and providing a difference of opinion occurs concerning any contemplated arrangement, how that difference is to be adjusted.

The letter ending on the following note:

In conclusion, we may be permitted to observe that the experience which the situation we have held has more or less given to us all, has served to convince us of the very serious detriment which the cause of education has received, in so far as the district schools are concerned, from the want of suitable buildings, from the multifarious duties which the one master is expected to discharge; and from the want of any library or of an apparatus for illustrating the elementary principles of Science. It has given us sincere gratification to observe that the Legislature by the recent act seems to have contemplated the removal of these deficiencies. Our wish, that, if we are to cooperate in carrying these desirable purposes into effect, we may be enabled to do so speedily and correctly, has prompted this communication, and will, we are confident, render it unnecessary to apologize for doing so, or for requesting your early attention to it.[55]

The legal question was referred to the Attorney General, C. A. Hagerman, who endorsed the following note on the letter:

I am of opinion that the recent act of Legislature does not annul the powers of the Trustees of the existing District Schools—but that they are to continue to exercise their authority until further regulations are adopted by the Lieutenant Governor in pursuance of the Act of the last session.

[54] P.A.C., Education Papers, Upper Canada, no. 686. The petition was addressed to S. B. Harrison and was signed by James Crooks, Alexander Gale, Mark Y. Stark, William M. Jarvis, and John Law.
[55] *Ibid.*

The legal quality of this opinion does not appear to be high and it contributed nothing to the resolution of the conflict between two pieces of legislation.[56]

It was not long before a substantive issue arose out of the legislative anomaly. In February, 1841, the Council of King's College issued a revised set of regulations for grammar schools.[57] The new rules did not leave much doubt about where the control over the grammar schools lay. Detailed instructions were laid down specifying the time the roll was to be called, the length of vacations, and maximum quarterly dues. The text of lengthy opening and closing prayers were prescribed. The curriculum was described for the six main forms as well as a partial form and a preparatory form. Quarterly and annual reports on the pupils were to be submitted to the parents and the Council of King's College on specified forms. A general register was to be kept to record all essential data about the individual pupils. In addition, the Council of King's College was to have the right to examine and appoint assistant masters in the grammar schools. This was a bitter dose for Rae and the Presbyterian trustees of the Gore District Grammar School.

There was a meeting of the trustees of the Gore District Grammar School on June 28, 1841, at which the lines were clearly drawn between the supporters and opponents of the Council of King's College and the Church of England. The meeting opened with the following resolution which was proposed by the Rev. John Gamble Geddes of the Church of England, minister of Christ's Church Cathedral in Hamilton, and seconded by William M. Jarvis, sheriff of the Gore District:

> That we, the Trustees of the Gore District School, having had submitted to us the Rules and Regulations prescribed by the King's College Council, for the Government of District Grammar Schools, according to the provisions of the late Provincial Act, (2nd Victoria, Chapter 10), do hereby express our entire concurrence therein, and agree to adopt the said Rules and Regulations for the government of the Gore District (Grammar) School.[58]

An amending motion was offered by the Rev. Mark Y. Stark, the Presbyterian minister in Dundas-Ancaster, and seconded by the Rev. Alexander Gale, as follows:

[56] The inquiry concerning the supervisory role of the Council of King's College was originally interpreted as a protest by the *Hamilton Gazette* which commented editorially on Nov. 25, 1839: "A majority of the Trustees, have it seems protested against this most salutary supervision, and appealed to His Excellency the Governor on the subject. A pretty system of education we shall have in the Colony, if the Trustees of our District Schools are to be allowed to manage them according to their own whims." The mistake was acknowledged a week later. *Hamilton Gazette*, Dec. 2, 1839.

[57] Hodgins, *Documentary History*, IV, 64–6.

[58] *Ibid.*, 157.

That the Trustees, previously to binding themselves to accept the proposition of the King's College Council, do petition the legislature for information as to the exact position which they as Trustees hold under the late Act, and as to the powers which are by it conferred upon the Council of King's College.[59]

Stark's amendment was defeated by one vote and Geddes' motion was carried by one vote. Allied with Stark and Gale was Dr. William Craigie of Ancaster and a member of the Kirk. These three Presbyterians recorded a series of bitter protests against the majority decision and against the educational system in general, commenting in part as follows:

We object to the management and control of grammar schools, instituted and endowed for the benefit of every individual in the country, without regard to sect, denomination or party, being invested in a Body of so partial and sectarian a character as that of the Council of King's College; and, because we can perceive evident marks in the steps which that Body have already taken, of a desire to grasp the patronage of those Schools, gain the control over them and organize them upon a particular system, not adapted to the wants, conformable to the wishes, or available for the benefit of a large portion of the people of the Province.

The final and most revealing protest was that

the assent to the above Resolution [approving the rules and regulations of the Council of King's College] was carried by the votes of the Trustees, who have not, for many years taken any interest in the School, or been present at the Examinations, and who thus appear to have been specially brought forward for a party object.[60]

The matter was not allowed to rest there, and on September 1, 1841, the Hon. John Hamilton presented to the Legislative Council a petition from the Rev. Alexander Gale and the other trustees of the Gore District Grammar School asking for a declaratory act to clarify and define the duties of trustees of district grammar schools and the Council of King's College.[61] Similar petitions were also submitted from Brockville and Kingston which indicates that dissatisfaction with the existing state of affairs was widespread. The sentiments of Stark, Gale, and Craigie were echoed in August, 1841, in a report by the Hon. William Morris, the Presbyterian spokesman in the Legislative Council, on behalf of a Select Committee which had been appointed to review the regulations of the Council of King's College. Morris expressed the Committee's view that the regulations "will have the effect of continuing disappointment and bad feeling in the Western portion of this province, instead of allaying the angry passions which a long continued system of mismanagement of the Educational affairs of the Colony had engendered."[62] There was no doubt

[59] *Ibid.*   [60] *Ibid.*   [61] *Ibid.*, 36.
[62] *Ibid.*, 30. The reference to "the Western portion of this province" means Canada West, now Ontario.

that angry passions had been aroused in the trustees of the Gore District Grammar School.

Once again Rae was in the thick of a controversy between the Presbyterians and the Church of England. Rae's allegiance had been made clear by various polemic attacks on the Church of England. In the course of time this was to cost him badly needed support. One should not suppose, however, that Rae's attention was devoted exclusively or even mainly to schoolteaching or educational problems in general. His interests were wide and he energetically pursued what he described as "my literary and philosophical speculations."

5

Rae's "Literary and Philosophical Speculations"

(1834–1848)

By the time John Rae arrived in Hamilton, it had many of the attributes of a rough, bustling frontier community. The bulk of the population were labourers, many of them Irish and many also with a propensity for drinking and fighting. A Board of Police had been established in 1833 and was attempting to improve the general tenor of social behaviour by establishing speed limits, controlling the incursion of pigs, and prohibiting bawdy houses, among other things. In other fields, considerable strides had been made in providing schools and at least one reading room had been opened to encourage more reading. The first newspaper, the *Gore Balance*, had started operations late in 1829 but lasted only about a year. In 1831 three other ephemeral publications were begun, the *Canadian Casket* (d. 1832), the *Western Mercury* (d. 1834), and the *Canadian Wesleyan* (d. 1835). In 1835, the *Hamilton Gazette* was started and it was to last for about twenty years. In 1834 a debating club for young men was formed by James Cahill, then the assistant master of the Gore District School.

The Methodists had already established a church in the 1820's and in 1833, the Rev. Alexander Gale arrived to take charge of the congregation of the kirk. A new church was built which was opened to public worship for the first time on August 3, 1834.[1] In the spring of 1835 the Church of England appointed the Rev. J. G. Geddes to Hamilton and adjacent charges, but an Anglican church was not built until 1839.

Dr. Thomas Rolph, in the course of an account of his travels, reported on the Hamilton scene in 1834. He estimated that the population in Sep-

[1] *Montreal Gazette,* Aug. 7, 1834.

tember, 1834, was 2,101 and noted that its cultural life was developing.[2] Rolph went on to refer to the existence of a literary society "at which scientific, philosophical and literary questions are discussed."

Rae was an active participant in the work of the Hamilton Literary Society, and probably its president in 1836. His role is indicated by a brief reference in the Journals of the House of Assembly late in 1836 to the reading of a petition "of Mr. John Rae and eighteen others of the Literary Society of Hamilton, District of Gore, praying that pecuniary aid might be extended to said Society."[3] The *Hamilton Gazette* was full of praise for this objective and commented editorially in January, 1837:

We perceive by the Minutes of the House of Assembly that an application has been made to the Legislature by the members of the Literary Society of this town for a grant of money to enable them to procure such apparatus as may be necessary for the proper illustration of the various subjects connected with science. We are happy to learn that it is the intention of the Society, in case of their application succeeding, to expend a portion of the money in the purchase of Books in order to commence a Circulating Library, to which they intend all persons, whether members of the Society or not, shall at all times have access by paying a small annual subscription.

As there are many gentlemen belonging to the Society who are well qualified to Lecture on Astronomy, Natural Philosophy or Chemistry, we hope that some of them will take upon themselves the task of delivering courses of Public Lectures on these subjects. From what we know of the inhabitants of this town, we have no reason to doubt but that such Lectures would be well attended, and that a competent Lecturer would be adequately rewarded both for this time and labour. Something of the kind is very necessary in this, and every growing town in the Province, to infuse into the rising generation a taste for science and books. As the greater part of the inhabitants of this country are destitute of the means of sending their children to institutions possessed of Libraries and Instruments for the practical illustration of scientific subjects, we sincerely hope the Legislature will adopt some efficient system for the establishment of Mechanic's Institutes with Libraries in every considerable town in the Province. As grants of money have formerly been made to similar Institutions in Toronto and Kingston, we trust the Legislature will not reject the application of the Hamilton Literary Society.[4]

At about the same time, a newspaper announcement invited the inhabitants of Hamilton and vicinity to attend a lecture to be delivered on January 4, 1837, by John Rae, A.M., "On the advantages to be derived

[2] Thomas Rolph, *A Brief Account, Together with Observations, made during a Visit in the West Indies, and a Tour through the United States of America, etc.* (Dundas, 1836), 215–16. By the summer of 1837, the population was reported to be 3,567, and if this can be believed, it points to an explosive growth in the community. *Hamilton Gazette*, Oct. 11, 1837.

[3] Referred to in Hodgins, *Documentary History*, III, 48.

[4] *Hamilton Gazette*, Jan. 11, 1837.

from the study of the natural sciences."[5] The notice was signed by Hugh Bowlby Willson, then secretary of the Hamilton Literary Society.

Rae's interest in political affairs in Canada continued unabated. Late in 1835 some residents of the Gore District had circulated some petition or protest indicating considerable sympathy with the reform group. In January, 1836, the sheriff of the Gore District published an answering petition drawn up by some of the loyal inhabitants calling for a public meeting to be held January 25, 1836, to permit them an "opportunity to testifying their unalterable attachment to their beloved Monarch." Among the petitioners was John Rae.[6]

Rae's career as a schoolteacher in Hamilton was decisively interrupted early in December, 1837, by the armed insurrection which marked the final crisis of the bitter political disputes of the 1830's in both Lower Canada and Upper Canada. When it was learned that the dissidents were gathering north of Toronto with the apparent purpose of seizing the seat of government, an immediate appeal was sent by Sir Francis Bond Head, the Lieutenant-Governor of Upper Canada at that time, to the sedentary militia for volunteers to repulse the rebels. Allan Napier MacNab, then Colonel of the Gore District Militia, quickly assembled approximately one hundred men from Hamilton and its surroundings and embarked for Toronto on the steamship *Traveller*, arriving in time to take part in the battle of Montgomery's Farm. Rae was in this first contingent, celebrated as the "Men of Gore."[7] The rebels, whose military abilities were insubstantial, were quickly dispersed and several of the leaders, including William Lyon Mackenzie, quickly departed for the United States. Some remnants of the rebels, supported by a group of American sympathizers, regrouped on Navy Island in the Niagara River and caused a number of disturbances in this area. In the spring of 1838, the Lieutenant-Governor, Sir George Arthur, Bond Head's successor, again appealed to MacNab for assistance in putting down the insurrection and the Gore District Militia set off for Niagara.[8] On this occasion also the force included John Rae, as well as some two hundred feathered and painted Indians. Rae took part in some of the skirmishes with the rebels on the Niagara frontier, but details of his

        [5] *Ibid.*, Jan. 4, 1837.
        [6] *Montreal Gazette*, Jan. 19, 1836. Among the co-signers were Alexander Roxburgh, John Law, Thomas Rolph, the Rev. J. G. Geddes, Dr. William Craigie, and Hugh Bowlby Willson.
        [7] Mixter quotes from a letter of MacNab: "He was among the first who accompanied me to Toronto on the breaking out of the Rebellion of 1837, and continued on duty at the Niagara frontier and elsewhere as long as his services were required." *Sociological Theory of Capital*, xxiv.
        [8] P.A.C., Upper Canada Despatches to the Governor-General, G.16, vol. 46, despatch no. 5, June 27, 1838, Arthur to Durham.

exploits are now lacking.[9] Whether Rae had a position of responsibility is not certain, but he later claimed the friendship of MacNab and the acquaintance of Sir Francis Bond Head as a result of "some passages in the Rebellion of 1837," so it is not improbable that he had.

Rae's continuing interest in scientific matters is illustrated by his account of an ingenious aeronautical experiment. In 1838, he wrote to the editor of the *American Journal of Science and Arts* describing an entertaining investigation of the effects of the heat of the sun in raising a balloon. Rae described his procedure in the following way:

Notice of the effect of Solar Heat in raising a Balloon, in a letter to the Editor, dated Hamilton, Upper Canada, April 17th, 1837, from John Rae, Esq.—

By the action of the sunbeams I caused a body of some pounds' weight to ascend and float in the atmosphere, certainly at the height of a mile, probably of several. I will not detain you with an account of previous speculations and experiments but state the simple fact. Of paper blackened with China ink, of which I enclose specimens, I made a bag—the body of a cylindrical form, one of the ends tapering to a cone. The length of the axes of the cylinder and cone together eighteen feet, the diameter of the former ten feet and three quarters. At the apex of the conical part there was left an opening of about a foot in diameter secured by a circular piece of wire and having suspended from its centre a string eight feet long with a weight of four ounces at the end of it. The whole weighed about three pounds. On exposing this apparatus to the sun's rays, the black paper absorbing them, the interior air is heated and expanded, and the whole rises as a balloon filled with hydrogen gas, or common air heated by combustion. It was on the 10th inst. at half past seven, A.M. that I made my final experiment. It happened, that just at the moment we were engaged at it, an eddy of wind came upon us, a small rent was made in the paper, and we were obliged to let go, though it seemed to be only half filled. It floated, nevertheless, and soon began to expand more fully and to ascend. The wind at the surface of the earth was then about W.S.W., but as it ascended, this new aerial voyager, which, if I may be allowed, I would name the Sun Flyer, getting into other currents, went first south, and then a little to the west of south, disappearing in about fifty five minutes, bearing due south.

Hamilton lies at the head of Lake Ontario, on the western extremity of Burlington bay and immediately beneath what is here termed the mountain—the limestone ridge that surrounds the head of the lake from Niagara falls to near Toronto. From the point where I stood, the summit of this was exactly three quarters of a mile distant and at least two hundred and fifty feet high. At some

[9] Mixter had a letter of Rae to his sister Ann Cuthbert Fleming describing his adventures on this expedition but it is now lost. *Sociological Theory of Capital*, xxiv. In an article appearing in the *Journals and Transactions of the Wentworth Historical Society*, there is an extract from a questionnaire submitted by John W. Bickle. "Dr. Gore [sic], principal of Gore St., Grammar School, and others, going off with the Volunteers to meet the rebels; and Sir Allan MacNab, in connection with the rebellion of '37 are among his recollections" (II, 146). Despite the confusion, the reference is undoubtedly to Rae.

distance above the trees which fringe the edge of the mountain, this new voyager of the air dwindled to a mere point and disappeared. The morning was very clear and our Canadian sky is very pure. I think therefore it must have been at least twenty miles off and therefore over a mile and a half high. I had calculated somewhat loosely, that it would rise, if no accident intervened, about six miles. These calculations were founded on previous experiments with a small cubical bag about two feet on the side, formed of similarly prepared paper. In this, when exposed to the sun's rays, the thermometer stood at 30°, 40°, 60°, or even 80°, higher than in the shade, (I mean Fahrenheit's thermometer,) and it weighed itself from three fourths to one and a half ounces avoirdupois less in the former than in the latter situation. I am unable to say what the precise buoyant power of the large bag may have been. In a previous essay I had attempted to ascertain this and other particulars by leaving a large opening in the bottom, into which I got, and keeping it fast with strings attached all round; but it then inflated so rapidly that before our preparations were completed the upper part tore away from the lower, and after ascending about one hundred feet upset and came down. It seemed to me from the strings, &c. broken, to have had a force of several pounds.

I have heard nothing of my apparatus since I dismissed it. In the course it took it would pass over a level, woody and thinly settled tract till it came near Lake Erie, then it would be at a high elevation, and might not catch the eye of many individuals. If I calculated its rate nearly correctly it would have gone over two hundred miles before sunset. This would carry it in a right line to the extremity of Ohio or Michigan. It may however have been tossed about by counter currents on Lake Erie and sunk there, or some accident may have happened to it from the rent, which however was near the bottom, and it may have had to come down in mid-course and landed in the woods unseen. I do not think it has been caught by any one in Canada or I should have heard of it, as my address was attached to it.

'*Cui bono.*' It is a new power and all such have at least become of use. But I think the Sun Flyer, if kept flying,—(and were its nature understood, this would be an easy matter, for, though it comes to the earth with sun set it would rise with him on the morning,) might be made to communicate to us interesting facts concerning the regions it visits—their temperature, currents, &c. Again, a large one, forty or forty five feet diameter, would easily carry up a man, and if made of proper materials would be safe and more manageable than a balloon, as by means of a value its power of ascent and descent would be almost unlimited, and all advantage might be taken of varying currents, and the effect of inclined planes, giving diagonal movements. It is also to be considered that sunshine costs nothing.[10]

The editor, Benjamin Silliman Sr., added a sceptical comment on the last sentence:

Clouds too come without cost, and the shading of the sky would of course bring down the voyager. Would this be prevented by artificial heat, or in what manner would the ingenious inventor propose to prevent a descent in dangerous circumstances—on the sea, or a dense forest, a mountain precipice, &c.?

[10] *American Journal of the Arts and Sciences* (*Miscellanies*), XXXIII, Jan., 1838, 196–98. Rae's letter is incorrectly attributed to John Rae, the explorer, in the *Dictionary of National Biography*. Rae's experiment with his "Sun Flyer" is believed to be the first aeronautical experiment ever to be conducted in Canada.

In mid-1839, Rae again entered the arena of religious controversy and wrote a prolix philosophical article entitled, "How Ought the Clergy Reserve Question to be Settled?" This article appeared in the *Canadian Christian Examiner and Presbyterian Magazine* in July, August, and September, 1839. The promised conclusion was not published but the extant text is given in item 8, Part III of this volume.

Rae developed at considerable length his conviction that there should be a state-supported church in Canada. He argued that the prosperity and happiness of a community was the aim of all government and that these were governed by the prevalence of moral virtues. Moral virtues, in turn, rested on the basis of religion and it thus followed that it was the duty of all governments to support religion actively. He rejected the principle of voluntaryism, in part on the grounds that individuals might benefit from the "security, tranquillity, and morality" of a religious community without defraying any of the expenses of maintaining a religious establishment. Also, he pointed out that it was generally one of the prerogatives of the state to transfer the burden of the support of religion to the rent of land.

Rae emphasized that it was not his aim to exclude from the benefits of state support the Methodists, the seceding Presbyterians, and other Protestant denominations. To qualify, however, they should subscribe to the doctrines of the Church of England and the Church of Scotland "insofar as these standards are strictly doctrinal." He would even concede to the Baptists the doctrine of infant baptism. A religious body should nevertheless have achieved a respectable size before claiming legislative aid, and he suggested, as a minimum, one-twelfth of the aggregate number of the other Protestant sects. He dwelt briefly on the desirability of state-supported theological colleges and he rejected the idea that the legislature should dictate the course of studies in divinity, proposing merely that a three-year term of studies might be appropriate. The precise methods by which funds were to be diverted or obtained to support his proposals were unfortunately in the concluding and unavailable part of Rae's essay and one can only presume that his views on the Clergy Reserves expressed in his "Letter to the Honourable Mr. Stanley. . ." had not changed materially.

Despite the numerous demands on his time in the late 1830's Rae did not abandon his projected work on the economic geography of Canada and in the summer of 1840, an announcement appeared in several Canadian newspapers that another book by John Rae entitled "Outlines of the Natural History and Statistics of Canada" would be published in England the following winter.[11] The text of the prospectus is a tantalizing sample of his work:

[11] *Hamilton Gazette*, July 27, 1840. The book was advertised frequently in the *Montreal Gazette* throughout the fall of 1840.

The object of the Author of this work is to place before the British Public, in a volume of moderate compass, a clear and comprehensive account of the Nature and Resources of this interesting Colony. Though numerous productions have already issued from the Press on this Subject, of which many have deservedly obtained an extensive circulation, there would still seem to be ample room for a work of the character here contemplated.

Almost all the Publications referred to, have been unsystematic—the result of the casual observations of travellers, noting such things as passed before them, and merely designing to convey to the reader the impressions made on themselves by the portions of the vast regions around them that came immediately under their view. Now whatever may be the merits of such works, and how much soever of real information they contain, without adverting to other causes of error, it is certain, that, from their partial nature alone, they are apt to mislead the reader concerning a Country, of the varied features and vast extent of Canada. At all events, every fresh arrival from Britain furnishes us with abundant proof, that it is far from being well understood, and that many erroneous impressions prevail concerning it.

Very soon after his landing in the Colony, it appeared to the author that the best mode of remedying the defect which then as now existed, and the only way indeed of conveying a correct idea of the Canadas to the British reader, must consist in tracing out the great natural causes, the operation of which has given to the country those distinctive features that both characterize it as a whole, and discriminate one portion of it from the other. That by showing how nature had moulded it into its present form, its real proportions and aspect would be clearly set forth. To this task he devoted a large portion of his time. As he proceeded with it, he had the gratification of finding, that those causes, to the agency of which may be traced the characteristics of Canada, are not numerous in themselves, and that their operations are very clearly and strikingly marked.

Thus, on examining the rocky ranges that form the bases of the several regions of the country, they are found to be distinct, and clearly defined, as well in their nature, as in the spaces they respectively occupy. The effects also of the comparatively recent operation of water on the surface, are very conspicuous, as might indeed be conjectured from the vast lakes which either skirt, or surround so large a proportion of the territory, and have evidently had a great agency in giving to it its present configuration and qualities.—The consideration of these phenomena shows that Canada is naturally divided into four great regions having each distinctive qualities.

There exist natural and well ascertained causes, the agency of which must render the climate of a country situated as Canada is, on the north eastern side of the western continent, very different from one placed like Great Britain, on the north west of the eastern continent, and the consideration of which shows exactly what the nature of the former is, and must be, and how it compares with the latter. Climate, again, has great influence on animal life, and therefore on the salubrity of these, and all other regions, and on the diseases that prevail in them, and, conjoined with the qualities of the soil, gives to vegetation the varied forms it assumes at various points, and determines its nature in these Provinces. On the climate, soil and consequent phenomena of vegetable life, depends the general aptitude of the country for the operations of the agriculturalist, as well as the peculiar fitness of its different sections for particular products.

A knowledge of all these particulars would seem to furnish a sufficient ground work for comprehending the real nature and capabilities of the country. And with advantage proceeding to detail the progress of settlement in it, and the extent to which its vast resources have hitherto been developed. This might be accomplished by enumerating its artificial divisions, tracing the natural regions, or regions to which they respectively belong; stating the progress of agriculture, commerce and population in each, the facilities of communication, either natural or artificial which it enjoys, its peculiar products and other statistical details.

Such is the general plan of the work now to be presented to the public. There will, however, be appended to it, some general notices on the effects of the prices of land, wages of labour, and profits of Stock, as modifying the operations of the Agriculturalist and Capitalist. A good map and copious statistical Tables of exports, imports, revenues and all other information that can thus be most conveniently embodied will be appended.

Though based on science it is the object and wish of the Author, to make the Book a practically useful and popular work. Science will only therefore be called in, when it clearly explains facts and phenomena of general interest, and care will be taken that all scientific principles introduced, be brought forward in a way that may make them perfectly intelligible to the general reader. Though specifically designed for the British public, it is hoped that the work will be of interest to the Canadian reader, by making him well acquainted with the peculiarities of the various sections of this important dependency of the Empire which he inhabits, and perhaps by calling attention to interesting phenomena, which he had not previously remarked.

It is believed that no work approaching in plan to the present, has been published by anyone personally acquainted with the country, with the exception of Dr. Dunlop's Backwoodsman, and Gourlay, Bouchette and Rolph's volumes. Had the Backwoodsman extended his slight but admirable sketches to full delineations, the author would never have attempted a description of Upper Canada. As he decided otherwise, the works are of a different character. With regard to the other books it may be remarked that Mr. Gourlay's book was published under so very unfavourable circumstances that the talent which portions of it evidently display, lies buried under a heterogeneous mass of uninteresting matter: that Bouchette is acknowledged to be chiefly valuable for Geographical details; and that Dr. Rolph's production scarcely obtained a circulation in Britain, and laboured under the disadvantage of its author being at the time himself only personally acquainted with a small portion of the Upper Province. It may be remarked also, that, with the exception of Bouchette, these Authors confine their observations to one Province, a circumstance which, owing to the intimate connection of the two, is, it is apprehended, of great disadvantages to clear views of the nature and resources of either.

For eighteen years that the author has lived in Canada, he has had this object continually in view, and been collecting materials for it. He has resided in various parts of the country, and traversed all the surveyed parts of it in every direction, from 50 miles below Quebec to Lake St. Clair. He has the happiness of possessing many friends in almost every section of it, who have afforded him their valuable assistance in his undertaking; and through the kindness of Lord Seaton[12] when

---

[12] Sir John Colborne became the first Baron Seaton in 1839.

Lieut. Governor of Upper Canada, he had the unreserved liberty of inspecting documents in the Surveyor General's and other public offices of that Province. He looks forward therefore with some confidence to public support, and he does so more especially, that his remuneration for the very considerable expenses of such an undertaking, will in a great measure depend, on the number of Subscribers he may obtain in Canada. The volume will be full sized octavo, and will not exceed 10s. c'y.

Hamilton, July, 1840.

On the day the announcement first appeared, the *Hamilton Gazette* commented in an editorial note:

We beg leave to call the attention of our Readers to the work of which a Prospectus appears in this days Gazette on the *Natural History and Statistics of the Canadas*. From the ability of the Author and the pains he has taken on the subject, we have no doubt it will merit that full support which we trust it will receive from the Canadian Public.[13]

Years later, Rae mentioned this work to some correspondent, saying:

As this [my work on Canada] was long and went to the bottom of things, my friends and the booksellers prognosticated that it would, like the former [i.e. *New Principles*], be too heavy a work to be read. I kept the manuscript by me, adding to my stock of information as occasion offered, still thinking of one day bringing it forth. Among other mischances that have befallen, these manuscripts, sent to New York, seem to have been strangely lost. So there is an end to that.[14]

Rae lectured to the Mechanics' Institute in Hamilton on a number of occasions in 1841. The minutes of the Institute for late 1840 and early 1841 describe negotiations with various prospective lecturers, including Rae. The minutes of April 21, 1841, show that Rae had given four lectures in geology during March and April.[15]

Among his other scholarly pursuits, Rae took some interest in literary affairs in Canada. One of the surviving examples of his work in this field is a brief essay entitled "Plagiarism," which appeared in the *Literary Gar-*

[13] The *Montreal Gazette* on Aug. 8, 1840, wrote a fairly detailed account of Rae's prospectus and concluded: "Of such a work we cannot but express our hearty approbation, as it will be attended with many beneficial results to the interests of these Provinces; and we therefore sincerely trust that, both at home and in the Colonies, it will experience the success which, we have no doubt, it will richly merit. Mr. Rae is already well and favourably known to literature and science and a work such as this coming from his hands, cannot fail to interest and instruct the public."

[14] *Sociological Theory of Capital*, xxxi. Mixter says the letter was to John Stuart Mill.

[15] The Minutes of the Mechanics' Institute for this period are in the possession of the Hamilton Public Library. The initial negotiations with Rae about these lectures were conducted by Mr. Thornton, who was later to become the School Superintendent for the Gore District.

land of Montreal in October, 1839.[16] Immediately above the essay it was parenthetically indicated that it was an original contribution. Rae's considerable literary power is illustrated by this essay, the text of which is given in item 9 of Part III of this volume.

In the light of Rae's views on plagiarism, it is not surprising that Rae was angered by the literary activities of John Sheridan Hogan.[17] In 1842 Hogan became the centre of an international incident which was to involve John Rae. When he was returning to Canada from a visit to Rochester he was arrested by the United States authorities at Lockport on a charge of being implicated in the destruction of the *Caroline*.[18] Rae was secretary of a protest meeting which arose from this arrest and forwarded a report of the proceedings to the Governor-in-Chief, including the resolution:

> That this meeting views with feelings of indignation and regret the repeated and unprovoked insults and injuries perpetrated upon the persons and properties of British Subjects in this province by citizens of the United States in conjunction with Canadian outlaws with the evident intention of involving the two nations in a calamitous war which it is the interest of both to avert by every honourable concession.[19]

Somewhat later Hogan undertook to become a writer on topical subjects. According to H. J. Morgan, "his attention having been called to the aspect of political affairs in Canada, he contributed some able articles on the subject to *Blackwood's Edinburgh Magazine*, which attracted considerable attention at the time, and, indeed, established Mr. Hogan's reputation as one of the literati of Canada."[20] Hogan's articles appeared in two parts, "Civil Revolution in the Canadas" (June, 1849) and "Civil Revolution in the Canadas. A Remedy" (August, 1849).[21]

Mixter quotes one of Rae's former pupils as saying, "J. S. Hogan made

[16] Plagiarism was a common literary form in Canada around 1840. There is an entertaining account of a plagiaristic fiasco in the *Literary Garland* of April, 1844 (p. 192), involving Susanna Moodie and Edmond Hugomont (Hugh E. Montgomerie). According to the editor's account, Mrs. Moodie accused Montgomerie of plagiarizing one of her short stories. Peace was restored when it was learned that Montgomerie had merely translated a story by some French writer who had translated Mrs. Moodie's story and passed it off as his own.

[17] For an account of Hogan's life see the Biographical Appendix.

[18] Edwin C. Guillet in his *The Lives and Times of the Patriots* (Toronto, 1938), 189n, suggests that Hogan's role in this episode was that of an *agent provocateur*.

[19] P.A.C., Governor-in-Chief's Registry of Letters and Dispatches Received, 1841–52. G20, vol. 280, no. 1306, March 16, 1842.

[20] H. J. Morgan, *Sketches of Celebrated Canadians and Persons Connected with Canada* (Quebec, 1862), 765.

[21] Pp. 133–262 and 637–768. Both articles were anonymous but were dated "Hamilton C.W."

use of portions of Rae's history of Canada to get up an article for Blackwood for which he received £40 sterling."[22] Rae's account of the matter
was given in a letter written some years later:

Some time before leaving Canada, a young friend came to reside with me, and
having something of a turn for politics was very free in his inquiries as to my
opinions and views of matters, which I gave him in full. On this foundation, for
he knew nothing of these matters himself, he goes and writes an article for
Blackwood. I just saw it before leaving America, and found it a reflection of my
own thoughts, though sometimes dim or distorted. Since landing on these shores
[Hawaii] I have had letters from Canada asking if I were the author and stating
that the article had had considerable success.[23]

In December, 1839, Rae contributed another attractive essay to the
Literary Garland entitled "Genius and Its Application." Although the
complete text is reproduced among Rae's miscellaneous writings,[24] it is
worth remarking here that this piece is a noteworthy example of his erudi-
tion, his literary ability, and what Mill was later to describe as "his considerable talent for philosophic generalities." True genius, Rae conceived,
was a gift of nature and not a quality to be achieved by education or industry. He cites Socrates, Archimedes, and Euclid as some of the great geniuses
of antiquity and gives as one reason for their greatness the fact that they
were unhampered by models and rules. This was in contrast to many of the
Romans whom he regards differently in part because of "the corrections
and restraints of art." He is almost ecstatic in his praise of the genius of
Shakespeare and, what is now not so fashionable, finds in Sir Walter Scott
a modern example of genius. In some respects Rae almost defies sum-
marization, but in this essay one can detect Rae's continued preoccupation
with innovation, with vanity, and with the importance of education, all
areas which are dealt with more prosaically in his *New Principles*. It is quite
evident, however, that this small nugget is a by-product or an expansion
of some of the work he had completed five years earlier.

Rae maintained his keen interest in the geological sciences, but the only
material appearing in print was a two-part article in the *British American
Journal of Medical and Physical Science* for July and August, 1845.[25] The
article was entitled "Remarks on the Rev. Mr. Leach's Observations on the
Previous Existence of a Fresh Water Inland Sea," and was a somewhat
patronizing attack on the views expressed by the Rev. W. T. Leach in an

[22] *Sociological Theory of Capital*, xxxii.
[23] *Ibid.*, xxxi.
[24] See item 10, Part III of this volume.
[25] *British American Journal of Medical and Physical Science*, July, 1845, 91, and Aug.,
1845, 119.

earlier article in the same journal.[26] Leach had come to Canada as a
minister of the Church of Scotland in 1832 and served for a period as
minister of St. Andrew's Church in Toronto. In 1842, he indicated his
intention of resigning to join the Church of England but was "solemnly
deposed" by the Synod of the Kirk. Possibly Rae's animus may not have
sprung solely from their differences on geology. In any case, in his article
Leach advanced the theory that no freshwater lake had ever covered the
North American continent, but rather an arm of the sea, out of which the
land mass gradually rose by successive upheavals. Rae granted that the
lake was originally salt, but contended that it had become fresh by the
run-off of sea water and the addition of rain and river water. Gradually,
he said, the great river valleys were formed as the water broke through the
mountain barriers and ran off to the sea, lowering the level of the lake. The
differences between the two men arose over the question of whether the
river valleys were in existence at the time of the original upheaval or were
formed by the bursting through of water from the inland lake. Leach was
inclined to attach undue weight to recent geological events, while Rae
pointed out correctly that geological developments were often to be
measured in terms of millions or billions of years.

In discussing the effects of erosion, Rae says at one point in his article:

Every large rocky mass has different degrees of tenacity. When, therefore, a
stream of water has to work its way through such a mass, it has a tendency to
form islands. Wherever a portion of the rocks, possessing greater hardness and
density than the adjoining parts, presents a firmer front to the stream, the action
of the water is diverted from the point, and turned to wearing out channels on
each side of it. Hence arises an island of an oval form. The force of the stream,
warded off from the upper end, being expended on the sides, and leaving the
lower end nearly in tranquillity, and consequently extending somewhat largely
down the stream.

Again, water in moving by such an island, impresses on it very distinct marks
of its action. We know that the velocity of a stream is always much the greatest
at the surface. It is on the surface also that ice and other matters are floated along.
There is, consequently, an intensity of action at this level, which impresses on the
rock a horizontal indentation or groove. The thing is to be witnessed in Norway,
and in that strange miniature alpine tract of granite and limestone, which lies
between Perth and Kingston. I am cognizant of the fact, as I know both regions
by personal observation.

Having thus formed a distinct perception of general principles, let us go to the
farm about two miles north of Cap Rouge, on which twelve years since the late
Andrew Stuart had his summer residence . . .

[26] William Turnbull Leach (1805–1886) became Canon of Christ Church Cathedral,
Montreal, in 1854 and, in 1865, Archdeacon of Montreal. He was Professor of Classical
Literature at McGill for many years and became Dean of the Faculty of Arts and
Vice-Principal. He was also the author of an article "On the Uses and Abuses of
Phrenology: A Lecture," which appeared in *ibid.*, 1846.

Apart from the mention of Rae's unexplained trip to Norway, this passage is of interest because it suggests that Rae may have been personally acquainted with Andrew Stuart. Stuart (1785–1840) was for many years a member of the Legislative Council for Lower Canada and Solicitor General in the period 1837–40. After a period of sympathizing with the reform group, Stuart became the chief opponent of Papineau in the Assembly. He was the author of a number of books,[27] and was clearly a man of considerable intellectual attainments.

At another point in his article Rae refers to his travels in Canada. He says, in referring to the banks of the Canadian lakes, " I have examined these margins from Kingston to Amherstburgh, Sandwich, and Penetanguishene, and at various points of the southern shores . . ."

Leach offered a two-part rebuttal in November and December, 1845, which suggests some irritation with Rae. He wrote, in part:

The language of Dr. Rae, in commenting upon the observations which I venture to have published in the British American Journal, breathed a tone, it then seemed to me, of unnecessary severity—I think of some dogmatism too. If I recollect correctly, my observations were offered with no arrogance nor pretension that could justify severity. It is difficult to see the validity of Dr. Rae's right to pronounce the observations of others, in matters purely scientific, heterodox or heresy. I distinctly refuse to plead to his jurisdiction, and stand upon my own right to differ in opinion on such questions from anybody I please, for all that he may think it such presumption to differ from so great a genius as himself. Seriously, the gathering and estimating of evidence being all that is concerned in the question, and the nature of the pursuit being happily exclusive of all contentious passions, let Dr. Rae and myself look to nothing but the evidence, and seek for nothing but the truth.

The controversy between Leach and Rae does not throw much light on the geological history of North America. However, it does appear that Leach's geological knowledge was sadly deficient and his deductive reasoning not much better. Rae demonstrates clearly a superior understanding of geological phenomena and particularly of the role of time. He appears to have been a competent observer of the physiographic characteristics and the geological deposits in Canada, but if Rae understood the rule of continental glaciation in North America he did not make this clear.

Rae continued to participate in the work of various literary and scientific societies until the time he left Hamilton. A notice dated October 20, 1847,

[27] These included *Notes upon the South Western Boundary Line of the British Provinces of Lower Canada and New Brunswick and the United States of America* (Quebec, 1830; 2nd ed., Montreal, 1839); *Review of the Proceedings of the Legislature in Lower Canada in the Session of 1831* (Montreal, 1832); *An Account of the Endowments for Education in Lower Canada, and the Legislative and Other Public Acts for the Advancement Thereof, from the Cession of the Country in 1763 to the Present Time* (London, 1838).

was published by Stephen J. Jones, the Secretary of the Mechanics' Institute, listing a series of lectures for the forthcoming winter season, including two by John Rae. Rae's lectures were scheduled for March 1 and March 8, 1848, and were entitled "On the Characteristics of the Modern School of History."[28] Most of the lectures in the series were published in the *Hamilton Spectator*, but Rae's unfortunately never appeared. He was probably too upset at the time by his personal misfortunes to fulfil his engagement.

[28] *Hamilton Spectator and Journal of Commerce*, Nov. 10, 1847.

6

Rae and the Presbyterians

(1838–1840)

John Rae was at least an interested bystander in the prolonged controversy over the sectarian character of King's College. A Royal Charter had been granted to King's College in 1827, largely as a result of the vigorous efforts of John Strachan and, while the regulations governing the college were more liberal than either Oxford or Cambridge at the time, it was required that all theological students subscribe to the Thirty-nine Articles. For this reason, the Presbyterians looked on the new university with considerable hostility.

In 1832, the newly formed Synod of the Presbyterian Church of Canada in connection with the Church of Scotland met in Kingston and considered, among other things, an overture from the Rev. William Rintoul on the problem of training young Presbyterians for the ministry in Canada. The Synod agreed that a Presbyterian theological seminary should be established and a committee was appointed to prepare a memorial to His Majesty praying for the creation of such an institution.[1] The next year, the Synod met in Toronto and represented to Sir John Colborne "their anxious desire to see the College proposed to be instituted in this place in early operation, under such a charter as shall render it generally available, and secure to it the confidence and support of all denominations . . ."[2]

In 1836, the Synod, meeting in Kingston, again declared that it would be

---

[1] "Minutes of the Synod of the Presbyterian Church of Canada, in connection with the Church of Scotland . . ." 1832, 26. This will be cited hereafter as "Minutes of the Synod."
[2] *Ibid.*, 1833, 44.

"highly expedient to employ every means in their power to obtain the establishment of a Theological College, at which young men may enjoy the means of preparing themselves for the work of the Ministry in this Church."[3] Then, in 1837, the Synod minutes record:

On a reference of several members of the Presbytery of Hamilton for advice in regard to the education of young men now looking forward to the Office of the Holy Ministry, it was resolved that Presbyteries in the mean time receive under their care such young men applying to them as they may deem fit to enter on a course of preparatory study, and direct their studies as they best can, in the hope that better means of instruction shall soon be obtained. . . .[4]

Shortly after this, the Presbytery of Hamilton arranged to have four young men begin a course of studies under Rae.[5]

At this time, the Presbytery of Hamilton was under the charge of the Rev. Alexander Gale. Gale's feelings are clearly illustrated in an excerpt from a letter dated March, 1838, to the Rev. William Bell, then minister of the Church of Scotland in Perth:

The true way to triumph . . . is to bring fact to bear . . . to exhibit an actual, living specimen of scholarship in all the preparatory branches required, literary, mathematical, philosophical, acquired in the Province without any aid from stone walls, far less from steeples . . . and yet fully equal, if not superior, to the average amount of learning required in Scotland previous to admission to Divinity Hall.

This I think we shall be able to do at no distant period, in the person of a young man by the name of McColl . . . He has now been more than a year and a half under the tuition of Dr. Rae our District Schoolmaster and under the inspection of the Presbytery of Hamilton . . .

If a respectable class of young men could be assembled under Dr. Rae, or any other competent teacher, we should very soon overpower all opposition whether among our brethren or in the church at home . . . Besides Mr. McColl, there are four other young men whom I expect within a few weeks to see under Dr. Rae's charge . . . I would respectfully but earnestly entreat you to send your son [George] . . . as soon as circumstances will permit . . .

I may mention that the whole charge for board and education per annum will not exceed £26, although this is no trifle compared with the ordinary revenues of a Canadian minister, yet I trust you will be able to make the sacrifice . . .[6]

In 1838, the Synod of the Kirk met in Montreal and received a report from the Presbytery of Hamilton on the four young men. This throws some light on the educational requirements of those days:

[3] *Ibid.*, 1836, 125.
[4] *Ibid.*, 1837, 146.
[5] Hodgins, *Documentary History*, III, 289.
[6] Quoted in Isabel Skelton, *A Man Austere: William Bell, Parson and Pioneer* (Toronto, 1947), 225.

At Hamilton the Eleventh day of July, One Thousand Eight Hundred and Thirty-eight, the Presbytery met and was constituted with prayer. Mr. Angus McColl, Mr. Stephen Balmer, Mr. John McKinnon and Mr. Robert Wallace appeared for examination. The Presbytery proceeded to examine them severally and minutely in the various Branches of Education in which they had been engaged. The Presbytery ordered the following particulars to be recorded respecting them as a result of this examination viz. that Mr. Angus McColl[7] is about nineteen years of age, and has been engaged for about three years preceding this date in prosecuting his education, during two of which he has been under the tuition of Dr. Rae, that he has read in Greek thirteen Books of the Iliad, the whole contents of the Collectanea Majora, in Latin, the Georgics, eight Books of the Aeneid, and the greater part of the Odes and Satires of Horace, that he has also read the first five books of Euclid, and in Algebra has advanced to simple Equations; and that in all these branches he has made a very satisfactory progress, not only as to extent of reading, but as to accuracy of knowledge; and moreover that he has manifested a very satisfactory acquaintance with the Holy Scripture, and just views of the Christian system, and, as the Presbytery has good reason to believe, decided tokens of personal piety.

That Mr. Robert Wallace[8] is about seventeen years of age, and has been under Dr. Rae's tuition for four months, during which period he has for the first time entered on the study of English Grammar, Latin Geography and Mathematics, that he has now given to the Presbytery the most gratifying evidence of his diligence in study and of his progress in all these branches, having construed a portion of Cornelius Nepos *ad aperturum libri* with readiness and accuracy, exhibiting a most satisfactory precision of grammatical knowledge, and having demonstrated several of the most difficult theorems in the first Book of Euclid with facility and easiness, and that the Presbytery have entire satisfaction as to his knowledge of divine truth and piety.

That Mr. Stephen Balmer,[9] who is twenty-one years of age, had made some progress in the Latin language before leaving Scotland but that these early attainments had been greatly diminished during the seven years he had spent in Upper Canada; that during the short period he has been under the tuition of Doctor Rae, he has made a respectable progress in the reading of Latin, in the Greek grammar, and in the Mathematics, and that the Presbytery have satisfactory evidence of his piety.

That Mr. John McKinnon[10] is about twenty-one years of age, and has been engaged in prosecuting his studies for about eighteen months altogether, during

[7] McColl was ordained a Presbyterian minister in Chatham, Ontario, in 1848. In a biographical note about McColl, Rose in his *Cyclopaedia of Canadian Biography* says, "He . . . attended the Grammar School in Toronto, where the Governor's prize was awarded him for his classical attainments. He then went to a similar school at Hamilton, which was then, and for sometime after, conducted by Dr. John Rae, well known for his varied attainments, and specially for his knowledge of political economy. His time, while under Dr. Rae's instructions, was devoted to the classics, to mathematics, and to the French language. Here also he began to study Hebrew but without a master. He acted for a short while as assistant to Dr. Rae in his school. . . ."

[8] Wallace later became the Presbyterian minister at Ingersoll, Ontario.

[9] Balmer died on Dec. 2, 1839.

[10] McKinnon was for many years the Presbyterian minister in Sydenham and Owen Sound, Ontario.

between two and three of which he has been under Doctor Rae's tuition; that he possesses a considerable knowledge of the Latin language—reading along with Mr. Balmer in Virgil and Horace—and has also made progress in the Greek grammar, and that the Presbytery having further examined him as to his knowledge and view of religious truth and of the sacred office to which he desires to dedicate himself, and having received highly satisfactory testimonials of his christian character from the Rev. Peter Ferguson of Esquesing, agreed to receive him as a student under his care.[11]

At the same session, the Synod resolved:

To tender their thanks to Mr. John Rae, Master of the Gore District School, for his valuable and disinterested services in conducting the studies of several young men who have view to the Ministry in this Church. The Moderator was instructed to communicate this to Mr. Rae.[12]

In July, 1839, the Synod in Kingston considered the report of the Committee on the Education of Candidates for the Ministry, and agreed:

To record their great satisfaction with the assiduity and progress in study, manifested by the young men studying, under the superintendence of the Presbytery of Hamilton, and enjoined that Presbytery to continue their superintendence of the studies of the young men. . . .[13]

The only additional reference to Rae's students occurs in the Minutes of the Synod in 1841 which merely state that "Statements by Presbyteries in regard to the young men prosecuting their studies for the Holy Ministry were read."[14] There is also a note that George Bell had asked to be transferred from the Presbytery of Hamilton, where he had studied under Rae, to the Presbytery of Bathurst which included Perth, the location of his father's church.[15]

By 1839, plans for the new Presbyterian College were crystallizing and in February, 1840, the legislature of Upper Canada passed an Act incorporating the University of Kingston.[16] This was disallowed by the imperial legislature shortly after on the grounds that it infringed on the royal prerogative but a Royal Charter was granted in 1841. The original legislative act provided that at least three professors should be appointed, a professor of classical literature, a professor of natural philosophy and mathematics, and a professor of divinity and moral and mental science. It also stated

[11] "Minutes of the Synod," 1838, 158.

[12] Ibid., 169

[13] Ibid., 1839, 195.

[14] Ibid., 1841, 24.

[15] George Bell (1819–1898) was the first Canadian-born graduate of Queen's University. For many years he was Presbyterian minister in Clifton, Ontario, and in 1883 was appointed Registrar and Librarian of Queen's. He relinquished his post as Librarian in 1888 but continued to be Registrar until 1896.

[16] The legislation received the vice-regal assent on Feb. 10, 1840.

that the appointment of the professors of natural philosophy and mathematics and of divinity were to be left to the Committee on Colonial Churches of the General Assembly of the Church of Scotland. The Board of Trustees, meeting in Kingston in July, 1841, nominated the Rev. Peter Colin Campbell of Brockville to be Professor of Classical Literature, provided there was any money to pay him after provision had been made for the other chairs.[17] In the meantime, the Rev. Thomas Liddell had been designated as Principal.

Finally on March 7, 1842, Queen's College opened with an enrolment of seven theological students. Four of them, George Bell, Angus McColl, John McKinnon, and Robert Wallace had taken at least some of their preparatory work under Rae in Hamilton.

Evidently unaware of the commitments to the General Assembly of the Church of Scotland, Rae came to Kingston in 1841 or possibly early in 1842, armed with testimonials concerning his ability as a teacher to offer himself as a candidate for the chair of natural philosophy and mathematics.[18] In view of the understanding with the Church of Scotland, Rae's application was either shelved or rejected. Although the trustees were apparently considerably concerned by the inability of the Committee on Colonial Churches to nominate suitable candidates, Rae was not reconsidered as a candidate so far as is known.[19] It was not until October, 1842, that the Rev. James Williamson was appointed to the vacant position.

In October, 1845, Rae again appealed to Queen's and offered himself as a candidate for the vacant position of professor of classical literature. He said that he had been advised of the vacancy by "my friend Dr. Craigie" but his application was phrased in a rather abrupt and resentful tone and contained a pessimistic observation, "It is however very likely that the Trustees have some other individual in view to enter into a competition with whom would be bootless."[20] Whether this was true or not, Rae was again turned down.

The tone of Rae's letter suggests that he felt the Trustees had not rewarded him very adequately for his efforts in the difficult days before

[17] *Montreal Gazette*, Aug. 17, 1841. Campbell returned to Scotland in 1845 and in 1867 became Principal of the University of Aberdeen.

[18] Letter, John Rae to the Rev. John Machar, Jan. 12, 1848. At this time Rae was uncertain whether he came to Kingston in 1841 or 1842, but says it was when Professor Campbell was appointed. Presumably he refers to the date of Campbell's actual appointment rather than his nomination by the Board of Trustees.

[19] In a letter from the Rev. P. C. Campbell to Alexander Pringle, Secretary to the Trustees of Queen's College, dated Feb. 4, 1842, the lack of a professor of mathematics was referred to as "the principal difficulty connected with the teaching department."

[20] Letter, John Rae to the Rev. James Williamson, Secretary of the Board of Trustees of Queen's College, Oct. 27, 1845.

Queen's opened. At the semi-centennial celebration of Queen's in 1889, the Rev. Dr. George Bell spoke of the history of the University and mentioned the classes of young men who had studied under Rae prior to the opening of the University in Kingston.[21] This modest honour seems to be the only recognition of Rae's place in the history of Queen's University.

[21] *Queen's College Journal*, Jan. 15, 1890, 55.

7

Rae's Dismissal from His School

(1847–1848)

There is a good deal of evidence to show that Rae was highly regarded as a schoolteacher at least during the early part of his tenure of the Gore District School. This conclusion is largely based on the semi-annual reports of the trustees which were legally required before a teacher could be paid. Although the reports which have been preserved are scattered, they were usually complimentary.

In July, 1835, the trustees reported to the Lieutenant-Governor "that John Rae has faithfully demeaned himself in his office,"[1] and also "that they found much reason to be satisfied with the general progress of the scholars and with the system of instruction pursued."[2] There were seventeen pupils in the school at this time.

Following the examination of the school and the pupils in December, 1836, the trustees reported to the Lieutenant-Governor, in part:

> The Trustees proceeded to the examination of the pupils in the different Classes and were highly pleased with the proficiency made by them in the several departments of learning.
>
> The Trustees have to express their great satisfaction at the accuracy which the Pupils evinced in the fundamental knowledge of the Latin and Greek languages, and the rapid progress made by them. . . .
>
> The Trustees have to report their highest satisfaction with, and approbation of Dr. Rae's conduct and management of the District School, and recommend it with entire confidence to the patronage of the public.[3]

[1] P.A.C., Education Papers, Upper Canada, no. 490.
[2] *Ibid.*, no. 492.
[3] *Hamilton Gazette*, Jan. 11, 1837.

In July, 1837, the trustees again said:

[They] were highly pleased with the proficiency evinced and the progress made by the pupils since the last winter examination, and consider the same as not only highly creditable to the diligence of the Scholars, but likewise evincing the abilities, the assiduity, and perseverance of Doctor Rae, their master. . . .

The Trustees have every reason to be pleased with the exertions and indefatigability of Dr. Rae in the discharge of his arduous duties, and have to congratulate him and the public in general in the acquisition which he and the District School have received in the assistance of Mr. Henry Lawson, A.M. in the School.

The certificates of conduct, character, ability and learning of Mr. Lawson are of the highest order, and when the Trustees consider what the exertions and energies of Dr. Rae will be combined, they anticipate the happiest results to the prosperity of the District School. The Trustees confidently recommend the Gore District School, to the attention and patronage of the public.[4]

In the Reports of the Grammar and Common Schools in Upper Canada submitted to the Legislative Assembly by the Lieutenant-Governor in 1839, there is a note about Rae's school:

The Trustees say:—that they have examined the District (Grammar) School conducted by Dr. John Rae, the Principal, and Mr. William Tassie, his assistant, and find the institution in a most flourishing and advancing condition. The progress of the numerous pupils in knowledge is great, and every credit is due to the diligence and attention of the Teachers.[5]

Rae's place as an educationalist in Hamilton was recognized by his appointment in 1843 as a member of the Board of Examiners for Hamilton established under the Common School Act of 1841.[6] In December, 1842, the Hamilton Board of Police which also acted as the Board of Education had divided the city into five common school districts under authority of the Act of 1841.[7] The Board of Police nominated a Board of Examiners whose main responsibility was to act as examiners for prospective teachers for the common schools.

The dispute over the control of the grammar schools or some other reason seems to have induced a note of coolness or formality in the reports of the trustees on the state of Rae's school. In July, 1844, the report of the trustees was more reserved:

We . . . beg to report for the information of His Excellency the Governor General that we have this day held the annual examination of the said School,

[4] *Ibid.*, July 19, 1837.
[5] Hodgins, *Documentary History*, III, 256.
[6] 4 & 5 Vic. c. 18. This appointment is noted in "Minutes," Hamilton Board of Police (1833–44), March 31, 1843, 325.
[7] J. G. Hodgins, *The Establishment of Schools and Colleges in Ontario, 1792–1910* (Toronto, 1910), I, 89.

that we have found it conducted in a satisfactory manner and that the pupils
exhibited a very fair proficiency in the various branches of Classical and English
education.[8]

A year later a similar report was submitted, this time by "The Committee
of the Trustees of the Gore District Grammar School appointed by the
General Board for the Special Supervision of that Institution" in which
they stated that they had "examined the said school and found it to be
conducted in a satisfactory manner."[9]

By this time there were three grammar schools in the Gore District and
nine trustees. There were schools in Ancaster and Palermo in addition to
Rae's school in Hamilton. Committees of three of the trustees were formed
to supervise each of the schools. However, by the end of 1847, one of the
trustees had died, one had moved to Toronto and one had resigned. Of the
remaining six only two, the Rev. J. G. Geddes and Dr. William Craigie of
Hamilton, were specifically concerned with Rae's school. From Rae's
point of view, the fact that the Rev. Alexander Gale no longer served as a
member of the committee supervising his school was of singular importance.

Gale's departure was a result of internal discord in the Kirk in Canada.
In order to understand this development it is necessary to digress briefly
to examine a momentous event in the history of the Church of Scotland.
"Presbyterianism," as Matthew Arnold once said, "is born to division as
the sparks fly upwards." Presbyterians, like bees, have shown a remarkable
tendency to hive off, a process which has often been accompanied by
extreme bitterness and protracted litigation. The sixth and most serious
schism was the Disruption of 1843, which arose out of a controversy over
the rights of congregations to control effectively the appointment of their
own ministers. This had been impaired early in the eighteenth century by
legislation which in effect had restored the right of patronage. In 1834, the
General Assembly of the Kirk passed a resolution giving the male heads of
families in congregations the right to veto the individual designated by the
patron. This "veto law" was considered by a Civil Court of Session in 1838
in connection with the famous Auchterarder Case, in which 287 out of a
total of 300 heads of families had vetoed a proposed appointment. The
Court of Session declared the veto law *ultra vires* which immediately raised
the question of the right of secular authorities to intervene in or set aside
the decisions of the church authorities. The upshot was that on May 18,
1843, 470 ministers severed all their connections with the Established
Church of Scotland to join the Free Church.

[8] P.A.C., Provincial Secretary's Office, Canada West, no. 8132, July 18, 1844.
[9] *Ibid.*, no. 12386, July 11, 1845.

So far as the Kirk in Canada was concerned, its Synod had been recognized by a declaratory enactment of the General Assembly of the Church of Scotland in 1833,[10] and there was a strong bond of sympathy between the parent Church and the colonial synod. The Canadian members of the Kirk watched with keen interest and sympathy the controversy over the relations between the spiritual prerogatives of the Church and the civil power.

Early in July, 1844, the Synod of the Presbyterian Church of Canada in connection with the Church of Scotland met in Kingston to consider *inter alia* the implications of the Disruption. On July 4, the Synod reviewed the following propositions, which are part of a longer list, and recorded their views:

5. There has been no interference whatever, on the part of the Civil Powers, with any of our Ecclesiastical Courts.
Agreed to by all.
6. There is not, at present, so far as can be reasonably judged, any prospect of such interference with the Ecclesiastical Courts.
Agreed to by all with the exception of Mr. Gale.
7. There is no external or legal let or hindrance to the extension of the Church in this Province.
Agreed to by all.
8. Therefore the alleged causes of disruption at home do not exist here.
Agreed to by all.[11]

On July 9, 1844, in a remarkable and baffling *volte-face*, an important group of the Presbyterian clergy in Canada indicated that they were unwilling to continue an association with the Established Church of Scotland which it now appeared had accepted an untenable and dangerous relation with the state. Accordingly, twenty-three ministers broke away from the Presbyterian Church of Canada in connection with the Church of Scotland and established an independent organization, the Presbyterian Church of Canada.

This event was of particular significance to Rae because it affected many of his friends and associates and particularly the trustees of the Gore District Grammar School. Both Gale and Stark switched to the "free" church while Dr. William Craigie remained with the Kirk.[12] The Synod of the Presbyterian Church of Canada, of which Stark was the first moderator, immediately took steps to create its own theological college and in November, 1844, what was to become Knox College opened in Toronto. A

[10] Gregg, *History of the Presbyterian Church in Canada*, 469–70.
[11] "Minutes of the Synod," July, 1844, 10.
[12] Craigie was an elder representing the Presbytery of Toronto at meetings of the Synod of the Kirk in 1835, 1839, 1840, 1842, and 1844. He became Presbytery Clerk in 1845.

preparatory school known as the Toronto Academy or sometimes Gale's Academy was established in 1845, and Gale came from Hamilton to be the Principal and in addition Professor of Classical Literature of Knox College. In this way, Rae lost one of his strongest friends and supporters among the trustees.

Rae's relations with the Rev. J. Gamble Geddes may have been strained ever since the disputes among the trustees in the early 1840's and may never have been cordial in view of Rae's role as a critic of the Church of England. The fact that Geddes opened his own private school in Hamilton in 1843 may not have improved matters. Geddes' school was in direct competition with the Gore District Grammar School, but in addition to the normal curriculum of English, classics, mathematics, French and German, emphasized religious instruction. Classes were devoted to the "Study of the Church Catechism, Church History and Christian Evidence."[13] Whether there were serious religious, occupational, or personal differences between Rae and Geddes must, however, remain conjectural. On one occasion, Geddes made some very generous comments on the work of Rae's sister, Ann Cuthbert Fleming. He wrote a testimonial about Mrs. Fleming's book, The Prompter:[14]

> I have much pleasure in bearing testimony to the success with which you lately instructed a juvenile class in the District School in the principles of English grammar on a new system of your own invention, and which, I understand you intend to publish.
>
> The proficiency which your pupils—most of them boys about eight years old, and many of whom were perfectly ignorant of grammar—exhibited in the short space of six weeks would have been incredible had I not witnessed it with my own eyes and ears.

One might judge from this that the differences between the two men were not of long standing.

Dr. William Craigie (1790–1863), a native of Aberdeenshire, had studied medicine at Marischal College and later at the Universities of Edinburgh and Dublin. He taught school for a brief period after his arrival in Canada in 1834, but soon began to practise medicine in Ancaster and continued after he moved to Hamilton in the mid-forties.[15] Craigie had been appointed a trustee of the Gore District School early in 1837 on the recom-

---

[13] A brief account of this school by the Rev. Canon George A. Bull is contained in Hodgins, *Documentary History*, V, 282. At first, the school had only five pupils but soon the enrolment increased to about fifty, necessitating the employment of an assistant teacher.

[14] Geddes' testimonial was published in the back of Mrs. Fleming's *The Prompter Containing the Principles of the English Language, etc.* (Montreal, 1844).

[15] He was licensed by the Medical Board of Upper Canada in April, 1835.

mendation of Sir Allan N. MacNab and had taken an intense interest in educational matters. In 1841, Craigie unsuccessfully applied for the position of Superintendent of Education in Canada West; he became a member of the Board of Trustees of Queen's in 1845.

Late in December, 1847, Geddes and Craigie decided to oust Rae from his position as headmaster of the Gore District Grammar School. Accordingly they submitted a petition to Lord Elgin, the Governor General, expressing their dissatisfaction with the state of the school, primarily on grounds of its "inefficiency."[16] They found it necessary to comment on the fact that there was some inconsistency between their earlier favourable reports and the "decided disapprobation" expressed in their report, saying:

They beg however to state in explanation that it will be found that their Certificates and Reports for several years have not gone beyond the bare letter of the law,—thus much they thought they could scarcely in justice withhold as past services were entitled to Remuneration; and they forbore to make any representation of the inefficiency of the school from motives of delicacy—from a desire not to act with harshness or severity—and from a hope which they continued to entertain that on obtaining something like proper School accommodation, subsequent improvement might render censure unnecessary, if a longer period of probation were given. A sense of duty, however, forbids them to be longer silent for although better school accommodation was provided, not only has no improvement taken place in the Classical and Mathematical departments, but there appears rather to have been a falling off. Of about twelve boys who were engaged in Latin studies the Junior Class was found ignorant of the very first rudiments of Grammar, and of the Senior Division but two or three evinced anything like satisfactory progress; while in Mathematics there was still less proficiency. If any proof were wanting of the inefficiency of the School as a Grammar School, it will be found in the fact that parents who wish to give their children a liberal education, are constrained to do so either by the more expensive means of private tuition, or by sending them away from home, so that what ought to have been the leading school of the District, has dwindled down to little better than a respectable Common School, in which however the Trustees feel it but common justice to say that the English branches are taught with much efficiency.[17]

The last sentence refers to the fact that William Tassie taught English reading and grammar while Rae taught the classical and mathematical subjects. The trustees adduced additional proof of the inefficiency of Rae's school by saying that the pupils of the other grammar schools in the Gore District had recently competed successfully with the pupils of Rae's school

[16] P.A.C., Provincial Secretary's Office, Canada West, no. 18698, Dec. 30, 1847.
[17] The Grammar School Amendment Act of 1819 stipulated that the trustees of district schools must submit certificates semi-annually stating that the schools had been conducted in a satisfactory manner and that there were more than ten pupils. The teachers were paid on the basis of these certificates.

"which has enjoyed the support of Government under the same principal
for a period of twelve years." The trustees then went on to say:

Under these circumstances the Trustees feel it a painful but imperative duty
to express their dissatisfaction with the present state of the School and their
persuasion that it will never answer the ends of its institution, until placed in the
hands of a more efficient Master. In expressing this opinion they do not intend
to throw any reflections on the Master's attainments in Scholarship, but merely
to express their sense of his inefficiency as a Teacher.

Although the report of the trustees dwelt on Rae's inefficiency as a
teacher, it also stated that there were between sixty and seventy pupils in
the school, which indicates that the situation was not bad enough to have
prevented a substantial increase in enrolment. Rae's shortcomings were
also discussed briefly in a letter written by Craigie which accompanied the
trustees' report.[18] Craigie noted that "the attendance of the Master is very
irregular and his observance of the rules adopted for the Government of
the Schools far from satisfactory."[19]

Considerable attention was devoted to the problem of school accommodation in the report of the trustees and in Craigie's letter:

The Trustees have made repeated appeals to the Municipal and City Councils,
as well as to the Inhabitants to provide suitable school accommodation, hitherto
without effect; and as the lease of the present building, the rent of which they
have great difficulty in raising, expires on the 1st February, and cannot be
renewed, they have come to the resolution of allowing the School to remain in
abeyance until suitable buildings are provided, and a fairer prospect presents
itself of rendering it useful and efficient.

Craigie explained in more detail the accommodation problem:

Prior to the last two years the School was kept in miserable apartments rented by
the Teacher, and the ready answer was, "Who could teach efficiently in such a
place as this?" After repeated and vain appeals to the local authorities and to the
inhabitants, to build a proper schoolhouse (and the failure of these appeals, they
doubt not, was owing to the general feeling that there could not be a useful
school till there was a change of Teacher), the Trustees rented two good rooms
and still more to rouse the energies of the Teacher appointed an annual examination of five scholars from each of the three Grammar Schools in the District.
At these examinations the inferiority of the Hamilton Scholars, except in English
Grammar and Geography, was very apparent.

It is clear from this that the school accommodation was desperately bad
and there is little wonder that the teaching was regarded as inefficient. To

[18] P.A.C., Provincial Secretary's Office, Canada West, no. 18698.
[19] This is a curious charge coming from Craigie since he was one of the trustees who
vehemently protested against the way in which the rules of the Council of King's
College were adopted in 1841.

teach between sixty and seventy boys even in "two good rooms" would doubtless have strained the most skilled and earnest pedagogue.[20]

The report of the trustees expressing their dissatisfaction with Rae was referred to the Attorney General for an opinion on the legal aspects of the issue. The Attorney General expressed the view that "the Government has no power to dismiss a Teacher of a Grammar School. That power is vested in the Trustees, and then only for a misdemeanour, or impropriety of conduct."[21] This opinion was relayed to Craigie by the Provincial Secretary, Dominick Daly, sometimes referred to as the "Everlasting Secretary," on February 21, 1848.[22] Craigie replied on March 10 that the trustees had unanimously resolved to dismiss Rae "for unfaithful demeanour and impropriety of conduct," adding a remarkable footnote:

In your letter it is stated that a teacher can only be removed for "a misdemeanour or impropriety of conduct." This might imply that misdemeanour was used in its legal sense. On reference to the Act, however, the trustees find that it is "any misdemeanour or impropriety of conduct," and taking this in connexion with the following clause of the act that the certificate must bear "that he has faithfully demeaned himself," they infer that "unfaithful demeanour" is a "misdemeanour" in the meaning of the Statute.[23]

The legal position of the trustees was weak in view of the faulty drafting of the legislation and they merely parroted the legal grounds for dismissal. In fact, since the trustees could prevent the payment of Rae's salary by refusing to issue the necessary certificate and since they had allowed the lease on the schoolrooms to lapse, their legal right to oust Rae was not very important.

In the meantime, Rae prepared a memorial to Lord Elgin seeking to rebut the charge of inefficiency. The text of Rae's document is curiously insipid, perhaps because he regarded it as a preliminary version of the more detailed and careful statement which he planned to prepare. His petition, dated February 16, 1848, was:

That some weeks since your memorialist was presented with a copy of a report of the Trustees of the school of which he is master, which it was intimated to him it was the intention of said Trustees to forward to your Excellency: that thereupon he immediately began to draw up a memorial to your Excellency to rebut that whole report; that however from various causes, in particular from individuals having been and now being absent from Hamilton whose evidence he conceives

[20] The problem of inadequate accommodation for the school was not a new one. In 1829, Stephen Randal complained in a return to the Private Secretary of the Lieutenant-Governor that the school room was only 20′ × 20′ and was too small to accommodate forty boys. P.A.C., Education Papers, Upper Canada, no. 152.

[21] P.A.C., Provincial Secretary's Office, Canada West, no. 18698.

[22] *Ibid.*

[23] *Ibid.*, no. 19547.

necessary with other documents fitly to support his position he has not yet been able to make up a full statement of his case: that he is exceedingly desirous of furnishing every information, and all documents necessary for the full investigation of the subject, as all important to himself, and as he humbly conceives to the general interests of education in Canada: but that he is unwilling to forward a memorial defective in any particular: that however the length of time which he has unwillingly allowed to pass leads him to fear that his case may possibly be prejudged and that therefore he herewith transmits a series of documents, sufficient as he humbly conceives to show that for a long course of years he has been reckoned by competent judges to have been deficient neither in talents, industry, or success in his occupation of teacher, and that he still retains the confidence and support of individuals quite as capable as the Trustees of forming a just estimate of his merits.

That your memorialist trusts these documents will be sufficient to suspend any action in his case until he shall be able to forward a complete statement of particulars, and that so trusting he as in duty bound will ever pray &c. &c. &c.[24]

The list of accompanying documents and Rae's comments on them throw some interesting light on Rae's friends and supporters:

1. Copy of Letter from the Revd Henry Esson 1827
2. ─────────────────────Revd Hugh Urquhart
   (The work referred to in the latter communication and too partially written about was reviewed at considerable length in various Journals among others in the Northamerican Review and Foreign Quarterly Review—in the former in the beginning in the latter about the middle of the year 1835.)
3d Communication from the Revd John Cook D.D. Moderator of the Synod of the Scotch Church in Canada.[25]
4th ─────────────────────from the Revd Daniel Allen Moderator of the Synod of Hamilton.[26]
   N.B. Only copies of these documents can be procured they are however in the handwriting of James Durno one of J R scholars who died six years since and which may easily be identified. The originals with other important documents were left in the hands of the Trustees of Queens College Kingston and have not been recovered.
5. Testimonial from Trustees May 1840
6. Letter from Colin Reid Esqr Barrister[27]
7. ─────Stephen J. Jones─────
8 ─────Richard Martin─────────[28]

[24] P.A.C., Provincial Secretary's Office, Canada West, no. 19325, Feb. 16, 1848.

[25] John Cook (1805–92), minister of St. Andrew's Church, Quebec City, Principal of Queen's College, 1857–58, and Principal of Morrin College, Quebec, 1862–92. Cook was Moderator of the Synod of the Kirk in 1838 and was instructed by the Synod to write to Rae to thank him for his work with the Presbyterian theological students. This is presumably the letter referred to.

[26] In 1852, Daniel Allen was minister of the Kirk in North East Hope, Presbytery of London.

[27] Colin C. Reid was a Hamilton lawyer.

[28] Richard Martin, Q.C. (1823–86), became a well-known lawyer in Hamilton.

9. Testimonial from scholars 1840 to which is appended the present position of said scholars in so far as known to J. R.

10. Letter from Rev. J Gamble Geddes Sep 1 1841

11. Communication for T. A. Gibson Esq second master of High School Montreal.[29]

12. Letter from Colonel Martin.[30]
    (It may not be irrelevant to state that Colonel Martin's father and brother are well known in parliamentary history as distinguished representatives of the County Galway Ireland.)

13. Letter from Henry Morgan Esq an English gentleman

14. Communication from Sir Allan N Macnab (It may be proper to note with regard to this that J. R. only applied to Sir Allan for a certificate of military service as a document along with others which would show the loss he had sustained in remaining in Canada in 1837—and that the testimonial as to his ability as a teacher is altogether voluntary.

15. Testimonials with regard to Alexr Roxburgh.[31]

Rae's memorial was briefly acknowledged by the Provincial Secretary who merely sent him a copy of his earlier reply to Craigie and returned his documents.[32]

From this account, it will be clear that Rae's dismissal climaxed a long period of bitterness between two opposed groups on the board of trustees. Their differences reflected the protracted quarrelling between the Presbyterians and the Church of England over the control of education in the province and other matters. Rae had unequivocally allied himself with the Presbyterian cause and his position was vulnerable when, for purely fortuitous reasons, he was left without support on the board of trustees.

Mixter quotes some evidence to the effect that Rae may have been dismissed because of his religious views: "A former acquaintance writing

[29] Thomas Adam Gibson was successively master of the grammar school of Wick, Scotland, master of Cauvin's Hospital (1834–38), Edinburgh, and rector of Tain Academy before he emigrated to Canada about 1840. He finally became first classical master of the High School Department of McGill College, the successor to the Royal Grammar School. He was the author of *Geography of Canada* (Montreal, 1855) and of a number of other books and editor of the 1836 edition of *Mair's Tyro Dictionary, Latin and English.*

[30] Richard Martin (1797–1878), the father of the Richard Martin referred to above. Martin, the father, was at one time Rector of Dunboyne, County Meath, but withdrew from the priesthood and emigrated to Canada in 1833. He became Sheriff of Haldimand County in December, 1850, and was also Lieutenant-Colonel of the Haldimand Militia.

[31] This probably refers to Alexander Roxburgh, Jr., one of Rae's pupils whose father (1774–1856) was at one time a Captain in the Glengarry Fencibles. He moved to Ancaster in 1832 and during the Rebellion of 1837 was Quartermaster-General for the loyalist forces on the Niagara frontier. Later he lived in Hamilton and became a magistrate.

[32] P.A.C., Provincial Secretary's Office, Canada West, no. 19325, March 1, 1848. Rae kept the various testimonials until his death. They were given to Mixter by Sir Roderick Cameron but are now lost. See *Sociological Theory of Capital*, xxv.

recently is of the opinion that undoubtedly the real reason for the action of the Trustees was Rae's religious views. He had become a good deal of a free thinker and most of the Board were clergymen."[33] This conclusion is completely untenable and probably arises out of Mixter's unfamiliarity with the Disruption in the Kirk in 1844. Although there is no positive evidence, it is very likely that Rae's sympathies were with the Free Church, i.e., the group that defected from the Church of Scotland. This group included such friends and associates of Rae as Esson, Gale, Rintoul, and Stark. It is indicative also that all of Rae's theological students with the exception of George Bell joined the Free Church. It may be surmised that Mixter's correspondent referred to Rae's adherence to the Free Church in terms which were wrongly interpreted by Mixter. It is nevertheless almost certain that Craigie and Rae were opposed on the bedevilled question which led to the Disruption. In general, there was great bitterness engendered by the dispute and many friendships and associations were ruptured by it.

There were undoubtedly points of difference between Craigie and Rae on educational techniques. Craigie is known to have held strong views on the place of religion in education. Writing to the Superintendent of Education, Canada West, in 1843, Craigie made the following old-fashioned comment on the Common School Act of 1841:

A system of education to be really useful and effective must be based firmly on Religion. No man who believes the Scriptures to be the Oracles of God, who believes in His promise to preserve and bless them and in his Omnipotence, which is pledged to give it effect, can reasonably hope, or expect, that a system of education, of which a primary object is not instruction in the momentous facts, and all-important doctrines of the Bible, could receive this blessing, or be attended, or followed, with success; and the mere politician, who knows anything of Government, and of the History of Education,—its signal success, where based on Religion, and its signal failure, where otherwise,—must inevitably arrive at the same conclusion.[34]

Geddes may have entertained similar ideas on the subject. Rae's basic conception of education would not have fitted in satisfactorily with these views.

There is some possibility that there were differences between Craigie and Rae, arising out of Craigie's scheme to build a central school in Hamilton, a proposal which he first made public early in December, 1847.[35] Possibly Rae had indicated his opposition to the plan for centralization or perhaps

[33] Sociological Theory of Capital, xxv.
[34] Letter, William Craigie to Robert Murray, Oct. 7, 1843, quoted in Hodgins, Docmenutary History, IV, 311.
[35] Hodgins, Establishment of Schools and Colleges in Ontario, 1792–1910, I, 70.

Craigie realized that it would not be possible to get Church of England support so long as Rae was the schoolteacher.

There may have been good grounds for the charges that Rae was neglecting his duties as a schoolmaster. Considering the deplorable conditions of overcrowding and the difficulties of dealing with sixty or seventy pupils at once this would not have been surprising. The unwillingness of the people of Hamilton to provide reasonably good classrooms must have been disheartening. It was also a disappointing period in Rae's life: the manuscript of his *magnum opus*, "Outlines of the Natural History and Statistics of Canada," had been lost, his application for a teaching post at Queen's College had been rejected and his contributions to political economy appeared to him to have been completely ignored.

One possibility that cannot be overlooked is that Rae had taken to drink in this period of his life. There is no information on this point except a casual reference in a letter to a friend in Hamilton written in 1850 in which he says, "I very seldom taste anything stronger than tea, unless with a friend; but I am become a confirmed smoker."[36] If, in fact, Rae had sought solace in alcohol he would have had a great deal of company in Canada of that period.

The report of the Gore District School Superintendent for 1848 has some relevant remarks on the question of the dismissal of teachers:

It not infrequently happens that mere caprice with regard to a Teacher, or Trustees, will set those whose rule of action is their own feeling actively to work to run down the Teacher of the School, without ever considering what a dreadful injury they are inflicting on the young. Of this, I had an instance last week. One of the best qualified Teachers in the District was condemned for not doing his duty while it was quite evident from the advanced state of the scholars under his care, that the accusers were unjust and had made no effort to ascertain the truth.[37]

Rae was not mentioned by name and the episode may be merely a coincidence.

Developments in the Gore District Grammar School in the ten years after Rae left do not throw much light on the episode of his dismissal. Rae's immediate successor in the Gore District Grammar School was James Windeat, a graduate of St. Peter's College, Cambridge, who had taught previously in the Johnston District Grammar School. Windeat resigned before the summer of 1848 and was replaced by George Elmslie, a member of the Church of England, who had been headmaster of the

[36] The letter is quoted in full in the following chapter.
[37] The excerpt is from a report by Patrick Thornton of Hamilton, the School Superintendent of the Gore District. Hodgins, *Documentary History*, VIII, 66.

Grammar School in Ancaster.[38] Elmslie was later replaced by William Tassie as headmaster. In the early 1850's, education in Hamilton was upset by the controversy over the construction of a central school which was so vigorously advocated by Craigie. After lengthy and heated discussion Craigie won his point and finally, in 1855, the Central School and the Gore District Grammar School were merged. When this occurred, Geddes resigned from the Board of Trustees in a stiff and unfriendly letter.[39] It was also at this time that William Tassie took over the grammar school in Galt which achieved great distinction under his guidance. One conclusion to be drawn from all this is that Craigie was a man of great determination who was willing to betray his friends and alienate his allies to achieve his aims.

Rae was headmaster of the Gore District School for a period of thirteen years. At the end of this time, when he was fifty-two years old, his career as a schoolmaster in Canada was terminated by his dismissal. Rae was no innocent victim of circumstances. He was not only an outspoken opponent of the Church of England but probably a dissident Presbyterian as well. Not long after his dismissal Rae wrote to his friend, Hugh Bowlby Willson, supposedly from Panama or California:

London, Paris, with a little capital in money and literary reputation have been my aim for years. There, with the assistance of libraries, museums, friends who could and might be induced to assist me, I have conceived I should have the fairest field for my literary and philosophical speculations, and for my mechanical schemes. The one would assist the other. Had it not been for those confounded Trustees, my plans were so laid that I feel pretty confident I should before this have been there, and it was this overthrow of my plans more than the mere ejection from the school that so nearly overset me, and but for you, I believe, would have given me my final quietus.[40]

Additional testimony concerning Rae's financial plight is contained in a petition late in November, 1847, from one John Coumbe to the Governor General asking that Rae's salary be garnisheed for rent. Coumbe explained his grievance: "Dr John Rae occupied my House but I am sorry to say he quited it having removed his goods unknown to me whereby I was deprieved of my Rent amounting with cost for repariation of Delapidations to forty two pounds."[41]

Rae appears to have left Hamilton sometime in the summer or fall of

[38] P.A.C., Provincial Secretary's Office, Canada West, no. 255; letter, William Craigie to R. B. Sullivan, Aug. 4, 1848.

[39] *Ibid.*, no. 1183; letter, J. G. Geddes to Provincial Secretary, July 24, 1856.

[40] *Sociological Theory of Capital*, xxxix–xl.

[41] P.A.C., Provincial Secretary's Office, Canada West, no. 18341, Nov. 23, 1847. The Provincial Secretary replied that Coumbe would have to refer his claim to "the ordinary legal tribunals of the country."

1848. Where he went immediately is not known but there is some evidence indicating that he paid a visit to Three Rivers. The evidence is in the form of the following two poems which were published in the *Literary Garland* in January, 1849.

TO J. R.

The Last o' November

The last o' November comes surly an' drear,
Wi' dark frowning clouds, near the close o' the year;
The trees are a' leafless, the birds fled awa,
An' mountain an' valley are covered wi' snaw;
Pale Nature looks wae as she hangs down her head,
O'er the beauties o' simmer a' withered and dead,
An' piercing an' bleak are the blasts on the lea—
Yet dear is the last o' November to me.

For aye when it comes it brings back to my min'
The hame that I left, an' the days o' langsyne.
An' where is the spot on the earth that's so dear,
The mountains so blue, or the waters so clear,
As my own native hills, with the heather in bloom,
Where the green thistle waves 'mongst the beautiful broom?
And to think on the lan' that I'll never mair see,
Brings the sigh frae my heart, an' the tear frae my e'e.

But o' there is something that's far dearer still
Than the fond recollections of valley an' hill;
'Tis the friends of my youth, my companions of yore,
Who have bade me farewell, ne'er to meet with me more;
The sense of whose friendship can never depart
Till the last throb of feeling is still in my heart.
My sleep shall be dreamless, in solitude drear,
When the friends of my childhood shall cease to be dear.

J. D.

Three Rivers, last o' November, 1848.

TO J. D.

A Flight o' Fancy

Your bonnie lines, an' cowe o' heather,
Made my auld heart as licht's a feather;
Sae off on fancy's wings I flew,
My native glen ance mair to view.
I thought it early morn in May —
Month o' the year maist blythe an' gay,—
I lighted on the warlock knowe,
Where stunted bushes only grow;

Then I had full within my view,
Baith crystal stream an' mountains blue;
The lambies bleatin' on the hill,
Some sporting'—loupin' o'er the rill;
The mavis perched on thorny spray,
In blythe notes welcomed in the day;
The linties on the whinnie brae,
Sent down their streams o' melody.
The laverock, soarin' high in air,
Poured forth sic dulcet warblins there,
As tunes the heart to praise an' prayer;
The auld kirk on the risin' knowe,
The mill mair distant in the howe;
The meadows clad in richest green,
Where comely youths an' maids were seen.
But a' my early friends were gane,
Some laid aneath the sod or stane;
Some perished on the stormy main;
But maist were in the battle slain.
The few that live were far awa,
"Pursuing fortunes slidd'ry ba'."
The Glen being lanely noo to me,
The tear-drop fillin' fast my e'e,
I shook frae aff my wings the dew,
Flew back to tell my wues to you.

J. R.

Three Rivers, last o' November, 1848.

The identity of "J.D." is not known for certain, but there is a possibility that it was James Dickson. Dickson (1793–1855) was born in Paxton, Berwickshire, and came to Canada from Scotland in 1818 as a young man. He became a dealer in lumber or firewood and was prominent in local affairs in Three Rivers being among other things a Justice of the Peace and Senior Church Warden of the Anglican Church.[42] In 1827 he married Henrietta Sawtell, the oldest daughter of Luther Sawtell, a well-known dry goods merchant in Montreal and likely to be a business acquaintance at least of James Fleming, who was also a dry goods merchant.

According to Mixter, Rae spent some part of 1849 in Boston and New York where he again took up school teaching.[43] By this time, Rae's friend,

[42] There are references to James Dickson in Benjamin Sulte, *Trois-Rivières d'autrefois*, fourth series (Montreal, 1934) [Mélanges historiques, vol. 21] and A. E. E. Legge, *The Anglican Church in Three Rivers, Quebec, 1768–1956* (Russell, Ont., 1956), and several notices of various official appointments in the *Quebec Gazette*.

[43] *Sociological Theory of Capital*, xxv. The New York City Directory for 1849 lists a John Rae living at 102 James Street.

Roderick William Cameron, was established as a broker and commission merchant in New York so Rae was not completely friendless.

In mid-1849, Rae received the sad news of the death of his wife, Eliza, who had remained in Hamilton. She died on August 16, 1849, of cholera, a disease which was epidemic in Canada that summer.[44] Mixter says of this episode: "Her death took place August 17, 1849, under particularly distressing circumstances, into the details of which it is not necessary to enter. Letters written by friends and kindred at the time show that this must have been a sad bereavement to the already sorely oppressed man. Rae himself once alludes to it as 'a great and soul-penetrating sorrow.' "[45] This melancholy event finally uprooted him and he decided, like many other discouraged and restless men, to head for California and a new life.

[44] There is a brief obituary notice in the *Montreal Gazette*, Aug. 28, 1849.
[45] *Sociological Theory of Capital*, xxv.

8

"Dr. Rae in California"

(1849–1851)

The discovery of gold in California in 1848 offered a stimulus and a challenge to many footloose and rootless men. Something like a hundred thousand men migrated westward by various routes often undergoing fearful hardships to reach the goldfields. To Rae, with his career as a schoolteacher in Canada shattered, his wife dead, and his hopes of literary achievement stifled, this golden land appeared to offer something new and exciting. He left New York in the steamship *Empire City* in December, 1849, bound for Chagres. This was one of the favoured sea routes which involved overland travel to Panama and thence again by sea to California.

Those who went by sea had their choice of the "Panama Route" or the "Cape Route." The first was favored by those who could pay $380, largely because they would reach the gold fields in weeks rather than months—or so they were told. The journey from New York to Chagres in Panama was novel enough to be exciting; travelers could wear their new flannel shirts and heavy boots, and pepper passing dolphins with their shiny new revolvers. But at Chagres, a steaming cluster of mud huts holding back the jungle, hardships began. First they haggled with natives for canoe transportation up the Chagres River. Then for two days they made their way inland amidst constant rainfall and oppressive heat, marched another two days through a snake-ridden jungle, and at last reached the ancient city of Panama on the shores of the Pacific, where they settled down amidst heat, moisture, and filth to wait a ship to San Francisco.[1]

Rae spent some time in Chagres, according to his own account. On December 27, 1849, he wrote a letter to Hugh Bowlby Willson from

[1] Ray Allen Billington, *The Far Western Frontier, 1830–1960* (New York, 1956), 224.

Chagres which was reproduced in part by Mixter.[2] The letter throws some revealing light on his frame of mind during this period:

I have now for many years been an exile from the land which I had chosen as my home,[3] and in which I had made up my mind to pass my remaining days, and within the present month, and in beginning old age, have become a wanderer and adventurer over the wide earth. You know the cruel injustice which had thus driven me forth. You partly know also the cruel sufferings thus entailed on me, and which have almost rent my heart. But this of good has resulted from all.[4] Nature under a new face, humanity under an altered aspect; a sense of danger, and a necessity for action, have, as it were, renewed my soul, and enabled me to look calmly on what I have been and what I am. Thus I see myself as in times past destiny seemed to have stamped me, I can analyze, as it were, the elements of my then existence, and taking my stand on what new has broken in on it, can measure and look on it as a thing apart from the present.

Fortune has not permitted me to be the student I would have desired. The study of such a one is in the spacious library where undisturbed and uncontrolled he can roam over the thoughts and read the souls of men of all times and countries; or else the wide world itself, with all conveniences to explore it and examine the various aspects of nature and of man which it exhibits—or better still, each alternately. Only partially, only scantily have I enjoyed these advantages. But every man has a world of study within his own soul, and in the workings of the passions of those around him. This I have not neglected. . . .

Alas for the student, ardent and feeling, and with hopes like mine, pursuing truth without dread as concerns self, and yet shrinking from it when at length grasped as a thing, though having within itself the energetic powers of a new and better order of things yet coming on the present world, if receiving it, like one of the phials of wrath of the apocalypse. I had determined that no important writing of mine should appear till after my death. Thus I could acquit myself to the Omnipotent for not hiding what He had allowed me to see of what at least appeared to me *light*, and avoid the suspicion of being actuated by personal motives. . . .

What now I may do is uncertain. I know not even if my manuscripts are safe. Certainly a new spirit is awakened within me, and may lead to a new course of action, if I be not cut down by some of the chances which I see fall to so many around me. . . .

Now as concerns Canadian independence, or annexation; that also as a thing interesting in itself, and more especially as one to be taken as a sign of other things of greater interest with which the present era seems pregnant, had occupied at least some little of my attention; but I had become accustomed to view it from a point and in a light different from that in which politicians of the hour necessarily regard it.

Let me explain myself. When one commences the study of history, it is generally under the apprehension that this study will serve as a master key to the problems of the day, and will enable him not only to form just conclusions

[2] *Sociological Theory of Capital*, xxxvii–xxxix.
[3] This may be a reference to France.
[4] Presumably this sentence should read, "But out of this, good has resulted from ill."

J.R. I—8

concerning them, but, if so prompted, to address his contemporaries with authority and power. But as he advances farther and farther in the pursuit, and if he has seized the philosophical spirit of investigating it which has begun to give its proper life to the inquiries of the age, he finds the eye of his mind conducted by it to a far higher elevation whence it takes in a great reach of the whole tide of humanity lying beneath, flowing on with unceasing current from the dim and cloudy mountains of the past in lengthened course to the immense and measureless future. Not only is his soul absorbed by the contemplation of the vast prospect, but he feels both the comparative insignificance of the immediate present and his own want of power to control it. What is a slight turning in the course or a little ripple on the surface of the huge stream which, under the guidance of energies so mighty is hurrying on so fast and so far? Not only do the questions of the day diminish before him to mere waves chafing the shore and serving little else but to mark the strength of the great feelings, sufferings, passions, or if you will, principles which, as it were blindly and confusedly, though doubtless under the real government of an Omnipotent hand whose workings pass his ken, impel the mighty mass along; but also he becomes sensible how insignificant individual efforts must be to control forces which he sees and feels bearing others and himself away with overwhelming energy.

To one having learned to view things in this light, it must be difficult, and I found it impossible in New York, to write a popular article such as the interests of your Journal[5] require on a question which if not in the temper in which it is agitated at least in the thing itself is profoundly significant.

Almost all that is known of Rae's adventures in Panama and California is contained in a letter to some friend, excerpts from which were printed in the *Hamilton Gazette*, December 19, 1850.[6] This letter together with the editorial introduction is given below:

DR. RAE IN CALIFORNIA

We are indebted to a friend for the perusal of a letter from Dr. Rae, formerly a resident of this city, but now in California, from which we have made several interesting extracts. A number of letters have been published from the land of Gold, but the Doctor's candid epistle more fully illustrates the climate, diseases, and state of the country, than any we have yet read. It also clearly shows the vicissitudes and shifts which the immigrant is compelled to undergo, even to obtain the absolute necessaries of life, and the fortunes are not to be made in a day, as some of our "ne'er do well" friends vainly imagine.

The following are extracts:—

"For my own part, I think that for some years to come there is a better prospect for a young man who can command $2000 or $3000 and can have a good

---

[5] The reference here is to the *Independent*, of which Willson was editor, a newspaper promoting the cause of annexation of Canada to the United States and the severance of political ties with Great Britain.

[6] Mixter says that the letter was to R. W. Cameron (*Sociological Theory of Capital*, xxvi, n.1), but it will be noted that Rae closes the letter with "Yours respectfully," a form which would not have been appropriate for Cameron, an ex-pupil and a much younger man.

correspondence in New York and St. Francisco, than in any other mercantile speculation on this continent. Towns are rising up all over the country, their support being altogether derived from supplying the miners, and profits are very large. By making choice of one of these, there is no question that there would be an immediate opening to a sale and very profitable business. In the larger cities, such as San Francisco and Sacramento, speculation is rife. In these, therefore, large fortunes have been made, and heavy failures constantly occur.

Mining is not so profitable as at first, still it is so much so as to be able to attract for many years as large a mining population as that now engaged in the occupation. I think the average here abouts is not under $7 to the hardworking man the year round, and he spends about $1.50 per day for food and clothing—I mean of course with reference both to gain and expenditure. I may mention some facts corroborative of this opinion. Chopping by the cord costs $4, and a good hand can make his two cords per day, for though the timber, chiefly oak, is more difficult to cut than in New York State or Canada, there is no underbrush. Carpenters' wages are from $10 to $14. Washing, $6 per dozen &c. As to other occupations, similar high rates prevail.

This place, Colloma, is the spot where gold was first found. I hear the clack of Sutter's Mill as I write, and close by is the Race where the two men, Marshall and Weeman, still inhabitants of the town, came upon the lump that may, by thus appearing to them, be said to have made a new era in the history of this continent. I live in the very log cabin they occupied. As I know not if you received any of my letters, it may be as well to give you a summary of what has hitherto been my fortune. The Macbeans left me at Chagres, frightened at the enormous prices to which tickets by the steamboat had risen. By the advice of Capt. Wilson, of the steamship *Empire City*, in which you will recollect I embarked, I commenced practising there and did pretty well, and have little doubt that, had I continued and lived, I should now have been worth a considerable sum. The question, however, of living for any time in Chagres is doubtful, so that although I enjoyed perfect health and pleasant times for the five weeks I remained there, I thought it prudent to take the offer of a friend to go as Surgeon of the *Brutus* a ship of 500 tons from Panama. Unfortunately she did not sail as advertised, so that I waited at Panama five weeks, and not having given myself out for practice, spent every cent I had and more too. Worse than that, some one made the captain, who was also mostly owner of the vessel believe that I was no doctor, but only an old schoolmaster; and I believe if he could he would have shaken me off. Being moreover a mean greedy fellow, he made my situation very uncomfortable. We had a great deal of sickness on board, and a passage of nine or ten weeks. On landing I pushed for the mines, and had difficulty to get here. About ten miles from this I was actually without a single coin in my pocket, when I found a half eagle in the middle of the road. Shortly after arriving here I fell sick, the remains of the Panama fever, with which I had been annoyed at Panama and on the route, and which I had only kept off by medicine. Here, after exposure to great fatigue, I had the bad luck to lose my way in the woods when walking to my camp after nightfall, and kept wandering most of the night. This brought matters to a crisis. I had violent fever for a fortnight, during a great part of which my brain was affected, my thoughts wandering in spite of me. How I got through I scarcely know. I got sick at an inn, and considering the low state of my finances, the people were very kind. Still, an inn in California is a confoundedly uncomfortable place of habitation even for one in health; to a sick man it is a painful purgatory or worse. No bedsteads, the floors never washed or seldom swept even, and you huddle pell mell on the floor, as you can. Progress, however is rapid, and things are mending. The fever left me extremely weak and thin. I did not know what to do, and as a last resort, set up school with eleven scholars, paying from $6 to $8 per month. The exertion I used to bring this about produced a violent and very difficult diarrhoea, which further reduced me. I still managed, however, to teach six hours a day, though so weak I could scarcely walk. The intense heat of the day, the thermometer for hours together many successive days together standing at 107 to 112 in the shade for four or five hours seemed to be mainly instrumental in making my case so obstinate. I kept school for two months, and only gained about $20. I then gave it up, bought a set of carpenter's tools, and rented this cabin. I might have done well at this trade, rockers and cradles for washing gold rose in price, owing to the great immigration, fetching $24. I could make one in two days, and the materials cost only about $5. Many carpenters at that time made two or three in a day. Unfortunately I over-exerted myself in a walk I took to see a sick man, and I was attacked by a combination of rheumatism and scurvy, so as to make me a cripple. I still fought away, however, with hard times as best I might, and have gradually regained my health. I am now beginning to make scales and weights for weighing gold; they sell here at from $5 to $10. I believe I can make a set at least per diem, and as my expenses are under $2, I trust to be able not only to live, but to accumulate. My intention is to give my whole mind to mechanics and civil engineering, for which I have always had a taste, and for which this region is about to open a wide field. *This country swarms with Doctors.*

I have lately become acquainted with a young man of the name of Henderson from Toronto—a lawyer from Archibald McLean's office.[7] He has only been here five weeks and has got together some hundred dollars, partly in the mines, partly by hunting, at which he tells me he often makes an ounce a day. Hares weighing 10 to 12 lbs., which are tolerably numerous, bring readily $5; quails $1 per pair. He wishes me to join him, and as James Cameron has been kind enough to offer me the use of his gun, I may take a trial of the sport. This puts me in mind that I have not mentioned the price of beef, it is 25¢; mutton, 40¢ to 50¢; liver, one of our dainties, 40¢ to 50¢; fish, 50¢; salt pork, 25¢; fresh pork, $1! A man in a year or two might make a large fortune by raising hogs; the hill sides are covered with acorns and nut-bearing trees, so that the creatures require no food, and being of the Chinese breed, are fat as they can be, to waddle about at all and shift for themselves winter and summer. There is one in town two years old, weighing about 300 lbs, an enormous fellow, for which $1000 has been offered and refused. In Canada hogs are filthy creatures, but here they turn up their noses with an indignant grunt at anything that is not savoury.

Society is in a strange state here. Sunday is the great market day, and then the shops are thronged and theatres opened. Gambling also goes on at a prodigious rate. I have been amused at the long faces which persons of what are termed religious professions make, on the state of affairs; still they go along with the

---

[7] At the time of this letter Archibald McLean was a Puisne Judge of the Court of Common Pleas in Toronto, but the identity of Henderson is uncertain.

crowd, buy and sell, and make gain, because they came to California to do so. One clergyman keeps a gaming house, another is a butcher, &c. Strange are the transmogrifications which meet the eye. One old lady was very kind to me when sick, sent me soup, &c., whether I would or not, and wished to be very friendly. I don't like such advances in any form, but on the verge of 50 it struck me as ridiculous. Think what I thought of things when I found out that she was Lady Abbess to a Bagnio. She was lamenting to me the necessity she had been under of keeping a *boarding* house; said she was of respectable connexions in New York, and was going back there. She has since gone, and I am told by a merchant here that she actually carried with her over 200,000 the results of her *laudable* exertions in St. Francisco, Sacramento and Colloma. I suppose she will get white-washed and become respectable. These women and the gamblers are the wealthiest of the population. The houses they build are the most showy in the town, two of which are in my vicinity. The effrontery of the inmates and fre-quenters is beyond anything I could have conceived. Sometimes bloody rows take place, and weapons are drawn, but no case of out-and-out killing since my arrival.

The country is beautiful to look at, and but for the great vicissitudes of tem-perature, very healthy. The air is pure as pure can be. All affections of the lungs vanish before it. Beef in the hottest weather does not taint, if preserved from the flies. The streams from the Sierra Nevada would flow clear as crystal but for the doings of the miners.

My health is gradually improving, and it seems to me not unlikely that it may become more robust than it has been for years. I very seldom taste anything stronger than tea, unless with a friend; but I am become a confirmed smoker."

Your's respectfully,

JOHN RAE

The explosive growth of the population in California naturally created an urgent need for increased supplies of foodstuffs of all kinds. The development of this new and wealthy market in 1848 and 1849 led to an agricultural boom in the Hawaiian Islands, a natural source of such staples as meat, potatoes, and sugar. Apart from this commercial inter-course, many Hawaiian natives joined in the search for gold. It was there-fore natural that interest in the Hawaiian Islands and their economic prospects was stimulated. John Rae, like many others, had found that life in the gold fields was hard and unrewarding. Spurred on by wanderlust, scientific curiosity, and the prospect of regaining his health, Rae sailed to the Hawaiian Islands in the spring of 1851.

9

Life in the Hawaiian Islands
(1851–1871)

Evidently Rae landed first in Honolulu, where he stayed briefly, and then moved to Wailuku on the island of Maui. Not long after his landing on the islands he wrote to Roderick William Cameron giving his initial impressions of his new home. Cameron sent the letter to the editor of the *Hamilton Gazette* who published the text and an introductory note on January 19, 1852:

LETTER FROM DR. RAE[1]

We give below an extract from a letter received from Dr. Rae, late of this city. As District School Master for a great many years, he was not only well known but highly esteemed by all the old residenters; we are sure that his letter will be read with interest by his old friends and acquaintances. The letter was received by Mr. R. W. Cameron, who has favored us with a copy.

Wailuku Maui
Hawaiian Islands, Aug. 23, 1851

My Dear Young Friend,
   It is now 21 months since I left New York. After a great deal of adventure and wandering, and some thing of danger and suffering, I have at length, I think, found rest to my feet and an abiding place . . . Things would have gone off well enough in California; but that excessive bad health, the effects of the Panama fever, made me for a long time helpless: I determined, therefore, to come to these Islands. I was not sure what I should do, and tried various schemes, and at length, at the recommendation of the member for Public Instruction, came here

---

[1] Some obvious errors in transcription in this letter have been corrected.

to take charge of a school vacant by the sickness of M——, our Missionary. I came here and found the gentleman busy surveying, and in the receipt then of $16.00 per day, and so not likely to take to school teaching. He could have no objection to my commencing; but would not give up his maps, globes, Philosophical apparatus, etc., all at the expense of quarter-dollars begged through the Union, to say nothing of his dwelling house and lands, worth I am told, about $10,000, which he holds, and will hold, as private property. I had run so far, however, that I determined to run no further; and by good fortune getting into the good graces of a petty chieftain and his wife, an old lady of sixty-five, he gave me a good house for a school-room, 36 feet by 18 feet, and did me other services; and I set about teaching the youth the English tongue, a rather difficult task for one knowing nothing of Hawaiian. However, I got on pretty well, beginning with 18, and in three weeks having over 40, at $1.00 per quarter— better paid, and in hard dollars, than I ever experienced before. I have been here over three months, and like things, on the whole, well. My medical talents are also coming into play, and bring in something.

I have just returned from the rising city of Honolulu, the Capital, where I was invited to give the Agricultural Society lectures on Geology. This introduced me to the notables of the Island, and I have promises of help from various quarters. Probably, in the course of a year or so, I shall be appointed Geologist for the Hawaiian Kingdom.

In the meantime I begin to enjoy new scenes. The climate of the whole Island, and especially of the part I live on is superb, the thermometer ranging from 60 to 82; for the whole year there has not been a day either too hot or too cold since I came, and the gentle rains that have fallen, with one exception, have been in the night.

There are splendid gardens, all the tropical fruits and flowers, and many of those of temperate climates flourish, bananas, oranges, melons most delicious and large, and grapes the finest I ever tasted grow in rich exuberance. The plant which is peculiar is the taro, the staff of life of the inhabitants. A small patch, half a rood, will maintain a family for a year, and take about six days' labour. It is between bread and potatoes, and I have become very fond of it. The pity is that content with this patch, the natives will not take the trouble, or but rarely will, to make any other garden.

Amid the world of novelty that surrounds me, I could fill many pages that would be of interest to you, but my paper warns me to be short. On the whole I like the people. Thoughtlessness, idleness and extreme license of life are the great defects, and will I fear make them melt all away from the earth; it is a pity for they are able, kind-hearted and really are an intelligent race, and one might travel through the midst of them all alone, and without a weapon, with his pocket full of gold without a fear, and if without a sou, find everywhere an open door.

I have said their licentiousness is extreme, in fact in the old times it was thought at times a religious duty to carry it to all possible excess. They have got a better light now; but though they own it a sin, it is not in their eyes a shame. I cannot go into particulars, it may suffice to say that it surprised even me, who am pretty well acquainted with old Greece and Rome.

Another thing against them is the doing away with the power of the chiefs, who of course governed their people for their good, as well as their own, and compelled them to work, before the people learned to govern themselves, but the topic would extend too far, so I stop. You would like better to hear of the capabilities of these Islands. I am on Maui, which is the second or third in size and consequence. It is divided into two mountains, one of which immediately to the west of me is very much broken and split up into deep glens. Its summits rise to six or seven thousand feet, and the scenery is at many parts exceedingly picturesque. Between it and Haleakala, (the halo of the sun) a sandy peninsula of 12 miles square, on which herds of beautiful cattle and a few horses feed, spreads out a level plain. Haleakala runs to 10,000 feet or nearly two miles in height, by an acclivity of 20 to 30 miles, and of a course so gentle that it seems as if a plough could go easily from top to bottom, as indeed but for occasional gullies it well might. Till you ascend 1,300 feet it is all adapted for sugar, the cane growing beautifully, and giving a ton an acre, even under the imperfect system of cultivation, with care it might yield two. The potato region comes next, giving two or three abundant crops every year. Then comes a belt of wood, above that is a region—according to my friend Dr. MacDougall, a Scotch sheep farmer's son, and long a resident in New South Wales, the best in the world for grazing sheep. The very summit is occupied by an extinct crater, some nine miles by three or four, and 2000 feet deep; here snow is occasionally seen in winter. This and about it is the retreat of packs of wild dogs, who ought to be all shot down. Not a twentieth of all this inviting field is put to any use, though sugar was until lately selling at 14¢ to 20¢ per lb., and potatoes at $3.00 the flour barrel. A change has come over this, however, the sugar selling at 5¢ and potatoes at $1.00, this from the fluctuations in the California market.

Money very scarce, and 3 per cent, a month.

Yours very truly,
JOHN RAE

The lectures on geology referred to in the letter to Cameron arose out of a misunderstanding. He had evidently written to someone in Honolulu offering to deliver a series of about twelve lectures, but his letter was lost in transit and in the confusion he was invited to deliver two lectures to the Royal Hawaiian Agricultural Society, the text of which has been preserved.[2]

Within a few months after his arrival, Rae, then living at Hana, Maui, was named as one of the persons entitled to distribute free medicines to indigent natives.[3] In the spring of 1853 a smallpox epidemic broke out in the Islands and in July Rae was pressed into service to vaccinate the natives. He was appointed as Medical Agent of the Board of Health at this time and in the course of several months walked over most of the island of Maui inoculating the natives and taking a keen interest in their speech and culture. One of the results of this was a "Journal of a Tour

[2] These lectures were turned over to Dr. T. A. Jaggar by Mixter.
[3] Archives of Hawaii, Board of Health Documents, no. 88, Dec. 16, 1850. This is the date on the folder, the list itself is undated.

around East Maui" which he retained until his death, but which has now been lost.[4]

During his first few years in Maui Rae seems to have recovered quickly from his unhappy experience in Hamilton and his illness in California. His energy and the range of his interests are quite remarkable. Writing to John Stuart Mill in December, 1853, Rae said:

I have been a wanderer in California, lost my health there, came to these islands to recruit about three years since, have been practising my profession, I am a medical man, and am now engaged in rather extensive agricultural operations, and some other material projects, which will, I expect, for several years very much occupy my time. I have, however, lately written an article unfolding some views in Geology, which are, I believe, novel, and even to myself somewhat startling, but yet, I think will ultimately be found true. Certain phenomena in these islands, and on this ocean, led me to them. This will probably appear in Stillman's [sic] Journal, though there may be some delay from an apprehended miscarriage of part of the manuscript. I have also written, for a medical friend in Canada, some observations on medical matters, which, it is likely, will find their way to the American press. I have, too, made some progress in a work on the condition and prospects of these islands, which I should like to publish simultaneously in England and America. I have besides an essay on hand on the Hawaiian language.[5]

At this time, Rae was living on a farm at Koali, Hana, East Maui, which he had leased for a ten-year period. Apart from his farming operations he seems to have devoted considerable time to providing medical care for the natives in his capacity as Medical Agent of the Board of Health. The arrangement was that the Board of Health would send medicines to Rae for distribution to the sick. No charge was made to the poor and the others were charged sufficient to pay the cost of the medicines. In a rather pathetic letter dated March, 1860, Rae wrote to the Secretary of the Board of Health: "I have had so many severe cases of syphilis in a protracted stage that the bottle of Iodide Potas. which you sent will soon be exhausted. You would much oblige me therefore if you would send me a fresh supply —as much as you can afford for the $1.00 I enclose."[6] Later in 1860, Rae wrote the following more detailed account of his medical problems to the Secretary of the Board of Health:

I shall very willingly take the trouble of dispensing such medicines as you may send me. Perhaps it may be as well to inform you that more than one half of the

---

[4] *Sociological Theory of Capital*, xxvii.

[5] The complete text is given in item 15 of Part III of this volume. On several occasions, Rae referred to "Stillman's Journal" by which he meant the *American Journal of Science and Arts* edited by Benjamin Silliman.

[6] Archives of Hawaii, Board of Health files, 1860; letter, John Rae to Dr. Robert M'Kibbin, Jr., March 4, 1860.

diseases which one meets with here are venereal. Nitrate of Silver mercury in its various forms and some of the preparations of Iodine were the remedies which when in practice here I most used. The other complaints are affections of the liver & Bronchitis. We also have usually every year an epidemic which the Missionaries I think set the example of denominating Influensa. The digestive organs and internal canal are always affected and with them either the lungs or the head, last year most who had it lost the hair of the scalp. Smart purgatives and Ipicac or squills with opium was the treatment I followed. What is called scrofula is also prevalent here as elsewhere. But I never saw a case of the scrofula of Great Britain on these islands. I have never seen here the serous curdy discharge & flabby pale granulations which mark it there. The sores look more like venereal ulcers than scrofula and I am inclined to think that some venereal taint is almost always conjoined with the original disease whatever that may have been. At all events I have found no case that did not yield to some combination of mercury & Iodine.

I write these things not at all under the supposition that you can send me all the medicines I have indicated or even any considerable portion of them but that if it be not too much trouble you would make such selection as might come nearest to what I want. I may add that sulp. of magnesia has the advantage of being cheap and readily taken by Kanakas and that aloes, also a cheap drug, seems indicated in congestion of the Biliary organs. I have by me some quantity of Nitric acid else on the same principle (its little cost) I should have requested you to send me a little of it.[7]

In 1859, Rae was made District Judge of Hana, a part of the island of Maui. He probably owed this appointment to his friend and patron, Robert Crichton Wyllie, one of the leading citizens of the Islands. It is likely that Rae's acquaintance with Wyllie dated from the time of Rae's lectures before the Royal Hawaiian Agricultural Society and it is evident that they became close and trusted friends. Wyllie had been born in the parish of Dunlop, Ayrshire, in 1798 and was educated at Glasgow University where he qualified as a surgeon before he was twenty. After several voyages to the North Sea as a ship's surgeon, Wyllie emigrated to Australia to become a sheep farmer. Later he went into business in Chile and became a wealthy man. He moved to London and was in business there for a period before travelling to Honolulu in 1844. He was made acting British Consul, but in 1845 he was appointed Minister of Foreign Relations by Kamehameha III, a post which he filled for twenty years, until his death in 1865. In a sketch of his life Manley Hopkins says, "His industry was prodigious; his foreign correspondence voluminous; his mind was omnivorous."[8] Wyllie lived at Rosebank, a villa in the Nuuanu valley, near Honolulu, where Rae was a house guest on a number of occasions.

[7] *Ibid.*; letter, John Rae to Robert M'Kibbin, Oct. 5, 1860.

[8] Manley Hopkins, *Hawaii: The Past, Present, and Future of its Island-Kingdom. An Historical Account of the Sandwich Islands* (*Polynesia*) (London, 1866, 2nd ed.), 501. Chapter xxx is devoted to a sketch of Wyllie's life from which this material is taken.

These two expatriate Scotsmen and kindred spirits were clearly drawn to each other by the similarity in their early training and background.[9] They were both men of great intellectual acuity and were united in, among other things, their contempt for the activities of the American missionaries.

By the end of 1860, Rae had also been appointed Coroner for Hana and Notary Public for Maui and was obviously something of a personage on the island. As early as 1857 Rae appeared to be exercising official duties of some sort, perhaps in his capacity as Notary Public for Maui, and some of his correspondence with the official responsible for the administration of lands has been preserved.[10]

By 1862, Rae had purchased an extensive tract of land in Hana totalling about 336 acres, for which he paid a total of $261.48.[11] He embarked on ambitious agricultural operations and as usual found that he was handicapped by lack of money. In the fall of 1862, Rae wrote to one of the land officials that he had forty acres prepared for ploughing and harrowing. He went on to say in his letter:

My land turns up very rich but very stiff. A piece of about 30 acres of lighter soil I intend for Indian corn the other ten for hill taro & awa both of which grow magnificently on the land. The best of my farm however lies over a certain round hill which you may have seen. There a chief and people dwelt in the olden time it is now over run with fern bananas & sugar cane and the abode of wild hogs so large that the natives will not go there unless in a body. I have got two stout dogs to hunt them and hope to rout them out and provide myself with some wild boar ham.[12]

At one point Rae's interest in his neglected inventions revived and he appealed to his friend Hugh Bowlby Willson to help him to market his devices. The following excerpt, from what appears to be a draft of this letter, has been preserved[13]:

A change has come o'er the thread of my life. You have perhaps seen a horse of a sort of sluggish temper, not deficient in any of the externals that denote some degree of power, but yet who seemed incapable of anything but a stubborn, shambling gait which whip or spur made only more uncomfortable. Well, gather your reins, feel that you are well in your saddle, and spare not but dig the iron well into his sides. You will rouse him; and if you keep your seat through his first plungings and boundings it may be that you will be astonished how well and fast and far he will bear you. Such is the change that has come over the temper of

[9] In a letter to Abraham Fornander dated Feb. 9, 1861, Wyllie wrote, "my general ideas harmonize wonderfully with Dr. Rae's. . . ."

[10] Archives of Hawaii, Interior Department land files, 1857; letters, John Rae to William Webster, July 5 and Sept. 3, 1857.

[11] Ibid., 1862; letter, P. Nahaolelua to His Highness, L. Kamehameha, July 16, 1862.

[12] Ibid.; letter, John Rae to S. Spencer, Oct. 15, 1862.

[13] Rae mss.

my mind. The iron has pierced deep into me, it rankles in my very vitals, and for aught I see will do so till the grave cover me. I must be doing something, I have relief in action . . .

I propose to lay before you such of these schemes as are connected with navigation. There are things which have occupied my attention at long intervals from almost my boyhood. Though myself convinced of the soundness of my general views and of the practicability of most of my projects I am far from sanguine that you will be able to put any of them in a train that will lead to success. Literary enterprises are hazardous but the fate of inventions still more so. I believe the world would be absolutely astonished could there be brought to its view the knowledge which its crowd have crushed out of form and trampled under foot so that it could never rise to open day light.

> Ah! who can tell how hard it is to climb
> The steep where Fame's proud temple shines afar!
> Ah! who can tell how many a soul sublime
> Has felt the influence of malignant star,
> And waged with fortune an eternal war;
> Check'd by the scoff of Pride, by Envy's frown,
> Or Poverty's inconquerable bar
> In life's low vale remote has pined alone
> Then dropp'd into the grave, unpitied and unknown![14]

Rae then proceeded to describe in detail his sounding device which he had first conceived when he was a university student and commented on the cool reception it had received from one of his university professors.

I was then under a very eminent professor of mathematics in the Marischal College, Aberdeen, the late Dr. [Robert] Hamilton, and showed it him. He allowed it sound in theory and ingenious, but smiled it down as impracticable. Though not convinced I was obliged to yield and let it go, as I did not wish to irritate my father . . . Dr. Hamilton's objection to my scheme was that it was very good on paper, but that in so boisterous an element as the ocean it was almost absurd to think it could be of any practical utility. He judged of the ocean from fanciful ideas he had got sitting in his elbow chair. I knew something of it then, and have lived on it many a long day since, and can see nothing absurd in the project. In fact, in weather in which a whale boat could live, there would be no difficulty in giving the globes their proper position in the water. In other weather, no attempt at deep sounding by the lead itself could be made with a prospect of success. Once a few feet beneath the surface all violent motion ceases.

I cannot but think, however, that the temper of mind which led him to object was one with which all inventions are commonly, one might almost say reasonably, met. Nine out of ten of all mechanical schemes are abortive. In fact, they generally take their rise in this way. Some idea new, or conceived to be new, flits by chance across the brain of a man unaccustomed to new ideas. The novelty of the thing, and still more so the novelty of its occurring to himself, sets it in a point of view that puts out of sight all other conceptions and magnifies itself so prodigiously that he can see nothing else. It becomes therefore

[14] Rae's poetic quotation is the first stanza of "The Minstrel: or, The Progress of Genius," by James Beattie (1735–1803).

his hobby, and he rides it, or rather it more often rides him to the D—. But the man who is consulted in such a case, especially if he has been in the habit of being so consulted, sees the thing in a very different light. He knows beforehand that these projects are almost all vanity. That some flaw in their conception makes them useless, or that a search would prove them not original. In short, that it is ten to one if this particular one succeed. If a man of any reputation in science, he is rather annoyed at such applications compelling him to give up time he thinks valuable to the labour of detecting the flaws which in every probability exist in the scheme and accordingly takes hold of the first that presents itself to his mind. This shortens his labour, and is a sort of charity to the would be inventor. It is in this way perhaps that the greater number of new inventions have not had the sanction of the learned. If given at all, it is given in a mightily cautious manner.

On this account I should myself have great difficulty at present to get anyone to take hold of a single one of my schemes, and I am aware I am putting your friendship to a severe test in asking you to attempt it. Your acquaintance however is pretty general and you are I think somewhat mechanically inclined yourself. Moreover I know you would help me if you could and therefore will do so if you can.

Mixter quotes another excerpt from this letter to Willson, or possibly from a different draft:

After a little reflection I have decided on sending you a summary of that whole past of my history which relates to progression *through* water. I am partly led to this from having the chance of sending a heavy packet with safety by my friend J. W. Austin, Esq. of Boston, who has resided for many years in these islands in a position somewhat analogous to our Attorney-General, and who now is returning to his native soil. He will write you and receive your instructions as to transmitting this and other papers he takes charge of.[15]

The friend Rae referred to was James Walker Austin (1829–1896), who had arrived in the Islands in 1851 and in the spring of 1852 was appointed District Attorney of the Second Judicial District, Maui. He lived for four years in Lahaina, Maui, and on April 1, 1856, returned temporarily to the United States. He came back to live in Honolulu where he was a prominent lawyer and later in life a Judge of the Supreme Court of the Hawaiian Islands.[16]

In 1862, the Hawaiian legislature authorized the establishment of dispensaries in the various districts under the direction of the Board of Health to provide medical care for the poor. Early in October, Rae's appointment as Medical Attendant to the dispensary in Hana was formally announced

[15] *Sociological Theory of Capital*, xxx, n.1. Mixter's footnote incorrectly gives "century" for "history" in the first sentence. Mixter also said in the same place that he had found among Rae's papers "considerable in the way of inventive speculation on the art of shipbuilding in general, and several essays on aeronautics." This material is no longer available.

[16] A biography of Austin—Walter Austin, *James Walker Austin* (Norwood, Mass., 1921)—does not refer either to Rae or Willson.

although Rae had agreed to undertake the work sometime earlier.[17] The *Polynesian*, in an editorial, remarked that the creation of the dispensaries "is one of the few bright leaves with which the last Legislature adorned their brows" and said of the appointments themselves: "The well known ability of the appointees, their long residence in the country, their perfect knowledge of the character and wants of the people, inspire the fullest confidence that they will succeed."[18] As Medical Attendant, Rae was to receive a salary of $250 a year in addition to his salary of $600 a year as District Judge.

In the meantime, Rae continued with his ambitious farming scheme. He explained some of his problems in a letter written in December, 1862, to one of the land officials:

You know I have turned farmer well my expenses have run a little beyond my calculations. The whole has been outgo and nothing coming in. I have planted several acres taro but that takes 10 months to ripen. I have cleared some fifty or sixty acres of *amaomao* and seeded down with grass for an additional run for my cattle and I have prepared some forty acres for planting with indian corn ten of which are ploughed over. In June or July I must have a considerable return from these as land and climate are well suited for that crop. I am told I ought to have 40 bushels an acre but even the half of that and say 30 acres should bring me from four to six hundred dollars. This would put me at my ease as I have got over the main expenses of building fencing &c. At present however I am short on my calculations from $50 to $100. This has arisen in the first place from my natives having smashed a plough and in the second from finding that my new employment of Government Dr requires me to have on hand a considerable & various stock of medicines for which the Honolulu prices are very high. Now would it be convenient for you to give me the loan of $50 to $100 for six months commencing on the 10th of Janr. It would be a great accommodation. It might either be by note on Bishop & co Bank or simply a loan paying the usual interest on such transactions. Please inform me if you can do me this favour writing me by return of post or better still by the manuokawai if she be in port when this arrives.

My land turns out better than I imagined. In the last week or two I have cleared or rather simply cut down 20 acres fern *amaomao* not a stone in it and easily ploughed when the roots are rotted out which will take twelve months. The soil apparently of the richest quality.[19]

Although Rae's anticipated appointment as an official geologist never materialized, his avid interest in geological questions continued unabated. The geological characteristics of the Hawaiian Islands had a special fascination for him and he wrote extensively on this subject. In one of his lectures there is a comment explaining his interest:

[17] Archives of Hawaii Board of Health files, 1862; letter, John Rae to Robert M'Kibbin, Sept. 21, 1862.

[18] *Polynesian*, Oct. 11, 1862.

[19] Archives of Hawaii, Interior Department land files, 1862; letter, John Rae to S. Spencer, Dec. 9, 1862.

Geology has ever been with a me a favourite study. It has so been both from its own positive utility; from the wide field it opens to the intellect to expatiate in; and from the new and magnificent views it presents us of nature in all her aspects, and the natural sciences make their connection and relations to each other and to the supreme ruler and governor of all.

So conceiving of it, it has been my endeavour in so far as my poor ability and the situation I have been placed in permitted, to attempt to spread a taste for its pursuit among those who happened at any time to be around me; and thus I have been led more than once to give a series of lectures on it.[20]

Most of Rae's geological writings were given to Dr. T. A. Jaggar, a distinguished authority on volcanology and Hawaiian geology, around 1904 and fortunately have been preserved. There is a brief reference to this in Mixter's biographical sketch when he says that Rae's geological writings "have been placed in proper hands and may in part be printed."[21] Jaggar wrote a brief assessment of Rae as a geologist at about this time which is quite generous:

JOHN RAE AS A GEOLOGIST

The papers left by Rae which deal with geological topics are as follows:—

1. An essay on the geology of Canada, containing a description of the Gulf of St. Lawrence, as observed by myself, as a new-comer in 1821.
2. A fragmentary letter of the hypothetical conditions which govern coastal oscillations, lava, volcanoes and tides.
3. A theory of tides, based upon the supposition of a mobile crust of the earth.
4. A description of the physiography and mineralogy of the Sandwich Islands—written about 1852.
5. Two lectures on general geology, delivered before the Royal Hawaiian Agricultural Society. The date is probably about 1860 or later.[22]
6. Fragmentary manuscript.

The essay on the geology of Canada was of course written at a time when very little was known about the region, and it is accordingly of interest only from an historical standpoint. It would be of great interest to one of the Canadian Geological Survey in Ottawa, and accordingly I have made a note on the cover of the manuscript, recommending that it be sent to Dr. Daly.[23]

The second manuscript concerns a subject which was evidently especially interesting to Mr. Rae. The origin of coastal oscillations, volcanoes and tides. His hypothesis of the fluid interior of the earth evidently came from observations of the Hawaiian craters and the relatively rapid changes in sea-level evident on the coast of the Sandwich Islands led him to suppose that some connection was

---

[20] Rae mss. Lectures before the Royal Hawaiian Agricultural Society.

[21] *Sociological Theory of Capital*, xxxiii.

[22] In fact, the lectures were given in 1851.

[23] Professor R. A. Daly, at one time associated with the Canadian Geological Survey and for many years Professor of Igneous Geology at Harvard. In a note to the writer Professor Daly said he had never seen the manuscript, so Jaggar's suggestion was evidently not followed and the manuscript cannot now be traced.

to be found between these oscillations of the land and the extrusion of lavas. His theoretical conceptions are visionary and insufficiently supported by sound mathematical, astronomical or physical data. On the other hand, however, he has an extraordinarily accurate mental picture of earth scale, and of the great effect of small changes on life and on the distribution of waters on the surface of the earth. This manuscript and the one which follows it on the tides might well be sent to Professor George Darwin in Cambridge. He would certainly be interested in the work from the point of view of an antiquarian, even if he found nothing in it of scientific value. Rae's tide theory simply extends somewhat further his doctrine of a thin crust, flowing on a fluid interior of the earth, and imagines that the tides of the ocean are occasioned in part by movements of the earth's crust. It is not altogether certain today that this may not be true.

The description of the physical geography of the Sandwich Islands which must have been written about 1852, is worth publishing. It shows keen insight and perception of atmospheric and the work of the winds, considerably in advance of his time. His perception of the development of the valleys of the Hawaiian Islands by the action of running water and the possibility of wearing the land down is all along the line of modern physiography and science, which has only been developed in the last twenty years.

The lectures on general geology give us some clue to Rae's sources of information. He was evidently a follower of Lyell, Dawson, Agassiz, and Hitchcock. The first lecture is a general résumé of the subject, and the second lecture presents much original material, including his own theories of earth movement. The papers are incomplete, however, and hardly seem to me worth publication. The fragmentary manuscripts in the last packet contain some notes on geology and religion that may give a clue to Rae's knowledge of geology, the man has evidently read extensively the British and American geologists of his day, and he was familiar with the work of glaciers, Dawson's theory of icebergs, Hitchcock's footprints in the red sandstone of western Massachusetts, and the beginning of Darwinism. In his letter on the Sandwich Islands, he calls attention with remarkable insight to the elevation of the coastal shelf, the power of stream erosion, the peculiar cauldron volcanoes of the island and the convectional circulation of the atmosphere which in combination with the rotation of the earth brings about the trade winds. He shows in all of his work much original insight, unbiased by books, and while some of his theories are bizarre, he has an extraordinarily accurate sense of earth scale and the relations of earth process to the oceans and continents. The two most characteristic and complete writings in the series are the one on the Sandwich Islands and the lecture on hypothetical questions. Both of these with the fragments that exist in the collection could probably be reproduced in folio and might be worth publishing as types of his geological writings.

Although Jaggar was quite sympathetic to Rae, the manuscripts he sent to Professor George Darwin of Cambridge University were returned inscribed with a note: "A remarkable and interesting letter—much that is erroneous. It does not form a contribution to knowledge worthy of publication." The proposal to publish a selection of Rae's geological writings was evidently dropped after this.

Apart from their scientific quality, Rae's views on geology were at least expressed with great elegance. In one of his lectures, he explains the fundamental aim of geology:

Geology assumes to itself the task of ascertaining and describing the structure of the earth for great depths often extending to miles beneath its present surface; and of revealing the mighty revolutions which have taken place in this surface in periods in general of very remote antiquity, sometimes reaching back to almost countless ages. These two things the actual present condition and the previous changes and revolutions are conjoined because as the one has produced the other we are thus enabled reasoning upward to deduce the cause from the effect; and again downward, the effect from the cause each mutually assisting in ascertaining and elucidating the other. Thus has the science advanced to important conclusions. To the geologist this our mundane planet is no longer what it seemed to old philosophy, a chaotic mixture of elements, fixed while in wild confusion, and moulded into the form of the globe which we now inhabit; and presents a beautiful order and progression of existences, one condition of things producing and ushering in another, and each in succession opening up new and astonishing prospects of the wisdom and beneficence of the almighty architect.[24]

In case any tokens of Rae's piety were required, one of his comments in a lecture will serve:

To some of my hearers thoughts such as these [e.g., the extreme antiquity of the universe] may appear to verge on impiety as in seeming opposition to the revealed word of God. I beg they will for a while withhold their condemnation as before I conclude I trust to be able to convince the most scrupulous even the most timid of believers that christianity has nothing to dread but much to hope from the progress of the sciences both of Geology and Astronomy.[25]

As an illustration of the nature of Rae's speculations on geology, one of his letters, written to Dr. Archibald Hall of Montreal, is given in item 20 of Part III of this volume.

Despite his busy life, Rae's intellectual fervour did not diminish as he grew older. In particular, he was greatly concerned by the plight of the natives and the damage which was being done to the native culture and moral standards by the impact of Western laws, customs and religion. Early in 1861 he completed a long and penetrating article with the title, "Thoughts on the System of Legislation Which Has Prevailed in the Hawaiian Islands for the Last Forty Years; on the Evils Which Have Arisen from It; and of the Possible Remedies for These Evils." The article was published in six instalments in the *Polynesian*, a Honolulu newspaper edited by Abraham Fornander.[26] The complete text is reproduced in Part III, item 11. What started out to be a protest against the stupidity of laws

[24] Rae mss. Lectures before the Royal Hawaiian Agricultural Society.
[25] *Ibid.*
[26] *Polynesian*, Feb. 2, Feb. 9, Feb. 16, March 16, March 30, April 20, 1861.

designed to curb the free and easy sex relations of the natives grew into an admirable analysis of comparative morals and comparative religions. Although the issue was a continuing and bitter one in the Islands, Rae's contribution may have arisen in part out of a report of the American Board of Commissioners for Foreign Missions for 1860. This report quoted with obvious approval some laudatory remarks of Richard Henry Dana:

It is no small thing to say of the missionaries of the American Board, that in less than forty years they have taught this whole people to read and to write, to cipher and to sew. They have given them an alphabet, grammar, and dictionary; preserved their language from extinction; given it a literature, and translated into it the Bible and works of devotion, science, and entertainment, &c. They have established schools, reared up native teachers, and so pressed their work that now the proportion of inhabitants who can read and write is greater than in New England. And whereas they found these islanders a nation of half-naked savages, living in the surf and on the sand, eating raw fish, fighting among themselves, tyrannized over by feudal chiefs, and abandoned to sensuality; they now see them decently clothed, recognizing the law of marriage, knowing something of accounts, going to school and public worship with more regularity than the people do at home, and the more elevated of them taking part in conducting the affairs of the constitutional monarchy under which they serve, holding seats on the judicial bench and in the legislative chambers, and filling posts in the local magistracies.[27]

Rae, in his analysis, vigorously opposed what he regarded as the irrelevance and bigotry of legislation sponsored by the missionaries which undertook in effect to restore a new system of *tabu* based on an alien culture and a severe theology. This time, at least, Rae was not without powerful friends. Wyllie wrote to him after the appearance of the first article in the series:

I haste to express to you the very great pleasure with which I read your "Thoughts on the System of Legislature" published in the Polynesian No 40 of 2d instant. . . .
You might have added with great truth, on the Authority of the Spaulding Club, that under the preaching of John Knox and his brother Bigots, the Number of Bastard Children in Scotland, increased beyond all former precedent; and precisely the same moral phenominon appeared in Geneva, under the teachings of Calvin.[28]

An outstanding example of the quality of Rae's mind was his essay on the "Polynesian Languages" which appeared in three instalments in the

[27] Dana's views were originally expressed in a letter published in the *New York Tribune* in 1860. This excerpt was reprinted in Hopkins, *Hawaii*, 199–200. Dana himself was a Boston lawyer and an Episcopalian.
[28] Archives of Hawaii, Foreign Office Letter Book, no. 28E, vol. II, Miscellaneous Internal Correspondence, p. 260; R. C. Wyllie to John Rae, Feb. 4, 1861.

Polynesian in the fall of 1862.[29] As a part of a general theory of human migration, Rae advanced the hypothesis that the Polynesian race had originated somewhere in southern Asia and, while intercourse with the mainland was cut off at some stage, the similarity of the Polynesian and Indo-European languages remained. In the course of this venture into comparative philology, Rae developed the theory that human speech originated in facial gestures. Certain pantomimic gestures evolved to represent the simple concepts of force, form, and movement and more complex ideas were gradually converted into speech by modification of the basic sounds. The text of this remarkable document is given in item 12, Part III, of this volume.

Shortly after, Wyllie sent a copy to John Stuart Mill, who commented:

The other paper [Polynesian Languages] will, I think, place Dr. Rae very high among ethnologists and philologists. After having reached by independent investigation the highest generalization previous made, namely, that all languages have grown by development from a few hundred words, Dr. Rae seems to have supplied the first probable explanation of the manner in which these primitive words may themselves have originated. If his hypothesis is made out, it is the keystone of the science of philology, it is *a priori* extremely probable, and the facts he brings forward establish a strong case of verification *a posteriori*. I hope that Dr. Max Müller has been put in possession of this important speculation.[30]

Mill's suggestion was evidently followed for, in 1863, Max Müller made some observations on Rae's speculations:

All who have had to examine the accounts of new languages, or families of languages, published by missionaries or travellers are aware how not only their theories, but their facts, have to be sifted, before they can be allowed to occupy even a temporary place in our handbooks, or before we should feel justified in rectifying accordingly the frontiers on the great map of the languages of mankind. Thus I received but the other day some papers, printed at Honolulu [footnote: The Polynesian Honolulu Sept. 27, Oct. 4, Oct. 11, 1862 containing an essay by Dr. J. Rae], propounding the theory "that all those tongues which we designate as the Indo-European Languages have their true root and origin in the Polynesian language." "I am certain," the author writes, "that this is the case as regards the Greek and Sanskrit; I find reason to believe it to be so as to the Latin and other more modern tongues, in short, as to all European Languages, old and young." And he proceeds: "The second discovery which I believe I have made, and with which the former is connected, is that the study of the Polynesian

---

[29] *Polynesian*, Sept. 27, Oct. 4, Oct. 11, 1862. In Fornander's book, *An Account of the Polynesian Race: Its Origin and Migrations and the Ancient History of the Hawaiian People to the Times of Kamehameha I* (London, 1878–85), he refers to "the late Dr. John Rae of Hana, Maui, who in a series of articles published in the 'Polynesian' (Honolulu, 1862), first called attention to the extreme antiquity of the Polynesian language" (I, xii).

[30] The complete text is given in item 23 of Part III of this volume.

language gives us the key to the original function of language itself, and to its whole mechanism."

Strange as it may sound to hear the language of Homer and Ennius spoken of as an offshoot of the Sandwich Islands, mere ridicule would be a very inappropriate and very inefficient answer to such a theory. It is not very long ago that all the Greek and Latin Scholars of Europe shook their heads at the idea of tracing the roots of the classical languages back to Sanskrit, and even at the present moment there are still many persons who cannot realize the fact that, at a very remote, but a very real period in the history of the world, the ancestors of the Homeric poets and of the poets of the Veda must have lived together as members of one and the same race, as speakers of one and the same idiom.[31]

Rae was doubtless pleased by the interest in his work and in the fall of 1862 he wrote to Spencer of the Interior Department:

Mr Wyllie writes me that my articles on the Polynesian language have been highly praised in high quarters I know not whether he means the King or the Bishop, also that he has sent copies to the great folks in England. So I suppose it likely that a little attention will be awakened to the subject in Europe. Should the Germans take it up they will follow it out. Mr. Fornander also writes me that after New Year he intends to bring out my various articles in Book form. Hence I shall I think have the honour of being the first author of a book in these Islands.[32]

Within recent years Sir Richard Paget and other scholars have praised Rae's concept highly and have pointed out that Rae anticipated modern formulations of the gesture theory of language by many years.[33] Paget wrote that Rae's essay was "so remarkable" that he had decided to reprint it verbatim as an appendix to his book, *Human Speech*, published in 1930. It has therefore been readily available to scholars in this field since that time. An Icelandic philologist, Alexander Jóhannesson, has recently indicated allegiance to the gestural theory, writing:

It is not unnatural to think, that homo sapiens has spread all over the earth and conquered it from a central area, but it is not less probable, that he has gradually developed from a lower degree, a Gibbon-like being, in many parts of the earth and under different conditions, as ethnology shows. But however this may have happened, it is sure that, as primitive man began to speak, his speaking organs spontaneously imitated his gesture which he had hitherto used to make himself comprehensible and to understand others, as the deaf and dumb still do in our own times. This theory, the gesture theory, was first put forward by Dr. J. Rae 1862 in three treatises on Polynesian, later by Sir Richard Paget in his book "Human Speech" 1930, and "This English" 1935 (in the first of which Rae's

[31] Max Müller, *Lectures on the Science of Language*, Second Series (London, 1864), 10–11.
[32] Archives of Hawaii, Interior Department land files, 1862; letter, John Rae to S. Spencer, Dec. 9, 1862.
[33] Sir Richard Paget, *Human Speech* (New York, 1930), 157.

treatises are reprinted), and finally by the author of this essay in his "Um frumtungu Indógermana og frumheimkynni" 1943.[34]

Some of the difficulties are suggested by Professor G. R. Driver, Professor of Semitic Philology, Magdalen College, Oxford, in a prefatory note to Jóhannesson's book:

... much work remains to be done in the way of recording the underlying primitive forms of the Semitic and especially of the Indo-European languages and, until these are satisfactorily established, investigators into the origin of language itself must perforce rely on relatively late and therefore often inadequate or misleading matter as the base of their researches. The enquiry is as important as it is interesting, and few will doubt that the present work is on the right lines; the origin of the forms of speech must be sought in the organs that produce the sounds of speech.[35]

It is fairly evident that Rae's views have not commanded any general support among the professional philologists, but it should be noted that his essay was in the form of a letter to Wyllie and was not initially intended for publication. He felt that it was incomplete and too abrupt in some of its conclusions. He continued to work on this project and accumulated a mass of material with the aim of publishing a book on languages. This was never done although he kept the manuscript until his death.[36]

Another fragment of Rae's literary output during his life in the Hawaiian Islands is his transcription of the legend of Laieikawai which he probably wrote in the late 1850's. This is a complex mythological tale concerning natural and human divinities which Rae transcribed with obvious sympathy and with a fine poetic feeling. His version of the legend was printed in the *Journal of American Folklore* in 1900,[37] and is reproduced as item 13 in Part III of this volume.

Rae was on friendly and intimate terms with his ally and champion Wyllie and evidently visited at his home on several occasions. In the summer of 1859 Rae wrote to Wyllie to say that he had written to his friend Sir Allan Napier MacNab to ask him to use his influence to procure him a consular appointment somewhere in the Pacific.[38] Rae asked Wyllie

[34] Alexander Jóhannesson, *Origin of Language: Four Essays* (Reykjavík, 1949), 31.
[35] *Ibid.*, 7.
[36] Robert Skakel Knight, Rae's great-nephew later wrote, "Sir Roderick Cameron examined the material, and said he was sure it could not be used, as no one but Dr. Rae could explain or arrange it." *Montreal Daily Star*, March 4, 1899. The manuscript is now lost.
[37] "Laieikawaii: A Legend of the Hawaiian Island," *Journal of American Folklore*, XIII, 1900, 241–60.
[38] Archives of Hawaii, Foreign Office files, 1859, Miscellaneous Local Correspondence; letter, John Rae to R. C. Wyllie, n.d., received Aug. 12, 1859. After serving as Prime Minister of United Canada in the period 1854–56, MacNab resigned his seat on Oct. 24,

to write to MacNab supporting his request, but Wyllie suggested that Her Britannic Majesty's Consul General would probably have more influence with Lord John Russell.[39] Although no details are available, Rae's petition to MacNab certainly had no results. Wyllie urged Rae to enter political life and in November, 1861, wrote to him: "I repeat my opinion, formerly expressed, that a man of your fine education, talent and enlarged views on matters of Civil Government and political economy, in the approaching Legislature would be a benefit to the Hawaiian Nation."[40] A few months later Wyllie wrote on the same subject, saying:

I am so sorry that you are not among the Legislators who are to assemble on the 1st of May. What we want are laws, taxation, education, amusements and industrial pursuits, fitted to the genius, temperament, taste and capabilities of the Hawaiian people. Having carefully studied all these for years, and being a well educated, sound thinking, close reasoning and benevolent man, you could not have failed to have been a very useful member.[41]

Several of Rae's letters written in the 1860's to the Board of Health dealing principally with leprosy and vaccination against smallpox have been preserved. In 1869, when he was seventy-three years of age, he sent a draft for $118 to the Secretary of the Board of Health, saying:

On a former occasion when Dr. MacKibbon was in office he required a list of persons vaccinated & of children the names of their parents also. I have kept such a list but was told by Drs Lee and Hillebrand that it is unnecessary. You will probably recollect that by my engagement with the Board I am to have 25c. for each successful case.[42]

It is difficult now to reconstruct many of the details of Rae's personal life in Maui. In some pencilled comments found among Rae's manuscripts there is a note that Rae lived with a native woman but no additional information was given.

One of Mixter's correspondents in Honolulu wrote that Rae lived "in a solitary place far back from the sea; and when he walked abroad his tall, spare form was seen always accompanied by two large dogs."[43] Rae's great-nephew, Robert Skakel Knight, wrote to Mixter:

1857, and lived in England from 1857 to 1860. He was evidently on friendly terms with Queen Victoria, but it is not known whether Rae was aware of the change in MacNab's political fortunes in Canada.

[39] *Ibid.*; letter, R. C. Wyllie to John Rae, Sept. 19, 1859.

[40] Archives of Hawaii, Foreign Office Letter Book, no. 37E, vol. III, Miscellaneous Internal Correspondence; letter, R. C. Wyllie to John Rae, Nov. 20, 1861. Wyllie expressed the same opinion to Walter Murray Gibson of Polawaii, Lanai, in a letter dated Dec. 24, 1861. *Ibid.*

[41] *Ibid.*; letter, R. C. Wyllie to John Rae, April 8, 1862.

[42] Archives of Hawaii, Board of Health files, 1868–9, Minutes of the Board of Health, Nov. 12, 1869.

[43] *Sociological Theory of Capital*, xxvii.

An Englishman who knew him in the Sandwich Islands told me that he could only compare him to some of the grand old Scotch gentlemen in Sir Walter Scott's novels. But he said he was quite incapable of taking care of money, so that other people had to look out for him all the time. Literary work was all that he cared for.[44]

Judging from the appearance of his surviving manuscripts one of Rae's problems was to keep a supply of writing paper. He evidently wrote on anything he could lay his hands on. On the back page of a child's exercise book which he used there is a note "Feby 20, 1855 one cow sent to pasture by manu" and below it some fragment of a composition, "Never have advocated any measure but from a settled conviction of its justice a profound feeling of its righteousness."

On at least one occasion in 1866 Rae had a bout of ill health. He explained in a letter to the Secretary of the Board of Health written in September, 1866, that he had not been able to undertake any vaccinations because of "the state of my health which since last Feby has been in a very precarious state. My eyes have also been affected & . . . I have no glasses I can use."[45]

At last, Rae heeded the urgings of his friend Cameron to return to live out his days at Sir Roderick's home "Clifton Berley" in Rosebank on Staten Island.[46] He sailed from Hawaii to San Francisco in the steamer *Ajax* and arrived in New York in the summer of 1871, old and enfeebled but still mentally alert. According to Mixter the unaccustomed severity of the climate affected him and Rae remained in his room the following winter and spring. On July 12, 1872, in the seventy-seventh year of his age, he died.[47]

Rae's grave is in an old section of Woodland Cemetery, Staten Island.[48] It is overgrown with weeds and unmarked. If there ever was a headstone it has disintegrated or disappeared. But it is a pleasant location and in the summer it will be green and warm, perhaps not unlike Hana.

[44] *Montreal Daily Star*, March 4, 1899.

[45] Archives of Hawaii, Board of Health, 11th folder, Sept. 24, 1866.

[46] Mixter states that Cameron had assisted Rae financially and quotes from a letter of Cameron's, "If you will come and spend your remaining years with me, I will defray all your expenses from Maui to my home." *Sociological Theory of Capital*, xxviii.

[47] Brief obituary notices appeared in the *New York Evening Post*, July 18, 1872, and the New York *Herald*, July 19, 1872.

[48] Mixter says, "He was buried in Woodland Cemetery, Staten Island, in a lot purchased by Sir Roderick, 'in which two others, one a faithful servant and the other a distant relative, are buried.'" *Sociological Theory of Capital*, xxviii.

BIOGRAPHICAL APPENDIX

RODERICK WILLIAM CAMERON (1823–1900). Cameron was born in Williamstown, Glengarry County, on July 25, 1823, the son of Duncan Cameron, a former partner in the North West Company. His early education was in Rae's school in Williamstown, but he finished his schooling at the Eastern District School in Cornwall under the Rev. Hugh Urquhart. He moved to Hamilton about 1839 where he was employed as a clerk by the firm of R. and J. Roy, wholesale and retail dry goods merchants. In 1847, after an unsuccessful venture into civic politics in Hamilton, Cameron moved to New York where he became a commission agent and broker and also engaged in the shipping business. Cameron, in addition to being a man of great personal charm, was astute in business, specializing in shipping between the United States and Australia. He operated a number of clipper ships including the famous *Flying Scud* and founded the Australia Pioneer Line. In 1849, he was a member of a Canadian delegation to Washington which was urging a reciprocity treaty. He later represented Canada and Australia at several international exhibitions and prepared some reports on Australia which were printed by the Canadian government. Cameron was Honorary Commissioner for New South Wales to the Philadelphia Exhibition, 1876, and to the Paris Exposition, 1878, and Commissioner for Canada to the Sydney and Melbourne Exhibitions in 1880 and 1881. In 1883, he was knighted on the recommendation of the Canadian government. In later life, he travelled widely and was greatly interested in horse racing, having imported from England a number of outstanding stallions including "Leamington," the sire of "Iroquois," a winner of the Derby and St. Leger.

DAVID CHISHOLME (1796?–1842) was born in Ross, Scotland, and studied law as a young man. He emigrated to Montreal about 1822 and in that year married Racheal Cuthbert, daughter of Captain John Robertson of the Inverness-shire militia. For a period he was editor of the *Canadian Magazine and Literary Repository* and in the period 1824–26 he edited the *Canadian Review and Literary and Historical Journal*, later the *Canadian Review and Magazine*. For a short time he was editor of the Montreal *Herald* but this ended in the spring of 1826. Late in 1826, he was appointed Clerk of the Peace for the District of Three Rivers and subsequently also became Coroner, Commissioner to administer Oaths, Postmaster and Agent for the Provincial Secretary. He was ousted from these positions in 1836 as a result of an address from the House of Assembly which he had offended by his ultra-loyalist sentiments. In 1837 he became editor of the *Montreal Gazette* and continued in that position until his death on September 24, 1842. Chisholme is supposed to be the author of a series of letters initially appearing in the *Kingston Chronicle* in 1828 and 1829 which were published in book form as *The Lower Canada Watchman* (Kingston, 1829). He also wrote *Observa-*

tions on the Rights of the British Colonies to Representation in the Imperial Parliament (Three Rivers, 1832) and the incomplete *The Annals of Canada,* an account of the Rebellion of 1837–38.

HENRY ESSON (1793–1853) was born at Balnacraig, Aboyne. He attended Marischal College in the period 1807–11, and graduated with the degree of M.A. in 1811, thus overlapping one year when Rae was a student there. The records of Marischal College show that Esson was first bursar and won a silver pen in 1808 for academic attainments. Ordained in the Church of Scotland, he became co-pastor of the St. Gabriel Street Church in Montreal in 1817. In 1822 he established the Montreal Academical Institution, a school for boys, where he taught for many years. He was active in the intellectual life of Montreal and was vice-president of the Natural History Society in 1829. He was apparently well educated and personally charming but was involved on several occasions in litigation and bitter disputes in the church and civil courts. Of him, Gregg says in his *History of the Presbyterian Church in the Dominion of Canada,* "He passed with great credit through the literary and philosophical classes at college, carrying off the higher prizes in the different departments, and securing at the same time the cordial attachment of his teachers and his fellow students." The Rev. Robert Campbell, the historian of Esson's church, described him as a "scholar, gentleman and brilliant talker." In later life Esson became Professor of Mental and Moral Philosophy at Knox College, Toronto, having left the St. Gabriel St. Church at the time of the disruption in 1844.

JAMES FLEMING (1778–1855) was born in Aberdeenshire and emigrated to Montreal as a young man where he became a successful business man. He was a communicant of St. Andrew's Church, one of the Scotch Presbyterian churches in Montreal, and frequently participated in church affairs. He was an elder of the church in the 1830's and on a number of occasions a lay delegate to the Synod from the Presbytery of Quebec. During most of the 1830's, James Fleming was very active as a committee member in promoting the work of such groups as the Sunday School Union Society of Canada and the Montreal Auxiliary Religious Tract Society. He died in Montreal on October 6, 1855.

JOHN FLEMING (1786–1832) was born in Aberdeenshire and came to Canada about 1803. He became a partner of Hart Logan and Co., a firm of general merchants, in 1815 and later its head. In the late 1820's he was a Justice of the Peace, Lieutenant in the Militia, member of the Legislative Council, a life governor of the Montreal General Hospital, and secretary of the Montreal Committee of Trade—a precursor of the Board of Trade which existed between 1822 and 1839. He was closely associated with some of the early banks in Montreal. He was a director and vice-president of the Bank of Montreal in the period 1826–30 and became the fifth president in 1830, a position he held until his death. He had also been president of the Bank of Canada from 1830 until it merged with the Bank of Montreal in 1831. In addition to his commercial and financial activities, he was involved in both literary and political affairs in Montreal. Even as a

young man, he had distinguished himself by winning the prize offered by the
Quebec Literary Society for the best English poem submitted in 1809, an ode
entitled "The Birthday of His Majesty King George III." He contributed on a
number of occasions to the *Canadian Review and Magazine* around 1825 and
published two pamphlets or books, both of which displayed considerable literary
ability as well as animosity towards the French Canadians. These were: *Some
Considerations on This Question; whether the British government acted wisely in
granting to Canada her present constitution*, a pamphlet issued in 1810 under the
pen name "A British Settler"; and *Political Annals of Lower Canada* printed in
1828. In 1831, he was a vice-president of the Natural History Society of Montreal.
Fleming accumulated a library of 11,000 volumes which was one of the largest
in private hands in Canada at that time. He died during the cholera epidemic on
June 30, 1832, aged 46 years.

JOHN RAMSAY FLEMING (1824?–1901). Fleming was the son of Ann Cuthbert
Knight by her marriage to James Fleming and was born in Montreal about 1824.
He was called to the bar in Montreal in 1847 and practised for many years in
Aylmer, Quebec, as a member of the firm of Fleming, Church, and Kenney,
Advocates. He was made a Queen's Counsel by the Province of Quebec in 1876
and by the federal government in 1887. He was *bâtonnier* of the Hull Bar in the
period 1889–93 and for many years Prothonotary of the Superior Court in Ottawa
County, Quebec. He died in Ottawa on February 6, 1901.

ALEXANDER GALE (1800–1854) was the son of John Gale of the Mill of Logie in
the Parish of Logie-Coldstone, Aberdeenshire. His mother was Jean Esson, a
sister of Henry Esson. Gale was educated at Marischal College. He was first
bursar in 1815 and received the degree of M.A. in 1819. After being licensed by
the Presbytery of Kincardine O'Neil, Gale emigrated to Canada in 1827. For
several years after 1828 he was the Presbyterian Minister at Amherstburgh and
then took over the charge at Lachine late in 1831, where he also ran a boys'
school. In 1833 he became the minister of the kirk in Hamilton and in early 1834
was named one of the trustees of the Gore District School. In August, 1836, he
married Margaret, the daughter of James Scarth of Kirkwall, Orkney, in
Brooklyn, N.Y. There was a daughter, Jane, by this marriage who later married
the Rev. Mr. Ingliss of Hamilton and a son, James, who became teller of the
Commercial Bank of Hamilton. Gale joined the Free Church in 1844 and moved
to Toronto where he became principal of the Toronto Academy for a period and
also Professor of Classical Literature at Knox College in 1846. He was Moderator
of the Synod of the Presbyterian Church of Canada in 1853. He died at his
home Logie-on-the-Mountain in the township of Barton on April 6, 1854.

JOHN SHERIDAN HOGAN (*c.* 1815–1859). Hogan was a native of Ireland who
emigrated to Canada as a boy. He ran away from his guardian in Toronto and
became a newsboy for the *Canadian Wesleyan*, a weekly newspaper in Hamilton
which flourished 1831–35. He became a reporter and then a clerk and bookkeeper
in the office of the Sheriff of the Gore District. About 1840 he began the study of

law and in 1844 became an attorney (not a barrister). In January, 1840, he opened a theatre in Hamilton. Later he founded the *United Empire*, a Toronto weekly and was parliamentary correspondent for a number of newspapers. Hogan added to the lustre of his reputation in 1855 with an *Essay on Canada* which won him first prize from the Paris Exhibition Committee of Canada. He later became editor of the *Daily Colonist* in Toronto and was elected as a member for Grey County to the provincial legislature in 1857. Hogan has been described by an acquaintance, William Gillespy, at one time editor of the *Hamilton Spectator*, as "unhappy, ill-starred, peevish and inclined always to take the gloomiest view of everything. . . . In spite of himself [he] was a good fellow at heart." He gained further notice in 1859 when he was mysteriously murdered by a member of the notorious Brooks' Bush gang.

JESSIE KNIGHT, the daughter of Ann Cuthbert Rae and James Innes Knight, was born in Scotland about 1814, but so far as is known never came to Canada. She married William Thurburn of Keith, Banffshire, probably about 1840. He was admitted as a solicitor in Scotland in 1836. According to the law list of 1842 he was a Justice of the Peace and Procurator Fiscal for the upper district of Banffshire as well as agent for the Aberdeen City and County Bank and for the Scottish Provincial Assurance companies. There was a son, Alexander Thurburn, born February 18, 1841, in Keith who was admitted as a solicitor in 1865 and was a member of the firm of Thurburn and Fleming. He would have been a first cousin of Robert Skakel Knight and the likely source of the information about the Rae family in Scotland referred to by Mixter on page xx of the *Sociological Theory of Capital*. Alexander Thurburn died in 1912 and his widow died in 1923. It is believed there are no direct descendants surviving.

ROBERT KNIGHT (1811–c.1863) was born in Portsoy, Banffshire, April 27, 1811, the son of James Innes Knight and Ann Cuthbert Rae. He was educated at the Royal Grammar School, Montreal, under Alex Skakel and at John Rae's school in Williamstown. As a youth he became an assistant teacher in a school in Chambly, Quebec, and studied for the Anglican ministry. He was ordained a deacon in 1835 and a priest in 1836, and was then appointed a missionary by the Society for the Propagation of the Gospel and assigned to Frampton, Quebec. He married in 1847 and moved to England where he became Perpetual Curate of Warton and later Vicar of Polesworth, Warwickshire. He wrote *A Critical Commentary on the Epistle of St. Paul, the Apostle to the Romans* (London, 1854), *The Doctrine of Scriptural Predestination* . . . (London, 1854) and *The Plurality of Worlds* (2nd ed.; London, 1878) and contributed to the *Journal of Sacred Literature* and other religious publications. He died in Polesworth, Warwickshire, about 1863. Some biographical information about the Knight family is contained in the preface to the second edition of Robert Knight's *The Plurality of Worlds*, written by Robert Skakel Knight, who quotes on page iv from notes of his father, "I also remember my two uncles John and Alexander, and used to designate them from this reminiscence big John and little Alexander . . ." There is a biographical note about Robert Knight in Thomas R. Millman, *The Life of the Right Reverend, the Honourable Charles James Stewart* . . . (London, Ont., 1953), 205.

ROBERT SKAKEL KNIGHT, the son of Robert Knight, was born in England sometime around 1850 and lived most of his life there. He was the author of a book, *Exercises in English Composition, with an Introductory Chapter on Analysis* (London, 1876). From 1876 to 1895 he was a Fellow of the Royal Society of Literature but resigned in the latter year upon coming to Canada where he lived in Lancaster, Ontario. Robert Skakel Knight had a daughter, Dorothy W. Knight, and both corresponded with Mixter. The former died around 1902.

JOHN MACKENZIE (1790–1855) was born in Fort Augustus, Scotland, and graduated from King's College in 1812. After a period of teaching school in Urquhart and Aberdeen he was ordained in 1818 as a Presbyterian minister. In 1819, he succeeded the Rev. John Bethune as minister of the kirk in Williamstown. He was the first Moderator of the Synod of the Presbyterian Church of Canada in connection with the Church of Scotland in 1831; in the same year he was appointed a trustee of the Eastern District School in Cornwall. He continued as pastor of the Williamstown congregation until his death in 1855.

JOHN RAE (1845–1915), the journalist and author, was born in Wick, Scotland, in 1845, the son of William Rae, Provost of Wick. He was educated at the University of Edinburgh, where he received a M.A. degree, and, in 1897, an honorary LL.D. He was a frequent contributor to economic journals, including the *Economic Journal*, on a variety of social and economic topics. He also wrote a number of books on economics including *Contemporary Socialism* (New York, 1884), *Eight Hours for Work* (London and New York, 1894), and a well-known *Life of Adam Smith* (New York, 1895). He died in England on April 19, 1915.

JOHN RAE (1813–1893), the Arctic explorer, was born in the Orkney Islands on September 30, 1813, the son of John Rae of the Hall of Clestrain, Stromness, for many years an agent of the Hudson's Bay Company. He began the study of medicine at the University of Edinburgh in 1829 and qualified as a licentiate of the Royal College of Surgeons in 1833. After completing his medical studies he became resident surgeon of the Hudson's Bay Company at Moose Factory where he stayed for about ten years. About 1843 he began his career as an Arctic explorer still in the employ of the Hudson's Bay Company and achieved great distinction in this field of activity. He found some of the remains of the last expedition of Sir John Franklin who had sailed to the Arctic in H.M. ships *Erebus* and *Terror* in 1845 and completely disappeared. This discovery won him considerable public attention and the lion's share of the prize of £10,000 offered by the British government for ascertaining the fate of Franklin's party. In the 1850's, Rae was a frequent visitor in Hamilton, Ontario, where he had two brothers, Thomas, a wholesale dry goods and hardware merchant, and Richard H. Rae, a merchant and later emigration agent. During his intermittent visits to Hamilton in the period 1857–59, Rae was actively associated with the Hamilton Association for the Cultivation of Science, Literature, and Art. Rae was awarded an honorary M.D. by McGill in 1853, an honorary LL.D. from Edinburgh in 1856, and became a Fellow of the Royal Society in 1880. He was the author of

Narrative of an Expedition to the Shores of the Arctic Seas in 1847 (London, 1850) and a great many scientific papers. He died on July 22, 1893. The introduction to *John Rae's Correspondence with the Hudson's Bay Company on Arctic Exploration, 1844–1855*, edited by E. E. Rich (London, 1953) contains a valuable biographical account.

JOHN RAE (1813–1893), the Australian, achieved considerable prominence as a civil servant, author, and artist. He was born in Aberdeen on January 9, 1813, and was educated at the Grammar School in Aberdeen and at Marischal College. He received his M.A. in 1832 and after a period of studying law emigrated to Australia in 1839. He was appointed town clerk of Sydney in 1843 and in 1861 became Under Secretary for Works and Commissioner for Railways. In 1888 he became a member of the Australian civil service board and retired in 1893. He led an active literary life and in 1842 wrote the text of a book *Sydney Illustrated*. In 1853 he published *The Book of the Prophet Isaiah rendered into English Blank Verse*. In 1869, he issued *Gleanings from my Scrap-Book*, which appeared in two series, and this was followed in 1874 by *Gleanings from my Scrap-Book: Third Series*. He died on July 15, 1900. See Percival Serle, *Dictionary of Australian Biography* (Sydney, London, 1949).

ALEXANDER SKAKEL (1776–1846) was born in Aberdeenshire and educated at King's College, Aberdeen, where he took the degree of M.A. in 1794. His early academic training was in preparation for the ministry of the Church of Scotland, but he was never ordained. He came to Canada as a young man and became a schoolteacher in Montreal in 1798. For over twenty years his school was a private institution, but in 1818 Skakel became headmaster of the Royal Grammar School in Montreal. He was closely associated with the Natural History Society in Montreal and was prominent in hospital affairs, being secretary of the Board of Management of the Montreal General Hospital for many years, as well as a life governor. Starting early in 1813, Skakel gave an annual series of lectures on natural philosophy which he continued for many years. He was a frequent contributor to various literary magazines in Montreal. In 1845, he was awarded an honorary LL.D. by the University of Aberdeen for his contribution to education. Skakel died on August 13, 1846. In the January, 1847, issue of the *Literary Garland* there was an anonymous poem, "An Elegy on the Death of Alex Skakel, L.L.D." Rae's sister, Ann Cuthbert, was a friend of Skakel's and her son Robert Knight was one of his pupils in the Royal Grammar School. As a mark of esteem for his teacher Robert Knight later named his own son Robert Skakel Knight.

HUGH BOWLBY WILLSON (1813–1880), born in Winona, Ontario, was the son of the Hon. John Willson of Saltfleet, the first speaker of the Legislative Assembly of Upper Canada, a member of the Assembly for thirty years, and a prominent figure in the political life of Upper Canada. In the Rebellion of 1837, Willson was a lieutenant in the 3rd Gore Regiment, and may have been one of the so-called "Men of Gore." In 1841, he was called to the bar and practised law for a time in Hamilton. In 1847, he was Secretary of the Upper Canada Mining Company and evidently interested in literary and topical matters. In January, 1848, he spoke before the Mercantile Literary Association on the subject, "On Canada: its rise, progress and capabilities," and in March on "Railways—their effects upon commerce and general superiority over other means of communication considered, particularly in reference to Canada." Willson became deeply involved in the annexationist movement in 1849 and became editor of the *Independent*, a newspaper devoted to the advocacy of severing relations with Britain and closer ties with the United States. Following the annexationist venture, he travelled about for a period writing a good deal. In 1852 he was in London, England, as a member of a firm dealing in American and Canadian securities. In 1864 a newspaper advertisement described Willson's occupation as "Barrister and Attorney at Law, parliamentary agent, solicitor of patents of invention, &c. &c." and showed him to be living in Quebec City. Among Willson's printed works are: *Canada and the United States* (a letter to the Editor of the *National Intelligencer*, 1849); *Reports and Correspondence on the "Patent Compound Rail"* (London, 1851); *Great Western Railway of Canada* (Hamilton, 1860); *Military Defences of Canada* (Quebec, 1862); *The Science of Shipbuilding, Considered in its Relations to the Laws of Nature* (London, 1863); *High Speed Steamers: or, How to Build a River Boat to Run Thirty Miles an Hour* (Albany, 1866); *The Science of Money Considered* . . . (Washington, 1869); *A Plea for Uncle Sam's Money: or Greenback versus Bank Notes* (New York, 1870); *The Money Question Considered Scientifically and Practically* (London, 1874); *Industrial Crises, Their Causes and Remedies* . . . (Washington, 1879); *Currency: or the Fundamental Principles of Monetary Science: explained and applied* . . . (New York, 1882). The last book appeared posthumously, for Willson died in 1880 in New York.

PART II

RAE AS A SOCIAL SCIENTIST

10

The Background of Rae's *New Principles*

Around 1820, there was a surge in the literary, religious, and financial life of Montreal which reflected, in part, a transfer of economic power. A news item in the Montreal *Herald* in May, 1821, is symbolic of the change:

Alexander McKenzie, Esq., left this city last Sunday morning in one of the North West Canoes in order to convey into the interior the news of the union of the two fur companies and the dispatches on that subject received from London.[1]

The end of the long and acrimonious competitive struggle between the North West Company and the Hudson's Bay Company meant that Montreal had lost its dominant role in the fur trade. Thus, the way was paved for the growth in the strength and influence of the merchant class in the economic life of Montreal. The changes in the social and economic structure of the community were, however, accompanied by bitter and violent controversy.

In the 1820's and 1830's, Lower Canada and particularly Montreal seethed with a struggle between two completely antagonistic social groups, one dominated by the French-Canadian faction, the *Patriotes*, and the other by the merchants, many of them Scottish Presbyterians. Culturally, the differences were evident; language, religion, and social customs were dissimilar and this produced distrust and dislike. From an economic

---

[1] Montreal *Herald*, May 9, 1821. Alexander McKenzie was a former partner of the North West Company, at this time acting as agent for McTavish, McGillivrays and Company.

point of view, the merchants were insistent on the paramount importance of their commercial relations with England, while the French-Canadian faction was primarily agrarian in its outlook and lukewarm if not hostile to the British connection. Politically, the French-Canadian faction found comfort in the radical, revolutionary, or merely democratic ideas which were current in England, Europe, and the United States at that time, while the merchants countered with loyal addresses to the King and protestations of devotion to the Mother Country. It is, of course, a severe oversimplification to suggest that there was any fixed relation between language or ethnic background and political attitude. One particular manifestation of the antagonism in Lower Canada was a series of bitter controversies within the House of Assembly. The result was that the business of the House was carried on only with the greatest difficulty. The period was marked by violence, abuse, and vilification, culminating in 1837 in armed insurrection.

A qualified observer, the Hon. E. G. Stanley, commented on the factional spirit in Montreal which he noted during his visit in 1824:

It [Montreal] is the head of the navigation of the St. Lawrence, ships of seven hundred tons being able to come quite up to the City, though about 700 miles from the Sea and it is in the direct line of communication with the United States by way of Lake Champlain. It is probably this circumstance among others that has attracted so great a number of American merchants to establish themselves here. Indeed the upper class of the population is chiefly composed of them & Scotch Settlers, the French population being here limited to the lower orders chiefly. Perhaps on this account the jealousies between French and English, Catholic & Protestant, and the spirit of party generally, high everywhere in Lower Canada, are particularly prominent at Montreal.[2]

John Rae was concerned in these controversies on both personal and philosophical grounds. In the first place he was intimately associated with the Montreal merchants and their friends and in due course was to become one of their philosophers and publicists. Rae's involvement stemmed partly from his associations with his sister, Ann Cuthbert, and her friends. Her boarding school catered to the daughters of the well-to-do merchant class in Montreal and her commercial connections were strengthened when she married into the Fleming family. Her husband, James, and his younger brother John were both successful in business in Montreal, but John also

[2] *Journal of a Tour in America 1824–1825* (Edinburgh, 1930), 80. He also recorded in his journal (81): "During our stay of a few days at this place, we met with the most marked attention and civility. The merchants of Montreal are indeed celebrated in America for their social disposition. Many of them are wealthy, and Mr. McGillivray in particular has a beautiful villa within two or three miles of the Town which displays in the interior as well as the exterior really good taste." He had also been a dinner guest at the Beaver Club.

had marked literary and intellectual gifts which were used with telling effect against the *Patriotes*.[3] The fact that John Fleming was a prominent official of both the Bank of Canada and the Bank of Montreal made him an object of hostility.[4]

Apart from his immediate family connections Rae had other associations with people prominent in both political and literary activities in Montreal. For example, Rae's friend, the Rev. Henry Esson, married Maria Sweeny, the daughter of a local merchant Campbell Sweeny, while her sister Jane married Dr. William Caldwell, a man of prominence in medical and literary affairs. Rae must have known at least some of the members of the Constitutional Society of Lower Canada, a select group of ultra-loyal pamphleteers, one of whose members was John Fleming.[5] It is almost certain that Rae had some associations with David Chisholme, whose attacks on Papineau and his followers were noteworthy for their virulence.[6] Rae in one place makes an incidental reference to Andrew Stuart (1785–1840), Solicitor General of Lower Canada in the period 1837–40, the gifted opponent of Papineau, which indicates he may have known him. All the available evidence suggests that this whole group were solidly united in their attachment to the Crown and to economic policies which would stimulate the growth of Canadian commerce and settlement.

Apart from Rae's connections in Montreal, it should also be noted that

[3] John Fleming's book, *Political Annals of Lower Canada* (Montreal, 1828), was referred to by David Chisholme as "that most valuable and learned work . . . that ought to be in the hands of every man who has any regard for the prosperity of this part of his Majesty's dominions." *The Lower Canada Watchman* (Kingston, 1829), 263. In contrast, it was described by Pierre de Salles Laterrière as "a work full of information as it is of prejudice against the French Canadians." Benjamin Sulte, C. E. Fryer, L. O. David, *A History of Quebec: Its Resources and People* (Montreal, Toronto, 1908), I, 302.

[4] The French-Canadian faction was suspicious of the influence of the Canadian banks, particularly the Bank of Montreal. Louis Joseph Papineau was quoted as saying, "Another most weighty consideration was, whether, by the control of £600,000 of the capital of the country, the Directors did not possess an alarming political influence. In fact the political influence had been felt in Montreal at the last election. The President of the Bank [of Montreal], accompanied by a Member of the Executive Council, had gone around to solicit votes . . ." *Montreal Gazette*, April 1, 1830, quoted in D. G. Creighton, *The Commercial Empire of the St. Lawrence 1760–1853* (Toronto and New Haven, 1937), 278–9.

[5] Those attending the first meeting of the Constitutional Society of Lower Canada were identified in the press as: Senex, Veritas, Nerva, Vindex, Denis, Constitutionalist, Horatio, Delta, A British Settler, and Junius. *Montreal Gazette*, Aug. 16, 1827. The use of such *noms de plume*, which was characteristic of this period, is maddening to a modern investigator.

[6] In an open letter to Papineau, dated Feb. 28, 1829, Chisholme wrote: "You are, indeed, Sir, a public criminal of no ordinary character. Intoxicated with impudence, there is no end of your rudeness: frantick with rage, there are no bounds to your malevolence. The high and the low, among such as do not coincide with you in opinion, are equally objects of your hatred and resentment." *Lower Canada Watchman*, 197.

he was associated with an unusual group of men in Williamstown. These Scotsmen from Glengarry were in general successful in their business affairs, well educated, and informed on the problems of the day and eager to promote the economic growth and the population of Upper Canada. For example, there was a meeting in Williamstown in November, 1822, whose chairman was Alexander McMartin, M.P., called to urge the union of Upper and Lower Canada. A committee was appointed to write petitions consisting among others of such men as Alex Fraser, the Rev. John McLaurin, Hugh McGillis, Duncan Cameron, John McGillivray, and Alpin Grant.[7] The secretary was Rae's friend, the Rev. John Mackenzie. It might be noted also that at a meeting of the Friends of the Re-union of Upper and Lower Canada in Montreal in October, 1822, the Hon. John Richardson was chairman and John Fleming was secretary.[8]

Thus Rae's friends and associates were embroiled in controversial problems of economic development right from the time of his arrival and it was inevitable that Rae should become involved to some degree. What is really extraordinary is that he was prepared to devote something like fifteen years of his life to the development of a definitive solution of Canada's economic and political problems. The man was obviously obsessed or inspired by the Baconian notions of inductive philosophy. He was later to quote with approval from Lord Bacon's *Novum Organum* in the course of chastising Adam Smith:

There have been, and can be but two modes of searching after truth. The one commencing the chain of reasoning with some familiar conception of things, flies from them immediately to general axioms, and from these, and their assumed incontrovertible truth, judges of all particulars. A way of philosophizing brief, but rash; easy and well fitted to conduct to disputes, but not leading to a knowledge of nature. This is the common mode. The other rises gradually and slowly from fact to fact and only at last arrives at the most general conclusions. These, however, are not notions, the products of the imagination, but real laws of nature, and such as she herself will acknowledge and obey.[9]

It must have been shortly after his arrival in Williamstown that Rae began his preliminary research into the resources of Canada. By his own account he had travelled extensively collecting statistical and other information. Rae's petition of 1832 to the Lieutenant-Governor for financial assistance, referred to earlier, outlines the nature of his economic, statistical, and geological research. This work had evidently involved him in some intellectual and conceptual difficulties which he explained in the preface to his *New Principles* a couple of years later.

[7] Montreal *Herald*, Nov. 20, 1822.
[8] *Montreal Gazette*, Oct. 14, 1822.
[9] *New Principles*, 333–4.

During my residence in this country [Canada], the field of my inquiries being much contracted, I again recurred to the disquisitions of Adam Smith, and of other European writers of the same school, in order to trace out more fully than I had hitherto done, the connexion between the phenomena attending the increase and diminution of wealth, and those general principles of the nature of man, and of the world, determining, as I conceive, the whole progress of human affairs. Though I was led to this study, simply from my desire to advance, as far as my situation permitted me, in a path of investigation which had, to me, a very lively interest, my prosecution of it had the effect of impressing me more deeply with a conviction of the unsoundness of the system maintained in the Wealth of Nations.

In this stage of my progress I became engaged in a work on the present state of Canada, and on its relations with the rest of the British Empire. These relations seem to me to spring from the mutual benefit arising to the colony and the empire from their connexion. The sect of politicians, to whom I allude, deny that any such benefit arises to either party. Were their reasoning correct, it would follow as a necessary consequence, that Canada is, in this respect, of no advantage to Great Britain, and would go far to prove, what, indeed, seems by many to be believed, that the sooner the connexion between them is dissolved the better.

Dissenting as I do, from the opinions of these theorists, it appeared to me that the work I had undertaken required me to state some of the reasons on which I grounded this dissent . . .[10]

Rae thus involved himself in an important political controversy. The agitation in Great Britain in the 1820's for the dissolution of all colonial ties was profoundly disturbing to the mercantile class in Canada. The disciples of Adam Smith and Jeremy Bentham were vociferously denying that there was any advantage in colonial possessions.[11] On the contrary, they were a bill of expense, a source of international discord, and a political nuisance. The *Edinburgh Review* was a leading vehicle for the anti-colonial group. This excerpt is a sample:

. . . the mere military expense attending the government of our West India and North American Colonies, costs the Treasury of Great Britain, *in time of peace, little less than a MILLION A YEAR, exclusive of the revenue collected in them.* And they have the farther disadvantage of multiplying the chances of misunderstanding and contests with foreign powers, and of making a vast addition to the expense of war.

Such being the case with respect to our colonial possessions, it is not easy to see how we could sustain any injury from the total breaking up of the colonial monopoly, or even from the total and unconditional abandonment of these dependencies.[12]

[10] *Ibid.*, v–vi.

[11] "The economists and the Benthamites exploded the old colonial theories, and informed the country that colonies were causes of war and of misgovernment and definitely pernicious; but the country was hard of hearing." W. P. Morrell, *British Colonial Policy in the Age of Peel and Russell* (Oxford, 1930), 2–3.

[12] *Edinburgh Review*, XLII, Aug. 1825, 292–3.

This point of view is not to be found explicitly in Adam Smith. In fact, Adam Smith had written in one place:

To propose that Great Britain should voluntarily give up all authority over her colonies, and leave them to elect their own magistrates to enact their own laws, and to make peace and war as they might think proper, would be to propose such a measure as never was, and never will be adopted, by any nation in the world.[13]

Subsequent refinements in the doctrine of international trade theory had fostered a cavalier attitude to the colonies among the economists. James Mill noted in discussing the advantages of trade with colonies: "It is needless to consider the case of free trade with a colony, because that falls under the case of trade with any foreign country."[14] The *Edinburgh Review* visualized the union of Canada and the United States in the near future, saying:

Every man of sense, whether in the Cabinet or out of it, knows, that Canada must, at no distant period, be merged in the American republic. And certainly John Bull discovers no very great impatience of taxation, when he quietly allows his pockets to be drained, in order to clear and fertilize a province for the use of his rival Jonathan.[15]

Such provocative remarks naturally stimulated a good deal of invective in Canada. Some examples are contained in Chisholme's *Canadian Review and Magazine*.[16] The final issue in September, 1826, started off with two reviews excoriating the political dreamers and the political economists of the *Edinburgh Review*. The first article reviewed two pamphlets supporting the value of the colonies, one of them by Mr. Justice Haliburton, otherwise Sam Slick. The second article dealt with a harmless booklet, *Sketches of New Brunswick . . .*, but provided the occasion for a polemic written by Chisholme himself. He wrote,

What renders these provincial histories of peculiar importance at the present moment, is the broad and conspicuous light in which they place the value to their inhabitants and the parent country of the rich and extensive province of which they treat; while a turbulent and malignant spirit has gone abroad to depreciate that value, and foment opinions and sentiments the most dangerous and destructive of the peace, the happiness, and the prosperity at once of the colonies and the parent state.

That spirit, conceived by disaffection, bred in the corruption of a party, and

[13] Adam Smith, *An Inquiry into the Nature and Causes of the Wealth of Nations* [Cannan ed.] (New York, 1937), 581–2.

[14] James Mill, *Elements of Political Economy* (2nd ed.; London, 1824), 204.

[15] *Edinburgh Review*, XLII, Aug. 1825, 292.

[16] In Feb., 1826, the name of the *Canadian Review and Literary and Historical Journal* was changed to the *Canadian Review and Magazine*.

disseminated by the trumpet of sedition, we are glad to find every wise and prudent man exclaiming against in language that does honour to the human heart and understanding. If ever patriotism had occasion to be indignant; if she ever found it necessary to resent any injury; or to lift her magnanimous sword to punish and repel an attack upon her virtue and purity, it is now . . .[17]

Apart from Rae's personal affiliation with the merchant class one additional influence on his intellectual convictions should be recognized. This was his close association with the Presbyterian Church.[18] To appreciate this influence two points should be noted. First of all the fate of the Presbyterians in Canada depended clearly on the preservation of colonial status. They wanted establishment, government subsidies for ministers' salaries and for the building of churches, and a share of the Clergy Reserves. Severance of the colonial tie would surely dash their hopes and aspirations. In the second place, there is no doubt that the dominant importance assigned to morality and education in Rae's writings on economics was strongly influenced by his Presbyterian background. The accumulation of capital in a community, Rae later wrote, was influenced by two factors, among others: "The extent of the intellectual powers, and the consequent habits of reflection and prudence, in the minds of the members of the society" and "the stability of the condition of the affairs of the society, and the reign of law and order throughout it." The Presbyterians, with a deep-rooted interest in education and an abiding respect for law and order in civil affairs, were clearly a beneficial influence in a capital-hungry country.

Evidently, Rae's *New Principles* was initially intended as an appendix or adjunct to his work on the present state and resources of Canada. He decided instead to issue separately his views on political economy. This development is referred to in a letter written to the Secretary of the Lieutenant-Governor of Upper Canada by the Rev. William Rintoul in mid-1833.[19] In part, this read:

I have a letter this morning from Dr. John Rae presently residing at Montreal in which he requests me to distribute a few circulars containing the prospectus of a new work which he is about to publish, and he informs me that he had transmitted to you for the perusal of His Excellency one of the circulars. I gather from

[17] Vol. III, no. 5, 21.
[18] This should be understood to mean, of course, the Presbyterian Church of Canada in connection with the Church of Scotland.
[19] William Rintoul was born in Clackmannanshire, Scotland, and educated at Edinburgh University. He arrived in Canada in 1831 and shortly after his arrival participated in the first Synod of the Presbyterian Church of Canada in connection with the Church of Scotland in Kingston. He became minister of St. Andrew's Church, Toronto, in 1831, was Professor of Hebrew and Biblical Literature at Knox College, and in 1850 minister of the St. Gabriel Street Church, Montreal. He died in 1852.

the train of his letter that he had not requested the name of His Excellency as a subscriber as indeed he requests me to seek that favour in his behalf. Now though I do not think there was any need for his employing my agency in this matter, or that His Excellency will be more ready to grant the favour on my account, I am unwilling to refuse Dr. Rae the little service he has sought at my hands; and so I make bold to give this plain account of the matter to His Excellency through you; and shall feel myself obliged to His Excellency by the kindly patronage of the work of a gentleman whom I esteem.

His Excellency may perhaps remember that Dr. Rae about 18 months ago was through the favour of His Excellency prosecuting statistical researches in the Surveyor Generals Office, with a view to a statistical work on Canada. At that time I believe he intended that his views on political economy should be embodied in an appendix to the statistical work; however it appears that they have so expanded as to warrant him to venture on a separate publication. I cannot pretend to offer any opinion of the probable character of either of the works which he projects; though I may take upon me to say, that from the enthusiasm with which he has been prosecuting them, and the acuteness and culture of his mind, I do think they will prove not unworthy of the patronage of His Excellency.[20]

The prospectus mentioned by Rintoul does not appear to have survived separately, but it is possible that it was the first preface to the *New Principles*.

Since Rae's *New Principles* was conceived as a by-product of his study of the Canadian economy, it is not possible to say precisely when it was begun. However, judging from the fact that the preface to the book is dated "Montreal, 1833," and that Rintoul had copies of the prospectus in July, 1833, a version of it was completed at that time. Rae had intended, according to the preface, to publish the book in England, but his plans changed for reasons unspecified and the book was published in Boston instead. In a postscript to the preface dated Boston, 1834, Rae explains certain alterations in the text arising from this change.

Rae made a lengthy visit to Boston in 1834 and it may be presumed that his reason was to explore the possibility of publication in Boston, but whether this was because his negotiations in England were unsuccessful or not is unknown. An unidentified reviewer in the Boston *Daily Advertiser* says on this question: "He [Rae] was induced to make some inquiries as to the probable success of the work here. The plan was communicated to some gentlemen of this city, under whose advice the publication has been made."[21] Rae's sister is quoted by Mixter as saying that he received "great attention from some literary and distinguished characters" but does not identify either the context or the characters.[22]

[20] P.A.C., Upper Canada Sundries; letter, William Rintoul to Lt.-Col. William Rowan, July 4, 1833.
[21] *Montreal Gazette*, Aug. 26, 1834.
[22] *Sociological Theory of Capital*, xxiii.

It is known, however, that one of Rae's sponsors was Alexander Hill Everett (1790–1847), the brilliant and erratic editor of the *North American Review*. This remarkable and able man, at one time United States Minister to Spain and a friend and protégé of John Quincy Adams, was an accomplished linguist, classicist, and scholar and a significant figure in the resurgent literary life in Boston in the early 1830's. Everett had written an anti-Malthusian tract in 1823, *New Ideas on Population with Remarks on the Theories of Malthus and Godwin*, and was keenly interested in the tariff question. The *North American Review* was an influential organ and Everett's editorial policy was to support "correct principles in taste, morals and religion.[23] In the political sphere, according to Van Wyck Brooks: "Its aim, as time advanced, was to keep the tariff up, to keep the Whigs in power for the sake of the tariff, and to keep on good terms with the Southern magnates, whose cotton fed the Northern factories, so that the tariff might serve the Boston bankers."[24]

Thus both Everett and his journal were vigorously supporting a protectionist policy in the United States. The clamour for higher tariffs had developed in the 1820's and had culminated in the so-called "Tariff of Abominations" in 1828. Despite this, the opponents of "the American System" could call on the formidable authority of Adam Smith to refute the crude arguments of the protectionists. It was therefore something of a coup when the Pennsylvania Society for the Promotion of Manufactures and the Mechanic Arts were able to produce the apostate Friedrich List at the Harrisburg Convention of 1827. List was able to clothe the protectionist arguments with a degree of intellectual respectability, but in other ways he was a disappointment. What was urgently needed was an elementary text for the dissemination of the true principles of political economy. This List was never able to produce. There was naturally widespread interest in economics in the colleges and universities of the period, but the works of Adam Smith and J. B. Say dominated the scene. The Pennsylvania protectionists advertised widely the need for both elementary and advanced textbooks to counter the doctrines of the "colonial" or "foreign" system of free trade but with indifferent success.

Thus it was that when Rae arrived in Boston with a manuscript entitled "Statement of Some New Principles on the Subject of Political Economy Exposing the Fallacies of the System of Free Trade, and of Some Other Doctrines Maintained in the *Wealth of Nations*," he was cordially received. Whether any of Rae's sponsors in Boston read his manu-

[23] Samuel Flagg Bemis, *John Quincy Adams and the Union* (New York, 1956), 230.
[24] Van Wyck Brooks, *The Flowering of New England, 1815–1865* (New York, 1936), 114.

script is doubtful, but his provocative title was full of promise.

It must have been an exhilarating experience for Rae to associate with the Boston *literati* after his long and relatively arid period in the backwoods. It is probable that he was swept off his feet by the flattery and friendship of Everett and his associates. Joseph Dorfman has a revealing comment on this episode.

The scene was reminiscent of the Harrisburg Convention of 1827. A great tariff convention had just been held in New York. Everett, as chairman of that body, prepared the memorial to Congress. Just as Ingersoll had thought he had found in the German, List, the theorist for his movement, so it seems Everett thought that the Scotsman, Rae, with a treatise ready for publication, was his man of the hour. Apparently Everett had not read the manuscript, but had been impressed by Rae's intellectual stature in their personal meetings in Boston.[25]

It is easy to understand how Rae, a country schoolteacher, might have succumbed to the blandishments of such a distinguished and sophisticated person as Everett. Rae's involvement with Everett was unfortunate, and some of the consequences were to cast a long shadow, as will be seen.

[25] Joseph Dorfman, *The Economic Mind in American Civilization* (*1606–1865*) (New York, 1946), II, 780.

11

Rae on Political Economy

In 1834, when Rae was thirty-eight years old, his book on political economy was published in Boston. Not only was this a major event in Rae's life, but his work was ultimately to exert a considerable influence on the development of the theory of capital. While it is desirable to examine certain aspects of Rae's contribution to political economy, it is not the intention to summarize or interpret the whole of Rae's book.[1] The immediate availability of the text makes this unnecessary. Nor does it appear desirable at this point to undertake an analysis of Rae's place in the history of economic thought. To some extent he borrowed and assimilated ideas from other people, but to trace such influences would involve a long digression and a great deal of conjecture. Instead it is proposed to single out some particular aspects of his work and to offer some explanatory remarks. The aspects dealt with will be limited to: (1) Rae's critique of Adam Smith; (2) Rae's theory of capital; (3) Rae on invention; (4) Rae on tariff protection; (5) Rae on luxury.

1. RAE'S CRITIQUE OF ADAM SMITH

In order to understand Rae's economics, it is essential first of all to appreciate his fundamental assumption concerning the growth of the capital or the wealth of a community. His contention is that there is a fundamental distinction between the factors governing the wealth of individuals

[1] Some aspects have already been dealt with elsewhere. See, for example, the admirable article by Craufurd D. W. Goodwin, "John Rae: Undiscovered Exponent of Canadian Banks," *Canadian Banker*, LXVI, Winter, 1959, 110–15.

and the factors governing the wealth of nations. His introductory remarks contrast two diverse policies designed to increase the national wealth. First, there is the policy founded on the view that the encouragement of commerce and manufactures leads to an increase in national wealth and naturally therefore to an increase in the wealth of the individuals composing the nation. "This view of the matter leads directly to a system of unceasing regulation and restraint."[2] Second, there is an alternative claim that increases in the wealth of individuals must necessarily lead to greater national wealth. Any restraint or hindrance which impairs the ability of individuals to become wealthy must therefore be avoided lest it in turn leads to a diminution of the national wealth. This, of course, was Adam Smith's heroic contribution to the political life of the Western world.

Rae argues that both these systems were based on the faulty assumption of the identity of individual and national wealth, but he singled out Adam Smith for attack. He explained:

My main object, in this book, is to show that that notion of the exact identity of the causes giving rise to individual and national wealth, on which the reasonings and arguments of Adam Smith all along depend, is erroneous, that consequently the doctrines he has engrafted on it, cannot be thus maintained, and are inconsistent with facts admitted by himself.[3]

There was nothing essentially new in Rae's argument. The same general ideas had been argued by the Earl of Lauderdale in his *Public Wealth* in 1804 and by Jeremy Bentham in his letter to Adam Smith on projects in arts written in 1787. Rae quotes from both these authors and was probably familiar with their criticisms.

Rae emphasized that individuals could become rich by the acquisition of larger shares of existing wealth while nations were constrained to create new wealth before they could become richer. Hard work and parsimony might help a person to become wealthy but the wealth of the nation as a whole could only grow with the help of the "inventive faculty." The implications of this view for economic policy were immediately clear. It was a cardinal requirement of policy to foster invention and to facilitate the transference of inventions from one country to another. This view further justified the intervention of the state in helping new industries by protective duties, bounties and other financial encouragement. Moreover, Rae believed that it was desirable for the state to encourage and support financially industrial research which would lead to new inventions. Rae's essential criterion for assessing economic policy as well as social behaviour was the effect on the accumulation of capital.

Rae's attitude to government intervention was in sharp contrast to the

<hr>

[2] *New Principles*, 7.   [3] *Ibid.*, 8.

views expressed by many of the followers of Adam Smith. He quotes as an example a comment by Dugald Stewart in his *Account of the Life and Writings of Dr. Smith*:

"Little else is requisite to carry a state to the highest degree of opulence from the lowest barbarism but peace, easy taxes, and a tolerable administration of justice; all the rest being brought about by the natural course of things. All governments which thwart this natural course, which force things into another channel, or which endeavor to arrest the progress of society at a particular point, are unnatural, and to support themselves are obliged to be oppressive and tyrannical."[4]

Rae conceived that governments had, in fact, a real obligation to undertake policies which would benefit the economic welfare of the community. He contended that there existed certain social or economic laws which could be determined by truly scientific analysis and that these could lead legislators to the adoption of wise and beneficial policies. Rae had a deeprooted belief in man's perfectibility and in the possibilities of improvements in the intelligence and morality of a society. In one place he says specifically:

... the result of a successful inquiry into the nature of wealth, would terminate in affording the means of exposing the errors that legislators had committed from not attending to all the circumstances connected with the growth of that wealth, whose progress it had been their aim to advance, and would so teach them, not that they ought to remain inactive, but how they may act safely, and advantageously; and that thus, it would maintain the analogy running through the whole of man's connexion with the trains of events going on about him, the course of which he governs by ascertaining exactly what it is. That here, as elsewhere, his advance in knowledge would show him his power, not his impotence.[5]

In part Rae's criticisms of Adam Smith stemmed from a fundamental difference in philosophic method. Rae was strongly influenced by the views of Francis Bacon on scientific method and argues vigorously that Smith's philosophy was not in accordance with the true inductive method described by Bacon. Rae claims that Smith's philosophy was essentially explanatory or systematic, saying:

To me it appears that his philosophy is that of explanation and system, and that his speculations are not to be considered as inductive investigations and expositions of the real principles guiding the successions of phenomena, but as successful efforts to arrange with regularity, according to common and preconceived notions, a multiplicity of known facts.[6]

Rae quotes from Adam Smith's *History of Astronomy* the comment, "A philosophical system is an imaginary machine invented to connect together in the fancy those different movements and effects, which are

---

[4] *Ibid.*, 358.   [5] *Ibid.*, 361–2.   [6] *Ibid.*, 331.

already in reality performed," and emphasizes that it is directly opposed
to the views in Bacon's *Novum Organum*.

Rae summarizes his dissent in the following trenchant paragraphs:

. . . in my opinion the disciples and followers of Adam Smith, in claiming for the
speculations contained in the Wealth of Nations, and for the doctrines they have
founded on them, the rank of an experimental science, the conclusions of which
are entitled to the same credence with other experimental sciences, act injudi-
ciously, and by insisting on pretensions which are unfounded, injure the cause of
that philosopher and conceal his real merits. If we view his philosophical system
of the Wealth of Nations, or indeed any of his philosophical systems, as he
views every such system, "as an imaginary machine invented to connect together
in the fancy those different movements and effects which are already in reality
performed," nothing of the sort can be more beautiful. A clear, orderly and
extensive view is given of a vast number of interesting and important facts,
connected by a few familiar principles. A great body of knowledge is thus brought
before the mind in a shape which it can readily grasp, and easily command. The
object being not to discover, but to arrange and methodize, all the subordinate
principles of the system are artfully bent so as to embrace the phenomena, and
care is taken that the imagination be not shocked by a view of matters that shall
seem irreconcilable to the aspect of affairs which the contemplation of the world
of life itself presents. Nor is it to be disputed that a general system of the sort,
besides the pleasure and the advantage derived from it, is likely to be nearer the
truth than speculations of the same nature, confined to particular parts.

The case, however, is completely altered, when the loose and popular principles
on which such a system proceeds, are adopted as demonstrative axioms, the discoveries of real science, and are carried out to their extreme consequences. Their
original purpose is then altogether changed, and instead of serving to bring
before the mind a collection of facts, they lead it farther and farther away from
truth and reality, into the barren and wearisome regions of mere verbal abstrac-
tions.[7]

2. RAE'S THEORY OF CAPITAL

Rae saw with great clarity the interaction of capital accumulation and
social conditions. His interest in this problem stemmed from his youthful
and ambitious scheme to study the causes which have made man
"what he is in various countries or has been in various times."[8] Even before
he emigrated, Rae obviously had some tentative views on the role of wealth
in society and he found in Canada many opportunities for observing different kinds of societies in several stages of development. He became familiar
with the primitive societies of the Indians, with the rough life in the backwoods, and with the characteristics of urban society in the colonial cities
of Montreal and York. Much of Rae's theory of capital was the product
of his own observations, confirmed by his knowledge of the writings of

Ibid., 350–1.   [8] *Ibid.*, iv.

travellers in other undeveloped countries. He shows considerable familiarity with social conditions among the Romans, the ancient Germans and particularly the Chinese. His principal purpose was to analyse the factors which determined the accumulation of capital. His analysis is notable for its generality, its subtlety, and above all for its essential correctness.

Rae's theory of capital accumulation will be summarized under three broad headings: (a) the nature of capital; (b) the supply of capital; (c) the demand for capital. It must be recognized in advance that any summary of Rae is liable to be inadequate and distorted. The lucid sweep of his ideas is lost as well as the excellent literary quality of his writings.

(a) The nature of capital

Rae's concept of capital was amorphous and all-embracing. He adopted the term "instrument" to describe durable capital and all other physical transformations whose use resulted in the occurrence of future events. He explained his choice of terminology in the following words:

. . . all those changes which man makes, in the form or arrangements of the parts of material objects, for the purpose of supplying his future wants, and which derive their power of doing this from his knowledge of the course of events, and the changes which his labor, guided by his reason, is hence enabled to make in the issue of these events, may be termed instruments.[9]

He explains that the term instruments as commonly used refers to mechanical devices such as levers, wedges, and more complex machines but that, despite the inconvenience, he needs a much more general concept. He gives an agricultural illustration and points out that the field, the wheat, the flour and the bread are all instruments. In short, any means to an end is an instrument. What are ordinarily treated as consumption goods are obviously instruments. Rae specifically refers to instruments which can easily be moved from place to place and exchanged. This class of instruments he calls goods or commodities.

All instruments have three characteristics in common. These are:

1. They are all either *directly* formed by human labor, or *indirectly* through the aid of other instruments themselves formed by human labor. . . .
2. All instruments bring to pass, or tend, or help, to bring to pass events supplying some of the wants of man, and are then exhausted. . . .
3. Between the formation and exhaustion of instruments a space of time intervenes. This necessarily happens because all events take place in time. Sometimes that space extends to years, sometimes to months, occasionally to shorter periods, but it always exists.[10]

Rae introduces two other terminological points in connection with instruments. First, he defines the *capacity* of an instrument as its power to

[9] *Ibid.*, 87.   [10] *Ibid.*, 91–3.

produce events supplying human wants or a quantitative equivalent of the events. Second, he uses the term *exhaustion* to refer to the process by which instruments are again transformed into materials or dissipated. Food and fuel are exhausted quickly while machinery is worn out or exhausted gradually.

He then considers the question of measuring the capacity of instruments. The idea that capacity can be usefully measured in physical terms is rejected. Instead he proposes to measure capacity in terms of units of labour cost. He reasons that an equivalence exists between the events emanating from an instrument and the labour necessary to produce the same events in the absence of the instrument. He assumes a highly simplified system in which real wages are constant and uniform in a given society but different in different societies. He disclaims any intention of investigating the principles which govern wage rates and their variations and emphasizes that his rigorous assumptions are intended merely to simplify the exposition.

The cost of production of instruments is also measured solely in terms of labour. Rae notes that labour alone seldom can be used to form instruments and that the co-operation of other instruments is necessary. However, he suggests as a further measure of simplification that the contribution of these co-operating instruments can be measured by an equivalent amount of labour. All this amounts to adopting a standardized and abstract daily wage as a *numéraire*.

There are thus three basic concepts in Rae's theory of capital accumulation. The first is their original cost measured in terms of labour inputs; the second is their capacity expressed as the equivalent of labour costs; and the third is the length of time elapsing between their formation and their exhaustion. He proposes to develop a method of classifying instruments which will express all possible interrelations of these three magnitudes.

This is done by arranging all instruments in a series, each term of which represents the number of years it will take for the instrument to yield double its original cost of formation. The place of an instrument in the series determines what he calls its *order*. He represents the series by the capital letters of the alphabet followed by the small letters and gives the following example: "Instruments in the order C, in three years issue in events equivalent to double the cost of formation; of the order D, in four years; of the order Z, in twenty-six years; of the order *a*, in twenty-seven years, &c."[11] He goes on to say that instruments in the neighbourhood of the order A will be said to belong to "the more quickly returning orders" while instruments around the order of Z or beyond will be classed as "the

[11] *Ibid.*, 101.

more slowly returning orders." His general rule is that the proximity of an instrument to the order A is inversely related to the cost of production and the period of exhaustion and directly to its capacity. Rae freely admits that an instrument may not yield double its cost of production in an integral number of years and states that the order may in fact be between two succeeding members of the series. He provides also for the case in which an instrument is exhausted before it has yielded double its original cost. Here he derives the order by assuming a prolongation of the period of exhaustion until the necessary increase in the yield has been attained. The converse case occurs when an instrument yields more than double its cost before it is exhausted. Under such circumstances, its order will be determined by the length of time it took for the returns to amount to double the cost.

Rae devotes some attention to the assumption that all instruments are formed at one point of time and exhausted at another. He admits that the process of formation and exhaustion usually extends over a period of time, but contends that some average point can be taken to represent either the time of formation or exhaustion.[12] Rae formulates quite clearly the notion of an average period of production and an average period of exhaustion, but he attaches no economic significance to them.

Rae's conception that all instruments can be assigned a certain order is merely another way of saying that all instruments can be ranked according to their rate of yield. Each of Rae's orders corresponds to some unique rate of yield and it is a simple matter to derive the relationship between orders and rates of yield from the formula $(1 + r)^x = 2$, where x is the order of the instrument, expressed in years, and r the percentage rate of yield. For example, the order A corresponds to a rate of yield of 100 per cent per annum, the order B to a rate of yield of 41–42 per cent per annum and the order N to slightly more than 5 per cent per annum.[13] It is now more usual to speak of rates of return, but it should be borne in mind that Rae's formulation was quite precise, though the terminology is unfamiliar and a little awkward.

To summarize briefly, Rae's concept of capital was that it consisted of instruments, each of which could be assigned to a certain order and each of which became exhausted and reverted to materials or simply disappeared

[12] Rae was influenced by the contemporary view that land had some special indestructible or inexhaustible quality which set it apart from other instruments. He stated that the act of clearing land or rendering it fit for cultivation transformed it into an instrument of indefinite life. The tilling and seeding of the land forms another instrument which is subject to exhaustion. The distinction is ingenious but specious. It is strange how he could have proposed this after living in Canada where he must have seen cleared land revert to the bush after a relatively short period of neglect.

[13] Rae shows the equivalence between orders and annual rates of return in *New Principles*, 195.

in a specified period of time. The durability of instruments, has a central place in his theory of capital accumulation, and his analysis of the supply and demand factors influencing durability is the core of Rae's contribution to economic theory. He first considers the supply factors.

(b) The supply of capital

Rae distinguishes conceptually between durability and efficiency, both of which affect the capacity of instruments, but he concludes that increased durability usually implies increased efficiency, except for certain types of wearing apparel and hand tools or utensils. He discusses the characteristics of dwellings for purposes of illustration, saying:

A dwelling-house is an instrument, aiding to bring to an issue events of various classes. It more or less completely prevents rain, damp, and the extremes of cold and heat, from penetrating to the space included within its area. It preserves all other instruments contained within it, in comparative safety. It gives those who inhabit it the power of carrying on unmolested, various domestic occupations, and of enjoying, undisturbed by the gaze of strangers, any of the gratifications or amusements of life of which they may be able and desirous to partake. Events of these sorts, it may bring to pass, for a longer or shorter time, or to a greater or less extent, within the same time. In the former case, the durability is increased, in the latter, the efficiency; in both, the capacity is augmented.[14]

He goes on to compare dwellings built of wood, lath, mud, plaster, and paper which would be habitable only for a few months or years with dwellings that might last for two or three centuries "by employing stone, iron and the most durable woods, and joining and compacting them together, with great nicety and accuracy." Assuming no change in efficiency, an increase in durability amounts to an increase in capacity which means that, in the case of dwellings in particular, durability and capacity can be extended indefinitely.

But, to give increased durability to an instrument requires the expenditure of additional labour. Rae then undertakes to examine the relation between the marginal return from an increase in durability and the associated marginal cost. His analysis is in terms of undiscounted marginal returns and marginal cost and he concludes that when these two magnitudes are equal, increased durability will shift the instrument to a more slowly returning order. He compares a dwelling built to last thirty years with a similar dwelling costing twice as much and lasting sixty years. If the thirty-year house is of the order O, the sixty-year house will be of an order lying between X and Y. As durability is increased, under conditions where the marginal cost and the undiscounted marginal returns are equal, the rate of yield declines. Rae concluded that the marginal cost of increased dura-

[14] *Ibid.*, 110.

bility must decrease in a geometric ratio if the rate of yield of an instrument is to remain unchanged. His own words are:

If, therefore, continual additions be made to the durability of an instrument, it cannot be preserved at an order of equally quick return, unless the several augmentations be communicated to it, by an expenditure diminishing in a geometrical ratio; that is, in a ratio becoming indefinitely less, as it is continued.[15]

Rae saw dimly the significance of the equality of discounted marginal returns and marginal cost, but unfortunately he immediately denied that the implied behaviour of cost was possible. He visualized the process of geometrically decreasing marginal cost continuing indefinitely and concluded that this was an absurdity. If he had not thought in terms of indefinite durability, he might have stated the marginal conditions governing durability correctly.

As it was, Rae stated clearly the reasons for the increasing cost of imparting durability to instruments. His reasoning was that men use the cheapest and most abundant materials first and then must turn to more expensive processes or rely on diminishing and more costly supplies. He says:

... as the stock of materials which any society possesses, is limited, its members, if we suppose them to acquire no additional knowledge of the powers of those materials, and yet to add continually to the amount of instruments they form out of them, must at length have recourse to such as are either operated on with greater difficulty, or bring about desired events more sparingly or tardily. The efficiency of the instruments produced must therefore be generated by greater cost; that is, they must pass to orders of slower return.[16]

To this statement of the principle of diminishing returns Rae added a comment on the influence of technological change. He explained that new processes were continually being developed and that the more durable an instrument the greater the chances would be that it would become obsolescent and unable to compete with more recently created and improved instruments.

[15] *Ibid.*, 112. This conclusion is challenged in Gustaf Åkerman's *Realkapital und Kapitalzins* (Stockholm, 1923). Åkerman, borrowing explicitly from Rae, conceives of the labour costs of manufacturing durable capital as consisting of a series, the first term being the amount required to make the capital last one year, the next term being the amount required to extend the life of the capital for another year, and so on. Åkerman states a rule that the average of the terms in the series must be decreasing before it is profitable to extend the life of capital. Åkerman's claim that Rae is wrong (pp. 22 and 118) seems to reflect some confusion between the average and marginal behaviour of the terms of the series. Rae's contention that the series must form a decreasing geometric progression is quite correct and at the same time a more stringent condition than Åkerman's. See also Knut Wicksell, *Lectures on Political Economy* (New York, 1934), I, 259–61.

[16] *New Principles* 113

He concluded that a fall in the rate of yield was inevitable when the durability of instruments was increased, provided that technical knowledge was unchanged and the kind of materials available the same. The influence of technical progress on the formation of instruments is, of course, profound. Rae notes that the ability of barbarous nations to increase their capital equipment is limited but in technically advanced societies there does not seem to be an assignable limit to the amount of new instruments that could be formed. He says:

One would not find it very easy to say, how much might be added, to the durability and efficiency, of dwelling-houses alone. The amount of the capacity for the facilitation of future transport, which might be embodied in railroads, returning ultimately much more than the cost of their formation, is incalculable; as is also, the degree to which mining operations might be extended. Even supposing all these, and many other instruments, to have acquired a vastly increased extent, both as concerns durability and efficiency; instead of limiting their farther increase, it would seem likely, rather to open up a still wider space, for the exertion of future industry in the formation of others.[17]

But, Rae says, so long as the state of the arts is stationary, the process of capital accumulation carries instruments gradually to the more slowly returning orders, that is, the marginal rate of yield falls. There is a limit to the willingness of individuals and societies to construct instruments of the more slowly returning orders and this is the decisive factor which retards capital accumulation. Rae then turns his attention to the circumstances which influence societies to halt the process of capital accumulation once a limiting rate of return has been reached.

(c) The demand for capital

Rae's central argument was that the formation of an instrument implied the sacrifice of a present good for a future good. Instruments characteristically yield future returns greater than present sacrifices; otherwise they will not be formed. The construction of instruments will continue in a society until a certain order is attained or alternatively until a certain rate of return is achieved. A point is finally reached where the willingness to make continued present sacrifices ceases and then the formation of instruments stops. Rae refers to the propensity to sacrifice present goods for future goods as the *effective desire of accumulation*. His explanation of this phenomenon deserves quotation:

Were life to endure for ever, were the capacity to enjoy in perfection all its goods, both mental and corporeal, to be prolonged with it, and were we guided solely by the dictates of reason, there could be no limit to the formation of means for future gratification, till our utmost wishes were supplied. A pleasure to be

[17] *Ibid.*, 116–17.

enjoyed, or a pain to be endured, fifty or a hundred years hence, would be considered deserving the same attention as if it were to befall us fifty or a hundred minutes hence, and the sacrifice of a smaller present good, for a greater future good, would be readily made, to whatever period that futurity might extend. But life, and the power to enjoy it, are the most uncertain of all things, and we are not guided altogether by reason. We know not the period when death may come upon us, but we know that it may come in a few days, and must come in a few years. Why then be providing goods that cannot be enjoyed until times, which, though not very remote, may never come to us, or until times still more remote, and which we are convinced we shall never see? If life, too, is of uncertain duration and the time that death comes between us and all our possessions unknown, the approaches of old age are at least certain, and are dulling, day by day, the relish of every pleasure.

A mere reasonable regard to their own interest, would, therefore, place the present very far above the future, in the estimation of most men. But, it is besides to be remarked, that such pleasures as may now be enjoyed, generally awaken a passion strongly prompting to the partaking of them. The actual presence of the immediate object of desire in the mind, by exciting the attention, seems to rouse all the faculties, as it were, to fix their view on it, and leads them to a very lively conception of the enjoyments which it offers to their instant possession. The prospects of future good, which future years may hold out to us, seem at such a moment dull and dubious, and are apt tobe slighted, for objects on which the day-light is falling strongly, and showing us in all their freshness just within our grasp. There is no man perhaps, to whom a good to be enjoyed to day, would not seem of very different importance, from one exactly similar to be enjoyed twelve years hence, even though the arrival of both were equally certain.[18]

Why then, Rae asks, do people save when the benefits of future goods are not only uncertain but probably inferior? His answer is that people are not guided solely by selfish interests but are influenced by what he calls the social and benevolent affections. Man's pleasures derive from his ties to "his kindred, his friends, his country, or his race." Even when he dies, his sacrifices will not be lost if they continue to benefit the living. Rae admits that these motives are sometimes feeble and that "the world is full of deceit, hollowness and unhappiness," but the existence of social and benevolent affections is nevertheless a real and important influence.

This influence is supplemented by reasoning and reflective habits arising out of the intellectual powers. The joys of the moment are tempered by reflection on the future and its prospects. The more man is concerned with the welfare of others, the more desirable it seems to make provision for the future. Intellectual power and affection for others strengthen and confirm the desire for accumulation.

Rae mentions a third influence—security. A healthy climate, a safe occupation, and expectancy of long life all make it more probable that the fruits of sacrifice will be gathered. Frugality is strongly influenced by geo-

[18] *Ibid.*, 119–20.

graphy and occupations. Sailors and soldiers are prodigals and so are the inhabitants of the West Indies, New Orleans, and the East Indies. The general prevalence of law and order and peace and tranquillity affect the habit of saving. On the other hand, "war and pestilence have always waste and luxury among the other evils that follow in their train."

Rae's own summary of the three circumstances governing the desire to accumulate are:

1. The prevalence throughout the society, of the social and benevolent affections, or, of that principle, which, under whatever name it may be known, leads us to derive happiness, from the good we communicate to others.
2. The extent of the intellectual powers, and the consequent prevalence of habits of reflection, and prudence, in the minds of the members of the society.
3. The stability of the condition of the affairs of the society, and the reign of law and order throughout it.[19]

Rae takes note of the contemporary and earlier view that self-interest is the principal motive for saving. He deals with this as a special case, saying:

If we confine our attention to the present times, and to particular parts of the globe, this may be readily admitted. Now, and in those places, a prudent regard to self interest would doubtless prompt many individuals to cooperate effectively in the increase of the general means of enjoyment. But there is nothing more apt to mislead us, when investigating the causes determining the motions of any great system, than to take our station at some particular point in it, and, examining the appearances there presented to us, to suppose that they must be precisely similar through the whole sphere of action. Because, in Great Britain, a regard to mere self interest, may now prompt to a course of action leading to making a large provision for the wants of others, we are, in reality, no more warranted to conclude that it will do so always, and in every place, than were the ancients warranted to conclude, because, in their particular communities, the pursuit of wealth commonly generated evil, that it must therefore do so always and in every place.[20]

Rae's discussion of these sociological influences on the accumulation of capital is a brilliant piece of analysis and is brightened considerably by his gift for descriptive anecdotes. He shows here the broad sweep of his mind and his understanding of human motivation. This is deservedly the best-known aspect of Rae's work. It is not usually recognized that it is only a part of an integrated theory of the supply and demand factors influencing capital accumulation. Because of its generality, his capital theory applied equally to the North American Indians and the ancient Romans.

Rae had the advantage of being able to observe the economic characteristics of an underdeveloped country at first hand and his knowledge of

[19] *Ibid.*, 124.   [20] *Ibid.*, 124–5.

Canadian conditions in the 1820's and early 1830's clearly influenced his views of capital formation. The construction of roads and other public works was of major economic and political significance to the backwoods communities of Upper Canada and the durability of such instruments an immediate and practical issue. Confirmation of this appears in the following statement in *Lord Durham's Report;*

I know, indeed, of no difference in the machinery of government in the old and new world that strikes an European more forcibly than the apparently undue importance which the business of constructing public works appears to occupy in American legislation. In speaking of the character of a government, its merits appear to be estimated by the public works which it has carried into effect. If an individual is asked how his own legislature has acted, he will generally say what roads or bridges it has made, or neglected to make, in his own district; and if he is consulted about changes in a constitution, he seems to try their soundness by calculating whether his neighbourhood would get more or better roads and bridges under the existing, or the proposed system.[21]

Rae's analysis of the role of durability in capital formation and the influence of sociological factors on capital accumulation is applicable with very little modification to the problems of underdeveloped countries in the middle of the twentieth century.

3. RAE ON INVENTION

The sections of Rae's book dealing with invention are a remarkable contribution to the literature of economics. From a purely literary point of view his work in this area is marked by lucidity and grace which is at least equalled by the generality and relevance of his economic analysis. Basically his concern is with the influence of invention on capital accumulation, a theme which he introduced in his early discussion of the difference between the wealth of individuals and the wealth of a society.

After a long and penetrating historical discussion of invention, Rae summarizes the relation of invention to capital in a few pages. In essence, he sees invention as a force which makes labour more effective and thus reduces production costs. This not only increases the return on specific instruments, but the benefits are diffused throughout society. The instruments of the society are carried to more productive orders and its absolute capital and stock are correspondingly increased.

Invention and improvement permit the use of "inferior or more stubborn materials" in production, and this process will continue until the total instruments arrive at an order corresponding to the effective desire of accumulation. The introduction of improvements leads to increases in the

[21] Lucas, ed., *Lord Durham's Report*, II, 90.

rate of return on capital and this contrasts with high rates of return associated with a low effective desire of accumulation in certain countries. He
suggests that profits will generally be high in countries which are becoming
wealthier and cites as an example the high rates of profit in North America
arising out of "the unintermitting transfer to that continent of European
arts, and from the generation of new arts in the country itself."

Rae is at his most eloquent in his comments on the personal characteristics of inventors. He speaks of the difference between "real inventers" and
"mere compilers and repeaters" and goes on:

It may be observed, too, that as of bards, so of authors, they who are mere compilers and repeaters, may be more successful than they who are real inventers,
they may better suit their productions to particular times, tastes, and exigencies,
and, besides, they can always find an audience prepared, by previous training, to
applaud.

The tendency of these pursuits is to withdraw those occupied in them, from
the daily business of society. They fill not the places open for them, and which
they are expected to fill; even when necessity pushes them for a time into them,
and compels them to mingle with the crowd, they are marked as not belonging
to it. Abstract and scientific truth can only be discovered, by deep and absorbing
meditation; imperfectly at first discerned, through the medium of its dull capacities, the intellect slowly, and cautiously, not without much of doubt, and many
unsuccessful essays, succeeds in lifting the veil that hides it. The procedure is
altogether unlike the prompt determination, and ready confidence, of the man of
action, and generally unfits, to a greater or less degree, for performing well the
part. He, again, who dwells in the world of possible moral beauty and perfection,
moves awkwardly, rashly, and painfully, through this of everyday life, he is ever
mistaking his own way and jostling others in theirs. To the possessors of fortune,
these habits only give eccentricity; they affect those of scanty fortune, or without
fortune, with more serious ills. Unable to fight their way ably, cautiously, and
perseveringly, through the bustle of life, poverty, dependence, and all their
attendant evils, are most commonly their lot.

> "Toil, envy, want, the patron, and the jail,"

are calamities, from the actual endurance of some of which, or the dread of it,
they are seldom free. These, however, they share with other men; there are some
peculiarly their own.[22]

The inventive faculty and the social and benevolent affections in a society
are likely to be associated.

. . . though, in the individual, manifestations of the inventive faculty imply a
superiority in some of the intellectual powers, they rather imply, in the society a
preponderance of the social and benevolent affections. It is this general acuteness
of moral sensation, and lively sympathy consequently with the pleasures arising
to the individual, from the success of exertions for purposes of general good, that
can alone excite, and nourish, the enthusiasm of genius.[23]

[22] *New Principles*, 213–14.   [23] *Ibid.*, 222.

The progress of invention and the principles governing the accumulation of wealth are thus related but there are opposing forces at work in periods of social disturbance:

Whatever disturbs, or threatens to disturb, the established order of things, by exposing the property of the members of the society to danger, and diminishing the certainty of its future possession, diminishes also the desire to accumulate it. Intestine commotions, persecutions, wars, internal oppression, or outward violence, either, therefore, altogether destroy, or, at least, very much impair the strength of the effective desire of accumulation. On the contrary, they excite the inventive faculty to activity. . . . Whatever, therefore, breaks the wonted order of events, and exposes the necessity, or the possibility, of connecting them by some other means, strongly stimulates invention. The slumbering faculties rouse themselves to meet the unexpected exigence, and the possibility of giving a new, and more perfect order to elements not yet fixed, animates to a boldness of enterprise, which were rashness, had they assumed their determined places. Hence, as has often been remarked, periods of great changes in kingdoms or governments, are the seasons when genius breaks forth in brightest lustre. The beneficial effects of what are termed revolutions, are, perhaps, chiefly to be traced, to their thus wakening the torpid powers; the troubling of the waters they bring about, undoes the palsy of the mind.[24]

4. RAE ON TARIFF PROTECTION

It would be difficult to improve on Rae's own summary of the factors influencing the growth of capital. Capital is increased, in his words:

I. By whatever promotes the general intelligence and morality of the society; and that, consequently, the moral and intellectual education of the people makes an important element in its progress . . .

II. By whatever promotes invention;
    1. By advancing the progress of science and art within the community;
    2. By the transfer from other communities of the sciences and arts there generated:

III. By whatever prevents the dissipation in luxury, of any portion of the funds of the community.[25]

The way in which "the legislator" can influence the growth of capital will depend on legislative influences on these factors, but Rae purposely limited his consideration of the influence of the legislator in two areas: (a) the transfer of foreign arts to his own country; (b) the diversion to useful purposes of funds which would otherwise be dissipated in luxury.

Early in his book Rae had already introduced the question of international transfers of technical knowledge in his critique of Adam Smith. In that place, Rae argued at some length that in certain instances advan-

[24] *Ibid.*, 222–3.   [25] *Ibid.*, 362.

tages in production could be acquired by borrowing methods developed in other countries. If by legislative action useful arts could be transferred from a distant country in such a way as to provide commodities at least as cheaply as they could be imported, there appeared to be ample justification for such a policy. The treatment at this place is fairly discursive, but near the end of the book his arguments become more succinct.

Here he repeated his contention that there were situations in which it was proper for the legislator to encourage the transfer of technical knowledge or "useful arts" from one country to another. He enumerates three advantages of such transfers: (*a*) saving of the cost of transporting commodities; (*b*) the stimulation of invention with its consequently beneficial effects on capital formation; (*c*) the avoidance of interruption in the supply of essential imports because of wars or other causes. He states his case carefully, warning:

> But, while the legislator is called on to act, he is also called on to act cautiously, and to regulate his proceedings by an attentive consideration of the progress of events. He is never justifiable in attempting to transfer arts yielding utilities from foreign countries to his own, unless he have sufficient reason to conclude that they will ultimately lessen the cost of the commodities they produce, or are of such a nature, that the risk of waste to the stock of the community, from a sudden interruption to their importation from abroad, is sufficiently great to warrant the probable expense, both of the transfer and of maintaining the manufacture at home. It is his business first to ascertain these points, and to regulate his proceedings accordingly.[26]

Rae refers to several historical instances of "injudicious conduct of the legislator," and goes on to emphasize two factors which should encourage the transfer of a foreign art, an abundance of raw materials and great strength of the accumulative principle.

As practical devices Rae mentions premiums, bounties, and duties, suggesting that premiums may be useful to test the practicability of a transfer. If the transfer appears feasible it then may become desirable to introduce bounties or duties.

> In this way real capital, and healthy enterprise are directed to the art, the difficulties attending its introduction overcome in the shortest possible space, and the commodities yielded by it are produced at less outlay, and afforded at a less price than that, at which they were before imported.[27]

It should be emphasized that Rae's comments are a thoughtful and sophisticated statement of what came to be known later as the "infant industry" argument for protection. It is, in fact, difficult to discover anything in Rae's detailed argument that is objectionable. Any reasonable person, no matter how ardent his free-trade convictions, would be compelled to agree with the justice of Rae's contentions.

Certainly Rae clearly recognized the advantages of freedom of trade. In one place, he says:

In regard to articles supplying real wants, the more easy and unconstrained the communication, the more extended the production, the freer the competition, the farther, as we have seen, are the stocks of instruments of the societies exchanging carried towards the more quickly returning orders. Every step in advance in the course is equivalent, subject only to the risk of the communication being interrupted, to a real improvement.[28]

What is really remarkable is that Rae in the postscript to his preface appeared to ally himself with some of the crude protectionist arguments current in the United States in the 1820's and 1830's. In a way belying the tenor of the material in the text, Rae said at the beginning of the book in the postscript to the preface:

The practical bearings of that system [protection] on the condition of things in this republic, have been discussed so often, and with so much ability, that probably few new arguments or facts concerning it can be brought forward by any one, least of all can they be expected from a foreigner. Although, therefore, I look on the effects of the policy pursued by the legislature of the United States, as affording the best practical illustration hitherto existing of the correctness of some of the principles I maintain, I have scarcely at all referred to them for that purpose, but have contented myself with showing how the benefits resulting from the operations of the legislature, in this and in other similar cases, are to be accounted for. I have thus omitted much matter that would have appeared, had the work been published in England, but which, it seemed to me, would be at least superfluous here.[29]

As will be seen, the mere position of Rae's carelessly phrased comments on the protectionist controversy were to convey an unfortunate and largely erroneous impression to some of his readers.

5. RAE ON LUXURY

Rae suggested that vanity was one of the mainsprings of human motivation and that it had a retarding effect on capital accumulation. The mere desire of superiority over others stimulates the desire for "commodities of which the consumption is conspicuous" and leads in some instances to an extravagant passion "to have what others cannot have." The social and benevolent affections and intellectual powers, on the other hand, counter and keep within bounds the indulgence of mere vanity. Rae suggests on the basis of historical evidence that vanity and luxury

---

[28] *Ibid.*, 310.   [29] *Ibid.*, ix.

are not usual in societies where the effective desire of accumulation is high. Conversely, in savage societies, there is a marked propensity to make great sacrifices "to have the means of decking their persons or habitations with something rare and costly."

The difficulty with luxuries, Rae pointed out, was that their production left the absolute capital of a society unchanged. For the superiority enjoyed by one person from the acquisition of luxuries would be balanced by a corresponding feeling of inferiority on the part of another. Nevertheless, vanity may have some beneficial by-products if it stimulates the spread of invention. He suggests that certain exotic luxuries have been found to have a "substratum of utility," and mentions as examples, soap, silk and cotton fabrics, and glass.

Rae explains that scarcity and high price are essential characteristics of luxury. His comment about the celebrated northern Duchess who is quoted as saying, "What a pity that eggs were not a sixpence the piece," is indicative of his view. He implies that the demand for luxuries is such that an increase in price may lead to an increase in consumption. Conversely, the demand for luxuries may fall with a decrease in price. On the basis of his findings Rae had some original and stimulating suggestions respecting the taxation of luxuries.

In essence, Rae's point is that taxes on pure luxuries might yield substantial revenues without imposing a burden on the consumer. His illustrations, which feature alcoholic liquors, are interesting:

In Great Britain rum is, I believe, at least double the price of whisky, and brandy still higher, the consumption, therefore, of the dearer article instead of the cheaper, must arise nearly altogether from vanity. In Canada, again, the price at which Scotch whisky is sold, is double the price of rum, and considerably above the price of brandy. The excess of its price above these other liquors must, therefore, be considered a luxury.[30]

In an accompanying footnote he explains that the price of Scotch whisky is ten shillings per gallon and Canadian whisky from two to three shillings. He recognizes that taxes or duties designed to fall on luxuries must be introduced very gradually:

Men have generally a high opinion of the reasonableness of their conduct, and the correctness of their taste. They are apt to fancy that there is a real and very great enjoyment in expenses, which, in truth, have scarce any thing to recommend them but the gratification they afford to vanity. In like manner, when any article rises suddenly and greatly in price, when in their power, they are prone to adopt some substitute and relinquish the use of it. . . . Hence, were a high duty at once imposed on any particular wine, or any particular sort of cotton fabric, it

[30] *Ibid.*, 372–3.

might have the effect of diminishing the consumption very greatly, or stopping it entirely. Whereas, were the tax at first very slight, and then slowly augmented, the reasoning powers not being startled, vanity, instead of flying off to some other objects, would be apt to apply itself to them as affording a convenient means of gratification.[31]

He concludes his argument with a sensible and clear statement:

As the great mass of commodities are in part utilities, in part luxuries, so, in transferring the manufacture of any of them from one country to another, it very frequently happens that, in as far as the article in question has real utility, the domestic soon equals the foreign variety. It is chiefly in a laborious finish, for the most part the result of the demands of vanity, that the former falls behind the latter. In such instances the operation of transferring the art from one country to another, by means of a protective duty, takes either very little, or nothing, from the revenue of individuals, and makes, it may be, a considerable addition to that of the legislator. Its general effects on the funds of the community, are directly, and indirectly, to advance the absolute capital of the society by the introduction of a new art, and, during the process, to give a considerable revenue to the legislator for the attainment of public objects, without encroaching at all, or but in a very slight degree, on the returns made by the industry or stocks of individuals.[32]

It is tempting to suggest, on the basis of some of Rae's comments, that he anticipated a great deal of modern economics. He did offer some surprisingly acute observations, but it may be unfair to emphasize Rae's overdone role as a forerunner of others. His work can be judged on its own merits. One point should perhaps be emphasized. Rae wove into his work erudite and interesting discussions of such things as luxury and conspicuous consumption,[33] the division of labour, taxation, the cost of production, and above all invention. But there is an essential unity about his work because nearly all his ideas are directly related to his theory of capital accumulation. The effect on capital accumulation of various modes of social behaviour including the activities of legislative bodies is Rae's touchstone.

[31] Ibid., 374–5.
[32] Ibid., 375–6.
[33] Rae used the phrases "consumption is not conspicuous" and "consumption is conspicuous" on pages 297 and 310 respectively of the New Principles. In this connection it is interesting to note J. J. Spengler's statement that "Veblen knew Rae's work but did not cite it." "John Rae on Economic Development: A Note," Quarterly Journal of Economics, Aug., 1959, 394, n. 6.

12

Reactions to Rae's Book in the Nineteenth Century

On the title page of his *New Principles*, Rae quoted from Hume's *Essay on Commerce*, "When we reason upon general subjects, one may justly affirm, that our speculations can scarce ever be too fine, provided they be just." This may indicate Rae's awareness that parts of his book at least were abstract and difficult and of interest to a limited group of people. He may have been disappointed, but he should not have been surprised when it became clear that his book would not achieve any great popularity. To some extent, this resulted from the nature of the reviews it received.

The book itself was obviously difficult to review in part because it dealt with some unfamiliar concepts and sometimes Rae's terminology obscured his ideas. It must be admitted, moreover, that Rae had been somewhat provocative in his criticisms of Adam Smith and it was this part of his book that drew fire. Among certain groups it was almost a matter of religious faith to deny the validity of Rae's attack on the dogmas of free trade. Some of the reviews concentrated on Rae's heresy with the result that the more important aspects of the book tended to receive little attention.

For example, a review which appeared in the *Athenaeum* late in 1834, reviled Rae in emphatic and sarcastic terms for his protectionist arguments. In its first paragraph, the review said:

It was originally the author's design to publish his work in England, where it would assuredly have dropped still-born from the press: luckily for himself, he has brought it out in Boston, at a moment when the New Englanders were sadly at a loss for some plausible reply to the demands of the Southern States. The time and place of publication has consequently invested Mr. Rae's speculations with an importance rather beyond their merits, and impose upon us the duty of examining questions which have been long since decided by the common sense of Europe.[1]

It ended with the following unkind remark:

We cannot conclude without noticing the gratifying progress which the principles we have endeavoured to advocate are making in England and France. A few Raes may indeed be found in both countries, who still advocate the old system of mutual exclusion with its consequent exasperation of national envy, national jealousy, and national hatred. But people have found that the pleasures resulting from the indulgence of such feelings are very few, and very expensive. There are, we fear, still many prejudices to be removed, and many interests to be conciliated, before a new system can be established with ease, or perhaps with safety; but the process of amelioration has commenced, and its pace is every day accelerated. We have hopes that America will not be left behind in the race of improvement, and that all such advisers as Mr. Rae will be discountenanced.[2]

A reviewer in the Boston *Daily Advertiser* was also sceptical but much kinder in his notice:

By the *élite* body of professed political economists, the annunciation of new principles in that study may be received with something of that watering of the mouth which affects the true *gourmand* on the discovery of some *bonne bouche*. The ardour of the literary epicure may however be somewhat abated, on perceiving that these new principles are connected with the exposure of the *fallacies of Adam Smith*. Fallacies of the Wealth of Nations! As if the work which has opened a new era in political science, which has been, as it were adopted as a text-book, which has been admitted to be true in theory, even by those who have denied its conclusions, could be treated as a book of fallacies.

He went on to say:

The general reader will find in it none of those paradoxes and fine spun theories which distinguish M'Culloch and Ricardo. It announces distinct principles in intelligible language. The style is pure, copious and harmonious. Its illustrations address themselves to every understanding, showing in the author great acuteness of observation, and a mind stored with the treasures of classic learning.

After suggesting that the book was "destined to produce a sensation in the literary community," he concluded:

It is true that the views adopted by the author lead him to discard the grounds on which the system of ultra free trade rests, as unphilosophical and untenable. But his arguments resting on general principles are equally worthy the attention of all whose pursuit is truth. The work may be particularly recommended to the attention of those who have adopted the *dicta* of the modern school of free trade as infallible maxims—we say to them especially, read the book.[3]

[1] *Athenaeum*, no. 374, Dec. 27, 1834, 933–4.   [2] *Ibid.*, 934.
[3] Reprinted in the *Montreal Gazette*, Aug. 26, 1834.

By far the ablest review of Rae's book appeared in the *Foreign Quarterly Review*, possibly written by the publisher John George Cochrane.[4] There were some waspish comments such as, "It was to be expected that if America entered into the field of contention, she would despise authority," but generally the tone of the review was sympathetic. Rae's views were summarized in a clear and fair fashion and in a number of instances the reviewer was full of praise, particularly for Rae's discussions of the psychology of primitive peoples.[5] The closing comment of the review may be worth quoting:

What we have already written, with the example we have given, is calculated, we think, to impress the English reader with a very favourable impression of American modes of ratiocination in reference to the high argument of Political Economy. Mr. Rae's book deserves especially study, as dealing not only with the means and appliances of production, but, by estimating duly the moral constitution of man, providing for corresponding consumption. Experience has shown us that more corn may be grown than can be eaten, more clothes manufactured that can be worn, and yet, by some fault of distribution, or some want of capacity, large numbers of the population may remain unclothed and almost unfed. Man is not a machine; and it is but just that the producers should be the partakers of wealth. But it has not always been so. It is wisely said by Mr. Rae that good laws or government can neither be established nor maintained without good morals. In fine;—where purely selfish feelings prevail, laws have no power.

"Quid faciant leges ubi sola pecunia regnat"[6]

The book was reviewed at some length in the *North American Review* by Alexander Hill Everett, the editor and one of Rae's sponsors. Judging from his comments, Everett had not read the manuscript in advance and expected a protectionist tract. He intimated that this was not quite what he had in mind in sponsoring its issuance in Boston, saying:

The title of *New Principles* ... is perhaps more appropriate to the state of public opinion in England, than in this country, where substantially the same ideas have been so often stated in speeches, reports, reviews and newspaper essays, that they have become in some degree familiar, although they have not yet been

---

[4] XV, no. 30 (1835), 241–66.

[5] In his original article on Rae, Mixter refers to this review as follows: "A reviewer in the *Foreign Quarterly Review* soon wearied in following Rae's close, abstract reasoning on capital, and broke off with a long quotation concerning an illustration from Indian life which, he said, formed a 'charming relief to the subject.' The quotation begins, 'The North American Indian in his canoe comes to an island in some lake or river,'—and so on. As the ingenuous reviewer presently adds: 'we love to accompany the writer in his analysis of the Indian mind ...' " C. W. Mixter, "A Forerunner of Böhm-Bawerk," *Quarterly Journal of Economics*, XI (1897), 164–5. This comment is both inaccurate and unfair and refers to a very minor remark in a detailed twenty-five page review.

[6] *Foreign Quarterly Review*, XV, no. 30 (1835), 265–6.

embodied among us in any single work of sufficient compass and authority to serve as a text book. Such a work is very much wanted. It is somewhat doubtful whether the one before us will entirely answer the purpose.[7]

Nevertheless, Everett paid tribute to Rae as an original, zealous, and honest inquirer after truth and to his pure, correct, and at times eloquent language. He suggested that not everyone would be in agreement with Rae's "peculiar theories," and went on:

Our author's leading principle is . . . that the economical condition of communities is regulated, in a great measure, by their social and political institutions. In developing this idea, he has exhibited great ingenuity, extensive reading, and a remarkable power of style, with no other prominent fault, than one, which is itself an evidence of high intellectual ability, a tendency to excessive refinement and abstraction.[8]

Everett referred again to Rae's purity of taste and power of style and continued:

With the ability which he possesses of communicating his discoveries to the public in so agreeable a form, we hazard little in predicting that our author, should he persevere in his researches, as we trust he will, is in very little danger of encountering the neglect and abandonment which he describes too correctly as the not uncommon reward of inventive genius.[9]

There were reservations about Rae's nomenclature. Everett admitted that "something, perhaps, is gained in precision by the use of the language he has employed, but on the other hand, the impression which a remark would otherwise make, is often much weakened by the introduction of phrases which wear a technical aspect, and are not distinctly understood till after a pretty strong effort of attention." Some measure of Everett's attention may be got from the fact that slightly more than one-half of his nineteen-page review consisted of quotations from Rae. Everett concluded with a recommendation that in another edition it might be desirable to omit Rae's discussions of the "influence of social and political conditions of communities on their wealth" to leave "room for treating in a more full and satisfactory way, within the compass of a moderate volume, the immediate subject which is the expediency of a legislative protection of domestic industry." He noted further, "A well written and well reasoned essay on this question, drawn up in such a form that it could be used with convenience as a text book for students at colleges, would be very useful, and would meet a ready sale."[10]

Years later, Rae commented on this in a letter saying:

[7] *North American Review*, Jan., 1835, 123.
[8] *Ibid.*, 129.　　　　　　[9] *Ibid.*, 138.　　　　　[10] *Ibid.*, 141.

Unfortunately, I was induced to publish [my Political Economy] in Boston, under the assurance from Mr. A. Everett that it would be appreciated there. He was, however, I believe scared at it. Could not make up his mind, nor could any one there, if I was right or wrong, and so passed it by with praise of its style, etc. This damned it.[11]

Doubtless, he was deeply disappointed in the reception of his book and must have been distressed by the uncommonly poor advice he had received from Everett and his associates.

Rae's book was not ignored in Canada. The *Montreal Gazette* reprinted the review from the Boston *Daily Advertiser*, and shortly afterwards an advertisement appeared stating that "a few copies" were for sale in two book stores at 12*s* 6*d*.[12] The *Montreal Gazette* also printed a letter to the editor praising the book in the highest terms; it was probably written by the Rev. Henry Esson. The letter shows that Rae's main contributions were appreciated:

SIR,—Allow me through your columns, to call the attention of the public to a work . . . lately published in Boston, and now for sale in this city.

It is from the pen of a fellow-citizen, and treats upon one of the most interesting subjects of human investigation. It is decidedly a clever work, and the learned author deserves the gratitude of the public.

The style is easy, clear and vigorous, and many passages rise to the highest order of philosophical writing. The distinguished peculiarity and in my estimation the chief merit of this work, lies in its treating Political Economy as an enquiry into the operation of human motives, and shewing the springs of action which operate under different states of society, in the production and accumulation of individual wealth, thereby estimating with greater accuracy the probable ration of increase of national wealth.

This, it will be perceived, is a very different starting point from that taken by Adam Smith, viz. that the natural desire of every man to better his condition, and the accumulation of capital, are the only sources of wealth; the fallacy consisting in the assumption of that as a cause which is only a condition.

Before there is an active desire to better one's condition, there must be a certain degree of civilization, and a certain amount of security from interruption in the efforts to accumulate, and before capital can be the means of augmenting productive industry, there must be found a profitable investment.

The arts and sciences, or the inventive faculty, are therefore stated by Mr. Rae to be a principal source of national wealth, and in the encouragement of these, Government may with propriety exercise its wisdom in legislation. To state, with sufficient distinctness to be understood, all the different points on which Mr. Rae differs from his predecessors, would necessarily occupy too much space in your columns, a reference to the work itself is therefore advisable for the critical

[11] *Sociological Theory of Capital*, xxxi. The letter is claimed by Mixter to have been to John Stuart Mill, but it is doubtful if Rae would have used such a colloquial style in writing to Mill.

[12] *Montreal Gazette*, Sept. 11, 1834.

reader. To the general reader, I would recommend the perusal of the tenth chapter of Book II, treating, "of the causes of the progress of Invention, and of the effects arising from it" and of "note G" at the end of the work "on Banking."

They may be read by any one with both interest and profit; the first, as a melancholy but faithful picture of the struggles of genius in paths of science; the second, as a clear statement of an intricate subject.

That Mr. Rae's work will become extensively known, I cannot for a moment doubt, and I most heartily wish its indefatigable author a suitable reward for his valuable labours.[13]

Fortunately, Rae found a reputable and enthusiastic champion in England. This was Nassau Senior who apparently discovered Rae's book independently and recognized the merits of Rae's theory of capital accumulation. It is not known precisely when Senior learned of Rae, but it appears to have been before 1847. Senior mentioned Rae's account of the improvidence of Indians in his series of lectures as Drummond Professor of Political Economy at Oxford in 1847-52.[14] It appears likely also that Senior was influenced by Rae's discussion of the factors influencing saving in his lectures dealing with the accumulation of capital. Dr. Marian Bowley quotes the following excerpts from one of Senior's lectures which is reminiscent of Rae:

In fact it is in general the average price paid for the purchase or for the hire of durable instruments, and, in particular, the average number of years' purchase of land, and the average interest of money, which decides, in every particular society, the extent to which a member of that society will carry his providence, or, in other words, what degree of future advantage will induce him to sacrifice for a given time a given amount of the means of present enjoyment.[15]

A revealing sidelight on Senior's interest in Rae is given in a comment by Sir Francis Hastings Doyle:

I must confess my faith in free trade was rudely shaken long ago. I was reading Mill in some uncertainty of mind, when I lighted upon a passage praising an American political economist with such extraordinary enthusiasm that I actually bought and read the book. This praise astonished me, and when I accidentally found out from Lord Dalmeny that he was a friend of Senior's, the Oxford professor of political economy, I put my difficulty before him, and asked him to sound Senior on the subject. The next time I met him, he came up laughing, and said, "Well, I did not get much out of Senior. The moment I mentioned the book, he also began to praise it furiously, declaring himself to be the man who had discovered it and shown it to Mill; but when I asked him, as I did, quoting you as my authority, how it came to pass that a political economist of that high class,

---

[13] *Ibid.*, Sept. 13, 1834. The letter was signed merely with the initial "E." but probably was written by Esson.

[14] Marian Bowley, *Nassau Senior and Classical Economics* ((London, 1937), 161 n.

[15] The excerpt is from Course II, lecture 9, of Senior's Lectures, 1847-52, which is quoted in *ibid.*, 161-2.

could have written a treatise for the sole purpose of upholding protection, and exposing the failures of free trade, he answered thus: 'Oh, I never looked at that part of the book; what I am referring to is a certain chapter on the accumulation of capital, and other discussions of a like kind.' " As soon as I got home I shut up Mill, and put him back upon the shelf. I thought that pedants who were so afraid of entangling themselves in the labyrinth of their own science, that they would not follow a man whose genius and power they admitted a single step off the beaten road, lest they should find no end, 'in wandering mazes lost,' were no guides for me, because it was clear that they could not have any confidence in themselves.[16]

Senior's discovery and his success in interesting John Stuart Mill in Rae, led to several interesting developments. The first of these was the fact that some of the main features of Rae's theory of capital accumulation were taken over by Mill and incorporated in his *Principles of Political Economy* in 1848. As the following quotation will show, Mill's acknowledgment of Rae's contribution was generous:

But the disposition to save does not wholly depend on the external inducement to it; on the amount of profit to be made from savings. With the same pecuniary inducement, the inclination is very different, in different persons, and in different communities. The effective desire of accumulation is of unequal strength, not only according to the varieties of individual character, but to the general state of society and civilization. Like all other moral attributes, it is one in which the human race exhibits great differences, conformably to the diversity of its circumstances and the stage of its progress.

On topics which, if they were to be fully investigated, would exceed the bounds that can be allotted to them in this treatise, it is satisfactory to be able to refer to other works in which the necessary developments have been presented more at length. On the subject of Population, this valuable service has been rendered by the celebrated *Essay* of Mr. Malthus; and on the point which now occupies us I can refer with equal confidence to another, though a less known work, *New Principles of Political Economy*, by Dr. Rae. In no other book known to me is so much light thrown, both from principle and history, on the causes which determine the accumulation of capital.[17]

Mill also mentioned Rae's obscurity and made some general comments on his book in a footnote:

This treatise is an example, such as not infrequently presents itself, how much more depends on accident, than on the qualities of a book, in determining its

[16] *Reminiscences and Opinions of Sir Francis Hastings Doyle* (New York, 1886), 133–4. I am indebted to Professor Jacob Viner for this reference. Doyle was an English poet and civil servant who worked for the British Customs in the period 1846–88.

[17] J. S. Mill, *Principles of Political Economy with Some of Their Applications to Social Philosophy* (London, 1927), Ashley edition, 165. It is interesting to note that Mill refers to "Dr. Rae," although there is nothing in Rae's *New Principles* to show that he was a doctor. This suggests that Mill may have learned something about Rae, possibly from Charles Buller or Edward Gibbon Wakefield. Alternatively, he may have noted that A. H. Everett referred to "Dr. Rae" in the *North American Review*.

reception. Had it appeared at a suitable time, and been favoured by circumstances, it would have had every requisite for great success. The author, a Scotchman settled in the United States, unites much knowledge, an original vein of thought, a considerable turn for philosophic generalities, and a manner of exposition and illustration calculated to make ideas tell not only for what they are worth, but for more than they are worth, and which sometimes, I think, has that effect in the writer's own mind. The principal fault of the book is the position of antagonism in which, with the controversial spirit apt to be found in those who have new thoughts on old subjects, he has placed himself towards Adam Smith. I call this a fault, (though I think many of the criticisms just, and some of them far-seeing,) because there is much less real difference of opinion than might be supposed from Rae's animadversions; and because what he has found vulnerable in his great predecessor is chiefly the "human *too much*" in his premises; the portion of them that is over and above what was either required or is actually used for the establishment of his conclusions.[18]

In other places Mill commented with approbation on Rae's treatment of the division of labour, the taxation of luxuries, and the use of protective tariffs.

It was not until nineteen years after his book was printed and five years after the publication of Mill's *Political Economy* that Rae learned of Mill's favourable mention through a friend in Canada, probably Hugh Bowlby Willson. Rae wrote to Mill expressing his pleasure and noted that "it is the only thing connected with that publication which has afforded me any gratification." Mill, in his reply, confirmed the fact that Senior had recommended Rae's book to him and indeed had lent him his copy before he bought one of his own in a book stall.[19]

As a result of Mill's laudatory references, Rae's book came to the attention of Professor Francesco Ferrara of the University of Turin. Ferrara translated Rae's book into Italian and included it in volume XI of the *Biblioteca dell' economista*, which was published in thirteen volumes between 1850 and 1856 in Turin. The other works translated in this volume were:

David Ricardo, *Principles of Political Economy*

Robert Torrens, *An Essay on the Production of Wealth*

Samuel Bailey, *A Critical Dissertation on the Nature, Measures and Causes of Value*

Richard Whately, Archbishop of Dublin, *Introductory Lectures on Political Economy*

There is nothing to show that Rae ever knew he was included in such distinguished company.

[18] *Ibid.*, 165 n.
[19] The complete text of the letters exchanged between Rae and Mill is given in items 15 and 16 in Part III of this volume.

Rae's *New Principles* appeared with the imposing title *Dimostrazione di taluni nuovi principii sull'economia politica, dimonstrante gli errori del sistema de commercio libero, e di altre dottrine contenute nella "Richezza delli nazioni,"* prefaced by a warm tribute from Professor Ferrara. Ferrara himself refused to accept the Ricardian views on the theory of value, being convinced that value was dependent always and almost exclusively on the cost of reproduction. Ferrara regarded Rae as the first economist to recognize "the unequivocal and fundamental aspect which he assigns to the principle of the cost of reproduction," and was inclined to look on this as more important than Rae's contributions to the theory of capital. In referring to Rae's book, Ferrara wrote:

This work is still almost unknown in Europe. I have not seen it referred to by anyone except Stuart Mill who praised ideas in it which certainly have some merit but in my opinion are inferior to those which are revealed by the clear and forth-right way in which the author expounds the theory of value. This as the reader will see occupies several pages ... in which I would find difficulty in contra-dicting a single word.[20]

Apart from Mill's *Principles* and Ferrara's translation, Rae's *New Principles* was almost entirely ignored in the body of economic literature which grew up during the remainder of the nineteenth century. Even such a compendium as McCulloch's *Literature of Political Economy* printed in 1845 did not refer to Rae.

In some instances, Rae may have had a real but unacknowledged in-fluence. For example, Mixter claims that W. E. Hearn, an Australian economist, author of a work entitled *Plutology*,[21] was indebted to Rae. He goes on to say: "This is seen not so much in particular passages as in the method and spirit of this admirable treatise. The high commendation which Jevons, Marshall and Edgeworth have bestowed upon Hearn's work, therefore belongs in part to another."[22]

So far as a potential North American audience was concerned there were a number of reasons for the lack of attention to Rae's book. In Canada it appeared at a most unfortunate time. Not only were there a very small number of people capable of appreciating Rae's economics adequately, but their attention was distracted in the mid-1830's by the intemperate political disputes of the period. It was a time for tocsins and clarion calls and not for closely reasoned and abstract works on political economy.

[20] *Biblioteca dell' economista* (first series), XI, xxv (R. W. J.'s translation).
[21] (Melbourne, 1863; London, 1864).
[22] *Sociological Theory of Capital*, xxxii. Dr. Craufurd Goodwin has told me that J. A. LaNauze in his *Political Economy in Australia* (Melbourne, 1949) suggests that Hearn borrowed heavily from Rae without adequate acknowledgment.

Similarly, in the United States, the usefulness of what was considered as a protectionist tract had dwindled somewhat by 1834. The tariff legislation of 1828 had provided sharply increased protection and provoked angry controversy. But, amending measures in 1832 and 1833 reduced some of the extreme tariffs and paved the way for a gradual future reduction in the level of protection. Thus, by 1834, the tariff issue had diminished in political importance compared to a few years earlier and Rae's book thus appeared too late. Besides, his arguments were a little too refined and attenuated for popular consumption.

Apart from this, Rae was merely a colonial in a period when colonies were associated with savages of various hues, with transported felons, and with primitive and picturesque living conditions. The notion that a mere colonial could make any significant contribution to political economy was far-fetched enough and it was more absurd to consider seriously any work which challenged the entrenched and authoritative views of Adam Smith. Even in Canada, the authority of Adam Smith was unchallenged. For example, the Hon. John Willson, the father of Rae's dear friend Hugh Bowlby Willson and a man of great political influence in Upper Canada and undoubtedly an acquaintance of Rae, made his adherence to the doctrines of free trade quite clear. In his obituary notice, it was said: "He never swerved from the opinion that, in an agricultural country especially, free trade, or the nearest practical approach to it, was the true policy. Adam Smith's 'Wealth of Nations' is one of the best worn books in his small but well selected library."[23]

In the early nineteenth century, there was a remarkable amount of trans-atlantic spitefulness in literary affairs. The scorn of the notorious comment in the *Edinburgh Review* "Who reads an American book?" was matched by many bitter rejoinders in the United States. For example, A. H. Everett's first essay after he became editor of the *North American Review* in 1830 on "The Tone of British Criticism," included some hard words:

The *Quarterly* reviles us, the *Edinburgh* sneers at us, the magazines show us up under no very brilliant colors in imaginary travels and journals from Kentucky:— even the poor bookseller's drudge who gets up that humblest of all periodicals, *Literary Gazette* can afford to be merry at the expense of Jonathan. In short, we are daily, weekly, monthly and quarterly, from one year's end to the other, accused before these self-created courts of sundry high crimes and misdemeanours.[24]

[23] "Obituary of the Hon. John Willson," in James J. Talman, ed., *Loyalist Narratives from Upper Canada* (Toronto, 1946), 367–8.
[24] *North American Review*, XXXI, July, 1830, quoted in F. L. Mott, *A History of American Magazines, 1741–1850* (New York and London, 1930), I, 394.

Curiously enough, the *North American Review,* upon occasion, was contemptuous of Canadian literary endeavours partly because they were colonial. The intellectual snobbery in England and the Anglo-American literary bickering had a double-edged effect on Rae's book. He was largely ignored in England. His status as a political economist was thus impaired and consequently his work tended to be dismissed or ignored in Canada. Moreover, he was either a Scotsman or a Canadian or both and this probably cost him the support, for what it was worth, of the literary chauvinists in the United States.

In Canada, the very slow development of universities was a factor in the neglect of Rae's work. As a result there was no adequate forum for the discussion of Rae and people like him, and even later in the nineteenth century when courses in political economy were introduced, the emphasis was naturally on the great classical figures. The lagging of higher education was another index of Canada's relative poverty in the nineteenth century and the consequent emphasis on the hard realities of life.

It is a matter of some interest to assess the extent to which Rae may have had some influence on the adoption of a protectionist policy by Canada in the late 1870's. Rae's name was certainly mentioned on a number of occasions, but, so far as is known, this is because it occurred in a famous paragraph in J. S. Mill's *Political Economy.* One example is to be found in the writings of John Maclean, a well-known advocate of protection:

The advocates of the promotion of home industry by duties on foreign manufactured goods are under incalculable obligations to Mr. Mill, for that paragraph in his works quoted both by the *World* and the *Leader* (the latter giving also a sentence which the former omits). With all the illustrious author's explanations— and explanations of these explanations again, by the writers—an admission of immense value has been placed on record; and a great many explanations will not neutralize its effect. . . . His further remark, endorsing Mr. Rae's, that "nothing has a greater tendency to promote improvement etc. . . ." is corroborated.[25]

John A. Macdonald quoted Mill's paragraph in full in 1876 in introducing a resolution which was the precursor of the National Policy of 1878:

The only case in which, on mere principles of political economy, protecting duties can be defensible, is when they are imposed temporarily (especially in a young and rising nation) in hope of naturalizing a foreign industry, in itself perfectly suitable to the circumstances of the country. The superiority of one country over another in a branch of production often arises only from having begun it sooner. There may be no inherent advantage on one part, or disadvantage on the

[25] John Maclean, *Protection and Free Trade* (Montreal, 1867), 51. The newspapers referred to are the *New York World* and the *Toronto Leader.*

other, but only a present superiority of acquired skill and experience. A country which has this skill and experience yet to acquire, may in other respects be better adapted to the production than these which were earlier in the field, and besides, it is a just remark of Mr. Rae, that nothing has a greater tendency to promote improvements in any branch of production than its trial under a new set of conditions. But it cannot be expected that individuals should, at their own risk, or rather to their certain loss, introduce a new manufacture and bear the burthen of carrying it on until the producers have been educated up to the level of those with whom the processes are traditional. A protecting duty, continued for a reasonable time, will[26] sometimes be the least inconvenient mode in which the nation can tax itself for the support of such an experiment. But the protection should be confined to cases in which there is good ground of assurance that the industry which it fosters will after a time be able to dispense with it; nor should the domestic producers ever be allowed to expect that it will be continued to them beyond the time necessary for a fair trial of what they are capable of accomplishing.

Macdonald then went on to add:

I say this extract I have now read applies to the circumstances of Canada. We are a young country, just emerging from the first struggles with the forest. We have but little realized capital as yet; the manufacturers of the country, with a few small exceptions, having scarcely taken root.[27]

Schumpeter has some interesting comments to make on the comparative neglect of Rae:

As a rule, a work presenting novel ideas will not elicit response if it lacks the support which comes from being written by a well known author. We ought, therefore, to be surprised at the response it met with rather than at the fact that it did not meet with more. J. S. Mill noticed it, and—perhaps in consequence of this—there was an Italian translation in 1856. How, then, can it have been necessary to 'discover' Rae, as Professor Mixter rightly claimed it was? ... The answer might serve as a motto for a chapter of the sociology of science. J. S. Mill was invariably fair and even generous. Sensing the quality of the work, he was glad to mention it in a friendly spirit, not only to accept from it a phrase that happened to fit into his line of thought ('effective desire of accumulation') but also to quote it copiously (Book I, ch. 11). He even went so far as to com-

[26] Macdonald said, in referring to this "celebrated passage" that "It has been repeated by him in the last edition of his book in the same words that it was in the first." Canada, House of Commons, *Debates*, March 7, 1876, 490. This is not quite so, since as Sir W. J. Ashley notes, the word "will' in the original 1848 text was changed to "might" in the 1871 edition and the words "it is essential that" were inserted after "But" in the following sentence. Mill, *Principles of Political Economy*, 922.

[27] Canada, House of Commons, *Debates*, March 7, 1876, 490–1. There is no evidence to show that Macdonald was aware of who Rae was, although they knew a number of people in common, including the Rev. John Machar, Archibald McLean, and Sir Allan N. MacNab. Macdonald had also participated in the agitation among the Presbyterians for the establishment of a school to train young men for the ministry. See Donald Creighton, *John A. Macdonald: The Young Politician* (Toronto, 1952), 74–5.

pare Rae's performance on accumulation with Malthus' performance on population. And all this, written in what was to be for forty years the most influential textbook of economics, was insufficient to introduce Rae to the profession or to rouse any curiosity concerning the rest of his book! Or, alternatively, if this impression is wrong and any considerable number of Mill's readers did take it up, there was not one among them to realize its true importance. However, it may be of some significance to note that Senior knew the book. . . .[28]

It may be, however, that Bagehot stated succinctly the reason for the tendency to neglect Rae in the nineteenth century in his comment: "Our Political Economy does not recognize that there is a vital distinction between the main mode in which capital grows in such countries as England now, and the mode in which it grew in all countries at first."[29] It now seems clear that the theory of capital was an unpopular subject among the academic profession in nineteenth-century England and it should therefore not cause great surprise that an author whose main contribution was in this field should have had little attention paid to him.

The late H. A. Innis of the University of Toronto was interested deeply in questions relating to the dissemination of knowledge and commented on Rae's case:

I have been thinking of [the neglect of Rae] and wondering how far it throws light on a problem which has worried me over a long period—namely that of borrowing on the dissemination of knowledge. I suspect that the wealthy powerful countries have the best social scientists and that the social scientists in small poorer countries have very little chance of making any distinctive contribution which will be accepted. Rae's story seemed to illustrate this point to an important extent. If he had been born in the United States we would have had several doctoral theses by this time.[30]

There was also a purely practical consideration which hindered the acceptance of Rae. This was the fact that the initial printing of the book must have been small and it very rapidly became scarce.[31] For this reason, a great many people had to content themselves with the commentaries of John Stuart Mill and others.[32]

[28] J. A. Schumpeter, *History of Economic Analysis* (New York, 1954), 469.

[29] Walter Bagehot, *Economic Studies* (London, 1905), 14.

[30] Communication to the writer, June 10, 1950.

[31] A number of the copies of Rae's *New Principles* in libraries are presentation copies signed by Rae. The recipients were Maurice Scollard, Toronto (New York Public Library), John McLeod (Hamilton Public Library), and James Fleming (Toronto Public Library). The copy in the Library of Parliament belonged to A. Buchanan, possibly Alexander Carlyle Buchanan.

[32] For example, Knut Wicksell refers to "the long-forgotten work of John Rae" and says, "unfortunately, I only know his work through Böhm-Bawerk's quite detailed and largely eulogistic description of it (in the *Geschichte und Kritik des Kapitalzinstheorie*)." *Ekonomisk Tidskrift* (1923), reprinted in *Lectures on Political Economy*, I, 259.

There may also be some clue to the neglect of Rae's book to be found in his own personality and activities. There is little doubt that he was sorely disappointed in the reception of his book and, in consequence, he seems to have shunned any further study of the theoretical aspects of economics. He appears to have had a curious diffidence about his own work. So far as is known he never spoke in public on economics after 1834, and appeared to be reluctant to advertise himself. In later years, he did not even own a copy of his *New Principles*.

There may also be some clue to the neglect of Rae's book to be found in

13

Rae's Views on Social Questions

One of the recurring themes pervading most of Rae's written work is his
emphasis on the social virtues of morality. In part this may have stemmed
from the influence of his family and his early teachers. One can detect the
same general approach in some of his sister's writings. The "Analysis"
prefacing part of her work *Home, A Poem* refers to "Dissipation and folly,
unconquerable obstacles to domestic happiness." In one of her stanzas,
she declaims:

> Yet not alone where Vice, where Folly sway;
> Through Hymen's bowers domestic sorrows stray;
> Spleen's dusky vapour, Passion's angry flame,
> The glance of Jealousy, and brow of Gloom, ·
> Too oft the op'ning sweets of life destroy,
> And blight the bosom's gayest hours of joy.

There can be no doubt that Rae's attitude was also moulded by the
Presbyterian Church. When Rae was a youth the influence of the church on
moral attitudes was much stronger than it is today and in addition religion
was a pervasive element of everyday life. Rae himself notes in one place
that the religious character of the people of Scotland was primarily the
result of the "Church in the house."

The importance of good standards of morality is emphasized time and
again in Rae's economic writings. Vanity, vice, and folly exerted a pernicious influence on capital accumulation in any society. He drove his point
home in his attacks on the Anglican Church when he accused it of tolerat-
ing Adam Smith's "liberal or loose system" of morality, a system which

was quite unsuitable for a young country such as Canada. In the course of his discussion of luxury he makes his views very clear:

All luxuries occasion a loss to the society, in proportion to their amount. .... Its amount cannot, for reasons already stated, be easily ascertained, nor is it necessary for our purpose that it should. It is sufficient to observe, that, in all societies which have hitherto existed, it has been considerable; and that it seems to be determined, in every society, by the strength of the selfish, and weakness of the intellectual powers and benevolent affections; and, consequently that it is inversely as the strength of the accumulative principle.[1]

When Rae discussed the factors influencing the "effective desire of accumulation" he emphasized, in addition to the prevalence of social and benevolent affections, the habits of reflection and prudence and the stability of social conditions. All these factors are obviously influenced by the moral characteristics of a society and it was clearly his preoccupation with these matters which ultimately lead Mixter to rename his edition of Rae's *New Principles* the *Sociological Theory of Capital*.

Despite his preoccupation with morality, Rae was in no sense narrow-minded or unrealistic in his approach. He had a broad understanding and tolerance of the frailties of human nature, and in his work dealing with the Hawaiian laws with "the purpose of suppressing disorders incident to the intercourse of the sexes," he specifically rejected laws as effective instruments for these irregularities, saying:

I believe it will be found that all attempts to amend the morality of any nation by legislative enactments have ever proved worse than useless. Human nature somehow rises up in arms against any forces from without that would compel it to be good or righteous after any particular fashion, and, in the tumult of rebellion thus excited, treads down and stifles those inward monitors to which the soul would otherwise have been inclined to listen.

One answer to the problem, according to Rae, was to raise the esteem in which Hawaiian women were held. He then asked,

How was this to be brought about?

"Tis education forms the common mind;
Just as the twig is bent the tree's inclined."

There can be no doubt of the truth of the poet's maxim, if we understand by the term not mere book learning, but education in its largest and true sense, comprehending all the influences which are brought to bear on the individual, from infancy to maturity. In that extended sense, the best education is undoubtedly that which most conduces to the prosperity and happiness of the individual, and of the community of which he or she is to be a member. As it comes short, or runs counter to this, it is defective or faulty.

[1] *New Principles*, 290.

Education, morality, and prosperity were, in fact, inextricably inter-
twined in Rae's view of society. Here again, his views were undoubtedly
influenced by the progress of popular education in Scotland. In the early
nineteenth century, education was much more widely diffused in Scotland
than in England, in part as a result of the influence of the Church of Scotland. In the General Assembly of the Church of Scotland in 1818, the
claim was made "that there was a school in every parish, competently
endowed as provided for by law, and in general supplied with a suitably
qualified teacher."[2] Rae emphasized on a number of occasions the beneficent role of the Church of Scotland in education and went on to attribute
many of the well-known virtues of the Scottish people to their admirable
educational system.

In one of his letters to the editor of the *Montreal Gazette* he began by a
succinct statement of his view.

Ignorance is the impure source from which almost all the miseries and crimes
of mankind proceed. Let a people become enlightened, and their virtue, happiness
and prosperity follow as a necessary consequence. We may search the records of
antiquity in vain for an instance of any nation that was ignorant and yet virtuous,
or of a nation that was enlightened and which yet continued to grovel in wretchedness and vice. The history of the world proclaims the truth of this remark.
During the gloom which overhung Europe in that period of her history, when
science sought for shelter on the plains of Samarcand, it was then that the empire
of vice was unbounded and that the moral and intellectual powers of man were
prostrated before the supremacy of an authority which was founded upon his
own ignorance and superstitious fears. When, however, the sun of science once
more arose upon the nations of Europe, the benign influence which he shed forth
called into being the energies of industry and wealth. As men became more
intelligent they hastened to break the bonds by which they had been so long
held in vassalage, and as knowledge was more widely diffused, their virtue,
happiness and wealth increased in the same proportion. The power of knowledge
in advancing the best interests of the human race is irresistible.

Later in the same letter, he waxed indignant about the inadequate qualifications required for teachers in Lower Canada.

Who but a fool would engage a man to build him a house, without enquiring
whether or not he was a good mechanic, and who but a scoundrel would engage
a person, with the information of a ploughboy or a coalheaver, to conduct the
education of his child, to form his character and habits and to lead him, by the
example of his own life, and the beautiful precepts of morality with which he
inclines his youthful mind to entertain an abhorrence of vice, and an admiration
of virtue.[3]

[2] Quoted from W. Smart, *Economic Annals of the Nineteenth Century, 1801–1820*
(London, 1910), 73, in P. Hume Brown, *History of Scotland to the Present Time* (Cambridge, 1911), III, 348, n. 1.
[3] See item 7 in Part III of this volume.

In the course of his discussion on the population question, Rae had some interesting comments on "the social instincts." He said of them that "they seem hammered into the race by repeated strokes often after it has been softened in the furnace of affliction." He developed the concept of "the effective desire of offspring" and undertook to explain the catastrophic decline in the population of the Hawaiian Islands on this basis. He noted that Captain Cook had estimated the population of the islands at 800,000 but at the time of his writing (c. 1854) it had fallen to about 70,000. Rae clearly had a laboratory for the study of population problems which was denied to the English theorists no matter how astute and penetrating. Rae could not, for example, agree that the population decline in the Hawaiian Islands could be adequately explained by the Malthusian hypothesis. What had happened rather was a breakdown of the social fabric with a consequent diminution in the effective desire for children. He explained that there was a relationship to the accumulation of capital.

Practically, the population question seems to me to turn on what I might call the effective desire of offspring. This runs parallel with the effective desire of accumulation (for at bottom they spring from similar causes) but often outruns it. That is to say, if there be no effective desire for offspring the accumulative principle falls; but the effective desire of offspring may exist where the effective desire of accumulation is small. The reason is that the desire of offspring is regulated, like some other things, by certain sentiments pervading the society, which we may term instincts of society. We have nearly as great difficulty in assigning causes for these, as for the instincts of animals.[4]

In general, it can be concluded that Rae never lost sight of his youthful aim of producing a true "natural history of man." Nearly everything that he wrote was influenced by his earnest conviction that man's behaviour, particularly his economic behaviour, was conditioned by prevailing social attitudes. These attitudes were not fixed but in his view could be changed and improved by the inculcation of proper religious and moral beliefs and above all by the beneficent influence of education.

[4] See item 18 in Part III of this volume.

14

Rae, Mixter, and Böhm-Bawerk

During much of the nineteenth century the discussions by economists of the earnings or returns to the human and other resources contributing to the production of goods were usually in terms of the wages of labour, the rent of land, and the profits of stock. The fact that these types of returns accrued to three fairly distinct social classes, the labourers, the land-owners, and the capitalists beclouded the problem of distribution with a number of ethical, moral, and political considerations.

In particular, the proposition that wages are paid out of capital, the so-called wage fund doctrine, attracted so much hostility that many writers on economics tended to skirt around the subject. The adherents of the classical tradition in England in the latter part of the nineteenth century concentrated their attention on other issues and a consistent and coherent theory of capital was not developed. More attention was paid to the economic problems of capital formation by certain of the Continental economists, notably Eugen von Böhm-Bawerk. Böhm-Bawerk's main contribution to capital theory, *Positive Theorie des Kapitals*, appeared in 1890 and was translated into English by William Smart and published with the title *Positive Theory of Capital* in 1891. The mere fact that his book was available in English attracted a good deal of attention to Böhm-Bawerk's views. Apart from this, Böhm-Bawerk had some basic contributions to make to the understanding of capital theory, particularly with respect to the influence of time on human preference.

One of Böhm-Bawerk's principal concepts concerned the notion of the period of production. On the assumption that a precise date can be assigned to the input of each factor contributing to a production process and that the resultant units of output or consumption can also be dated, the period of production is the time interval between the average date of the inputs and the average date of output or consumption. Böhm-Bawerk was impressed with the importance of variations in the length of the period of production and argued that increases in the capital used in production involved a lengthening of the period of production. The productivity of incremental additions to the period of production diminishes, however, and ultimately the length of the period is adjusted in such a way as to balance the supply of labour and the corresponding demand for labour. Some features of Böhm-Bawerk's capital theory almost at once invited critical comment and there was naturally keen interest in his writings in academic circles.

About 1896, Charles Whitney Mixter, a graduate student in economics at Harvard, became interested in John Rae, probably at the suggestion of Professor F. W. Taussig, whose seminar on economics Mixter attended. He saw a close resemblance between the theories of Rae and Böhm-Bawerk, although it is not clear whether this notion was original or was suggested to him by Taussig. In any case in 1897, Mixter had published an article about Rae in the *Quarterly Journal of Economics* entitled "A Forerunner of Böhm-Bawerk,"[1] in which he drew attention to Rae and his work.

Böhm-Bawerk had clearly been unaware of the nature of Rae's contribution to the theory of capital although he obviously knew something of Rae from the quotations of John Stuart Mill. In Böhm-Bawerk's *Geschichte und Kritik der Capital-zinstheorien* first published in 1884, he makes no reference to John Rae.[2] However, his attention having been called to Rae by Mixter's article, Böhm-Bawerk included a new chapter on Rae in the second edition of his *Geschichte* published in 1900.[3] Böhm-Bawerk was very generous in his appreciation of Rae, and remarked on the fact that Rae, like a number of other first-rate economists, had been almost completely ignored by his contemporaries and his significance had only been appreciated when later generations had recognized and rediscovered his significance. Böhm-Bawerk emphasized that one of the difficulties was the extreme scarcity of Rae's book and suggested that Mill had not done Rae complete justice despite frequent and lengthy quotations. Mill had, according to Böhm-Bawerk, not reproduced the essential kernel of Rae's theory but had drawn attention to the "ornamental incidentals,"

[1] Vol. XI, Jan., 1897, 161–90.
[2] Eugen von Böhm-Bawerk, *Geschichte und Kritik der Capital-zinstheorien* (Innsbruck, 1884).
[3] *Ibid.* (2nd ed.; Innsbruck, 1900), 375–428.

J.R.I—13

which did not reveal its special quality. There was a remarkable similarity both to his own views and those of Jevons, but Böhm-Bawerk made it clear that Mixter was not quite correct in his estimate of the similarity of the theories of Rae and Böhm-Bawerk, Böhm-Bawerk's interest in Rae can perhaps be measured partly by the fact that he devoted a chapter of fifty-four pages to him. If it did nothing else, this assured Rae a place in Continental economic literature which abounds in references to him.

Shortly after the appearance of the *Geschichte* Mixter wrote a commentary on Böhm-Bawerk's chapter dealing with Rae which was published in the *Quarterly Journal of Economics* in 1902. In it he admitted that he had overstated his claim for Rae as a precursor of Böhm-Bawerk.[4] He was hostile to Böhm-Bawerk's critical comments on Rae and wrote towards the end of his article: "I am at a loss to understand why one who has such a complete grasp of Rae's 'theory as a whole' can, nevertheless, continue to urge again and again inconclusive objections to particular parts of it, unless it be by reason of confusion of thought growing out of a one-sided theory of value."[5] Mixter was also instrumental in publishing some of Rae's letters in the *Quarterly Journal of Economics*[6] and the *Economic Journal*.[7] This correspondence has been reproduced as items 17 and 18 of Part III of this volume.

In the meantime, Irving Fisher made the first of his many generous appreciations of Rae as an economist. In February, 1897, he published a brief note on Rae in the *Yale Review*:

A neglected Economist. In the January number of the *Quarterly Journal of Economics*, Mr. C. W. Mixter brings to light a remarkable book by Mr. John Rae, published in Boston in 1834 and entitled "Statement of some new principles on the subject of political economy, exposing the fallacies of the system of Free Trade and of some other doctrines maintained in the 'wealth of nations'. " The subtitle is apt to repel many readers and perhaps has contributed to keep the book on the dusty shelf for so long a time. But Mr. Rae was in reality a free trader, and stated the arguments on that side with much precision. The limitations which he emphasized are such as most candid economists will admit. The bulk of the work is devoted not to the free trade controversy, but to the theory of capital or "stock." In this the author has almost completely anticipated the brilliant work of Böhm-Bawerk in "The positive theory of capital." The time element and the relation

---

[4] C. W. Mixter, "Böhm-Bawerk on Rae," *Quarterly Journal of Economics*, XVI, 1902, 385–412. On the first page of the article, Mixter says in a footnote: "I plead guilty to the charge that to a considerable extent on a former occasion I read Böhm-Bawerk into Rae, and that I represented a greater likeness to exist between them than is actually the case."

[5] *Ibid.*, 409.

[6] "Fragment of an Unpublished Manuscript by John Rae (1796–1872)," *Quarterly Journal of Economics*, XVI, 1901–02, 123–5.

[7] "Letters of Rae to Mill," *Economic Journal*, XII, 1902, 111–20.

between the length of the production process (or, as Mr. Rae puts it, the rapidity of return of instruments) and the rate of profits and interest, are developed with a clearness and insight which entitles the author to a place in the front rank of economists. He was not possessed of the modern idea of marginal utility, but in other respects his work is equal to or even superior to that of Böhm-Bawerk. In particular his distinction between "accumulation" of capital at a given state of knowledge and an "augmentation" of capital through progress of invention is one which Böhm-Bawerk had not worked out. In this and in many other points Mr. Rae's book contains results which cannot be found elsewhere. No economist who is interested in the theory of capital in any of its aspects can afford longer to let Mr. Rae's investigation go unread. His work is a magnificent specimen of true scientific method and a rare example of orderly and convincing exposition. His style too is easy, forceful and captivating, and his fund of ready illustrations commands instant admiration. Not the least remarkable feature of this many-sided work is the clear conception of *sociology*, or "Natural History of Men," which it contains. It is difficult to realize that Mr. Rae wrote before that science was definitely founded. In short, the "New principles of political economy" is truly a masterpiece, a book of a generation or a century. It was written before the world was ready for such painstaking analysis. Now that its merits have been pointed out by Mr. Mixter, it is sure to be accorded a high place among the classics of economic science.[8]

At the time Mixter wrote his original article on Rae and Böhm-Bawerk in 1897 he knew nothing of Rae's life except the scanty facts revealed in the *New Principles*. With the encouragement of Professor Frank W. Taussig and Professor Charles Franklin Dunbar, Mixter later undertook to learn more about Rae. With this in mind he wrote the following letter to the editor of the "Notes and Queries" column of the *Montreal Daily Star*:

I am told by a student of McGill University that you may be able to give me some information as to the life of John Rae, author of "Statement of Some New Principles of Political Economy," published in Boston in 1834, the preface being dated "Montreal, 1833."

Rae is now recognized as one of the greatest economists of the century but absolutely nothing is known about his personality except a few things which he tells in the preface of his work, where one learns that he was a Scotchman who emigrated to Canada, but that is about all. This John Rae is sometimes confounded with John Rae, M.D., the Arctic explorer, but they are not the same. I do not wish to put you to any trouble, but if you could give any information as to this distinguished Canadian, it will be very much appreciated.[9]

Shortly after, replies were published from Henry J. Morgan, the author of *Bibliotheca Canadiensis* and a well-known Canadian literary figure, and

---

[8] *Yale Review* (old series), V, Feb., 1897, 457. The note was unsigned but is attributed to Irving Fisher by Mixter. *Sociological Theory of Capital*, xxxii.

[9] *Montreal Daily Star*, Feb. 25, 1899.

Robert Skakel Knight, Rae's great-nephew, both of whom were frequent contributors to the "Notes and Queries" column.[10]

In this way, Mixter was led to Sir Roderick William Cameron, who had known Rae all his life and was his devoted pupil, friend, and benefactor. Most of Rae's personal papers as well as a good deal of manuscript material which had been preserved by Cameron were turned over to Mixter. On the basis of this material, Mixter was able to identify a number of Rae's pupils who were still living and who could provide him with additional information about his life in Canada. Through relatives of Robert Skakel Knight living in Scotland, Mixter obtained additional information about Rae's early life in Scotland.

Because of the great scarcity of Rae's book, Mixter decided to reissue the book together with a biographical sketch. Thus it was that Rae's *Statement of Some New Principles on the Subject of Political Economy* reappeared with the title *The Sociological Theory of Capital* in 1905. As well as adding the invaluable biographical information which he had assembled, Mixter rearranged Rae's text with the intention of producing what he considered to be a more coherent account of Rae's theory of capital. He added a number of footnote comments and a small amount of additional material which he had found among Rae's papers.

Reviews of *The Sociological Theory of Capital* appeared in almost all the economic journals of the world. James Bonar, writing in the *Economic Journal*, commented:

Cantillon and Rae bid fair to take a far more prominent place in economic history since their resuscitation than they had secured in their own century. They are no longer saved from oblivion by a mere reference of Adam Smith and a mere quotation of J. S. Mill. Their own books will henceforth speak for them.[11]

Adolphe Landry, the French economist, was most generous, saying:

En lisant Rae on ne sera pas seulement frappé de la richesse des aperçus, de l'ingeniosité et de la fertilité d'esprit de cet auteur on sera frappé surtout du caractère moderne de l'oeuvre.[12]

Böhm-Bawerk also reviewed the book, relatively briefly, and pointed out that he had already devoted a long chapter to Rae in his *Geschichte*. He reiterated many of his generous tributes to Rae:

With a remarkable striving for fundamentals, Rae attempts to trace the problems of capital back to their very roots, which lie in the fields of production technique, psychology and sociology. At the same time he develops points of view and lines

---

[10] *Ibid.*, March 4, 1899.
[11] *Economic Journal*, March, 1906, 97.
[12] *Revue d'économie politique*, XXI, May, 1907, 380.

of reasoning which, on the one hand, are reminiscent of his no less original contemporary, von Thünen, who wrote on this side of the ocean, and on the other, appear again several generations later with Jevons and which also play a role in the attempts made by the author of these lines towards a solution of the problems of capital.[13]

There were many tributes to Mixter's editorial labours. L. W. Zartmann, in his review, said:

Concerning the present reprint, Professor Mixter deserves much credit for the labor he has bestowed on the original work to make it more readable. He has corrected the punctuation, which was extremely bad.[14]

Adolphe Landry did raise some objections and closed his review with some critical remarks on Mixter's editorial liberties:

Il y a donc lieu de remercier vivement M. Mixter de nous avoir rendu Rae accessible. Regrettons seulement que M. Mixter, au lieu de réimprimer les *New principles* tels qu'ils ont paru, ait eu l'idée, quelque peu singulière à mon sens, de distribuer le texte de Rae selon un plan nouveau. M. Mixter a voulu attirer l'attention du lecteur sur la théorie du capital que Rae a exposée; était-il nécessaire pour cela de détacher les passages de son livre qui contiennent l'exposé de cette théorie, et de faire du reste des appendices et des "residua"?[15]

Bonar noted that "the editor has taken the liberty of rearranging the book," but went on to say that "if the author could in very deed come to life again, he could not fail to be grateful for the unwearied labours of an editor in every way worthy of him." This was at least a nice compliment to Mixter, but it is difficult to be sure what Rae, resurrected, would have thought.

True to his appreciation of Rae in 1897, Irving Fisher continued throughout his life to acknowledge Rae's contribution to the theory of capital. Fisher's *Theory of Interest* is dedicated "To the memory of John Rae and Eugen von Böhm-Bawerk who laid the foundations on which I have endeavoured to build," and in the preface, in speaking of his theory of capital, Fisher says, "Every essential part of it was at least foreshadowed by John Rae in 1834."[16]

Rae has also played some part in the development of capital theory in Sweden. Knut Wicksell, in writing a review of Gustaf Åkerman's *Realkapital und Kapitalzins* in 1923, says in one place, "As the author himself admits, the real starting-point, if nothing else, of his own treatment was

[13] *Zeitschrift für Volkwirtschaft, Sozialpolitik und Verwaltung*, Band 15, 1906, 273 (R.W.J.'s translation).

[14] *Annals of the American Academy*, XXVII, March, 1906, 444.

[15] *Revue d'économie politique*, XXI, May, 1907, 381.

[16] Irving Fisher, *The Theory of Interest* (New York, 1930), ix.

discovered in the long-forgotten work of the Scottish-American, John Rae."[17] Wicksell at this point introduces an interesting footnote on Rae:

Unfortunately, I only know his work through Böhm-Bawerk's quite detailed and largely eulogistic description of it (in the *Geschichte und Kritik der Kapital-zinstheorie*). Böhm-Bawerk's criticism is in effect identical with his celebrated objection against all "productivity theorists", who in his opinion constantly confuse physical and value productivity. As I have already attempted to show in *Uber Wert, Kapital und Rente*, at the very most this confusion is nothing more than a methodological error. In the first approach to the solution of the problem of production and distribution, it is permissible, if not advisable, to consider the prices of commodities as constant (which in the last analysis is essentially what Böhm-Bawerk himself does); in the same way, we regard production as constant in the first stage of the solution of the problem of pricing. It is only at a later stage that we should combine both these approximations in order to obtain the final solution of the problem. Once this is grasped, then, as far as I can see, Böhm-Bawerk's objection loses its force.

Åkerman's acknowledgment is not quite as pointed as Wicksell suggests, although he does say:

Rae considers buildings as a sum of equal increments of durability each of which arises out of a certain increment to the construction labour. This way of looking at it is very interesting and fruitful and will be used in what follows.[18]

This notion that the cost of construction of capital equipment may be regarded as a series, each term of which represents the cost of adding a year to the life of the capital good was developed, with bewildering arithmetic detail, in Åkerman's capital theory.

More recently, Rae has been the subject of a detailed study by Helmut Lehmann, whose book *John Raes Werk, seine Philosophischen und Method-ologischen Grundlagen*, published in 1937, contains an analysis of the influence of Bacon on Rae and of Rae's methodological approach to the social sciences and particularly his emphasis on the inductive method.[19]

No attempt has been made to provide an exhaustive account of all the writers on economics who have commented on or analysed Rae's contribution to political economy either on the basis of the *New Principles* itself or the citations by Mill and Böhm-Bawerk.[20] However, brief reference

---

[17] *Lectures on Political Economy*, I, 258–9.

[18] Gustaf Åkerman, *Realkapital und Kapitalzins* (Stockholm, 1923), 21–2 (R. W. J.'s translation).

[19] Lehmann's book was a doctoral dissertation submitted to the University of Leipzig and printed in Dresden in 1937.

[20] Among others, the list would include: J. B. Clark, Luigi Cossa, Karl Diehl, F. Y. Edgeworth, Walter Eucken, Joseph Garnier, Lewis Haney, Eduard Heimann, J. K. Ingram, E. A. J. Johnson, Julius Kautz, Paul Mombert, Franz Oppenheimer, Wilhelm Roscher, Rudolph Streller and Horst Wagenführ. Some of the references are, of course, quite fleeting.

should be made to the admirable accounts of Rae's work contained in recent studies by J. J. Spengler and Craufurd Goodwin.

Professor Spengler has given a valuable account of Rae's theory of economic development in the *Quarterly Journal of Economics* in 1959.[21] He outlines three main aspects of Rae's views. The first is that there is a slow but continual diminution of the return on capital under static conditions unless new technical knowledge is being gained and incorporated in inventions. The second is that capital accumulation varies in relation both to the rate of return and the effective desire of accumulation in a community. The third is that "in the longer run, it is upon the cumulation of relevant knowledge and its expression in invention that both capital accumulation and the improvement of man's lot ultimately depend."[22] Spengler then goes on to consider Rae's discussion of economic policy and his general argument that state intervention could often be justified, particularly in underdeveloped countries, to stimulate economic development. He summarizes the various avenues of state action proposed by Rae as: "rouse the inventive principle; augment capital formation; promote science and art by encouraging the discovery of new arts and improvement of the old; introduce arts and industries from progressive foreign countries; enable private individuals to produce domestically, when feasible, various goods formerly imported, thereby effecting a saving in transportation costs."[23] Altogether Spengler's article is a most valuable brief summary of some of Rae's most important economic ideas. Spengler has also commented on Rae in another place where he discusses the relation of Rae to Thorstein Veblen, Bernard Mandeville, and others.[24]

Dr. Craufurd Goodwin has given an excellent and sympathetic account of Rae in his book, *Canadian Economic Thought: The Political Economy of a Developing Nation 1814–1914*. He concentrates his attention on Rae's place in the development of economic thought in Canada and notes that "Rae made original contributions to theory which were far superior to those of any other writers in Canada."[25] Goodwin's comments on the indirect influence which Rae may have had on the introduction of the National Policy are of particular interest.

Despite the revival of interest in Rae around the beginning of the twentieth century, and the more recent commentaries mentioned above, he continues to be a lonely figure in the history of economic thought.

[21] "John Rae on Economic Development: A Note," 393–406.
[22] *Ibid.*, 399.
[23] *Ibid.*, 403.
[24] "Veblen and Mandeville Contrasted," *Weltwirtschaftliches Archiv*, LXXXII (1959).
[25] p. 122.

Even the Mixter edition of his work has now become relatively scarce and expensive. If it were more readily available, it might be wondered whether it does not convey a distorted impression. There is an essential unity and coherence about Rae's original book arising from the fact that it stemmed from a specific series of economic and political problems which convulsed Canada in the period 1820–40. The same kind of economic problems have occured many times since in undeveloped territories of the world and are of particular significance in the mid-twentieth century. There is little evidence to show that Rae's profound and perceptive analysis of the economics of new countries has had any appreciable influence.

15

Conclusion

It is possible to arrive at some definite conclusions about Rae's intellectual
qualities. He clearly had brilliant insights into the workings of society and
a remarkable ability to synthesize and generalize his observations. But it
ought to be emphasized that Rae was a very learned and scholarly man
and not in any sense an untutored genius. The composition of his book on
political economy while living in the back concessions of Glengarry or
Huntingdon County was a prodigious feat, but it should not obscure the
fact that Rae was thoroughly familiar with the existing literature of political economy and that his basic studies had been carried out in Aberdeen,
Edinburgh, and Paris. He is therefore distinctly different from those who
have contributed heavily to the literature of economics without troubling
themselves about the traditions of the subject or the rudiments of scientific
reasoning. Rae was perhaps unnecessarily polemical, in places, but it must
be remembered that his book was produced in an atmosphere of violence
and excitement in both Lower and Upper Canada and he saw in the doctrines of the slavish adherents of Adam Smith serious threats to the
cherished attachment to Britain and to the Crown. He was, in
effect, writing a pamphlet or a tract for the times and neither he nor
his associates appeared to recognize that he was making a fundamental
contribution to the theory of capital. And this was done, not only
correctly in its essentials, but in language so compelling and eloquent
that its literary quality will bear comparison with anything in the literature
of economics.

He commented himself on the inability of people to judge their own capacities in one of his essays in the *Literary Garland*,[1] saying:

It is indeed very difficult for any one to form a correct judgment of his own abilities, or of the channel in which they ought to be employed. The esteem of self, common to all, prompts men to over-rate their talents, and the love of singularity allures their minds into a fondness for vain-glory, and incites them to attempt objects whose exterior pomp and dignity, like the deceptive caskets of Portia, fascinate the view.

Even though a good deal is known about Rae's life and work, the man himself emerges dimly. No portrait of him has been found and, apart from the information that he was "tall, rather slender and dignified" and may have worn a wig, even his personal appearance is a mystery. He was a formidable polemicist and yet evidently kind and loving to the pupils in his school. How curiously it strikes one now to see in the obituaries of two of his pupils who died as old men around 1900, notes to the effect that they had been educated under Dr. Rae. There is no doubt that he had many friends and they loved him dearly.

He suffered some cruel misfortunes in his personal life and yet apart from some periods of dejection and apathy he pressed on with his schemes and conjectures, fired with remarkable ambition and optimism. Only a few months after he was wandering in California, sick and literally penniless, he wrote to his friend Cameron, "Probably in the course of a year or so, I shall be appointed Geologist for the Hawaiian Kingdom." He appeared to be questing all his life; in the offing there was a fortune to be made or a literary reputation to achieve or a scientific idea to formulate. His youthful verve never seemed to leave him, even in his old age. According to Mixter, among his papers he left a note written in a wavering hand, and presumed to date from his final illness:

If we regard the generous impulses, the ennobling hopes, the lofty aspirations, that swell the breast of youth, we should say that the human heart was a soil in which the heaven-wafted seeds of every virtue might germinate and grow and flourish, and spread a paradise over the earth. But alas, when the time comes when each has to cast himself into the stream of actual life, the movements of whose impetuous current have come down from places and times far remote, the first plunge awakens him to the absorbing necessity of putting forth all his energies to maintain himself in the whirling tide. He loses sight of those landmarks which were to have guided his course. Progress, Progress, is his cry; and on he dashes, pushing aside and thrusting down.[2]

---

[1] "Genius and its Applications," reprinted as item 10 in Part III of this volume.
[2] *Sociological Theory of Capital*, xliii.

His faults or inadequacies are difficult to identify, although perhaps it is clear that he was handicapped by a deep-rooted inability to compromise. In one of his scraps of manuscript he did indicate a revulsion against courses of action intended to publicize himself or to gain some monetary or other advantage. Mixter refers to some obscure episode in which Rae was encouraged to pursue some endeavour by his friends. Rae wrote, in reply:

Now this was the way to make me sit still. Even the fancying to myself that personal advantage was in reality the end of my efforts was sure to confound me, and the holding this up to me as their true aim and object completely paralysed me. . . . It may seem incredible to you, but it is the real fact that these dinnings in my ears always brought a similar chaos over my thoughts, and if fool enough to try, I only floundered on from one instability to another. This may seem to you a strange, unnatural, almost mad humor of mine. So perhaps it was; it was at least what doctors call abnormal, the result probably in part of my peculiar organization, in part of cruel mental suffering in early youth, the fruits, the avengers perhaps, of a momentary yielding to violent passions. This gave to the world and all it holds a real air of mere vanity and vexation of spirit.[3]

Probably one of the unluckiest things ever to happen to Rae was the loss of the manuscript for his "Outlines of the Natural History and Statistics of Canada." This together with the lukewarm reception of his *New Principles* must have discouraged him from further ventures in political economy. In any case he appeared to devote an increasing amount of his time to geological speculations. Never content with a superficial view, he had to probe to the very foundations of the science. His hypotheses were audacious and despite his talents as an observer and a brilliant intuition he lacked the basic resources in terms of scientific instruments and precise data to progress very far. He was not content with following in the footsteps of others but felt constrained to strike out for himself.

He saw himself as an inventor and innovator even while he was still a boy and he understood and wrote feelingly of the role of such bold spirits. In one place he wrote a fitting epitaph for himself while he described the role of innovators in society:

Pursuing objects not to be perceived by others, or if perceived, whose importance is beyond the reach of their conceptions, the motives of their conduct are necessarily misapprehended. They are esteemed either idlers, culpably negligent in turning to account the talents they have got, dullards deficient in the common parts necessary to discharge the common offices of life, or madmen unfit to be trusted with their performance; shut out from the esteem or fellowship of those whose regard they might prize, they are brought into contact with those with whom they can have nothing in common, knaves who laugh at them as their

[3] *Ibid.*, xli

prey, fools who pity them as their fellows. Their characters misunderstood, debarred from all sympathy, uncheered by any approbations, the "eternal war," they have to wage with fortune, is doubly trying, because they are aware, that, if they succumb, they will be borne off the field, not only unknown, but misconceived.[4]

But this would be a sombre memorial. Perhaps the words of Henry Adams are more fitting:

A teacher affects eternity; he can never tell where his influence stops.

[4] *New Principles*, 214.

PART III

SELECTED PAPERS AND LETTERS

A. ARTICLES AND ESSAYS

1

Sketches of the Origin and Progress of Manufactures and of the Policy Which Has Regulated Their Legislative Encouragement in Great Britain and in Other Countries;— to which will be added

*An enquiry into the expediency of establishing some new branches of industry in the Canadas, more particularly with a view to the employment of women and children in the cities of Quebec and Montreal**

According to the natural course of things, the greater part of the capital of every growing society is first directed to agriculture, afterwards to manufactures, and last of all to foreign commerce.

Smith, *Wealth of Nations*, Book 3, chap. 1.

The wants of mankind are few when population is small; but they gradually encrease with the numbers of the species and with its progress in civilization. New desires, the offspring of new wants, in their turn, give birth to new arts, which mark the advancement of society, introducing the conveniencies and elegancies of life by the agency of mechanics and manufac-

* *Canadian Review and Literary and Historical Journal*, no. 3, March, 1825.

turers who prepare the rude produce of the earth for the use and gratification of their fellow men.

Among a people chiefly agricultural, in the early stages of human society, some persons, more ingenious than the rest, make discoveries and improve the natural products in a variety of modes, whence gradually arise the division of labour, the difference of professions, and a new distribution of wealth among mankind. From making clothes and utensils for his family, the man of an inventive mechanical turn will be led by degrees to a profitable employment of his time and talent in working for others; and an interchange of the fruits of mechanical and agricultural labour will take place between ingenious artisans and laborious husbandmen. The utility of this division of labour in process of time will establish the distinction; and the natural propensity to imitation will transmit the arts from father to son, or preserve them otherwise, according to the peculiar circumstances of the society.

When the useful arts have made this progress, competition begins to appear; the artisans emulate each other in improvement and in recommending their works, on the principle of œconomy, to the husbandmen; while the latter, acquiring a decided taste for the conveniencies of life, redouble their exertions in agriculture to enable them to command the labours of the former. A surplus of agricultural produce may thus be raised, and a superfluous assortment of artificial products prepared for exchange; in which circumstances, security of property will become an object of greater importance, the protection of law and government will be required, villages, towns and cities will be built; public fairs and emporiums in eligible situations will be established, and the use of money to facilitate commerce will be adopted.

From such a state of inland trade a transition will naturally take place, on the first opportunity, to foreign commerce, which will be either active (a) or passive, according to the circumstances of a country and the character of its inhabitants. If it have only a passive commerce, manufactures will never be carried to that extent, variety and perfection of which

(a) By active commerce is understood the purchase and transportation of the produce or manufactures of one or more countries to others by land or water, and exchanging them for some equivalent, in specie bills or merchandise. Active commerce has chiefly originated in countries convenient for navigation, but comparatively poor; the Phenecians and Tyrians among the ancients, and the Venetians, Dutch and others among the moderns were at first mere carriers for other nations. Those who inhabit the most fertile regions of the world are satisfied generally with a passive commerce; and they regulate their exertions in agriculture and manufactures chiefly by the internal demand, though the presence and encouragement of foreign factors have doubtless some effect on their industry, notwithstanding the reluctance observable among such people to vary their produce or manufactures.

they are susceptible in a state that has an active universal commerce. But there is a progress in human affairs; and in most countries of temperate climate, improvable soil and situation, we, at an early period of their history find such manufactures as the following dispersed in different quarters: coarse woollens and linens; provisions and liquors; hides and leather; vegetable and fish oils.

When a country advanced thus far is frequented by foreign merchants and by ships engaged in active commerce, its inhabitants gradually acquire confidence in their own abilities; and dispersed manufacturers of goods from native materials are united together in large towns conveniently situated. This progress has been particularly observable in the United States of North America, where foreign merchants, with foreign capital, have facilitated the establishment of manufactures, while pursuing very different objects. They first encouraged the raising of produce suitable to their respective markets, by offering in return the comforts and luxuries of manufacturing nations. This commerce, while it cherished the industry of an intelligent people, could not fail to excite in them the natural ambition of rendering their enjoyments independent of accident or caprice. So soon, therefore, as emigration from Europe and the encrease of native population became adequate to supply that division of labour which manufactures require, and when the riches acquired by the sale of produce had provided capital, the class of American manufacturers arose and pressed forward for legislative encouragement. The place first occupied by foreign artisans is now assumed by the native citizens; and, notwithstanding the errors of injudicious zeal, the United States must speedily obtain all the advantages which the useful arts, applied to the extensive resources of that country, are calculated to procure.

But we proceed to state the circumstances and political principles which appear to have regulated the legislative encouragement of manufactures in European countries, keeping more particularly in view the progress of events and of commercial legislation in Great Britain.

1. In the state of society which has long prevailed in modern times, some particular manufactures are absolutely necessary to secure the independence of a nation. The manufacture of gun-powder, cannon, small-arms and other munitions of war should claim the first attention of every wise government. In a maritime state, the building and equipment of ships of war are objects of primary importance; and, if native materials be deficient, a large stock of foreign stores should be gradually collected. History informs us that such was the policy of the Dutch, whose depots of arms and naval stores were long the envy and admiration of the world. The kings and statesmen of Britain have likewise been celebrated for

zeal in providing arms and naval stores; and they have steadily encouraged at home manufactures from iron, steel and other metals, flax, hemp, &c. while they have promoted the importation of raw materials from the colonies and from foreign countries for the same purpose.

2. When the chief materials of a manufacture are native or colonial, and when workmen, machinery and capital can be obtained at rates which promise successful competition with foreigners, such manufacture, if not otherwise sufficiently attractive to individuals, should be encouraged by government. In such circumstances was the woollen manufacture established in England. The impolitic conduct of the Count of Flanders, in the reign of Edward the Third, and long afterwards the tyranny of Philip of Spain, in the reign of Queen Elizabeth, having driven many able workmen to England, wool was no longer exported, but became one of the staple articles of British manufacture, both for domestic supply and for colonial and foreign demand.

3. When agriculture and its kindred avocations; manufactures requisite to support the national independence, and those which are fabricated from native or colonial produce leave part of the population unemployed and the wages of labour below their rates in neighbouring countries, then a manufacture from foreign materials may be safely encouraged. This frequently took place in Holland, particularly when its skill and population were so much augmented by the industrious French Protestants who fled from persecution after the revocation of the Edict of Nantz in the year 1685. Many of those refugees, skilled in the manufacture of silks, gold and silver stuffs and embroidery, settled likewise in England, where the silk manufacture quickly rose to importance. But, during half a century, Britain has been eminently successful in rivalling foreign nations in manufacturing foreign materials; because her wonderful improvements in machinery and in various inventions which facilitate the fabrication and transportation of materials, have greatly diminished the expense of labour, and the British commercial marine no sooner became extensive than competition between ship-owners began to prevail; and in the pursuit of active commerce it frequently happened that to secure a full freight homeward, much produce on ship's account was necessarily purchased, and this additional supply of materials is no small inducement to attempt manufactures from foreign produce. The same vessels that conveyed the materials brought likewise new workmen; and the fabrication of many articles is thus communicated from one nation to another.

4. The peculiar circumstances of some nations influence the manufacturing industry of others. When any country for example or its colonies has very productive mines of gold and silver, it will probably be idle in

proportion to its native riches, and inclined to resort for manufactures to more industrious nations, whose labour will in this manner receive a powerful stimulus. Spain and Portugal while they possessed South America, were very deficient in manufacturing industry; and their American treasures were employed in purchasing the labour of the Dutch, the English and the French. The Spanish and Portuguese colonies having now become independent States are nevertheless commercially dependent, and they will long continue to give the produce of their mines for the comforts and luxuries of manufacturing nations. In the competition for the supply of those markets, more particularly since they have been relieved from the restrictions of European sovereignty, the manufacturing interest of Great Britain has made extraordinary efforts; and the decay of the French, the Dutch, Spaniards and other nations has left English manufactures unrivalled in the Empire of Brazil and in the new Republics of Spanish America. (*b*)

5. When the colonies of a manufacturing nation hold forth a growing market for its manufactures, the efforts of individuals to furnish a complete assortment for colonial supply should be encouraged by government. In such a connection, the admission of colonial produce into the ports of the mother country for sale at all times without restriction, has been considered by political œconomists as an essential part of that implied contract, which on the other hand has given to the parent state the exclusive supply of manufactured goods and freight. On these principles, Great Britain and her splendid colonial empire on the American continent long conducted their intercourse with mutual benefit; and in this manner may her progress in manufactures be accounted for, from the reign of Queen Elizabeth to that of his late Majesty George the Third.

6. When foreign wars have interrupted the accustomed supply of foreign manufactures, it will frequently be good policy to encourage the establishment of substitutes at home before the public taste for them be weakened. Thus partly from necessity as well as from national rivalship, Britain has displayed much ingenuity in imitating and improving the manufactures of foreign nations. She has gradually obtained the manufacture of many articles long exclusively supplied by Germany, France and Holland; (*c*) and till the late convulsions in Europe had almost des-

(*b*) The revolutionary calamities and wars of France, which destroyed her manufactures and active commerce, and the decline of Holland, are circumstances which have contributed essentially to the variety, extent and general consumption of British manufactures in every quarter of the globe.

(*c*) Such as manufactures from metals in general; refined sugar, linen, paper, brandy, silks, laces, glass, porcelain and earthenware, distilled liquors and made wines, &c. &c.

troyed manufactures on the continent, she was daily adopting in every art the inventions and improvements of her neighbours.

7. When machinery as a substitute for human labour is introduced, a new era takes place in manufactures. Since the application of the power of steam to the manufacturing machinery of Great Britain, her inexhaustible mines of coal have given her a decided superiority over all nations in that species of labour. One of the first consequences of the introduction of manufacturing machinery into Britain, was seen in the establishment of the cotton manufacture on such a footing that the consumption of imported cottons is superseded. The cotton manufacture as now carried on in Britain, ranks next in national importance to that of woollens, exceeding it even in variety of use and facility of execution, and supporting many arts and subordinate labours such as mechanics, bleaching, printing on cloths, &c.

From this review of the progress of Great Britain, we may venture to draw the following inference of general utility, namely,

8. In a well peopled country, when all the means of inland and foreign communication are at command, and when tranquility at home and respect abroad are secured by the necessary display of moral and physical force, then all the manufactures suitable for domestic supply, and foreign and colonial commerce may be encouraged, and when, with those advantages, the elements of useful knowledge are generally diffused, enlightening the great body of the people and directing their genius, talents and industry to the improvements of the useful arts, the patronage of the government may be no longer necessary, but the progress of manufacturing industry may be left to the sagacious superintendence of private interest.

We shall now consider various methods of encouraging the establishment and progress of manufactures, directing our view to the practice of the free instead of the despotic governments of Europe: (*d*) and this part of the subject will admit of several divisions: 1. capital; 2. materials;

(*d*) In many European countries, the profession of a merchant and consequently that of a manufacturer, has been considered as degrading; and in such a case the first measure of encouragement by government is to confer respectability upon those professions by diminishing old prejudices originating in feudal and warlike times. In France under Lewis 14th, much was done during the administration of Colbert, to rectify public opinion in this respect; and many of the nobles were persuaded to employ both their capital and their personal attention in manufactures and wholesale trade. But in despotic governments, an uniform policy seldom regulates the œconomy of the state, and it occasionally happens that after one monarch has expended millions upon manufacturing establishments, his whole plans are neglected by his successor. In free governments, such discouragements being unknown, less expensive encouragements are necessary; and to England and Holland, where no impolitic laws prohibited their entrance, numbers of active industrious artisans continued to emigrate, attracted by religious and civil liberty, and that security of property which is the parent and reward of industry.

3. workmen, implements and machines; 4. subsistance; 5. abundance of fuel and facility of transportation; 6. education of the people or a general diffusion of elementary knowledge; 7. customers or a market.

1. *Capital.* No manufacture of importance can be established without expending very considerable sums in buildings, materials, wages, &c. In the infancy of manufactures, therefore, governments have generally assisted the design by granting charters of incorporation. So little indeed was public opinion in favor of the employment of money in trade and manufactures, in the beginning of last century, that hardly any new manufacture could be established in Britain except by joint stock companies. Those corporations obtained confidence; and after accumulating capital from every quarter, their general success diffused a spirit of enterprize throughout the country, paving the way for the more œconomical and better managed undertakings of private associations and individuals. In latter times, Banks of deposit and discount, incorporated by government, have been enabled to command the wealth dispersed through an educated population; among whom their notes, circulating to a great extent, afford extraordinary accommodation to manufacturing establishments. Much of the progress of Scotland in the cotton manufacture, may be ascribed to the confidence enjoyed by the Banks, and the extent to which they are thus enabled to circulate their paper. Their common practice of granting Bank credits or cash accounts, as described by Adam Smith, may encourage a manufacturer to employ his whole property and credit, with less risk of ruin from accidental fluctuations in the money market than is encountered in other countries. (*e*)

2. *Materials.* An abundance and variety of materials, native or colonial, are the only safe and lasting foundation for manufactures; and this principle is supported by the fate of Holland, which country derived but a transitory advantage from her manufactures, because she depended for her chief supplies of materials upon foreign nations. Those nations whose more extensive territory and more fruitful soil, produced raw materials in sufficient abundance and variety, were by her illustrious example roused to industry; and, instead of continuing to exchange produce for manufactures, they attempted to encrease their national income, by a new distribution and application of national labour. England sold great part of her valuable materials, such as tin, iron, lead, wool and hides to foreigners 'till the reign of Queen Elizabeth, when being disturbed in her commercial relations by the troubles in the Netherlands, she began to perceive the vast advantages to be derived from her insular situation, and her soil pro-

(*e*) A Scotch Bank, credit or cash account, has been described already in the Canadian Review, No. 2, article 8th, page 357.

ducing materials for the most important manufactures. In modern times, her active and universal commerce has introduced from foreign countries the culture of flax, hemp, and other valuable materials; and great encouragement, both honorary and pecuniary, is held forth by public societies for the cultivation of useful produce at home and in the colonies. With similar views, the government has admitted the importation of sheep's wool, cotton wool, undressed flax and hemp, raw silk, undressed hides, flax and hemp seeds, and various drugs and dye-stuffs from foreign countries upon payment of the lightest duties. In the commercial annals of Great Britain, instances occur of bounties being allowed for the importation of certain materials, found absolutely necessary, in particular emergencies for the support of staple manufactures. One of the principal benefits which arise from the establishment of chambers of commerce, in the manufacturing and trading cities of Britain and Ireland, is the facility with which information may be thus collected respecting the crops and stocks of materials throughout the kingdoms.

3. *Workmen, implements and machines.* In the infancy of manufactures, the principal workmen are exempted from militia service or any other public duty which would interfere with habits of steady industry. If the manufactory be placed at a short distance from large cities where there are many poor people, not fully occupied, many workmen of an inferior description may be thus obtained on reasonable terms. But with the view of encouraging manufactures, most governments have been accustomed to admit and naturalize foreign artisans; and, on the other hand, to punish severely the seduction of such useful persons from their native land, as well as the exportation of such materials and machines as are considered the basis and the means of national superiority, in manufacturing industry. But the example of Britain tends to show, that a variety of regulations and restrictions in favor of the capitalists who first establish manufactures may be dispensed with in the progress of that species of industry, more particularly when machinery becomes the great competitor of human labour. While England was gradually raising up that astonishing fabric of manufactures which now exists, various expedients of a temporary and subsidiary nature were adopted, serving the purpose of ladders, frames and scaffolding, which she can now with safety and advantage throw down and forget. But the memory of such regulations remains for the instruction of other nations in the commencement of their manufacturing career. The British laws being the result of the long continued appeals of manufacturers for protection, well deserve the study of those statesmen who are entrusted with the introduction of the useful arts into new societies. The improvement and extension of manufactures so much depend upon the invention

of implements and machines to facilitate and abridge labour, that the generosity of government as well as of various societies in Britain, has been long steadily exerted in rewarding excellence in practical mechanics. Upon the inventors of those wonderful machines, which by the agency of water or steam, perform both night and day the labour of hundreds of human beings in every process of the cotton manufacture, the British government have bestowed honors and pecuniary rewards. A patent, comprising an exclusive right for a reasonable number of years is readily obtained for every new invention; and occasionally the extensive utility of the discovery has induced the government to render the benefit free to the public at once by granting an adequate compensation; in all which cases it becomes expedient to consult men of science capable of duly investigating and estimating the value of the invention.

4. *Subsistence.* Having encouraged a part of the population to detach themselves from the soil, the government of a manufacturing country should be particularly careful to facilitate their subsistence, and to protect them from extravagant prices for provisions by a liberal admission of the grain of their own colonies or that of friendly nations. This important branch of political œconomy was admirably administered by the Dutch. Depending chiefly upon commerce for provisions, they gradually established such a system of supply as enabled them at length to sell grain occasionally to the very countries from which they had imported it. To enable a government to execute the important trust of securing the adequate supplies for a manufacturing population, the most correct and extensive information respecting the fertility of the soil and the course of the seasons is necessary. The British government, aided by agricultural and commercial societies, have made many experiments to reconcile the landed, colonial and commercial interests on the subject of the provision trade; and the results which have taken place will probably show that a monopoly which stimulates agriculturists to waste capital upon poor soils is in process of time as hurtful to themselves as to the commercial and manufacturing population.

5. *Abundance of fuel and facility of transportation* are objects of great importance, in countries extensively engaged in manufactures. Fuel so essentially necessary in former times for the working and refining of metals has become a new source of wealth since the application of steam to manufacturing machinery. The boundless forests of North America, and the still more valuable coal mines of Great Britain, are of primary importance, as fuel can rarely be procured in sufficient quantities for general purposes except from native resources. Britain in this respect has improved her natural advantages in an exemplary manner; and, of the canals, roads,

iron-bridges and railways, which are there seen on every side, not a few were originally projected to facilitate the transportation of fuel. But those useful works are likewise the principal means of encouraging the establishment of manufactures in remote and inland situations, where abundance of materials or cheapness of labour, may be the natural attractions; and the capitalists of a country may be induced to co-operate with government in the introduction of new branches of industry, by a liberal encouragement to roads, canals and other means of communication with maritime towns.

6. *Education of the people, or a general diffusion of elementary knowledge.* With respect to a manufacturing population, education is to be viewed as a preventive of evil as well as productive of good. Great manufactories furnish more dangerous opportunities, particularly to young persons, for the contamination and practice of vice, than the less constant assemblages of the sexes, in agricultural industry. The manufacturing population of Britain, were indeed long deprived of education, though its value and advantage were by many admired; but 'till the introduction of mutual instruction, by Dr. Bell and Joseph Lancaster, it had been found extremely difficult to contrive a mode of education, requiring that moderate expense of time and money, which the interest of employers could permit. Machinery, set in motion by water or steam, having superseded the use of men and horses as merely instruments of strength, intelligent superintendance and direction are now more required than bodily force. Owing chiefly to this change, the weaker sex is not only employed in vast numbers in the cotton manufactories, but likewise many thousands of children, of the tender age of five years and upwards, who can only receive education by means of some establishment peculiarly adapted to their circumstances. Every proprietor, therefore, of a manufactory should be encouraged to erect a school for the instruction of the children employed by him; (*f*) and it is to be hoped that private interest will prompt his exertions to the same purpose; because he might thus reasonably expect to provide a future supply of intelligent artizans, able to second his efforts for the improvement of the useful arts. As in a regiment of soldiers, properly organized and commanded, there grows up a zeal for the credit of the corps; so among the persons employed in an extensive manufactory, there may arise and be cherished a general enthusiasm for the celebrity of the establishment; and a due proportion of well disposed and reasonable men may on most

(*f*) The proprietor of an extending manufactory, having the means of giving education and employment at the same time, can do more good to the children of the poor than either the government or any benevolent individuals who merely provide instruction by the erection and endowment of charity schools.

occasions be found, to counteract the machinations of the turbulent, provided the character and conduct of the proprietor may have been always calculated to inspire respect.

The last division of legislative encouragements to Manufactures, comprises various means of obtaining customers or a Market. This Market may be either domestic or foreign; and the first as well as the surest aim of native manufactures is domestic supply; a monopoly of which has been frequently facilitated by the measures of governments eager for the establishment and rapid growth of manufacturing industry. With such views, they for instance enact, that every article required in the equipment of their fleets and armies, and in every other branch of the public service, shall, if possible, be supplied from native manufactures. And, pursuing their object beyond the limits of the military, naval and civil departments, it may be necessary to stimulate the efforts of private individuals by imposing duties on the importation of foreign manufactures, and thus rendering taxation not merely the means of raising a revenue but an ingenious device for the introduction and protection of the useful and liberal arts of life. There is also a species of encouragement less authoritative, though perhaps not less efficient, and which ought not to be neglected in facilitating to the native manufacture the exclusive supply of the home market: we mean the influence of example held forth by the higher classes of a community. When the Court and the people of fashion give a preference to home manufactures, public opinion is gradually strengthened in their favor; and nothing but a very considerable superiority in the quality of the foreign goods can long prevent their being driven from the home market, leaving a wide field to the national ingenuity which should be exerted in finding substitutes for imported luxuries. (g)

As nothing however but an extensive exportation trade can call forth the united energies of a nation for the advancement of Manufactures, a wise government, contemplating their encouragement, must naturally look beyond domestic supply. For this purpose, they will make commercial treaties with foreign nations, stipulating various reciprocal advantages and sending public Agents as Consuls to protect and countenance the Merchant in his distant establishments. Among the modern nations of

(g) Among the earliest means of encouraging manufactures as well as commerce should be mentioned the establishment and proper regulation of fairs or public markets; where the most decisive measures for the protection of person and property were taken by the magistracy. In the first stages of European civilization, the incorporation of cities and of different mechanical trades, so liable to abuse, was nevertheless the most ready and decisive expedient for creating a new class of subjects, restraining the pretensions of the agricultural population, and establishing that emulation between the town and the country which a politic government can turn to the greatest advantage as an engine of public prosperity.

Europe, the earliest attempts to provide a foreign market, have been made through the medium of joint-stock, regulated or exclusive companies; whose constitution and privileges have been frequently altered or annulled, at the will of the legislature, in accordance with the varying interests and exigencies of trade. Among the bold pioneers of British manufactures and commerce should be mentioned the Russian, Turkey or Levant, African and East India Companies. Many such establishments, which have become invidious in our days, and unnecessary to the support of British commerce, were originally the only means of uniting the capital, talent and respectability, requisite for laying the foundation of an active foreign commerce. Governments of well peopled countries, and of an enterprizing disposition, may also provide a growing market for their manufactures, by planting colonies in countries whose soil and climate may be favorable to the production of those raw materials and surplus means of subsistance, which the mother country may be willing to admit at all times, without burthen of duties for home consumption. The colonial policy of Great Britain was long regulated on this principle; and no nation more fully experienced its advantages; for it is easy to prove that much of her wonderful progress in arts, manufactures and commerce, during the eighteenth century, was owing to the stimulus given to her manufacturing industry by the wants of the American colonies. Among the more direct encouragements afforded by governments to the exportation of manufactures, bounties and drawbacks are of primary importance. The bounty may be strictly described as a premium for the exportation of the manufactured article, and the drawback as an allowance on the duties previously paid upon the foreign materials employed, and both have been used with success by every manufacturing nation in the commencement of its career.

We shall conclude this part of our essay with earnestly recommending the strictest inspection, by legal authority, of all staple articles intended for exportation. The general tendency of commercial legislation should be to enforce the practice of justice and good faith on the part of manufacturers and merchants in their dealings at home and abroad; for it has been long remarked that fraudulent measures and weights, counterfeit stamps and false names, are more destructive to a nation's trade than formidable rivalships and wars.

End of Part First

2

On the State and Prospects of Education and Learning in the Canadas*

There is no single object of such vast importance to a community—none in which its great and permanent interests are so deeply involved, as education. On this depends the improvement, intellectual and moral, of the minds of the people—and what improvement can be compared with this, either in its immediate or remote effects! The general prosperity and happiness of a community, are most effectually secured, when due provision is made for training up the youth by the generous discipline of a manly and enlightened education. If we take a general survey of the nations of the world, we shall find that their rank in the political scale, corresponds invariably with the degree in which knowledge is diffused, and the blessings of education extended to the population. A well educated nation, however barren its soil, or ungenial its climate—however inconsiderable the extent of its territory, or the number of its inhabitants, will always evince and confirm the truth of the famous maxim of Lord Bacon, that "knowledge is power." Witness Scotland, which has risen mainly, we are persuaded, in consequence of the superior excellence of the national system of education, to a rank in the scale of nations, which the proudest and mightiest States might well envy. Nor have the inestimable benefits of a manly and virtuous education conferred upon her people, been circumscribed within the narrow limits of her own territory—of the British Islands, or even the wide extent of the British Empire. She affords glorious evidence that the power of education is not more beneficent than it is diffusive.

* This essay originally appeared in *The Canadian Miscellany; or, the Religious, Literary & Statistical Intelligencer*, May, 1828, vol. I, no. 2, 33–45.

What region of the earth, accessible to man, or opening any field for adventure or enterprise, have her sons not visited, imparting to it the blessings of civilisation and improvement, carrying, wherever they go, the invaluable gifts of art, knowledge, science and religion. It were much to be wished that some person qualified for such an interesting inquiry, would undertake the task of unfolding a view of the influence which Scotland, intellectually and morally, has exerted on the rest of the world, and the degree in which her power in these respects, may yet be extended and made subservient to the advancement of the Empire and glory of Britain. Such an inquiry, we are persuaded, would exhibit results of which even few Scotsmen are fully aware. What a fine comment would it furnish on the celebrated axiom above quoted. How strikingly would it evince to all unprejudiced men the vast power of education, by shewing that one small nation, which has not been favoured by nature, either in her soil or climate, has been to the rest of the world more than any other of the British nations, "the little Leaven that leaveneth the whole Lump."

Of what moment, therefore, must it be to a young and rising country, to secure the unspeakable advantage of a liberal and effective system of education. It is beyond comparison, the first and most important object of legislative attention. To make provision for giving it to the people on the cheapest and easiest terms, without any restriction or shackles imposed that are not absolutely necessary for the safety of the state, and the protection of religion and morality, is, we conceive, the first and most sacred duty of every legislature or government,—nor can a greater reproach be attached to the rulers of a nation, in as much as there cannot be any neglect of their high trust, more fatal or more difficult to be remedied, than that of education. Without a due attention to this most vital interest of the State in the first instance, all other legislation will be vain and impotent. "*Quid vanae proficiunt leges, sine moribus.*" Education, co-operating with habit and example, is the great former of individual character; and therefore it is evident that ultimately it must fashion and determine the spirit and the character of nations. An enlightened education is the corrector of errors and prejudices, the parent of all right opinions, of all sound principles, the very fountain of truth and virtue. It is the former and enlightener of that public opinion which is above the "sceptered sway;" and while it is the just object of terror to all arbitrary power, to all dominion and influence not founded on right and administered with justice and beneficence; it is the true basis and the sure guardian of the throne that is "established in righteousness." It may be truly regarded as the palladium of a free state, the ark of rational liberty, and will avail more for protecting and securing all rights public and private, than even a free press; for, without education, a free press could do nothing, even supposing, what is scarcely conceivable, that it could exist in such circumstances. In fine, it is scarcely hyperbolical to say, that it is a panacea or universal remedy for almost all the distempers and derangements which can affect or assail the body politic.

But while it is thus omnipotent for good, it is scarcely less so for evil. It may become a powerful engine in the hands of a party or a faction, and be perverted to the worst and most dangerous purposes, to the destruction of civil and religious liberty, to the support of bigotry, superstition and arbitrary power. It is like the lever of Archimedes; the party which can grasp and wield it, if—(which we fear is rare and almost unexampled in the history of the world)—their virtue, patriotism and love of liberty, do not get the better of their ambition and party feelings, may, and at the long run, inevitably will lay prostrate all opposition, and mould to their views and interests, the whole community. The very foundations of truth and liberty are sapped and subverted when this potent engine is usurped and engrossed by the ambitious, the bigotted, or by designing men, whatever may be their party and views. What a melancholy example of the malignant and fatal power of a perverted education with regard to the genius, learning, religion, and liberties of a people, does the present condition of Spain, Italy and Portugal exhibit, and what a lesson do they impress on the minds of the statesman and legislator, of the patriot and the philosopher. It is true, these are examples of its most extreme abuse, but they suggest a warning which observation and experience will amply confirm, that whatever, in any degree, tends not only to pervert and corrupt the spirit of national education, but even to contract its power, and to diminish its influence and efficacy, is an evil of the greatest magnitude. In every country, therefore, which is qualified to appreciate and not unworthy to enjoy the blessings of freedom and education, the legislature will not only provide means for its support on an adequate scale, but will watch with the most jealous vigilance and circumspection over the administration of its funds and institutions, and adopt every possible precaution against all usurpation or intrusion on the part of those who may have any temptation to enlist its agency in their own cause. As nature, by her universal and perfect laws, has communicated and diffused alike to every part of the creation, the indispensible blessing of air and light, so the supreme power in every state should provide that education not only be not intercepted from any, even the humblest member of the community, but that it be communicated to all in the fullest extent of its advantages. It should, as much as may be, preclude all possibility of any individual, of any faction or body, narrowing, intercepting or perverting, in any measure, this most needful and beneficent provision for the intellectual, moral and political life, health, soundness and vigour of the social system.

The principle now universally admitted after a long and violent opposition, that the diffusion of knowledge is a blessing to society, and that therefore it becomes a political as well as a moral and religious duty to promote education, we regard as one of the greatest triumphs which truth has gained in our day, indeed, we might have said, in any period of the world. But, notwithstanding this triumph, we must not flatter ourselves that the cause of education is not exposed to some danger still, from the selfish machinations of designing and ambitious men. However they may have been compelled to abandon their old ground, and to renounce, if not the spirit, at least the appearance and profession of hostility to its cause, they are too deeply impressed with a sense of its mighty power, as an engine of party, not to endeavour, by all arts, to draw it entirely into their own hands, and to wield and exert it for their own purposes. They have not changed their spirit or their principles, but merely their language and mode of reasoning. Though they may not openly avow it, they have the same end still in view, but they pursue it by a new path. They have not abandoned the field, but merely shifted their ground, and changed their mode of attack. Those who formerly looked, or had they lived half a century earlier, would have looked, as we shrewdly conjecture, with aspect malign on the progress of popular education, and on all who were in earnest to promote it, are now either persuaded or shamed into an abjuration of this obsolete heresy. But still they are ill at ease on this subject. They seem to forget that if education is free and unfettered, its progress is the progress of knowledge, and therefore of truth, and can never do hurt to any party, to any system, of which the spirit and tendency are in harmony with truth. Or if they do not forget this, they at least betray a consciousness that they cannot safely trust their cause to the strength of its own merits, or suffer education to operate with its free, full and uninfected influence.

Accordingly, they now contend that though it is the duty of the state to promote education, it is bound to place its administration exclusively in the hands of certain bodies, and to incorporate with it certain principles political and ecclesiastical. They assume a principle or axiom, the truth of which must be admitted, but reason from it after a fashion not uncommon with them, according to which, almost any conclusion may be deduced from any premises. Religion, say they, and we most cordially assent to the proposition, ought to form a main object of attention in the education of youth. But we deny absolutely the conclusion attempted to be drawn, that a certain establishment, or particular body or order of men in the community, be exclusively invested with the government of seminaries of education, and the instruction of youth. From the proposition that religion ought to form a prominent part of education, it can never be deduced on any principles of legitimate reasoning, that the whole management and controul of it should be vested in the hands of the Clergy of a particular Church. But this, so far as we are able to discover, is the purport and amount of Dr. Strachan's reasoning in favour of the exclusive character of the University, for the erection of which, he has lately obtained a charter from his Majesty. Does the Doctor seriously believe that languages, science, and philosophy cannot or ought not to be taught without engrafting upon them the theology or politics of some religious establishment? Is there not a time and a place for everything? Would it not produce utter confusion and perplexity of ideas to the professor and to the pupils, to jumble together things so remote and heterogeneous as Chemistry, Mathematics, Physics, and the Ecclesiastical Polity or Theological Peculiarities of a certain Church? If this is not implied in the Doctor's argument—if it merely imports that the professor ought to have a general sense of Religion, to be a believer in the Gospel, and to inculcate and enforce wherever it is natural or seasonable in the course of his instructions, sound principles, moral and religious, on his pupils, we readily concur in the truth of the position, but cannot perceive what connection it has with the conclusion which it is brought to support, namely, the vesting of the exclusive controul of education in some one Church or Ecclesiastical Body. We readily admit that the Professor should not be a Deist, much less an Atheist; we think he ought to be a Christian in the strictest sense of the word, one heartily attached to Religion, and in earnest to patronise and promote its faith and influence among his pupils, so far as it may, without any violence, or any departure from his appropriate functions, he in his power so to do. But while we admit all this, we do think it would be altogether from the purpose of his office and the nature of his duties, to become ex-cathedra, the advocate of any particular set of doctrines or form of worship, or to endeavour directly or indirectly, to make impressions on the minds of his pupils in favour of any Church, or in any manner or degree to set himself to prepossess the minds of the youth under his charge, for or against any system of Religious Faith, in a College which was professedly open to pupils of all denominations. And if it were in such circumstances unwarrantable and inconsistent with the design and constitution of the University to tamper with the religious faith and principles of the youth who might attend it, we would be glad to be informed what necessity demands, or what utility recommends, the exclusion of loyal, learned and able men of whatever sect or party, who are firm believers in the truth of the Christian Religion.

The youth ought to be instructed in the peculiar doctrines of their respective Communions, by their Pastors; any attempt to interfere more or less, with their religious principles, would, as we conceive, be inconsistent with the spirit of the Charter: a University or a College, erected wholly or even principally for the purpose of proselytising, we hesitate not to say, would be an enormous evil, an intolerable nuisance; and we are struck with equal astonishment at the folly and the assurance of the man who avows and publishes broadly to the world, a project so monstrously ridiculous! If any one reads the speech of Dr. Strachan, and is unacquainted with the sentiments and views which he has revealed, perhaps with more frankness than discretion, in his various other publications, he may, peradventure, be deceived into the charitable supposition, that the only view of that venerable personage in framing the charter, was to protect the Christian Faith, and to guard against infidelity and irreligion, and that he, simple hearted generous man! was grieved in spirit, when his utmost exertions in favour of a liberal constitution, could only avert the yoke from the necks of the Students, but not prevent its imposition on the Members of the Council—What will be the surprise of such persons when they learn that the Doctor has elsewhere avowed and published to all the world that, for half a century to come, the business of proselytising will afford a sufficient occupation for the academical body over which he presides. Philosophy and learning will be meanwhile laid on the shelf to sleep in peace, until this religious renovation is accomplished, and doubtless will awake from their long slumber with a youthful vigour and renovation in the year of Jubilee.—But, to resume our subject, the Doctor's plot is an excellent plot, and has the merit of being perfectly intelligible, even to the shallowest. Open wide the portals of the University—admit all the youth—invite and encourage them to come in—come in, but how return—how come out?—Proselytes to the true Faith. The raw uninstructed youth under the discipline of this proselytising College, very appropriately placed under the direction of a president, who is himself an illustrious proselyte, will have their minds industriously imbued with the principles of his adopted Church, and to Episcopalise *Sectarians* and *Dissenters*, will employ the wisdom and the zeal of this learned body—while the ostensible and professed object of their Establishment—the care and the culture of Literature, Science and Philosophy are to be suspended for half a century—a period declared to be not more than sufficient for the completion of the great and good work.

"But in vain is the net spread in the sight of any bird." The people of

Upper Canada, who are not of the Communion of the Church of England, will have only two alternatives presented to them, either to deprive their children of a University Education, or to send them to King's College, with the hazard, if not the certainty, of having their religious Faith and Principles shaken or subverted. Rather than incur this danger, they may be inclined to send them to a College in the United States, deeming the peril of political Heresy, less formidable than, as it may be viewed by them, *a religious perversion.*

The people of Upper Canada, who are not of the Episcopal Communion, will, we presume, be disposed to regard the Doctor's University with jealousy and fear, and to say of it as the Fox did when he excused himself for not having paid a visit to the Lion's den with the other animals, who dutifully went to congratulate their monarch on his recovery from a fit of sickness—"I see all the footsteps pointing towards your den—none from it."

We have long beheld with regret, and not without some alarm for the ultimate consequences, symptoms by no means ambiguous or disguised, of a disposition on the part of those who are now vested, almost exclusively with the superintendance and management, or who, at least, exert a paramount influence and controul over the funds and institutions for Education in both Provinces, to make them subservient to their party views.

This we regard as an evil of no ordinary magnitude, and if it be not speedily and effectually remedied, it will assuredly be productive of much excitement and discontent. However painful, it has now become the unavoidable duty of those who have been with the most palpable injustice excluded from all share in the direction of education, to disabuse his Majesty's Government on this very important subject, and most respectfully but earnestly, to solicit the redress of those grievances under which they have hitherto laboured, in consequence, as they firmly believe, of misrepresentation and intrigue. When we consider that the population of these Provinces is made up of almost all the denominations of the Christian world—that the great majority are Catholics—that the remaining population is composed, not only of different religious persuasions, but of different nations, Scotch, Irish, American and English, and that the Episcopal Communion embraces but a very small proportion of the mixed population, it would seem incredible that such exhorbitant pretensions should be avowed, or that they should even have been conceived.

Such pretensions are utterly at variance with all maxims of sound policy, and we cannot but add, of common sense. They are wild and impracticable. They will not, they cannot succeed in such a country as this; and the only effect of urging them, must be to discredit and weaken the Church of England, to excite opposition, disaffection and disgust, and thereby to render their ultimate failure more certain and complete. The advancing of claims so antiquated and obsolete, so repugnant to the spirit of the age in which we live, and so incompatible with the interests and the feelings of this country, seems to reverse the comparison of our Saviour— it is attempting to sew a piece of *old* cloth on a *new* garment, which will inevitably be rent in pieces by the strength and the straining of that to which it is applied. But the advocates for introducing into Canada, the exclusive system with regard to Religion and Education, very prudently forbear from arguing the principle on general grounds of reason or expediency; and in order, as it would seem, to hide the weakness of their cause, and to find some shelter and defence against the assault which they cannot meet directly, they appeal to the Religious and Literary Establishments of Great Britain, and are fain to fight behind the walls and battlements of those venerable and time-hallowed Institutions.—And if we could give them credit for a true sympathy with whatever is valuable and venerable in these noble establishments, we would regard them and their projects with much less distrust and jealousy than we can, with our present sentiments, afford to do. We are so uncharitable as to think that they have set their eye and their heart more on the blemishes than the beauties, more on the defects and imperfections, than the real excellencies which are to be found in these Establishments. We think, to adopt the characteristic expression of Miss Edgeworth's Scotsman, that "it may be doubted" whether the gentleman of whom we speak, sympathise with as lively sincerity with all that these great Institutions bear in their character and design, that is in unison with the liberal wisdom of Bacon and of Locke, as we shrewdly suspect they do with certain relics of Monkish superstition and gothic ignorance.

Now, were we even to admit that the Establishments of Great Britain, Academical and Ecclesiastical, were incapable of any amelioration, and that viewed in relation to the circumstances of the Parent Country, they were absolutely perfect—while we see them gradually, and in some late instances, very rapidly divesting themselves of ancient prejudices, and rubbing off industriously the rust of ages—while we see them wisely availing themselves of the lights of time and experience, nay, adopting the boldest and most decisive measures for the correction of errors and abuses, and the introduction of new and better principles and methods*—

* On this very interesting subject, we beg permission to recommend to the attention of Dr. Strachan, and those who favour his views, a very masterly article in the Quarterly Review, No. 71, in which the Reviewer has compared, and indeed contrasted, the system of the English Universities, with that of the Scotch.—This article is remarkable also, as

waiving all this, we might still ask, are these Establishments to be imitated without any reserve or exception—are they to be applied without any qualification or change to a country, in many respects, very differently circumstanced? If the British Parliament had to devise a new system, Academical or Ecclesiastical, is it perfectly certain that they would resume, without any modification, the old model or pattern framed in times of ignorance, when political philosophy was in its infancy, or at least, in times destitute of many of the lights of enlarged knowledge and experience which we now happily enjoy? The practice of reasoning in this confident and unqualified manner, from the Institutions, whether Academical, Religious, or Political, of the Parent Country, is not, we apprehend, quite so legitimate and trustworthy as it is common. Change of place and of time, almost invariably demands a corresponding change in policy.

But we will not rest the cause on a rejection, *as inapplicable to the case*, of the precedents and examples which Dr. Strachan, we fear, somewhat rashly and imprudently has pleaded in favour of his exclusive system. He has appealed to the Constitution of the Church of Scotland, and of her Universities, as an authority in his favour. This may be regarded, so far as we are concerned, as a sort of argumentum ad hominem, and we shall therefore be somewhat particular in answering it. We will, in the first place, therefore, beg leave to differ altogether from the venerable Archdeacon in his assumption, which is indeed a very sweeping one, that to the exclusive principle in question, Scotland owes the worth, piety and learning of her Sons—for we are bold to aver that it is not merely because Scotland has an established Church, and Universities, Schools, &c., under the superintendance and controul of that Church, with tests, subscriptions, &c., that she has risen to her present eminence, moral and literary—but it is because her Establishments are in spirit and in practice liberal, tolerant and mild—it is because their exclusiveness is scarcely perceptible, scarcely felt—it is because the good sense, intelligence and liberality of the people of Scotland, have in effect exploded these "prisci vertigia ruris," and would be inclined to laugh to scorn this plea which the Doctor has built on the Constitution of her Church and Universities, with no other view than to bolster up a system in most palpable and extreme repugnance to their character and spirit; and with an ingenuity which we cannot but admire, while he applauds their excellence and efficiency, ascribes it wholly to a principle by which he would proscribe her children, in a British Colony, from having any place or portion in the establishments of the Country—

affording a striking example of the rapid progress of enlightened and liberal opinions in the Parent Country, of which any reader may satisfy himself, by comparing this with other articles on the same subject, in the preceding numbers of the work.

and stigmatise them as not worthy to be entrusted with an equal measure of power, privilege and influence with the Sister Establishment.

The Doctor, we perceive, is but little acquainted with the actual state and practice of our Scottish Universities, and still less with their spirit. We do not know that he could have adduced another example more fatal to his cause. For while, in Scotland, the vast majority of the people are attached to the established Church, and the vast majority of the Dissenters are now scarcely to be distinguished from the Members of the Establishment, it is a fact, that there are no tests, and so lightly does the power of the Church, in regard to the exacting of subscriptions to her Creed, bear on our Episcopal Brethren who, let it be particularly noted, are, as soon as they plant a foot on the north side of the Tweed, really and absolutely Dissenters—that, in the Universities of Glasgow and Edinburgh, there are and have been not a few professors of that persuasion who, it is perfectly understood, continue to adhere to their own creed, enjoy a most perfect toleration, and go without any let or impediment to their own chapels—nay, are accustomed to give to their classes holidays on certain of the grand Festivals of their Church, while, meantime, the Presbyterian professors attend their classes, and the general business of the College goes on as usual. Such is the practical liberality of the Scottish Universities, and it affords a most decisive and satisfactory answer to those who allege that harmony and unity of sentiment could not be maintained in an academical senate or council composed of professors differing in religious faith and sentiments. As it is not one of the objects contemplated in the constitution of our Scottish Universities to make converts to Presbytery, there is no more peril of any discord or collision, in consequence of any difference in religious faith, in our College senates, when the interests of education and literature are brought under deliberation, than in any committee of merchants or bank directors similarly composed, who never dream of allowing religious and ecclesiastical questions to be mixed up with the proper business of their respective boards. Of one thing we feel confident, that out of Spain, Portugal or Italy the Doctor would not find a single specimen of an academical establishment to match his proselytising University; and, indeed, such is the spirit of *liberalism* that has now spread abroad, at least through all the Protestant parts of Europe, that we are persuaded they would receive with incredulity or laughter the tidings that a venerable Archdeacon of the Church of England had erected a University in the metropolis of a British Province in North America, for the sole purpose of converting—not the Aborigines to the Christian Faith, not the Catholics to the doctrines of the Reformed Churches—but of bringing over to the communion of his adopted Church the members of the Sister Establishment, to which he himself continued to be attached for a considerable period of his life— and that large sums of money and extensive tracts of land were appropriated, under the same auspices, for this pious and charitable purpose.— But, to resume the subject of our Scottish Universities, we congratulate ourselves and the country on the Doctor's approval of their system; and if he will only take the trouble, in the first place, to inform himself of their true character and actual practice, and frame his College with an enlightened liberality and a just discrimination of local circumstances, with more regard to the spirit than to the letter of his patterns, we could have little doubt that the result would be as honourable to himself as it would be satisfactory and beneficial to the Country. As the vast majority of the population of Canada are not of the communion of the Church of England, and as the members of the Scottish Church, notwithstanding all letters, charts, pamphlets and circulars to the contrary, we are bold to affirm, do greatly outnumber her *bonà fide* adherents, even after all that the zeal of proselytizing has achieved in times past, let the Doctor be counselled to give up his exclusive system, if not on the score of its illiberality, at least of its impracticability; but, at all events, if he would hide from himself and others its weakness and its deformity, let him not bring it into comparison with our Scottish Universities, for this is to aggravate by contrast its illiberality.—We can assure the Doctor, that the religious character of the people of Scotland, so far as we have been able to discover, is not owing chiefly, or even in any considerable degree, to the discipline of our public Schools and Universities, or to the attention paid to it in them; we have, indeed, known some of our youth forget their religious knowledge, and abandon their religious principles there—and with all due respect for the religious character of our Schools and Universities, in which view we doubt not, as in every other, they will be found second to no other Seminaries in the world, we do not give them the credit of producing the religious character of the people. No—we believe that Scotland owes this, much more to the universal and religious observance of the Sabbath day, to the regular attendance of all the people on the services of the Church, and the ordinances of Religion, and above all to her domestic discipline, the pious care of parents and heads of families; she owes it primarily to the *Church in the house.* If we are asked what has produced and diffused this religious character, which, however it may tend to preserve and to perpetuate itself, must have been formed by influences and institutions, external and independent of itself, we would reply, that it seems to us that the primary and grand agency by which this character has been formed, may be traced to the constitution and discipline of our national Church, which is admirably calculated to promote and secure the respectability and usefulness of the Clergy—whom it strictly precludes from all secular offices—prohibits their holding pluralities, obliges all of them to preach and to go through all the duties and labours of the pastoral office, so long as they hold any living in the Church; and while it secures most effectually their temporal provision, has, by establishing the parity of all her Clergy, and forbidding any one to hold more than a single cure, cut off all the temptations that wealth, ambition and the prospect of rising through a long succession of dignities and promotions, present to try the virtue and the self-denial of the Clergy of some other Churches: in short, instead of dazzling her ministers by a display of outward splendour, and intoxicating them with a love of ecclesiastical promotion and advancement, she has taken every possible security that they may have no temptation to forget the simplicity, humility and laborious zeal which alone can form an Apostolical Church or Clergy, and has left them, in fact, no other sources whence to acquire reputation, honour and dignity, than learning, piety and worth.

To all this it may be added that the enlightened and liberal character of her institutions, academical and ecclesiastical, have given to the whole of her population, to the Dissenters, in as large a measure, (certainly with as ample an improvement on their part) as to the immediate members of the Church, all the freedom of conscience and of worship, all the blessings of learning and education, and a competition on almost equal terms with the establishment itself.

The great and happy effects which have resulted from the liberal Constitution, and still more liberal administration of her Establishments for the support of Religion and Learning, are universally known; and we are persuaded that all impartial men who inquire into the causes of that pre-eminence to which Scotland has risen, in the past and present century, in knowledge, learning, piety and moral worth, will agree with us in ascribing it to the manly and enlightened principles which guided our reformers in framing our public institutions, and which, through their operation and influence, have imparted to the national character and spirit, that good sense and liberal tone by which it is distinguished; and which, like a vital influence, has preserved their healthy and vigorous action, and provided for their progressive expansion and improvement.

We cannot forbear to remark in the present instance, that it seems somewhat inconsistent and ungracious, that in a College established by the suggestion, and under the auspices of a Scotsman, who received his education, and is indebted for his learning and usefulness to the Institutions of his native land, the charter should be so framed as to exclude from official dignity and emolument, the honest and attached Members of our Church. Surely the Doctor must have felt himself strongly impelled by the feelings of gratitude, as well as by the pride and the spirit of a Scotsman, to protest against a proscription so illiberal, ungenerous, impolitic, and unjust. What, would you exclude, might he have said indignantly, to those illiberal and bigotted persons, whoever they may have been, who, thwarted and counteracted his enlightened and generous views with regard to the Constitution of the University—would you exclude in a British Colony, the natives of the Sister Kingdom from an equal participation in all the rights, privileges and honours of British subjects—of the natives of the Colony? This, under any circumstances, would be palpable and flagrant injustice. But, in the present case, the grievance is peculiarly aggravated, for it affects a people to whom, of all others, the British Colonies are most peculiarly and deeply indebted, and none of her Colonies more remarkably than the Canadas. To omit all consideration of any part which Scottish valour and spirit bore in the acquisition of this Country to the Empire, it is a fact, notorious to all the world, that the natives of Scotland, chiefly in consequence of their intelligence, learning, and good morals, have contributed, in the most signal manner, to extend, to establish, and to perpetuate the power, the influence, and all that is most excellent and valuable in the character of their Country and her Institutions, as well in Canada, as in the other dominions of Great Britain. They form a most numerous portion of the whole population, perhaps inferior only to the natives who are of French extraction, and if we take into account their intelligence, wealth, learning and consideration, they are, without all question, the most important and respectable part of the British population. Without them, and without the manly spirit of intelligence and enterprise which they carry with them into every part of the world, what would the Colonies of Britain have been at the present day? Our Legislative and Executive Councils are filled with them—our wealthiest merchants, our most substantial and prosperous agriculturalists, our most sober, industrious and well-doing settlers, are Scotsmen; nay, many of the most extensive, populous, flourishing and, we must add, loyal settlements, are purely, or by a vast majority, Scottish. But this is not all. To Scotsmen education in this Colony, owes every thing. Its very Patriarchs and Apostles in Canada, of whom the Doctor might have claimed to himself the well merited honour of being the first in point of time, if not in point of merit, have been almost exclusively Scotch. We might challenge the Country to produce, at this day, any individual of conspicuous merit, who, if he received his education in this Country, did not owe, at least the most important part of that invaluable acquisition to a Scottish Preceptor, or to some learned disciple of some learned adventurer from that land of learning? We could almost fancy that we see the Doctor under the warm inspiration of his Scottish feelings rising into a strain of indignant eloquence, and demanding, in all the "preferved spirit" of his country, of those who would stigmatize her and her sons, by a proscription so basely ungrateful to their merit and their services to the Empire—what would be the consequence of this exclusion? If you shut the door of honourable preferment in your Colonies, against the natives of Scotland, you will inflict a cruel wrong on a most meritorious people, as well as a serious calamity on your Empire. What, (might he have demanded,) would be the condition of your Colonies, if ye were to debar from them, the knowledge, the spirit, the talents, the virtues of the people of Scotland? This would be to strike out the very eye and soul of your foreign dominions; for to Scotland, at least hitherto, they have been almost exclusively indebted for the light of knowledge and learning. To your foreign Empire, Scotland has been the one eye of the Cyclops—deprive it of this organ of intellectual light, and where will ye find the means of replacing or repairing it. It may be wise to consider, ere it be too late, whether there would not be some hazard that the foreign and distant dominions of Great Britain might suggest to our minds, a comparison with the fate of the blind Polyphemus, "Monstrum, horrendum, [informe] ingens, cui lumen ademptum."

(*To be continued.*)

3

Letter to the Honourable Mr. Stanley, on the Relative Claims of the English and the Scotch Churches in the Canadas*

SIR,

Religion and country are sacred names. The love of them is natural to good men, and is so connected with the best feelings and affections of the heart, that to be wanting in them, throws a shade over the whole character. Unhappy must be the condition, or debased must be the spirit of the man, who can calmly and unresistingly stand by and watch the progress of measures inimical to the interests of either. Unhappy must he be, if the circumstances of his lot have left him no choice, but that of patient endurance; base and debased, if, having the means to avert the evil, he yet wants the will to employ them.

With what sentiments then, can my countrymen, can Scotsmen, regard their present situation in this Province. We leave our native land to come to a British, not an English, Province; and therefore with the assured confidence, that we are there to enjoy equal rights, privileges, and advantages, with those possessed by the natives of any other part of the British Empire. But we find here a party, a powerful, and hitherto an all prevailing party, who tell us a very different tale, who tell us we must submit to bear the burden, and wear the badge of inferiority and subjection.

We have a national Church, and a national form of worship, to which we are sincerely attached. If we adhere to them, we are regarded with

* This letter took up the entire issue of August, 1828, of the *Canadian Miscellany; or, the Religious, Literary & Statistical Intelligencer* and some of the accompanying notes were included in September, the last issue of this magazine. The letter itself was not dated in this version. The complete text of the letter and notes is included.

the jealousy, and stigmatised with the name, of dissenters. Is a teacher of our persuasion to be appointed? He finds the powerful interest of a dominant religion arrayed against him. Is an university to be established? Men of Presbyterian principles are incapacitated from holding office in it. Our Clergy can perform the marriage ceremony, even among their own flocks, only through the licence of the magistrate; and the very rites of sepulture have been denied us, unless at the purchase of submitting to the ceremonies of a form of worship at variance with our own. Meanwhile, the English styles herself the Established Church, is protected, and her Clergy paid by the British Government, is laying plans for her future aggrandisement and extension at our expense, and has taken possession of a seventh part of the country as her own.

Surprised at the unexpected aspect of affairs, we seek, but seek in vain, for any thing in the circumstances of our country or Church, that ought in reason or justice to have produced it. Were we in truth the natives, as we seem to be thought, of a conquered and degraded Kingdom, of some subject Province of England, though we might bear these things in sorrow, we should yet bear them in silence. But we have been accustomed to think with honest pride, on our past history, and present state, as evincing, that our country is entitled to all the privileges that belong to a free and independent nation. The pages of our earlier annals paint us contending for ages with a nation, warlike and far richer and more powerful than we, yet sinking not under the conflict; and England accustomed elsewhere to conquer, turning at length away with blunted sword and torn banner from our borders. Is there aught in our subsequent history, that has destroyed that equality which the swords of our ancestors were able to maintain in the field? Not, surely, that our rival consented to receive from us a king, or sought to be incorporated with us as a nation. Have we yielded in the contest, since English and Scottish has been lost in British feeling, and since the rivalry that led us to meet opposed in the hostile plain, has been converted into the more generous emulation of who shall best promote the prosperity and glory of the United Empire? Europe answers for us. When her people record those by whom they have been benefited or delighted, what names are more frequent in their mouths than those of Scotsmen? The whole world can witness in our favour. In what corner of it, have not Scottish enterprise, and Scottish valour, contributed to exalt the glory of the British name? Whose were the hardy limbs, whose the firm hearts, that planted the standard of the Empire on the summits of those very cliffs, that now afford shelter and protection to some, who would oppose the just privileges of their sons? The country speaks for itself, and proves, that its existence adds no mean strength to the British Empire, or lustre to the British character. Let the lover of the human kind search the whole globe—where will he find a spot on which his view can rest, with greater pleasure—where will he find, take them all in all, a more intelligent, a more industrious, a more moral, or happy people than in Scotland?

We seek, equally in vain, for any thing in the national worship itself which should cause it to be so depreciated. Were our attachment to it but lukewarm—had it, as unpropitious to the happiness of mankind, proved itself undeserving the support of those, who might have had the misfortune to have been educated under it; —as the fosterer of sedition, and disloyalty, were it justly regarded with suspicion and jealousy by our rulers; —shame would then shut our mouths, and prevent our advancing aught in its defence. But, on the contrary, we love, we honour our religion —and were it allowed to pride to mingle in such a sentiment, we might well be proud of it. It is the religion of our fathers; that religion, in the cause of which, they toiled and bled; which they raised up amidst suffering and persecution, and left to us as a rich inheritance. Its worth our national character itself speaks, in all that is good and honourable, in which it enters as a vital element. If we are to judge of the tree by the fruit, we need not shrink from a comparison with any Church under the sun. Teachers and taught, alike evince the excellence of the institutions of our own. In learning, in diligence, in virtue, in all those attributes that fit a set of men for becoming the moral and religious instructors of a people, the Clergy of the Church of Scotland are acknowledged to stand pre-eminent. And, if pure religion, the religion of the Bible, that religion which rests in the heart, and displays itself, not in vain parade and empty show, but in subduing evil passions, and traning up its votaries to virtue here, and happiness hereafter, exist on earth, it is to be found among the people to whom they minister.

Or, were our relative numbers and respectability small, when compared with those of the rival sect in this country, we should submit even to a compromise of our rights with more patience, and should feel unwilling, that the interests of an inconsiderable part should disturb the harmony of the whole. But what renders the injustice done us the more galling, is the undeniable fact that, were the numbers of Scotsmen and Englishmen, who, in Canada, wish to adhere to their respective Churches, fairly estimated, we shall be found to outnumber and outweigh our opponents in a seven-fold proportion. If, again, we turn to the recorded principles of national union, we find nought in them on which our adversaries can build their extravagant claims; on the contrary, we find a full equality throughout; we find ourselves guaranteed in all rights, privileges, and advantages, which do, or may belong to the natives of the sister Kingdom.

When I reflect on these things, Sir, I am so far from acquiescing in the justice of the charges of heat and animosity which have been brought against us, that I feel we have hitherto exerted a very remarkable forbearance—a forbearance that can only be well explained, from our habits of deliberating with caution, as of acting with energy. Had we longer stood aloof, and allowed our adversaries to follow out their plans without complaint or remonstrance, we had ill performed our parts towards ourselves or posterity. In taking measures to place the question fairly before the legislature of the Empire, we have done but our duty. Having done so, we have no cause to dread our final success. The British Government has too high a sense of honour and justice to seek to deprive us of our evident rights; it has too much prudence, by an act of manifest injustice, to do aught to alienate the affections of a loyal and spirited people.

But our opponents seek to place the question on other grounds, and to found it on policy and expediency. Our claims rest on national faith; on solemn treaties; on the fitness of our religion, to lead its followers in that path, which the revealed will of the Deity has marked out as the road to eternal happiness; and doubtful indeed, must any policy be, which would run counter to these firm principles. But, I assert, and I am prepared clearly to prove, that did our claims rest on no other basis than that of simple policy and expediency, every enlightened principle of both would give us a decided advantage over those who oppose us.

Let me then, Sir, solicit your attention to this view of the subject, and let us consider what are the relations of Great Britain and Canada, which, constituting the bond of their political union and government, must therefore regulate the principles on which that government is conducted, and determine the expediency of whatever measure it may be called on to adopt.

A community of interests is the firmest basis of union among Governments, "*idem velte, et idem nolle, eademum firma amicitia est*," is a maxim as true, in regard to states, as parties. It is happily on these grounds that the connection of Great Britain and Canada rests.

Britain, a great manufacturing and commercial nation, abounding in capital, redundant with population, finds her own welfare connected with that of a people, who take from her the products of her manufacturing industry, who offer an asylum to her superfluous population, and who supply her with the raw materials, which she cannot so easily raise within her immediate territories. —We, again, may esteem the prosperity of the mother country our own, while that prosperity sends us the finished productions of human labour far more cheaply than we could manufacture them—while it gives us in return, a market for the produce of our fields and forests, and while it sends capital to the country to enable us to call forth its abundant resources. While these circumstances in the relations of the two countries continue, and it is impossible for us to assign a time, when they shall cease, so long will it be for the benefit of both to remain under a common government. Capital will then flow more plentifully from the one country to the other, because it will flow far more securely; the commercial relations of the two countries will run no risk of being interrupted, and thence destroyed; and, above all, that lamentable but unavoidable jealousy of separate states, which leads to mutual seclusion and privation, because one will not embrace a good, least it should prove a greater benefit to its rival, can have no place while we form a common people.

To these ties which connect Canada thus intimately with Great Britain, there is added yet this other, that great part of the population of the country is of British descent, and that consequently their manners, feelings, and habits, partake to a certain extent of those of the parent state. While there is no separation of the interests of the two countries, this circumstance must also be allowed most powerfully to cement their union.

These things then—an ultimate connection of interests, a similarity to a certain extent of manners and feelings—are the basis of our union with Great Britain. Besides these, there seems not any other. Force forms not any of our relations with the mother country. We are not held together, either by the necessities of geographical situation, by the right of conquest, or by any other of those compulsory circumstances, which have place in the union of some parts of this great Empire. Ireland is separated from the neighbouring island by but a narrow firth; its destinies must therefore be connected, and must, in a measure, depend on those of its more powerful neighbours.

The bravery of our armies has given us the command of a vast territory in the East Indies, and has put it in our power to adopt what system we please in its government, and to impose on its inhabitants the laws that to us seem best.—The sins of our fathers have put under our controul the unhappy beings who till the soil of the Western Indies; and while our troops are the instruments that maintain the influence thus acquired, it is fit that we should regulate the concerns of them, and of the masters who keep them to their task, according to our pleasure.

In all these cases, force may, and in some of them it must be employed; but it enters not into the national relations of Great Britain and Canada; nor, I believe, will any one be hardy enough to affirm, that it ought to make a necessary part of the system which connects them.

From these principles, three tests, for determining the relative expediency of protecting the one or the other of the rival sects, may be deduced.

1st. Which form of worship is best calculated to promote the prosperity of the colony?

2d. Which will most effectually diffuse among us British habits and feelings?

3d. Which is most congenial to the state of society that exists in Canada, and therefore least requiring the aid of adventitious power?

1st. The excellency of any religious system, considered merely as a means of promoting the prosperity of society, is chiefly to be estimated by its tendency to restrain offences against the laws, against the state, against morality. If experience then be a fit guide—if from what has been, we may safely infer what is to be—we may form a judgment of the effects likely, in this respect, to flow from the operation of the rival systems in Canada, from those which they have produced, in those parts of the British Empire, where they have been already long established. In England and Scotland, where they exist apart—in Ireland where they are mingled together.

Compared with the population of the two countries of England and Scotland, what then is the relative amount of those offences between man and man, which occur in them, and of which the laws take cognizance?— of murders, of robberies, forgeries, fraudulent bankruptcies, and the long list of criminal delinquencies? What is the amount, estimated in the same manner, of those transgressions which are not directly under the controul of the laws; of licentiousness, of intemperance, of debauchery? What, for instance, compared with their respective population, is the proportion of illegitimate births in the two countries?

Or, to what extent have offences against the state, seditious opinions, principles, actions, combinations to destroy the public tranquillity and established government, prevailed in the southern, compared with the northern part of the Island?

We may safely leave the answer to those questions with our opponents.

Nor will their cause be in the least advanced by a reference to Ireland. There they will find, that obedience to the laws, tranquillity and happiness, have kept equal pace with the progress of the Presbyterian faith.

I am willing to admit, what may undoubtedly be urged, that other causes than the influence of their religious institutions, have operated in enabling the inhabitants of the northern parts of the British Isles, to derive more happiness from their lot, and therefore to be more contented with it, than those of the south. But, with all those admissions, there is a mass of facts remaining, sufficient to show very evidently, that experience does by no means hold forth the Episcopal form of worship, as more fitted than the Presbyterian, to promote the wellbeing and tranquillity of a British population.* As far then as the mere prosperity of the colony itself is concerned by the relative measures in question, I hold that we have a decided advantage over our opponents.

We have now to consider which of the two measures is best calculated to diffuse among us, in Canada, British habits and feelings. And here, at the first blush of the question, finding Episcopacy the established religion of the most extensive and powerful part of the mother country, I am willing to allow, that we might be disposed to conceive, that as far as religious institutions form the habits and feelings, it were better suited than Presbyterianism to give a British tone to the sentiments and affections of the Canadian population. But this first impression is dissipated by a more attentive consideration. It must be admitted, that it is only so far as Episcopacy prevails in fact and reality, not so far as it is established in form and name; so far as it is seated in the heart, not so far as the outward behaviour may be bowed to its observances, that it can in reality be said to enter into the composition of British feeling and character. Now, if, as I believe to be the case, Episcopacy is even in England the religion chiefly of the higher orders; if it is largely dissented from by those in the lower walks of life; and if, even they who, in this class, submit to its ordinances, do so, not so much from choice as from necessity; if so far from being really established in Ireland, the attempt to establish it has been a chief of the real or nominal causes of the discontent and confusion that pervade that unhappy country; if, again, on the other hand, Presbyterianism is in truth and not in form established as the national, I may say, as the sole religion of Scotland, an integral part of the Empire; if, in spite of the very different encouragement which the two have received in Ireland, its votaries there outnumber those of the other Protestant Church; and if in England, the ministry of the pastors, either of the dissenting or established Churches, is beloved and followed by the mass of the people, nearly in proportion as it assimilates itself to the tenets and doctrines of Presbyterianism; if, these things be, as I believe they must be allowed to be, truths—then, surely, it cannot in candour be said, that Episcopacy has any claims very superior to Presbyterianism, to form a constitutent part of the British character, or to frame our modes of thinking and acting to a similarity with those, which regulate the habits and feelings of the population of the mother country.

But besides the power which the mere institutions of religion exert in forming the character of a people, there is an influence, apparently

* I might here advert to the comparative expense which has hitherto attended the two establishments, but they have so often, of late, been contrasted on this point, that I believe it unnecessary.

less direct, but perhaps more important, which arises from the particular feelings, manners and bias of the Clergy who preside over these institutions. These, from the rank which they hold, and from the respect which is paid to their opinions, give a certain tone and character to the judgments and inclinations of the society with which they mix. If, then, it is desirable that our partialities and affections should in Canada incline towards Britain, it is also desirable that as great a proportion as possible of men placed in the influential station of ministers of religion should be Britons. Dr. Strachan has himself stated that the late Bishop of Quebec found that "gentlemen of education and zeal in his Church, refused to forsake their homes and the endearing associations of early years, to come to so distant and inhospitable a colony."

This statement seems perfectly correct, and hence the proportion of Englishmen, by birth and education, who, in this colony, form part of the English Church, is altogether trifling. The deficiency is supplied, by educating in the colony, native Canadians for the Church, and by making proselytes among the Clergy of other Churches.

On the contrary, the Scotch Clergy of the national Church are, to a man, Scotsmen; and, from the cheapness of education in Scotland, and the more moderate views of her Clergy, there is no doubt, that suitable encouragement in Canada, would readily attract from thence, any additional number of Clergymen, of respectable abilities and character, that might be necessary. Now, though it would be both prudent and just, to place the native Canadian on the same footing with these, and although this is a measure, which I am satisfied the Scotch Clergy in Canada are most anxious to bring about, and which I am assured they have every prospect of accomplishing, still it can scarcely be supposed, but that a fair competition would leave a large opening for native Britons to establish themselves in the respectable and influential character of popular Clergymen. These are the men who, perhaps, of all others, have most power to promote that community of habits, feelings and affections, which bind us to the parent country, by the strong ties of mutual sympathy and esteem; and that Church which promises to establish, throughout the colony, the largest proportion of such men, is in a particular manner deserving the protection of government.

I have now, in the third place, to consider which of the two systems is most congenial to the state of society that exists in Canada, and therefore least requires the aid of adventitious power for its support. For, I assume it as a principle that, as our connection with the mother country arises not from any compulsatory circumstance, but from the reciprocal benefits that flow from that connection, force does not form any of the bonds of our political union, and must always, when introduced, have a tendency to lessen the stability of that union, and can therefore never, with safety, be brought extensively into action, nor ought ever to be employed but in cases of the most urgent necessity.

I am persuaded that the Church of England is not naturally adapted to prevail in Canada, and that it can only obtain an extensive footing among us through compulsion; whereas that of Scotland is suited to our desires and wants, and requires but little encouragement to spread wide throughout the Colony, and to take firm root among the population of British descent in Canada. To establish the former part of this conclusion, it is not necessary for me to enter into any discussion concerning the suitableness of the present state of that Church, to the people of England. Even admitting that she suits the state of that country, it follows not thence that she is adapted to the order of things in this.

We have seen that there are many circumstances in the nature of things which tend to cement the union of Great Britain and Canada, and the operation of which, if we seek not to establish it on less secure grounds, must long, very long preserve that union entire. But it cannot be denied, that there are others, and founded in an equally immutable basis, that tend to separate the character of the people of the two countries, and which render institutions and establishments that may be suited to the people of the one, totally at variance with the habits and feelings of those of the other. We shall be satisfied of this truth, if we attend to the different elements of which society is composed in the one country and the other.

In Britain there is a wide diversity of ranks, arising partly from the vestiges of the feudal system, partly from the immense accumulation of wealth, which successful commerce and manufactures have heaped up. There is a proud and powerful Aristocracy, a persevering and substantial middle class, a lower order, industrious indeed, but needy, and compelled to make their wills bend to their necessities, and submit to the mandates of their superiors. All substantial power is in the hands of the first class— the influence which the others exert, is indirect and precarious. It is widely different in Canada. Here, moderate industry and prudence secure to every man competence and independence. Every man thus feels, that he has power to exert that wish which is natural to all men—to have a voice in what concerns their interest or feelings. Nor is there any thing to keep this natural propensity in check.

Landed property is not of that value, and is not so divided; neither has wealth so accumulated in the hands of a few, or is likely so to accumulate, as to train up a powerful class, who may lord it over those beneath them. We are all here very much on a level; and our conditions and habits are rapidly and inevitably approximating us to that system of liberty and equality, which prevails in that portion of this continent formerly colonised by Great Britain. This conclusion, it is vain for the politician either to deny or regret; let him only endeavour, and let us hope and trust, that we may ever retain kindlier and better feelings for the country of our common origin, than it has been the fortune of events to give to our Southern neighbours.

There is not, in truth, a prouder man than the Canadian farmer. He has no superior; he is not dependent on the assistance, scarcely on the co-operation, of a single individual.

His own land, by the moderate exertions of his own family, supplies him with all the necessaries, and with many of the luxuries of life.

The materials of the house that shelters him, and the fire that warms him, he has found on his own property; the clothing that protects him from the winter cold, and summer heat, has been made from his own flax and the wool of his own flocks, by the hands of his household; the vegetables that supply his table, the animals he slaughters for it, the cider that refreshes his meals, the very sugar that sweetens his tea, and all that variety of fruits, that would attract the most fastidious appetite, are the produce of his own fields, and orchards, and woods. He feels and enjoys those comforts—nor is it the least of the gratification they afford him, that he can contrast them with former privation, and reflect that they are all the fruit of his own exertions. He has raised himself and his family from indigence to abundance, and placed them beyond the fear of future want; he has done so by his own successful enterprise and persevering industry; he is to be excused if these contemplations raise him in his own eyes, until he scarcely thinks there is a wiser or better man in existence than he. Hence arises a spirit which some would characterise as high and independent, others as self-conceited and self-important, but which, how-ever it might by different people be designated, must be allowed by all to give the possessor a due sense of his own consequence, and to lead him to resist the assumption of every sort of pretension and authority, of which he cannot clearly see the grounds. It is not difficult to perceive, that the feelings which thus pervade our society, and the form which it is assuming among us, are totally opposed to the principles and spirit of the Church of England. A very slight examination of her most prominent features will satisfy us, that she is in fact only suited to a country where there is a wide diversity of ranks—a class powerful enough to govern—a class weak enough to be governed.

She boasts that popular violence had no hand in her reformation; and her present condition well declares, that the people had no vote in determining the form she was to assume; for, it is such as kings and nobles would alone be pleased to bestow. These have divided with her the riches and influence, of which she once had the sole possession; they have purified her of the gross superstition and extravagant pretentions of her parent, but it was no part of their plan to give any influence to the inferior orders: the interests of the people were therefore entirely forgotten, their only part is to pay tithes and listen to him, whom their superiors set over them.

What is the result? If we look into the condition of the Church of England, in England, we shall find its members possessing much curious and elegant learning, men of polished manners and fine feelings; having, in short, all those qualities which are esteemed in the upper walks of life; but taken as a body, though to this as to all other very general conclusions, there must be many exceptions, they will be allowed to be wanting in that simple eloquence and strenuous exertion, which are valued by the body of the people, and which it is necessary that he should possess, who would make an effectual impression on them.—While human nature is human nature, we may rest assured, that he who has been trained up to the prospect of the patronage of men of rank and learning, will seek chiefly to become the fine gentleman and scholar, while he who knows that the success of his future prospects, must be measured by his reputation among the bulk of his hearers as a preacher, and his ability to excite among them religious feelings, will seek chiefly, and therefore most successfully, to acquire the qualities, which characterise a useful and popular preacher—a flowing and commanding eloquence, and a habit of readily expatiating on the truths and promises of revelation. But not only is this state of things little favourable to the growth of eloquence, but it renders that eloquence of a sort, that can only be relished by those of superior rank and refinement. He who understands how to impress his audience with the importance of the truths of revealed religion, will mould his harangue to the habits and conceptions of those whom he chiefly addresses; as St. Paul himself, when discoursing to a Grecian auditory, did not disdain to quote from one of their own poets.—If seeking to win the attention of men of refinement and taste, whose minds have been trained to contemplate the whole course and operation of nature; to consider the relations of its various parts, and their mutual connections and dependencies—the duties which his condition, as a moral agent, seems to impose on man,—and the beauty and excellence of virtue— he will hold up the gospel as a means of reconciling the conflicting principles of good and evil, with the perfections of the Deity,—as pointing to that virtuous and honourable path, which reason itself indicates, as assuring to those who tread in it, a far more certain and splendid reward, than unaided reason dared to promise. He, again, who addresses himself to those who have had no leisure to devote to those contemplations—who, but for the gospel, would be left to commit, whatever their desires prompted and their opportunities permitted, will enlarge on the guilt of human nature, the boundless love of God, in devising and executing a plan for the salvation of creatures, so fallen and depraved, and, by dwelling on all those topics, which address the heart, rather than the understanding, engage the affections on the side of religion, seek to give it a place in the soul, and raise it up, as a barrier to the approach of surrounding evil.—Thus, in seeking to attain the same end, the preacher will naturally vary his mode according to the condition of those to whom he directs his discourse. But besides this diversity of manner in attaining the end, the end itself is not exactly the same.

Moral delinquencies assume a lighter or darker shade, according to the degree of evil that results from them, and are consequently measured to a certain extent by the rank which the agent holds in society. It has been remarked by a celebrated author, "that in every civilized society, in every society where the distinction of ranks has once been completely established, there have been always two different schemes or systems of morality, current at the same time; of which the one may be called the strict or austere; the other the liberal, or if you will, the loose system. The former is generally admired and revered by the common people: the latter is commonly more esteemed and adopted by what are called people of fashion. The degree of disapprobation with which we ought to mark the vices of levity, the vices which are apt to arise from great prosperity, and from the excess of gaiety and good humour, seems to constitute the principal distinction between those two opposite schemes or systems. In the liberal or loose system—luxury, wanton, and even disorderly mirth, the pursuit of pleasure to some degree of intemperance, the breach of chastity, at least in one of the two sexes, &c., provided they are not accompanied with gross indecency, and do not lead to falsehood and injustice, are generally treated with a good deal of indulgence, and are easily either excused or pardoned altogether. In the austere system, on the contrary, those excesses are regarded with the utmost abhorrence and detestation. The vices of levity are always ruinous to the common people, and a single week's thoughtlessness and dissipation is often sufficient to undo a poor workman for ever, and to drive him through despair upon committing the most enormous crimes. The wiser and better sort of the common people, therefore, have always the utmost abhorrence and detestation of such excesses, which, their experience tells them, are so immediately fatal to people of their condition.—The disorder and extravagance of several years, on the contrary, will not always ruin a man of fashion; and people of that rank are very apt to consider the power of indulging, in some degree of excess, as one of the advantages of their fortune, and the liberty of doing so without censure or reproach—as one of the privileges which belong to their station. In people of their own station, therefore, they regard such excesses, with but a small degree of disapprobation, and censure them either very slightly or not at all."*—We must admit these observations to be, in general, just, and to have some truth, even when applied to the Professors and Preachers of Christianity.

From all these causes, two sects exist, and must exist throughout christendom. Hot and unreflecting men in each, have applied harsh terms to designate their opponents. The name signifies not very much; it will, however, be allowed that the Protestant Church, in the British dominions, is divided into two parties, and that the Church of England is at the head of what Smith calls the liberal or loose system, and is opposed to that which, both from its doctrines, and its manner of inculcating them, will ever have most favour with the people.

Such is the Church of England, and with all her imperfections—in possessing her share of which, I am by no means disposed to allow that she has escaped the lot of all terrestrial things—yet, as the Church of England, and when confined to England, I willingly admit that her existence produces many beneficial results, and that even her defects may be tolerated. Her Clergy form a link, an imperfect one, no doubt, but still, one that cannot well be spared between the lower and higher orders. They excel in all the gentle and conciliating virtues of charity and benevolence—and were the people of England, or even Ireland, questioned; though, I believe, they would not assent to their being the men whose ministry they preferred to all others—they would yet, I am sure, bear willing testimony to their being a race of good and benevolent gentlemen, and kind masters, whom they respected and loved, who soothed the sufferings of their lot, and aided them to bear its hardships without repining or murmuring. And as to the pomp and power that wait on the higher order of her Clergy —it may *there*, with reason, or at least, with some share of it, be said— the Church must have, at her head, men of wealth and influence, that she may maintain her rank and estimation among a proud aristocracy— and that, if the body of the people have no choice in their spiritual guides, they may the more readily submit to this, seeing the government of their temporal concerns is held by their superiors.

Yet, even in England, it cannot be denied—that this state of things

Wealth of Nations, B. 5, C. 1.

has raised up against her a very numerous and powerful body, who regard her riches and influence with evident jealousy and envy—that the acknowledged incapacity of her teachers to meet the wants of the people, has caused dissent to prevail, to an extent that alarms her friends, and is only kept within its present limits, by the poverty of those among whom it would else have place. I am, then, utterly astonished, how it could possibly be thought, by any one acquainted with the spirit of that Church, and the character of the population of British extraction in Canada, that she is calculated to take firm root in the soil of this country. I have had little success in my attempt to delineate them, if it be not at once perceived that they are completely opposed. The Church of England is given to pomp and splendour, and the higher orders of her Clergy have all that haughtiness and manner and life, and those aristocratical habits and propensities, which the possession of wealth and power, and the associating with those who do possess them, infallibly create. The British Canadian, again, feels highly his own importance, and is jealous of the least assumption of superior consequence, or of authority for which he cannot see an adequate foundation.

The grounds of the superiority which mere birth, science or learning would claim, he cannot understand, and, therefore, will not admit. He allows the power of wealth but as adding to the enjoyment of the possessor; feeling his own independence, he bows not to the riches of the rich man, he would look on any assumption of superiority on that account as a mere usurpation; an usurpation which could not be too strenuously resisted, or speedily overthrown—and which would be doubly galling to him, were he to imagine, that the means of maintaining it were unjustly drawn from funds, of which he alone ought to have the disposal. Were it possible to suppose that a few of the dignitaries of the Church of England were settled in Canada, and supported at the expense of the Colony, in any thing like the power and splendour, which they possess in England, I am satisfied that they could not be maintained in their situations for many years. To preserve tranquillity in the Colony, it would be absolutely necessary that they should be removed. Hitherto, it is true we have seen but little of that body. Hitherto, that Church has been able to assume but little of that rank and consequence, which she has acquired at home; nor has she yet been able to bear forward the higher ranks of her Clergy, to that commanding station which they there maintain. From the little that we have seen, however, we may form an estimate of what a future day may witness, should the plans of aggrandisement, which she is now forming, be realized. What then has been the consequence of that union of Church and State—of that ambition to direct the affairs of the one as well as the other—to mingle with the great as companions—and to be men of political importance, which the English Church claims as a right for those at her head—what has been the consequence of this line of conduct in Canada, in the only instance, where there have been both the power and the will to follow it out? Has such conduct been popular—has it conciliated our goodwill and esteem? Could the question be put over the whole Province, I fear there would be but one answer of dissent. On the contrary, it has been universally reprobated, and has excited the most unequivocal marks of public disapprobation and dislike. True it is, the individual in question, may be unworthy of the hostile feelings which the mass of the population entertain towards him—and that, warmly supported by all ranks of the Clergy of his Church, and by his numerous party of friends and followers—he affects utterly to despise them. So, no doubt, might his more wealthy successors. The existence of such feelings, however, proves that such men are very dangerous to the tranquillity of the Country, and to the peaceable rule of the government that supports them.

Nor does the appearance of the Church of England seem better calculated to win our esteem, when we view her in another light.—No form of Church Government can naturally flourish in Canada, which does not give to the people the power of choosing their own pastors. What would be their feelings then, were their pastors appointed as in England? how would a man accustomed to have a voice, at least in all that affects his interests, and believing himself perfectly competent to form a judgment of the preacher, who is best adapted to his wants, bear to be told, Mr. A. is to be appointed, he is brother to Lord B., or he is said to be a man of most gentlemanly and engaging manners, and a great favourite of Bishop C., or even, he is an excellent classical scholar, or an admirable mathematician, and went through all his classes and trials with great eclat? Did the individual possess all the other qualities which his people would deem desirable, yet, I may safely say, that the feelings of jealousy and dislike which his being so appointed, must infallibly generate, would blast his future success, and mar all his utility. But we have seen that the qualities, which the discipline of that Church tends to call forth, are not such as make a preacher successful, and popular, and useful, to the class of people among whom he would have to minister in Canada. They would therefore feel such an appointment as a gross oppression,—an oppression to which they would not long be disposed patiently to submit. Let us recollect that this is no light matter—they feel their need of an efficient preacher—one whose words reach their hearts—whose zeal and industry are indefatigable—who may be able to awaken in their breasts, and in the breasts of their families, a sense of the importance of the things of another world, and to raise them above the frailties and sufferings of this. You give them one, who, we shall admit, is learned, respectable and pious, but whose discourses seem to them dry, cold, and unintelligible, and from whose ministry they can reap little either of benefit or delight.

He thinks he has discharged his duty when he has gone over the ritual of his Church, and read a learned and orthodox discourse, and is disposed to lay the blame on the unhappy prejudices of his flock, if they hear him without attention or pleasure. They, again, naturally contrast the feelings with which they listen to him, and the effects on their conduct and happiness, which his labours produce, with the happier results that flow from the ministry of some one whose acquirements are more fitly adjusted to their habits and wants; they feel the great diversity; they impute the cause of it to the preacher; can it be supposed that they would not resent his being placed over them without their consent, as a grievous injury; can it be believed that they would not seek, by all means in their power, to do away with the system that produced it.

The history of the Reformation in Scotland, is the very reverse of that which had place in England. The Church of Scotland was founded on the complete overthrow of superstition and spiritual tyranny, and was raised up amid the principles of civil and religious liberty, when these were in all the vigour which success and recent origin could give them. Its original constitution and form declare the elements from whence it arose. These proclaim freedom within and without—they give to the people the choice of their own pastors, and establish an equality among the pastors themselves. The Clergyman is chosen by those, who are most interested in obtaining one, who may satisfy their wants, and who best knows what their wants are; he looks only to God and his people, and, while he discharges his duty to them, dreads the frown of no superior.

This form of Christianity, so much more simple and less costly than that of Episcopacy, shows, by the condition of the people among whom it prevails, how well it is adapted for the diffusion of genuine religion, and the promotion of general happiness and peace. There can be no question that it is well suited to the state of society in Canada.—Its doctrines have been characterised as calvinistical, austere, puritanical; these terms seem to imply that it is the religion of the people. Accordingly, wherever a similar form has been established, it has commanded their suffrage. Adam Smith remarks that "the Presbyterian Clergy have more influence over the minds of the common people than perhaps the Clergy of any established Church, and that it is accordingly, only in Presbyterian countries that we ever find the common people converted without persecution, completely, and almost to a man, to the Established Church."* Its original form, giving the election to the congregation, suits our liberal notions. It is indeed true, that this original constitution of our national Church, exists now, generally, only in name, having in reality, been nearly done away with by the preponderating influence of the higher orders, and by the inconveniencies found to arise out of a popular form, from the licentiousness of a people not trained to the use of liberty. In this country, however, it would naturally resume its original spirit, which in Scotland has not been extinguished, but is merely kept in subjection, by a sort of legal ingenuity, the form remaining as of old.

In a word, whether we regard the happy effects, which experience warrants us to draw as resulting from the prevalence of Presbyterianism among a people, or the additional strength of attachment to the Parent Country, which its diffusion would create, or the facility with which it might be spread among us, I see not any other form of Presbyterianism, that can be at all put in competition with it, and least of all, can that of the Episcopacy of the Church of England.

Experience has hitherto served fully to confirm all that I have advanced. The Church of England protected, and her Clergy liberally paid by the Parent State, has hitherto made but an uncertain and feeble progress—while that of Scotland, under the pressure of the slights and neglects of the powers that be, has been well supported by the people—has obtained a firm hold of their affections, and even in nominal adherents out-numbers her rival. While, so far from the spread of Episcopacy having added to the stock of British feeling, and increased our attachment to the Parent State, it has been only remarkable for the discontent and murmurings, which its progress has excited. Whereas, on the other hand, where the religion of the Church of Scotland has greatest sway, there is the firmest seat of loyalty and devotion to the cause of Britain—there the principles of her government have been held in the greatest respect, and the enemies of her ascendency, have even met the most determined opposition.

It has indeed been asserted by the advocates of the Church of England, that the encouragement given to that Church, must create in the people, a feeling of attachment to the Parent Country, and that her actual progress in Canada shews, that there is a disposition on the part of our population, to place themselves under her banners. Both assertions may, without difficulty, be refuted. It would indeed be a phenomenon, unprecedented in history, if the attempt violently to impose a system of religion on a people, who should conciliate their regard, and no one who has had an opportunity of observing the spirit which the attempt has generated in

* *Wealth of Nations*, B. 5, C. 1.

Canada, and which now so clearly manifests itself, can, for a moment, believe that this country is likely to form an exception to a general rule. And as for her progress, if we arrange her adherents into classes, and analyse in each the motives that have influenced their choice, we may form an idea of what that has actually been. These classes may be reckoned four:—

1st. Those who may be called her natural followers. The population of English, or Irish birth, or descent, who have preserved their adherence to the Established Church of the Mother Country. This class cannot be numerous, for the proportion of settlers of English birth or descent is but small, and of these many are dissenters. The great body of the Irish, are Roman Catholics.

2d. The second class consists of those who may be called her natural proselytes, because their feelings and principles have made them so. It has been said, that the Church of England, when compared with other forms of Protestantism, is the religion of a gentleman. The remark savours of illiberality; yet, we have seen that the form and doctrines of that Church do, in truth, render it more attractive, than its severe and more rigid rivals, to those whose station in life gives greatest latitude to the pursuit of pleasure, and whose minds the refinements of science and taste have rendered more fastidious. The numbers of this class of her votaries, are determined, by the increase of abundant wealth and refinement; I suspect it must, therefore, be long confined within very narrow bounds.

The next two classes have been produced by the direct operation of wealth and power.

3d. There are men whose religion sits so loose about them, that they change it as a garment, according to the caprice or convenience of the hour;—for these, what is said to be the Established Religion, being the most fashionable, and sometimes the most lucrative, will always have charms. The causes which tend to increase this class, must cease to act, should the Church of England be put on the same footing with that of Scotland.

4th. The fourth class has been formed, and is measured by the direct influence of the funds which the wealth of the Church, aided by government, enables it so easily—to scatter over the wilds of Canada—the seeds, as it hopes, of an abundant harvest in future.

£200 sterling, a year, is the sum which the Church is enabled to give her missionaries. This certain income, with the prospect of some addition, is fully sufficient, in Canada, to induce respectable men to accept the office. These are placed in the remote and thinly scattered settlements, where the scanty means of the inhabitants have not enabled them to provide for a pastor, and even, though the form of protestantism, which they profess, may not be that which the people would prefer, nor the pastors themselves of the stamp they would desire—they must still, to a certain extent, attract congregations.

This state of things can only have place while the means of settlers are limited; it must cease when their increasing prosperity enables them to provide pastors more suited to their tastes and necessities; it is, in fact, so ceasing;* and it would cease immediately, were the incumbents to be thrown on the unaided resources of the population. No candid observer will assert, that the attachment of this class, whose members constitute the main body of her nominal followers, is very strong or secure to the Church, whose ministry, the force of circumstances now leads them to attend.

Thus, then, it appears that the Church of England is naturally contracted within the narrow limits of the first and second classes, and is indebted for the nominal footing, she has obtained among the others—not to any qualifications or merits of her own, but solely to the influence of adventitious circumstances. And, with all the aid, which these circumstances have afforded her, it is well known to every one, acquainted with the state of the country, that the ground she occupies among us, is contracted and insecure.

The most conclusive evidence, that can be produced on these points, is that which was given to the select Committee of the House of Assembly of Upper Canada. That Committee examined no less than 51 gentlemen of all parties, on questions arising out of the policy which the Church of England has hitherto successfully pursued in this Province. The result of its labours is highly deserving the attention of all, who are interested in ascertaining the real state and sentiments of the people on religious matters. I select two of these questions, and give a summary of the answers.

Question 4th. Is the tendency of the population of this Province towards the Church of England? Is it spreading over the Province?

Answer, by Elder William Case. I believe but a very small portion of the population (comparatively speaking) is attached to the Church of England. The progress of her establishment is very slow, compared with that of some other denominations. This may arise from various causes—as

1st. From a dislike in the people, to her ceremonies and forms of worship.

2d. From the matter and manner of preaching.

3d. From a want of proper exercise of discipline among her members and professors; and, in some instances, from (as the people consider it) the unchristian-like conduct of her Clergymen.

* Dr. Strachan's Sermon on the death of the late Lord Bishop of Quebec, p. 19.

Answer by the Rev. James Richardson. I believe, from what knowledge I have, that but a small portion of the people of this country are members of the Church of England, compared with some other denominations— and though it has increased in the number of its Churches and Ministers, yet, I believe, it does not increase in its number of members, in proportion to the increase of the population of the Province. To my certain knowledge, many of her members have withdrawn themselves from her communion, and joined themselves to the Methodists.

This may arise from several causes, principally from the want of a christian discipline being exercised, and a dislike to certain practices of some of her Ministers.

Answer by Dr. Dunlop, Warden to the Canada Company:—

In the first part of the question, I would say, certainly not—because, among the Catholics, proselytism is very uncommon. The Presbyterians and Methodists are averse to a set form of worship: and to the former, sponsors in Baptism form a bar to their uniting with the Church of England. I have known more instances than one, when Presbyterians, living at a distance from a Clergyman of their own communion, have attended the Church of England, and even received the Sacrament of the Lord's Supper, after her forms, who came upwards of 80 miles to have their children baptised by a Minister of the Kirk of Scotland.

To the second part of the question, I would say, that the Clergy are spreading over the Province; but that their congregations are not large, nor could they, without assistance, support their Clergy.

James Lyons, Esq., M.P. I am decidedly of opinion, that the tendency of the population of this Province, is not towards the Church of England, and it is not spreading over the Province.

The Honourable Thomas Clark. The tendency of the population of this Province, is not towards the Church of England, the Pastors of which are spreading in the Province.

The Honourable Thomas Baby. I have not ascertained that the tendency of the major part of the population of this Province, is towards the Church of England. There are, already, many English Churches erected in the Province; but, except in our largest towns, I believe they are but thinly attended.

There are forty-four answers given—all in a similar strain, with the exception of—1st., The Attorney General of the Province, John B. Robinson, Esq., who states that he has observed that, whenever a pious and kind Missionary of the Church of England is stationed in any populous part of the Province, he speedily acquires a numerous congregation, and that many individuals join it, who were, before, considered as belonging to other religious denominations." But adds, "How far this might be the case, if such persons had, at the same place, pious and enlightened Ministers of their own, I cannot pretend to say." And further—"The Church of England is rapidly increasing."

This latter assertion is best explained by the answer of John Rolph, Esq., M.P.

If by the "tendency of the population of this Province towards the Church of England," is meant that a greater number, in any given time, become members or communicants of the Church, than of others—I decidedly think there is, at present, no such tendency. But I think the Church of England, as it is called, is increasing—and, in my opinion, from its intrinsic worth and excellence, will increase, if not made an object of jealousy and disgust to christians of all other denominations.

The other exception is that of P. Van Koughnett, Esq., M.P. He states that—"in his own district, (the Eastern,) the tendency towards the Church of England is great. Its members are increasing fast." I am disposed to question the accuracy of that gentleman's statement, both from my own knowledge of that district, and from the general opinion there entertained, that on this point, he has been mistaken.

Question 9th. "What proportion, in your opinion, do the members of the Church of England, in this Province, bear to the whole population?

Answer by Elder William Case. "If we consider those only as her members, who receive the Sacrament of the Lord's Supper, in the Church of England, the proportion of them to the population of the Province, is exceedingly small—perhaps about 1 to 243; but, if we embrace the number composing the congregations of the Church of England as her members, they would bear, in my opinion, the proportion of about 1 to 100 of the whole population of the Province. Estimating the population at 170,000 souls, the proportion of the communicants of the Church of England, to the communicants of other denominations, is, in my opinion, about 1 to 18."

In about this latter proportion of 1 to 18, the number of her adherents is fixed, by taking the average of the amount given by the others answering the question, some rating them as high as one-sixth, others as low as one-twenty-fifth of the whole population.

Answer by Charles Fothergill, Esq., M.P. "It has always appeared to me, that the Episcopalians, properly so called, are the least numerous of christian denominations in the Province."

Answer by Dr. Dunlop Warden of the Canada Company. "So far as my data go, they are not—they are but limited. I would say from one-tenth to one-eighth."

Answer by P. Van Koughnett, Esq., M.P. "I cannot tell."

By John B. Robinson, Esq., Attorney General. "I do not know, nor do I think any body else does."

Honourable Thomas Clark. "A small proportion, perhaps one-fifteenth to one-twentieth."

Every one well acquainted with the state of the Protestant population of Canada, must allow that the Presbyterians, if not the most numerous, is one of the most numerous of the sects into which they are divided. It is true, that of the Presbyterians, many are dissenters from the Church of Scotland; but when it is considered that the tenets of both are the same, and that the only ground of separation, is a difference of opinion on the subject of patronage, a question that can never have place in this country, it will appear to be owing to casual circumstances, that any such body exists, and that there can be little doubt that it might easily and naturally be comprehended within the limits of the national Church. On this point, the evidence given to the Committee of the House of Assembly, is also decisive.

The 10th question is—"What denomination of Christians, in this Province, do you think the most numerous?"

The witnesses are here divided between the Methodists and Presbyterians, the majority inclining to the former, but uniformly giving their answers in favour of the one or the other. Indeed, there seems little question that, if left to its unaided resources, this Province would present the same appearance in religious matters, that the United States do. There, I believe, the Methodists form the most numerous sect, and the Presbyterians rank next—the former acting as pioneers, and spreading themselves over all the newly settled countries—the latter coming after them, and gradually gaining ground as the people become able to support regular Preachers. This state of things naturally takes place, where no funds are provided by the State, for the religious wants of those, whose situation prevents them from maintaining Clergymen of education, from their own unaided resources. There the Methodists rapidly diffuse themselves, and though many of them are, of course, devoid of any pretensions to learning, and are actuated merely by a sort of blind zeal—yet, unquestionably their labours are, on the whole, productive of great good. They, however, who are best judges of human nature, will, I believe, agree with me in thinking that the advantages which morality and religion would derive from the state giving moderate support to preachers of a higher order, who would avoid exciting that spirit of fanaticism and delusion, which too often subsides into total apathy, would amply repay the expenses attending the measure. With this support, I believe that Presbyterianism would take the lead of any denomination of Christians in North America.

I conceive that I have now fully proved my third head of argument, and have established, that the feelings of the Protestant population of Canada are as decidedly opposed to the pretensions of the English Church, as they are naturally disposed to yield to the more moderate claims of that of Scotland; and that to give the reins to some church politicians and render the Colony, as they express it, English, by forcing over us a church establishment, like that of England, were a policy no less unwise than dangerous. It has already been acted on to an extent that has alarmed every true friend of Britain, and of Canada, and if persevered in, every succeeding year will, I am satisfied, serve further to demonstrate that it is both impracticable and unsafe. Could we ever suppose its supporters to be ultimately so far successful as to establish it in Canada as the dominant religion, I am persuaded that their triumph would be but of short duration. Let us just carry forward our views a little till the period when the dreams of our sanguine projectors are to be realised. Let the Church of England thrive and prosper among us, let her clergy rule over us, and let them be put in possession of such a portion of the good things of the Land, as may be consistent with her dignity, and with the share she claims in her native England. We shall admit that as a body they might be learned, and respectable; but then, by the constitution of their Church and the care of Government, they would be independent of the people, and therefore feeling, and unavoidably showing that the opinion of their flock is of little consequence to them, and, as they are men, allowing the besetting sins of power and affluence to have dominion over them.

Would such a body be able to guard against the progress of dissent? If among the needy and pampered population of England it has made alarming progress—if, already, here, we find churchmen complaining, that, "even where Churches are erected, the persons who give regular attendance are so few as generally to discourage the minister, and that his influence is frequently broken or injured by numbers of uneducated itinerant Preachers, who, leaving their steady employment, betake themselves to preaching the Gospel, from idleness, or a zeal without knowledge,"* what would be the case then? Assuredly the number of these would mightily increase, and they would be of a higher order; the increased prosperity of their hearers would call to the station men of more talent and education; their cause would prosper—dissent would advance with rapid strides—and what a scene would the aspect of affairs then present— a clergy supported in affluence, by the resources, of which Government had put them in possession—a people—disliking their Ministry and withdrawing themselves from it.—Such a state of matters could be supported

* Dr. Strachan's Sermon on the Death of the late Lord Bishop of Quebec, p. 19.

by nothing but absolute force.—The population would demand, that the resources of the country should be expended for the benefit of the country, and not for the support of a clergy, whose labours they neither wanted nor accepted. Government might think itself pledged to support them; discontent and murmuring would arise; confusion would follow; the burden of Episcopacy would be thrown off, even at the risk of casting off along with it, the allegiance to the Mother Country—Canada is not England; Episcopacy can never be the dominant religion of this Colony.— To imagine that it will be so, to image forth Bishops and Deans and Doctors, in due gradation of dozens and hundreds and thousands,† reposing, in state and security, on the abundant produce of four or five millions of acres, and on the dutiful obedience of the flocks, over, whom they preside, is no doubt a goodly vision to a churchman's eye—but it is a mere vision.—To attempt to render it a reality, would assuredly at no distant period produce discontent, commotion and separation of interests and affections—perhaps of Governments.

But it may be urged—you draw a picture of things which we never contemplated; we mean not to raise our church to that height of prosperity, which she has attained at home—we mean not to say that her positive advantages ought to be here, what they are in England or Ireland.‡

But let me ask you, why thus limit her pretensions? you cannot surely mean to say that she has assumed a rank in those countries to which she is not entitled, and which she ought not to maintain.—You are accustomed to hold her up as a venerated example of all that is faultless in discipline, and perfect in doctrine; and if you have any regard to consistency, you must confess that it would be your wish and endeavour to assimilate her condition in Canada, to that full perfection she has attained in the parent state. The only consistent answer you can give is—"We cannot." "We know alas! that we are unable to accomplish it."—The force of this reply I admit; I am at least as well satisfied of its being incontrovertible, as you can be yourselves. But what I assert is, that, as far as is in your power, you will endeavour to compass, what to you seems an end so desirable.—Your prejudices blind you to the danger of the attempt; your personal interests prompt you to it; motives which, with your belief, are blameless, even praiseworthy, hurry you on till you would put to the hazard the tranquillity of the Colony and the interests of the Parent State. It is to the wisdom of the British Government, not to your prudence, that we must look, for *restricting* you to that rank, with which the interests of Britain and Canada alike require, that you should be contented.

† Dr. Strachan esteems two thousand a very small number.
‡ Letter of the Bishop of Quebec.

Having now I trust shown, that, even setting right and justice altogether aside, and regarding the question as one of expediency, the claims of the Church of Scotland to the support of the British Government, are superior to those of the Church of England, I have proved what I undertook to establish, and I might here conclude. It has, however, been the unhappy, but natural tendency of the overbearing spirit and pretensions of the Church of England, to produce a prejudice in the minds of many, against all church establishments, and to cause many respectable individuals to believe, that it were for the interests of Canada, that no Church should receive more protection than another from the Government of the Country. The near neighbourhood of the United States—which, following up this system, connects not the church establishment with the state, and is yet without question the most prosperous, and is rapidly rising to be one of the most powerful of the Empires of the civilized world—has also much increased the numbers of those, who hold these sentiments. Were this opinion correct, it would at once settle the question, by establishing the propriety of Government's withdrawing its support from both Churches, a measure which they, who hold it, seem to urge. As I cannot, however, acquiesce in this conclusion, you will allow me to state very shortly, the reasons which lead me to dissent from it.

In my opinion, several very considerable and substantial advantages arise from the Ministers of Religion being connected with the state, and, in part, supported by it.

1st. Great part of the expense necessarily attending their maintenance may in this way be drawn from sources, which are least burdensome to society. The Ministers of Religion may be ranked among that class, to which some political economists have given the name of unproductive labourers. The labour of the farmer, the manufacturer, the mechanic, by producing things necessary to man, or by giving those already existing more useful forms, creates the means of maintaining other manufacturers, farmers or mechanics. The labour of the preacher of Christianity, though highly useful, even viewed merely with relation to its political advantages, as a means of instructing the people, has no immediate tendency to create funds, from whence it may be maintained. "Like the declamation of the actor, the harangue of the orator, or the tune of the musician, his work perishes at the very instant of its production." The maintenance therefore of this class is a tax on the common funds of the Society.—Of these funds, the *revenue arising from the rent of land*, seems that, of which the abstraction of a part, *least retards the general prosperity*. Without recurring to the theoretical reasonings, which would establish this conclusion, its correctness will be sufficiently shown, by attending to what occurs, where such an arrangement has place. In Scotland for instance, the Clergy are chiefly paid by the proprietors of land. The sum, which is thus collected, may, perhaps, be nearly £150,000. Now the levying of this sum on them, has little other effect than that of taking from them the means of supplying themselves, with so great a share of expensive luxuries. It perhaps reduces to nearly that amount the quantity of rare wines, or of costly silks, or the number of horses or menial servants, which that class afford, and this is the only evil resulting from it. But were this sum levied on the farmer, manufacturer and labourer, it would have the effect to reduce the accumulation of capital by the two former, and hence the general prosperity of the society; and it would tend to make the latter content himself with a small share of comforts or even necessaries and, by thus sinking him in the scale of social life produce a result, the evil of which, will not now a days be disputed. In England again and Ireland, the Clergy are themselves, to a great extent, proprietors of land; but had the property, they thus hold, not been set apart to the Church, it would have been possessed by the gentry, there being no reason to suppose that it would have gone to the common good of the Society. It would therefore merely have supported a class probably more luxurious and less conciliatory in their manners than those, whom it now maintains. The evil which arises from the church establishment of England and Ireland, if any evil does arise, is not that they hold property so extended, but that they hold it for a purpose, to which they do not apply it—they might have held it by some such service as delivering a dozen pepper corns yearly to the King, and then they would hold it as quietly as any of the gentry; but as it was granted them for the service of instructing the people, if they do not instruct them, or if they do not give them that sort of instruction they wish, the people look on them as possessing riches to which they are not entitled, as unjustly holding the reward of the discharge of duties, which others must be paid to perform. Hence dissention, discontent and commotion arise, evils overbalancing the advantage of the expense of the clerical establishment being in a great measure defrayed by the funds, which are most easily spared for the purpose. But it is only to the misapplication of the principle, that any objection can be made; the principle itself is sound; and hence the establishment, on funds arising from the revenue of land, of a body of men, who would truly perform the duties of Christian instructors, would be a real good. Some may doubt, whether the Church of England is a benefit to England, and others may regard her, as of the greatest evil to Ireland; but no one, well acquainted with Scotland, will deny that her Church has been productive of a great share of all that is good and lovely in the land.

2d. An established Church seeks to preserve its respectability, by admitting none to take upon them the Ministry, who have not made a decent progress in learning and science. Hence the general advancement of science and learning is promoted, and the interests of religion and morality do not suffer at the hands of unskilled and injudicious defenders.

3d. A body of men, from education and habit, friendly to the prevalence of peace and concord among mankind, and prompted by interest to avoid all causes of commotion and civil controversy, as endangering an order of things, which secures to them comfort and respectability, seems a useful alloy to the violent operation of those principles, which govern the motions of states, where the chief power is in the hands of the people; such a body, like oil thrown on the stormy waters, calms the turbulence, and diminishes the danger of popular commotion.

I do not think, that the United States can fairly be brought forward, in opposition, as an instance of good, arising from a system which throws the care of religion and its Ministers entirely on the people. Many circumstances, quite unconnected with this, have united their influence, to give to the inhabitants of that extensive country, an unequalled degree of prosperity and power. So far from the want of a religious establishment having proved beneficial, it is, I am persuaded, a defect in the constitution, and has checked the diffusion of concord and happiness. In this opinion I am joined by some of the most liberal and zealous defenders of the rights of mankind.*

The interests of religion and virtue must suffer, when the exertions of their defenders are cramped by the fear of approaching indigence and distress. The ministers of religion ought surely to be preserved from all harrowing anxieties, concerning temporal affairs, and, though removed from the vanities of the world, to be exempted as much as possible from its cares. In the States they are merely the hired servants of their Congregations, holding their situations from one term of years unto another, and consequently, exposed to be thrown loose upon the world, whenever their own infirmities, or the caprice of their hearers may lead to the belief, that they are less fit than formerly, to discharge the duties of their office. If we take, in conjunction with this, the very limited extent of their incomes (averaging I am assured less than £150 currency per annum) we shall be disposed to allow that they can scarcely possess that independence, or hold that rank in society, which would draw men of education into the ministry, or give full effect to the exhortations they deliver.

Besides, I am led to believe, that the burden of maintaining a well qualified Clergyman, has been felt to be so severe, when it had to be borne chiefly by the poorer classes of society, as in many instances to have kept

* Mably.

the people without Pastors, or to have contributed to the appointment of pastors of less respectable acquirements than were to be wished. From these causes, our North American neighbours have, I believe, a greater sprinkling of fanaticism, and are somewhat less moral and less religious, than if the ministers of religion had been connected with the state, and supported by it. They may shortly feel other evils arising from this defect in their constitution. That rivalry of interest and feeling, which every day is increasing, between the sections of their extended empire, must be met by a spirit of mutual forbearance and concession, or must ultimately terminate in the dissolution of the confederacy, and the conversion of that fair portion of the globe into a scene of commotion and bloodshed. The ministers of an established church, forming a bond of connection between the remotest parts of the most extensive dominions, and prompted no less by interest than duty, to maintain that connection, to allay the heats of civil controversy, and to cherish peace and good will among the people, whose devotions they direct, would have been the natural guardians of the unity of their Empire.

For these reasons, I must think, that, in this case, the United States hold forth to us an example, not to be imitated, but avoided; and it seems to me, that the only fit answer, that they can make, who most admire the character and maxims of their legislators, is not, that in this case they have acted wisely, but that they acted, as they were unavoidedly compelled to act. At the time of the separation of her North American Colonies from the Mother Country, all controlling power being withdrawn, it was impossible for any one of the numerous rival sects to be raised over all others. It is very different in Canada; this country is in the very act of assuming a form, and the people of acquiring a character. That form and character must, in some measure at least, be determined, by the influence which Great Britain exerts, nor does it seem to me, that that influence can be, in any way, more powerfully and beneficially exerted, than in the formation of those religious establishments, which may be raised up, by its fostering care. In this case, the circumstances of the times, and the principles of justice and sound policy seem to point out one course.

The two National Churches claim with justice the protection of the National Government: it is the interest of that Government to protect them, and there are at present, at its disposal, funds, in my opinion, fully adequate to meet every expense, to which this protection may expose it.

It seems to me that the Clergy Reserves, if put under proper management, would yield a revenue perfectly adequate to this purpose.—Hitherto, it is true, they have been almost entirely unproductive; but I am disposed to ascribe this circumstance to the system, which has been adopted in their management, having been formed, without due regard to the circumstances of the country, and the character of the settlers. Hitherto these lands have been offered to lease, for terms of only 21 years. Now this period, though sufficiently liberal in Great Britain, is altogether too short to meet the views of the Canadian Settler. Those, who seek to occupy wild lands, in this country, have made many sacrifices, and encountered much distress, ere they could even place themselves among us; they are prepared to make still greater sacrifices, and to task their endurance yet more severely, but they bear without repining the hardships and privations, to which they expose themselves, because they regard them as the price they have to pay for ultimate comfort and independence. Were they to give up the hopes of one day securing these to themselves and families, they must look on all they have already done, as thrown away, and would lose the chief incitement to future exertion. It is evident therefore, that leases of uncultivated land, for a term of years of which most who come with an intention of settling in Canada, have a prospect of seeing a conclusion, at which time were they to accept them, they and their families would be again thrown—unprovided for on the world, are not very likely to be eagerly sought after. Besides this, if any one takes a lot of wild land in Canada, with the intention of living on it, and drawing his subsistence from its cultivation, 21 years is a period in general too short to repay him for his necessary trouble and expense. He must build a house to dwell in, a barn to secure his grain, and stables for his cattle; his lands must be fenced, and perhaps they may require to be drained. These improvements absorb the greater part of the capital, which his yearly labour accumulates, and, at the period when he is just beginning to reap the benefit of them, he is required to surrender them to another. For these reasons, no man of prudence and perseverance will accept of any of these lots, for the purpose of settling upon them; and such of them as are leased, are therefore held by those, who own adjoining farms, and who, by obtaining a lease, can more conveniently pillage these lots, of whatever valuable timber, or other natural productions they contain. Instead however, of leases of 21 years, were these lands offered for terms of 70, 80, or 100 years, I am persuaded that a very large portion of them would, in no long period, be taken up by actual settlers. There is a certain class of settlers to whom such leases would be invaluable.

There are many individuals from Ireland, Scotland, and England, whose finances are exhausted, ere they reach Canada, and who are burdened with large and young families. It is impossible for these men, immediately to pursue, what has probably been their original plan, and directly push into the wilderness. They absolutely require to have previously provided some small sum for the expense of the journey, some necessary tools and utensils, and provisions for themselves and families, until they can reasonably expect to draw subsistence from the land, they come to occupy. To obtain these indispensables, their only resource, in general, is to betake themselves to some town or village, or to its neighbourhood, and then, from what they may be able to save from their wages, to collect a sum sufficient for their purpose. Years are thus inevitably consumed by the emigrant, and very often, ere he has attained his purpose, old age presses on him, or he yields to the temptations to intemperance, which new habits and foreign manners expose him to, or he sets out prematurely, and sinks under the united pressure of severe toil, want, and disease. On the contrary, were these reserves open to him, on terms that he would choose to accept, he might proceed there immediately; his labour though not so constantly in demand would be more liberally paid when required—provisions would be cheaper, and every hour not otherwise occupied might be employed most profitably on his own farm. The possession of any property for the term, I speak of is, in arithmetical calculations nearly equivalent to the absolute property; in the estimation of the poor emigrant, it could not be very different; it would provide for himself and for his children's children, and further than this his care and ambition do not commonly extend.

By the calculations of Dr. Strachan, there are at present, in Upper Canada, 18,000 reserved lots of 200 acres each. Of these, many are in parts of the country which are well settled, or are immediately contiguous to them. Were these leases granted for the periods I have mentioned, and were proper means taken to inform those interested, of the existence, situation, and capabilities of the vacant lots, for at present, every thing is ignorance with regard to them, I am persuaded, that, in a few years a considerable proportion of them would be leased. To make the most moderate calculation, I shall say, that in five or six years, 1500 of these lots would be occupied, by tenants paying an average rent of £5 per lot; this would make a sum of £7,500, from which I shall deduct £1,500 for the expense of management; the remainder, £6,000, would, in my opinion, form a revenue, fully sufficient for all the aid, which a Protestant Clergy, in this Province, will, probably, for some time require, or have a right to expect—and which, properly applied, would be productive of the most important advantages. The good that might result from it, however, would entirely depend on the manner, in which it were expended, as there can be no question that, if misapplied, it would be productive of more evil than benefit.

Two principles seem to present themselves in determining the manner in which any Clergy should be established, so as to be most useful to the community. They ought to be so far dependant on the people, as to stimulate them to render their labours acceptable—they ought to be so far independant of them, as to give them a respectable station, and to add to the authority of their counsels. The interests of each congregation, more particularly, require the former of these conditions—the general interests of society, the latter.

These principles, in general correct, are especially so, when applied to the Protestant population of Canada, nor do I think, that although a measure, which should embrace them, might be somewhat difficult to form, it would by any means be impracticable. It is chiefly to show this, that I venture to suggest the following schemes.

Each Township in the Province of Upper-Canada, averages about 66,000 acres, giving thus 660 lots of 100 acres each, the usual size of farms. It may be presumed that two Protestant Clergymen will, for a long time, be sufficient to meet the wants of the population of each township. I would, therefore, propose to limit the number to that, and, whenever, in any township, 100, owners, or upwards, of lots of 100 acres, or upwards—each living on their lots, and having cleared, at least, 15 acres on them—came forward and produced proof that a Protestant Clergyman of the Church of England, or of Scotland, was settled among them, and that they paid him the sum of £125 currency—then £125 currency, should be given them from the general fund, arising from the rent of Clergy Reserves. This would secure each Clergyman an income of at least £250 currency, or about £200 sterling—a moderate—and yet, perhaps, a sufficient revenue as a minimum, in such a country as Canada. A minister thus settled, ought not to be subject to be removed, but by the proper authorities, in the Church of which he might be a member. Further, for every six Clergymen, of either Church, so established in the Province, I would propose that one missionary, travelling from place to place, as he might be directed—by the Bishop, if of the Church of England—by the Presbytery, or Synod, if of the Church of Scotland—should have an allowance of £200 currency, from the general fund. After providing for these objects, any overplus that might remain, should be applied to the purposes of general education. There are said to be about 240 townships actually surveyed; these, were Clergymen placed throughout them, on this plan, would ultimately require 480 settled Ministers, and 80 Missionaries. 480 Ministers, at £125, would amount to £60,000—80 Missionaries, at £200, would require £16,000—altogether £76,000. The whole reserves, in the townships, contain upwards of 2,200,000 acres—and let us suppose that these, when the population of the Province has filled up the townships now surveyed, are rented at only one shilling per acre—this would give a revenue of upwards of £110,000, leaving a balance of more than £34,000 for the expense of collection, &c., and for the purposes of general education.

It is probable, however, that long ere this period could arrive, many changes would take place in the Province, which would render it necessary to modify any plan that might now be formed. I have only made these calculations to show—and for this reason, I have made them very low— that, as far as we can at present discover, the scheme I propose, seems perfectly practicable.

I own, that to me, some such plan would seem to possess many advantages, and not to be exposed to the objections of any party. It affords a prospect of establishing one or both of the Churches, on a firm and extended basis, an event which, I believe, would be of the greatest good to both Canada and Great Britain. It regulates the progress of both, by what each maintains or possesses—of the affections of the people. As far as they possess these, it must be allowed by all, that they ought to be supported—and if they do not possess them, the funds in question go to a purpose of the greatest acknowledged utility. It throws a great part of the burden of supporting the Ministers of religion on a fund, the revenue arising from the rent of land, on which I have endeavoured to show, it is most advantageous for the society that it should fall. By rendering the lands reserved, of advantageous occupancy to many settlers, it removes, in a great measure, the chief objection to their being retained, namely, their being a bar to improvement.

An opinion, I am aware, has gone abroad, that these lands have been of the greatest detriment to the Colony, and that they ought to be sold off by government. I must observe, however, that though, as presently managed, they operate to the prejudice of the Province, the evils arising from them, have been considerably exaggerated from causes which I shall state.

1st. Having been taken possession of by a Church, whose pretensions are very unpopular, they have shared in the odium, with which her exorbitant claims are regarded.

2d. Every one remarks the much less rapid progress that we make, than our American neighbours, in improving and enriching the Country. Truth and candour would lead to the conclusion, that this must mainly arise, from our population not having yet attained that spirit of enterprise, and that knowledge of the best mode of proceeding, which so admirably fit the American, for extracting every possible good from the materials, which nature has spread over the continent. But, the vanity natural to man, throws the blame of any falling off, from his own shoulders, to those of others—and the Canadian cultivator is thus inclined, to accuse the government, as the sole cause of that short-coming, of which, at least a great share ought to be attributed to himself. Of all the measures of government, that he can conceive to operate to his prejudice—that of reserving a seventh part of the lands unoccupied, most meets his eye, and receives, therefore, its full share of abuse.

3d. Many wish that these lands were brought to the market, as they hope to make advantageous purchases of some of them—and such reasonings are of sufficient weight to determine political opinions.

Some such plan as that which I have proposed, would obviate any reasonable objections to retaining them, and I should be sorry, therefore, to see them alienated, as they form the only fund, from which a permanent provision can be made for the Ministers of religion. The Colony would not consent to be directly taxed for this purpose, because many would thus be obliged to pay for the support of those, from whose labours they were not directly benefited. Nor can it be supposed, that the Mother Country will bind herself always to support an extensive religious establishment, in a distant Colony. These lands were set apart for the maintenance of a Protestant Clergy—no measure can be adopted to divert them from this purpose, but must be attended with important effects to Canada, and greatly influence the fortunes of a country, probably destined to contain, through succeeding generations, many millions of intelligent and enlightened freemen. Surely then, before being adopted, its consequences ought to be well weighed—and all its bearings on the future, as well as the present, attentively considered.

It is this deep conviction of the importance of the subject, in every part, that must plead my excuse for having so long trespassed on your attention.

I have the honour to subscribe myself,

Sir, your most obedient and very humble servant,

JOHN RAE.

The arguments I have brought forward, might be well illustrated, and receive a signal confirmation from what occurred in the Provinces of North America, which were, last century, under the dominion of Great Britain. It was then the policy of government to support the Church of England, and depress other denominations; the result is well known to all versed in the history of the period. Through the kindness of the Rev. Dr. Proudfit, Salem, I have the advantage of giving it in the words of the Rev. Dr. McLeod, New York:—

"I may state," writes that gentleman, "from recollection, on the authority of the worthy Dr. Rogers, supported by the assent of Dr. Livingston, to the fact that, for some years before the revolutionary war, great excitement existed, on account of the power employed by the Episcopal

Church, in this country, in the suppression of dissenters—especially the Presbyterians. The friends of the Church of England, were striving to obtain an American Episcopate—and the Presbyterians endeavoured to present such a complex establishment—an association was formed for the purpose of publishing, from time to time, against the claims of the hierarchy, as injurious to the liberties of the Colonies. The eloquent Governor Livingston, was the chief writer and editor of these articles; and the controversy certainly prepared the minds of many for the stand, afterwards taken in the revolution, which established the independence of the United States—Drs. Rogers, Laidly, and Mason, were of the association."

We live in more liberal and more enlightened times. I trust our policy will partake of the spirit of the age, and that not acting in opposition to the natural propensities of the people, but on the contrary, founding its operations on these, it will raise up a body of men, a blessing to those, whose devotions they direct, and a firm bond of unison between Canada and Great Britain.

The length of Mr. Rae's excellent letter, prevents us from being able to give, in this number, some notes accompanying it. They will appear in our next.

Notes to Mr. Rae's Letter*

The author's reasonings on the comparative adaptation of the two Established Churches of England and Scotland, to the state of society in this new world, are strikingly illustrated, and amply confirmed by the actual condition and progress of each in the United States of America. According to Bristed,[†] the Clergy of the American Anglo, or Protestant Espicopal Church, might, in 1822, be counted, in round numbers, 300; the Clergy of the Presbyterian Church, since their late junction, 1300, or more than four times the number of the Episcopal Clergy. It is also important to remark, that in doctrine and form of worship, the latter are so assimilated to the Congregationalists and Baptists, that it is by no

* *Canadian Miscellany*, vol. I, no. 6, Sept. 1828.

† John Bristed (1778–1855), author and Episcopal clergyman at Bristol, Rhode Island, 1829–43. He was born in England but emigrated to the United States. His published works show that he was greatly interested in economic problems, history and religion.

means improbable, from the superior excellence of their Church policy, they may ultimately draw a great portion of these, and even of other denominations, within their pale. The Congregationalists, or Independants, whose Clergy number 1600, have already some appearance of approximating towards the Presbyterian Church. They have their associations, or regular meetings of the Ministers of the District, which are virtually Presbyteries, in which candidates for Holy Orders are tried, and the general interests of the Churches brought under deliberation; and, as the great objections which were alledged against the Presbyterian mode of Church government, and which originally led to the formation of the sect of Independents in England, are obviated by the political constitution of the United States, we may reasonably hope that this body will ultimately coalesce with their Presbyterian brethren. We believe that where differences of doctrine do not exist between them, it is regarded, in general, as a matter of indifference, both by the Clergy and people, to which of the two denominations they attach themselves. However this may be, whether we regard the number, the learning, or the zeal of the Presbyterian Clergy— the unquestionable efficiency of their system of Church government, and its happy adaptation to the condition and feelings of the American people, or the ample funds, and numerous and well endowed establishments which they already possess for the education of their pastors and the advancement of their Church—we must needs wonder at the rashness and ignorance manifested by the Clergy of the English Church in Upper Canada, who, in a document lately published, appear to have asserted that the Presbyterian Church is not fitted for extension out of Scotland. Had these Rev. Gentlemen been a little better acquainted with the state of religion in the neighbouring Country, and especially, with the very remarkable and striking change, which the Episcopal Church has undergone there, we are confident they would have avoided touching on grounds so perilous to their own argument. We hesitate not to affirm that Episcopacy, in the states of America, has departed so far from the constitution and spirit of the Church of England, and approached so near to the characteristic features and principles of Presbytery, that we are warranted to pronounce it more assimilated to the order of the latter, than to that of the former Church. The following extracts from Bristed, will shew that the Bishops of the American Anglo Church are nearly on the same footing as the superintendants, which were appointed in the early periods of the Scottish Reformation; Laymen are admitted into the general and state convention, and the primitive simplicity of the Christian Church is restored, not only by the circumstance of their Bishops officiating as parish Priests, but by the exclusion of that complication of offices and dignities which are found in the Church of England—Archbishops, Archdeacons, Deans, &c., and above all, by the right of electing the Clergyman being vested in the members of the congregation. See Bristed, Introduction, page 23.

"By the fourth article of the constitution of the American Anglo Church, it is enacted, that the Bishops, or Bishops, in every state, shall be chosen agreeably to such rules as shall be fixed by the Convention, which consists of both Laity and Clergy, of that state. And the second canon ordains, that no diocese or state shall proceed to the election or appointment of a Bishop, unless there be, at least, six officiating Presbyters, or Priests, residing therein, and who, agreeably to the canons of the Church, may be qualified to vote for a Bishop; a majority of whom, at least, shall concur in such election.

"At present, there are *nine* Bishops in the American Anglo Church, to wit: of the eastern diocese, including the states of Maine, New-Hampshire, Massachusetts, Vermont, and Rhode-Island; of the states, respectively, of Connecticut, New-York, New-Jersey, Pennsylvania, Maryland, Virginia, South Carolina, and Ohio. There are two dioceses, the state of Delaware, and the state of North Carolina, which have no Bishops. Every state in the Union may become a diocese, whenever its Protestant Episcopalians are sufficiently numerous, and deem it expedient.

"The whole Church is governed by the General Convention whose power pervades every diocese. It sits regularly once in three years; but may be specially convened in the interval. It consists of an upper house, composed of all the existing Bishops; and of a lower house, containing a delegated portion of Clergy and Laity from each diocese. The state Conventions are held, for the most part, annually in each diocese, and consist of Clergy and Lay-delegates from every separate congregation. These bodies legislate for their respective dioceses; but their canons must not contradict the constitution of the general Church.

"The liturgy, articles, and homilies of the Anglican Church, are adopted, with some few slight local alterations. No particular revenues are attached to the Episcopate; and the Bishops, generally, are parish Priests, in addition to their bishoprics. But efforts are making, in several dioceses, to raise a Bishop's fund, in order to disengage the diocesan from parochial duty, and leave him at leisure to perform the services that are deemed more peculiarly Episcopal. Archbishops there are none, nor Prebendaries, nor Deans, nor Archdeacons, nor a long list of et ceteras, to be found in the Anglican Church; the only orders are three, Bishops, Presbyters, and Deacons. The senior Bishop presides in the house of Bishops, during the session of the General Convention.

"The parish Priests are elected, according to the charters of the congregations. Some Churches choose their Minister by the vestry, consisting of persons elected annually by the pew-holders. Others by ballot—the whole congregation voting. The Bishops have no *direct* patronage—no livings in their gift. The Clergy are settled by the choice or call of the people to whom they minister; and the stipend is fixed by compact, between the pastor and the congregation; and the common law enforces the fulfilment of this contract on both sides, whence all undue dependence of the Clergy on the people is prevented."

In the scheme which the author has given for the disposal of the Clergy Reserve, though he has made his calculations for the Upper Province, it is to be presumed that a similar plan will suit equally well in Lower Canada. See pages [248–9].

The comparative paucity of crime in Scotland, is a matter of general notoriety. We have not at present beside us, the official return of capital convictions, in the three Kingdoms, for a series of years; but we know that, during the last twelve months, only three were sentenced to death in Scotland, two of which were Irish. See page [226].

4

Loyal Address to the King*

To the Editor of the Montreal Gazette.

SIR,—The Petition to His Majesty has just arrived in this remote and unfrequented corner of the Province, and I am sure you will be gratified to learn that it has been received with the highest enthusiasm, by every member of the community, who is at all capable of forming a correct judgement, upon the very important objects contemplated by it. It grieves me, however, to be obliged to state, that even here the effects of the Anti-British faction have so far succeeded, as to have created the suspicion among certain individuals, that more is meant than meets the eye by the Petition, and that it is to be considered, as the first step to the introduction of *taxes and other abominations into this Colony*. I need hardly mention, that this idea was entertained only by a class of politicians, with whom Lower Canada is rife—men, whose ignorance of reading and writing, prevents them from judging for themselves, and that it owed its origin to a few individuals, whose station in society should have rendered them incapable of advancing the interests of their party by allegations so utterly absurd, so despicable and malignant. This ridiculous misconception having been nearly removed by the counter-statements and patient explanations of the more intelligent portion of the inhabitants, I believe, I may safely say, that almost every man of the English, Scotch and Irish, and even of the *enfans du sol!* as they have been invidiously, and most foolishly called, has come forward, and with alacrity and enthusiasm, to

* *Montreal Gazette*, Dec. 24, 1832.

take advantage of the opportunity afforded him, of testifying his unalterable attachment to the British Government, his entire satisfaction
with the present Constitution of the Colony, and his resolute determination to resist any attempt at innovation upon a Government, by which
the interests of all classes of the King's subjects are so justly and equally
attended to. A meeting of the inhabitants of Godmanchester is to take
place on Tuesday, the 18th instant, for the purpose of taking into consideration the best means of testifying their attachment to the Government of Great Britain, and of preserving its Sovereignty over this part of
the Empire. No one can rejoice more than I at the opportunity thus
presented, of holding up to public scorn and detestation, the pitiful proceedings of the factious and unprincipled grievance-mongers. A fair and
honorable opposition is an object of interest and admiration, and is in
some sort necessary by the discussion it creates, to preserve the purity of a
Government, just as storms and tempests are necessary to prevent the
atmosphere from becoming vitiated or corrupted. But when men so far
forget themselves as to advance the interests of their party by gross misrepresentations, infamous falsehoods and horrid blasphemies, it is full
time that their proceedings should be opposed by other means than argument or reasoning. So long as the wretched men who now agitate and
mislead the minds of their ignorant and undesigning countrymen, were
contented with venting their spleen upon matters which did not vitally
affect the Government, their narrow-minded policy was regarded by some
with pity and regret, and by others as by myself, with the most unutterable
scorn and contempt. But neither pity nor contempt will stop the strong
tide of revolutionary principles with which this interesting Colony is
apparently about to be inundated and ruined. The banners of imperial
justice must be displayed, else in a short time will the reign of terror be
attempted in Canada.

"And red ruin ride triumphantly."

From the sort of fermentation which takes place in all political bodies,
there are generally some unhappy individuals, who are thrown to the
surface of society to make themselves conspicuous by their follies or their
vices. In England, the *profanum vulgus* has for many years been excited
and misled by the impieties and falsehoods of Cobbett, Hunt, and Carlile;
and it was quite natural that in Canada we should have similar characters
to rail against the Just providence of God, and to misrepresent the best,
and the justest government towards her Colonies, the world has ever
witnessed. Had the Canadian demagogues been dealt with as their arche-

types in England, their impiety and sedition would have been silenced long ere this by the treadmill or the iron bolts of a prison. But the forbearance of Great Britain has been abused, and so far from shaming the men to whom I allude into obedience to the laws and respect to the government, it has rather acted as an encouragement to them to pursue their mad career, and to such an extent have they now proceeded, that they have had the audacity to insult the Majesty of England in the person of his Lieutenant, they have calumniated the Law Officers of the Crown, and they have even dared to attempt the overthrow of this well balanced and happy Government. Seeing then that matters have come to such a crisis as this, it is surely time, that every loyal and well affected subject in the Province, should declare his abhorrence of the principles and proceedings of the Canadian agitators, and their readiness to sacrifice life, fortune and all to support the supremacy of a power, under which they enjoy so many blessings, and by the perpetuity of which they hope to enjoy so many more.

Had Canada been like Ireland, and the demagogue like O'Connell, there would have been a plausible reason for the discontent and sedition which at present overspread the land; but the circumstances of the two countries are as dissimilar as the characters and talents of the men. O'Connell is possessed of gigantic powers of mind, his historical and political knowledge is profound and varied, and he wields at will the most resistless powers of a commanding eloquence.—Besides all this, O'Connell is an honourable man and a patriot; he has made great sacrifices for his country's good, and to his exertions are mainly to be attributed the important boons which were lately granted her, and the few blessings she now enjoys; but the virtues and talents of the Canadian agitator must be exhibited before they can be acknowledged: hitherto we have seen nothing to convince us of his mental acquirements, but his acquaintance with the crafty and unprincipled policy of Machiavelli, and no claim or title to patriotism, but what he has in common with the renowned Thistlewood, or any of the celebrated, though *less elevated*, Paisley Radicals. But again, Ireland has many grievances to complain of, she has two orders of priesthood to support, she is taxed beyond the possibility of endurance, a great proportion of her population is in absolute starvation and the energies of the nation are paralyzed by the erring policy which has been so long pursued towards her. Such a man therefore as O'Connell was really wanted in Ireland, and the circumstances of that unhappy country called him and his coadjutors into being; but what the political grievances of Canada are, I am totally ignorant. She possesses every political privilege she could desire, she enjoys a just and equal government, laws of her own choice, which are administered with even-handed justice, and she sits in security and peace under the fostering care and protection of the most powerful nation upon earth. As the consequence of all this, the country is in the most flourishing condition and bids fair in future years to become a great and prosperous nation. It is evident then, that the seditious proceedings of the Canadian demagogues are quite uncalled for, and that the public good can by no means be the object they have at present in view. If they in reality burned with one spark of patriotic enthusiasm, their ambition to distinguish themselves in their country's cause might be gratified with objects which would be conducive to the public good. Instead of misleading their ignorant countrymen by disseminating principles of dis-affection to the Government of England, and forming dark cabals against the present constitution of the Colony, they would find a far more mag-nanimous employment in pointing out to their countrymen the happiness they now enjoy, they would endeavour to rivet their affections more closely to a nation which relieved them from the iron grasp of despotism, and bestowed upon them all the privileges they now possess, they would tell them of the vast sums of British gold which are yearly poured into this Colony, and the thousands of a strong, hardy and warlike population who are crowding to its shores. But strange to say, these men have chosen to themselves a task which fills every virtuous mind with horror and disgust. In place of gratitude for the benefits so liberally bestowed upon this coun-try and the generous intentions of England towards it, they encourage their countrymen to return the bitterest animosity and the deadliest hate. The more compliant the Imperial Government has been in redressing their imaginary wrongs and grievances, the more rapacious are they taught to become in their demands, and to such a height have their foolish imagina-tions been raised, that I really believe nothing short of the overthrow of the government, a separation from England, and a declaration of Canadian Independence is contemplated. But this faction has been allowed to pro-ceed too far; it ought to have been crushed in embryo, and doubtless so it would, had it been thought possible that the ingratitude and malignity of man could have proceeded to such an extent. Canada has been treated with a degree of indulgence unprecedented in the history of conquest; one boon has followed another in rapid succession, since the British standard first floated over the ramparts of Quebec; but since these benefits have been made use of, only to strengthen her arm against her benefactor, it is time that England should rise in the majesty of her power, and declare what she has a right to expect, and that all true and loyal subjects, whether of Eng-lish, Scotch, Irish, American or Canadian origin should avail themselves of every favourable opportunity, but more especially that presented by the

recent proceedings of the loyal meeting in Montreal, to express their unqualified detestation of the headlong and destructive course pursued by
the Canadian agitators. I am, Sir, your most obedient servant,

J—— R——.

Godmanchester, Dec. 10, 1832.

5

The Opposition to Emigration*

To the Editor of the Montreal Gazette.

SIR,—The object which I propose in the following communication is to make a few remarks on Emigration, and to point out the egregious folly which they are guilty of who endeavour to impede or suppress it. It was my intention to have addressed them to Mr. Papineau or Mr. Rodier, but as I entertain very strong doubts, whether either of these gentlemen would find leisure to attend to them in the midst of the important but ungracious and unconstitutional proceedings in which they are now engaged. I have deemed it preferable to give them publicity through means of your paper, in the idea that they may meet the notice of a few at least of the Anti-British faction in the House of Assembly, and thereby accomplish the benevolent purpose which I have in view. It may be thought presumptuous to address these gentlemen on a subject, with which they in particular ought to be so well acquainted, but when I think upon the few advantages which many of them have enjoyed in prosecuting the study of Political Economy, and upon the laws which in consequence they have passed in direct opposition to the clearest and most obvious doctrines established by that science, I am emboldened to proceed in the task I have imposed upon myself. Nor let it be thought inconsistent with the dignity of our Canadian Legislators, occasionally to lay aside the violence and rancour of political debate, to attend to discussions which humanize the mind, and dispose it to reason with accuracy, and decide with justice

* *Montreal Gazette*, Jan. 19, 1833.

and truth upon the important subjects which come under their consideration. The proudest and most learned of English Lawgivers, have thought
it no compromise of *their* dignity, to acknowledge the obligations they owe
to the lessons which have been read them through the public press by
such men as Ricardo, Bentham or M'Culloch; and I trust that no one of
our Canadian Legislators will suffer degradation in his own eyes, by
bestowing a few minutes attention upon the subjects which may occasionally
discussed by him who now addresses them.

That labour, whether morally or physically considered, constitutes
wealth is a principle which has been long established by the most irrefragable arguments. I thought this truth had been as firmly believed by all
well informed men, as the Axioms of Euclid, or the Principia of Newton.
It seems, however, I have been mistaken in the opinion I entertained, since
the public acts of the Anti-British faction, and the statements of Mr.
Evans, in a late number of the *New Montreal Gazette*, go to shew either
their total ignorance or disbelief of this truth. What idea the faction entertain of the origin and nature of wealth I know not, but the gentleman whom
I have just mentioned, declares that it is the earth. Now he might just as
well have said that it was air, fire, or water; because any one of the elements of the obsolete philosophy of Thales, would have suited his purpose
just as well. The means of supporting life cannot well be produced without
land, neither can they be produced without air, fire or water, and indeed I
maintain that the component principles of the atmosphere are far more
necessary to the support of both animal and vegetable life, than land of
any quality however good. A beetle has been known to live for six months
upon air alone, and there are certain plants which may be suspended from
the roof of a greenhouse, and which will yet in spite of their extraordinary
situation, continue to exhibit all the phenomena of a healthy vegetation.
If land constituted wealth, then must Canada before the conquest have
been the richest country upon earth, when each *enfant du sol* owned his
hundreds of acres of forest land, could sit in security and peace under his
own butter-nut tree smoking his eternal calumet, when ignorance of the
happier lot of others made him entirely satisfied with the comparative
wretchedness of his own, and when no cares intervened to disturb the
tranquillity of his repose, but the trouble of wheeling the produce of his
stable and barn-yard into the waters of the St. Lawrence. Land then is not
wealth; neither is gold, nor any of the precious metals wealth, as certain
late writers seem to think. If gold constituted wealth, then should Spain
have been the richest country in the universe; and yet strange to say,
shortly after the discovery of what were then called the Indies, when
every peasant had utensils of gold and silver in his cottage, that country

became crippled, beggared and reduced. Gold then is not wealth, but labour is wealth, and land and gold are only valuable, in as far as labour has been bestowed in obtaining them, and in working them up to their highest state of excellence. I need not pursue this argument farther, since what I have said must have made the truth sufficiently obvious; indeed to a mind trained to habits of just reasoning, the enunciation of the proposition must have carried conviction along with it.

If labour then is wealth, it follows that in the same proportion in which an industrious population is increased in a country, must the prosperity of that country be advanced. The prosperity of France and England is estimated not by the numbers of broad acres, but by the millions of industrious, hard working and scientific men they contain. The faction, however, seems to entertain a very different opinion upon this subject. Their idea seems to be that the prosperity of the country is in an inverse ratio to its population. They do not indeed make so paradoxical and startling an avowal as this; but judging from their harangues and their parliamentary proceedings, the inference is unavoidable. This being their opinion one naturally wonders how Mr. Rodier could have been so inconsistent with his principles, as to have railed against Divine Providence for permitting the Angel of Destruction to thin the ranks of our meagre population, and give so fearful a display of the preventive checks of Mr. Malthus. But I tremble while I write this sentence; the anger of an avenging God is too dreadful a subject to be spoken of but with reverence and awe. The idea, however, was forced upon my notice, and I must say, that had the faction been true to their principles, any conduct would have been more becoming than the unmanly prostration of feeling they exhibited, and the ignominious complaints they uttered, making themselves the scorn of the Christian world by their pusillanimity and inconsistency. One man, however, exhibited a firm adherence to the principles of the myrmidons over whom he reigns, by sternly withholding all the charities and sympathies of life, from the thousands who were falling around him.

That labour is wealth, or what is nearly the same thing, that an increased population is wealth, is a truth which has been acknowledged in every corner of the habitable earth, but that in which we dwell. Our neighbours in the United States, whose prosperity, intelligence, and liberality of sentiment, begin to be better known and more highly appreciated, receive emigrants from Great Britain with open arms. It is not so much the gold they carry along with them which induces the Americans to welcome them to their shores, as the skill and ingenuity they possess in agriculture, manufactures, commerce, and their intimate acquaintance with all the more recondite departments of art and science. I need not point to Chili, Peru,

Columbia, or any other of the South American governments, for an examplification of the truth and power of my principle, nor need I ask by what instrumentality these interesting republics were first called into being, and by whose enterprise and exertions they are now enabled to advance in the glorious march of improvement which seems to have begun upon earth. Let me ask, however, by what remarkable circumstance it was, that Russia in so short a time shook off the slumber that had hung upon her for ages, and awoke in all the strength and glory of the oldest and most enlightened states. This wonderful event was accomplished chiefly by British emigrants, a class of individuals whom the faction regards as a curse to Canada, but who were rightly considered by Russia as the only means of raising her dominions from barbarism and insignificance into the possession of wealth and importance. Emigrants from Great Britain erected foundries, mills, distilleries, and manufactories of all sorts, they constructed arsenals and navy yards, they assisted in establishing schools and colleges, and set a going the wonderful moral, political, and physical machinery which is now at work in that colossal empire. But were these men taxed on their arrival at Petersburgh, treated with inhumanity and injustice, or scowled upon with looks of malignity and hate? Did the arbitrary Autocrat of all the Russias behave towards them as the arbitrary Demagogue of Lower Canada would behave, if he dared, towards us? No, but he welcomed them to his dominions with cordiality and joy, he settled them in happiness and comfort, and heaped upon them honours and rewards which his keen discernment could never think too great.

The Pashwa of Egypt too has been so thoroughly convinced of the same truth, that even he has had the magnanimity to oppose the most inveterate prejudices presented by the religion, the character, and the habits of his people, and has encouraged the settlement of British emigrants in his Pashwalik, and the introduction of all the arts of industry and the pursuits of science. The rapidity with which he has succeeded in carrying his projects into effect, for the civilization and improvement of the circumstances of his people, is almost incredible. The wisdom of a thousand ages looks down from the eternal Pyramids in wonder and astonishment, at the moving masses which float along the Nile like things instinct with life conveying the means of subsistence and enjoyment to the remotest corners of the kingdom. Should the powers which are at work at present in Egypt continue long to operate, there can be no doubt but that in a few years she will far surpass her ancient glory under the Pharaohs or the Ptolemies; she has already so far exhibited what the wealth of labour, or the power of knowledge can accomplish, as to have despised the terrors of the bowstring and made the descendant of the Prophet tremble beneath the gilded domes and minarets of his impregnable Seraglio.

What a humiliating circumstance it is, that we are obliged to turn from the contemplation of the rapid strides which every nation and kingdom upon earth is making towards aggrandizement and wealth, and to consider that in Canada a faction of ignorant, bigotted men should be permitted to exist, whose object it seems to be to crush in their birth every generous aspiration after wealth, knowledge or honor, and to oppose the settlement of those individuals among them by whose means the country's advancement could be so much accelerated! What a horrid state of prejudice and ignorance does it argue, that men should continue, wilfully and perversely, to oppose their own and their country's best interests. They have the example of savages, semi-barbarous, and civilized nations, to shew the benefits arising from the influx of British principles and British arts and yet these men strain every nerve to oppose their introduction into Canada, and shew the most resolute determination to remain in happy contentment with "the wisdom of *their* ancestors;" while the whole world besides is going on apparently to realize the dream of Condorcet, respecting the infinite perfectibility of the circumstances of man. But that nothing may be wanting to fill up the measure of our contempt for this pitiful faction, we have only to consider the fact, that poor, helpless, unaided and alone, and with a miserable population of only 500,000, they have had the unheard of folly and presumption to talk of Canadian independence, and have really and truly acted, as if they meant to throw off their allegiance from a power, which rules over one hundred and fifty millions of living souls.

Before taking leave of this part of my subject, I cannot avoid mentioning as another and most satisfactory exemplification of my principle, the prosperous condition and flourishing aspect of the properties of such men as Charles Penner, Esquire, and the Lachine farmers, who have made themselves so obnoxious to the Honourable the Speaker of the House of Assembly, by returning a verdict according to the dictates of conscience, law, and justice, and for having acted throughout the whole of the proceedings connected with the affair of the 21st May, with the high honour and rectitude of purpose which uniformly characterise the conduct of British gentlemen. But perhaps the very best illustration of the truth, that labour is wealth, is to be found in the fact, that several hundreds of settlers who arrived in Upper Canada last spring, without one sixpence in the world, are already possessed of a stock of produce and cattle which would be incredible, were it not authenticated by the testimony of Mr. Ritchie, the Agent for the settlement of Emigrants on Lake Simcoe. I detest comparisons, but when I see examples in my immediate neighborhood of certain of the *enfans du sol*, who have resided on their own farms for fifty years, who have not in all that time cleared twenty acres of land, whose houses are in ruins, whose children are clothed with rags and pinched with want, and whose total ignorance of the first principles of agriculture, or their unwillingness to practice them, prevents them from raising the most necessary articles of life,—when I see all this, I cannot but say, that surely even the pauper population of England must be a blessing to Canada, whatever Mr. Evans may advance to the contrary. Indeed, so thoroughly convinced am I, that the prosperity of Lower Canada depends upon continued emigration, that I have no hestitation in saying, I consider it would be for her interest to receive a yearly importation of 20,000 emigrants, did they even come with nothing to cover their nakedness, but the clothes upon their backs. They bring with them the bone and muscle, the power of knowledge and the rectitude of principle, which would render them a blessing to any state, but especially to so poor and thinly inhabited a country as this. It is needless to talk of framing laws to prevent or obstruct continued, nay increased emigration to this Colony.—No legislative enactment, without the grossest violation of the right of the subject, can prevent him from going to any part of His Majesty's dominions he may be pleased to select. There are thirty or forty thousand Irishmen settled in Glasgow, and yet no one ever thought of applying to Parliament for an act to prevent the inhabitants of any of the three kingdoms from leaving their respective countries. Every enlightened statesman has considered that the more intimately the elements which compose the British Empire are mixed up, the better does the compound become, and laying all other considerations aside, I certainly think that the condition of Lower Canada would be greatly improved, by having a dash of pure British blood thrown into its composition.

One more word and I have done,—the faction may continue to prosecute their villainous machinations, and they may succeed for a time by their wicked stratagems and violent harangues to baffle and confound the generous intentions of Government, but they *will not, cannot, shall not* succeed in preventing the onward career of this British Province to the plenitude of human grandeur, and from becoming the brightest gem that shines in the Imperial diadem. An increased influx of the enterprising, wealthy, and enlightened inhabitants of Great Britain *will* continue to take place, and no law can prevent it, without it be attempted to put our bodies in fetters, still stronger than those which the greatest reformers have succeeded in striking from our minds. Would to God, that the blessings of knowledge were more widely diffused throughout this Province, and then sure am I, that the simple minded, kind hearted peasantry of Lower Canada would not permit themselves to follow at the chariot wheels of the Arch Demagogue who now reigns over them, and makes use of them only to swell the triumph of his inglorious ambition. Would to God that he could be brought to know that his present proceedings can bring him nothing but wretchedness, misery, and scorn; and must sooner or later, lead both him and his unhappy followers into consequences, which the imaginations of all good men must shudder to picture forth!

> Oh thou eternal Mover of the Heavens,
> Look with a gentle eye upon this wretch!
> Oh beat away the busy meddling fiend
> That lays strong seige unto this wretch's soul.

J——. R——.

Godmanchester, Jan. 5, 1833.

6

Emigration—Mr. Evans' Letter*

To the Editor of the Montreal Gazette.

SIR,—I have just seen a letter from Mr. Evans to the Editor of the *Montreal Herald*, containing remarks upon my letter to you of the 5th January, and an attempt to defend the principle that "land is the sole source of all wealth." Taking into consideration the *tout ensemble* of Mr. Evans' letter, I must say of it that it presents as formidable a front, as the production of any polemic, with whom it has ever been my lot to wage war. In making this acknowledgment, however, I intend the gentleman no compliment. The difficulty with which I have to combat, in replying to his letter, arises entirely from my inability to comprehend his meaning. His language is so vague and unsatisfactory, and the opinions he advances so contradictory and irreconcileable, that in attempting to thread the maze of his hazy argument, one is unavoidably led to conceive that the gentleman's ideas when he wrote it, were, to use one of his own expressions, "quite in a wilderness state." He does not grapple with the proposition that labour constitutes wealth, nor does he substantiate the truth of his own doctrine, that land is the sole source of all wealth. Had he reasoned upon the principle, that it is impossible for two contradictory statements to be both true, it would have been very easy for him to overthrow my proposition, by substantiating, had it been possible, the truth of his own; or by substantiating the truth of mine, to overthrow his own, and thereby settle the matter in dispute between us at once. But Mr. Evans pursues neither

* *Montreal Gazette*, Feb. 26, 1833.

the one line of conduct nor the other. In fact, he first assents to my proposition, then he qualifies his assent, by and bye he edges off still farther, and lastly he totally denies, but does not disprove my doctrine, by boldly stating that land is the sole source of all wealth. The truth is, Mr. Evans is fairly placed between the horns of a dilemma, and is situated, with respect to these two propositions, pretty much like Macheath, when he sung out in the agony of his soul,

> "How happy could I be with either,
> "Were t'other dear charmer away."

The two doctrines are as irreconcileable as the two inamoratas of the redoubted hero of the opera. The one or the other must be abandoned: I cannot reconcile them, I shall therefore leave that task for the gentleman's amusement during the leisure hours which this winter may afford him.

At the imminent hazard of being considered a *proser* or a *bore*, I shall consider Mr. Evan's remarks *seriatim*, as this is the only manner in which justice can be done to them. Mr. Evans writes:—

"This gentleman appears to imagine he proves my total ignorance, in having stated land to be the sole source of all riches."

This assertion Mr. E. will permit me to contradict. I never did imagine that I had proved his *total* ignorance by such means, neither was it my object or desire to bring such an accusation against him. I am not so uncourteous as to wound the feelings of any man by taxing him with ignorance, and though I am free to confess I have seen little to induce me to form a high estimate of Mr. E.'s mental acquirements, I entertain too favourable an opinion of the intellectual capacities of many of the members of the Agricultural Society, to suppose that they would compromise the respectability of their institution by appointing a Secretary who was totally ignorant.

Mr. E. says:—

"This gentleman appears to imagine he proves my total ignorance in having stated 'land to be the sole source of all riches,' that I might just as well have said, that it was air, fire, or water; and in a most philosophical manner, goes on to instruct the ignorant, by informing them that though the means of supporting life cannot well be produced without land, neither can they be produced without air, fire, or water, and that the component principles of the atmosphere are far more necessary to the support of animal and vegetable life, than land of any quality, however good, &c. &c. What valuable information this may prove to the community —particularly in a country like this, where men may lose themselves in the forest occasionally. There may be an opportunity of proving the experiment that men may exist on air alone, like the beetle and the certain plant suspended from the roof of a green-house. I can assure the gentleman that notwithstanding all his learned argument, I should wish him to prove the experiment, before I should be subjected to such a trial, and that I am sufficiently acquainted with the influence of air, fire, and water, on animal and vegetable life, for my profession as a farmer."

In all this paragraph there is not the shadow of an argument, but in its place we find pointless wit, ill conceived and badly supported ridicule, and a sort of sneering superciliousness of tone, which is still more injudicious and still more perfectly misapplied than even my unhappy quotation from the bard of Avon, which gave so much offence to the fastidious taste of Mr. Evans. I would remind this gentleman that ridicule is not the most approved method of treating a philosophical question, that the subject must be absurd indeed which admits of such a mode of procedure, and that there is nothing in the question under consideration which justifies the application of such an epithet. Surely the doctrines which have been supported by the brightest names of ancient and modern times, are not becoming subjects for the buffoonery or vulgar wit of even such a man as Mr. Evans. He sneers at me, forsooth, for remarking that air, or fire, or water, was as much the source of wealth as land. I say so still, for I have seen nothing in all his letter, which could induce me to change my opinion or even entertain the slightest doubt of its truth. When seeds are moistened and placed in the exhausted receiver of an air pump, they swell but do not vegetate; the leaves of plants absorb carbonic acid gas from the atmosphere, and Sir Humphrey Davy remarks that some plants, such as the house leek and different species of the aloe, increase in weight when suspended in the atmosphere and unconnected with the soil. From a consideration of these circumstances then, together with others familiar to all acquainted with the physiology of plants, many have been led to believe that atmospheric air contains all the principles from which the food of man is derived.

To show how necessary the mechanical and chemical effects of heat are to the due performance of the functions of plants, I need only refer to the known influences which the changes of the season have upon all the phenomena of vegetation. Again, the Egyptians, and from them the Greeks, observing how necessary water was to vegetation, considered that it was the productive element from which all plants were capable of being composed; and in later days, Van Helmont advanced the same idea, that all vegetable products were capable of being generated from water. Lastly, Sir Humphrey Davy, certainly the most elegant and profound chemist who has ever existed, expressly states, that "though neither water, nor air, nor earth supplies the whole food of plants, yet they all operate in the process of vegetation." From what has been stated then it would appear that I am not singular in the idea that air, fire or water, is as much the source of wealth in the sense in which Mr. Evans uses that word, as land of any quality however good. In the latter part of the above quotation, Mr. Evans evidently attempts to be humorous at my expence, but he has rendered his pleasantry so mystified and unintelligible, by the language in which he expresses himself, that I feel inclined to leave this part of his letter in its own glorious uncertainty. Still, however, to judge from the number of points of admiration with which he has so liberally bespattered his page, there must be something very good in it at bottom, if one could only get at it. If I may be allowed a rough guess, I should say that he unwittingly attempts to throw ridicule upon the very subject which the most illustrious philosopher of modern times introduced in his lectures to the most en-lightened audience in Christendom.

Risu inepto res ineptior nulla est.

Mr. Evans proceeds:—

"This gentleman, after proving to his own satisfaction that land was not the source of wealth, says labor is wealth. I have never said or thought otherwise where labour could find employment."

Indeed! With what shadow of consistency then, can Mr. Evans after-wards assert, in the most emphatic terms, that "land is the sole source of all wealth." Certainly this is not in accordance with the logic of Aristotle or Locke.

Mr. Evans proceeds:—

"But I should wish to know how labour could find employment in Canada if not on land." He afterwards says, "were this population to be transported to Canada how could their presence produce wealth here un-less they were to be employed on land."

Why then I can inform Mr. Evans, many thousands could find employ-ment on WATER, as for instance the fisheries of Gaspé. Many might be employed very profitably in the iron works and forges, and in the various departments into which manufactures and commerce are divided.

Before I proceed further, I may remark that I do not think Mr. Evans has a very definite idea of what is meant by the word wealth. He seems to me to think, that it is merely the abundance of the vegetable produce of the earth; whereas wealth, according to the definition of one of the most eminent French political economists, is that it consists in "the surplus of produce over consumption, or of income above expenditure." Now the question among the learned has not heretofore been, whether this surplus is exclusively produced by the application of labour to agriculture, commerce or manufactures, but whether agricultural, commercial, or manufacturing labour has the greatest share in producing wealth. The English writers very naturally assign the first rank to manufactures and commerce; the French again, with whom Adam Smith agrees in this particular, place agriculture above both commerce and manufactures, while the Italian authors entertain different notions upon this subject, according as they inhabited maritime or interior provinces. From all this it would appear that the French, Italian, and English writers on political economy agree in acknowledging that agricultural, commercial, or manufacturing labor may all become the source of public wealth, and that they only differ with respect to the productive powers of each kind of labour. Mr. Evans then stands *alone* in the opinion that land is the sole source of all wealth. Mr. Evans continues,

"What has produced near ten millions annually of poor rates in England, but want of employment? were land to be had there in plenty, and at a cheap rate, could such a state of things exist? Labourers could be had there and in Ireland, if they could find employment, and what is the consequence of the want of it? a redundant population of paupers—the greatest evil that can afflict any country. Were this population to be transported to Canada, how could their presence produce wealth here, unless they were to be employed on land? Of no country in the world, I maintain, can it be more truly said that 'land is the source of all wealth' than of Canada."

This argument is quite nugatory and irrelevant. If it proves any thing it is only that England must be indeed a very rich country, since she can afford to pay ten millions annually for the support of her poor. But I deny the assertion that want of employment is the sole cause of the magnitude of the English poor rates. Many become paupers from misfortune, which human prudence could neither foresee nor prevent; and many from sickness or dissipation, the most productive cause of all human misery and crime. There can be no doubt, that many industrious and deserving individuals are reduced to poverty by want of employment, but however deplorable the fact may be, it is not the less, true that there cannot at all times be a uniform demand for all the productions of industry, and that if one kind of labour is in *great* demand, it will generally be found to be at the expense of another. The rest of the above quotation proves nothing. I may mention in reference to it however, that although labour may not at all times be employed in producing wealth, it is not the less on that account the cause of wealth. The steam engine does not lose its power when it is not at work, nor do the coffers of Baron Rothschild lose their value, when unemployed in relieving the wants of a needy State. Mr. Evans is quite mistaken in supposing that there is not plenty of land to be had in England. There are no less than fifteen millions of available, and fifteen millions of unavailable land in that country, and it was in consequence of this circumstance, I believe, that Mr. Rowland Hill was induced to advance the philanthropic suggestion which has been so much agitated of late. If there be so much unemployed land in England, I may be asked, why so many should think of emigrating to Canada. I am not in the habit of scanning the private motives of people's conduct: I know, however, that it is the birthright of every Englishman to go where he pleases, and to do what he pleases. Some men may think that they can turn their labour to more account in this section of the empire than in the Metropolitan State; others may be induced to gratify their migratory propensities by strength of purse; and very many, I do not doubt, come to Canada, because they imagine it resembles the Utopia of schoolboys, where the houses are built of gingerbread and plum cakes, and thatched with pancakes, where the roads are paved with apple dumplings, and roasted pigs run all over the country with knives and forks stuck in their sides, crying "come eat me, come eat me."

"Without labour, I admit," says Mr. E. "this land would be unproductive; but how could labour be supported here or elsewhere, without the produce of the earth to support it, (unless this gentleman's new theory is correct.)"

I willingly admit, that the means of supporting life were co-existent with labor, nay, that they existed in the order of events before labour, but I by no means admit, that wealth existed anterior to labour. Wealth, it will be recollected, is the surplus of agricultural, commercial or manufacturing produce above consumption or of income above expenditure, wherefore I infer that labour is antecedent to wealth.

"The earth at the command of the Almighty, originally produced grass and herbs, plants, corn and trees, in their lovely verdure and amazing variety, whose seed was in themselves for the use of man and other animals; and from this spontaneous production has all seeds, &c. been derived, and continued to the present day. All the labour or ingenuity of man could not produce a single new seed or plant, that did not originally grow spontaneously in this or some other country."

This whole passage, flattery apart, contains one of the most beautiful displays of the *bathos* I have ever met with. Had it been penned during the Augustan age of English literature, it would no doubt have entitled its author to make a conspicuous figure in that immortal poem the Dunciad. Here we have the most contradictory ideas mixed up in one incomprehensible sentence. In the first member of the sentence, we are treated to a version of the simple yet sublime account of Moses, respecting the creation of vegetable substances, which equals anything to be found in the creation of Sir Richard Blackmore, a Knight whose banner waves over the first niche in the temple of dulness, and in the very next member of the same sentence, we are told that all seeds, &c. derive their origin from spontaneous production—a doctrine which is as incompatible with the Mosaic account of the creation, as with the principles of truth and reason. Really this gentleman has a most wonderful talent in reconciling the most paradoxical or rather contradictory propositions. I have no doubt, but that he would be able to give a better account than even the late Sir John Leslie of the hyperbola and its asymptotes, could he be persuaded to direct his attention to that subject.

"If" says Mr. E. "the support of men and animals must incontrovertily be derived from the produce of the earth alone, on what principle can it be denied that land is the sole source of all wealth."

To shew the fallacy of this process of reasoning, I need only throw it into the form of a syllogism—The food of man is wealth, the earth alone produces the food of man, therefore the earth alone is the sole source of all wealth. Now though I were even to admit the truth of the first proposition, which I am very far from doing, the truth of the syllogism would be destroyed by the error contained in the second proposition. The earth alone does not produce the food of man, for a very great proportion of it is derived from the WATER; wherefore the reasoning of Mr. Evans is obviously false.

With respect to the last paragraph of Mr. Evans' letter, I do not think it merits notice. For the truth of what I have stated respecting the Emigrants on Lake Simcoe, I refer Mr. Evans to the *Montreal Gazette* of the 15th ultimo.

In taking leave of Mr. Evans, I may mention, that it was my intention to retire under cover of a quotation from Shakspeare, but as I might again offend the critical acumen of that gentleman, I shall only further add, that I trust I have made it appear, that my principle stands upon a basis as immutable as any other moral truth, and that Mr. Evans has totally failed in defending the position that "land is the sole source of all wealth."

————————————————ibi omnis
    Effusus labor————————————————

                                                J.—— R.——

Godmanchester, January 29, 1833.

7

Remarks on the Education Bill*

Ignorance is the impure source from which almost all the miseries and crimes of mankind proceed. Let a people become enlightened, and their virtue, happiness and prosperity follow as a necessary consequence. We may search the records of antiquity in vain for an instance of any nation that was ignorant and yet virtuous, or of a nation that was enlightened and which yet continued to grovel in wretchedness and vice. The history of the world proclaims the truth of this remark. During the gloom which overhung Europe in that period of her history, when science sought for shelter on the plains of Samarcand, it was then that the empire of vice was unbounded and that the moral and intellectual powers of man were prostrated before the supremacy of an authority which was founded upon his own ignorance and superstitious fears. When, however, the sun of science once more arose upon the nations of Europe, the benign influence which he shed forth called into being the energies of industry and wealth. As men became more intelligent they hastened to break the bonds by which they had been so long held in vassalage, and as knowledge was more widely diffused, their virtue, happiness and wealth increased in the same proportion. The power of knowledge in advancing the best interests of the human race is irresistible. Whenever men become enlightened and begin to think and reason upon the circumstances in which they are placed, and the relations in which they stand to each other and the whole body of society, the first decided step towards the melioration of their circumstances has been taken. As their attainments in knowledge are

* *Montreal Gazette*, March 19, 1833.

increased, their moral energies are strengthened and expanded, they become acquainted with their proper station in the universe and hasten to vindicate their claim to it. No moral degradation, no tyranny nor political grievance, can long exist in an enlightened state. What an intelligent people wills, is and must be law, though the chains of their rulers were strong as adamant. Had the inhabitants of Turkey been permitted to think or to reason, the Mahmouds would long ere this have ceased to reign, the grievous taxes, the open robberies, the cold blooded murders to which that unhappy people are subjected, would long ago have terminated, and the flaming scimitars of the turbanned host of Janizaries would not have continued so long to carry terror and dismay to the hearts of men, who knew the just value of freedom and were determined to obtain its enjoyment. The strength and power, the happiness and wealth of the British Empire are all founded on the intelligence of the people. Being enlightened, they are acquainted with the true sources of happiness and wealth, and are perfectly aware of the best means of turning their productive powers to greatest account in the various arts of industry. Being in the habit of thinking and reasoning upon the nature of the government under which they live, they are capable of appreciating its excellencies and detecting the defects which change of times and circumstances have created in it. But in place of checking the freedom of thought or strictly prohibiting all enquiry into the complicated machinery of the state, as was done during the dark period of Papal domination and as is still done by some tyrannical governments of modern times, the British Legislators promote and encourage both. They are too deeply read in the principles of good government not to know, that a power whose object is the happiness and prosperity of the people, has nothing to fear from the scrutiny of an enlightened mind. They know that its melioration and not its destruction will be the consequence. There we find them exerting their utmost efforts for the education of youth and the diffusion of useful knowledge among all classes of the people. Indeed if there be one thing more admirable than another in the paternal government of England, it is the deep interest it takes in the instruction of the people. In no quarter of the earth can knowledge be more easily obtained than in England. There is not a town, hamlet or village, but can boast of its Schools, Libraries, Reading Rooms, Mechanics' Institutions or Societies, where information upon all subjects may be obtained, and where the minds of men are trained to habits of reasoning and thinking which would qualify them to fill any situation of life with credit and honor. In such a state of society as this, it is impossible for any species of corruption long to exist. The people know their strength and their rulers do so too. Circumstances must bend to meet the will of the majority of the inhabitants of any state. A great proportion of the wealth and pride of England was arrayed against the Emancipation of the Catholics and the Reform of Parliament; but the people demanded both, and their will was law.

If the factious men who are now dominant in the House of Assembly of Lower Canada, really and truly possessed one moiety of the patriotism they profess, and if it were their object to emancipate the people from the real or imaginary wrongs by which they say they are oppressed, they would begin the accomplishment of their object by educating and instruct- ing the people; they would endeavour to elevate them in the scale of rational and intellectual being, they would rouse up their dormant energies and teach them to think freely and fearlessly upon all those subjects which concern their unalienable rights. But it is not the object of the faction to enlighten their Canadian brethren. They have too much crafty policy not to be aware that their plans are of too dark a dye to stand one glance of the searching eye of truth. They know that tyranny and oppression are supported only by ignorance and fear. They know too that were education to become general, and the press capable of exerting its full power in Lower Canada, their usurped authority would end upon the instant, and they themselves would sink into the insignificance or mediocrity, beyond which the most ambitious of their number were never meant to rise. Hence we find them putting forth their utmost endeavours to suppress and discourage education, and thereby prevent that class of individuals, over whom unhappily they have at present too much power, from en- quiring into the true motives of their conduct, and detecting the abandoned principles by which they are actuated. Had they rendered it penal in any one to learn to read, or to exert his reasoning and thinking powers, the wickedness of their intentions would have been at once made evident to all. It was necessary, therefore, in conformity with their iniquitous policy, that an Act should be passed, whose object should ostensibly be the encouragement of Education, but which should yet, by the operation of the clauses it contained, tend directly to counteract that object. The Law to which I have alluded sets forth "that it is expedient to appropriate certain sums of money for the encouragement of Elementary Education in this Province, and to make further and more ample Legislative provision for the same purpose." It is not my intention to animadvert upon every clause contained in this most Jesuitical law. I pass over all the puerilities it contains, as for example that in Sec. XI, where it is decreed, with all the pomp and solemnity of Legislative wisdom, "that all children attending such Schools shall be equally taught in classes, and that the name of each pupil shall be written in his or her book by the Teacher, &c." Nor shall

I say one word respecting the cumbrous and unwieldy nature of the machinery necessary to be set agoing anterior to the establishment of an "Elementary School." My object will have been sufficiently accomplished, if I succeed in proving that the direct tendency of this law is to suppress, not to encourage Education, to perpetuate the reign of ignorance and vice among the youth of this Province, not to expand their intellectual faculties, nor to refine, purify and elevate their moral powers.

In Sec. IX, Chap. 26, it is decreed "That no child or person under five or above fifteen years of age shall be admitted as a pupil at any Elementary School during the hours established by this Act," &c. &c. The direct tendency of this clause is to prevent the children of Canada from deriving any benefit from education at all. Let the talents of a child be ever so precocious, it is not to be permitted to receive any instruction until it is five years of age, and let them be ever so backward, the doors of the school are to be for ever closed against it whenever it is turned of fifteen. It is Mr. Stewart, I think, who says, in his "Elements of the Philosophy of the Human Mind," that all the faculties of a human being are not fully developed until its fifteenth year. My own observation, however, would lead me to differ from so great an authority, and to entertain the idea that the sixteenth or seventeenth year was nearer the truth. But whether Mr. Stewart's opinion or mine be the correct one matters not, since the wicked intent of the above clause would be made sufficiently obvious by either, in as far, as according to it, a child must be removed from school at or before the very time at which he begins to derive any benefit from it. If there were academies over all the Province, at which a more extended education could be obtained, the clause referred to would be the less objectionable. But no such institutions can yet be boasted of in Lower Canada, and accordingly the poor aspirant after knowledge must be driven from the further enjoyment of instruction, whenever he has attained his fifteenth year, and his young faculties must be crushed or blighted at the very period, when they bid fairest promise of expanding in beauty and in strength. In England, where education is conducted upon the most extended scale and upon the most enlightened principles, the years which are to be devoted to education are never interfered with. In that country, boys of all ages, and of the most various attainments, may be found in the same school, and even on the same form, and yet, thank God, the Imperial Parliament has never yet made itself odious or ridiculous, by attempting to prevent the people from enjoying the benefits of a liberal and extended education, to fetter and confine the energies of the teacher, or to arrest or impede the enquiries of the pupil. Had the faction been as anxious to enlighten the people, and elevate them in the scale of rational existence, as they are to preserve them in ignorance, and perpetuate their degradation, they would have rendered it imperative upon all to devote the time, which is now wasted upon the pipe and the glass to the acquisition of useful knowledge. The one law would have been as just as the other. And in their rage for legislation, they might have taken a leaf out of the History of Iceland, a history which should cover every *enfan du sol* with shame and confusion, and have declared that the Clergy should have the power of preventing any marriage, where the woman was unable to read: they might have gone a step farther, and in place of voting away the public money, to reward one or two of their especial favourites for the silly books they have published, have imitated the same interesting people, when, about one hundred and thirty years ago, they ordered a man to be publicly whipped, for the errors he had committed in a translation of the book of Genesis.

In Sec. VIII. Chap. 26, it is enacted that the teacher shall produce a certificate that "he is known as a person of sober life and conversation, and has been examined and found qualified to teach reading, writing, and arithmetic." When a merchant is desirous of engaging the services of a porter to his warehouse, he generally requires such qualifications as those enumerated in this Act, and, accordingly, it is no unusual thing in this Colony, to observe him who may be carrying about a load of goods on his back today, employed tomorrow in guiding and directing the studies of the future Legislators of this Province. I have just heard of a person who was first a porter in a store in Montreal, then a waiter in a tavern, and who is now a teacher in one of the district schools of Lower Canada. What can shew the wickedness or absurdity of the Act more emphatically than such a circumstance as this. If it had been the intention of the faction to enlighten and instruct the people, and to raise the character of education throughout the Province, they would have framed the law, so that none but persons fully competent should be engaged. All, however, that is required of a teacher is that he be acquainted with reading, writing, and arithmetic, and that he do not drink or swear. It is not necessary that he should have had experience in the difficult art of teaching, that he be skilled in the workings of the human mind, that he be a man of patient and industrious habits, and above all, that his moral character stand fair and unspotted in the world. None of all these things is requisite and hence it would be no difficult matter to fill up every school in Lower Canada, with teachers taken from the labourers employed on the canals, and other public works now in progress throughout the country. Who but a fool would engage a man to build him a house, without enquiring whether or not he was a good mechanic, and who but a scoundrel would engage a person, with the information of a ploughboy or a coalheaver, to conduct the education of his child, to form his character and habits, and to lead him, by the example of his own life, and the beautiful precepts of morality with which he inclines his youthful mind to entertain an abhorrence of vice, and an admiration of virtue. If any thing could convince me more than another, that the suppression and not the encouragement of education, was the object contemplated by the faction, it would be the enactment contained in this clause. For suppose a boy had obtained all the instruction which one of these Government teachers was capable of communicating, the business of his education would not yet have begun. His reading, writing, and arithmetic are of no use, unless he be capable of employing these acquirements to some useful purpose. His reading ought to be rendered serviceable to him, in obtaining a knowledge of the principles of grammar, history, and geography, his writing, in noting down those truths or circumstances which he cannot well trust to his memory, and his arithmetic, in solving questions in land-surveying and mensuration, and in any of the thousand questions which present themselves in the transactions of every day life. But all this the teachers employed by the Parliament of Lower Canada are totally incapable of assisting him to do, and hence, however anxious a parent may be to give the child of his body the benefit of a good education, it is rendered totally impossible for him to do so, by the operation of this most cruel, most unjust, and most Jesuitical law.

Again in Sec. VIII, Chap. 26, it is enacted "that the allowance (£20 per annum) shall not be paid for any such school, unless open school shall have been kept at the rate of one hundred and ninety days in the year, nor unless twenty children at least, between the ages of five and fifteen, inclusively, have actually attended such school, nor if any higher rate shall have been demanded or paid at such school than two shillings currency per month, unless by previous agreement, signed by the parent or guardian of such child, &c. &c." and in Sec. X of the same Chapter, it is declared "that the trustees may admit a number of poor children gratuitously, not exceeding ten, &c." By this law then, it is decreed that every school shall contain at least twenty scholars, one half of whom may be free, and the other half of whom may each pay no more than two shillings per month. In all the country parts of Lower Canada, it is almost impossible to get even twenty pupils to attend any school regularly, who are of the age prescribed by the Act of Parliament; we may conclude therefore, that twenty is the average number attending the Government schools. Now supposing the teacher had been able to comply with all the frivolous and vexatious regulations of this Act, he would be entitled at the end of a year to receive the parliamentary allowance £20, and from his ten pupils

£12 more, a sum which in all amounts to £32. A common labourer receives £2 per month, and his board, which is generally estimated at £1 10 per month more, this in all amounts to £42 per ann. A carpenter receives five shillings per day, and his board, which in all amounts to £100 per annum. From this calculation then it appears, that he who holds the important office of an instructor of youth, receives only three fourths of the wages earned by a common labourer, and only three tenths of those gained by an ordinary mechanic. But suppose the schoolmaster have failed to comply with every one of the conditions of the Act, suppose, for example, he has been unable to keep up the number of his scholars to twenty during the whole year, that the want of clothes, or the whim or caprice of the parents, have prevented the children from attending the school, in that case the Parliamentary allowance is peremptorily denied him. The bright visions of temporary wealth, which for many a long month had floated before his fancy, and cheered him amid the arduous duties of his thankless office, is suddenly withdrawn from before him, the debts he has been compelled to contract, now press heavily upon him and the merciless creditors, whom he is unable to satisfy, either forcibly possess themselves of his meagre library and scanty wardrobe, or give him leisure ere long to reflect amid the darkness and gloom of a prison, upon the unprincipled laws by which he has been led to devote his time and talents to obtain a pallet of straw in jail, and to become a beacon to all others of the danger there is in attempting to counteract the ambitious projects of the dominant faction, by instructing or enlightening the inhabitants of Lower Canada. With such an example as this before his eyes, (and extraordinary as it may seem, the picture is not too highly coloured.) what man of sound mind would devote himself to the business of instruction. Men generally expect to be rewarded for the exertion of their talents, and accordingly it happens, that as the profits arising from the cultivation of any branch of industry are great, the numbers of clever men who follow it is great also. When a nation is litigious there is no lack of lawyers; when it is bilious or hypochondriacal, there is no scarcity of physicians; when it is ignorant and superstitious, there is no dearth of ghostly advisers; and when it is determined to be enlightened and free, men of learning and worth will readily present themselves as candidates for the honors and rewards, which are to be obtained by the education of youth and the diffusion of knowledge. But it would not have suited the purposes of those who framed this Act, to permit virtuous and learned men to put to work the powerful machinery of which they are possessed, for the complete emancipation of the people from the state of ignorance in which they are now held. It was necessary, therefore, that all encouragement should be withdrawn from learning, that the people might continue the passive and unresisting instruments of the men who now rule over them. Hence it was enacted by the combined wisdom of the generous and liberal minded majority in Parliament assembled, that learning, virtue and honor shall be discountenanced in this Colony, that the occupation of an instructor of youth shall be considered disgraceful, that he who follows it shall be ranked among the Pariahs or outcasts of society, that he shall be prevented from associating with any but the poorest and most wretched of the people, that our children shall be taught to regard him with pity and contempt, and that all men shall be constantly reminded that superior attainments are dangerous to the best interests of him who possesses them, and hostile to the objects contemplated by the majority of this House for their own individual aggrandizement and power. This is most assuredly the only interputation which this law will bear, and it has so well accomplished the purpose for which it was originally framed, that there is now hardly one competent Teacher to be found in the District Schools of Lower Canada. Many respectable Teachers, rather than submit to be fettered and confined by the restrictions imposed upon them by this Act, or to be controlled by the regulations drawn up by illiterate and uneducated Trustees, have resigned their Parliamentary allowance altogether, and have established schools upon their own responsibility. Others again of an inferior caste have abandoned the occupation to become day labourers, bar-keepers, boatmen or pedlars. Many of the School houses erected within the last few years are rapidly going to premature decay, and the Teachers, who are employed in the remainder of them, are generally speaking woe-begone, God forsaken creatures whose laziness and ignorance render them unfit for any other employment, and by whom therefore, notwithstanding all its accompanying contumely, insult and neglect, it is considered a most desirable occupation. So admirably then has this law operated to affect the purposes of those who framed it, that they now proceed in perfect security to prosecute their favorite schemes, without the slightest fear of detection from the encreased knowledge of those, whom it is their anxious wish to retain as the passive instruments of their will, they plunder the public treasury by votes of money to themselves, they deprive British Officers of worth and respectability of their situations, upon the most frivolous pretences, to make way for themselves and their own base hirelings, they attempt to blast the fair name of the meritorious individuals, who refused to advance their unhallowed objects by the abandonment of all the principles dearest to men of honor and integrity, they even go the length of imitating the infidel philosophers of Revolutionary France, in proposing a Convention of the people to accomplish beyond doubt what

they have already so well begun, they encourage their unsuspecting countrymen to regard their British fellow-subjects with hatred and distrust, and to
look forward to the time as at no great distance, when the smiling fields
and verdant plains of this beautiful and interesting Colony shall again
become the arena, on which the great question of British or French ascendancy shall be again decided. All this they now do, and much more they
have it in contemplation to effect without the slightest fear of their wicked
designs being penetrated by the men, whose thoughts and feelings they
have contrived to subdue to their utmost wish. But let them beware of the
reaction, which their own wickedness and folly will ere long excite against
them, let them beware of the steady and unerring operation of those
principles, which now sap the very foundation of their power, and which
will ere long reveal the real intent of their dark imaginings, in characters
clear as the noon-day sun, when they and their hateful authority shall
sink together in the dust, when the soul of the Canadian "shall walk
abroad in her own majesty, his body swell beyond the measure of the
chains, that burst from around him, and he shall stand redeemed, regener-
ated, and disenthralled."

J. R.

Godmanchester, Feb. 25, 1833.

8

How Ought the Clergy Reserve Question
to be Settled?*

We need not tell our readers that the subject of this article is one which, if
we can worthily treat of it, is deserving of all their attention. It is one of
too engrossing importance, it too sensibly affects, it too largely affects all
who have made this province their home—more than this, perhaps it is
too universally felt so to do, to need any such preface. We would fain hope
that we shall be able so to treat of it, as to carry along with us the great
majority of our readers of that church, which, planted in these transatlantic
regions by our brethren, we have clung to and endeavoured to uphold—so
too to treat of it as to satisfy such of our readers as are not of our communion that we aim at nothing but what is consistent with the well-being
of Canada, nothing but what is consistent with those germs of firm, and
liberal, and righteous principle, which even under the darkness of the
cloud that has overshadowed us, we have rejoiced to see rising into prominent view amidst the workings of the passing storm, to the present glory
of the land, and we trust in augury of its future prosperity.

While we thus speak, however, we are not by any means insensible to the
difficulties which environ the subject. It is one indeed which has been long
present to our thoughts, one, too, to which we have given much consideration, which we have viewed under all the aspects that change of personal
circumstances could induce, and which has yet always seemed to us the

* This article was published in *The Canadian Christian Examiner and Presbyterian
Magazine* in three instalments in July, August and September, 1839. Despite the note
that it was "to be continued," the remainder of the article did not appear in this publication, which ceased in December, 1840.

same. But it is one also that comes on us, bearing with it its full share of those conflicting arguments and opinions, and obstinate preconceptions, which encumber most practical questions of importance. It may be said to be essential to the nature of such questions to generate prejudices. In nine cases out of ten, the attention of individuals is first drawn to them by the practical experience of some actual good or evil resulting from the mode in which they have been determined in the society to which they belong. Such individual experiences generally strike us more forcibly than whatever else can be presented to the intellect. They are probably the first things connected with the subject which have caught the attention. They are known to be realities. And thus, instead of being viewed as only single instances out of a mass of facts that ought to be examined, compared and generalized, they are held as prime truths. They become the centre round which the whole opinions of the man cluster—the common point of union of his arguments and reasonings, from which he issues to the field of controversy, and to which, when pressed by opposing instances and arguments, he retreats, as to an impregnable fortress, from which no force of logic can ever have power to drive him. "This," he says, "I have seen and felt, and cannot be in error about. Here you cannot shake me." He may be brought to doubt whether it is that you really wish dishonestly to deceive and lead him astray, or whether you are not yourself deceived; or, he may be even led to admire the art and seeming show of reason with which you support what he esteems a fantastic hypothesis; but to doubt of his own principles, to question the stability of the particular point on which he has taken his stand—that no more enters into his thoughts, than it came into the conceptions of our simple fathers to imagine that the earth was other than a solid plane, round which sun, moon, and stars performed their appointed circuits.

Hence it is, from this tendency of mankind to shut up their senses to all but one-sided views of such questions, that they come to us surrounded by a multitude of conflicting sentiments, and so encompassed by prejudices, that the light of truth with difficulty penetrates to them, and is scarcely ever able to show them to us under a perfectly clear and unchanging aspect. Hence it were vain, in any such questions, to expect perfect unanimity of sentiment. The most we can hope for, is the concordance of a considerable majority. To this extent do our hopes reach as to the assent to be given by our readers to the opinion which we are to place before them on this question. We trust that such of them as may entertain different views, will not at once start off from us; that they will ponder our reasons, and, should our general conclusions after all differ from theirs, that they will consider whether or no the particular cases to be determined, are not to be held exceptions to *their* general rules, while we, perhaps, should hold the cases they bring forward, as exceptions to *our* general rules. If so, it must be admitted that the dispute is really not about things, but about names; and we shall have liberty to apply what the one calls *rules,* and the other *exceptions* to rules, to the particular cases before us.

Our convictions on this subject are embraced under the two following heads. *First,* there ought in these Provinces to be a provision for the support of religion. *Secondly,* there is a scheme devisable for disposing of the funds already set apart for this purpose, that ought to satisfy all parties.

I. The former of these presents itself naturally to us as the result of the more general principle, that the state or community ought to provide for the moral and religious instruction of its members. This again is a principle which we hold directly deducible, in the first instance, from what is essentially embodied in the very notion we have of what we call a state. Let us see whether this conclusion can be fairly drawn from the premises, by considering first what a state is not, and secondly what it is.

In the first place then, it is apparent that we cannot, by this term, mean to indicate any body of individual men. This is obvious, because, even while we are speaking of a state, the chances to which humanity is subject have, in all probability, changed the individuals composing it. Death or expatriation has taken some out of the community; some have been born into it or have come into it from other communities. A twelve-month brings a considerable alteration over the individuals whose agency is prominent in the conduct of affairs. In twelve years, or, at most, in twice twelve years, a society is no longer recognizable by the sameness of its members. A new race has arisen, the old has passed away, or, if we see some of them remaining, time and fortune have so wrought on them that they are no longer the same men.

Tempora mutantur et nos mutamur in illis.

What things then are recognized as the same? We answer the institutions and manners of the people, their modes and principles of action. These constitute the real identity of nations. They make England, England, and France, France.

The simile is an ancient one that likens the race of men to the trees of the forest. If we conceive, as is the fact, that each bud is an individual—is capable of separation from the parent stem—has a life and death of its own, and if we take as an instance a tree from some clime where there is no season of torpor or lifelessness, it will furnish a good illustration of this notion of a state. There we see on the same plant, buds and blossoms, fruits and off-dropping leaves—individual life in its stages of infancy, maturity, and old age—a continuity of existence preserved throughout the body though the individuals making it up are changed. As years hold on their course so the old pass away, the new come on; but, throughout, though leaves, flowers and fruit change, the tree is still the same. A similar view meets the Nestor who contemplates the identity of nations through successive generations. He sees amid rapid individual change and death, identity and continuity of existence remaining; nay, as it were growing out of them.

The next question is, what is it, that uniting individuals into one body politic preserves that body, and preserves in it that identity of manners, morals, feelings, modes and principles of action, which make up and preserve its distinctive character and life. We answer—the existence of reciprocal obligations, the discharge of reciprocal duties.

There is no member of any society or body politic, who is not under large obligations to that society. He has been indebted to it, from the first moment of his existence, for protection from the wrongs and injuries to which the selfish passions of his fellow citizens, or the citizens of other states, might have subjected him; he is indebted to it for the growth and propagation of the arts of civilized life, and for the accumulation of capital —their result, the benefits arising from which each member of the society partakes; he is indebted to it also for the amount of intellectual, moral, and religious instruction which he has received. Were the directing and controlling force of the state to cease, were its protecting power to come to an end, the reign of security and order would terminate, and a sense of anarchy and violence commence, in which neither life nor property would be safe, neither intellectual, moral or religious culture could have place.

The obligations are mutual: as every citizen has received benefits from the state, so every citizen has duties to perform to the state. He is bound to obey its laws, to bear his share in supporting the expenses of its various institutions, and, when occasion requires, to peril life and fortune in its defence. As each bud in a tree, in return for having been fed by the juices, and supported by the substance of the stock, on attaining maturity, and its leaves unfolding, elaborates its share of the circulating fluids, and fits them for making the secretions necessary for the growth and preservation of the plant, so every citizen, high and low, rich and poor, is called on to contribute his share to the prosperity and permanence of the commonwealth. To the fulfillment of this great duty there is no exception. It may be—in well regulated communities it often is—that he lives unconscious of the functions he discharges; but, in all communities, every citizen in active life, whether he revels in wealth, or that the sweat, daily starting from his brow, day by day, earns for him his daily bread, does in fact contribute a share for the support of the state.

These reciprocal duties and obligations must be fulfilled. It is essential to the well-being, to the existence itself, of every community, that they be discharged. In well regulated communities, it often—indeed it generally—happens, that they are so discharged; that what we may call the mere machinery of the state carries on the necessary processes without any prominent agency of the individuals whose lot it is, for the time, to hold the position either of governors or of the governed. It is always either from some defect, or from some sudden emergency, when the preconcerted machinery failing, recourse of necessity is had to the elementary principles of things, that the power of this principle is so tested, and its force felt, that all men perceive and acknowledge its reality.—The territory is invaded by a hostile army. Every citizen becomes a soldier; however little the preceding course of his life may have fitted him for encountering the hardships and dangers of warfare, he quits the comforts, breaks from the ties of home, and marches to the field; and were he to refuse so to do, he would justly be esteemed guilty of a crime, and worthy of the severest punishment. Some foreign power, again, maltreats a citizen; forcibly, for instance, seizes on him within the territory of the state, removes him to its own, and there arbitrarily deals with him. His country is on the instant ready to take up arms on his behalf. It signifies not what rank he has held; he may have been of the lowest, he may have been at actual beggary; but, no matter who or what he is, he is a citizen, and the whole state is pledged to redress or avenge his wrongs. Were it to fail in this—were it unhappily from internal or external weakness, to fail in its clear duty, the procedure were not only disgraceful, but almost ruinous; the state would not only immediately lose caste among other states, not only externally would it sink in rank, but internally its strength would be diminished. The bonds of brotherhood among its members would be sensibly loosened. Every man would feel that his own rights had been compromised—that he was no longer under the shelter, he had conceived—that the state would give him less, and that therefore he owed it less than he had thought. A national war were preferable to the degradation, disgrace and positive weakness induced by such a procedure.

When we recur to such like instances, to instances in which states, in their actions, are brought before our view, as it were under a process of experiment, the fact that the state and the individual are bound to one another by the strongest reciprocal duties and obligations clearly appears to us.

Our readers, we suspect, will think we dwell too long on truths so plain that none would seek to controvert them. We do indeed, as we think, speak only of plain truths, and of such only would we wish to speak; but, at the same time, they are truths of so great moment, that, in what we say concerning them, we had far rather be esteemed tedious than felt to be obscure. Yet must we take care not to insist on what is plain, to very weariness. It will then be granted that the state does not consist of the given number of citizens at any particular instant acting in it. These represent it indeed, for the moment, but they do not make it up. That which makes it up, is that from which they themselves sprung, from which others like them are rising, and which when their ephemeral earthly existence is over, is, they trust, to send forth numerous, nay, innumerable successions such as they— that great trunk, out of which they have grown—that congregated mass of institutions, capital, manners, morals, feelings, modes and principles of action, that gave form and life to the tide of previous population, out of which the individual existence of each has proceeded, and though of which, to the observer, it be now the eye-meeting token, it is yet only in so far so, as the wave glancing in the sun-beam before him, is of the ocean from which it, with its fellows has been upheaved to roll along for the moment on its surface, but within the depths of which it and they are to be immediately re-absorbed.

When, then, the statesman, and by this term we would now understand, each man whose voice has a directing power in the state, a term in our empire nearly equivalent to every reflecting man within it—when such a one truly seeks to discover what, concerning any particular question, ought to be his conduct as an honest representative for the time of all that is embodied in the vast meanings of the word country, we conceive we are justified in telling him that he cannot reasonably hope to do so, if he set before him the immediate benefit of himself and his compeers as the mark at which he ought to aim. In adopting such a standard, he confines himself to the mere surface of things, and if therefore in the affairs on which he sits in judgement, he catch the true and right, it is as it were by chance, and not from his view compassing the real principles, forming them, and dividing them from the false and pernicious. For it necessarily follows from the very simplest idea of what we term a state, that questions concerning it do not hinge on what is to advantage the present living and acting men; but on what tends to produce successions of men, having all that is possible of what we esteem good in and about these, and divested of all that we esteem evil.

When one thinks he has fathomed the depths of the question, and exhausted it, by considering the immediate effects of any determination of it on the men of his particular period, he deceives himself in two ways. He takes not into account the things that have produced these men and all that belongs to them, and the effects which the measure he advocates would have had on these things. When asked, therefore, what would have been the consequence had such a measure been introduced at some distant period—say two hundred years ago—would we of this generation have been the men we are—or, if it had changed us, how would it have changed us? he is either unable to answer, or he answers at random, without any recurrence to history, without any attempt to trace out effects to their causes. Again, he deceives himself in not considering, that, inasmuch as it alters the constitution of society, it must alter the men, in after days to have being in the society, and that until he has traced out what would be the nature of the alterations it would produce on the generations thus progressively changing under its influence, he has by no means ascertained what really is in it of good or evil. Thus, let us suppose a society of correct morals, industrious habits, and prosperous condition, in which the instances were exceedingly rare where men sought to get what they had not earned, and where, seeking to earn a return for labour or capital, they were not disappointed. In such a society the distresses of destitution and poverty would be rare; but though rare they would still exist; there would be individuals even there, whom infirmity of body or mind, or disease, or misfortune had brought to want. These indeed might not experience the extreme miseries that in less happy conditions poverty brings with it; for there would be hands ever ready to relieve them. Still they would be experienced. There would be individuals whose distresses no one knew; even whose persons were unknown. These would silently have to endure the horrors of want, or to feel the painful sensations occasioned by soliciting charity—soliciting charity, it might be, from strangers. Even after these had been endured, they might have been endured in vain, for application might ignorantly be made to individuals, nearly as poor as they who sought aid. There would also be the injustice of an unequal burden imposed. In such a state of things, the very charitable would sustain the whole load, those of less zealous benevolence would bear none of it.

Suppose now, that, in such a state of things, some one were to propose a measure to the legislature to end as he conceived all this suffering and all this unfairness. Suppose that he were to propose, that a small general tax should be levied, such as literally to meet the wants of all individuals whose means of living had failed. He might argue that thus what all acknowledged a duty, would be discharged by all in common, and would not press on individuals: that thus it would be effectually discharged, and that thus too the waste of time and distress of mind occasioned by going about soliciting assistance would be prevented. It cannot be said that such arguments might not prevail. They might seem sound to the majority; and they would be sound, as concerned the men at the moment existing in the society. Their falsity would lie in their not taking into account the men to exist in after times, and the conditions of whose existence would be modified by the very measures under consideration. We put not, as our readers are doubtless aware, a merely hypothetical case. In the reign of Elizabeth, the English legislature came to such a conclusion, or formally acknowledged it had previously come to it. Hence the English poor laws. The evils connected with that system of laws were not felt, or were not sensibly felt for a lengthened period; but, as is indeed the nature of such things, advancing with a velocity at first slow, but continually accelerating, they have within this century spread throughout the land, pressing heavily on the resources of the state, and sensibly deteriorating the character of the people. Many who have looked into these matters most closely, and are best entitled to speak on them, affirm that the evils resulting from these poor laws, are greater than those that have been brought on the country by any other cause. That the whole force of Europe, wielded for the ruin of the Island by the greatest military genius of modern times, produced not the mischief that has arisen from mistaken legislation in this matter. This view of the enormity of the evil may or may not be correct. We believe it is perfectly correct; but it is at least allowed on all hands, that either by the original poor laws, or by the rules adopted in their management, a great calamity was brought on the nation, the mischievous consequences of which it will be, to say the least, exceedingly difficult to eradicate. An unlimited fund was established to succour misfortune; to ward off the dread of destitution from honest industry; it may be, to manifest the greatness of a nation holding forth a loaded table to its very paupers; that fund has been perverted to the purpose of supplying the demands of dissolute prodigality; of snatching its just reward from toilworn industry; of humbling the moiety of a noble people to the posture, and, alas! to the feelings of out-worn beggars. It will also be allowed that this momentous error has arisen from the fallacy we have been endeavouring to point out—from the fallacy, of which they are guilty, who, holding the office of statesmen and legislators for the period, look merely at what is right for the existing men of the period, and conceive that this is of necessity good for the country; not discerning the confusion of terms, nor reflecting that, as these laws must produce a change in society—a change in the generations coming after them, they are in truth legislating for an order of things, which, it is probable, will be very different from that around them—from that which these laws are suited to operate upon.

Though many other instances press on our mind, of errors arising from this source of fallacy, the space we have occupied on this one, warns us that it is the only one which the limits of the patience of our readers, and of our own pages, will allow us to adduce.

The next truth that we have held forth as very evident is, that the great bond of commonwealths and individuals—the great cementing principle, uniting all into one whole, and connecting the men of the present with the men of the most distant ages, past and to come, consists in an existing reciprocity of duties between the state and the existing generation. It is on this, we conceive, that the soundness or unsoundness of any legislative measure mainly depends, and by it that its fitness is to be tested, rather than by any rash assumption that what may be good for the existing men of the period, is necessarily good for the state. It very often, indeed, we may almost say, it generally happens, that what is for the real good of the state is opposed to the immediate interests of many individuals. The real interest of the state requires the maintenance of great principles and motives of action, of expensive institutions, and of rights often not to be made good without severe contests with rival nations. These things demand sacrifices; they demand a yielding up of property, or of prejudices, a devotion of self to the general good, to the good of men far separated from the individual, not only by distance of space, but by distance of time. By a succession of generations of men imbued with such a spirit, each reaping the fruits of what was sown by their predecessors, and, in return, themselves sowing for posterity, nations become great and glorious. By a defect of such a spirit in successive generations, they inevitably fall to decay. The true patriot has ever, therefore, held it his part zealously to maintain whatever the state may rightfully claim of individuals—whatever individuals may of right claim of the state.

If on this question, we are to act on such a principle we would ask, in the first place, if the prosperity and happiness of the community be not the aim of all government. This we presume will be granted. Then would we ask if it be not essential to the prosperity and happiness of communities, that they be virtuous; nay more, if the prevalence of the moral virtues is not actually, visibly, seen to confer that prosperity and happiness. In the case of individuals indeed, the reverse of this sometimes strikes us. We see the worthiest men, in all that meets the outward view, amongst the most unhappy. But as concerns nations, search the whole earth, and we give up the argument if you find not that every state in which the moral virtues prevail, seems prosperous and happy; nay, if compared with each other, *caeteris paribus*, the prosperity and happiness of states is not exactly proportionate to the extent in which the moral virtues do prevail. Again we ask if morality is not grounded on religion. The mere intellect of man may be exercised on the contemplation, and may grow strong in contemplating the things presented to it by the world of matter alone; but we see not that there is any soil on which the moral virtues can flourish, or even any foundation on which they can rest, if his powers comprehend not something beyond this—if they do not lay hold on the truths connected with that eternity out of which he sprung, and to which he hastens. Does any one affect doubts on this subject. We would appeal in proof of it to his own real belief. Let him make choice of any existing community with which he is well acquainted, and suppose that by some miracle of evil, the belief of aught religious—of aught beyond what strikes the senses, is blotted out; and that no man has a conception of any being but what meets the eye, or of any existence but what is bounded by the epochs of birth and death. We would ask him to ponder the matter well, and then to say if he would not have just reason to dread that such motives to good, such restraints on evil being removed, hopes so ennobling being destroyed, a host of malignant and licentious passions would not be let loose that would devastate society. If an experiment so terrible could be made, would any reward bribe him to make his home among such a people? Would he not be in dread even to pass through them?

If then it be granted, as it necessarily must, that the prosperity of states is the great aim of the governors and the governed; if experience shows us that all which in states bears even the outward show of happiness, is commensurate with the prevalence of the moral virtues; if our knowledge of man makes it evident to the most sceptical of us, that these moral virtues do not thrive—do not even subsist but on the basis of religion—then, assuredly the active support of religion must be laid down as the duty of all governments. But in the present instance, we have stronger ground than even this. We speak not only of what might *a priori* be proved to be right to be done, but what actually has been done. In Great Britain, religion has ever received the direct support of the state, it has constituted a part of that great and glorious whole out of which we have grown, and to which we pride ourselves to belong. On what principle then can any of us, the men of a day, the present representatives of mighty interests stretching before and behind us for centuries, seek to tear out that which has come to us embodied and wrought into that great fabric which it is our part to transmit to posterity, at least unweakened and unimpaired. Is it because there are defects in this part of the edifice? There ever have been defects in every part of it, there ever, we may venture to say, will be defects in it. But if there are defects, are there not also things admirable? Is not a large portion of what has been, and is, excellent in the empire directly deducible from its religious establishments, and shall we affirm that here, as elsewhere, it is not the part of the patriot to correct, rather than to destroy, to build up rather than to demolish?

But some one says, in these days of great discoveries, we have come on one that altogether overturns your arguments. It has been found, that governments are established for the preservation of life and property, and not for any other purpose. They have nothing therefore to do with religion. As concerns it, their safest policy is to let it alone. We doubt the truth of this discovery. We doubt the truth of any discovery, that would separate the intellectual from the moral man; because we conceive they are not, and cannot be separated—that the lives and properties of men are, and can alone be, safe in any society, through the sustaining and restraining power of morality and religion. We maintain also, that, practically, you do, and must hold this to be a fact, and act accordingly, that every society is bound together by the truths of religion, and that in the daily working of its machinery, a belief in the truths, and the influence this has on the moral man, cannot be dispensed with for a moment. On what, in fact, does the decision of the majority of cases involving the lives and properties of men ultimately depend, but on testimony? and on what else than religious belief is the validity of testimony rightly made to rest? When an individual is brought into court to give his testimony, are the only questions that can there be put to him, those that concern life and property? or may he not be questioned concerning death and eternity? Nay, if he cannot give a satisfactory answer, both as to his knowledge and belief, in the latter, is he even permitted to speak concerning the former? He will not be heard on the question, though it may intimately concern his own property, or the lives and property of those dearest to him. He is debarred from the privileges of other citizens, and held an out-cast in that community, for the benefit of which he is nevertheless compelled to devote labour or property, or it may be life itself. Nor can such a procedure be justly censured. We know and feel that our whole civil rights, our lives and fortunes are protected, and can only be protected by the sanctity of an oath that comes from the lips of one who has some just conceptions of his relations to another world than this. It were gross neglect therefore in the laws, were all that is dear to men entrusted to him, who by some singular unhappiness in his lot, or perversity in his nature, has not been able to attain to any such conceptions. If the state requires its citizens to respect the property of others, it must be able to protect each one whose property is invaded, or it can expect nothing else but that, as in some parts of Italy, the population will be converted into disguised hoards of banditti. If it require them to leave to the laws the punishment that murder demands, then must it take care to inflict that punishment when due; else may it confidently anticipate the revival of a state of society like that which prevailed, when the right of private war was formally recognized.

If the state require its citizens to know and feel the great truths of religion, then must it assume that these truths are taught them. But some one again says—it is needless for the state to take this office on itself, because, though it might be its duty, were it not otherwise discharged, yet it is very certain, it will be effectually discharged by the *voluntary principle*. Could we persuade ourselves that this so named principle would indeed discharge, as well as the state, those functions which it is the duty of the state to see performed, we acknowledge, that it were a matter of indifference, whether the Government were an actor or an onlooker. But before we can assent to the propriety of the state, in this matter, becoming a mere spectator, we must be well assured that this principle will indeed perform the duty in every particular. Now, after looking into the matter with some care, we confess we cannot satisfy ourselves that such will be the case. On the contrary, it seems to us that there is a fallacy at the very bottom of the representation, that any so named principle is efficient only as it belies its name, and nearly in proportion as it is not voluntary, and that besides there seem to be defects in the churches, that arise from its operation, which we have reason to fear will one day produce serious evils.

There seems to us a fallacy at the very bottom of the matter, because we have neither seen nor heard, nor read, nor, unless the age of miracles were to return, can we form a conception of any body of men uniting to form themselves into a religious community, of their own mere motion, without some impelling cause from without. Let us take a case, the most resembling real voluntaryism that can occur. Say that, in some quarter of the world, there exists a community having no knowledge of any thing deserving the name of religion—heathens, we shall say—but, who would embrace religion, if worthily presented to them. It is clear that this mere disposition on their part will effect nothing. There must be a miracle, or there must be some human means, to bring religion before them. Say that what is wanting is completed by the arrival of a missionary or missionaries among them, of talent, and intent, and zeal, commensurate to the enterprise, whose labours result in these men forming themselves into a religious body— themselves defraying the expenses arising from the support of their clergy and other contingencies. This is probably the nearest approach that can be made to a purely voluntary church—to a body of men defraying by their voluntary contributions, the expenses of the religious privileges they enjoy. Yet, even in this case, it is apparent that this religious body only does so in part. Without the missionaries, its religion had been a blank; and in so far as it pays not the pecuniary outlay necessary to the existence and sending forth of these missionaries, its own voluntary contributions defray not the expenses, of the system of religion which it enjoys. What now have these missionaries cost? The question is difficult to answer. It were a fallacy to reckon the mere expenses alone of the maintenance, and education, and sending forth, of the individual missionary. To approximate to the actual expenditure, we must consider, to how many thousands, hundreds of thousands, nay millions, the gospel must be effectively preached in any land, before you can reasonably expect to gather out of the community, men possessed of the zeal, and talent, and patience, necessary to form, and send forth the successful missionary. We will not attempt such an estimate, but in so far as it is brought before us in what we have next to remark. If missions to the heathen be held to belong to the voluntary system, because the contributions to their support, either by churches or individuals, are voluntary, it must be confessed that the system is deplorably deficient. The fact, though a melancholy one, cannot be denied, that though more than five sixths of the earth has long been overspread with people destitute of religion, and though for the last two or three hundred years these regions have lain open to missionaries, yet do they still remain unchristianized—points only, here and there, appearing illuminating the deep gloom of heathenism that darkens so many lands.

To turn however from a case necessary to be stated, but which is only distantly connected with the matter in hand, to cases that are immediately connected with it—to churches such as the Independents and Methodists in England, and the Seceders in Scotland, who are held forth to us as examples of the efficiency of the voluntary system. And let us enquire, in the first place, how far the men who in these cases united to form themselves into religious communities, actually themselves paid the expenses of that religion which was among them, when so united. Now, it is notorious that the majority of these had been members of one or other of the national churches, and from them had imbibed their religious knowledge and feelings. Their religion was consequently the offspring of these national churches, and not of any voluntary system. Some indeed in England—for in Scotland there was scarce one—joined themselves to these bodies at their first formation, over whom religious feelings and convictions had not previously had any perceptible sway. Yet even these had learned something of what religion was, and had been prepared for embracing it, by the national churches. They had known speculatively, but still they had known, the great religious truths, which long radiating from these sources, had fixed themselves in the general convictions of the land, and were known to be recognized as verities by the mass of the good and great throughout it. These dissenters from the national churches sought not to make a new religion, but to improve the old. Either, as the Methodists in England, they thought that there was a deficiency of zeal in the administrations of the church, or, as the Seceders in Scotland, and the Independents in England, they conceived that some point in the government of the church was wrong and tended to corruption. But it is very certain, that when any of these bodies first met, had they asked themselves the question, whence is the material, the substantive medium through whose agency we received that religion which is among us, though they might have looked round in various directions, they must have at length turned themselves to the national church. They could not then be styled voluntaries; if by that term we mean to designate those who pay by voluntary contribution the pecuniary outlay that has been incurred by the infusion into them of the religious knowledge and feelings they possess.

Again, from the moment that any of these formed themselves into a separate religious community, the operation of the system into which a regard for their well-being led them, has in reality been continually more and more divesting them of that voluntary character which they probably believed they were assuming. No sooner have they seriously turned their thoughts on what is for the good of a church, than they have unavoidably been led to do all that in them lay, to form themselves into great *establishments*—into systems intending to operate, and therefore providing the means for operating, on successive generations. They have provided churches and parsonages as commodious and durable as possible, calculated to last not for one, but for many ages. Their educational establishments have been on a similar plan. If they have not become national churches, it is not because they have not endeavoured to become such, but because they have not been able to make themselves such. Each of these churches believed that it was the most conformable to the word of God of any existing church. Suppose this to have been really, prominently, the case; with regard to some one of them, and that this particular church had also possessed what all aimed at—the possession of superior zeal and prudence—had these things been so, we may suppose that this particular church might have been specially favoured as an instrument for the diffusion of the gospel; that it might have spread over the land, and have gradually absorbed within its body, not only other dissenting sects, but the established church itself, which losing their votaries would at length be obliged to relinquish the funds placed in their hands for religious purposes, and become altogether extinct. Such a church, if not a government church, would at least be a national church, and would naturally seek to make its funds as effective as possible for what would stand out before it as the great object of its existence—the training up the people in religion. Its churches would be large, numerous, durable: so would the houses of its clergy. As it would be economical, so, to avoid waste of its means, it is likely that in country places small glebes would be attached to these dwellings. The educational establishments of such a church would assuredly be extensive in their facilities, and liberal in their endowments. Nor, surely were there any portion of the people unable from poverty to procure for themselves the ministrations of religion, would it neglect to provide these for them. In this case it would hold it out to the rich, as their duty, to provide for the necessities of their poor brethren. Such a church could not be called voluntary, in the proper meaning of the term—in the sense of each individual in the community paying the pecuniary outlay, which the religious advantages he enjoyed actually cost. On the contrary, each really religious man, in as far as money was concerned, would owe the religion he enjoyed to contributions paid in years or ages before; and he himself in his contributions, would be making provision for religion reaching generations then unborn.

Such a church would approach in many particulars very nearly to our conceptions of an established church. It would differ from these in others.

The members of the community, neither as united into a whole civil body or state, nor as individuals, would be obliged in any shape to contribute to the support of the generally professed religion. The essence of its voluntaryism would consist in this, that any one who chose to stand altogether aloof from the church, might avoid contributing towards it. We conceive that this is by no means a desirable distinction. It seems to us contrary to the plainest principles of justice, in as much as these require an equivalent to be given for every advantage received. Now, in the first place, in such a community, there might be many individuals before whom religion was continually brought, and all its comforts presented, who yet defrayed not in the smallest degree the expenses of the establishment. Until they united themselves to the church, they would not contribute to its support. But besides this, whoever lives in a religious community, though he himself may live without religion, draws yet advantages— worldly advantages—from it, in the security, tranquility, and morality existing around him. The truth of this is manifested in the cause which men of this stamp have assigned for the existence of religion—in their assertion, that it owes its foundation to the wisdom of legislators, who have established it as a check to keep the passions of the multitude in salutary restraint. On these two accounts, therefore, it seems to us that it were an injustice—a thing essentially, and in itself wrong for individuals or a religious community not to contribute to the support of that religion. But, injustice is of a contagious nature. Where wrong is permitted among men, it seldom fails to breed wrong. We fear experience shows that such would be the case here. That the fact of many untaxed reaping the advantages which religion bestows on a community, would have the deplorable effect of turning the religious feelings of the community to perform the office of the tax gatherer. Men without religion would be marked, and so marked, that they would find their worldly prosperity and comfort injured by their apparent neglect of religion. Some would be driven into the fold in the garb of hypocrisy, others would stand out, exclaiming against, and conceiving themselves to be the victims of what they would term, priestcraft. Nothing more injurious to the cause of true religion can, we think, be conceived than such results. It saps the very root of the religion of love, when other feelings than pity predominate at the view of those who are void of religion. The evils and disorders which the being devoid of it may in this world give birth to, may indeed be the proper subject of indignation, but, at the contemplation of the condition itself, christian charity smothers every feeling but commiseration. On this head therefore, giving to what is termed the voluntary principle all the extent, and all the success conceivable, we apprehend it would be seriously defective.

There is another head also on which it seems to us that a church established under this so named principle is naturally defective. When a church is established by a whole community or state, it is generally in the power of the state, to throw the main burden of the support of religion upon the rent of land. This we conceive, in an economical view, is a very decided advantage. The reasonings of political economists, or, if these are not held convincing, the results of universal experience, demonstrate, that as society advances, a part of the annual revenue of the society is absorbed in the payment of the claims of the landholder. In the course of events, and the progress of time, certain individuals become proprietors of the land forming the territory of the state, and draw from those who till it a variable but large revenue. Now these landholders are not in ordinary called on to perform any service to the community. They may do so; there are many examples of illustrious benefits conferred on their country by individuals of this class. But they are not required to do so. "*Fruges consumere nati;*" their condition is to live and enjoy. It is then, we think, a clear advantage, when a portion of this fund is appropriated to support the expenses of the religion of the people—when it is bestowed on those who labour, not on those who sit idle. Thus it is well known that in Scotland the parochial clergy are supported from this fund. Their whole incomes arise from a small fixed amount yearly paid by the landlord—an amount we believe which is never begrudged them. We shall say that this is equal to a fortieth part of the yearly rent of that part of the kingdom. Were this taken from the clergy, and given to the landlord, it is clear that the community instead of gaining, would lose by the transfer. It would lose that portion of the revenue of the industrial classes, which the support of the clergy would necessarily absorb. In so far then, as the operation of what is termed the voluntary principle, takes from the wages of the labourer, and the profits of the capitalist, what a church supported by the state draws from the rent of land, it would seem to be disadvantageous to the community. But the truth is, that every church, as it establishes itself in a society, is desirous of placing whatever funds it may possess on land, because this species of property is felt to be the most secure of all. In this respect therefore, it is likely that such a church as we have been considering would assimilate itself to a church established by the state; and, just in proportion as it did so, would this disadvantage disappear.

In those particulars, therefore, in which a church supported by what is called the voluntary principle, is held by some to excel a church supported by the state, it seems to us, on the contrary, that it is inferior to it; and that it is inferior to it, in proportion as it differs from it. There remain to be pointed out two inherent defects—the probable sources of considerable evils.

The former of these comes very perceptibly in to view, when we consider that such a church, rising up within any community unconnected with the system of government which that community has adopted, and standing apart from it, must be regarded as a separate element—an element moving within the circle of the social compact, but having a motion of its own, not by any means necessarily in union with the other parts—a distinct principle—an 'imperium in imperio'—one existence operating largely on another, but for whose reciprocating action there is no machinery arranged. Such a condition of things might obviously lead to many evils. For brevity's sake we will only point to one; and, for the same reason, it shall be one connected with the second defect to which we would allude. It is we know very possible for a church, however excellent, to fall away from that excellence. However high therefore in the religious scale we may place any church, it is by no means impossible that in the course of ages it may descend to the lowest degrees; that its clergy may no longer be possessed with a truly religious spirit, and the efficacy of their ministry may cease. Now in the case of a church established on the voluntary principle there seems no constitutional remedy for this evil. The whole society may have contributed largely for successive generations to add to its means, trusting that by so doing they would add to its utility. But those very means, by giving its independence and wealth, may have fostered the pride of its clergy—may have made them careless about the effects of their ministry, and at length incapable of being effective ministers. The people fall away from them, but they heed not the declension; or, if they do, it is but to chide at what they term the growth of popular prejudice, not to lament over the decay of clerical zeal. Retired within their establishments, all uneasy reflections die away in the learned ease, and leisure, and pleasures, which these establishments afford. For such a condition of things there would be no constitutional remedy. A voluntary church owes the state nothing; for it has received nothing from it; nor can it be called on by the state to discharge duties to which it never pledged itself to the state. A great social grievance might exist for which there would be no remedy but in a great social wrong—in a violent inroad on the part of the state, on property which it had never granted, or never had had under its control. In protestant countries, the voluntary system has not any where continued for a space of time sufficient to mark by actual observation, the growth of such evils. Institutions only operate by degrees. The changes they produce are progressive, as generation succeeds generation. It is not until the lapse of ages, that we can expect fully to trace the real course any one of them shapes out for those subjected to its agency. We may however analogically refer to the effect of this system in the times of Romanism. Now, we apprehend, that were a Roman Catholic called on to instance those who gave the most eminent examples of the power and beauty of his religion, he would draw them from the voluntaries of his church—from the founders and early supporters of the monastic orders. Were he, on the other hand, called on to make known the source of those evils which, he will allow, overran the church for centuries preceding the era of the reformation, he would point to the same monastic orders, their corruptions, licentiousness, and ambition. If asked how it could be that good and ill flowed from the same fountain, he might probably reply:—they who founded these orders, they who laboured at their establishment, were holy men—men who zealously and disinterestedly devoted themselves to the highest duties of religion—to cleansing the church from the corruption of the times—to the instruction of the people—to the protection of the weak from the wrongs of the strong; and who, renouncing the pleasures of the world, were content to trust for the supply of their scanty personal wants, to the voluntary offerings of whose who benefited by their labours. Lives so spent procured for them the esteem of most men—the veneration of many. Numbers every where eagerly aided them with their substance in the prosecution of these enterprises, and the wealth that thus flowed in on them, was at first scrupulously applied by them to carry out the purposes for which it was given. They extended themselves in all directions; their missions penetrated to every land; they formed a great and respectable body in the church.

But, as time advanced, while the riches which the fervent spirit of their founders had procured to their respective orders remained, the spirit itself died away. Their successors, from age to age, became cold and colder. Men sought the shelter of these establishments for their own selfish ends. They turned to ease, and enjoyment, and sensual gratifications. They became the flatterers of the great, the despisers and deceivers of the multitude, the opprobrium of the church of which they had once been the ornament, the restless and ambitious agitators of communities, of which they had once been the benefactors.

We trust none of our readers will so far misunderstand us, as to conceive we are holding up, what a Roman Catholic, speaking according to his real belief, might state, with regard to the course of affairs in his communion, as being an exact parallel to what the operation of similar causes may be expected to produce within the pale of protestantism. When the difference is so great the analogy can only be remote. Still there is an analogy —an analogy which in the absence of other means of forming an opinion must have, and ought to have, considerable weight with us. We cannot but conclude, that there is danger in all churches, of funds set apart for the service of religion being diverted from it, and abused in the prosecution of worldly and improper objects; nor is the danger in any degree diminished by the fact of those funds having been originally procured by voluntary offerings. Now, in the case of churches established on the voluntary principle, it is impossible for the state to provide against this danger. Each of these churches grows out of the wealth and prosperity which the social condition, and the institutions of the community, in which it exists, have procured for it; and yet, in that tacit social compact, which takes a beginning with beginning institutions, and gathers strength with their progress, there is no provision made against those evils which its very possible perversion of those funds may occasion. This we conceive to be a great inherent defect in such churches. But it may probably be said in reply, "Your conclusions are all drawn from the supposition, that there is only one church within the state, and there may be a plurality." We made this supposition, it is true, but, it was for the sake of simplicity of explication. Whatever defect applies to one applies with equal force to two, three, or half a dozen churches, supported on this voluntary principle. In one important particular indeed the danger of defect is increased by a plurality of churches. It is obvious that a plurality of churches would add to the risk of large portions of the community being left destitute of religious instruction and ordinances. A single church, embracing the great mass of the community, and supported by them, would naturally think it a duty to extend its ministrations to those who were unable, or, for the time, disinclined to contribute to its support. But, where the responsibility is divided among several sects, there might be—we may say it is the natural condition of things that there should be—large masses left uninstructed, because none of these sects can conceive that it is its particular duty to extend its ministrations to all. It may indeed be supposed, that many of the evil consequences, otherwise likely to arise from the prolonged operation of the voluntary system, would be checked, because under the operation of this system, such a variety of sects and fluctuation of religious opinions would be produced, that no one sect could spread to a sufficient extent, or maintain itself for a sufficient time, to permit of the birth or growth of these evils. If any one should think this consideration a sufficient answer to the objections to which the system is liable, we certainly would not agree with him. Though some variety in religious belief be perhaps unavoidable, yet it is far from desirable; and such a continual fluctuation and successive overthrow of sects and opinions, from age to age, as is here contemplated, would be one of the worst evils that could come on a people, as it would tend more than any other circumstance to uproot religion altogether from among them. To hold that up as a remedy for evil, which is in itself the greatest evil, were therefore, it seems to us, an absurdity. But we trust, that, under any system, such a state of things is unlikely to have long continuance. It is we think not only contrary to reason and revelation, but opposed to fact. It seems to us that, when we take into view the whole protestant world, we shall rather see reason to rejoice that charity more and more prevails; that the bitterness occasioned by extreme views is softened; and that there is an approach to general unanimity of sentiment on religious matters; than to dread that protestantism will be still farther divided and weakened by increasing diversities of belief, and dissentions on these all important subjects.

But, finally, the answer to all which we have brought forward, that will most readily present itself to an advocate of the voluntary principle will we doubt not be, "The predominance in churches established by the state, of some of those defects, which, you assert, will develope themselves in the progress of the voluntary system, is the very cause of our separating from the establishment and becoming dissenters and voluntaries. We deny not these defects. On the contrary, were proof wanted, we would set *them* forth as proofs, of a very melancholy character, of the tendency of wealth and independence to produce pride and a neglect of duty, in all religious establishments. But we assert, that, in a church owing its support to the state, there is a check on this abuse, and a remedy for it. Such a church cannot conceal from itself the fact that it exists, and is paid, for the religious instruction of the whole people. If it fail in this duty, every one within it who has a sense of right and wrong, feels the failure as a sensible reproach. This feeling acts as a constant stimulant to the zeal of the church, and has a continual tendency to excite it to recover any ground it may have lost. Again we hold, that, if a church supported by the state, for the religious instruction of the people, fail in this its duty, it is the business of the state, either directly, or indirectly, to remedy the abuse. In this case, we hold that it is called on either to effect the removal of the defects that diminish the utility of the establishment, or to withdraw the funds that support it. In this, in our conception, lies the great advantage of establishments, and, notwithstanding the length to which we have already run, we must be indulged with a few words on what, in the apprehensions of very many, lies, we believe, at the root of the whole matter.

We believe it may be affirmed as a general and well known fact, that a majority of the advocates of the voluntary system are to be found in the ranks of what is termed the liberal party, and that they conceive in their advocacy of this system, they are following out the aims of that party. In this, in our opinion, they err. We also are liberals. We believe that the reign of feudality is over, and that the traces of its existence will gradually be obliterated; that consequently the hopes of humanity centre on the triumph of the people, on the rise in moral and intellectual worth, and on the ultimate ascendancy which is the inevitable consequence of their possession of these. To the furtherance of the sacred cause we would cheerfully contribute to the utmost of our ability in any way that our humble abilities might be useful. Farther still, we will say, that at the present moment, from many causes, chiefly as it seems to us, from the rapid progress in recent years of science and art, the people have outgrown their institutions, and that these are often constraining, cumbrous, and needing reform, to suit them to the actual condition of the elements of society. But while we willingly go thus far, we will not consent to take another step to which the efforts of some reformers would heedlessly press us. These feel the defects of existing institutions, but seem to feel these alone. Hence their cry—"*away with them.*" We protest against being hurried on to any such measures. We do not think that reform is synonymous with destruction, or liberty with lawlessness. On the contrary, we would be, not only for amending, but for extending our social institutions. It seems to us that as society still advances, as capital still further accumulates, as land becomes more valuable, as communities become more intellectual, and better able to appreciate the benefits of general union in carrying on schemes that tend to the good of the whole, or of great classes, and sections; so must our social arrangements and machinery become both more extended, and more complicated. Some men seem to believe that our energies are cramped by great national forms and institutions. Their idea of liberty seems to be, a power to break through these, and burst away from their pressure, as the *papilio* escapes from its envelope, and emerging into a new element flutters free from flower to flower, from sweet to sweet. We have no such extravagant, such aerial expectations. If the reader will pardon the comparison, we should say, that our condition more resembles some of the crustaceous tribes. The lobster we know has a thick and a heavy shell, and one, which, as he lives and thrives, at length begins to fetter and confine, and would at last squeeze him to death. He is therefore occasionally compelled to reform matters, and, though at risk of life, to throw off his case and give room to his limbs. But wise instinct is too strong with him to let him think of remaining in this free and shelless condition: he feels that this is not the life for him, and retreats to some shelter, nor is at ease till another shell incases him, larger, thicker, and therefore heavier than the former; but which is nevertheless necessary to give strength to his moving powers, and security to his existence. A similar necessity seems entailed on the social condition of man. While man is man, universal experience demonstrates that it is essential to the safety and even to the existence of society, that it be encompassed by a great frame work of institutions, which might be called burdensome, were it not necessary for its well being and security. We cannot therefore join with those, who, because they think—and perhaps truly think—they perceive great defects in existing national churches, would therefore have all national churches abolished, or, because some evils can be traced to the union of church and state, proclaim that these ought never to be united. We think that such sweeping assertions bear on the face of them a presumption of being erroneous. They are contrary to the general principle guiding us to social amelioration—reform, not destruction. They are false as to the particular case. As religion is a necessary element in the existence of civilized man, it must make a necessary part of the frame of society in every civilized community. Religious institutions and establishments will grow out of, and along with, every civilized community. They may grow symmetrically with the great stem, a part of it, giving and receiving strength and harmony as they rise and spread together, or standing out from it, unshapely and cumbersome, exposed to be severed by some passing blast, to the ruin of trunk and offshoot. As it can never be a matter of indifference to the community how these things are arranged, we maintain that when government or people have the power of modelling the religious frame-work, so as to suit it to existing circumstances, they mightly err if they neglect the opportunity. They have indeed only to do with the frame work, but, it is exceedingly important that that frame work be well fitted, and aptly joined, and capable of sustaining the fabric. It is surely the interest of every community to provide religious instruction for *all* its members. It is its interest that the ministers of religion have a competent education, and that they be so paid and maintained that they have neither the temptations of wealth or poverty to struggle against, but, without flattering the passions of either high or low, be prepared to devote their whole energies to the sacred cause in which they engage.

Shortly to speak, we are ourselves voluntaries; but, we are systematic voluntaries. So far from being opposed to what is called the voluntary system, we believe, that, as religion must have an existence in every civilized community, so that existence must be voluntary. We believe that every civilized community must in somehow *will* to sustain an establishment for the maintenance of religion—that this is a necessity of its existence, as a civilized society—but we assert that this *will* ought to be exerted in a systematic form; and that they who affirm that the whole community, though *willing* to support religion, ought not as a community to give it this support, would impose on us a principle false in theory, inefficient, injurious, and dangerous in practice.

We are aware that, as a reply to facts and reasonings on this subject, it is usual to refer to the example of the United States. We have no objection. In the history of that people we have an example of systematic voluntaryism, and of unsystematic—of a community *willing* as a body to establish religion, and carrying the will into action, and of other communities, not so uniting for this purpose. The fathers of New England crossed the wide Atlantic for these western wilds, for the express purpose of there establishing their religion, and they succeeded in their object. As their abodes spread along each stream, and throughout each valley, religion was settled with them. It was a distinctive feature of their polity, that provision should be made for its support, and care taken that every member of the community should be trained up in the knowledge and practice of its precepts. In the other sections of the territory now forming the union, no such purpose was carried into effect. They trusted to unsystematic voluntaryism. Here then the experiment has been tried—let us look at the results.

Whoever knows new England, knows that its population are a church provided and church-going people. Universal testimony tells us that in point of moral character they excel. It is apparent, that in other respects, their social condition must surpass their neighbours, for, under their management, a comparatively barren territory is the richest, most populous and flourishing in the union. It must be conceded also, that, as you recede from these states, and advance to the west and south, you find the externals of religion less apparent, the grossness of immorality more evident, and even the development of the natural resources of the territory less complete. These undeniable results require no comment. But, it is said the opinion of the people of the United States themselves, is in favour of what you call unsystematic voluntaryism; and they must be the best judges of what is most advantageous for themselves. We acknowledge the fact, but deny the conclusion. Whoever is acquainted with the course of public opinion in the United States, will see that there are two circumstances sufficiently accounting for the predominance there, of what is called the voluntary principle. In the first place their natural vanity—those exultant feelings that naturally arise with the consciousness of the fresh energies of national youth—inspire them with a persuasion that theirs is the best possible condition of humanity—that whatever *is* with them *is right*. Now at the time of their declaration of independence, the voluntary system was the general system. It therefore naturally became the universal system. But again, the tendency of all their political movements has been to give predominance to what may be termed *ultra* democratic views and principles. They conceive not, that liberty is to be preserved and perpetuated by the increasing power and sway of the moral principle throughout the community, rendering it possible for man to trust man still more and more, as the complications of society render such confidence more necessary; but that their only safety consists in trusting no man, and making the whole movement and mechanism of their polity depend on the immediate will of the immediate majority.

We think this principle erroneous. We think events show that it is so. We trust it is so; for if admitted, it would put a speedy limit to any great ameliorations in the condition of civilized man. But having been adopted it is a natural consequence that it should be carried out through the whole social system, religious as well as political. It is also to be considered that the adoption of any general principle of the sort generates a practical aptitude in working on it in all cases. This is especially observable in the present instance. No where will you find a set of people so ready to combine for carrying into effect any object of general and immediate interest as the population of the United States. The general interests of religion partake of the advantages of this national apitude for combination, and without any general organized system, are usually provided for in a manner which it were in vain to hope for in any other nation, were they in this matter to be given up to the mere promptings of popular impulse.

In so far, therefore, as in the history and condition of the United States we can trace effects to causes, it seems to us that the evidence is decidedly in favour of the state systematically providing for the support of religion, instead of leaving to accidental individual efforts what, it is the general persuasion, is the duty of all to provide for. The contrary method has not yet had time to work out all its effects; but, in so far as we can see, it is far from producing the same degree of good, and there is reason to fear that evils one day to become apparent are now growing out of it.

As we conceive therefore that it is the duty of the state in all instances to see that the religious wants of the people are provided for, so we think this a duty incumbent on all who legislate for this Province—the general principle necessarily includes the particular case. The contemplation indeed of the particular case presses home on us very forcibly the propriety of the general principle. The mother country conceives herself bound to uphold and protect the infant communities she settles in so many different regions. She spares not blood or treasure in defending their rights, or redressing their wrongs. Such a course is worthy of her. The cost is indeed great, but it is by a disregard of such immediate sacrifices, that her greatness has proceeded, and the world gives her credit for pursuing in this matter the path of true policy. Now while she thus unhesitatingly runs, in this matter, to the expense of millions to secure the existence of these embryo states, is it not wonderful that she should sometimes hesitate to contribute an amount, comparatively inconsiderable, to ensure the permanent growth among these of an element of that existence, which, merely politically speaking, is so essential to its happiness and security, as religion proves itself to be. She settles her sons far from their fatherland amid pathless woods and by lonely waters, and though the whole course of her policy is based on the notion that they will grow up to a resemblance of their ancestors, she takes no care that they be supplied with that which was essential to the growth of all that was great and ennobling in the bosoms of these their ancestors.

We ought now to speak of the mode in which the state should proceed in making this provision so that it may be effective and not liable to abuse. We perceive however that to attempt here to trace out general principles would protract our observations to an inconvenient length, and will therefore merely state what in the particular case ought, as it seems to us, before this to have been done, and what ought now to be done by those who legislate for Canada.

From what has been previously said it seems to us, that it was the duty of Great Britain to provide the means of religious instruction to the colonists whom she settled in these provinces. It also seems to us that she ought, for this purpose, to have employed the services of the two national churches, and that, if, after a fair trial of them, they were found incapable of discharging the office, it would have been her duty to employ any other instrumentality, not inconsistent with her protestant character.

She did early engage, or endeavour to engage, by every reasonable encouragement, the services of the church of England in this great work. To such of the clergy of that church as would enter on the arduous, doubtless, but glorious labour of missionaries to the infant province, she gave the countenance of the government of the colony, and afforded an ample provision against pecuniary want. Besides what their flocks might contribute, £200 sterling was secured to each missionary of that church. Unfortunately, for a long period, these her efforts had but very partial success. It is in reference to these times, that Dr. Strachan was wont to complain of the difficulty of inducing gentlemen of education to leave the comforts of England, and encounter the privations of a Canadian wilderness. The consequence was that they who had dispersed through this wilderness to give to it the beginnings of fertility and civilization, neither saw nor heard of the church of England, and what her missionaries might have accomplished, had they come among them, was unknown. It was also unfortunate, that, to supply this want of English missionaries, a system of proselytizing from other churches was adopted by which to fill her ranks. On this subject we may refer to the evidence of the Rev. Crosbie Morgell, chaplain to the Bishop of Quebec, given before the committee of the House of Commons, on the civil government of Canada 14th June 1828. "Question. Is there any difficulty in procuring persons to serve as clergymen in Canada, who have been educated in the doctrines of the church of England? Answer. Certainly. I should say there is difficulty in procuring them in Great Britain. Q. Is not that the reason why they have been induced to take so many persons into the service of the church who have been formerly belonging to other denominations of christians? A. When a mission becomes vacant, it is very desirable to fill it up as quickly as possible, and if we were to exclude all who have not been regularly educated in England, we should have to wait several months, and in the mean time sectarians would come in and perhaps disperse the congregation. Q. To what circumstance do you attribute the cessation of so many clergymen from their own church, and their conversion to ours? A. I must hope they are the purest motives, but I cannot dive into men's thoughts——." Concurring with Mr. Morgell in our hopes it must nevertheless be admitted that this circumstance, in conjunction with the conduct of prominent individuals thus brought over to her, has had great effect in giving a character of worldliness to the English Church, of which it is to be hoped she is undeserving, but which has been greatly injurious to her usefulness in the land. It is only of late years, that her clergy have really spread themselves through the country; and we believe it will appear that the numbers of her real adherents, make but a small proportion of the population of the colony.

As to the Church of Scotland the unhappy policy of the state has rather been to discountenance than to encourage it. It is unnecessary to remind the readers of the Examiner of what privileges this cruelly injudicious policy has deprived us, what grievous privations it has inflicted, what mighty evils it has entailed on us. Had the same encouragement been given to missionaries from our church, as from that of England, or even far more moderate encouragement, there cannot be a doubt, to one acquainted with the particulars of these times, that there would from the first have been an abundant supply of our clergy to minister to the spiritual necessities of our countrymen throughout the province. To what extent their ministrations might have been acceptable among others than those originally belonging to their church, how far they might have succeeded in supplying the religious blank which the province long presented, and yet, unhappily in so many directions continues to present, are questions not now to be satisfactorily answered.

All must at least admit that a deficiency so much to be lamented would thus in a great degree have been supplied. Meanwhile religious bodies not connected with either establishment have laboured in this field with zeal and with success. Of these the Methodists have been most prominent in their exertions, and most successful also. In the number of their congregations and ministers, and in the amount of their annual contributions for religious purposes, they exceed, and we should conceive in the number of their real adherents, they equal any other denomination of christians. Hence because one of the national churches was incompetent to the labour; because, as we perhaps think another was not encouraged to engage in the work, nay was held back from it—or, as others may conceive, because she too was not fully competent to it—there are actually established among us various protestant churches, having a strong and a just claim on the affections of the people. In one sense we somewhat regret this circumstance. We had rather, we freely confess, that the whole ground had been occupied solely by the two recognised establishments. But as that was not to be, we rejoice that the vast void these have left has been, in some measure, so well filled by others. Bigotry must indeed have blinded him, who is not sensible of the vast amount of good that has resulted from the zealous and effective labours of the methodists, the seceding presbyterians, and other protestant denominations, whose energies have been devoted to the extensive field of labour which the wide-spreading settlements of Upper Canada present to christian zeal. Fellow labourers with them for nearly half a century, sharing with them the toils, sharing also with them the joys of the hallowed work, far be it from the church of Scotland to urge the legislature to alter the relative situation of parties, to place one workman over another. Our principles—the principles we have in these pages advanced, forbid us to advocate any such measure. What is in itself good, what has grown with the growth, what has gathered strength with the gathering strength of the province, ought to be encouraged. It forms a part of the established order of things; and this it is both wrong and vain for the legislator to attempt to overturn. Such an attempt recoils on himself. It is his part to make the best of what is really established; provided it be not inconsistent with the general harmony of the whole. Now there is nothing in the professions, and in the standard of faith of the protestant sects that have established themselves in this province, inimical to the maintenance of peace and order within it; or to its advance in general prosperity. In essentials they all indeed closely resemble one or other of the national churches. We conceive therefore that it ought to be the aim of the legislature to form out of these a great provincial church—a church which would indeed have subdivisions of christians within it, conscientiously differing among themselves in many matters of government and in some points of doctrine, but professing to agree, and really agreeing, in the great fundamentals of protestant christianity. For the admission of any sect within this body there would seem to be only two things necessary. First—that it adhere to a sound standard of doctrine. Secondly—that it be really established in the hearts of a considerable body of the inhabitants of the province.

The first point would seem to be obtained by its being required that the clergy of every religious body recognized by the legislature, and provided for by law, should subscribe to the doctrines of the church either of England or Scotland, as contained respectively in the articles and confessions of faith, in so far as these standards are strictly doctrinal but not in any thing having reference to church government. We do not conceive that the members of any of the protestant sects now established in the province would object to this test of the soundness of their doctrinal views, with the exception of the Baptists. We think that what relates to infant baptism might be conceded to them as not being a matter which protestants hold among the essentials of religion; but we are not, we confess, very decided on this head, as any innovation to a general rule carries something of danger with it.

The next point would be gained by its being required of every religious body, claiming legislative aid, that it should satisfactorily show that its members amounted—say to one twelfth of the aggregate number of the other protestant sects, and that its contributions in support of religion also amounted to one-twelfth of the general contributions of the rest of the protestant church in the province. It seems to us very evident that there should be some limit to the number of sects to be admitted; nor does there seem any other practicable than the relative proportion which the numbers of the adherents of a particular sect, and the amount which they contribute bears to the general mass of protestantism within the province. Unless some limit be set by the legislator, he must admit every sect however insignificant in numbers, or however little substantial diversity there may be between it and other bodies. Such a looseness of legislating would, as it seems to us, be greatly inconvenient in the practical working of any plan, and would tend too much to foster that restless spirit, prompting a very small party to break off from the religious community to which they have belonged, on the most insignificant grounds which, as we have hinted, seems to have a tendency to spread widely and injuriously under the voluntary system.

Supposing that out of that religious body, gathered in this way from these primary elements, ought to be formed by the legislator that efficient protestant church which it is his aim to establish; the question which next arises is, how that real efficiency is to be brought out and secured.

To make teaching efficient and successful two things are requisite. The teacher must thoroughly know and comprehend what he proposes to teach; and he must be heedfully listened to.

The first only of these requisites the legislator can in this case partially secure. The main point—the rendering those who teach truly and deeply themselves religious—lies not within the scope of human laws. Yet he can employ the means in his power, and is as culpable, if he neglect them, as is a parent who neglects the religious education of his child under the pretence, that that education will not suffice to make him religious. Now what ever enlarges the mind, and gives greater scope and force to the moral, intellectual, and reasoning faculties, makes the man who is religious more deeply so: enables him to trace out more clearly the wonders, and to avoid entangling himself in the difficulties of religious truth; and vastly increases his power of impressing his convictions on others. On this account—on account of the increased energy it gives to the intellectual powers, and the weapons with which it furnishes the christian advocate, secular learning the study of the languages and sciences, has ever been held by all sound thinkers to be a most desirable, if not an essential part of the education of the professional divine. We conceive therefore that it is the duty of the legislator to make such provisions as may secure that the clergy whom he supports be a learned body. For this purpose we would propose that a fit proportion of the annual appropriation granted by the province to each religious denomination, should be devoted to the support of a college to be under the superintendence of that particular denomination; that, in case this sum were insufficient, two or more different sects might unite in support of a common institution. To secure the efficiency of these institutions in the secular departments of education it would be requisite that they should be placed under the superintendence of a general board qualified to exercise such superintendence, the constitution of which we shall afterwards consider. After a certain period—say five years from the commencement of the schemes being put in operation, no clergyman should be appointed as a minister in any of the churches who had not gone through with credit the established courses of general study. It would obviously be altogether out of the legislator's place to attempt to dictate in any way as to the particular course of divinity studies which the student for any church should pursue; but a provision might we think with propriety be made as to the length of time to be devoted by him to this exclusive object—perhaps the term of three years might be a reasonable period.

(To be continued.)

9

Plagiarism*

"Scribimus indocti doctique ————"

It has been well observed by Juvenal, that "the curse of writing is an endless itch." There is no hemisphere, into which the *cacoethes scribendi* has not made its way; there is no man, acquainted with the common mechanism of writing, who has not, at some period of his life, been under its dominion; nor have the Aesculapian fathers, with all their ingenuity and learning, been able to discover any remedy for this phlogistic distemper. Intellect has indeed pursued a glorious career, and the effulgent lamp of philosophy has shone forth with a heavenly splendour,

"At once the wonder, terror, and delight
Of distant nations,"

piercing the depths of ignorance, and chasing darkness from earth's farthest verge—exploring the arcana of every science, and revealing, to an astonished world, many hidden mysteries—dissipating many obscurities, and making known the errors of former generations—exhibiting the wisdom of the Deity in the grandest of his works, and manifesting discoveries in every department of the moral and material world. Serene philosophy has shed a lustre over the ennobled mind of man—it has enabled it to gain the heights of science; and the goal of perfection appears almost within its compass. But alas! the *scribendi cacoethes* is still as virulent in its effects as it was in the days of Homer's Machaon or

* From the *Literary Garland*, Oct., 1839, 561–2.

Virgil's Iapis; nor has any panacea been discovered by which it may be eradicated.

But to drop the allegory before it become cumbersome: There are innumerable kinds of scribblers; and they are all actuated by the same ruling passion—a desire of distinction. Fame is their guiding-star; and the words of Cowley they mentally repeat at every offering:

> "What shall I do to be for ever known,
> And make the age to come my own?"

Nor is there any thing reprehensible in a moderate ambition: on the contrary, when it displays itself in an honest mind, and meets with eminent abilities, it is of infinite service to the world; but when a man only thinks of distinguishing himself, without being qualified for the undertaking, he becomes a very ridiculous, and, not unfrequently, a very pernicious creature. Of all species of writers none are so offensive as the plagiarists, for none are so abject in their practices. Plagiarism is a low cunning, than which nothing can be more characteristic of an ignoble mind; and the *animus furandi* is as strongly evinced in a plagiarist as in the pilferer of the purse that "has been slave to thousands." The plagiarist, moreover, purloins in the most subtle manner, and no one is secure from the snares of his villainy. Works which have cost their artists many an anxious hour, when perhaps

> "Deep in ocean sunk the lamp of light,"

and whose fame has covered their memories with immortality, are the game of this impious crew. How often do we see the labours of some ancient, or modern philosopher—of a Socrates or a Bacon, of a Plato or a Newton, for instance, sacrificed at the altar of plagiarism! Plagiarists are indeed *angues in herba*. With serpentine cunning they insinuate themselves into the secrets of the learned; and the fruits of the genius of a philosopher may be ushered into the world as the productions of some senseless blockhead, who hesitates not to dignify himself with the title of author. But, like every thing else, plagiarism has an end; and, when it is once detected, loses its force, and makes a man incapable of bringing about even those events which he might have done had he passed only for a plain man. The reputation of one addicted to this vice, if perchance he should ever acquire any renown, will be as transitory as a morning cloud. Sooner or later,

> "The self-convicted bosom which hath wrought
> The bane of others or inslaved itself,"

will be discovered in its delinquency, and merited contempt will be the reward of its baseness.

> "——*Miserum est alienae incumbere famae,*
> *Ne collapsa ruant subductis tecta columis.*"

Not only is plagiarism in its effects, most hurtful to society, but its influence is a curse to man. Captivating in its appearance, it soon beguiles many followers, who avidously seek to acquire the praises of their fellows, but are yet unwilling to exert the talents bestowed on them by a beneficient Creator, or are incompetent for such tasks as they may have undertaken. Besides, plagiarism dulls the mind, and renders it incapable of exercising its legitimate functions; for no sooner has the soul become wholly subject to its power, than it relinquishes all idea of acquiring a merit by its own industry. It is an observation of Bacon, that, in a numerous family of children the eldest is often spoiled by the prospect of an estate, and the youngest by being the darling of the parents; but that some one or other in the middle, who has not perhaps been regarded, has made his way in the world and over-topped the rest. A similar remark will apply to plagiarism. Those who allow themselves to be mastered by it, become the votaries of a passion which disqualifies them from enlarging their capacities, and exercising their thoughts and judgment in studies in which they might have excelled, while, on the other hand, the man of an honest and moderate ambition, who is satisfied with "less noisy praise," and strives not to procure, what may be termed, a precocious reputation, will, very often, become a proficient in arts and learning. The mind, it is true, has a certain active power which cannot lie altogether idle, but its faculties are not to be forced in the same artificial manner that a skilful horticulturist may produce a bulbous plant; and in nothing is the dignity of human nature more remarkably villified than when man preposterously attempts the attainment of objects beyond his sphere of action.

The mind devoted to plagiarism exhibits an imbecility, and want of moral principle, which makes its possessor a very unworthy member of society, and ought to convince all of the paramount necessity of guarding against so disreputable a disposition. If it once gain an entrance, it insensibly advances, and, finally becomes a habit impossible to be overcome. "Man is a bundle of habits," says an eminent philosopher, "and the art in which the secret of human happiness consists, is to *set* the habits in such a manner that every change may be a change for the better." It is very certain, also, that plagiarism proceeds from vanity, from the improper exercise of that natural passion that that man has for distinction—a passion which, when governed and restrained by reason, gives motion to the latent powers of the soul; but, when not disciplined by philosophy, is detrimental to mankind. And as this love of fame is implanted in every bosom, and is capable of doing great good or incalculable mischief, it ought to be the watchful care of education to infuse into the untainted mind of youth, such early principles of morality and religion as will repel and overcome the passions that obstruct it, and fortify it against the ways of wickedness. The soul is a spacious and prolific garden, whose fruits depend upon the industry and skill of its cultivator—education; for if there be not care and science in its management, weeds will soon shoot up their rank heads and choke the precious seed whence springs virtue. It is very true that all men are not alike capable of shining in learning; but let it be remembered as a certain maxim, that every member of the human species is indispensable in the immensity of creation, and that, although there is a diversity in the powers of intellect, yet every man, if he do justice to himself, is capable of excelling in something.

> "While the claims
> Of social life to different labors urge
> The active powers of man, with wisest care,
> Hath nature on the multitude of minds
> Impress'd a various bias; and to each
> Decreed its province in the common toil.
> To some she taught the fabric of the spheres,
> The changeful moon, the circuit of the stars,
> The golden zones of heaven. To some she gave
> To search the story of eternal thought;
> Of space and time; of fates unbroken chain
> And will's quick movement. Others by the hand,
> She led o'er vales and mountains, to explore
> What healing virtue dwells in every vein
> Of herbs or trees. But some to nobler hopes
> Were destin'd: some within a finer mould
> She wrought, and temper'd with a purer flame.
> To these the sire omnipotent unfolds,
> In fuller aspects, and with fairer lights,
> This picture of the world. Through every part
> They trace the lofty sketches of his hand:
> In earth, or air, the meadow's flowery store,
> The moon's mild radiance, or the virgin's mien
> Dress'd in attractive smiles, they see pourtray'd
> (As far as mortal eyes the portrait scan,)
> Those lineaments of beauty which delight
> The mind supreme. They also feel their force,
> Enamour'd; they partake the eternal joy."

J. R.

10

Genius and its Application*

> In the soul
> Are many lesser faculties that serve
> Reason as chief; among these Fancy next
> Her office holds; of all external things,
> Which the five watchful senses represent,
> She forms imaginations, aery shapes,
> Which reason joining or disjoining, frames
> All what we affirm, or what deny and call
> Our knowledge or opinion; then retires
> Into her private cell when nature rests.
>
> *Milton.*

Of all the popular opinions that have made their way into the world, there is none more erroneous than that entertained by many persons with respect to genius. It is a prevalent notion, that it is a thing within the reach of every man; and, to adventitious circumstances, to the accidents of art and knowledge, is often ascribed the character of genius. A writer of verses is called a genius; a smatterer in the languages of the ancients is named a genius; and not unfrequently does the tone of a man's voice acquire for him the distinction of genius. In a word, genius is, by many, considered synonimous with learning; and as often as a person of any acquirements is mentioned, are we likely to hear the term genius applied to him.

A refined and cultivated mind does not properly constitute genius; but it consists in a gift of nature, which, without any assistance of art, notes its possessor to be a remarkable character, and enables him to produce works,

* From the *Literary Garland*, Dec., 1839, 33–6.

alike the admiration of their own times, and the astonishment of subsequent generations. Education may embellish the mind; it may refine the conversation, and set rules for our instruction; but there is something noble and majestic in a great natural genius, that places it immeasurably above a mind polished by learning. There is something divine in a true genius that raises the soul above itself, and enables it to attain objects beyond the sphere of intellect. "Genius," it has been observed, "resembles a proud steed, that whilst he obeys the slightest touch of the kind hand of a master revolts at the first indication of compulsion and of restraint." One of the best critics of antiquity, Horace, remarks of genius, that no one can claim that distinction who does not enjoy a superior imagination, and is not master of high flights of fancy.

> "—— Cui mens divinior atque os
> Magna sonaturum des nominis hujus honorem."

"Genius," says Reynolds, "is supposed to be a power of producing excellencies, which are out of the reach of the rules of art; a power which no precepts can teach, and which no industry can acquire." "It is the invention," observes Pope, "that in different degrees distinguishes all great geniusses: the utmost stretch of human study, learning, and industry, which masters every thing besides, can never attain to this. It furnishes art with all her materials, and, without it, judgment itself can at best but steal wisely: for art is only like a prudent steward, that lives on managing the riches of nature. Whatever praises may be given to works of judgment, there is not even a single beauty in them to which the invention must not contribute: as in the most regular gardens, art can only reduce the beauties of nature to more regularity, and such a figure, which the common eye may better take in, and is therefore more entertained with. And perhaps the reason why common critics are inclined to prefer a judicious and methodical genius to a great and fruitful one, is, because they find it easier for themselves to pursue their observations through an uniform and bounded walk of art, than to comprehend the vast and various extent of nature." Fancy, which is nothing else than invention, Milton declares to be the eye of the soul; and

> "—— In her absence *mimic* fancy wakes
> To imitate her; but misjoining shapes,
> Wild work produces oft."

The heathen world exhibited several great natural geniusses, not disciplined by any rules of art. But of them all—Solomon excepted—Homer affords the most striking illustration. His was an imagination above all artificial aid; and his mind a Paradise of the richest soil. The "*vividi vis animi,*" he possessed; and there is that divine fervour in his works that captivates the soul of every reader of any degree of poetical susceptibility. Demosthenes is another remarkable instance of genius. His indomitable spirit and wonderful perseverance enabled him to overcome constitutional defects; but it was the splendour of his imagination, the greatness of his invention, that produced the eloquence that astonished the Athenians, and may be said to have resembled

"The big thunder o'er the vast profound."

Socrates, of whom it was remarked, that he brought philosophy from heaven, to inhabit among men; and Archimedes and Euclid, were all powerful geniusses. They had no models from whom to borrow their theories—they were the imitators of none. The Romans were not void of genius. They produced many great men, whose memories we reverence, and whose works we admire; but, for the most part, they formed themselves by rules, and submitted the greatness of their natural talents to the corrections and restraints of art. The genius in both these classes of authors may be equally great, but exhibits itself differently; and, for the purpose of distinction, is classed separately. The one may be compared to a most prolific soil, whose fruits spring up in abundance without any certain order: in the other, art supplies the skill of a cultivator. Under this second head of genius may be classed Plato and Aristotle among the Greeks, Cicero and Tully, Juvenal and Horace, Virgil and Ovid, among the Romans, and Milton, Bacon, Newton and some others among the moderns.

Without derogating from the fame of the ancients, it may be remarked, that antiquity afforded a golden era for the display of genius. That irregular manner of life, and those manly pursuits from which barbarity takes its name, were most favourable to the free and unrestrained exercise of the nobler passions of the mind. In advanced and civilized society the characters of men are more uniform and disguised; and the powers of the soul have not the same opportunity of exerting themselves. "In the infancy of societies," says Dr. Blair, "men live scattered and dispersed in the midst of solitary rural scenes, where the beauties of nature are their chief entertainment. They meet with many objects to them new and strange; their wonder and surprise are frequently excited; and by the sudden changes of fortune occurring in their unsettled state of life their passions are raised to the utmost. Their passions having nothing to restrain them, their imagination has nothing to check it."

A more noble exemplification of human genius the world has never witnessed than in the Bard of Avon—the immortal Shakspeare, who has been most aptly compared to the stone in Pyrrhus' ring, which is represented to have had the figure of Apollo and the nine muses in the veins of it, produced by the spontaneous hand of nature, without any help from art. Born of humble parents, Shakspeare's education was limited, but his genius was indeed gigantic; and it has cast a deathless celebrity on the history of his country. The genius of this mighty magician, which diffused such glory around it, may be admired, or rather adored, but can never be measured.

> "A genius universal as his theme;
> Astonishing as Chaos, as the bloom
> Of blowing Eden fair, as heaven sublime."

In the whirlwind of his scene, Shakspeare bears the imagination of his audience along with him. He

> "Carries them here and there; jumping o'er times;
> Turning the accomplishment of many years,
> Into an hour glass."

"The English stage might be considered equally without rule and without model," writes Scott, "when Shakspeare arose. The effect of the genius of an individual upon the taste of a nation, is mighty; but that genius, in its turn, is formed according to the opinions prevalent at the period when it comes into existence. Such was the case with Shakspeare. Had he received an education more extensive, and possessed a taste refined by the classical models, it is probable that he also, in admiration of the ancient drama, might have mistaken the form for the essence, and subscribed to those rules which had produced such master pieces of art. Fortunately for the full exertion of a genius, as comprehensive and versatile as intense and powerful, Shakspeare had no access to any models of which the commanding merit might have controlled and limited his own exertions. He followed the path which a nameless crowd of obscure writers had trodden before him; but he moved in it with the grace and majestic step of a being of a superior order; and vindicated for ever the British theatre from a pedantic restriction to classical rule. Nothing went before Shakspeare which in any respect was fit to fix and stamp the character of a national drama; and certainly no one will succeed him capable of establishing, by mere authority, a form more restricted than that which Shakspeare used." The celebrated critic, Jeffrey, observes of that remarkable man, Sir Walter Scott, that, "even in his errors there are traces of a powerful genius." With a mind as versatile and creative as that of Shakspeare,

Scott, by an extraordinary force of nature, power of thought, and indefatigable study, amassed to himself such stores of knowledge as we cannot regard without amazement as having been acquired by any one man in the compass of the longest life. As a philosopher, historian, poet, and novelist the fame of "The great unknown," is equally imperishable. Time, in his ceaseless course, may consign the royalty of sovereigns to dark oblivion; "the race of yore who danced our infancy upon their knee," may be blotted from our remembrance; and nations may cease to exist; but the name of Scott will never die. A learned reviewer has truly remarked that "never has the analogy between poetry and painting been more strikingly exemplified than the writings of Scott. He sees every thing with a painter's eye. Whatever he represents has a character of individuality, and is drawn with an accuracy and minuteness of discrimination, which we are not accustomed to expect from verbal description. Much of this, no doubt, is the result of genius; for there is a quick and comprehensive power of discernment; an intensity and keenness of observation, an almost intuitive glance, which nature alone can give, and by means of which her favourites are enabled to discover characteristic differences, where the eye of dulness sees nothing but uniformity." Burns was a genius; and despite the pedantry and perverseness of those whom the bard himself styles, "cut throat bandits in the path of fame," a great one too. Burns may be well termed "Fancy's pleasing son;" and it may be said of him, what was observed of Ossian, that, "he did not write to please readers and critics. He sung from the love of poetry and song. His poetry, more perhaps than that of any other writer, deserves to be styled 'the poetry of the heart.' It is a heart penetrated with sublime and tender passions; a heart that glows and kindles the fancy; a heart that is full, and pours itself forth; and, under this poetic inspiration, giving vent to his genius, no wonder we should so often hear and acknowledge in his strains the powerful and ever-pleasing voice of nature—

> "—— *Arte natura potentior omni* ——
> *Est Deus in nobis, agitante calescimus illo.*"

How simple is the poet's description of himself! While he invokes, "a spark o' nature's fire," he despises "your jargon o' your schools."

> I am na *poet*, in a sense,
> But just a *rhymer*, like, by chance,
> An' hae to learning nae pretence,
> Yet, what the matter.
> Whene'er my muse does on me glance
> I jingle at her.

Your critic-folk may cock their nose,
And say, how can you e'er propose,
You wha ken hardly *verse frae prose*
    'To mak' a sang?'
But, by your leaves, my learned foes,
    Ye're maybe wrang.

What's a' your jargon o' your schools,
Your latin names for horns an' stools;
If honest nature made you *fools*,
    What sairs your grammars?
Ye'd better ta'en up spades and shools,
    Or knappin-hammers.

A set o' dull, conceited hashes,
Confuse their brains in college classes!
They *gang in* stirks and *come out* asses,
    Plain truth to speak;
An' syne they think to climb Parnassus
    By dint o' Greek!

Gie me a spark o' nature's fire,
That's a' the learning I desire;
Then tho' I trudge thro' dub an' mire
    At pleugh or cart,
My muse tho' hamely in attire,
    May touch the heart.[*]

It is impossible to reflect on those extraordinary instances of genius without being raised into a contemplation on the wonderful force of nature on the human mind; and of the great disparity observable in the intellectual capacities of men. It is indeed very surprising, when we remove our thoughts from such instances as have been mentioned, to consider those we so frequently meet with, who seem to have few ideas above those of sense and appetite; and when we compare them with persons of the most exalted attainments in arts and learning, we find it difficult to believe that they are members of the same species. But, whatever constitutes this first and incomprehensible inequality, it is very certain that the next great difference between men, in their several acquirements, is attributable to accidental circumstances in their education, their fortunes, or their course of life. Labour and time are requisite to mature the faculties of the soul; and without which many a genius lies unfashioned, like a jewel in the mine.

The application of genius is a subject worthy the deepest consideration. The many instances that are witnessed of the abuse of laudable talents,

* This is Robert Burns' "First Epistle to John Lapraik."

manifest the importance of consulting, in the care of youth, the natural disposition to any particular art, science, profession or trade; and, above all things, of studying impartially, in the formation of any scheme of life, the capacity of the mind. It is indeed very difficult for any one to form a correct judgment of his own abilities, or of the channel in which they ought to be employed. The esteem of self, common to all, prompts men to over-rate their talents, and the love of singularity allures their minds into a fond-ness for vain-glory, and incites them to attempt objects whose exterior pomp and dignity, like the deceptive caskets of Portia, fascinate the view. But it is not so difficult a thing to form an estimate of the attainments of others; and at no period of life are the powers of the soul more susceptible of examination than when the mind is in the May of youth, "a stranger to the savage arts of life." Historians relate of Scipio, that having been asked by some flatterers what the Romans would do for a general after his death, replied, "take Marius." Marius was then a very boy, and had given no instances of his valour; but it was visible to Scipio, from the manners of the youth, that he had a soul formed for the attempt and execution of great undertakings. The greatness of spirit that distinguished the conqueror Alexander, he early exhibited. Being asked, in his youth, to contend for a prize in the Olympic games, answered scornfully, that he would do so if he had kings to run against him. Innumerable are the instances that might be mentioned of the early dawning of greatness in men whose after lives evinced them to be extraordinary characters; but it would be useless to relate them.

The protection of genius—the encouragement of talent—is a subject that claims and deserves the solicitude of a generous spirit and liberal scholar. For want of cherishment, merit frequently languishes in silence; for, as the accomplished Pliny forcibly remarks, "*neque cuiquam tam statim clarum ingenium est, ut possit emergere; nisi illi materia, occasio, fautor etiam, commendatorque contingat.*"

> "But let us haste.—Night rolls the hours away,
> The redd'ning orient shows the coming day,
> The stars shine fainter on the' etherial plains,
> And of night's empire but a third remains."

J. R.

11

Thoughts on the System of Legislation

Which has prevailed in the Hawaiian Islands for the last forty years; on the evils that have arisen from it; and on the possible remedies for these evils*—by John Rae, *A.M., M.D., S.S.R., M.E.,*† *District Justice and Coroner for Hana, Maui, Notary Public for Maui, author of* New Principles of Political Economy, *&c., &c., &c.*

[I. February 2, 1861]

SIR:—I am desirous of endeavoring to call the attention of the public, and of the Legislature, to certain—as they seem to me—errors and defects in some of our laws, or rather in the principles of legislation which have given origin to these laws.

* This long article was published in instalments in the *Polynesian* in 1861 on February 2, February 9, February 16, March 16, March 30, and April 20. The editor prefaced the first instalment with the following note:

We commence to-day, on the first page, a series of communications from Dr. Rae, of Hana, Maui, touching the legislation of these Islands. His view of things, in their bearing upon this people, if not new to those who have had eyes to see and unprejudiced minds to consider, is at least well set forth, and the interest deepens as the narrative progresses.

Rae himself opened with the following explanatory letter to the editor:

I am sensible how little authority my name can here give to any arguments I may bring forward, and should, therefore, have preferred the modesty of an anonyme, but that the facts I wish to state would not permit my hiding myself under an *incognito*.

As it is so, I may be permitted to state to your readers why it is that I conceive I may, without presumption, endeavor to call their attention to the subjects I take upon me to discuss.

The character of the native Hawaiian has always been to me an object not only of mere curiosity, but of great and, I trust, intelligent interest. I have had ample opportunities for studying that character, and have used all proper means to avail myself of them. I have resided in these islands for over ten years, surrounded by natives, most generally without a white man within miles of me, and in my various capacities of pedlar, doctor, schoolmaster, farmer, and magistrate, I have necessarily seen them exhibited before me without disguise, and in various lights. To say that I fully comprehend them is more than I, or perhaps any white man, could do with justice. But at least I know something of them, and of the mode in which laws devised for their benefit have really operated.

The laws to which I wish specially to refer are those established with the purpose of suppressing disorders incident to the intercourse of the sexes—laws, or rather the want of laws, for repressing the diseases which spread from irregularities in that intercourse—and, finally, the law which has been passed to regulate the traffic in *awa*.

I would first speak of the laws which have been passed to suppress irregularities in the commerce of the sexes. And the first observation I would make is, that I have very great doubts whether the framing of any such laws, or at least their rigorous enforcement, be a measure that is ever either wise or expedient. I entertain these doubts, not because I dis-

---

SIR:—You are aware of most of the causes which have retarded the publication of these letters. It is only necessary that I should inform your readers of some of them.

When I entered on the subject I conceived that what I had to say would only occupy two, or it might be three, columns of your paper. As I proceeded, however, the subject expanded before me, so that from the time occupied in writing on it and other circumstances, the last session of the legislature had commenced before I had come near a conclusion. I thought it better, therefore, to wait until that session had closed, that I might see what new measures might be carried before giving my manuscript to the Press.

I have to add that the delay has led me to give greater expansion to my ideas than the preamble of my first letter would suggest to the reader.

I am yours very obediently,

JOHN RAE

HANA, January 10, 1860. [*sic*]

† Presumably S.S.R.M.E. stands for Socius Societatis Regiae Medicae Edinburgensis.

believe in the paramount importance of the purity of domestic life to the happiness and prosperity of individuals and nations. I am, on the contrary, convinced that it is the only true foundation for both; but because I believe it will be found that all attempts to amend the morality of any nation by legislative enactments and governmental action, have ever proved worse than useless. Human nature somehow rises up in arms against any force from without that would compel it to be good or righteous after any particular fashion, and, in the tumult of the rebellion thus excited, treads down and stifles those inward monitors to which the soul would otherwise have been inclined to listen. The thing has been often tried and always with bad success.

Louis the 14th closed a long life of license by an old age of devotion. He had been the model by which all around him had hitherto shaped their course of life, and he determined that in this also they should follow his kingly example. He was obeyed, for his iron will had a force more stringent than our laws. Decorum of manners, books of devotion, religious exercises seemed a fashion. But was there any good in this? Was there anything real? Quite the contrary. All these things felt as galling fetters, which they who wore them longed to shake off. This the event proved. With ill-dissembled joy was the descent marked of the old monarch to his tomb. Then all those disorderly passions that had been unwillingly pent up, having gathered tenfold force from restraint, burst forth exultant. In their fresh vigor, as they showed themselves at the Court of the Regent Orleans, they rivalled the orgies of the Roman Emperors. Under his successor, Louis 15th, exhausted but not satiated, they sank into the disgraceful debaucheries that tainted all the higher ranks of France during that reign, and cast so vile a stain on her nobility that the deep gulph dug for them by that terrible revolution, which these excesses had so largely contributed to excite, scarcely hides it from our eyes.

But it will be said by some: This is no fair instance; Louis 14th was a bigoted Roman Catholic, and the imperfect teachings of that faith can never be expected to serve as a firm foundation for national morality. Be it so. Let us then take an instance from another and opposite quarter.

Every one will acknowledge that the Puritans of England, the brethren of the pilgrim fathers, were an eminently religious people. I speak not of the correctness of their belief, nor of the just conformity of their practice to the revealed will, but of the sincerity of their faith, and of its influence on their lives and actions. That was tested in destitution, adversity, persecution and bore them stoutly through many a battle field, so nerving their arms to the combat that at length their good swords won for them the supremacy over England. They laid hands on the Kingdom as their rightful possession, and, in accordance as they conceived with the course manifestly marked out to them by the hand of God, they determined to make it a privilege worthy of His Saints to purify it of wickedness, purge it of all incentives to guilty folly, and exalt godliness in its midst. Vice was to be put down with a high hand. Death, therefore, was the penalty of proved licentiousness. All recreations and sports withdrawing the mind from the worship of God and Heaven by contemplations, were voted sinful and to be done away with. The theatres were, therefore, closed, and sports and recreations even more innocent abolished. None but men of acknowledged piety and godliness could aspire to office. Others were scowled down as opposers of God's work.*

The intent of these men was perhaps good, but nothing could have been more calamitous for themselves and England than the project they set about. It overthrew them. Its mischievous effects on the Kingdom were so great and manifold that their traces yet remain.

Religion, with all its graces and virtues, is from above, heavenly. The instruments with which rulers work, and alone can work, rewards and punishments, are of the earth, earthly. No government, therefore, can manufacture religion. When it sets about it, the article it turns out is sure to prove that rascally counterfeit, hypocrisy.

The world is mainly made up of worldlings, men who would rise and thrive, and are ever ready to adopt the mode by which they see others rising and thriving to seize the weapons that then and there may best serve them in the battle of life. Such men readily assume the externals of a prosperous religion. Is a readiness in extempore prayer demanded, their sharp wits and a little of the imitative faculty soon enable them on all needful occasions to rival, and even surpass, professionals in the wordy abasement of self, in the warmth and energy of their beseechings. Are a sanctimonious demeanor and a sober suit of clothes esteemed ensigns of inward piety, both can with almost equal ease to be put on. Is regular attendance at church requisite, they are there. Neither wildness of doctrine nor prosiness of manner can weary them out. Are cards, dice and other more enticing pleasures to be given up, they are abandoned, or only indulged in when a safe secrecy can be bought.

All this is no doubt something of a heavy price to pay, and, accordingly, were not the reward proportional, they would account themselves very ill-used men. Of consequence, every office of trust or emolument, whether they be fitted for it or not, must be theirs. Theirs too must be all governmental windfalls, and advantageous contracts. Means are to be found for

---

* See the enactment, "No person shall be employed but such as the House shall be satisfied of his real godliness."

gratifying worse propensities with impunity. Complaints against debaucheries, extortions, calumnies and frauds that would wither the reputation of other men, must be put down with the cry "He is a godly man, we know him to be incapable of such things." Woe, then, to the accuser! He is a marked and blasted man.

All this the puritanical party experienced, and evil were the consequences both within their camp, and without it. Within, even the really pious were contaminated by the bad example when they saw that men of the same religious standing as themselves were, according to the phraseology of the day, *self-seekers*, they also became self-seekers, entered into the common scramble, and contributed to bring disgrace on their party. So universally predominant had self-interest become, so far had the contagion spread, that, as is well known, Cromwell could not find men enough in his party sufficiently untainted by it, to enable him to carry on a constitutional government. He was actually compelled to be a despot.

Outside of the camp again, honest men who had stood aloof from the peculiar religious views and civil policy of that party, now looked on them with absolute detestation. They felt wronged by the state of political and social depression, and consequent insignificance, in which they had been so long compelled to exist. They were exasperated at the debarment from harmless sports and recreations, at the sabbatarian gloom in which the land was plunged, at the fines and sequestrations under which it groaned, all to gratify the tastes, and fill the pockets, of a set who had proved themselves not a whit better, but rather a little worse, than their neighbors. A settled indignation pervaded the minds of men, the forerunner of the revolution that ensued. They fell, and Charles was brought in. Then was seen what they had done for themselves and England.

As for them, their fall was complete and utter. The multitude regarded them as pharisaical hypocrites, more wicked at heart than publicans and sinners. How widely this sentiment prevailed in England may be gathered from the reception Butler's celebrated satire met with. To use the picture he draws of times

> "When pulpit drum ecclesiastic,
> Was beat with fist instead of a stick,"

seems too grossly exaggerated, and deficient both in probability and decorum. But then it convulsed the nation with laughter, and from sea to sea they clapped their hands with all the delight which people feel when they see a lash well laid on upon a rabble rout of scamps. As a party they were completely sunk; the really good among them finding it impossible to extricate themselves from the mire of the slough into which good and bad had been together hurled. How unlike was the fortune of that vast body of English Puritans, once so famous, to that of the handful of them who took refuge in a corner of North America, and, happily for themselves, had no opportunity to attempt to domineer over others. The one sunk in obscurity—the other revered and celebrated, as having so largely contributed to lay the foundations, and give solidity and strength, to the fabric of a mighty Empire. This was what the unhappy project of the English Puritan had done for himself; what he had done for the English people was still more calamitous.

He had found them at least decent. Piety and virtue among them had their praise. Vice had been for a reproach, not an honor. Now, as men ever go to extremes, because harmless mirth had been held a sin, they flew into the embrace of licentious folly. Because an air of piety and devotion had been used to cloak wickedness, they conceived, whenever they saw them, that they covered a knavish hypocrite. To be openly licentious, to mock at religion and virtue, was to be an honest fellow. Drunkenness and debauchery overran the nation. It is not unusual to lay all this on the head of Charles, but that is to ascribe greater power to him than he had or could have had. No single man can change the morals of a nation. Charles, indeed, willingly headed the frothy stream, and, as he gaily sailed along it, caught with delight at the glittering bubbles that floated on its surface, but the polluted tide itself had far deeper sources, and flowed from the diseased and corrupted national heart. In proof of my assertion I might cite the whole recorded history, the whole extant literature of the nation during the two periods, the one immediately preceding, the other following the Civil War, but I content myself with one particular. In those days, before the existence of newspapers and the currency of what is termed light literature, the playhouse was the great resource for daily intellectual delectation. It necessarily reflected the feelings, sentiments and tastes of the age. Now, if we take up any of the dramatists who flourished during the reigns of Elizabeth, James and Charles I., Shakspeare, for instance, or Ben Johnson, or even I think Fletcher, we find indeed a free picture of life and manners, but nothing vicious. The picture, on the contrary, is that of vice punished and virtue rewarded. To our tastes indeed some of the scenes are not very decorous, but it is an indecorum which we excuse as we do that of an infant gamboling on the carpet. In some of his tumbles we might wish perhaps that he wore something else than a petticoat; but he means no harm. That was the drama which the puritans had denounced and prohibited. The drama which came in with Charles, and which that education had given the nation a taste for, was of a different stamp. In it, as we see it in the pages of Congreve, Dryden and Wycherly, the hero is always a profligate, and is rewarded for his profligacy. The Puritan had made adultery death; the plot of these dramas generally turns on a successful adultery. He had made a serious offence of that free wit which only aims at a laugh. In the drama that followed his reign, so coarse is the ribaldry, so indecent the profligacy, as to be disgusting. We ought to recollect, too, that it was not the unwashed multitude alone that took delight in these representations, but the wit, the fashion, the nobility, and the beauty of the realm. Stately dames and high born maidens listened with complacency to what it shocks us even to read. I might continue, but I must have some respect for the patience of my reader. It was very long before England cleansed herself from the foul leprosy with which crude humours, unwisely pent up till they became vitiated, had thus defaced her fair form, and yet some scars remain.

We may then, on the one hand, set it down as a great truth that, as virtue springs from the heart, morality, or peculiar forms of morality and religion, can never be made to take root and flourish among a people by a force operating from without—by compulsion. The attempt is ever prejudicial, if not fatal to the real interests of both. Were it necessary, I might proceed to cite other examples in proof of this principle, for modern history is full of them, but I have written enough, perhaps more than enough for my purpose.

Again, on the other hand, it is, I think, an unquestionable fact that the course of governmental and legislative action in these Islands for nearly the last forty years—that is both before and after the framing of written laws, has run counter to this principle. There has been a constant attempt to bring in the Christian religion and the morality founded on it, or rather the peculiar views of Christianity and Christian morality entertained by a particular sect of Christians, through the influence of rewards and punishments. I do not know what name the religious body would prefer for the system to which they are attached, but by the rest of the world it would be most readily recognized as *Puritanic*.

Now, here there is something which I should really like to know. I should like to know to whom we owe the course of legislative action to which I refer. But I can find no one to inform me. I am everywhere met by a disclaimer. This only is apparent; it was not of Hawaiian growth. It has an unmistakable over sea air about it. As for the rest, it seems an enigma not to be solved, a mere *mythos*, myth, report, fame, *lono*, a something or somebody which we might wish or expect to present itself, but which will not come before our eyes. Had then my imagination power to "body forth" some shape of it—what the Greeks called an *eidolon* or visible form of that which has no form perceptible to sense, and could I roll back the course of time for forty years from this 1860, I would thus speak—the gravity of my matter would lend weight to my words, however humble he who uttered them.

[II. February 9, 1861]

At a great crises in their history an interesting and trustful race have placed in your hands, to mould into the best form of which they may be susceptible, not only their whole material interests, but all the capacities of their moral and intellectual being—all that makes or unmakes a people the very life of their nation. Hitherto, bounded in by the unbounded ocean, they have lived apart in a little world of their own. Masters of the elementary principles of most of the more necessary arts, these have sufficed them, with light but unremitting labor, to bring out the wealth of the land and sea of these their islands, blest with genial skies and no ungrateful soil, and to replenish them to their remotest corners with swarming and life enjoying multitudes. Possessed of a language, rudimentary in form indeed, but of singular capacity and power, and whose structure and connections may with confidence be pronounced to present by far the most curious and interesting philological problem of the age, they have known how to turn it so as to shadow out their imaginings in lays of heroes and demigods, in songs of mirth and wailing, of joy and sorrows—an infant poetry that has shed its light of varied hues over their labors, their ceremonies, their rejoicings, their mournings, and has lent a more vivid life to the whole current of their social existence, by the fascination of the coloring which it has spread over all its scenes. And thus, in the midst of the great Pacific, of others all unknowing and unknown, have they lived for centuries more than we can number.

But now a great change is coming over them. The days have arrived when the uttermost parts of the earth are to meet together, when that vast ocean, which hitherto has separated them from the rest of mankind, is to be the highway, conducting its various races to their shores. Manifold are the gifts these strangers bring—Arts and sciences, almost as superior to their own as the reasoning procedure of the man to the simple instinct of the animal; a religion of love and peace, bringing life and immortality to light to them, to replace the cruel rites by which they had sought to propitiate their divinities; new and vast fields of knowledge and power in which all their faculties may have room for unlimited expanse. Great gifts these, and containing, doubtless, the elements of much happiness. Yet, as their acceptance implies, a change not without their drawbacks; for all changes are dangerous. They all require fresh adaptations of materials and adjustment of parts, and it depends on the fitness of the mode in which these processes are conducted, whether they result in failure or success. You see by the side of some remote mountain torrent a young tree whose bright leaves and crimson blossoms you admire, and whose fruit, though it has some touch of wildness in it, is yet grateful to your taste; you transplant it to your garden, with the thought that the rich soil in which you place it, and the care with which you tend it, will cause it to shoot up in luxuriant beauty, and impart a more luscious flavor to its produce; but, it dwarfs; it withers and dries up under your fostering care; and at length you pluck it up, and cast it forth as a worthless thing, that has but ill rewarded all your pains. My friend, it is you yourself, and not the luckless plant, that is in fault. Nature, or the God of Nature, made it to grow and flourish out its time. You stretched forth your hand with intent to benefit, but, in act, to destroy. Perhaps in your haste you heeded not the delicate root-springing fibrils with which it sought out its nourishment in the clefts of the rocks, but, though they were its life, you rudely tore it from them; or the juices of the plot into which you put it were too rich, and acted as a poison to its unaccustomed system; or you neglected so to water it as to make up for the moisture that abounded in its original site. Some great error you must have committed. Its death under your hands is a proof not of the worthlessness of the plant, but of your own want of wisdom. Had your procedure been more judicious, had you suited the new position you gave it, to its needs, it might, in turn, have learned to adapt itself to it, and long have flourished to beautify and adorn the spot.

The process of moving a plant into richer soil and a warmer sun is not without its analogies to the giving new arts and new and better principles of action to a nation. In both, the new life is to be made to grow out of the old, and both must be conducted understandingly and with caution. In the case of this nation there is need to redouble that caution, for there are not wanting circumstances prejudicial to success. The gifts which the strangers bring are not all good; some are evil. Disease and provocatives to vice are among them.

Nor does this alone constitute the great difficulty of the procedure. The vastness of the change is a far greater obstacle to its success. For, first, as respects the new religion itself, it stands so opposed to the ancient belief of that process of uprooting the one, and implanting in its stead the other, implies so complete a revolution in the first principles of human action, that the contemplation of its magnitude may well induce a dread lest it fail, and by its failure the minds of the people be so unsettled, the ties that bind them together so weakened, and the foundations of their social system so shaken, that their very national life itself may be endangered.

For no people can exist without a religion! Human society seems incapable of maintaining itself without a belief in the existence of a superior, invisible, superintending power, or superintending powers, governing the course of human affairs, and dealing vengeance on all who transgress those lines, which each society has marked out for itself, as dividing the right from the wrong. Everywhere, all over the world, both ancient and modern, the atheist, he who denies the existence of a God, or of the gods, the avengers of broken oaths, has been held incapable of being a veritable member of society, because he is cut free from the bonds that unite men in each social system.

Hitherto the Hawaiians have not been without a religion. They have, on the contrary, been an eminently God-fearing people. A belief unhesitating, undoubting, in the existence of their several deities, in their agency in all the events of life, both public and private, and in their absolute control over them, has held firm possession of their souls. To them they have been constantly addressing prayers; to them they have been continually offering up sacrifices; to their propitious influences they have attributed all their successes; to their hostile agency all their misfortunes.

Utterly to extirpate this ancient faith, and to implant the new in its place, can assuredly be no easy task; for the beliefs of the old and the new are completely at variance. Setting aside the consideration that one is true, the other false, they differ essentially in this particular; under the ancient superstition the prospect of any after life was so dim and dark that it exercised no practical influence on the lives of the race. All the judgments that fell on them from their divinities were temporal and immediate. Sickness, the being swallowed up by the shark, the being smothered by the pestiferous breath of Pele, or impelled by her to cast one's self from some precipice, or death suddenly coming down on the springs of life, and stifling the offender in his sin, have hitherto been daily occurrences, visible to all who have dwelt among them. They have hitherto lived in constant dread of these swift ministers of the vengeance of the superior powers. But that they should live after death, and in that other life be rewarded or punished for deeds done in the flesh, scarcely entered their imaginations.

Now this belief in an after life is the very foundation of the Christian system. To that future life all its rewards and punishments had reference. In this it agrees with the religions that prevailed before it in Europe, Asia and Africa. Though the edifices erected were of very different character, they were all based on one common ground. Hence the comparative facility with which Christianity was there propagated. Hence the apparent difficulty of building it up here. The very foundation on which it is to be raised has first to be established. Were it, as it appears to the mind of the Hawaiian, a mere change from Gods having little power, to Gods having vast power, over the things of this world, over its arts and means of living, the transition were easy. But to assent to this misconception of its essential nature were a base deceit soon discovered, and of fatal after consequence to faith in either man or God.

It is absolutely necessary that not only one but two new and strange beliefs be established. It is necessary that Hawaiians be brought to believe that they have immortal souls, and no less immortal bodies, and that this life is but the portal by which these pass into abodes of everlasting bliss or endless woe, according as it shall be adjudged them at that great and awful day which awaits all the sons of men. On this belief, strange to Hawaiians, but which, unless so far as the resurrection of the body is concerned, is common to Christianity, with so many other religions, the whole superstructure of faith, worship and doctrine that is peculiar to the Christian system is to be built up. How is this to be accomplished?

If you would have me believe something new and wonderful, you must show me that you have had the means of ascertaining that it is a fact, and you must convince me by your conduct that you yourself believe it to be so.

You tell me, who am poor and ignorant, and who have never been away from this, the place of my birth, that beyond the distant mountains you have discovered vast deposits of gold to be had by merely removing the few inches of soil that covers them. You say to me: "Out of the great love I bear you, I have come here to inform you of this in order that, so soon as the snows of winter have passed away, we may together go and gather riches to our hearts' content." The tidings seem to me so strange and wonderful as almost to surpass belief. But I know that you are wise, full of knowledge, and are of far travel. They may, therefore, be true. I have at least no means of contradicting you. Still my faith on you may not be exactly such as to induce me to abandon my present pursuits, connections and enjoyments to go a long and toilsome road in quest of what seems almost too good to be true. While thus hesitating it occurs to me to ask you how much money will be required to take us two there. You answer four hundred dollars will be amply sufficient. "And how much have you in your purse?" "Six hundred dollars." "That, then, is much more than enough. Give me, I pray you, fifty dollars for a friend of mine, who is in great distress." If you refuse, and if, still further, I see that day after day you are planning and toiling from early morn till dusky night in order to add a few dimes to your store, no words of yours will convince me that you have yourself any confidence in the treasures of which you vaunt. Your conduct belies it. And, though I may not be sure that you have come with a prepared lie of love and kindness in your mouth, with which to cheat me out of something you covet, yet I cannot help having a strong suspicion of it. Had I, on the contrary, seen that your heart was so set on that distant wealth that you despised all the petty gains within your reach, I must needs have believed you, and placed confidence in what you told me. While human nature is human nature, so will men think and act. What concerns religious belief forms no exception. In order to inspire a lively faith, one must not only have it himself, but he must have the means of proving that he has it. If men see that one is so completely possessed with the belief of an eternal world of happiness that he esteems as naught all the possible evils and accidents that may befall him in this; if they see, moreover that his heart so overflows with love for them that he counts as nothing all the sacrifices he may be called on to make in order that they may be partakers in that happiness, they cannot but believe in the sincerity of his faith, in the reality of his love. And if, in addition to this, they know that he has had means far superior to theirs for ascertaining the truth of what he preaches, they almost necessarily become his converts. It is thus alone that Christianity has ever been successfully propagated. If we look to the early history of the Church, it is to the toils, the hazards, the martyrdoms of its early apostles, that the success of their labors is to be ascribed. So wide was the plenitude of the faith possessing the breasts of these men that it left no room in their hearts for other considerations. Heaven, with its eternal delights, was open to their eyes. Hence their triumph. As had been predicted, a great fight was before them—a fight to be carried on between the visible and the invisible, between the things of this life and the things of the other, between the ruler of this world, the Caesar, before whose image all men fell down in adoration, and the Lord of the other, the Christ who had ascended to Heaven before his followers, there to prepare for them mansions eternal, where they were to enjoy with him delights unspeakable forevermore. That full faith in their Lord was necessarily victorious. Through it the martyr, whether a gray-bearded man or a tender virgin, when borne onward to be a witness to its truth went joyously, joy-sparkled in the eye, and spoke through every bodily member, joy that he had been deemed worthy to be decked with the only earthly crown he coveted, the crown of martyrdom, a thing too little indeed to satisfy his longing aspirations, but which yet he might bear with humble thankfulness to the feet of his Captain, his Redeemer, his God, fully assured of the greeting awaiting him:—"Well done, thou good and faithful servant. Enter thou into the joys of thy Lord."

With soul thus prepared, the teeth of the wild beast, the sharp steel of the soldier, the consuming fire, had no terrors for him. Protected by that broad shield able to quench all the fiery darts of the evil one, he felt them not, but couched himself on the red hot iron, and the lapping flame, as on a bed of roses, a short repose on which was to waft him far away, for evermore, from all pain and suffering to regions of bliss eternal as the Heavens.

It was thus that the whole power of imperial Rome succumbed to the new belief. The most cruel of her tyrants, the wisest of her Emperors, in vain made war against it. He whom they marked out as a base criminal, conspiring against her sacred institutions, rose in the estimation of all who beheld him to the dignity of a witness for the truth of the new faith. The blood of her martyrs became the seed of the Church.

Now, this, the vast power of an absorbing faith, is not a thing of this or that age. Beliefs dominate over mankind, and he that has a strong faith, and the means and the courage to make it manifest, possesses a true power. But if he want the means, or lack the courage to use them, his faith will be dead within his own breast; it will never go forth as a living force compelling the wills of men. He need never hope to enlarge the circuit of Christendom by his conquests over the lands lying in darkness beyond her borders. I might cite examples through all history, but content myself with the contrast which two present.

Three centuries ago the heart of a man, a noble, of what was then perhaps the noblest Kingdom in Christendom, so burnt within him with zeal for the spread of his Redeemer's Kingdom, so swelled with the high courage with which a living faith inspired it, that it sent him forth, a new Apostle, to gather in remotest Heathendom to the fold of the Catholic Church. How went he forth? The King, having then the greatest power in the remote Indies, wished to speed him on in fitting pomp and honor. But he knew that the Kingdom of which he had become the soldier was not of this world, and could not be extended by a conformity to this world's ways. So he, a man who had from infancy been tenderly nurtured, and daintly served, went forth alone. During all that long voyage the bare deck his couch, the scraps that fell from the sailors' table his food. Yet went he not forth all alone. Truth, hope and charity were the companions of his voyage, and that glad sisterhood shed such a lustre round him, that, demeaning himself as the lowliest of the lowly, he was esteemed as the highest, for he was held as the undoubted servant of the Most High. The triumph of his cause, begun on ship-board, extended itself on shore. That living faith that glowed in his own breast burst forth all around, swift as the electric flash, powerful as the whelming flood. His converts were reckoned not by pitiful tens and hundreds, but by thousands, tens of thousands and hundreds of thousands. As he moved along Christianity took visible root in all the regions around, and the spires of Christian churches arose to greet his passage. But not content with the Indies, the vast and populous Empire of China attracted his regards. Thitherward he directed his steps, in the same lowly guise, with the same high hopes. But he reached not what stretched out before his mental vision as the promised land, rich with abundant harvests. The Angel of death arrested him on his transit. How did he meet his approach? One would have thought that some touch of human infirmity would have led him to regret being thus suddenly snatched away from the splendid triumph which he had not doubted was awaiting him. But no! Stretched on that lone shore, with none but the master of a wretched pinnance to tend him, his last moments seemed the happiest of his life, for they were filled with the joy of being called by his Master so much sooner than he had expected to the regions of eternal bliss; so lived and died Saint Francis Xavier.

Quite recently another man has made the same Indian tour, a Bishop he of the Church of England, noted for fervid piety, for great talent, profound learning, and winning manners. But he made it as he conceived was becoming a dignitary of that somewhat haughty Church. Government officials surrounded him; a long train accompanied him; he travelled as a prince; and as a prince and equal was he met by the princes and nobles of many ancient kingdoms. Everywhere respectful homage was paid him; everywhere he held high converse with those having the most extended reputation for learned and religious lore. But everywhere he was merely regarded as bearing his part respectably in the governmental pageant of a conquering country. Everywhere the memory of him passed away with that pageant, and he has left no more permanent impress on the hearts of the men of the vast Empire transversed by him than have the hoof-prints of his horses on their soul.*

[III. February 16, 1861]

Such is the difference between a faith self-relying, self-dependent, rendering no divided homage to the Lord of Heaven, and unencumbered by earthly ties, pressing ever onward on His service, and that faith which halts between two masters, longs for the coming of the heavenly kingdom, and yet cannot shake itself free from the entanglements of the earthly. You must prove to men that you are in earnest, before you can make them believe that what you preach is earnest. If you would have them take up the cross, you yourself must carry it aloft, not sinking under the heavy load, but bearing it forward with a countenance elate with the joy that you have been deemed worthy to sustain the precious burden.

Who is so to bear it to Hawaiians? Who is so to bear it to them that their

* There is, I believe, a slight anachronism in this. It is not, I think, quite forty years since Bishop Heber made his Indian tour.

unenlightened minds may be opened to receive, and sincerely believe, in all the great truths of which it is the emblem?

At this very moment New England sends out a band of men engaged for this work. They have taken up the cross; they have vowed vows; devoting their lives to the conversion of the heathen; and this is the field of labor assigned them. How are you to treat them? Let them alone. You cannot hinder, still less can you forward their work. If they are equal to their undertaking; if they are true to the vows they have vowed; if in singleness of heart and of purpose they turn their whole souls to the enterprise they have entered on; if fully possessed themselves by those high hopes they would awaken in others, they are well pleased to spend and be spent in the work, then it will prosper under their hands; for Hawaiians are but men, moved, like other men, by their hopes and fears, drawing their convictions, like other men, from what they see and know. If, then, after, it may be, years of painful toil, these, the messengers of the new faith, can say to them: "Ye are witnesses how holily, and justly, and blamelessly, we have lived among you; that we have so proved our love to you as to make it manifest to you that we have come to seek not *yours*, but *you*; not *your dollars* for ourselves, our wives, and children, but *your love*, for Christ," then will they be prepared to receive the written word, not as the word of men but of God, for they will be convinced that it is only a firm belief in its truth that could have animated to such sacrifices. Then will they in sincerity and truth embrace the sublime doctrines of Christianity, and with them the pure morality which it inculcates. Then many things in their former course of life will seem criminal, many odious in the eyes of the majority of the people. Then will come the proper season for the action of you the legislator, for then you will be called on to make laws in conformity to the will of the changed minds of a majority of the nation; for the legislator is but the embodiment of the moral sense of the nation. It is vain for him to run before it. It is wrong for him to lag behind it.

If, then, the messengers of the new faith are prepared to act, and do act in this spirit, happy for the prosperity of Hawaii the day of their arrival. If they lack the necessary strength of mind; if they faint in the path, or step aside from it, they had better have staid at home. Let not, at least, yours be the hand that would draw them aside from it by any prospects of worldly power, or honor, or riches, held out to them. That were on your part a fatal error, though one into which you may easily fall. That were on theirs a strong temptation, and one by which they might perhaps be led astray.

For it is not unnatural for you the chiefs of the race and their natural legislators thus to reason: "These men have come out as the teachers of the nation. Let it then be entrusted to them. Let everything be done as they direct; let no step be taken without their sanction; let them be in effect the rulers and law-givers of the people." And, such is the deceitfulness of the human heart, such the propensity of men, when, in their imaginations, a great good lies before them, to break through the line that fences them from it, though in so doing they commit a positive wrong, that it is not impossible that they may yield to the temptation, and that the very men who left home to unfold the things of another world may here immerse themselves in the affairs of this.

Dark were the day, and black the hour, for Hawaii that should witness such a compact. For evil, as well as good, exists in all things on earth. Even religious sects have their dark as well as their bright sides. The puritanical sect especially, of which these men are the messengers, changes mightily its aspect according as you view, if from this quarter or that. For while from one point of view it must be allowed the praise of being pure in morals, great in doing and in enduring, a noble defender of what it has esteemed the right; from another it shows itself puffed up with spiritual pride, narrow in its compass of vision, greedy of power and of gain.

There are characteristics which render that sect very unfit to rule over and legislate for Hawaiians; for, if they stand in the place of power, blinded by their self-sufficient spiritual price, instead of waiting till the changed hearts of the people demand a conformable legislative action, they may think themselves called on to constrain them, by legal enactments into that condition which in their conception a perfected Christianity produces. Now the narrowness of their views renders them incapable of conceiving any excellence of Christian civilization but in the precise form in which they have seen it existing in New England, or rather in which it would exist there had they the power to purge that land from what they conceive its defects. New England, thus purified, will consequently be to them the *beau ideal* to which they will seek forcibly to mould the Hawaiian race. They will be unable to understand that the essential difference in the characteristics of the two peoples renders the one incapable of receiving the form of the other. That, assuming that the Hawaiian race has within itself energies capable of causing it to grow up in fresh strength, and grace, and beauty, under the new day that has dawned on it, still, to force that growth into a form foreign to its nature may be to tax these energies so highly as utterly to exhaust them.

These will be the errors of the intellect, but there will be errors of the will accompanying them, sins all the more dangerous that they can cloak themselves under the guise of virtues—the lust of power—(they will term it the wish to do good)—the lust of gain—that will pass under their own eyes, and they will hope to make it pass under the eyes of others, as only a laudable desire to provide for the well-being of their households.

From what has been, we may certainly gather what will be. The same sect, two hundred years ago, gained the supreme power in England. What they did there, they will do here. The pictures will be the same, with this difference; that while this will have a more contracted compass, it will have a greater depth of color than had that. Look on it, I pray you, for a moment. And, first, as to the foreign population, it being proclaimed throughout the land that none but the godly can have part or portion in the good things of the Hawaiian kingdom, a host of those who call themselves such, and put on what are esteemed the signs of godliness, will fill the Puritan camp. The same indecent strife for offices of power and emolument that had place in England will have place there. There will consequently be such a scramble to mount into these high places over religion's back, her garments will be so defiled by foul feet that her best friends shall no longer be able to recognize her. Meanwhile, without the camp will remain those who are too openly profligate to make any religious pretences, and those who, conceiving religion to consist in something else than long prayers and solemn faces, are too honest to assume the puritanic livery from any prospect of gain or advancement.

Two parties will consequently be formed directly opposed to each other, and so heated by the animosities which such strifes engender that neither shall be able to see any good in the other. Those without the camp will rail at those within as a set of designing hypocrites, who have no other purpose than to filch from the natives their dollars. Those within will rail at those without as a set of godless men, misleaders of the natives, and bringing multifold evils upon the land.

Under these suppositions, what will befall the native population? It may be answered, many circumstances will cause them to come within the camp, and to be numbered as inclosed within the puritanic fold. For, in the first place, their former idolatrous worship will assuredly be put down, and those who continue to practice it be held guilty of an offence against the laws. Their old gods being thus taken from them, they will turn to the God of the strangers, for in their eyes he will have manifested His greater power by His having overthrown these idols, and they will hope that by rendering themselves to Him He will bestow on them benefits equal to those with which He has enriched the stranger. And not only will they turn to the new God, but, as, in their imaginations, all the powers which men possess over nature come from some God, they will seize with eagerness the books He has given the strangers: they will industriously strive to acquire the power of reading them: they will search them diligently, to find somewhere within them those sources of knowledge from which drinking the foreigner has grown to a stature so vastly superior to their own? Again, they have ever been used to obey the commands of those in authority. There will be nothing in that outward observance of religious ordinances, which consists in keeping the sabbath as a day of rest, going to church, &c., that will seem oppressive to them. They will soon see too that to make a great profession of religious convictions is a sure road to preferment for themselves and their children. Hence, there will not be wanting those who not only read but lay up in their memories many scripture passages, to be applied as occasion may direct; many, also, who, turning the copious fund of language which these islanders possess into that channel, may make long prayers not devoid of Bible imagery.

But how much of real Christianity may lie under this outward show, it will not be very easy to judge, for it will be difficult to see how the very foundation for a sincere conviction in its truths can have been laid. Christianity rests on the belief of a future life. This world is of no account; the other is the great matter. But while Hawaiians see the actions of all around them apparently proceeding from a regard to this, and not to that world, how shall that absorbing idea of the all importance of things eternal, which is necessary for even a true understanding of the Christian system, be implanted, and become established in their souls?

Nevertheless, led on by the genuine Puritanic spirit, those in the seat of power will deceive themselves into the belief that their preaching has made true Christians of the whole population, or, at least, that it ought to have done so, and they will proceed to mete out punishments against transgressors of what they conceive to be Christian morality, with all the severity of their fathers in the days of the blue laws. A code of coercive morality will be established, which would not be submitted to by any European or American community, but which the Hawaiians, accustomed to bend to the will of their superiors, will not *resist*, but will *evade*. From this source a tissue of lying and deception will spring up and spread among them, pushing its poisonous meshes through every household, and every where contaminating and destroying the native virtues of the people. For, it were altogether a mistake to imagine that virtue, though that virtue may be of the earth earthly, does not exist in this race. They have ever had a right and a wrong, a *pono* and a *pono ole*, no words are more frequent in their mouths—and then their native virtues have hitherto sufficed to give prosperity to the land, to give industry to the man, fecundity to the women. Destroy them—give nothing better in their place, and you take from their social system every substaining prop, and cause it to fall to the ground in, it may be, irremediable confusion.

Other circumstances will add to the disastrous effects of thus placing the destinies of your nation in the hands of a foreign and sectarian Priesthood.

Many foreigners without the camp, believing or feigning to believe, that all within are designing hypocrites, eager only for the *dala*, will take every opportunity to proclaim this their belief among the native population. A fresh source this of distrust in the new teachings, and an aggravation of the evils.*

On the other hand the contemplation of the native Hawaiian Church will be productive of anything but good to the free livers without. They will see within many so much more free living than themselves, that they would be ashamed to associate with them, but, because protected by a shield of false oaths they have hitherto lived unconvicted, received by the pastor as belonging to the sheep, not the goats, partaking of all Christian privileges and sacraments, no one daring to lift his voice against them. All this cannot but have the effect of spreading still further among the outsiders the belief that the whole is a juggling trick to conjure cash into needy and greedy pockets, to increase their boldness in denouncing it, and still further to shake any confidence the native mind may have reposed on it.

Under the supposition that a system of government and of legislation so unsound as that we have been looking at becoming the rule of the land, one other consideration would remain to deepen the gloom which the aspect of futurity would then present. How is it ever to be got rid of? There can be no doubt that the true Puritanic temper, proud of its own spiritual gifts and confident in their potency, would seize with avidity the seeming vantage ground which these Islands would then present to blazon before the world the extent of its conquests. It would be *veni, vidi, vici*, we came, we saw, we were victorious. Finding words for itself by the mouth of this missionary or that, it would proclaim to the world, "We have come here, we have preached the gospel, the idols have fallen; over all these Islands extends the reign of a Christian government, of Christian morality, of peace and of prosperity." The glad news would be received in full faith and find an echo over all Protestant Christendom. From all

* I may here take the license of a note to observe that I do not recollect having been in any mixed company in these Islands where the subject of the Protestant Mission was introduced without hearing either a sneer, a sarcasm or a reproach against it. On the other hand wherever I have been and with whomsoever I have met, I have never encountered one, except in controversy, who did not speak in terms of respect of the Catholic Priesthood. Some have expressed their surprise that men could be found, at this time of day, thus to sacrifice their lives: some have spoken of their *culte* as savoring of superstition, but all have granted them the praise of sincere self-devotion, all have expressed a desire that their labors might benefit the natives. I simply note a fact—it is for the reader to draw the conclusion.

Europe and America many an eye would turn exultant with triumph and with hope to the lands that rise out of the midst of the North Pacific. How destroy the pleasing picture! How proclaim that beneath the fair surface all is decay and rottenness! The endeavor will rather be to shun every measure that might lead to a suspicion of the truth. Hence a backward step will be almost impossible.

Such, Mr. Editor, it seems to me, are the consequences that might have been foreseen and predicted by one knowing the disposition of these Islanders, and the spirit of the Puritanic sect, should these become in effect the Legislators of Hawaii. How far they have been so and how far these consequences have followed I leave to your judgment and that of your readers.

[IV. March 16, 1861]

To me three things are apparent:

The first—That the system of legislation which has had place in this country for the last forty years is a system directly opposed in its spirit to the lessons of experience and the dictates of true political wisdom.

The second—That if it has not had its origin from that body of puritanic missionaries, who about that time chose these islands for the scene of their operations, it is at least such a system as one might *a priore* have conceived would emanate from them.

The third—It has wrought great mischief, and been productive of the most unhappy results to the native population.

As to the first head, I would observe, that the spirit of the constitution and laws of every nation naturally springs from, and ought to be in conformity to, the spirit of the people. This is the truth which it was the main object of Montesquieu's great work to prove, and, had it wanted farther confirmation, the course of events since he wrote would serve abundantly to confirm it.

I shall first make a few observations on the Constitution itself. It is established, and has been for years established. To essay to change it would, consequently, be, in my opinion, an unwise attempt to disturb the settled order of affairs. To examine, therefore, whether it is, or is not, the best form of Government that could have been devised for Hawaiians, comes not within the scope of the intent with which I publish these papers. I have practical, and not theoretical, objects in view. But, it is necessary to see the manner in which it might have been expected to operate, and in which it has in fact operated.

What is called constitutional government had its rise in England, and the primary idea of it was derived by the people of that kingdom from their Germanic ancestry. The British House of Commons, it is now allowed, is legitimately descended from the Anglo-Saxon Wittenagamot, or assembly of wise men. The principle of liberty dominated in all the Germanic races. The famous preamble, "*All men are born free and equal*" had never foundation in fact but to the German. To him it was an absolute reality. The liberty it was his own to assert; the equality was provided for by the laws, which established an annual and equal re-apportionment of all the lands of the nation. Among a pastoral people, where cattle make the general wealth, this effectually prevented the riches of one much exceeding that of another. In a race where this perfect liberty and equality had prevailed for innumerable generations, and among whom consequently all public measures were canvassed and debated by each, the right of every man to form an opinion on all public questions, and his duty to give utterance to it, became so deeply implanted in their souls, that it seemed to them a principle innate in human nature itself.

The cruel contest of the Saxon race in England with their Norman conquerors, and their miserably depressed condition under these haughty nobles, led them to cast longing eyes toward their ancient state, and kept ever alive in their breasts that feeling of the innate right of all men to have a voice in the management of their own affairs. This right they began gradually to assert, and were at last able, after a long struggle, to make good. Constitutional government in England and America may thus be shortly described as an attempt to reconcile the ancient Germanic principle of perfect liberty and equality, with the actual circumstances of modern society, where great wealth and great poverty exist together among the citizens of the same state.

It is characteristic of that Anglo-Saxon race to vaunt the excellencies of this form of Government, and whenever they have the power to endeavor to spread its sway. The attempt has not always had the most happy success, as France, Spain and the Spanish colonies may witness. To assure it success the people must not only have the ability to form a judgment on the course of public affairs, but they must acquire the habit of doing so, and they must have energy to give influence to their opinions by the choice of delegates who will give them expression and force. If they are deficient in these requisites, they will have no real weight in the constituted order of things, and the power which they ought to wield will fall into the hands of others. The Hawaiian race were in this predicament. They had neither such habits of thought or of action as fitted them to exert influence in the government of affairs. Whether they shall ever acquire them is a question which time alone can determine. That power naturally, therefore, fell into the hands of those to whom they looked up for direction—the puritanic clergy. That these seized it, and have exercised it, is generally asserted, and the acerbity with which their organs have attacked the Minister for Foreign Relations, since his attempts to set some bounds to their political influence, would seem to justify the belief that they have sought to guard it with jealous care.

On the one hand, therefore, I conceive it would be unjust to affirm that the constitutional scheme was devised by the puritanic clergy, in order that, without holding any recognized and responsible position in the Government, they might, unseen, influence and direct all its movements. It would be unjust to affirm this, because it is one of the characteristics of that Anglo-Saxon race to establish that form of civil polity wherever they have the power so to do. Yet, I think, on the other hand, it must be allowed that had that clergy set about to contrive a plan by which they might in effect rule, without being seen to rule, they could not have hit on one better suited to their purpose.

Passing the constitutional question with these remarks, I proceed now to the proof of the assertion I have made, "That the system of legislation which has had place in this country for the last forty years is a system directly opposed in its spirit to the lessons of experience and the dictates of true political wisdom." I include, of course, under this censure, both the period before, and that after the establishment of the present Constitution.

I have quoted Montesquieu's maxim that the spirit of the laws ought to spring from and be in conformity to the spirit of the people. What, then, were the disposition, propensities and conditions of those for whom the Hawaiian legislator was called on to form laws? As regards the native population, two circumstances may be mentioned very favorable to successful legislative action. These islands had all come under the rule of one regal family, and peace and order, therefore, reigned throughout their whole extent; and, again, all the people were eager to receive and docile to obey instruction in the ways of the new civilization that had dawned upon them. As a race, like the inhabitants of tropical climates in general, they loved ease and enjoyment, and were prone to yield themselves unrestrained to sensuous delights. The natives, indeed, of all the Pacific islands have long been noted by voyagers as of extremely licentious habits. The fable of the Paphian Goddess rising from the sea would almost seem emblematical of these isles beaten by the mid-ocean waves. This was their national vice. But be it observed they were perfectly innocent of the conception that it was a vice. On the contrary, their creed was:

> "Take the goods the gods provide thee.
> To enjoy is to obey."

It is so with all national vices. They so sink into the hearts of men that they come at last to pass for virtues. Hence the difficulty of eradicating them. This the history of the Anglo-Saxon race, with which they were destined to come in contact, sufficiently proves. Sprung mainly from the ancient Germanic stock, there have come down to us with that blood, much of the hardihood of body and mind, and energy of character, for which they were distinguished. Energetic action is essential to our happiness. We spurn inglorious ease, and despise those who give themselves up to it. But with these characteristics, there has also come down to us another trait, which, though we ought not as Christians to pride ourselves upon it, yet most of us, I suspect, are rather inclined to do so. The ancient German was a blood thirsty being. War was his business, his occupation, his pastime, his delight, *"gaudentes caede"* as Horace has it, to him no joy was to be compared with the *"joy of the battle."* How long was Christianity mitigating and restraining this war passion, and how much of it yet remains? The Germans of mid and southern Europe were Christians for many ages before Charlemagne, when tribe waged exterminating warfare against tribe. They were Christians in those dark ages that ushered in the Feudal rule, when the hand of every man was against his neighbor, and constant combats, onslaughts and battles so raged everywhere, that science, the arts, christianity itself, seemed about to be blotted out over all that region. They have been christians since petty warfare has ceased, and given place to the great wars of nations. How often has the magnificent chant *"Te Deum Laudamus,"* "Praise we the Lord" been sung for the victories of one Christian nation over another, and have men dared to lift up their voices in exultation to the God of righteousness and peace, because they have heaped the wide plain with the bloody corpses of their fellow worshippers? Now, are there any signs of this war passion ceasing? Read the productions of the peace society, and see how contrary to right reason all this is, how fatal to social prosperity. It is in vain. The thirst for combat and martial renown is in the blood that courses through our veins, and we yield to it. Even now, over all Europe, the eyes of men are sparkling as they burnish their arms for some coming fray.

If then we would look into ourselves, we might learn to judge more fairly of the failings of others; for surely this passion for fight and bloodshed is as repugnant to the gospel of peace and love as is the passion for licentious pleasures. And if in Europe it has taken twelve centuries for that gospel to mitigate the one, it was unreasonable to have expected that, even if fully accepted in Hawaii, the subduing the other would here be for it only the work of a day. This the Hawaiian legislator ought to have well considered.

Another circumstance ought to have been present to his mind when considering what laws he ought to frame, what regulations he ought to enforce for the two races here coming in contact. I allude to the very elevated position which woman holds in Europe and America. If we turn over the pages of the Old or New Testament, if we search all Roman, or Greek, or Sanscrit literature, we find nothing—not even in the widest stretch of fancy in their poets—that comes near the just conception of the idea comprehended in that now somewhat abused word, *lady*. How came woman to attain this high ground among us, and how is it possible to give to her something like a correspondent rank among Hawaiians, are questions which ought to have been put, and answered by him.

We owe much to ancient Germany, and for this also we are indebted to it. Elsewhere, obedient submission to the will of her lord and master, man, was held to be a woman's highest excellence. The German, on the contrary, conceived that she was nearer the Divinity than he was, held her in corresponding worship and honor, and when he himself came forth from his woods, brought her with him, to maintain and prove the true dignity of her sex. And she has done so. We think of her—and rightly think of her—as holding a place purer, holier, nearer the angels than our own grosser natures can attain to. We trust to her, and give her range of thought and action. Hence mainly the superior grace and polish, the purity, the happiness of modern society. Man did not before know what was in man, for he had so depressed one half of his nature that it lay hid from his eye. Before the lady came into being, the gentleman obviously could not exist.

In contemplating, therefore, the condition of the Hawaiian woman, we ought in fairness to view her rather as she compares with the woman of former times, or of countries where the Germanic race have not yet infused their peculiar sentiments with regard to the sex, than to conceive of her as an essentially degraded being, because she falls so far below that higher standard which is before our eyes. How to raise her to that higher standard ought to have been a primary object with the wise legislator. His duty, in short, towards the whole race of both sexes required him to endeavour to devise means by which they should acquire the arts and gradually mould themselves into a conformity to the more refined sentiments and purer morals of the white man to that strictness of life which his religion inculcates. This, a regard to their prosperity as a separate people demanded, and it became a necessity for their permanent existence, as a nation coming in immediate contact with the white man, and living in the same land with him. For, if they could not be raised to something like an equality with him, it ought to have been foreseen that they must neces-

sarily, in process of years, sink beneath his sway as an inferior and degraded race. How was this to be brought about?

> "Tis education forms the common mind;
> Just as the twig is bent the tree's inclined."

There can be no doubt of the truth of the poet's maxim, if we understand by the term not mere book learning, but education in its largest and
true sense, comprehending all the influences which are brought to bear on
the individual, from infancy to maturity. In that extended sense, the best education is undoubtedly that which most conduces to the prosperity and happiness of the individual, and of the community of which he or she is to be a
member. As it comes short, or runs counter to this, it is defective or faulty.

What then, it should have been considered, has hitherto been the education, or what have been the influences that have been brought to bear on
Hawaiian youth of both sexes, and how can these be ameliorated or more
beneficial ones be introduced in their place?

From all I have been able to gather of the ancient condition of the Hawaiian people, there seems to have been a remote approach among them to
that division in castes which exists in India. Each had his separate occupation. One tilled the land; another was fisherman; another a maker of
canoes, and so on. The sons followed the same division of labor as their
fathers, grandfathers, and probably remote ancestors had done. They
accompanied their fathers to the scenes of their labors, first as on-lookers;
next they were permitted to assist in such light matters as they could
manage, gradually as they acquired skill and strength, they became efficient aids. No coercion was used; the imitative propensity of our nature,
the knowledge that the better workmen they became the more they would
be esteemed, and the spirit of emulation, were the only stimulants, and,
as labor was never pushed to fatigue, they were sufficient. This course of
life could not fail to invigorate the frames of the youth, and to train them
to habits of persistent industry. They knew but little, but they knew it well.
They learned to take a pride in their proficiency in their particular avoca-
tion, and a pleasure in practising it. It also drew strongly together the ties
of paternal and filial affection. The father rejoiced to see his boys around
him striving to aid him in his toils, and they could not but regard with
daily increasing love the being who was hourly before them, endeavoring
after the means comfortably to maintain them, at once their parent, master
and friend. As the sons followed after the father, so did the daughters
after the mother. What I have said to one applied with equal truth to the
other. It must be obvious that while all thus mutually aided each other in
procuring the means sufficient for their simple needs and enjoyments,

a small family was but little of a burden, and soon became a help. To be a parent was, therefore, a thing generally desired.

I come now to another point. I have said that the ancient Hawaiian manners were very licentious. Yet it is certain that the women were very prolific; that the injunction to multiply and replenish the earth was fully obeyed by them. Nay, that, in spite of the wars, diseases and human sacrifices that were continually making gaps in their numbers, the population was so redundant that the practice of infanticide was permitted in order to restrain it. How were the two reconciled, for great fecundity and licentious manners are generally and rightly esteemed incompatible?

This is a delicate matter to handle. They who know what these ancient manners were, and what in fact they still remain, will perceive that there are some parts which I cannot at all approach; others I will touch as lightly as possible.

There must, it is obvious, have been some restraints, else mothers would have been rare. Like most other countries where the position of woman is inferior to that which she has with us, she was, with few exceptions, conceived to be under the protection and guardianship of man. The girl was carefully watched, so as to prevent her having any intimate connection with the other sex until she was of mature age. In this respect there was an analogy between her position and that of the Gypsey girl in Spain, as described by Mr. Burrows. There was no moral purity, but there was physical restraint, and from physical considerations. It was supposed, or rather known, that irregularities at an earlier period would prevent her frame from attaining full womanly perfection. Nor could she at any time take a temporary or permanent companion without the consent of her parents, or rather perhaps of the family to which she belonged. Her person was not her own, but theirs. In the same way, when she passed to a particular man, her person was his, nor could she dispose of it otherwise without his consent. There was great indulgence, it is ttrue, on both sides,

— "hanc veniam damus petimusque vicissim,"

but it had its bounds.

This low social position of the woman had nevertheless one advantage attending it. From her inferiority, and from her peculiar organization, she was supposed to be scarcely capable of resisting the closer approaches of the other sex. In the case therefore of a fault the shame alone fell upon her. And she dreaded the shame—not so much perhaps on her own account as for the sake of the disgrace which her conduct was conceived to bring upon her family and friends. The blame and the punishment fell chiefly on the male. He who had been guilty of leading astray a young girl, or seducing away another's acknowledged woman or wife was held to have been guilty of a very grave offence. The custom was for the family thus injured in the person of girl or woman, to go against the injurer and strip him of all he possessed (*hao*); or if a minor, to proceed in like manner against his father. A rude sort of justice this, and no doubt often success-fully resisted, but yet so powerfully seconded by the general sentiment that it seems to have been pretty effective.

These being perhaps the circumstances in the condition and prospects of the Hawaiian people which should more particularly have engaged the attention of their legislators, at the time to which I refer, I come now to consider the course of action which they ought to have suggested to him. And as to this, I shall confine myself to general principles. It were useless to enter into details, since the time for action has passed.

First, as to the establishment of schools and school education.

It is, I think, a principle in which all who have maturely reflected on the subject will agree with me, that we ought to form a judgment concerning any school, or system of schools, not so much from what is actually learned in it, as from the discipline to which the mind is subjected, and the habits of thought and action which are there acquired. A man may forget most, or nearly all, which he has learned during five or six years schooling, and yet the time he has spent there may be the most profitable to him of his whole life. If during school hours he has been ever busy, if tasks have ever been set before him such as have tried his mental powers, but which he was yet capable of accomplishing, if a sense of his growing energies, and the feeling of generous emulation fostered in his breast, have led him to be victor over them, whether crabbed Greek, or musty algebra, have formed the main subject of his studies, it matters not; the faculties of his mind have been developed; he has learned the noble lesson of having confidence in himself, and in his power to meet and master difficulties, and he comes forth to the world a resolute and energetic man. If again he has at school been under a crude and capricious ruler; if he has been con-tinually set to do things beyond his power, and been flogged and punished because he could not compass the impossible, his mind will be agitated by conflicting passions; he will lose all calm strength of soul; he will learn to distrust himself and others; and, if some happy out-school influences do not counteract the evil, he may be made for life a wavering, suspicious, and unhappy mortal, incapable of daring or doing anything.

[V. March 30, 1861]

If it has been the youths' ill fortune to fall into the hands of a lazy ignora-mus, a man who knows next to nothing, and cares not to learn anything;

who has no idea of discipline other than that of keeping each scholar in his place, and no other notion of teaching than that of hearing each drawl forth his lesson as best he may; or, if he get a dull perception that things are not going fast enough, of endeavoring to quicken the progress by a general application of the rod, the case is perhaps still worse. Condemned to remain for all the weary hours, his thoughts fixed on vacancy, and his body to one spot, young body and spirit begin to droop together, and to him his schooling is converted into an engine to reduce him, so far as its powers can compass it, to the condition of an idle moonstruck driveler.

If you would end well you must begin well. At the period to which I refer, when the nations had awakened to a just sense of what, and how important education is; when Prussia and France were doing so much for the school; when, in the latter country, the most original philosophic genius it has had to boast of since the days of Des Cartes, had not disdained to turn all the powers of his comprehensive mind to the work of regenerating her school system, one would have thought that an intelligent legislator would have understood all the importance of a right commencement.

To me, therefore, it seems unquestionable, that whatever means the legislator could have then commanded for that purpose, should have been employed to render the first school, or schools, as effective as possible. The numbers taught should have been a consideration altogether secondary to that of their being taught well; for it was from these that were to issue the future teachers of the nation. It was all-important, therefore, that they should have received the very best education possible—that is, that they should have been trained to turn all the energies of their minds to the acquisition of the particular branches of knowledge or art assigned them, and that they should have known them thoroughly and well. If one is to introduce a new plant into a country, it is of little consequence whether he take five seeds, or a hundred, or two hundred, but it is all-important that they be of the best species, and the best variety of that species. School education was to Hawaiians precisely like a new and—if of a right sort— most excellent plant, to be spread over all their islands.

Another thing, about which there ought not, I conceive, to have been any doubt in the mind of the legislator, was that of having separate schools for the different sexes. This may be a debatable question in some countries, but to any one knowing the manners of Hawaiians, there ought to have been no question about it here.

I think, also, that some European language—and that language naturally was the English—ought to have formed a prominent part of the course of study. So alone could the native Hawaiian be placed on anything like an equality with the white man; so alone could any portion of delicacy, purity and elevation of sentiment be infused into the natural loveableness of the native female character.

There is another branch of education, the introduction or non-introduction of which could only have been determined by circumstances. I allude to instruction in the arts, such as carpentry, blacksmith work, &c. Two things would have made it very desirable; 1st, the importance of a knowledge of such arts to the social progress of the nation; 2nd, that these arts are much better suited to the natural bent and capacity of many youths than are the languages and sciences. But the means of such instruction might not have been at hand.

Come we now to consider the propriety of positive enactments with respect to particulars pertaining to the commerce of the sexes. These I conceive ought to have been simply supplementary to the general sentiment. There were two points on which that sentiment was unanimous. The man who, without the consent of the parents, had any connection with a young girl, was universally thought to have done an injury to them, for which he ought to make them large reparation. It was the same thing with regard to the acknowledged wife of any one. Now as the old system, of each family righting its own wrongs must necessarily be suppressed, it ought to have been replaced by some law exacting from each delinquent an adequate compensation.

As to positive laws concerning marriage, adultery, &c., I conceive that the then state of morals and feeling in Hawaiian society did not authorise them, and no law ought to run counter to public opinion; neither ought it to go much before it, or to lag far behind it. It is quite clear that where there is no positive standard of right and wrong, to which all men are prepared to appeal, this prevailing sentiment ought to govern, and indeed will govern. Here, as in words, general usage is the rule.

To oppose it is always wrong and generally useless.

Take the example of decency in dress. What is decent in one country is indecent in another. A Hindoo could not with propriety walk on the banks of the Thames in the garb with which it is quite decent for him to appear in on the banks of the Ganges. He therefore in England conforms in that respect to the ideas of Englishmen. In India he re-assumes his native attire, and were the Queen of England to require that he and all his countrymen and fellow subjects there should wear an English dress, she would be guilty of a piece of legislation absurd, unjust and impracticable.

It is the same in cases where there is a standard but where men differ in their interpretation of its requirements. Here, also, the general acceptation in any particular society or country becomes the rule. Take as an example the disputed point of the marriage of Priests and Bishops in the Church of England. It is well known that Queen Elizabeth was opposed to it and would not suffer the Bishops' wives to appear at Court, regarding them as mere concubines. The opinion within and without that Church was, however, against her, and though the head of it, she was far too sagacious a ruler to enact any law opposed to that general sentiment.

There has more than once been an attempt made more closely to assimilate that same English Church to the Catholic and Roman Church. At present this marriage of Priests is one of the matters concerning which they are at variance. Both parties appeal to scripture, to authority and to right reason, but they cannot settle the point. Now let us suppose, that without any change of sentiment in the mass of the clergy and people, what is called the Puseyite party were to gain over to its side the Crown and its ministers, together with the higher dignitaries of the church, and that these were to pass an ordinance declaring that the marriage of Priests was contrary to right rule and the discipline of the Church, forbidding it therefore altogether, and commanding all married Priests either to repudiate their wives and children or to resign their benefices. Such an ordinance would certainly be one impracticable to be carried into effect, and therefore both unwise and unpolitic, but it would also be unjust. The priests might say—"Prove to us that you are right and we yield without a murmur to the sacrifice you demand; but to compel us to it, while we and our people believe that the error is not on our side, but on yours, is a manifest wrong. To constrain the will without satisfying the understanding or convincing the reason, is sheer tyranny." To take now another case nearer to our subject, but which ought surely to be determined on the same grounds. Suppose that at the time when the regulations and laws to which I refer were being carried into effect, the legislator of the day had taken corporeal form, and had gone about among the natives to make their propriety apparent to them, and that these had spoken out their minds without fear. He comes to a certain house and the following is part of the dialogue which he holds with one of them: *Native*: "I maintain it is wrong." *Legislator*: "But it is the law." *N*: "So you say, but if so it is a very cruel law. What! you will have it that I am wrong, because when my chief, my friend, came to my house last night, I gave him my daughter as a companion! Could I have done less? Has not such been the custom of us and our fathers? Was she not honored by his embraces? and should she happen to bear a child to him, would not it, whether son or daughter, be the most esteemed of all my family? And for this you tell me I must either pay a fine of fifteen dollars, or my daughter be sent to work for months on the public roads. It is iniquitious." *L*: "But you know all this is contrary to what the new teachers who have come among us say is right. You have been to hear these teachers; you ought to have listened to them, and not have done what they condemn." *N*: "Yes, I know I have been to hear these men; I wished to know what they had to say, and truly strange things have I heard. They tell us that all our old ways are sins, and that if I continue to practice them, I am a sinner and shall be punished for my sins; that after death I shall be raised up, soul and body, and thrown into a pit of burning fire—not for an hour, or a day, that were trouble enough; not for a month or a year—but for years, and years, and years never to end; always burning, burning—never consuming. Can anything be more awful! Were I to believe this, do you think I would continue in our old ways? Not for an hour. I would sooner put my right arm into the fire and burn it off. It would be much wiser. There would be no need then of your fines and punishments. What would a pitiful fifteen dollars be in comparison of these things? I and my daughter, and my whole family would then, day by day, be at the feet of you and the teachers, praying you to instruct us how we might avoid a doom so terrible." *L*: "Why are you not there now?" *N*: "Should I ever be able to reconcile my mind to the possibility of things so new and strange, and find reason to believe them, I will be there, but not till then. I am willing to listen to the teachers, I am willing to help them, for I think they mean well—but not as yet to obey them, and they professed to have come here to teach, not to govern." *L*: "I see you are incorrigible; you must pay the fine immediately, or I will send men to take off your daughter to the work."

But further, such laws are not only inefficient and unjust, they are demoralizing. For, as it must be out of the people themselves that the agents for enforcing the law are chosen, if that law be generally thought unfair or oppressive, there will be a conspiracy to evade it between those who ought to enforce it and those on whom it should be enforced. In order to escape from it, all sorts of tricks, devices, deceits, will come into play, and, if need be, perjury itself will be resorted to; and the feelings of the great majority being in favor of those who thus strive to nullify it, these will serve to gloss over and excuse, as really not blameworthy, whatever means they employ for the purpose. Hence deceit, lying and false oaths will come to be held up to the people as sometimes not only free from guilt, but actually praiseworthy.

Thus, at the beginning of this century the people of England thought the criminal law too severe—that the punishment of death was awarded in crimes not deserving that penalty. Accordingly, juries in these cases were in the habit of acquitting, even when the evidence was conclusive.

J.R. 1—24

They thought the guilt less to swear falsely than to take life, where life ought not to be taken. Public opinion ran strongly in favor of the course pursued by these jurors, until at length the laws were rendered more lenient.

It was at the beginning of this century also, that Napoleon issued his famous decrees interdicting the continent of Europe from all trade with England, and stationed officials in every port to see that they were enforced. Nevertheless, the prohibition was ineffectual. Means were found to evade it, and these means were forgery and perjury. A vessel sailed, we shall say, from Bergen in Norway, clearing for Rotterdam, Holland. In a few weeks she returned, having, apparently in some mysterious manner, escaped all the British cruisers. Her cargo, indeed, had a marvellous air of being goods of English manufacture, but captain and mate swore they had been in Holland; there were the papers, all regular, with the signatures and seals of the Burgomaster and other officials, and, if sent to these personages they could not indeed swear that they recollected signing them, but allowed they might have signed them; they were so like they could not pronounce them forgeries. What could the poor Imperial Envoy do? Nevertheless, the ship had discharged in a British port, she had had papers protecting her from British cruisers, and the whole thing was a mass of complicated perjuries and forgeries. Yet such was the detestation which the arbitrary measures of the French Emperor excited over Europe, that men looked on with a very lenient eye, and scarcely blamed those who were implicated in them. Two things were observed: Norwegian logs, &c., were not wanting in Great Britain, nor British goods in Norway, and also, that though the salaries of the Imperial officers were not large, yet they some how or other contrived in a few years to amass considerable wealth.

All clergymen of the Church of England must profess their belief in the 39 articles, yet the great majority preach a doctrine not in accordance with them. They were excused. Public opinion acquits them. It is thought that so few can readily believe in all these articles, that were not this latitude winked at, the bulk of the pulpits must stand empty. Yet surely this is a scandal which it were well if possible to do away with. It cannot but have the effect of somewhat blunting in the clergy the clear sense of the righteousness of pure and simple truth, and of lowering them and their cause in general estimation.

I have one more serious objection to make to laws and I have done. They act counter to the cause which they are intended to promote. They can only be firmly based on a preponderating, an almost unanimous public sentiment in their favor. But the attempt to force any of them on a people where many are opposed to the principle on which it is based, necessarily excites into action that counter sentiment, and gives strength to it. Thus in the United States, thirty or forty years ago, the vice of drunkenness was rampant and destructive. A party arose to diminish or put it down. After the first burst of ridicule which any novelty of the sort naturally produces, their efforts came to be very generally applauded, even by those whose practice was opposed to their teachings. Most confirmed drunkards were inclined to curse the hour when they first tasted a drop of liquor, and scarce one of the more moderate drinkers but must have felt, from all that he saw around him, that he was swimming and disporting himself on the edge of a mighty whirlpool, which, some heedless day, might suck him into its embrace, and clasping him with a force overmastering all his struggles, might bear him away within its rounding sweep, still down, and further down, till lost forever in its dark and dismal depths. Though, therefore, among the advocates of the new doctrine there were of necessity many ignorant men, making the strangest and most absurd blunders in physical science and historical fact, no one of any consideration raised his voice against them. Approving the thing itself, wise men were content merely to smile at the palpable errors of many of its supporters. The temperance cause therefore gained ground very rapidly. But no sooner than what is called the Maine law passed, than the face of affairs suddenly underwent a change. The cry of tyranny was raised; men of ability began to expose the fallacies of some of the leading principles on which the teetotal system is grounded, and the cause has, within the last few years, encountered so much opposition that it is doubtful whether it has recently advanced or receded.

From these considerations, or others analogous to them, it doubtless has arisen that, in Christian countries, the laws practically may be said to take no notice of offences against chastity of conduct. Marriage alone is fenced in by law, for it is both a religious rite and civil contract. As to other matters, they are left to the unfettered action of public opinion, the rebukes of which are always most severe when it stands alone.

The natural course of things here would have been, that the binding union of two persons of different sexes should have been first introduced as a part of the new religion, and so soon as the rite became general, that it should have received the additional authority of the civil power, and here the law should have stopped. If in Europe and America the attempt to compel the sexes to a more strict morality by civil penalty has been abandoned as both unwise and impracticable, the project of making any such effort here, where the ideas of the people concerning the sexual commerce were so much more loose, ought never to have been entertained. That should have been left to the efforts of the new teachers, and to the nicer sense of moral and corporeal purity, which it was to be hoped their efforts would gradually infuse into the minds of the people.

Of two things one must happen. Either the efforts of the preachers succeeding, purer morals would prevail. Law could do nothing to forward this movement; on the contrary, by rousing into stronger action the opposing sentiment, it was sure to retard it. Or again, the efforts of the preachers would fail, and sexual vice be as rampant as ever, and then, if the hand of the law were stretched forth, while vainly attempting to grasp offenders, it would only succeed in stirring up other disorders. It ought, therefore, to have remained quiet. In confirmation of the prudence of such a course, I may advert to the fact that in minor matters, which fortunately the law has not taken on itself to regulate, the native of these islands has made a sensible advance. In dress, and in many of his habits he takes a pride in assimilating himself to the white man; he assumes the virtue if he has it not, and in time it becomes, or will become, part of his nature.

But though it is vain for the Legislator to set himself in opposition to the general sentiment, he may often succeed, by wise enactments, in turning that sentiment into proper channels, and thus indirectly bring about much which it would be injudicious for him to attempt to effect by positive law. This consideration brings me to a part of my subject which the necessity of the case leads me to discuss. It were selfish fastidiousness to pass it by.

[VI. April 20, 1861]

The general tradition of the natives is that the voyages of Captain Cook to these islands first introduced syphilitic affections among them. Than that disease no greater scourge afflicts humanity. Often insidious even in its first approaches, abating and seeming to disappear and yet lying dormant in the system, and after the lapse it may be of years breaking out with fresh and fatal virulence, passing to the unfortunate spouse and the hapless children and children's children, it was sure among a people like these islanders, if left, to itself, to spread widely and ravage terribly. And yet there is perhaps no disease which is so much under the command of medical treatment as this one, if then, "*salus populi suprema lex,*" and if the lives and well-being of the people were of weight in the consideration of the Legislator he ought to have strained all his efforts to procure such medical succor as might stay the ravages of the malady, and if possible eradicate it. An hospital or hospitals ought to have been established, and such other means resorted to as might have been most likely to bring about a result so desirable.

But farther, there was danger of a fresh inbreak of the malady from another quarter. Forty years ago foreign vessels were every now and then arriving at these islands. Their number has been continually increasing, and for many years they have been reckoned by hundreds. Now the habits of sailors are notoriously licentious. They sail to every port over the wide world, and at whatever port they arrive, even in the capital of moral New England itself, they find abundant means awaiting them for gratifying all their natural appetites. They have only to conform to the special regulations of the port at which they touch, and the law of the land interferes not farther with them. Was Hawaii to be made an exception in this respect to all the rest of the world? and, if not, was it proper, or was it not, to enforce such regulations as might prevent the intercourse referred to from introducing fresh disease among the people? These were questions to have been seriously debated and definitely settled. And it seems to me that a conclusion might very soon have been arrived at. This, I think, would have been the common sense view of the subject. Situated as Hawaii is, it is impossible to prevent sailors from landing. If they land, from the general experience of all countries, and from the known feelings and habits of Hawaiian females, they cannot but find some who will associate with them. These are things which no laws can prevent. It were worse than useless, therefore, to make laws the object of which should be to endeavor to prevent them. This being the case, how was disease to be prevented from being diffused by them among the native population? A pretty effectual regulation would have been to have had proper officers appointed to see that no sailor capable of communicating the contagion should remain on shore, unless in the hospital, he paying, when discharged, a sum sufficient merely to defray the expenses of his cure; and again that all foreign sailors should have had a certain quarter in the vicinity of the ports at which they landed marked out for them as a residence, if found beyond which, between sunrise and sunset, they should have been subject to fine or imprisonment.

Sailors are so much accustomed to discipline that, so far as I have seen, they readily yield obedience to regulations which do not seriously interfere with their propensities. Besides, they have the sense to see that whatever tends to lessen or eradicate disease turns ultimately to their own benefit. Nevertheless, it may be a question if such regulations as the above were practicable, or were the best practicable. But there can be no question, if we consider what Hawaii then was, that some regulations of the sort were urgently demanded.

Foreign sailors having been subjected to certain rules, it would have naturally followed that all women who frequented their quarters should also be subject to rule. It seems to me that these rules should have been framed with a double purpose, the one to guard against the advance of disease, the other to affix some stigma of opprobrium on the females pursuing this course. A law similar to that which has recently passed would *then* have had both these effects. At that time such intercourse was a comparatively new thing; Hawaiians had not yet quite made up their minds about it. A very little matter might then have turned them against it, and led them to regard females who had been publicly known as the companions of foreign sailors as having thereby degraded themselves. Perhaps additional point might have been given to the sentiment by obliging such women, (*femmes publiques*) as in France, to wear a distinguishing dress—not such a one as would make them glaringly prominent objects wherever they appeared, but sufficiently marked to let them be known to all.

Such, Mr. Editor, are, as it seems to me, the leading principles that, at the period to which I refer, should have guided the Legislator in his treatment of the matters in question. How has it happened that all his measures seem to have been framed and carried out in a spirit directly opposed to them? How has it happened that, in spite of the numerous evils of which they have been the apparent source, these measures have still been persisted in?

How, for example, has it happened that the schools, instead of having been instruments for awakening the intellect, and invigorating all the faculties, by training them to healthy exercise, have in reality been abodes where idleness may be said to have been expressly taught, and where drowsy indolence, pressing down and benumbing with its leaden weight all the powers of the soul, has reigned supreme? How has it happened that, instead of having been the seats where, well sheltered from every withering blast, the nascent virtues of the young heart might expand, and open themselves to each kindly influence of Heaven, they have in truth been seminaries as it were prepared to give unrestrained scope to the utmost depravity of premature licentiousness?

How has it happened that laws for the suppression of sexual vices have been so unwisely framed that they have raised such a universal spirit of opposition to their execution as not only to have exasperated the disorders they were intended to have subdued, but to have nearly broken down all the bulwarks that fence in human virtue—the sense of shame, by pity for the sufferer, even sympathy with her—the fear of God, by the multitude of false oaths which they cause to be daily uttered with impunity—almost the fear of man, by the shield which perjury, thus hardened into brazen boldness, holds ever ready with which to screen the guilty?

How has it happened that a fell disease has been permitted, almost without check, so to extend itself as to have permeated into every household, and year by year to be carrying off by hundreds the flower of the people? How has it happened that no part of the plentiful influx of wealth into the public coffers, arising from the commerce of foreigners, though that commerce was the origin of the bane, has been suffered to be diverted to procure some efficient antidote for medicating to the plague which it had generated? How has it happened that the single house which has at length been erected as a shelter for the destitute sick, where their maladies might be properly tended, owes its origin to no legislative action, but to the bounty of right royal and loyal hearts?

While thus disease ravages, while thus the women, struck with the curse of barrenness, both by its blighting influence and by premature excesses, are unable to fill up the fearful gaps it is making, and we see the unhappy race melting away before our eyes, even as in other lands I have seen a snow drift, on some mountain side, melting away beneath the rays of an April sun. How is it that the system under the sway of which the fearful decadence has had place is still resolutely kept up? How is it that every effort after some salutary change is obstinately opposed? How is it that, when a slight amelioration has been at length effected, every means are resorted to to counteract its beneficial operation, its supporters traduced and villipended, to the finger pointed at them, while the insensate, the positively blasphemous cry, is attempted to be raised against them, and has in fact passed in feeble echoes from island shore to island shore, "Behold the enemies of Jehovah! Behold the men leagued with the foul spirits of the pit to do battle against the Lord of Hosts! War, then! War! Rise ye up in force against him! Up with ye, and down with God's foes! Down with the impious ones! Down with them!"

Farther still, and yet more strange, how is it that we find among the supporters of all this cruel folly men not destitute of intelligence, not in other matters devoid of the kindlier feelings of humanity, not wanting in some tincture at least of liberal knowledge and learning?

The phenomenon is assuredly one of the most singular which the history of humanity presents. Its strangeness might well excite our highest curiosity, were it not that this feeling is swallowed up and lost in that of strong indignation at the long series of baneful consequences which our eyes witness as having followed in its train. I have an hypotheses to propound, which may perhaps serve in some measure to explain it, and to show how it is that men can have been found to lend themselves as agents to lead on a train of events so singularly and culpably disastrous. But in order that I may do so, I must mount to a little higher ground. For this purpose it is necessary to attend to some of the peculiarities of Protestant, or, to speak more correctly, of Puritanic doctrine.

1. Puritans affirm that their christianity rests solely on the Bible and the preached word.

2. As a seeming consequence of this that the reading of the Bible, and the hearing of the preached word, are all the human means necessary to make men Christians.

3. That Christianity is the parent of modern civilization.

4. That modern civilization has made greater progress in Protestant than in Catholic countries.

5. As a consequence of the two last, that thus the superior excellence of their form of Christianity, viz: that which is built solely on the Bible and the preached word is evinced.

It seems to follow from these premises, as a necessary consequence, that, if you find a nation in search of a religion, you have only to send Puritanic preachers to expound the Bible to them in their own tongue, to teach them to read it in that tongue, to scatter profusely among them copies of it translated into that tongue, and you not only make them Christians, but bring them to a state of very high civilization. Now all these, considered as merely a set of Puritanic dogmas, are harmless enough. If they who profess them choose to believe them, it is scarcely worth the while of the rest of the world, unless in the way of polemic controversy, to call them in question. But it is a different thing when they are assumed as the basis of action in our doings with a whole people. Before allowing them quietly to take this position, it were reasonable to inquire what foundation they have in fact, or in the records of history. The question is capable of being reduced to narrow limits.

It is undeniable that Christianity was first promulgated verbally. The Redeemer himself left nothing in writing. It was the inspired word, issuing from the lips of the Apostles and Disciples, conjoined with their miracles and martyrdoms, that began the conversion of the Roman world. Thus Christianity existed for many ages before the scattered writings which form the New Testament were collected. Both the Old and New Testaments, therefore, were regarded in the primitive ages not as being themselves Christianity, but as supplementary to Christianity. It was the miracles and martyrdoms, and the inspired eloquence of the Apostles, and their immediate Disciples, that was the foundation of the firm, unwavering faith of these ages. Now all faiths are propagated from generation to generation. What the father reverently believes, the son receives uninquiringly as sacred truth. So the strong faith of the primitive church flowed down from age to age till the period of the Reformation. When at that time Protestants left the Catholic Church, they took out of it with them two things: Faith in the great truths of Christianity, faith on the Bible as the very word of God. What was peculiar to them, and more especially to the Puritanic sects, was the rejection of all that was in the Church except the Bible, and the belief that each man was capable of interpreting that book for himself, and had the right to do so.

Granting, then, that by a special providence of God, all that is essential to Christianity has been preserved in those once scattered writings, which in the primary ages were regarded as merely supplementary to it; granting that the Bible is the foundation of modern civilization, knowledge and science, even, as one of the advocates of that system once had it in the *Polynesian*—even of Political Economy itself, this further question remains: Whence is derived to Protestants their existing measure of faith in the Bible as the inspired word of God? Does it proceed solely from an examination of the Historical evidence, and of the Book itself, having convinced them that it is verily the oracle of the Supreme Being; or is it partly at least traditional and hereditary, and ultimately derived to them through the Catholic church from the primitive ages?

If the former supposition be correct, then there are reasonable grounds to expect that the diffusion of the Bible among a heathen nation, and the preaching to them, with the ordinary zeal and ability of Protestant clergymen, will be followed by their real conversion, for they will have had all that Protestants have; and what has made white men Christians may be presumed capable of also making Christians of those of another shade of color. But if the latter, if the faith of Protestants is in part a transmission from the primitive ages through the Catholic church, then these have something which is wanting to the heathen, and, until this is somehow supplied, we have no reasonable grounds to hope that their preaching the word and diffusing the scriptures will insure a real conversion. Until this point is settled, Protestant missions to any heathen nation can only be regarded in the light of an experiment, which, among its other results, will go far to prove whether or not the puritanic dogma is correct. I will illustrate my meaning by a reference to natural philosophy: Water, you tell me, and tell me truly, is composed of oxygen and hydrogen. I assume, therefore, that by putting these gasses in just proportions into a bottle, and shaking them well together, I shall have water. But shake them how I will I cannot produce it. To bring the dissociate atoms into combination something more is wanted. They will not unite without heat. Raise some of them to a very high temperature and then they will combine, and will give you a power by which, if you conduct the process aright, the seemingly discordant natures of both the two shall be completely blended into one apparently simple element. In the same way the Protestant missionary, when he goes among the heathen with the Bible, brings near two very discordant elements. Within the boards of the Book which he holds in his hand are truths, which if he could make them penetrate to, and be blended with, the hearts of those around him would completely change their nature—but, has he succeeded in doing so? On the contrary, has not the experiment hitherto nearly altogether failed? Have not the Bible and the heathen been shaken—not irreverently be it spoken—been well shaken up together by aid of missionaries in every possible form, and has not the result been *nil*, or next to *nil*?

Ought not, therefore, this result cause us to doubt of the truth of the puritanic dogmas concerning the all sufficiency of the Bible and the preached word, and to show us, that to convert the heathen something more is requisite, something that may make up to them for that hereditary and reverential faith, which, perhaps, unknown to him, is the cause of the missionary himself cherishing the book. Does it not in short require an amount of self-sacrificing and fearless zeal, and disinterested love for the heathen, which it is almost unfair to expect in a Protestant Missionary? For the Protestant clergy are bound to the world in which they live, by ties which mingle them with it and make them part of it. They can scarcely be expected, therefore, to rise much above it. What the Rev. Malcolm says, towards the conclusion of his missionary travels in the East, when endeavoring to account for the little success of Protestant missions in India, &c., is quite pertinent to the subject. I condense his observations, but do not change a word:

"Streams rise not higher than their sources. None but extraordinary persons rise above the level of their times, and it is in vain to expect all missionaries to be extraordinary persons. As they come from the mass, so they must resemble the mass. If one come from a religious community pervaded by a love of ease, elegance and gain, what reason have we to expect that an appointment as missionary should, as by a charm, at once raise him to a fervor of piety, contempt of earth, courage in dissenting from custom, and a readiness to endure privations, which none of his church at home have maintained, and for which he has neither training nor example. In vain we harangue departing missionaries upon the necessity of a holy weanedness from the world and contempt of ease, if we have no more ourselves."

If then the truth of the great New Testament and Bible doctrines, and therefore of the Book itself, was first demonstrated to the old heathen world by astounding miracles and heroic martyrdoms, if some portions of the faith thus generated has flowed down to us in a hereditary and traditional stream, and makes in reality a part of Protestant Christianity, then it were unreasonable in us to expect that the Bible, and the mere expounding of its doctrines, will themselves serve to convert the heathen of the present day. We must have something to come in the place of that primitive, heroic zeal, and if our missionaries are of a class not able to supply it, it were as absurd in us to exclaim against the hardness of the heathen heart, when we see them cast away the Book as repugnant to them, as it were for a blundering chemist to rail at the obstinacy of his oxygen and hydrogen for not becoming water, though he had shaken them together in a bottle till his arm was tired. What signifies it then that you have erected a cumbrous, expensive and powerful looking apparatus, if it be so clogged by the cold damps of earth, that, turn it how you will, all your labor shall not be able to draw from out of it a single spark of celestial fire, by which to ignite and combine the two discordant elements that you desire to blend together.

12

Polynesian Languages*

Hana, Maui, March, 1862

To His Excellency R. C. Wyllie, Esq., &c., &c., &c.

MY DEAR SIR:—I wish to give you a very brief sketch of what I have been doing about Hawaiian, or, rather, the Polynesian language, in its connections with language in general, and with the Asio-European languages in particular.

My motive for this is two-fold: First, I know the subject, as connected with our Insular Kingdom, is of itself of interest to you, and also that the kindly feeling you have for myself will make you anxious to know what I have accomplished already, and what I expect or hope to accomplish, in an inquiry, the importance of which cannot be doubted. The second is, that it has more than once already happened to me, to have reached important and brilliant discoveries, and that, while waiting to follow up their details, some blast of adverse fortune, hurrying me to other scenes, has prevented my attaining that fullness of proof I desired, and I have seen what I had treasured up taken, as it were piecemeal, out of my hands, by those who were more propitiously circumstanced than I.

* Rae's essay on the Polynesian languages was published in the *Polynesian*, in the issues of September 27, October 4 and October 11, 1862. It was prefaced by the following comment by Abraham Fornander:

Polynesian Languages

The following Essay on the Polynesian languages, was written by Dr. J. Rae, of Hana, Maui, author of "Political Principles," etc., etc., and addressed to His Excellency R. C. Wyllie, by whose permission we now publish it.—Ed. Polynesian.

The briefness to which I must necessarily confine myself must, I am aware, prevent you from seizing altogether my thoughts, but you will be able to gather something of what I believe I have attained to, and something of what I think it, to say the least, very probable, I may presently reach; and should death, or some other mischance overtake me, what I write to you may serve as a record of the things really done by me in this matter. Without farther preface I commence.

There are two inquiries running parallel to each other, and having intimate relations, but which are capable of being separated.

The first of these is, from whence did the Polynesian race come, and at what period of the world's history did they take possession of these islands? The second, what is the nature of their language; what light does it throw on the original formation of language itself; and what connections has it with other tongues?

As to the first; Asia is the acknowledged great mother of Nations. Her vast dimensions, her generally warm, yet varied, climate, and the original fertility of her soil, even yet but partially exhausted, mark her out as such; all recorded history assigns her this honor; ethnological inquiries prove it. How many distinct civilizations may have arisen there, how many may have either partially or wholly dominated over, and nearly, or perhaps altogether, extinguished preceding civilizations, we know not, nor, at present at least, have the means of knowing. There is every reason however to believe, that they have been numerous. Everywhere we see traces of various races. Many questions here arise. I will only notice two. 1st. What has given rise to the various races, and has successively enabled one to dominate over the other? I answer, a main cause has been the progress of invention. We, for instance, the dominant civilization of the day, may be said to be a steam-using people. We have been so for only half a century, yet what superiority has it given, is it giving, and will it give us? and how much (if other and still more important inventions do not come into play) will it alone change us in two or three centuries? I shall take another example. What steam is doing to and for us, the taming and domesticating of sheep, cattle and horses, must have done for those who first subjugated them. We may see this in North America. The Indians who have troops of horses are essentially different, and altogether superior, to the Indians of two or three centuries since; live in greater comfort, are gathered together in larger bodies, and are far more formidable. We see the same in Africa, where the black Caffres and other herding races rise greatly above the original Negro both bodily and mentally. There are very many facts going to prove that this was a cause which operated largely in Asia, in founding new races, and enabling them to subdue and extinguish others.

This succession of race to race seems to have been one of the main causes of the progress of mankind—the superior always overcoming the inferior, and either absorbing or exterminating it. It (the superior) has then gone on, by its own proper force, gathering new powers as it advanced, until some internal disease attacking it, it became either stationary or retrograded, and was in turn subjugated, and sank under the advance of some people having more of the elements of vigorous social life within them.*

It may be thought that Asia itself is opposed to this theory, showing in the main, with the exception of China, only as it were the *residua* of numerous peoples once powerful and prosperous, but now prostrate, imbecile, without the energy to advance a single step. In reality it is a strikingly exemplative of its correctness. Look at the facts: Geographically as we look on the map, Europe seems, and really is, but a part, and a small part, of Asia—a little northern nook, outshotten from that great continent. Some three or four thousand years since, our ancestors, Celts and Germans, pressed probably by the redundant population of their native Asiatic seats, begun to move into this Europe, and take possession of that hitherto neglected region. Necessity, that severe but excellent schoolmistress, taught them many things in their northern advance; for, to encounter and overcome difficulties, gives strength to nations as to individuals. The sterner the trial the greater the vigor. Accordingly, the farther north the stronger the men. The northmen, or Normans, have given Kings and Nobles to almost all Europe. That force and strength, and vigor of character, which we thus acquired, now renders us the dominant race of the whole globe, and as such we are spreading ourselves over all its more inviting parts, over Central Asia among the rest. There seems at present every probability that, in two or three centuries, all that region will be possessed by the Anglo-Saxon, and perhaps other European men, the pure blood occupying the higher, more cool, and healthy parts, a mixed race the lower and hotter portions; and that the English language, arts and literature, will be things giving a new fashion to society and obliterating the ancient forms. But in doing all this, we shall only be returning to, and repossessing our ancient seats; we shall be but enacting on a grander

* "As the race of trees so is that of men." The analogy might be carried farther than Old Homer thought of. Nature scatters widely the seeds of life, and each, whether of plant or animal, has a struggle for existence. Those best adapted to their position—that is, in our phraseology, the stronger crowd out the weaker. If particularly strong, the peculiarities which gave them their strength harden in them and their descendants into what we call first a variety, and then a species, which dominates over others and presses them out of being. Hence what have been termed centers of creation in the vegetable world, have, as it seems to me, their analogies in the world of man, and these make so many starting points for the true philosophic history of our race.

scale, one scene of the great drama of human progress, of which many similar have preceded, and others may possibly follow.

Some such change was probably wrought on the aspect of society in Southern Asia by the domestication of cattle. When these began to multiply and be collected in herds, men would pass with them into the rich northern pastures, the abode before of the wandering hunter. At first they would exist as separate tribes, otherwise there would be strife between the herdsmen, to avoid which, as in the case of Abraham and Lot, one would say to the other: "Is not the whole land before us? If thou wilt go to the right, I will go to the left; and if thou prefer the left, I will go to the right." But in the course of years, cattle and men would multiply, tribes would become nations—nations battling with each other—for herdsmen are naturally, we may say necessarily, the fiercest of warriors. Ages of this sort of life would beget a numerous, vigorous, and warlike race in the north, requiring only to be united under some able and ambitious chief, to pour down on the South, and stamp it with a new impress. I think there is evidence of such a revolution, or perhaps of a series of such revolutions having had place there.

The other question is this: When one people or race is vanquished and overrun by another, or by its arts, where are we to expect to find traces or remnants of it? I answer, the new force always strikes at the rich central parts—at the heart of the Empire. The fragmentary outer parts often remain untouched. Thus, there is no doubt that the Laps are the remnants of a race once occupying at least the Northern parts of Europe. They now, therefore, exist only on the outskirts of their ancient domain. The Celts came next, and once occupied the larger part of that continent. The Germans, including in the term both the Teutonic and Gothic divisions, came next, and, with the Romans, subjugated the Celts. Where, now-a-days, do we find the Celts? In the uttermost borders, on the Westernmost shores of Ireland and Scotland. Classic and French literature and science have operated as a foreign force over the Teutons and Goths, in all the richer parts of Northern Europe. Where do the learned, now-a-days, go for the pure idiom as it was probably spoken in the time of Christ? To remote, cold and barren Iceland.

If, then, as there is reason to believe, these Islands were peopled by a race once dominating over a small, or great part of Asia, all analogy would lead us to conclude, that, while that race must there have been over-run, and its original characteristics crushed out by foreign forces and arts, they remained in these Islands very much in their primeval form. They must, it is true, have undergone some modifications, either greater or less. Were these for the better or the worse?

When Cook and his companions gave to the world their account of the condition of this new people, the conclusion to which men came was, not that they were savages, not that they were barbarians, but that they had a civilization, though that civilization was rude.

Guizot defines civilization as advance. That cannot be accepted as a just definition, but we may with truth affirm that civilization, implying the practice of various arts, and these arts in their play on each other begetting new arts, and rudimentary sciences, there ought always in all civilizations, regarded only from this point of view, to be an onward progress. The want of it, therefore, marks a disease in the body politic, which must ultimately bring on decay and death. It is natural for a tree to grow, and some we know have been growing for thousands of years. If it does not grow, it is because there is disease in the trunk, or roots, and decay is at last certain. So it is with man in society. He either advances or recedes.

Had the movement here been forward or backward? I believe it had been retrograde, though slow, and spread over many, many centuries. Many facts with which you are no doubt acquainted demonstrate this. I will refer to only one, viz., the decline of the art and practice of navigating long distances. It is quite clear from various circumstances and traditions, that, in the ancient times, the natives of these Hawaiian Islands frequently sailed to all the kindred groups. When Capt. Cook arrived they had no canoes fitted for such voyages.

If then, the arts had been in a declining state, we may conclude, with great probability, that such as were found existing here, had come to these Polynesian Islands with the original settlers, and hence we may draw some conclusions as to the time of the settlement, and the character of the people who formed it, and from that character as to their *habitat*. The arts in which these islanders excelled were fishing, navigation, irrigation. These would, I think, indicate that the parent stock had inhabited a warm climate, a country near the sea, and traversed by rivers. Again, there are some arts of which we find no trace here, which we can scarce suppose to have perished had they ever been introduced. First, written language. Had writing been known to the colonizing race, most assuredly that knowledge would have been kept up, if by none others, at least by the priests. Again, cattle. Had these been largely domesticated among the parent people at the colonizing period, I can conceive no cause that could have prevented their being brought here. The young could certainly have been transported.

It is, indeed, impossible from these circumstances, to fix the exact epoch of the emigration, but it certainly must have been at a very remote antiquity. It also must be allowed that the present Hindoostan has characters that would accord with the country indicated by the circumstances I have mentioned. There are many facts, which add to the probability of the supposition, that I pass by.

It seems to me, therefore, that from the considerations alone which I have briefly stated, the following might be maintained as a probable hypothesis:

At a period antecedent to the invention of letters, antecedent also to the full and general domestication of cattle, there was a great people inhabiting some part of Asia, very probably Hindoostan, who, for those remote ages, had carried navigation to a pitch of great excellence. That this people colonized the Polynesian groups. That they were subjugated, and their nationality, language and institutions obliterated by some other race, probably by one of shepherd warriors. That this revolution caused a complete break to the intercourse of the islanders with their mother country, which, for purposes of trade and government had before been frequent; isolated them from the rest of the world, and gradually sank them lower in the scale of civilization. That this deterioration, somewhat retarded by the intercourse of group with group, became more rapid as that intercourse ceased, and was most marked in the smaller and more detached islands.

For the sake of brevity I omit to notice the fact of the irruption of a black race from the West, and the support it gives my suppositions.

I propound this hypothesis, not as of itself being a matter of great consequence. Without something of more certain import, it were only one of curious speculation, or perhaps of unprofitable disputation. But my investigations into the structure of the Polynesian language, and its connection with the Indo-European tongues, have led me to two discoveries, which, if their truth be allowed, must be granted to be of very great and decided importance. One of these implies that the original seat of the Polynesian race was in Central or Western Asia. I believe it will be found that all those tongues which we designate as the Indo-European languages have their true root and origin in the Polynesian language. I am certain that this is the case as regards the Greek and Sanscrit; I find reason to believe it to be so as to the Latin and other more modern tongues, in short, as to all European languages, old and young. The precise relation which these bear to it is not so easily traced, but it is that of filiation; they are not cognate. The Polynesian is *parens*, whither *pater, avus, proavus, abavus*, or *atavus*.

Now, this, you will allow, is one of those discoveries which startle, and which are altogether so contrary to previous conceptions, that they are apt to be thrown aside without looking at, as bearing on their very face the impress of ridiculous paradoxes. Had a race been found in Central Asia whose language was thought to have these pretensions, men would take up the inquiry as one connecting with their preconceptions. But to seek for a solution of the great problem in these, the uttermost parts of the earth, seems, at the first glance on it, to be an absurdity. The question is removed from the rank of absurd paradoxes, if it can be shown that altogether apart from the consideration of language, there are reasonable grounds to conclude that these people are the remnants of a race inhabiting, in ancient days, some central point in Asia, and subsequently blotted out from the light of day, by the irruptions of more warlike tribes.

The second discovery which I believe I have made, and with which the former is connected, is, that the study of the Polynesian language gives us the key to the original formation of language itself, and to its whole mechanism.

I commence with this latter. I can only give you the heads, mostly mere titles of what would require separate chapters.

1. Man is an imitative animal, and all his arts have had their beginnings in this propensity.

2. Language has its origin in the same source.

3. We do not now make absolutely new words, but when we would express thoughts and feelings too deep for utterance by the common diction, we have recourse to poetry. The principles, therefore, guiding the creations of poesy, must have an analogy to those which guided the original inventors of language in creating names for things. These depend in part at least on the imitative propensity. Not to speak of its imagery, power by simile, &c., we have the precept, "the sound should seem an echo to the sense."

4. But whatever be the principles on which poetry is based, it is not a knowledge of them that makes a poet. No one can be educated into a poet, as he can to be an engineer or surgeon. The delight of the poet is to have bodied forth his thoughts in such form that their full depth may be fathomed by other minds. Neither he, nor the men who listen to him, think of, or care for, the mechanism by which the feat has been accomplished. He and they feel that it has been done, and that is all. Hence the notion of poetic inspiration. To analyze poetry itself as an art, and endeavor to trace its principles, is a later business. Homer and Sophocles came before Aristotle.

5. It is reasonable, therefore, to conclude that, as in poetry, so with the first framers of speech at each separate invention, they only felt that through means of the breath and the organs called into action, they had given utterance to something, that to themselves, and consequently to others, would serve to bring before the mind the object or event which it was wished to note. Neither the inventor, nor they who profited by the

invention, would at all attend to the mechanism by which this was brought about.

6. It is reasonable, however, also to conclude that, as in poetry, so in the first sounds giving names to events or objects, there was really something suggestive by analogy of the things they were intended to mark.

7. Language is defined articulate sound. Its general progress therefore would be from the slightly articulated to the strongly articulated. That is to say, from being but little broken by what we term consonants, to being greatly broken by them; speaking in the general therefore, the fewer the consonants the older the language. This conclusion, however, is modified by the fact that the farther removed from the equator the greater seems to be the tendency to insert consonants.

8. Men first discern in the concrete; the abstract, whether real or verbal, is later of being seized. Hence the conclusion may be drawn that, at first the distinctions we make between noun, adjective, verb, &c., would be little observed. (To make this clear, I should have to run into metaphysics.) The inflections also to which we give the name of declensions, and conjugations, not being essential to language, seem not likely to have had a place in the primitive tongues. And, as to the words we term verbs, as an action is not such till it is done, the primitive form would express simply the complete action, or would stand for what is termed the aorist tense. The present, the future, and the connections of the complete action with other events, would naturally be expressed by additions to that primitive form. In the first language or languages, the aorist would thus seem likely to be the simple form.

9. Mere sound, by its very nature, is very confined in its capacity to suggest ideas of external objects, because it has no resemblance to them. It would seem almost limited to the representation of the cries of animals, and therefore also of the animals uttering them. (Other considerations which I omit go to prove this bounded capacity of sound considered apart.) But, when we utter an articulate sound, we call into play the breath, and all what are termed the organs of speech, the lips, the tongue, the cheeks, &c. Now, these being things of which the nature and action are cognizable to the senses, they have resemblances, more or less near, to the objects making up what we call the visible world. They may possibly therefore have analogies to many of these, sufficiently close to indicate or suggest them, and to serve to recall them to the mind. They differ in this from any sound the voice can emit, for it obviously can have no resemblance to anything but some similar sound, and can only therefore suggest to the mind bodies which give a sound. Of the organs of speech, the larynx is the chief, but its action lies concealed, and would not be known to rude un-

cultured men. They would know only what they felt, that something issued as a stream from the mouth, when they uttered a sound. Accordingly, the more ancient Greeks, whose language was comparatively little broken by consonants, conceived of the voice as a stream. Now, a stream is capable of being variously modified, so as to have a resemblance to many things. It may be broad and shallow, or deep and narrow; it may flow slowly or swiftly; it may be made to pass rapidly through a contracted opening, or in a jet up or down; or sideways, or straight forward, &c. The lips, the tongue, the whole mouth, assume different forms in the utterance of different syllables, and all these forms may have resemblances to objects and actions external. It is to be observed, however, that this stream, its modifications and adjuncts, are only capable of representing force, form and movement.

Three consequences follow:

First, That the primitive significant sounds were all monosyllabic.

Second, That these primitive, articulate and significant sounds only expressed force, form and movement; on these, other significations were subsequently engrafted.

Third, That the nearer we come to original language the more scanty the nomenclature as to things remote from force, form and movement—as, for instance, colors.

10. Language either advances or recedes. Its natural tendency is to advance.

It has always been a great power, as well in what we call savage life as in civilized. Hence men who, from position or talent, hold an eminent place as speakers or writers, seek for what seems to them the forms which are best suited to give the most powerful expression to their thoughts. Most men of mark have a style of their own. If the community be large, and there be many who have made language their study, it is only such innovations as have real merit that become permanent. If it it be small, a single eminent man, especially where writing is unknown, may make great changes. There being no one to challenge the propriety of the innovations, they become first fashionable and then lasting. The old and better vocabulary drops. If, for instance, England had been a small country, and scarce a writer of distinction in it but Carlyle, he without doubt would have much altered the language. As it is, though he has his imitators, it is little probable that he will have a perceptible influence over the common diction. Hence, where writing is unknown, if the community be broken up into small tribes, the language very rapidly changes, and for the worse. An offset from an Indian tribe in a few generations has a language unintelligible to the parent stock. Hence the vast number of languages among the small hunting tribes of Indians in North and South America, which yet are all evidently of a common origin, for their principles are identical, The larger, therefore, the community, the more permanent the language; the smaller, the less it is permanent, and the greater the degeneracy. The smaller the community the more confined the range of ideas, consequently the smaller the vocabulary necessary, and the falling into abeyance of many words.

11. When we have to compare two languages in which similar words with similar meanings occur, it may be a question which is the parent and which the offspring. Thus, if the times to come are to be like the times that have gone by, a period in the world's history may possibly arrive, when the annals of modern Europe may have been so obscured by antiquity that men shall not know whether what then may remain of the Latin and English languages were spoken by contemporaneous people, or whether by races existing at different epochs; and if the latter, which was antecedent to the other? The question, were it to arise, might be thus determined: See if there be any words common to both which are compound in the one, and not so in the other. The one in which they exist as compounds is the primary tongue. The reason is plain. The materials existed in it, out of which to form the word. They did not exist in the other. Thus, omnipotent in English, has the same signification as omnipotens in Latin, but the parts of which it is made up *omnis* and *potens*, are significant words in the Roman tongue, but are not to be found in English, and so with hundreds of others. The Latin, therefore, might be confidently pronounced to have been the elder tongue.

The Polynesian language has every sign indicative of antiquity. It abounds in vowels, the proportion of these to consonants being twice or thrice that of the average of other languages (see above, 7). In it the same word may be verb, adjective, noun, or adverb, and the simple form of the verb is an aorist (8). It is monosyllabic, that is to say, every syllable has its own proper significance and force, even in the longest words. It is very scanty in its nomenclature as to things to which force, form and movement cannot be attributed as characteristics. Thus in colors there are but five or six names. Black and blue and dark green are not distinguished, nor bright yellow and white, nor brown and red, &c. This proceeds from no obtuseness of sense, for the slightest variation of tint is immediately detected by this people, and they have a very keen and just perception of what is called the harmony of colors. In the same way those affections of the mind which have no relation to external objects, and which do not manifest themselves by external signs, have a very scanty nomenclature. Thus, for love, friendship, gratitude, benevolence, esteem, &c., they have but one term, *aloha*. Those affections of the mind, on the contrary, which have relation to

external objects or which exhibit outward tokens, are pretty fully represented; thus, *huhu*, anger—literally, swelled out; as we say, swollen by rage,
&c. (9). Very many words which are compound in Polynesian, are held as
primary roots in languages which we term ancient, as for instance Sanscrit
and Greek (11).

Its simplicity (the Hawaiian language) gives great facilities for analysing
it. Every syllable is either a vowel, or a vowel preceded by a consonant. In
no case does a consonant close a syllable. This distinctive peculiarity may
partly have arisen from the greater difficulty of articulating a syllable
closing with a consonant. Ask an adult Hawaiian, knowing no language
save his own, to pronounce the syllable formed by the two first letters of
our alphabet, and he will be sure to pronounce it as if written ab*a*. And, in
reality, if we pronounce the same syllable slowly, and attend to our pronunciation of it, we shall be sensible that we ourselves have a slight tendency to add to it a feeble *a* sound. As the lips open, after being closed
upon the *b*, there issues out a faint breathing like that vowel. It is quite a
task for a native to avoid giving a distinct vowel sound, after any consonant. It would thus seem likely that this perfect cutting the current of the
voice, this distinct *articulation*, was a thing not existing in rudimentary
speech, and which had not entered the conceptions of those who framed
the Polynesian language.

There is, however, another possible explanation of the peculiarity. For
the fancy to be able to form any image of things external, out of the
current of the voice, it may be necessary that it should be felt as flowing (I
omit details). However we account for it, the circumstance shows, or goes
to show, that the Polynesian language ascends far up towards the times
when human speech was in a rudimentary condition.

The Protestant missionaries to these islands, following the judicious
advice of one skilled in these matters, made the Hawaiian alphabet as
simple as possible. The letters as given by them are twelve. First come the
five vowels, a e i o u, pronounced after the manner of the Scotch, and of
most European nations, and not after that of England. These therefore
unconnected with consonants form five separate syllables. There remain
seven consonants, and as each consonant can take any of the five vowels
after it, and $7 \times 5 = 35$, there would be altogether only forty possible
syllables in the Hawaiian dialect of the Polynesian. I believe, however, the
matter is not quite so simple; some of the vowels have more than one
sound, and the variation serves to mark distinct conceptions. Thus *a*, in the
first syllable of *Hana*, this place, and in that of *hana*, to work, has different
sounds; in the former, *ha* signifies a gap or opening, answering to the
Greek xa, or cha, from whence our chaos, chasm, &c.; whereas in the

latter it means personal, bodily effort. I shall not, however, pursue this part of the subject. I will only make one or two observations necessary to elucidate what follows.

In the first place, then, the Hawaiians often give a slight ruffling or roughening to their enunciation of vowels, which is in effect a nascent consonant. Thus in pronouncing the letter *a*, an *r* seems often to accompany it. That this is so appears by the fact that foreigners hear this faint *r* sound, and in consequence in their first attempts at pronunciation give it full force. Thus you will hear men who have picked up a little smattering of the tongue, pronouncing *aikane* as if it were written high carney; and, indeed, I have seen it so written. I might give many other examples. It is probable, therefore, that in the progress of language, these nascent consonants would become more marked, and pass into written language. Thus, according to my interpretation, ka denotes a forcible action proceeding from a definite point. Add to this another *a*, which marks continued action, and you have a forcible and continued movement, commencing at a definite point. Now, the only movement of this sort familiar to rude men, would be a rolling movement. Accordingly, a stone or a tree on rolling down a hill is said to 'kaa;' so a horse when he rolls on his back, so a man when rolling from his sleeping place, &c. When the Hawaiians saw a wheel carriage, they naturally called it a 'kaa'—a thing that rolls—thus 'pipi' being ox, a 'kaa pipi' is an ox cart. This root 'kaa' passing into the sanscrit become 'char,' which, in that language, means a movement onward from a definite point; hence probably 'caravan,' a word of Persic origin. Passing into the German it became 'karre;' into the Celtic, karr. Caesar Romanized this by adding an 'us' (carrus), but in French it is still 'char.' We write it car; and yet, though they have come down to us by a very long detour, were a stranger to these islands—say a Hungarian—to hear first one of us pronounce the two words "a car," and then a Hawaiian "he kaa," he would probably discern no difference, but that the latter were uttered after a more raucous fashion, like Hawaiian speech in general.

As there seem nascent consonants on many of the vowels, so great part of the consonants themselves may be said to be only incipient. Hence the diversities in writing; the Protestant missionaries printing with a k, the French with a t. It takes months of patient labor to teach a Hawaiian youth to know the difference between d, g, k and *t*; l and r also are not to be distinguished. All this may be referred to the same general principle, the further up you trace language the less articulate it is. That is to say, the less seldom, and less completely, is the current of the voice broken. The Hawaiian pours out a stream of sound, in which, to the unpracticed ear, vowels and consonants seem blended together. Hence the strange mistakes the first voyagers made, writing the same proper name in half-a-dozen different manners.

From a consideration of this circumstance, we may draw the conclusion that the different dialects of the Polynesian language are not really so far apart as they seem from printed books, because in writing, some have put down very lightly pronounced consonants as if distinctly uttered, and some have chosen one letter, others another, to represent sounds nearly or quite identical. Add to this that with us perfectly articulating Europeans, the consonants are esteemed the fixed points, the vowels the easily inter-changeable, whereas the contrary is the case with the Polynesian, and you have a cause for the misapprehension. European philologists of eminence, their view obscured by this erroneous apprehension, and giving the subject probably only a cursory examination, have authoritatively, but very falsely, pronounced the different dialects of the Polynesian to have but little affinity to each other. A European in seeing in one written dialect 'koki' and in another 'hoi,' in one 'kela' and in another 'tea,' would not think they were the same words, only probably slightly different in their pronunciation. In effect if you show the New Zealand Testament to a Hawaiian he will say it is a book written in a foreign language, but if you take it up, give a slight turn to the pronunciation of the words, and here and there substitute others, you will find that there are many passages quite intelligible to him.

In the same way, as there are many words in the Polynesian which require only a very slight turn in the pronunciation to become Sanscrit, Greek, Latin, &c., I think it is a conclusion authorized by analogy to the above, and by the practice of philologists in general, to affirm that they are either cognate or that one has sprung from the other.

To have recourse again to the syllable 'ka.' I have said that it denotes a forcible action proceeding from a definite point, a repetition of it has much the force of what is termed frequentative in grammar, denoting a recurring action, and, according to the nature of that action, either intensi-fying it or diminishing its force. Thus 'ka ka' denotes any quick repeated movement proceeding from a definite point, say from the hand, as for instance in extinguishing a fire in grass by striking repeatedly with a branch is 'kaka wela,' or splitting firewood is 'kaka wahie.' When reference is made to the action itself, the place being indefinite, a 'la' is added, as denoting place generally, something like the French 'la,' there. Hence 'kakala' comes to signify the breaking of the surf, the striking of a cock with his spurs, and hence again the spur itself. Now compare 'kakala' with the Latin calcar or kalkar, which is also a cock's spur, and you perceive it requires but a very small twist of the voice in the pronunciation to convert the one into the other. So it is with very many nearly Polynesian words in Greek, Latin and all other languages with which I am acquainted.

There are, then some forty or fifty possible syllables in the Hawaiian language. Is it possible to conceive that these are all, as it were, random sounds, having no connection with the nature of the things which singly, or in combination, they serve to denote? I think not. Everything, as it seems to me, must proceed from some cause, and therefore everything, even the slightest breeze that blows, has a cause, could we only find it out. Take, for instance, a parcel of these syllables, say ma, mi, no, ke, hi. Why should the one be used instead of the other? What is there in 'no,' why it should be employed in any word rather than 'ma?' Or, let us take a collection of words in which any syllable, say 'mi,' occurs, and see if we can discover anything in them which makes it appropriate, and which would render any other, say 'la,' 'li,' 'ha,' &c., unfit for the purpose. Here is a short list. 'Umi or 'mi,' a rat-trap; umi, infanticide; 'umi,' the number ten; 'emi,' to lessen; 'emiemi,' in the New Zealand dialect, to assemble; 'umiki,' to wrinkle; 'umiumi,' the beard; 'mimilo,' a whirlpool; 'omimi,' to wither; 'milo,' to 'spin;' 'mio,' to flow, as water through a narrow passage; 'mihi,' to sigh, New Zealand, 'mihi,' to repent; 'mimi,' to make water; 'amiomio,' to be giddy, New Zealand, 'amiomio,' unsettled, Tahiti dialect, 'romiromi;' 'romiromi,' to hide from approaching visitors, T.D.; 'lomilomi,' to chafe the limbs; 'minomino,' rumpled; 'milomilo,' to regard with curiosity, 'minamina,' to pity, 'umiumihah ehahe,' the white billows of the sea, T.D.; 'umiumihahehahe,' an undaunted warrior, T.D.

Now in reading over this list it is impossible to doubt that there must be some cause for the syllable 'mi' entering into all these words. It is impossible to conceive that it is mere accident which has brought it there. It must, so to say, have some inherent *force* of its own which renders it appropriate, and would render other syllables less appropriate for the place. Yet, utter it as often as I will, and give it any inflection I can, I find nothing in its mere sound indicative of any suitableness it has for giving the meaning of any one of the things or actions which we know these several words represent. Furthermore, the matter acquires additional difficulty from the consideration that whatever this appropriateness of the syllable 'mi' for filling the place it holds in any one of these words may consist in, it must be a something adapting it to them all; and yet the several things and actions represented by the words I have written down would seem to have nothing in common. What, for instance, can have less apparent connection than a rat-trap, infanticide and the number ten?

This is the problem which my theory, or system, or what you like to call it, proposes to attack and solve. I repeat the main points in it:

1. When the syllable 'mi' was first uttered as a name for any thing or action. Society was in a very rude and elementary condition; the perceptions of men were formed from their immediate sensations, and language was in its infancy.

2. The voice was conceived of as a current, flowing from the mouth, and capable of being bodied forth by the sensible organs of speech into this or that form.

3. These organs themselves being material, and flexed into different shapes in uttering, or attempting to utter, different sounds, might have analogies as thus modified, this way or that, to material things and actions.

Now place yourself in this condition. Suppose your language is syllabic, and very meager and scanty; that you hear some one utter the syllable 'mi,' and, never having heard this exact sound before, that you endeavor to give utterance to it yourself. We may separate the two letters and consider them apart; i, that is the English e (as in bee) takes for its utterance the smallest opening of the mouth of any of the vowels. The stream of the voice is therefore confined. To give the modification to this stream implied by the letter m, the lips are first compressed through their whole extent, and then slightly opened through that extent, to allow the i to escape. You have thus a broad, but thin stream flowing through a wide orifice whose sides approach. There is, therefore, nothing impossible in the supposition that the effort to pronounce the sound in question might be suggestive of that idea.

It is likely that the natural evacuations would be among the first things to which men would give names. I shall, therefore, take the Polynesian word used to express the voiding of urine as the first example. Suppose, then, that in the rudimentary state of things we are considering, some one, imagining he has found a proper term for the act, calls the attention of another to it, uttering at the same time the two syllables 'mi mi,' and that this other individual attempts to re-produce, and succeeds in re-producing, the sound. Would not the two actions, the one which he was performing by means of the organs of speech, the other at which he was looking, have a certain resemblance to each other? Would they, in effect, have any essential difference, but that in the one there was an aerial, in the other a liquid stream? Is there anything, therefore, impossible in the supposition that he might instinctively feel that the utterance of the sound mi mi had in it some certain appropriateness to the act of urinating? That the uttering it had some connection or other, unknown probably to him, and which he would not think of tracing out, with the thing; was, in short, a fitting name for it, as serving, on again hearing it, to recall the act to his memory? Is not this supposition much strengthened by the fact that this double syllable has, in truth, become the name for the thing in question over islands scattered for many thousands of miles over this ocean; that the same syllable is found in other languages for that evacuation, as in Sanscrit, 'mih;' in Greek, 'omicho;' in Latin, 'mingo;' and that we shall in vain search for any other syllable, the utterance of which produces in the organs a movement having any, or equal, analogy to the thing?

I proceed to the other words. In this I shall simply point out the analogy. They are mostly compounded with other syllables; these I will translate, not with critical accuracy, but shortly, by the English word coming nearest the idea.

First is 'mio,' in which o may be rendered on. The lips here are represented by two rocks nearly meeting, and, pressing through them the stream flows on. A correct enough representation this for a mountain torrent confined by rocks, for which the words 'mio' stands.

2. 'Amio'—is applied to denote a current of air passing through a door, or between rocks, with force. This force is indicated by the a prefixed, and the whole word may be translated—a gust of wind.

3. 'Amiomio.'—Subject to sudden gusts of passion—Tahitian.

4. 'Amiomio.'—Nearly the same in N.Z. dialect. These two may be from ami, a hinge; in this case they may be translated easily—moved hither and thither. 'Ami' and its cognates I have not put down.

5. 'Milo'—To spin. In this case the fingers take the place of lips, and the thread that of the slender current. 'Lo' is for long. If I might coin a word, one might say it 'mees' long—it is spun out long. This action gives a whirling movement to the thread, hence the next.

6. 'Mimilo'—To whirl, and—

7. 'Mimilo'—A whirlpool. Here the meeting of the opposing currents takes the place of the lips or fingers, and the whirl that of the stream or thread.

8. 'Umi,' or 'mi'—A rat-trap. Look at it! Have not its firmly closed serrated lips, which, however, may be opened, some analogy to the compressed human lips as they prepare themselves to utter the 'mi?' The u, strictly, a jutting out, when prefixed, stands for the other part of the trap.

9. 'Umi'—Ten. Think of the mode in which men, who have no other mode of reckoning but their fingers, denote this number. With extended arms they first stretch out all their digits, and then suddenly close them on the palms. The former action is the u, the latter the 'mi.'

10. 'Umi'—Infanticide. This was generally done by compressing the windpipe with the fingers.

11. 'Umiumi'—The beard. The Polynesians plucked it out by means of two pieces of shell, used in the way of pincers. These shells represent the

'mi,' viz., the compressed lips; the *u* the action of applying them. From this daily pluck, pluck, plucking the thing plucked, the beard, doubtless received its name.

12. 'Umiki'—To pinch; to stretch out the arm and press the thumb and fingers forcibly together. The ki denotes the forcibly.

13. 'Lomilomi'—To chafe the limbs; a pressing of the thumbs and fingers together here and there—'lo-lo.'

14. 'Romiromi' (the same word, with the Tahitian *r* in the place of *l*).— To hide suddenly. This is done by placing the things to be concealed, here and there (lo-lo) under the mats, and *pressing* these down on them.

15. 'Minomino'—Wrinkled; a cloth pinched by the fingers or something else into wrinkles. The *no* is passive; the cloth or paper having been operated on, not itself operating. I may remark that our word crumpled seems to me to have had a similar origin in a verb in the ancient German, signifying to compress with thumb and finger, of which we have a trace in our word *crumb*, a morsel broken off by thumb and finger.

16. 'Umiki'—To wrinkle; pinch.

17. 'Omimi'—Withered; as leaves corrugated into wrinkles.

18. 'Emi'—To lessen. Here the 'mi' is to squeeze, and the *e* out. Now, to squeeze out implies a lessening of the thing squeezed.

19. 'Emiemi'—To assemble. We speak of an assembled multitude as a press. Thus, in the New Testament, "he could not come to him for the press." Now, emiemi may here be translated a pressing together from all quarters, which is a sufficiently just conception of the idea implied in the word assemble.

20. 'Umiumihahehahe'—The white billows of the sea. In a storm when the waves of the sea are large, we see here and there their crests or project-ing lips elevating themselves on high. Sometimes this movement goes so far that some of these overshoot themselves, go beyond the perpendicular, break, and fall down on the body of the billow, making what we call a breaker. The *u* the projecting of the lips or crest; the mi the closing down of it upon the body of the wave. 'Hahehahe' may, I think, be shortly trans-lated tumultuous. Thus we should have the phrase—"The waves tossed into breakers over the tumultuous sea."

21. 'Umiumihahehahe'—An undaunted warrior. We speak of the *press* of the battle—mi. The *u* pushing broadly, that is boldly, forward. Thus we have "pushing boldly forward through the tumultuous press of the battle."

Matter and movement being all that the organs of the voice can be moulded to represent, it may be said to have been impossible for the Poly-nesian race to form words to express those emotions which give no external signs. All those emotions, however, which give manifestations of their existence by visible signs, however slight, have a place in the language. The eye, as changing its appearance under the influence of shame, rage, &c., has furnished names to several of these. We must seek elsewhere, however, for the three following:

22. 'Mihi'—repent. If you hear one Kanaka ask another what he should do concerning his wife, who has been guilty of a grave fault, the question will probably be put, "Ua mihi anei ia?"—"Has she repented?" Now what is the thing implied in the *mihi*? It is this: she has fallen down before her husband, moaning out the "uwe!" her visage contracted into wrinkles, down which, if she can force them out, the tears roll. The *mi* has reference to the wrinkles, the *hi* to the flow of tears. This is the full "mihi," but the term is used more frequently as a simple acknowledgment that wrong has been done.

23. 'Minamina'—to pity. Strong pity or compassion, such, for instance, as felt when looking at a ghastly wound inflicted on the person of a friend, produces a deep furrow in the middle of the forehead, and draws back the mouth so as to cause a fold at the corners. So at least the emotion is depicted in plates of the passions. This is, I think, a probable derivation of the term for the emotion in its stronger form. It is used, however, generally for much more trivial matters in the sense of to spare, and may then be nearly equivalent to giving out a thing in mere pinches, *mi*. It is opposed to 'Minomino,' the *na* being active and implying that the *mi* is produced by the act of the person spoken of.

24. 'Milimili'—a curiosity or to regard with curiosity. Observe how a native acts when something curious, and which he has never before seen, is presented to him. He takes it up, grasping it with his fingers, and turning it from hand to hand. The repeated *mi* is the grasping; the *li* the passing from hand to hand. Or, if you ask a native what is the meaning of 'mili-mili" the chances are he will endeavor to explain it to you by putting his hands through these movements.

I think you will admit that our problem has been solved—that we have found a reason why *mi*, in the several words, is more appropriate than any other syllable would be in the place it occupies. That we have also discovered a certain bond connecting these several names of things, seemingly so altogether unlike, this same *mi* indicating forms or movements, or both, existing in all these things, and through which each has certain analogies to the others.

I could easily more than quadruple the list, giving you, after the same fashion, a true, or at least a probable explanation of the sources of the forces which the same syllable *mi* has in all the terms.

I could in a similar manner take up, one by one, all the syllables of which the Polynesian language is composed, dissecting each, and showing how its force depends on the configuration of the organs at the moment of pronouncing it, and that thus we have a clue to unravel the most intricate mysteries of the language, and to guide us to a point of view whence the sources of its very considerable powers and beauties are disclosed to us. That, moreover, we are thus furnished with a sufficient cause for the phenomenon, otherwise inexplicable that words identical, or nearly identical in form, are used as the names of things seemingly utterly different in nature. In any such attempt to display its whole mechanism, no doubt one more thoroughly versed in its use, and better acquainted with the feelings, habits and customs of the race than I am, or can be supposed to be, would detect many inaccuracies, but he would also, I am convinced, see under them a solid substratum of truth.

You are probably inclined to ask me if I can thus decipher all the words in all the dialects. No. About two-thirds or three-fourths of those in the Hawaiian Bible, and one third in the other dialects. But you will best understand what I can do by my telling you the difficulties yet before me.

When chance threw me on these shores I could not forget that, many years before, when engaged in collecting materials for a rather ambitious work I then meditated, on what I may call the history of civilization, I had come to the conclusion that the Polynesian race were a remnant of some very ancient Asiatic civilization. Arrived here, therefore, I had a great desire to make myself acquainted with the language of these islands. Two obstacles met me—my innate inaptitude for acquiring any language, for, though I have attained some knowledge of several, it has been at the expense of three-fold the labor most other men require, and then I had arrived at an age when the sounds of new languages strike dully on the ear. By plunging directly into the midst of Kanakanism, the flood of strange sounds in which I became immersed found gradually a passage into that organ; but yet, when spoken rapidly or by a stranger, I often miss great part, or all that is said. I am thus far from that mastery of the tongue which I might have acquired had I come here at an earlier period of my life. With books it is different. We have the Bible, on the whole in so far as I am capable of judging, well translated. But, then, there are many Hawaiian words not there, and such as are, are not readily come-at-able. This requires a dictionary, and we have no good one. About three years since I got from Judge Andrews a pretty copious manuscript of Kamakau's, but presently afterwards, on coming here himself, he told me it was of little value, having been written when he was very young, and advised me to see and get one which he had made afterwards. About the same time I saw notice of an appropriation to aid Judge Andrews in publishing his dictionary, and concluding it would soon appear, and thinking he must have had all the aids which Kamakau and others could furnish, I have been waiting for it, and have not made that use of the manuscript I otherwise might.

As for the other dialects, although from your kindness and that of others I have Bibles, New Testaments and Prayer Books in several of them, and two dictionaries, one a New Zealand and the other a Tahitian, I am sorry to say they have very grave defects. It would seem as if the writers had not themselves well known the language into which they were translating. I cannot otherwise account for the very great number of English, Latin, Greek and Hebrew words which are introduced. Thus you have tavana, governor; tavani, servant; anatole (Greek), east; orebi (Hebrew), a fly; paleke (Greek), a concubine; osa (Hebrew), a moth, &c. &c. It is impossible that such things as these have no names in Tahiti. The most scanty languages have some word to denote the most of them. The veriest savage has always a name for the sun, and for the quarter in which he rises. In the Tahitian dictionary there is a list of 400 foreign words, and these are not all. There are, I am certain, a great many more introduced into the Bible, and which are not to be found in the dictionary. For as there is at least a third of the apparently native words used in the Bible not to be found in the dictionary, we may conclude that this is also the case as to the foreign. Indeed, I am certain of the fact, though to what extent this foreign invasion goes I am unable to say. Now this is very puzzling to the etymologist. Take any word, say orama, it has a Tahitian look about it, and even a good Greek scholar might not think of its being Greek, for it is of rare occurrence in that language. About the same may be said of the New Zealand Bible and dictionary. One is tempted to think that the translators knew but imperfectly the language, and, when their memory failed them, turned over their Hebrew, Greek and Latin dictionaries till they found a word easily pronounced by natives, and so clapped that down. What makes the matter worse for me is that Hebrew seems to have been the great resource, possibly because as I have been told by those I have met with here having some knowledge of that language, there are striking analogies between it and the Polynesian. Now I know nothing of Hebrew. All this renders these books of far less value to me than they otherwise would be, for it is only such words as being connected with the Hawaiian dialect, and therefore evidently Polynesian, that I dare venture to use.

I have, however, been enabled to make a sufficient study of many different dialects, to arrive at the conclusion that they all most certainly took their rise from one great mother tongue, and that they have all more or less degenerated from it. Thus you find words used in one dialect in some secondary and accidental sense, you find the primary sense in another. Now, it is plain that the word in its primary sense, must at one period have existed in that dialect in which its secondary signification now alone remains. It being then a fact that the use of some words in their more extended sense has been lost in certain islands, it seems to follow that others are likely to have altogether died out, and that probably the majority of words found now in only one or two groups, have belonged to the original language, which therefore must have been far more copious than any remaining dialect. I say nothing of what may be termed corruptions, the changed pronunciations, the contractions, the coining of new words, or the more extended and strained use of others, though all these would naturally take place and have seemingly done so. Viewed merely on the side of copiousness, and judging from the printed language, I should say that, of the various dialects, the Hawaiian is the most copious, and therefore most probably the nearest the original. This no doubt may be partly owing to the different ability or care of translators. Nevertheless, these islands, as having had the largest population, ought to have had the dialect least degenerated.

This great mother language must have been an original one. It is impossible to conceive it to be the corruption of any other tongue. Its structure forbids this supposition.

It is eminently a natural language. It may be said to be natural, because every sound, in every word, has significance, and denotes something having a real connection with the thing or things denoted. The pronunciation of each separate syllable induces a certain configuration of the organs, and that particular configuration has positive analogies, direct, or indirect, with the actions or objects indicated. There is thus a real connection between the sign, and the thing signified.

Again, it is natural, because, if we view speech as an invention of man, it must have commenced like other inventions from the simplest beginnings. Now, we can conceive this language existing in its rudimentary state in two, or three, or four syllables, and out of these growing by the laws regulating the progress of other inventions into its perfect form. No change would have been required in its original elements. The process would have been one of simple, though very skillful, agglutination.

If again, without yielding ourselves to the interpretation of the phenomena before us, by the established laws of the inductive philosophy, we rest on a literal following out of the history of the affair as given in Genesis; then, considered in itself, as it existed at one time somewhere on the great Asiatic continent, it has, I think, a better claim than any other of which I know to be held as the original universal language of the earth, before men attempted to construct the Tower of Babel. For

—————"the great first cause
Acts not by partial, but by general laws."

And this language, being the most natural, is consequently most in accordance with the great plan of the God of Nature.

Such being its innate claims to our attention, another question would seem to arise out of its very structure and constitution. For, its being a natural language, ought to have given it a tenacity of life superior to that of others. Do, then, any traces of its existence remain in the great Asiatic-European continent, in some part of which it once had its seat? This is a question to be determined by those learned in the languages ancient and modern, that flourish, or once flourished, in these vast regions. I myself am but poorly fitted for the inquiry, for I am no great linguist. Latin I have studied and read pretty largely. But the original Roman tongue seems to have grown out of the coalescent speech of various races, and that ancient tongue was unintelligible to Cicero. Few words therefore retaining much of their original form, can be supposed to have come down to us. Yet in the Latin tongue, as we have it, there are a very considerable number of words seemingly of Polynesian descent. In Greek I am but moderately skilled; that is to say, I read Homer and the more easy prose writers with tolerable facility, yet not without occasional difficulty. I have, however, found in that language, a great mass of words, amounting probably to hundreds, which are, I conceive, of undoubted Polynesian origin, and had I the Odyssee (I have only the Illiad by me) could considerably augment the number. Of Sanscrit I never had but a smattering, and I have not seen a Sanscrit book for more than twenty years, yet from my recollections, and from occasional Sanscrit words picked up in dictionaries, &c., I can trace out a Polynesian origin for so many that I have no doubt had I the books by me, I might make out a long list. Once I knew a little Gaelic or Celtic; of the very few words that remain to me, a considerable proportion are identical with the Polynesian. Of German I know next to nothing, yet there too there are many Polynesian looking roots. I am a tolerable Frenchman, but though in that language there is much that smacks of Polynesian, yet, as it is mainly compounded of Celtic, Latin and German, and I have no French dictionary with the supposed derivations, I cannot put anything French to account.

Yet notwithstanding the scantiness of my resources, my researches warrant me in saying that the Polynesian has been the prototype of some of the Asio-European tongues, and that therefore, to say the least, it is not impossible it may have been that of all, for their is an appearance of consanguinity in them all that seems to mark their having had a common parent.

That you may see I have good grounds for so affirming, I subjoin a list of words expressing ideas the most frequently recurring in all languages, and which, while they are likely to be most permanent, afford also the surest proof of identity of speech. The name of a particular thing—tobacco, for instance—may easily spread with the thing itself over many distant countries, but general names are very different.

I have therefore made choice of the four following classes of words, as being most general, and affording therefore the fairest criterion for you to arrive at some judgment on the matter:

1. The sexes—man and woman.

2. The elements—fire, air, earth, and water.

3. Those affections of the mind which seem primarily at least to have regarded material objects—as to see, to know, &c.

4. Words relating to speech itself. I put them down in two columns— the Polynesian to the left, the Indo-European on the right.

As I am not sure if you are familiar with the Greek characters, I put down the corresponding letters in English, but suppose them to be read with the broad sound. I use the letter *h* for the asperate ('), but would remark that this seems too strong for it. Its exact force, like other questions of the exact pronunciation of extinct languages, is a matter difficult to decide, but it seems to me to have been generally much slighter than that indicated by the letter *h*.

I take some liberty with words; that is, in some cases I assume a likeness to exist where perhaps that likeness may not be very apparent to you. But I go not half so far as most etymologists. The just principle seems to be this: When we see a series of words evidently passing from one language into another, or into a set of kindred languages, we are warranted in assigning a similar origin to others, though their likeness be not so apparent, provided there be no other source for them known to us.

Thus when we see that No. 2 has passed into general European speech, we may be allowed to assign a probable, though only a probable, passage of No. 1. And though the resemblance of 'karl' to 'kane' be far from close, yet as the ancient Germans and Greeks were seemingly of one parent stock, we have a right to expect that the words in both languages expressive of masculine vigor, would show tokens of affinity, or that if they were different words, that we should be able to trace their origin into some other language, or into some two or more of the words of these respective tongues compounded into one. But 'aner,' in Greek, and 'karl' in German, are both esteemed primitives, nor can we find any father for either but 'kane' which they both more resemble than they do each other. I may illustrate this by the analogy of the features of the face.

If curious in genealogies, you may have observed, in a long gallery of family pictures, that often brothers, first cousins, second cousins, &c., struck you at first as having little or no resemblance to each other, but, on looking at father and mother, grandfather and grandmother, or perhaps much farther back, you would be able to trace a certain cast of countenance, or perhaps some particular feature, appearing now distinctly, and now but just perceptible, but still running through the whole, and marking them as one race. You may perhaps have heard the late Dr. Gregory, of Edinburgh, in his lectures expatiating on this subject. He was accustomed to do so. So it is with languages, and the proofs of their relationship by their likeness to a common parent.

CLASS I.—MALE AND FEMALE
Man as a Male

No. 1.—A.
Kane, the male

Aner, (Greek)
Karl, (German), a man, *vir*.

In Greek, 'aner,' plural 'aneres,' is a man by excellence, as in the often repeated phrase in Homer, 'Oh my friends, be *men*'—'aneres.' In German, 'karl' seems to have marked a man by excellence—thus, 'Karl magnus,' the great karl, Charlemagne. In broad Scotch there is much old Saxon and Danish or Gothic. Carl is not only an old man, but also a male, as 'carl cat,' and *manly* energy, as when Burns speaks of resolution as the stalk of carl hemp in man.

B.—*Wi*, (Hawaiian,)
Vi, (Tahitian,)
Viri and *viri alo*, (Tahitian,)
   the front rank in battle,
Iwi, (New Zealand,) the men
   of a tribe.

Vis, ⎫
Vi, ⎬ (Latin,) force, strength,
Vir, a man,
Viri, the men.

In my interpretation, 'wi' or 'vi' in the Polynesian language, in one of its senses, denotes a strait, a difficulty, and consequently the force necessary to overcome it. Thus, 'wi,' scarcity of food, famine. Therefore 'wi' or 'vi' is nearly equivalent to the Latin 'vis' 'vi' and 'viri,' as also 'viri alo,' Tahitian, (*alo* or *ano*, front,) to 'viri,' (Latin) the men. 'Vir,' in Latin, being a man in the sense of 'aner' and 'karl,' hence 'virtus,' manliness, and 'virtue.'

No. 2

Wahine, (Hawaiian,)
Vahine, (Tahitian,)—woman,
Vaine, ⎫
Fifine, ⎭ Other dialects

Favini, (Sanscrit,) woman,
Femina, (Latin,) female, woman.

From 'favini,' (Sanscrit,) Latin etymologists derive, and that without any hestitation, the Latin 'femina,' a woman, or an animal of the female sex—hence our 'female' and 'feminine.' I may remark that as 'wahine' is undoubtedly a compound word in Polynesian, denoting the physical characteristics of the sex; if what I have advanced be admitted as correct, this single word would be alone sufficient to prove the priority of the Polynesian to the Sanscrit.

CLASS II.—THE ELEMENTS, FIRE, AIR, EARTH, WATER

No. 3.—A.   FIRE

Kapura, (New Zealand,) fire.
Mapura, „   „   „
Pura, (Tahitian,) to blaze as a fire.

Pur, genetive *puros*, plural *pura*, fire or fires.
Pura, (singular), a fire, a funeral fire; hence *pyra*, (Latin,) a funeral fire, and hence our *pyre*.
Für (Ger.) fire; hence probably the French *feu*, fire; *foyer*, a place for fire, a hearth, and hence probably our *fire*.

B.

A, action; hence the most powerful of agents in early states of society—fire.
Aa, to burn on.
Ahi, a fire, the flame, bursting forth.
Ai, the same in some dialects.

Daiō and *Kaiō*, to burn. Etymologists derive *kaio* from the Sanscrit *cush*. I think it more reasonable to consider the *d* in *daio* and the *k* in *kaio* as strengthening additions to the root; and thus, as *ō* is merely terminal, there remains *ai* or *ahi* for the root.
Agni, (Sanscrit,) fire; hence Latin *ignis* is said to be derived, and hence again our *ignite, igneous*, etc.

C.

La, (Polynesian,) sun.

La, (Celtic,) sun.
Alea, ele, ēlios, (Greek,) sun.

D.

Ao, (Poly.) sunrise or dawn.

Aōs, eōs, auos, (Greek,) dawn, hence *aurora*, etc.

E.

Lama, (Poly.) fire in motion, a torch.

Lama,

Lampas, a torch, a lamp; Latin *lampas*, lamp.
Flamma, (Latin,) flame; Spanish, *llama*.

No. 4.—A.

AIR

Ea, (Poly.) breath.

Ear, aer, (Celtic,) air.
Aar, (Syriac,) air.
Ayer, (Arabic,) air.
Aer, (Greek,) air.
Aer, (Latin,) air.

I think it is doubtful if the Polynesians had any definite idea of air when at rest. Kamakau, however, thus defines *ea*—"He makani ku malie, oia ka makani e hanu nei kakou, e pukka ana iwaho, e komo ana iloko." "Wind at rest, which we breathe, which issues out from us and comes within us."

B.

Puhi, (Poly.) the breath.

Psyche, (Greek,) breath, life, the soul; hence many Greek words and some English derived from them, as *psychology*, etc.

C.

Puhi, (Poly.) to blow.
Akapuhi, (Poly.) blow gently

Psychein, (Greek,) to blow.
Eka psychein or *aka psychein*, (Greek,) to blow gently, as did Minerva, when she blew aside the spear of Hector.

No. 5.—A.   EARTH

Aina, (Poly.) the earth as furnishing food, *ai* being food.

Aia, gaia, gē, (Gk.) earth,
land, soil.

B.

Honua, the earth as extended.

Chthon, accusative, *chthōna*, the
earth as extended.

C.

Kainga, aina, in New Zealand
means a place or time of
eating, and hence an abode.
Ngai, in Rorotonga, a place of
abode, a place.

Naiō, (Greek,) to inhabit.

D.

Mauna, (Hawaiian,) a mountain.
Maunga, (New Zealand,) a moun-
tain.
Moua, (Tahitian,) a mountain.
Mouna, (Tahitian,) a mountain.

Mount, mountain.
Saxon, *mount*.
Latin, *mons*.

E.

Pii ana, (Hawaiian,)

Ben, (Celtic,) a mountain. I do
not know how the Celts write
ben, but in the deep and long
pronunciation of the Scotch
Highlanders they bring the *ben*
to have a near resemblance to
pii ana in all but the final *a*.

F.

Awaawa, (Hawaiian,) valley.

Awn, is, I think, valley in Gaelic.

G.

Avaava, (Tahitian,) valley.

Valla, (Gothic,) valley, as *thing
valla*, in Norway and Shetland,
the valley where popular assemblies were anciently held. *Valles*,
Latin.

No. 6.   WATER

Wai (Hawaiian,) water.   *Agua* (Latin), water.

                                            Vari (Sanscrit), water.

A. Water having no constant form, the organs cannot assume a form having any analogy to it. In the Polynesian Language its name was necessarily derivative. It is generally seen as a body moving or flowing. This property seems to have furnished one name for it. In Polynesian, 'wa' is a space, or what fills a space, as 'wa-onahale,' the space where trees grow wild, wilderness; 'wa-nanalua,' the space that looks both ways, the eastern most point of this land, whence you look north and south over the ocean; 'waa,' a space to which action is an attribute, a canoe. The notion is analagous to Byron's "She walks the waters like a thing of life." So '*i*' being here like the Latin '*i*' in '*eo*'—to go—'*wa i*' may be translated, the space, or the body that goes or flows—water.

An interrogation is put, partly by the accent of the voice and partly by some conventional arrangement of words. Should a person put his head into the door of a house, and cry out, 'Any body here?' he would be understood to be asking a question. In the Polynesian idiom it is not 'any body here,' but, 'any body goes,' *wa* being space, or what fills space, as matter or body, and seeming at the early stages of the Polynesian language to have been used as we use 'body' for person. 'Wai,' therefore, is equivalent to 'any person goes, the form being, however, '*o wai*,' and thus, as it seems to me, it is that water and the interrogative pronoun have, in Polynesian, the same form. Now, not having the authorities by me, I cannot speak with certainty; but through many, and I believe through most of the Indo-European languages, the two words expressing *who*? and *water*, run with all the look of being first, second or third cousins. Thus we have in Latin, 'quis,' 'quae' and 'qua'—who, or *owai*; and 'aqua'—wai, water; in Scotch, 'wha' and 'whae'—owai—('water' equal to 'wai;') in Danish, 'wie'—owai; and Saxon, 'waes'—wai; &c., &c. Now whence shall we take a common progenitor, for them, if not in the Polynesian? I believe no other can be found.

B.

Another word to express a fluid, and so to denote water, was found in the connection between milk and the female breast; and hence a set of correlative terms running through various languages.

U—the projecting nipple of the
   female breast; hence

U—milk; and hence

U—to be damp or wet, and moisture.

Ulu—wetted, (Hawaiian)

Ua—the action of wetting—rain. From *u*, the nipple, comes

Uma—(N. Zealand)—the female breast—that is both the *u* and the broad seated gland or organ which supplies the secretion.

Umauma (Polynesian)—the two breasts, that is, the whole front of the chest in man and woman.

Uda—Sanscrit, wet; Latin, udus-wet; uveo, old verb—I am wet; uvedus, &c.

Uo, ue, uei, I rain, he rains, it rains. That *a* was in the original root, appears probable from the compounds 'ualos'—glass, from its transparency, and 'uades'—the watery stars Hyades.

'Huetos'—wet; 'Hudor'—water.

'Hydra'—water-serpent.

'Hygros'—wet, &c. &c., Latin, *udus, uridus*, &c.

———

The Greek and Romans rejecting the *u*, took *mamma* for the fleshy substance, and *mazos* for the breast in woman; the *u* remained for the inferior animals. Sanscrit, *udara*; German, *uder*, English, *Udder*; Latin, *uber*; Greek, *onthar*, &c.

N.B. I find that this analyzing of each word is more tedious than I thought it would be; I shall therefore confine myself to putting down the words with only a few notes.

CLASS III.—WORDS RELATING TO AFFECTIONS OF THE MIND, CONNECTED PRIMARILY WITH EXTERNAL OBJECTS.

A.

Ike, he saw, or he knew.

Ide (Gr.) he saw, or he knew.

Vidit, (Lat.), he saw.

B.

Manao, I think.

Mnao (Gr., obsolete form).

C.

Noo, I perceive at a distance, or I endeavour to see at distance.

Noonoo, the habit of reaching far in thought; wise, prudent. As a verb and a noun, the signification is similar.

Noonoo ole, without sense.

Sanscrit, *Man*, I think.

Mnaomai, (Gr.), I think.

Noos (Gr.) judgment, discretion, sense.

Gnoeō (Gr.), participle *gnous*; the latin *nosco*, the French *connoitre*, and Eng. *know*, seem all to come from this root.

D.

Oiaio, truth.

Parek noon (Gr.), without sense.

$\left.\begin{array}{l}\textit{Oiomai,}\\\textit{Oīo,}\end{array}\right\}$ (Gr.), I believe it true.

CLASS IV.—WORDS RELATING TO SPEECH.

A.

Leo or *reo*, the sound of the voice.

Reo, (Gr.), old form, I speak; changed afterwards to *ero*, I speak, hence 'rhetoric,' &c.

B.

O, a single utterance of sound, by the voice, a shout, as at night on hearing this shout one might say, 'Oh, that is a Kanaka passing, I know his O.'

Os (latin), genitive, *oris*, the mouth.

C.

Orero or *olelo*, a continuous speech, or to speak continuously.

Oratio (Lat.), a speech; *oro*, I speak continuously, I entreat.

D.

Kala, I strain my voice that the will of the chief may be known —I proclaim.

Kala kalare (old Latin), hence the 'kalendae,' calling out by the priests of the feast days.

Kaleo (Gr.), I call; Sanscrit, *kal*; Swedish, *Kalla*; Dutch, *kallen*, &c.

E.

Kalanga or *karanga*, is used in N.Z. and Rorotonga for 'olelo,' a continual speech.

English, *harangue*, Spanish & Portuguese, *arenga*; Celtic, *harencg*.

F.

Kani and *kakani*, to make a sharp sound, to play on a musical instrument, to sing.

Latin, *cano*, *cecini*, to make a loud noise, to play on a musical instrument; hence 'canto,' to sing frequently, and our *cant*.

G.

Mele, a chaunted poem.   *Ta mele* (Gr.), lyric, poetry,
                                     especially choral songs.

I said I would attempt no further analysis of these words, but leave them to speak for themselves. I must however make a partial exception as to one of them, *oiaio*, as I see it will enable me to illustrate two or three points. The first of these is, that no syllable in the Polynesian language is superfluous, but that each, by its peculiar force, contributes to give its proper significance to the term. In fact, if we consult the real genius of the language, what we call a word ought rather to be considered as a short sentence descriptive of the idea which it is desired to indicate. Hence natives, even those who have been most carefully instructed to model their writing after our system, seldom write a page without grouping some syllables after a fashion that we think faulty; and those who have not been so taught, seem to have no other rule as to the syllables that should be united to make a word than the idea uppermost in their minds at the time of writing.

My analysis of the word must be partial—even that I fear will be tedious. If we make a verb of it, it appears under the form *hooiaioai*, to testify. Now a European, on looking at it, would be apt to think it altogether barbarous, and that such an assemblage of vowels can have been only put together to make a sort of cry that might give strength to the affirmation by sheer noise. On the contrary, each of the eight vowel syllables has its own force, and helps to point out the full image. To see this we must begin at the middle, at the second *i*. I must therefore give you some such partial explanation of its force and of that of the accompanying *o*, as may lead you to apprehend the part they play here.

In uttering the *i* (the same sound as *ee* in bee) the breath is compressed into the smallest and seemingly swiftest current possible. It represents therefore a swift and what we may call a sharp movement.

Of all the vowels *o* is that of which the sound goes furthest. We have it therefore in most words relating to distance, as in *holo, lo, long,* etc.

In joining the two the sense is modified by their position. If we wrote *oi*, it is an *o* going on with an *i*. This is exemplified in *oi*, lame. Observe how a lame man advances. Standing on the sound limb, he puts the lame one leisurely out and sets it to the ground: this is the *o*. But no sooner does it get there, and the weight of the body begin to rest on it, than, hasting to relieve it of the burden, he moves the other leg rapidly forward, lessening the pressure at the same time by relaxing every joint he can bend, and thus letting his body sink as far as possible: this rapid sinking movement is the *i*.

Again, *oi*, a passing in advance, excellency. Here, *o* is the general advance, *i* is the going ahead of some particular one.

If, again, we write *io*, it is an *i* going on with an *o*. That is to say, it is a rapid, penetrating movement—*i*, and that movement long continued. Thus it is a rapid, penetrating movement—*i*, and that movement long continued. Thus we have in Hawaiian *io*, a chief's forerunner. He would be a man rapid in his course—*i*, and of good bottom—*o*. In Greek, *ios*, an arrow, and *Io*, the goddess who went so fast and far. Hence *io* is anything that goes quite through; that is *thorough*, complete, real, true. Like Burns, 'facts are chields that winna ding,' that is, cannot be forced out of their course. Hence, *io*, flesh, real food, in distinction to bone, etc., and reality or fact, or truth generally.

Ia is the pronoun that, analogous to Latin *is, ea, id*. Putting together these we have *o, ia, io*—Oh, that is fact. Prefixing the causative *hoo*, we have 'make that to be fact;' affix *ai*, completion of the action, and we have 'make that completely out to be a fact,' that is testify to its truth.

It is to be remarked that the stress of the voice is loud on the second *i*, the *oia* being pronounced very lightly, and that in Greek the *i* is always strongly accented, a mark of the contraction the word has suffered.

13

Laieikawai:
A Legend of the Hawaiian Islands*

INTRODUCTORY NOTE

Dr. John Rae, the recorder of the following legend, was born at Aberdeen, Scotland, in 1796. He studied at the universities of Aberdeen and Edinburgh. In 1821 he went to Canada, where he lived until 1849. From July, 1850 to 1871, he made his home in the Hawaiian Islands. He died in July, 1872, in Staten Island, N.Y. Dr. Rae was especially occupied with geological studies. His only published work is the "Statement of Some New Principles on the Subject of Political Economy," Boston, 1854 [sic]. The notes left by Dr. Rae do not include further information in regard to the folk-lore of the islands.

The material here given appears to have been included in a discourse, the date and place of which are not apparent. The manner in which a work of Sir George Grey is noticed would lead to the opinion that the period of the lecture was not much after 1855. The legend here treated has been given in its entirety, but also in abstract, in "The Legends and Myths of Hawaii," by King Kalakaua, New York, 1888, pages 455–480. The story appears to have been obtained by the editor of that work, Hon. R. M. Daggett, who presents the account as the condensation of the legend as more elaborately told by Haleole. The version of Dr. Rae, obtained a quarter of a century before, is not so much a variant as a different edition and abstract of the same tale, is apparently translated from the Hawaiian, and perhaps may have proceeded from the same narrator. The account of Dr. Rae is only a fragment, extending perhaps to less than a third of the tale, which must evidently have been very voluminous. In the portion which it does cover, however, it is more full and literal, and appears to give a clearer idea of the literary character of the heroic legend. The two versions serve to complete each other, and Dr. Rae's narrative therefore forms a welcome addition.

* Rae's transcription of the legend of Laieikawai was found among his papers by Mixter and turned over to the *Journal of American Folklore* where it appeared in the October–December issue of 1900 (241–60). The article is reproduced here as it appeared along with the introductory and concluding notes.

As will appear by the conclusion, the legend belongs to mythology in the strict sense, as dealing with persons who have actually received divine worship, and as connected with a lost ritual. It is concerned also with divinities of nature, with spirits of the moon, sun, and mountain. But these appear and act as human personages. How far the story is founded on elements of natural symbolism, how far it is only a fanciful elaboration of tribal life, is difficult to determine; in this respect the legend presents the difficulties which belong to all mythological systems, even the most primitive. Most striking is the manner in which virtue and faithfulness exalt the human agent, not only into the place of the gods but above them. The way in which earth and heaven are finally left in feminine control savors of the matriachate; to women belonged at least an equal share in magical knowledge and consequent authority; clearly in old Hawaii there could be no question concerning their rights.

From a literary point of view, the story, possessing the compass of a modern novel, is remarkable. It is easy to understand what obstacles are thrown in the way of comprehending the excellence of a tale known only by outlines, and where even the force of the significant names is lost, to leave only long and unintelligible appellations for the understanding of the foreigner. Yet among the barbaric ideas and practices belonging to all ancient (or mediaeval) thought, a spirit of gentleness and culture seems to breathe. To this amiable race the course of modern change brought a people of sterner and more energetic quality, whose iron hand brought them into subjugation, who dispossessed them of their territory, and who forced on them a civilization, manners, customs, and modes of thought for which they were unprepared, and which they may be unable to survive. Their language at least will perish, and the loss of language is the loss of everything. There will be no descendants to regard these histories with the honor which a German concedes to the poems of the poetic Edda, or which modern scholarship, nourished on the literature of Greece, accords to Hellenic myth. Yet surely in fulness of imagination and delicacy of conception the Hawaiian legend need not fear comparison.

It can only be hoped that now that the islands are definitely connected with the United States, as a matter of national honor, steps may be taken to complete, so far as possible, a record still unhappily so imperfect. Perhaps at least a full and correct text can be obtained of the present narrative.

My hypothesis that the Polynesians are the remnants of a people who were great in the remote day in which they flourished, and from whom other races have sprung seems to be receiving support from various quarters. I hear that the Governor of New Zealand has published a book,[1] in which he traces many analogies between the rites, superstitions, and habits of thought of the Maori, compared with the Greeks and other ancient nations. Viewed in this aspect, the old legendary tales and poems of the Hawaiians have considerable interest. I cannot doubt but that they bring down to us much derived from a very remote antiquity. It is also to be remembered that before the introduction of writing, the brains of living men were the

[1] The *Polynesian Mythology* of Sir George Grey was published in 1855. The manner of reference would lead to the opinion that the lecture of Dr. Rae could not have been delivered very much later.

only records that nations had. There were deposited the genealogies of the chiefs, there alone were to be found the chronicles of their wars, the boundaries of their possessions, and everything which it was desirable to secure from oblivion. A diligently cultivated and retentive memory, therefore, gave a man position and abundance; the memory was diligently cultivated, and became capable of performing feats which to us who lean on writing and books seem very surprising. Maui, one of the Hawaiian islands, is about seventy miles long, and from thirty to forty wide, with some deep indentations proportionally extending its seaboard. At the beginning of this century, the whole coast, and much of the interior, was cultivated and inhabited. Then tracts were divided into lands of one hundred or several hundred acres. I have known a man who could begin at any part of the island, and go round the whole of it, naming each possession in its order and giving its boundaries. We must not, therefore, wonder at the accurate knowledge of the geography of Greece which Homer displays in his catalogue of the ships and leaders. That strength of memory was rather an attribute of his age than a merit peculiar to himself. It is more than probable that many of his contemporaries could have performed the same feat.

Furthermore, we find that when the imagination has once shaped a picture in which men delight, that picture is subsequently taken as the model from which after ages copy. Virgil is not Homer, very far was he in time, farther if possible in position, in the habitual feelings and actions of the men among whom he lived. But Virgil is so full of Homeric ideas, that had the Greek poem perished we should yet have been able to have conceived from the Aeneid how men conducted themselves in what are termed the heroic ages of Greece. Nay, such has been the mastery of the Homeric lay over the minds of men, that its form, which we term epic, and the train of ideas running through it, has been taken almost to the present day as the model for every lengthened poem. Even in Milton's "Paradise Lost" the Christian God figures as a sort of Agamemnon, great in his might and the prince of Hell is an Achilles unconquerable in his pride.

Still more pertinent, perhaps, is it to remark that in an advancing society new ideas are continually springing up from within or finding their way from without and overshadowing and obliterating the old. Men pride themselves on being superior to their fathers and consequently are inclined to look down on them and on their works. Whereas, when a people has ceased to advance and are going downhill and degenerating, they feel that all the strength that is in them has come down from the great and glorious olden time, and it is their ambition to preserve as much of its influence as they possibly can.

These considerations induce me to think that, as I have said, the old legendary tales and poems of the Hawaiians bring down to us much of a very remote antiquity. Unfortunately, in very recent years they have been somewhat vitiated and corrupted. Before the arrival of the missionaries the recital of these tales was a great source of amusement both to chiefs and people. All flocked to hear them. But as the names of the ancient gods were frequently mentioned in them their recital appeared to these reverend gentlemen an act of idolatry, a grievous sin, and was strictly prohibited. Nevertheless, there were here and there ungodly people who secretly indulged themselves in listening to them and thus, though they were banished from what might be termed polite society for more than forty years they maintained an obscure existence among these outcasts. A rational curiosity and more enlightened views have recently drawn them out from the obscure shelter they had found, and through the medium of the press have presented them to the view of all who sufficiently understand the language. As was to have been expected they have come forth from the lowly abodes in which they have lurked somewhat mutilated and defaced. For nearly two generations they have passed out of the hands of skilled reciters, receiving honor and reward for their labor, and subject to intelligent criticism, and as floating waifs have been taken hold of by men unskilled in their use and careless in their preservation. Hence the old language has been somewhat altered, as is shown in the number of English terms introduced, and hence, also, as I conceive, many episodes have been appended foreign to the main thread of the story, and often of a different character. Still, that main thread stands out, and to us foreigners the change in language in itself probably is of trifling importance.

These *kaavs* are not merely short snatches of song, they are lengthened narrations with a plot running through them, requiring prolonged attention. The race seems always to have had a great taste for these recitals. The bard, as in the days of Homer, was an attendant on the banquets of his chief, and the people, for night after night, eagerly listened to the tales he told them of the heroes and demigods of old. In the larger islands and groups of islands these audiences were very numerous, for until a comparatively recent period the population was dense. They were also critical, for the chiefs prided themselves on preserving the purity and expressiveness of their language.

The object of the bard is to give pleasure to those who listen to him. He must bestow his rewards and punishments in a measure and manner that may seem to his audience according to desert. In the tale of which I am about to make some abstracts, the actors are dealt with pretty much as they deserve.

I have one word to say before I begin. We are in the habit of speaking of the naked savages of the Pacific as if the form of their garments or want of garments of necessity placed them in the lowest ranks of humanity. This is a prejudice, and one of which I myself was only disabused shortly after arriving at the Hawaiian Islands. I will tell you how that came to pass. I had taken up my abode at a tavern in Honolulu, and dined at the public table; he who for a day or two sat next to me was one whom, from his darkish complexion, I took to be a Portuguese, of whom there are many on the islands. He was of robust proportions, dressed in black broadcloth and black hat, after the general fashion of Englishmen, and spoke English passably well, so that we had some little conversation. I had the curiosity to ask the landlord who and what he was. He told me he was a native, a man of some property in houses and land in Honolulu, and that he had been in town for a day or two, collecting rents and the like. Meantime I had formed the acquaintance of a young American, who told me he lived a couple of miles out of town, and invited me to call on him. I went accordingly, and having followed his directions, I thought I must have arrived near his residence, and was looking round for it. I felt myself overcome by the heat, the thermometer being nearly ninety degrees in the shade, and thought I would shorten my search by going to one of the clusters of native houses and seeing if I could get information. I went to the door of one, and knocked. I was answered by a voice from within, and as I was pursuing my inquiries by the aid of the few native words I had picked up, I heard a second voice apparently giving directions. Tired of standing in the sun, I thought it better to abridge ceremony, and open the door. I found myself in a tolerably large chamber; before me stood a boy of about twelve, with a feather fan in his hand. He handed me a chair, so I took a seat and began to look around. My attention was attracted by the figure of a man stretched out on a mat, with no clothing but the *maro*. I was struck by the massive and regular proportions, and fully developed muscles, and the smooth, marble-like surface of his body; he seemed a fit model for a statue of Hercules. When casting my eyes on his face, I felt certain that I had seen it before, and a smile coming over it, I recognized my friend of the tavern. "Ah," he said, "I was waiting to see if you would find me out. I cannot think how you foreigners contrive to live in the clothes you wear; they have nearly killed me by having them on only for a day or two, and I have kept the boy fanning me ever since I have come home, to see and get the heat out of me. But come, I will myself show you the house of him you are inquiring for; I know him well." So saying, he rose, and taking hold of a large oblong square of white native cloth,[2] and arranging it about

[2] The *kihei*.

his person in the form of a Roman toga, or rather perhaps of the Greek pharos, he led me out. Near the door his people were beginning to prepare a native oven. He said: "Perhaps it is worth your while to see the way in which we cook our food, so different from yours;" and accordingly showed me the preparations and explained the whole process. Then he walked on before me to show the path, which led through a grove of the pandanus tree, taking care to point out to me that its long leaves were sharply serrated, and might cut me badly if I rubbed face or hands incautiously against them. While thus employed, I could not help envying the ease and freedom with which he moved, and comparing it with my own sweltering garments confining every motion. On emerging from the pandanus grove he carefully pointed out to me the house I was in search of, and then bade me good day. When he was gone I said to myself, so this is a native savage of the Pacific islands; why, he is clad far more sensibly, and therefore better, than I am. His garments are made for ease and comfort, allowing the free play of the limbs, and are really graceful.

That you may have a complete idea of what these are, I must describe the *maro*. It is a strip of cloth some yards long, and six or eight inches wide, passed several times between the thighs, and round the hips and waist with one end hanging down in front for eight or ten inches. It was *de rigueur* that in the male sex all this should be covered; there was no conception of impropriety in the exposure of other parts. Women, besides this, had the *pau*, formed by one or more pieces of cloth,[3] so arranged as to jut out all around the waist, and cover about a fourth of the person.

It is evident that this fashion of dress was suited to a tropical climate, and is there convenient and healthful. But when men came to live nearer the poles, they required garments adequate to cover and protect the whole person. Hence there is a natural reason for the different modes of dress. That there is anything in itself indecent or indelicate in either, I cannot see. A more liberal exposure of the person seems only a greater extension of the region we call face, and the conception of this region has been so various among different races and at different times, that it seems to be regulated by fancy rather than by reason. Among the Turks and other Oriental nations it was confined to one eye; with us it comprehends that part of the head not covered by hair, but in full dress of women in capital cities apparently extends to about a fourth of the person; at the same time, a man appearing in a similar state would be considered to offend against decency; yet the Scotch kilt is admitted to such assemblies, and, as far as my observation goes, the "philabeg aboon the knee" seems rather to attract

---

[3] Invariably five thicknesses, according to King Kalakaua.

rather than repel the fair sex. In the beginning of the last century, a man showing himself in such attire would have been considered odious and speedily expelled.

I conceive, therefore, that the matter of dress is an affair of climate and fashion, and consequently constitutes no legitimate criterion of the character of any people. It seems, therefore, unjust by calling the people inhabiting the Pacific islands naked, to assume that they were of necessity savage.

In illustration of what I have said, I am tempted to give you a specimen of what is to be found in the tales, by sketching the merest outline of a story and citing more at length the parts of the legend having some relation to ancient beliefs known to us through Greek and Hebrew narrative. It is entitled, from the name of the heroine, *Lai-e-i-kawai*. It must have been composed at least three hundred years ago, taking as the element for this computation the time necessary for the sea to effect the changes of the coast line which have occurred since it was framed. It cannot have a very remote antiquity, for Tahiti, which was once frequently visited by Hawaiians, had then receded into the region of the supernatural and of fable.

LAIEIKAWAI.

Once on a time, there was a chief living in Oahu, who held the low lands on the north of that island, named Koolauloa and Kaulanpoko. This chief took to himself a wife, and soon after their union, at a favourable moment when they were quite alone, said to her: "Listen, my wife; as yet we have been living happily together, but there is something more which I have to tell you. Should you have a child, and should that child be a boy, it would be a happy thing; he would aid us when we are old, cover our bones when we are dead, and portion out our boundaries, and if you had daughters he might protect them.[4] But if a daughter is your first-born she must die, or if you have two or more, they also must die; only when you have borne a son, shall the daughters who may afterwards be born be allowed to live." Some time afterwards, the woman became with child. It was born when the chief was absent fishing, and was a girl. From her surpassing beauty, the mother thought that the chief might change his mind and allow it to live; so she had it wrapped in the clothes usual for

---

[4] We see here the reason for the decision of the chief. An unprotected maiden would be dispossessed. In the Middle Age, the protection of damsels who might chance to be "uncounselled" (whence by misconception our modern epithet "disconsolate") was a duty of the true knight, a duty which implies the existence of the same state of things. The situation may probably imply a primitive custom of exposing the daughters.

infants and waited his return. But when he came, he gave it into the hands of the executioner to dispose of. Afterwards, she bore several children, all girls, and beautiful; but they, according to the relentless will of the chief, were all put to death. When she found herself with child for the fifth time, she went to the priest, and said to him: "Look at this body of mine, for exhausted am I from bearing children only for death from the exceeding sternness of my husband; four children have we had, four children only for death. Look, then on me, and tell me how it is, for if I am to bring forth a female, it is better for me to destroy it while yet in embryo than to allow it to come to the full time. But if I am to have a male child, its fate will be different."

The priest replied: "Return, and when you are near your time, come back to me, and I will then see about this birth of yours." Accordingly, when she was near her time, once more she came to the priest and said: "I have come as you commanded. I am near the birth; tell me now about the child I am to have." The priest said: "I must have a sign from you; give me what I ask, give me your hand." In reply, she stretched out her left hand, and as it happened, with the palm upward. Then he said: "You have given me your left hand with the palm turned up; you are to have a female child."

Hearing this speech, she was exceedingly grieved, for she lamented the former children whom her husband had caused to be put to death. Therefore she begged of the priest to reflect, and devise some plan by which this fresh misfortune might be averted, and the child might live. He replied: "Attend to what I tell you: return to the house, and when your pains come on say to the chief that you have a great desire for the fish called *ohua*, and further tell him that it is only caught by himself that will satisfy your longing; for your husband is skilled in the taking of that fish, so he will go fishing, and will not know when the birth is; and when the child is born, it shall be mine to take charge of it, so that when he returns it will be under my care, and when he make inquiry you must tell him that the birth was deformed, and that you had it put away."

This communication over, she returned to her home, and shortly afterwards the first pains of childbirth came upon her. So soon as she felt them increasing, she called for the chief, and said to him: "Oh, my husband! I see before my eyes the fish called ohua, therefore go you with all speed to fish, for it seems to me if I had one, the child desired would soon be born. Never before have I had a difficult delivery, never before have I so longed for an ohua. Therefore go you the fishing with all speed along with your men." This fish the chief was skilled in catching; it is taken in numbers, and requires the combined efforts of many hands to make sure of it.

On the instant the chief left the house, and set out with his men. While they were absent a child was born; it was a girl and was given in charge to Waka, the grandmother, who gave to her the name of Laieikawai; but while they were attending to her another child was born, also a girl, and the latter passed to the priest, who named her Laielohelohe. When these two had departed with the infants the chief returned, and asked his wife how she now felt. She answered: "I have been delivered of a helpless, deformed thing which they have put away." But the chief already knew that this had happened, for while he was at sea it had twice thundered.

Waka and the priest had now proceeded some distance from the house, when she said to him: "What shall we do with the infants that have fallen to us, in order to conceal them from the chief?"

By the advice of the priest, Waka, who has supernatural power, makes choice of a place of concealment for her charge. This hiding-place belonged to a class of which there are many instances in the Hawaiian islands, which have arisen from the peculiar structure of the volcanic rocks of which these are composed. The ancient flows of lava, piled one on another to a height of many thousand feet, which make the mass, have been very extensive and regular, stretching out in smooth sheets for miles, and sloping very gradually and usually seaward at an angle of about seven degrees. These strata differ greatly in composition; for example, the uppermost may be of a firm basaltic rock having a thickness of but a few feet; the one next below may be composed of partially rounded stones, held together by a claylike mass, and much thicker than that above it. The frequent rains of the upper regions form themselves into a stream, which gradually works out a channel in the upper rock, however firm. Still excavating downward, it penetrates to some chink, down which a portion of its waters sinks, and aided by the great pressure slowly forces an underground way to the sea in the form of a tiny rill. Time, the great agent in all such changes, enlarges its volume, so that a large, perhaps the larger portion of the stream, passes that way. The original chink becomes enlarged to a great hole and then to a wider chasm, the solid rock operated on below by the failure of the foundation on which it rests, and above by occasional floods rolling along its surface, is shaken, breaks up, and gives way. The stream, which originally flowed smoothly, is transformed into a mass of troubled waters rushing through a deep, wild, and broken channel. Meantime, all above the original orifice may remain as before, and then the waters run evenly until they reach the great chasm, over the upper lip or brim of which they glide in a thin sheet, and fall like a curtain into the large and deep pool which they have been hollowing out for themselves. No one who passed, unless on attentive examination, would suppose there was anything more than the large deep pool bounded by steep, rocky banks and the curtain-like waterfall, but in reality there is something hidden from his view, for in their process of excavation the rushing, whirling waters have dug not only downward and sideways, but also upward, and formed a large cave beneath the smooth basaltic sheet which now roofs it in. This the screening waterfall quite hides from view. I myself was for years in the habit of passing a small cavern of this sort almost daily, and never suspected its existence, until informed by a native. We entered it together when he said: "I once lived here for a long time, with some others; it was perfectly dry; we could spread our mats and live comfortably,—stay, I put by a stone pestle, and did not take it away; I may as well have it," and stretching his hand over a ledge of rock he took it up.[5]

Such was the place of concealment in which Laieikawai was nurtured by her grandmother, Waka, until she was approaching womanhood. About that period, the great seer of the island of Kauai, in making a circuit of the island, ascended a high mountain, and observed a rainbow hanging from a particular spot of the island of Oahu. He watched it for a day or two, and saw that it did not depend on the weather, for it was there whether the day was misty or in clear sunshine. To fully satisfy himself, he made another tour of the island, and on returning and again ascending the mountain, saw that the rainbow retained its place. He became convinced by his art that the rainbow marked the abode of some one who was or would become a great *alii* (king or chief, queen or chieftainess), and on whom his own fortunes would in a great measure depend. He therefore resolved to visit Oahu, and discover who this *alii* might be. He does so, and, guided by the rainbow, comes to the deep pond and waterfall. "This," he exclaims, "is no place for an *alii* to inhabit; what can be the meaning of what I beheld?" At this moment he observes in the smooth waters of the pond a swirl like that left by a swimmer or diver, and con-

[5] Early in the spring of 1885 the pool of Waiapuka, said to be connected with other legends beside that of Laieikawai, was visited by Mr. Daggett, editor of the *Legends and Myths of Hawaii*, with a party of ladies and gentlemen, accompanied by a number of natives. One of these plunged into the pool and disappeared in the cavern, after which his eyes were visible through an orifice. It is said that none of the party had ever before seen the passage attempted, and that the natives were overjoyed at the discovery. The visitor cast mystery about the method of his entrance. The pool is described as follows: "Entering the district of Koolauloa the next day, and approaching the coast over a broad stretch of grassy meadow but slightly above the level of the ocean, our party was suddenly brought to a halt beside a pool of clear water, nearly round, and perhaps a hundred feet in diameter. The surface of the pool was ten or twelve feet below the level of the surrounding plain, and its even banks of solid rock dropped almost perpendicularly into water of unknown depth. The volcano of the pool is affected neither by rain nor drought, and the native belief is that it is fed by springs at the bottom, and has a subterranean drainage to the ocean, some two or three miles distant."

cludes that such a one had been present, and fled at his approach. He therefore resolves to wait and watch. In reality, Waka had just visited her grandchild, and had reached her by diving under the waterfall, the only passage to her habitation.

I may observe, that according to the ancient belief of the Hawaiians, a rainbow was an attendant on great chiefs, especially such as were descended from the gods, and that to my mind it seems a probable supposition that the halo with which painters encircle holy persons had its rise from this superstition.

After a while Waka set out on her return; but while still under the surface of the water, she sees a man on the top of the precipice bordering the pond, and fearing that it was the father of Laieikawai, who had obtained some inkling of the deceit practised on him, she retreats. Toward evening she makes a second essay, but finds that the stranger retains his place, and defers any further attempt until night, when she manages to escape together with her grandchild, and begins a search for a more secure abode. She has a great charge, but by this time Laieikawai has grown to be a young girl of surpassing beauty, and with the Polynesians of that period beauty was all powerful. With them Mr. Darwin's principle of natural selection seems to have reigned supreme. Waka is therefore conscious that in her grandchild a great treasure has come to her, and when she shall have come to riper years is ambitious to wed her to the head chief of Kauai. In this scheme she is aided by the priest who has undertaken to care for the twin sister. Her first object, therefore, is to find a safe retreat, her second to conceal Laieikawai from all eyes. The seer of Kauai again determines to follow the great alii, *in esse* or *in posse*, whom the rainbow has discovered to him. This pursuit Waka dreads, and aided by the priest of Koolau, who appears to her in dreams, manages to throw him out and to establish herself on the southeast of the island of Hawaii, the largest of the group, at Paliuli, the dark precipice.[6] The seer does not abandon the pursuit, but continues to move from place to place, continually offering sacrifice and

[6] Hulumaniani, the prophet of Kauai, after having observed the rainbow for twenty days, has obtained a canoe and fifteen men from the chief of Wailua, provides himself with a black pig, white fowl, and red fish for sacrifice, and sets sail at the rising of the star Sirius. After the departure of Waka, he ascends Mount Kaala, and sees the rainbow over the island of Molokai; Waka is finally advised in a dream to remove to Hawaii, and dwell at Paliuli. The seer arrives at Hana, and there erects a shrine for the worship of his patron deity; in the seventh month of the year he sees the rainbow on the windward side of Hawaii. On the third day of the next month he offers fervent prayers in his oratory, and sees the shadows of Waka and her charge, whom he is informed by his god are living in Paliuli, in the forest of Puna, in a house thatched with the yellow feathers of the *oo*; he reaches Kaiwilahilahi, where he remains some years without being able to obtain further information. It is during this sojourn that takes place the episode of the wooing of Aiwohikupua. Such is the course of the story as related in *Legends and Myths*.

praying to his god. Waka, however, had not effected her retreat without misadventure, for in passing from one island to another, the man paddling the canoe had caught a glimpse of the face of Laʻeikawai, and admiring her extreme beauty, had besought Waka to bid her lower a little the mantle in which she was muffled, in order that he might see something of her person. Waka replies that it is the girl's own desire to be hid from the sight of men, and that she cannot interfere. This being not at all in accordance with her real inclination, Laieikawai contrives to unveil so much of her charms as to dazzle and astonish the man, who sets out to proclaim everywhere her surpassing charms. The fame of her beauty goes abroad, and suitors go in quest of her from various parts. The legend is chiefly occupied with the account of the pursuit, and the adventures thence arising.[7] I give you such fragmentary portions as seem more particularly illustrative of the beliefs and manners of the time.

Aiwohikupua, a chief of the island of Kauai, had vowed never to form any intimate connection with a woman of the islands, inasmuch as he had been deceived in those on which he had already entered, and concluding from information which he had received about her, that Laieikawai must be from Tahiti, this was one great motive for his desire to form a union with her. Her reported beauty was the other. He therefore selects one of his followers as counsellor and companion, and embarks in a double canoe with a crew of twenty to make the voyage. They arrive at Kipahulu on the island of Maui, where he lands, and determines to proceed by land to Hana, a distance of about twelve miles.

His counsellor accompanies him, while the canoe goes on by sea. As he walks along, his great personal beauty attracts all eyes, and gathers round him a throng of followers. Arrived at Haneoo, at that time the harbor of Hana, which has since been laid open by the encroachments of the sea,

---

[7] While the seer is at Kaiwilahilahi, the king of Kauai returns from his wedding journey and holds a great feast. At this festival he describes his meeting with the princess of Paliuli, and extols her supernatural beauty. The extraordinary circumstances of the visit are related. The kings sends his *kahu* or counsellor with a request for a meeting. The approach of the princess is announced by the singing of the bird *iiwipolena*. Here the account becomes literal: "Then a shadow fell on the door, and we were enveloped," said the king, "in a thick fog, and when it cleared away, the princess was seen in her glorious beauty, borne on the winds of birds." It is by listening to this story that the interest of Aiwohikupua is awakened. Again, when the sisters of the latter have finally reached the bower of Laieikawai, they find her resting on the wings of birds, with two *iiwipolenas* perched on her shoulders. The sisters are received as her companions, and fed by birds. In the case of the seer, a bird also appears to take the place of a chariot.

According to the glossary of *Legends and Myths*, *kahu* signifies "a nurse or guardian of a child." It would seem, therefore, that, as in mediaeval romances, the "governor" (we still say governess) remains with the full-grown lord or lady as servant, advisor, and friend.

they find all the people engaged in the sport of *hunalu*, "gliding on the waves," which they generally do on surf-boards. Among the players is a lovely girl, the daughter of a chief, Hinaikamalama by name. While they are admiring her, the counsellor whispers to his chief that it would be better to withdraw a little, lest they be entangled by her charms into some adventure prejudicial to their main enterprise, but when they are about to do so, Hinaikamalama, who seems to have been fascinated by the manly beauty of Aiwohikupua, calls the two distinguished strangers to join in the sport, and afterwards partake the hospitality of her father's house. This they consent to do, and when the hunalu is over, Hinaikamalama invites the chief to play with her a game of chance called *Kanane*. Before beginning, she asks him what the stakes shall be. He proposes to venture his double canoe; she objects and says: "Here is an easily managed stake, our persons. If I gain them, you must do whatever I command, that is not inconsistent with propriety. If I lose, then I shall be in like manner under your command. He agrees. They play, and he loses. Finding himself in difficulty, he endeavours to escape by speaking as follows (but I abridge his words): "I am well pleased with the issue of our wager, but I cannot now remain and be your servant, for I am under oath to make the circuit of the island of Hawaii before entering into any engagement with any woman. When I return, I will be your servant. Until then, I require of you to keep yourself secluded from all intercourse with men, else I shall hold that you have forfeited your claim on me." He then takes his leave, and on the day after arriving at Kauhola on Hawaii, he sees a great concourse of people gathered together at a place far upland. On inquiring the cause, he is told that they have assembled to hold a boxing-match. He desires to look on, and, having had the double canoe made secure, ascends to the spot, together with his counsellor and attendants. On his approach the assembly breaks up, inasmuch as all present are anxious to obtain a view of his handsome person. Presently they assemble, and in an orderly manner, take their places in a circle, while Aiwohikupua remains standing under the shade of a near and widely branching tree. Presently a chief named Ihuanu steps into the ring, and boastfully challenges any one present to the combat. None dares accept. While moving about inside the ring, he sees Aiwohikupua standing under the tree, and calls out to him: "Oh, stranger, shall you and I have some sport?" "Yes," replies Aiwohikupua, "if you take two others with you, then I shall think it worth while to engage you." Hearing this, a man approaches him from behind, and says: "Speak not thus to Ihuanu; no one has ever contended with him without serious injury." Aiwohikupua turns round on his interlocutor, and gives him a slap with the open hand, which, however, lays him dead on the earth. On seeing this, the friends of Ihuanu crowd round him, begging him not to engage an opponent of such force. Their prayers only further excite the boastful humor of Ihuanu, who answers angrily, and on looking round, sees Aiwohikupua approaching, and also observes a boy on the outskirts of the assembly who has taken an indecent attitude. Him he points out to Aiwohikupua, saying: "Here is your fit opponent." So enraged is Aiwohikupua at the grossness of the affront, that his blood rushes to the surface of his body, and reddens the skin all over. He steps aside, kneels down, and naming his gods, offers prayer to them. "Oh ye heavenly ones, this day look down on me your child, the flower that remains to you on earth, shed down strength upon me! Cause Ihuanu's sport to pass harmless by, and I pray you give me his head for my men to sport with, that all this assembly may see that I am the conqueror (*amama*)! May it be accomplished quickly and with power!" He then stands up, and facing Ihuanu, tells him to strike first. This Ihuanu does, aiming at the face, but Aiwohikipua, by a swift movement, eludes the blow, feeling only its wind on his cheek. Instantly follows the return blow of Aiwohikupua, which falls of the chest of his opponent with such force as to break through it, and fell him dead on the spot. Then ensues a great crowding and lamentation for his death, in the midst of which Aiwohikupua cuts off the head and gives it to his attendants, as he had prayed he might be able to do.[8]

This, you will say, is exceedingly savage; but the Greeks scarcely fall behind in that respect, as you may see in all the battles of the Iliad. It appears to me that the prayer has a certain likeness to the straightforward petitions which are found in Homer, nor is it undeserving of notice that the whole crowd of spectators, though bitterly lamenting the fate of one who had become their hero, make no attempt to prevent the mutilation of his body, apparently from a chivalric principle which holds it dishonorable to come between the victor and his rights.

Aiwohikupua reembarks, and coasting along, sees another numerous assembly, which also turns out to be a boxing-match. The fame of his mastery, however, has preceded him, and the chiefs, instead of combat, propose intimate friendship, an offer which he accepts. Still proceeding, he unexpectedly meets the seer of Kauai, who, in the course of his wanderings, was at that time resident on the coast of Hawaii. Unexpectedly he finds all things prepared for his reception; in fact, the seer was endowed with second sight. I now translate *verbatim*. On that evening, before the setting of the sun, the seer was sitting at the door of the house looking at the vapor resting on the clouds which were arising out of the sea, as is the custom of seers, and has been so from old times downward. He suddenly

---

[8] This interesting episode is barely noted in *Myths and Legends*, p. 461.

spake aloud: "The canoe of a chief this, nineteen men and a great chief; it is also a double canoe." On hearing him those around him were startled, as they could see no canoe, and asked him: "Where is that canoe of yours?" "It is not a real double canoe," he replied; "I only saw in the cloudy vapor; to-morrow we shall see a chief's canoe." During the night he had another and more distinct vision, and knew that it was the chief of Kauai who was approaching. He therefore made a sacrifice for his god. Being questioned as to these preparations he said: "I am making ready for my chief, him of whom I told you last night, and there is his double canoe on the sea, enveloped in the mist you behold." As Aiwohikupua approached the harbor, it thundered twenty times.[9] This brought the people together, and they saw the double canoe, the awning overhead, and the chief as the seer had foretold. As the canoe touched the shore the seer stood up, and offered prayer and sacrifice to the god of Aiwohikupua. As he was thus employed, his chief recognized him, and was moved with strong affection toward him, and so soon as the prayer was over, told his counsellor to present the gifts to the gods. The seer ran, embracing the limbs of the chief, and leaning his head on the neck of the latter, begins to wail. In like manner, the chief embraces the shoulders of the seer, and wailing recounts his many virtues. When this ceremony was over, which is customary with Polynesian friends who have long been separated, and who pour forth the *aloka* which had filled their hearts during the period of separation, the two turned to converse with each other and to enjoy themselves.

Aiwohikupua did not tell the seer what was the real object of his voyage, but pretended that he was merely making the circuit of Hawaii. After a stay of a few hours he resumes his route, and in no long time, directed by the rainbow, reaches the dwelling of Laieikawai, which he finds far upland, and only to be approached by a long and difficult path. He is struck with astonishment to see that the house is covered with thatch, as were all houses of those days, but instead of the grass called *piti*, or the long and broad leaves of the pandanus, it is formed of the feathers of the bird named *oo*. Now these feathers were the riches of the land. Only chiefs of consequence could afford to have cloaks made of them. Such a cloak he had brought with him as a magnificent present that would serve to propitiate his lady love, and behold! it must appear contemptible in her eyes, since the walls of her house were formed of the same material. It was as if a lover of our own days had provided himself with a bracelet of gold to present to his mistress, and had found that all the furniture of her house

[9] According to *Myths and Legends*, here much less definite, he sacrifices with black pig, white fowl, and bunch of *awa*, after which follows the thunder.

was of gold. He cannot think of offering a thing that must in her eyes seem too paltry to produce a favorable impression, and notwithstanding the remonstrances of his counsellor, determines to return to Kauai without attempting to obtain an interview. As they are coasting along Hawaii and near its north shore, he falls asleep, and is startled from his slumber by the loud outcries of his people; when he wakens and demands the cause of the uproar, they point to a woman of exceeding beauty seated on a cliff overhanging the sea, and robed in a white cloak. He orders them to advance toward her. As they approached the shore, he learns from some fishermen that it is Poliahu, who has come down from the mountains. As he approaches, he beckons, inviting her to descend. She does so and steps on board his canoe. He then addresses her: "Oh, beautiful woman of the precipice, most fortunate am I in having met with you. Thus have I the happy chance of praying you to accept me as your spouse, and your servant, who executes all the commands you give him. I entreat you to come with me to Kauai." She replies: "I am not from the precipice; I am from the peak of the far-off mountain, which is always clad in white, as myself am. As for your desire that I should take you for my spouse, tell me, are not you the chief who stood up and swore by his god that you would never unite yourself with any woman of the islands from Hawaii to Kauai, but would seek a wife in foreign lands? Are not you he who has entered into engagements with Hinaikamalama, the beauty of Hana? As for your desire to form a union with me I will say this, if you free yourself from all the entanglements in which you are involved, and then come for me, I will consent." Aiwohikupua is overwhelmed with wonder and confusion. At length he replies: "What you say is true, I cannot deny it; but tell me, whence have you all this knowledge, and who has informed you?" "I am descended," she answers, "as you are, from the gods, and they have given me power to see things afar off, as if they were close by. I consent to accompany you in your voyage along the coast, provided you give me a seat apart, and do not approach or touch me. I also will keep separate from you." He willingly agrees; she sails with him for about twenty miles, and then returns to her mountain, leaving him to strike off, and pursue his way to Kauai.[10] But he seems born to exemplify the maxim, "Men are deceivers ever," inasmuch as he makes for Hana, but does not land, keeping his canoe afloat in the harbor of Haneoo. Hinaikamalama perceives him approach, and is rejoiced at the thought of meeting him, but seeing him remain on the canoe, she goes to the shore, and asks him why he does not land. He replies that he cannot do so. She tells him he must, for

[10] She changes mantles with him, as sign of betrothal. Her own mantle is snow-white. She evidently impersonates the snowy mountain.

he has become hers by the issue of the game at Konani, and that if he does not come ashore, she will send a party to capture him. He replies: "Not so, O lady; I have no intention of breaking the contract I have formed with you, but the time is not yet come for fulfilling it. I have not yet been able to make the island of Hawaii, for a messenger was sent after me, to inform me that a disturbance has broken out at Kauai which requires my immediate presence. I have turned out of my way to inform you of this, that you may remain as we agreed, in expectation of my arrival." Hearing this Hinaikamalama is pacified and he departs. Before he arrives at Kauai, feeling that he would be put to shame if the ill success of his voyage became known, he warns his followers, on pain of death, to keep silence concerning their journey. Toward evening he arrives at Kauai, calls together his five sisters, informs them that he has been at Hawaii, and what was his object in going there, and tells them that he has returned in order to request their assistance in gaining the object of his desire, and to return with him to Hawaii, to employ whatever influence they may acquire over Laieikawai in furtherance of his suit. They consent, and returning to that island, ascend with him the stark precipice of Paliuli to the abode of Laieikawai. The four sisters derive their names from different modifications of a sweet-smelling shrub called *maile*, the youngest and wisest is known as the Breath of Many Flowers. The four first, one after the other, make the attempt to gain admittance to the abode of Laieikawai,[11] but are repulsed, the latter loudly declaring that she will never wed Aiwohikupua. Hearing this, he is irritated at the repulse, resolves immediately to return to Kauai, and vents his vexation on his sisters by declaring that he will leave them behind until they can move Laieikawai to accept his suit. Breath of Many Flowers protests against the wrong, more especially in her own case, as she has had no opportunity of using her influence over Laieikawai. Aiwohikupua tells her that she may come with him if she likes, but that her sisters must remain. She refuses to leave them. On this he and his counsellor depart. The sisters follow in hope that their brother will relent and take them on board the canoe when they reach the seashore, but he leaves them behind. They follow him along the shore, each in turn composing and chanting such an appeal as she thinks may best move him. They are much alike. I give the greater part of that sung by Breath of Many Flowers:—

> Brother ours, and chief all-hallowed,
> Are we thus to part for aye?
> Leave you us to wander wildly
> On this strange and distant shore?

[11] They send forth at night the fragrance of the flowers whose names they bear.

Has then love your breast foresaken
That you know not you are followed,
Followed over all the seven seas,
Over small seas, over great seas,
Over short waves, over long waves,
Over long-backed waves of ocean?
Turn you then with gentle visage,
Hear my outcries, hear my wailing,
Look upon your sisters mourning,
Far away fly rage and passion,
Far away each angry thought,
Once again embrace your darlings,
And with circling love enfold us,
You would we return to look on,
Look upon our parents' faces,
See them seated close beside you,
Bear my deep love to my island,
And to small and great upon it,
There return to those I love best,
To my darling sisters four.[12]

John Rae.

At this point the manuscript of Dr. Rae comes to a conclusion. The sequel of the history may be indicated after the abstract given in the work of King Kalakaua. After the conclusion of his second voyage, Aiwohikupua returns to Kauai, and at a feast, under the intoxicating influence of *awa*, is so imprudent as to reveal his suit to the princess of Paliuli. A young chief of Mana wagers that he will succeed where the other has failed; but in the end he loses his land, which is restored by Aiwohikupua. The latter now undertakes a third expedition, with the resolution to obtain Laieikawai by force. He is repulsed, however, through the efforts of his own sisters, who are supported by their patron god (familiar demon, as would have been said in the Middle Age), a huge lizard. The frustrated wooer prepares to console himself with Poliahu, and performs expiatory ceremonies in order to release himself from his vow never to wed a lady of the islands. He meets Poliahu, accompanied by mountain goddesses, and as the company of Aiwohikupua suffers from the cold of the upper regions, the bride and her friends remove their white mantles, which has the effect of lowering the snow on the summits.

It has so happened that the birds whom Aiwohikupua had sent as messengers to his inamorata had mistaken their road, and arrived at the house of Hinaikamalama, to whom, as already related, Aiwohikupua had

---

[12] This is the *mele* of the sisters only alluded to in *Legends and Myths*. The chief is willing to take with him the youngest sister, but she refuses to desert the others.

lost in the game, and who possessed the right over his person. Enraged at the unfaithfulness of her debtor, this lady makes a visit to Kauai, and at the wedding feast, in a game, becomes the prize of the bridegroom. She then openly declares his perfidy; Aiwohikupua is discredited, and the angry Poliahu returns to her mountain.

Waka now conceives a plan for uniting her granddaughter to the newly made king of Kauai; it is arranged that the couple shall meet in the surf, use one surfboard, float on one roller, and touch noses (such contact being symbolic of continued union), after which the great birds of the heroine are to carry the pair to the feather-house in Paliuli. A young libertine, Halaaniani, who has a sister gifted with magic powers, desires the beauty, by the help of the sorceress is able to take the place of the king, and is taken up to the feather-house. The enraged Waka casts off her granddaughter, and turns her attention to the sister who has been left with the priest, Laielohelohe, on whose behalf she makes a similar contract with the king of Kauai. The new lover of Laieikawai, not satisfied with one success, endeavors to obtain also this lady but is finally foiled. Laieikawai retires into obscurity, while the dissolute youth is left to general contempt.

The sisters of Aiwohikupua, who are now devoted to Laieikawai, consider in what manner they can restore their mistress to honor, and determine to wed her to another brother, Kaonohiokala. Now this family is divine, the father living in the moon, while the brother last mentioned has his residence in the sun, his name signifying Sun-Eyeball. The youngest sister, Kahalaomapuana by name, but who may here be called by the translated title given by Dr. Rae, Breath of Many Flowers, undertakes a pilgrimage to heaven. She is carried on her lizard, who swims with her for four months, until at the ends of the sea she finds her uncle, who takes her to the place of ascent. He utters a call, and a ladder composed of spider's web is let down on which the lady mounts to the moon. Here dwells the aged man who is her father; she follows directions, finds him asleep, leaps on his back and grasps his beard, then chants the *mele* of supplication in which she is instructed. She and her mother mount on a great bird, by whom they are carried up to the sun, where they find Noon acting as porter, Noon admits her, disperses the clouds, and she sees her brother, whose brilliant body gleams like flowing lava, asleep in the centre of the orb. He is awakened, accepts the proposal of Breath of Many Flowers, and his descent to earth is heralded by various signs. To Laieikawai, as betrothal present, he sends a rainbow robe. At rising of the full moon he descends, and the couple mount to heaven on a rainbow. Waka is killed by a thunderbolt, and Aiwohikupua reduced to merited poverty and scorn, being now placed in the tutelage of Breath of Many Flowers; the sisters are made regents of the other islands, the king of Kauai and his wife being left undisturbed in their possessions.

One would think that the story might end here, with the heroine exalted, not merely to a throne, but to the central glory of the celestials. But apparently Hawaiian thought, like Hellenic, had little confidence in the permanence of sexual attachment. The Eye of the Sun, in the course of a tour of his earthly domain, casts eyes of desire at the fair sister of his wife, while the king of Kauai, on his part, roves after the beauty of Hana, who of the three rival ladies alone has not yet been mated. On this intrigue he descends to earth, and consoles the foresaken spouse. The jealous Laieikawai, by gazing in the bowl of knowledge, is able to observe the conduct of her husband, and reports his offences to the father and mother! These descend on a rainbow, and pronounce sentence on Eye of the Sun, who is banished from heaven, and condemned to live on butterflies as a wandering ghost. Breath of Many Flowers is exalted to his place, as heir apparent of the solar realm. Laieikawai, at her own petition, rejoins her sister on earth; but the government of the group of islands is intrusted to the faithful prophet of Kauai. Laieikawai, it is to be presumed, gave birth to a child, for she continued to be adored by certain gentes under the title of The Lady of the Twilight.

B. MISCELLANEOUS LETTERS

14

John Rae to Dr. Archibald Hall*

APRIL 15, 1852

April 15th
Maui, Wailuku
Sandwich Islands

DEAR SIR

I have been on these islands more than twelve months. I have often thought
of writing you a general sketch of such things as I have seen in them or met
with in my previous wanderings as might possibly be of interest to you
as a medical man and a giver of information on scientific subjects in general
but have doubted whether any thing I might communicate would be new
to you. On this account I stopped short in penning a letter I had designed
for you a sort of jotting down of experiences & it has been lying by me for
many months. A speculation however has occurred to me which I am
really desirous of having inserted in some scientific periodical. My reasons
are that more than once I have entertained views which I was well satisfied
were substantially correct and which were important enough to have
revolutionised some of the sciences but which for want of time or means I
was not able [to] follow out with the persistence I desired . . . I waited so
long that others more favourably situated forestalled me and had deservedly all the credit of the discovery. I have at this moment more particularly in eye the advance that has been made in the conjunct sciences of
physiology and medicine. This has I take it been twofold more philosophical reasoning and experimenting having led to great and positive
results & these results having in turn given fresh impetus to a spirit of

* Rae mss.

sober rational & persevering inquiry. Thus the old senseless and irrational mode of speaking about things under the names of irritability debility &c. &c. &c. thus raising up phantasms which, under the name of vital powers all the old plastic nature of the ancients were supposed to move and mould all things, has been done away or is in process of being so. This was a task which at one time, more than thirty years ago, I had proposed to myself & it is surprising to myself how moved by a better and juster spirit of inquiry I had anticipated so much of what has been done. The progress of chemistry & optics has unquestionably however had much to do with the advances made. To return to what I have on hand. It is a geological and geographical problem which my residence on these islands has brought before me and of which I think I can give at least a probable solution. I will put it down on a separate sheet & request you will publish it with whatever imperfections it may have in its head in your journal which I hope & expect is flourishing or should any accident have befallen it in any of the scientific periodicals of the States. I shall then extract from my notes and gather from my recollections what has occurred to me as possibly of interest in the medical way. Should you think any of my experiences worth extracting you may use your discretion in the matter . . .

15

John Rae to John Stuart Mill*

DECEMBER 5, 1853 and JANUARY 9, 1854

Koali, Hana, Maui, Hawaiian
or Sandwich Islands, Dec. 5, 1853.

SIR,

I am induced to write you from having some months since perused an extract from your work on Political Economy, in which you notice a previous work of mine on the same subject. A friend in Canada sent me the extract, and you will believe it afforded me considerable gratification. Indeed, I may say, it is the only thing connected with that publication, which has afforded me any gratification. I had in truth given up the hopes of my work making any impression whatever, unless I should happen to attract public attention by other efforts, in some other sphere of literary enterprise. In that case I meditated, and still meditate, writing a treatise on Banking and Currency, the true principles regulating which I have long conceived can be clearly deduced from what I may venture to call my doctrines, and scarcely otherwise. I regret that I have had no opportunity of perusing your work, and so know not how far our ideas coincide, or diverge, on this and other matters.

I have been a wanderer in California, lost my health there, came to these islands to recruit about three years since, have been practising my profession, I am a medical man, and am now engaged in rather extensive

* This letter and Mill's draft reply were found among the papers of the "Mill–Taylor Collection" in the Library of the London School of Economics and printed with an introductory note by Professor F. A. Hayek in *Economica* (n.s.), vol. X, no. 39, Aug., 1943, 253–5.

agricultural operations, and some other material projects, which will I expect, for some years, very much occupy my time. I have, however, lately written an article, unfolding some views in Geology, which are, I believe, novel, and even to myself somewhat startling, but yet, I think, will ultimately be found true. Certain phenomena in these islands, and on this ocean, led me to them. This will probably appear in Stillman's Journal, though there may be some delay from an apprehended miscarriage of part of the manuscript. I have also written, for a medical friend in Canada, some observations on medical matters, which, it is likely, will find their way to the American press. I have, too, made some progress in a work on the condition and prospects of these islands, which I should like to publish simultaneously in England and America. I have besides an essay on hand on the Hawaiian language. It is this latter labour that is the occasion of my presently addressing you.

In my endeavours to get as nearly as possible to the root of the matter, I have found my way to, or I have stumbled on things that seem to me new and strange or, rather, which will appear such to others, for to me they only seem confirmatory of certain notions I have long entertained concerning the real history of Man, which you will probably put it down as a grave heresy in me to say, seems not to me to have been hitherto treated of, in the true and comprehensive spirit of Baconian philosophy. At all events the subject as it presents itself to me, besides being really curious, seems to open up glimpses at least, of paths stretching far away into the recesses of long antecedent time, which well deserve to be explored. I am somewhat nervous, and you will allow I have a little reason to be so, about bringing this forth. I conceive it is not likely to be well judged, or at all indeed appreciated, but by men of somewhat large and reflective minds. Fancy not that this is vanity. It is my knowledge of its probable imperfections that makes me feel the need of such judges. Were I writing in a well stored library, and with ample leisure, I should not be at all uneasy, but I do not relish that, for want of full development, or a slip here and there, views, which, though novel, have I conceive, truth and philosophy for their basis, should be thrown aside as merely fanciful or phantastical, or perhaps absurd and ridiculous. I am desirous therefore of audience fit, though few, and this has led me to take the liberty of addressing you. It is perhaps, therefore, proper, at all events it seems to me not unmeet, for me to tell you what I really have been and am about.

I have long entertained a project, partly literary and partly practical, which, as I advance, wears more and more a definite shape, to which all I have hitherto done or attempted, or that I have indicated to you, are mere toys. It must in fact either fail altogether, or must give a new impress to humanity itself. As a means to this end I desire a certain literary and philosophical reputation, and a certain amount of capital. I went to California hoping there to find the latter, and the means to the former. To gather gold and matter for a book. I imagined that a series of geological notes, a science of which I have long been a votary, and some account of the scenery and scenes the country exhibits, might make a volume which would have a certain circulation. But my health gave out, and I nearly died. On recovering, in these islands, I thought that it was but changing the scene of my operations, and that they might serve me to make money and write a book. This is what I am attempting. It was far from my wishes to go very deep into things, for that is voted heavy, I merely desired a light volume, somewhat tinged with the spirit of philosophy, that might have a certain popularity. But the bent of my mind, or some fatality has ever opened up to me large though sometimes misty views of things others have passed by, in every subject I have studied, and, against my will it has been so here. Hence my separate Geological and philosophical essays. There is this comfort, both will be short.

Koali, Jan. 9th, 1854.

I have been detained in this quarter of the island much longer than I anticipated and as I have to deliver this letter to the post office Lahaina myself the delay has given me leisure for some farther reflections on the mode of appearance in type best suited for my purpose. The result of these is embodied in the following request. Would you do me the favour of superintending, or rather get someone to superintend, the printing in London of a pamphlet or small volume of 80 to 100 pages, a sort of epistle to the eruditi, the viri graves et docti of the European republic of letters. The issue not to exceed 200 and to be considered strictly private. I would remit the funds necessary to defray the expense. In this production I could open myself more freely than in any publication, and I should hope from some quarters to receive advice and criticism that might be of much service to me in the specific philosophical problem and on others connected with it and might prepare the way for a real publication. It would be necessary that I should be edited and thus receive the approbation of some one in its own department of science for his name to secure attention. Have you any friend in the literary circles of London or of Paris or in Germany who could do this, and if so, would you be willing to ask him to do it?

I have been so long out of Britain that absence or death has taken from me all literary or other acquaintances within that Kingdom. This will, I hope, be handed you by my particular friend Hugh B. Wilson, Esq., of Canada west, whom, if you think well of it, you can inform as to the expense of paper, printing, etc. I write shortly on this subject to Sir Francis Bond Head, who may perhaps have an interest in my doings from some passages in our Canadian Rebellion. To Dr. Neil Arnott, who was once tutor to my elder brothers, but whom I fear death or indisposition may have withdrawn from the world, and to Dr. William Beattie, who is, I think, a native of the same town with myself, Aberdeen, and whom if so I knew in Edinburgh.

I shall hope to hear from you as soon as may be and you will oblige me by informing me how my work happened to fall into your hands. Very few copies went to G. Britain. Mr. W. will forward any letter from you.

With much respect

I am,

your very obedient servant

JOHN RAE.

John Stuart Mill, Esq.,
England.

16

John Stuart Mill to John Rae (draft)*
SEPTEMBER 19, 1854

SIR,

Your letter of Jan. 9th has reached me within these few days. I am glad to hear of the various literary enterprises you have in hand or in contemplation, as I feel assured from the character of your work on Pol. Ec. that your speculations in any subject to which you have applied yourself will contain (whether I agree with them or not) enough both of knowledge and of originality and ingenuity to more than justify bringing them before the world. I have made more use of your treatise than you appear to have been informed of, having quoted largely from it, especially from your discussion. of the circumstances which influence the "effective desire of accumulation", a point which you appear to me to have treated better than it had ever been treated before. I have already published my opinion that nothing was wanting to your book except favourable chances to have gained you the reputation you desire, and which I hope you may acquire by other writings.

You could not, however, have addressed yourself to any person less capable than myself of giving any useful assistance in bringing out your speculations on the Hawaiian language. My own pursuits do not lie in the direction of comparative philology nor have I any acquaintances in this class of érudits (chiefly to be found in Germany) from someone of whom you desire a recommendation and his name as editor. Nor do I think this would easily be obtained for the preliminary pamphlet which you contemplate whatever might be the case with the completed work. Even to get the pamphlet printed is more than I am able to undertake, not only from pressing occupations, but because the state of my health renders my resi-

* *Economica* (n.s.), vol. X, no. 39, Aug., 1943, 253–5.

dence in England, at the time when your MS could reach me, extremely uncertain.

Dr. Arnott, whom you mention as an old acquaintance, is alive and flourishing and may possibly have it more in his power to promote your object than myself.

You ask me how your book became known to me. I first heard of it from Mr. Senior who recommended it to me as a book of which he had a high opinion, and after I had read it through his means I picked up a copy in a stall.

I hope your health is quite re-established.

I am, Sir,

very faithfully yours,

E[ast] I[ndia] H[ouse], London, Sept. 19, 1854.

17

John Rae to John Stuart Mill (draft)*

c. 1854

You have done me the honor of adopting my views with regard to the laws regulating capital. Would you have the kindness to inform me how your exposition was received, and what is the condition of political economy in England just now, with regard especially to that part of the subject? Also in France and the Continent in general. Have the Germans entered on the theme? In my opinion they have more real mind than either France or England; and I am curious to know how they handle this matter, if they have at all entered on it.

Were I visiting in England, what chance would there be of my making an impression by publishing there a new edition of my *Principles*, or by breaking the book up, and giving it a more practical form? Suppose I were to put forth my views on capital, on money, currency and banking, on rent, on the wages of labor, and, perhaps, on population, each in short works,—stating only obvious facts, and venturing on no excursive reasoning,—what chance of success do you think I would have?

I do not know that I differ very much from Malthus on the population question; and it is a very delicate one to handle, in so much so that, were everything else favorable, I might give it the go-by. Still, I think he scarcely states it fairly . . . I do not think that Ricardo's theory of rent is sound. Things that measure each other do not, therefore, necessarily stand with relation of cause and effect; else in Kepler's theorem the equal times would be the cause of the equal spaces or conversely, whereas they are both con-

* This draft letter was found by Mixter among Rae's papers and was reprinted by him in the *Quarterly Journal of Economics*, Nov., 1901, 123–5.

comitant results of gravity and motion. In the same way, increased rent and the cultivation of inferior land are both concomitant results of certain causes. I also think that the question of the wages of labor has been dogmatized and placed on wrong grounds by a sort of jargon derived from superficial views on the nature of capital.

I was careful to say nothing on these heads in my book, because I did not wish needlessly to blazon the full extent of my heterodoxy; but I believe it was, a sense of the real social wrongs and consequently, evils that have arisen from a contracted view of this question that gave me that animus against Adam Smith which you, perhaps justly, condemn me for showing in my speculations. But in reality he is a sophist. Perhaps the greatest of them, I trust the last of them. The art with which he covers this makes his greatness. He is a sophist in the same way in his *Moral Sentiments*, which, followed out, sap the foundations of morality. And read his principles of philosophy in his minor works. They are the very opposite of the inductive philosophy of Bacon. I forget whether I brought this forward in my book. I have not looked at it for many years, and have no copy of it. However, I despair of getting the world to go with me in any such view. The British mind has, in my opinion, been contracting and narrowing itself for years, so that it cannot grasp great questions.

I ought to state that I have read very little on the subject of Political Economy since writing my book, and that little chiefly on monetary questions. I think that the whole subject of banking is capable of being treated in so demonstrative and accurate a manner that there would subsequently be no room for hasty and unsound generalizations and random schemes. I have taken measures to procure a copy of your book, which will probably reach me within the year, and give me a correct idea of the present state of the science.

18

John Rae to John Stuart Mill (draft)*
c. 1854

FIRST LETTER

I do not know that I differ very much from Malthus on the population question ... Still I think he scarcely states it fairly. The view he takes is precisely similar to that of the elder Mirabeau. He assimilates Man to the lower animals which is not correct. You will see the distinction stated in the Memorabilia where Socrates is showing the superiority of Man. There is besides this, a radical difference in that the one is guided by mere instinct, the other by reason, fancy, that changeful thing we call moral feeling. Malthus, indeed, puts down vice as one of the checks, but this scarcely covers the whole ground.

In reality the rapid diminution of population by which empires have become extinct is a very curious subject on which I suspect we are apt sometimes to take one-sided views because we only see one side, now, in the present phases of civilization. Were you where I am, you would find it more of a puzzle than it strikes you to be in Great Britain.

I suppose it will be allowed that many vicious practices have been put down among the natives here. I may give you a list of some of them. There were no permanent marriages; parties separated whenever they chose. When a woman married, she married the whole family of brothers.

* These two letters were compiled by Mixter from various versions found among Rae's papers and printed in the *Economic Journal*, vol. XII, no. 45, 1902, 111–20. Mixter suggests that they were written about 1863, but it is more likely that they were written earlier. There is no evidence that a finished copy of the draft was ever sent to Mill. In this version, Mixter's insertions in the text have been deleted.

So much was this the case, that they have yet no name for father distinct from uncle. She married, too, the friend of her husband: I mean his particular friend, as among the Greeks Aristogiton and Harmodious— a relation once in high honour here. Then child murder was very frequent. There are many women still alive who have killed six or eight of their off-spring. All this has been put down. Then there were constant and murder-ous wars. These have ceased. Epidemic diseases sweeping off multitudes are also among the traditions. Notwithstanding all this, in the joyous existence of those days vitality had a spring that brought up in exuberance a youthful population to fill up every gap. Now the race are dying away in a peaceful and fertile land, which everywhere for two hours daily labour gives a man abundance for himself and a large family.

Ask a native why this is, and he will tell you that if in old times a woman wishes for a family and had not one by her then partner, brothers of course included, she changed till she had her desire fulfilled. The same way with the man. Now single pairs are tied together for life, whether they suit or do not suit each other. There was another thing, also, which they are not so ready to tell of, but which doubtless had its effect. When a chief, or man raised any way above the common level, saw a child whom he thought might grow up to be a desirable woman, he signified his wishes to the parents and she was uniformly preserved intact for him. When she became of sufficient age, he cohabited with her for a day or two and *perhaps* she became one of his wives. There is no such thing as an intact girl now.

Admitting for argument's sake that these things cover the whole ground (which they do not, but leave a considerable vacancy), and we have a positive diminution of what we call vice, followed by an equal diminution of population. Capt. Cook reckoned the population of these Islands 800,000. It is now not more than 70,000; mainly because there are so many barren marriages. It requires, I think, some straining of terms to bring this state of things to be comprehended within Malthusian principles. The difficulty may, in my opinion, be said to arise from man's being the child of art, of phantasy, and of reason full of freaks,—the inferior animals of nature. Though this also, like all attempts to solve intricate problems by curt sayings, is also false; for, as "all nature is but art unknown to thee," so all art is but nature.

However, as I have said, I have little thought of writing on this question, because the English mind is not given to what would be termed abstract or curious speculation; and the Essay on Population does somehow or other embrace the whole question,—though viewing it, as I think, some-what on one side. Should a day arrive, which I think not impossible, when population is actually diminishing, then the nonperfection of the actual state of things will be an astounding question, and a cry will arise like that which the disasters of Sevastopol have made to be uttered and men will see that they have been blind. Then, also, they will exclaim against blind guides, though these guides have not been so very blind. The nation where men do not wish for children, is on the borders of a gulf that may swallow it up; for, if they take one step more, they may cease to have them.

You tell me, perhaps, of the benign influence of Christianity. Well, here the population are all Christians, and the very girls who are but so-so are every day searching for texts to expound next Sunday before the congregation. You think this monstrous, incredible. How can they, you say, reconcile their conduct with their professions? How—let me ask you—does a London baker who mixes his sour and sweet flour and corrects the compound with this and that drug, go to church and hope to be saved? In his heart he confesses he sins, but it is a very venial sin, and he is no worse than his neighbours. Well, this is the way of thinking of this people. Try as I have done to bring them to a juster sense of things by having recourse to Scripture, and they turn the tables on you and quote more passages in favour of charity, for they are great Bible readers, than I can for chastity. Now they hold us whites to be monstrously deficient in the former virtues, which to do them justice they are not. They think these sort of transgressions, especially in females, very venial. They are directly opposite to us in this respect and give physical reasons for it. They blame the male, if any one . . . Here a woman may confess to the sin, but she thinks no shame; on the contrary, she rather glories in the number of her lovers.

I am tempted to give you an instance. A young girl of fifteen, not more, used often to come to me asking me to marry her. I am often besieged this way—such is the fashion. One day she was sitting with some of her companions playing cards, and in an interlude of the game I asked her how many lovers she had had, *kané*, the expression is not ambiguous, and began numbering them on her fingers. She had got the length of perhaps a dozen, when she became puzzled and gave it up, and throwing her hands over her head with as innocent a laugh as you would wish to see, exclaimed "I can't, I forget, a million perhaps—'he miliona paha.' "

The sister of this girl, no better than she, was lately drowned. Her father and mother, church members of high standing, came to my house to meet a missionary from Lahaina. They were lamenting their daughter, and describing her Christian graces, and were comforted with assurances of her having gone to a better place. Sure enough, both women were to be seen, in storm or fair, brushing through the grass at early dawn to go to prayer meeting, and both would have thought it wrong to eat meat without saying grace. Everything has two sides. Yet this is pre-eminently a Christian land if you consult missionary publications; and assuredly in the amount of contributions to the church and to christianising other lands, in the attendance on public worship, in the verbal knowledge of the Bible, in the number of schools, and in some other respects, such as the rarity of crimes of violence, it contrasts favourably with Europe and even America, and a stranger might be imposed on. Still there is this great rottenness at the core.

You think this abominable and are inclined to blame the missionaries. They are but men and are inclined to hold up the fair side. Yet they know, they cannot fail to know, the real state of things, I have had many proofs of this.

In my days of school keeping, when I first landed, I had occasion to consult a lady, the wife of a missionary, how I was to conduct myself in a certain emergency. She candidly advised me to make no useless fuss [that] would break up my school,—that the girls were all bad, every one of them. "I assure you, when I think of what old and young are, I cannot see what all this is to come to. My pillow is wet every night with bitter tears as I pray that their hearts may be changed, and I feel that this daily struggle, with thoughts that overwhelm me, is shortening my days." Subsequent events confirmed all this very estimable woman said, even as to fate, for she died a few years afterwards, a victim, I do believe, to distress of mind. I am persuaded that the missionaries know that a large proportion of their incomes is derived from what we would call the wages of prostitution. Yet they say nothing; and if attacked, turn around on the white men and accuse them as the cause of the evil. Certainly these are generally a set of scamps—runaway sailors and escaped convicts—but the evil is deeper. One cause of this is their diminished desire for children. They cannot welcome their offspring to a joyous and proud existence as of old.

This brings me back to what I set out—the danger of that feeling. So fell Rome—Christian Rome. All the eloquence of the Fathers (and they were eloquent, though after a fashion of their own) could not bring back that hallowed feeling of the blissfulness . . . The dark cloud of despotism overshadowed them; a coward fear of death haunted them. They had no genuine pleasure in contemplating creatures coming into a state of being like their own. The pure joys of the domestic hearth had vanished. In its stead they sought to lose the present sense of evil by grasping at every vanity within their reach, and in this wild struggle after every exciting enjoyment drained or poisoned the springs of life. The history of the downfall of the Roman Empire, in my opinion, turns on the population question and its concomitants—on the low effective desire of offspring and on the hence necessary low effective desire of accumulation.

SECOND LETTER

It is impossible with propriety publicly to discuss the question of population. Hence, perhaps, what I conceive to be the failure of Malthus. As a philosophical question it must be taken in its whole length and breadth; if any particular be shirked it is weak and the conclusions consequently uncertain. We must enter on it in a temper indicated by the saying of Bacon. The sun shines on all places and is not himself contaminated by the filth of any. So discussed it might, in my opinion, run somehow thus.

Man is an animal. As such he must have the capacity of propagating his species else his existence would be limited to the individual. He must have the power also of multiplying his numbers, else accidents would diminish and ultimately destroy the race. In these respects he agrees with the inferior animals . . . The inferior animals, however, do not know the consequences of the act; and so, led on by pleasure, may be said to be under the necessity of multiplying. Man, knowing the consequences of the act, may be induced to refrain and hence has the power of reducing the numbers or annihilating the race. Were all mankind, for instance, to adopt the principles of the community of Shakers, men would universally perish from off the earth with this generation.

But man differs further from the inferior animals in this, that he . . . may refrain from procreation without diminution, or without material diminution, of sensual enjoyment; and so his numbers may indefinitely decrease. Socrates in the Memorabilia is made to tell his sons, when enumerating the benefits he had conferred on them, that the act of begetting them was a sacrifice on his part of other and better pleasures.

But man may in this be restrained by what we may shortly call reason or by revelation. These determine certain acts to be vicious; but then they vary in their decisions. The severer casuists condemn all sexual enjoyments that do not immediately tend to procreation. And, indeed, unless stopping at this point is impossible for mere reason to assign another—all being equally against nature if we take the inferior animals as representatives of her. The question becomes complicated from the fact of the sexual embrace being one of the strongest means of conciliating and confirming the sentiment of love between the parties. A woman of any refinement of feeling yields only to this sentiment; she would be shocked by being regarded as a mere machine for producing children. Christianity preaches certain precepts, but how few walk by them. In general you find men pursuing conduct which in some respects accords, in others is at variance with these; excusing sins they feel inclined to by damning those they have no mind to.

It is impossible, therefore, to predict what its precise influence may be on any people.

Practically, the population question seems to me to turn on what I might call the effective desire of offspring. This runs parallel with the effective desire of accumulation (for at bottom they spring from similar causes) but often outruns it. That is to say, if there be no effective desire of offspring the accumulative principle falls; but the effective desire of offspring may exist where the effective desire of accumulation is small. The reason is that the desire of offspring is regulated, like some other things, by certain sentiments pervading the society, which we may term instincts of society. We have nearly as great difficulty in assigning causes for these, as for the instincts of animals. We may rest on this, without attempting to go further,—that these in any particular species of animal and in any particular society conduce to their respective well-being in some particular phase of their existence. What reason can we, for instance, give for visiting with such terrible penalties the transgression of a young woman and being so very lenient to the man? The New Testament condemns both alike; the Old is more lenient to the woman. The Hawaiians are quite opposite to us. For plain physical reasons they lay the blame, if blame there be, on the man. So when a girl was tabooed for a chief, if there was a fault the woman escaped the man was put to death. These people would think our procedure cruel and barbarous to a degree.

Again in European Society and in well regulated minds, the intercourse between males is regarded with horror and is not to be spoken of. We shrink, as we say, instinctively from the subject. And this is true; it is an instinct. True, it is forbidden in Scripture; but the feeling is, I think, equally strong with those who are sceptical as to the Bible. The feeling among the Greeks was opposite. As for women, they said, she knows nothing of true love. The influence of this way of thinking on their national character is a curious problem. I believe it had much to do with that sudden bursting forth of that blaze of intellectual greatness, which burnt so bright and shone so far, and also with the quick degeneracy of the race. Whatever abases woman ultimately degrades man, for we must have two parents.

In the inferior animals instincts are capable of being modified and changed. Thus the shepherd dog and the pointer are from the same stock. They are born with separate instincts derived from the training of their progenitors often scarce require the aid of education to perfect them. It seems the same with the social instincts. They seem hammered into the race by repeated strokes often after it has been softened in the furnace of affliction. Thus with the half-breeds on these Pacific Islands. It is remarkable, here in Hawaii, that marriages between half-breeds are very rarely prolific. The whites generally assert that they cannot be so, more than can a race be propagated from mules. The opinion, of course, is absurd, but marks the universality of the circumstance that has given rise to it. In fact, I know of but one exception, the case of a half-white twice married and having children by both women; but he had passed his youth in England. This rather proves the rule, the cause of which is the greater licentiousness of the half-caste. Now the same race at Pitcairn's Island are quite prolific, having overstocked it. Their history, as you are aware, is this—Adulteries, drunkenness and other disorders threatened them with destruction. The fate staring them in the face changed their character and gave to them social instincts preservative of the race. In the inferior animals we find that a race of more vigorous instincts destroys a weaker. It is the same in societies.

I am getting tedious, and yet I am not, I fear, explaining my ideas sufficiently to be intelligible. I cannot within any reasonable bounds tell you how I conceive these social instincts germinate, flourish, and die; and how the effective desire of offspring lives and dies with them. It is an important chapter of what I conceive to be the real philosophy of History which has not yet been written. I shall, however, put down one or two examples which may serve to show the drift of my reasoning.

Compare the pagan north with Christian Rome—the Roman Empire just Christian. These barbarians of the north, especially the Germans, were warriors such as the earth has not elsewhere seen. They rushed to battle as to a joyous revel; they reckoned death a trifle when compared with the slightest spot on their good name. Hence were they prodigal of life. Hence on the battlefield or in duels they mostly perished young. Hence the necessity for a supply of youthful warriors. Hence all the social instincts tending to the fecundity of the race were carried amongst them to the highest pitch. Hence their love of offspring. They welcomed them to their own bold, free, glorious life and to a death if glorious not to be lamented. Hence the severe chastity of men and women, and the high rank which the latter assumed. There was nothing of what we call vice among them, unless in the number of wives which the great men had—which the greater proportion of women justified, and of which a curious survival remains in the left-handed marriages of German princes. Consider that for a thousand years these wars had been going on; that tribes were continually being exterminated and new ones springing up; that in this game those in which the supply of young warriors was most plentiful, had the best chance and would in the long run win; those in which any sexual vice prevailed would be weeded out by the sword, and you will see the process must have had great results. It was hence that the north became the officina gentium.

[Whatever] therefore, goes to weaken or destroy those social instincts which tend to generate love of offspring, is a crime against society. In this respect I think the English poor laws have operated very injuriously; and you will pardon me for saying that the notion they are a proof of high civilisation and the cramming them down the unwilling throat of Scotland and Ireland, seems to me a piece of egregious John Bullism. I know nothing of England personally, but I think I have observed among English emigrants to North America of the labouring class, that the family affections are feebler than among other people. From this and other symptoms, I apprehend the condition of the masses there is very unsatisfactory. When men begin to think children a burden, they may wish not to have them, and then it needs but a step to their ceasing to have them. All depends on public sentiment—the manifestation of social instincts.

In the middle and higher classes there are men who are recognized as not marrying men. Now though all the world knows—to use the expression of Mrs. Willson to Morton in Scott's Tales of my Landlord—that if they do not marry they must do worse, yet the world in the main thinks they are right. Suppose that some national disaster pressing severely on the people should produce among the lower orders a class of no family men and no family women and that legal or illegal unions should be formed on that understanding what would be the consequence? All social vices are contagious. For my own part I should not be surprised at any enormity getting a root and spreading fast and far among the masses. A little learning is a dangerous thing.

But I must have done without saying half my mind on this subject. Our social instincts are Germanic and hence the pressing of population on the means of subsistence; but they may change.

19

John Rae to H. B. Willson*

DECEMBER, 1856

If you would really help a man you must know how to help him. You
must know in what his well-being and happiness consist, what therefore
are his objects and aims. My earlier friends in Canada could not conceive
or at least understand what were mine. They thought me foolish in burying
the attainments and ability they were pleased to give me credit for in the
subordinate position of a village surgeon, or still worse in that of a country
schoolmaster. They could not conceive that my main need was quiet, to
think out my thoughts. When after ten years of this sort of life I had
sufficiently mastered my subjects and digested my problems and wished
to put some of them before the world, they had changed their notion of me,
and viewing me now as a mere schoolmaster stood aloof from me and my
projects, and would give me neither effective countenance nor support.
Some hinted that had I taken their advice I might have been in a very
different position, while the prudent said, 'What are your chances of gaining by this? How much will it put in your pocket? Sit quiet.' Others again,
looking on me as a mere adventurer, and measuring me from my humble
place and comparing it with the magnitude of my enterprises seemed to
say, 'What, you a village teacher, think you can master such high themes?
The man is mad: we will have nothing to do with him.' I have found all
men, even my most intimate friends, measuring the probable success of
my schemes not from what they inherently were, but from the position of
myself, the one bringing them forward. This I recollect well when I projected publishing my work on political economy, my friends were quite

* *Sociological Theory of Capital*, xl–xli.

incredulous of my ability to controvert the doctrines of Adam Smith in any particular, and smiled part in pity, part in wonderment, at the presumption of one who had not been able to raise himself from the position of a country schoolmaster embarking on so hopeless an enterprise. Now had they known motives for contenting myself with what seemed to them so inferior a station, they might or at least they ought to have come to another conclusion. It was in truth because I was engaged in important speculations for which school life though a drudgery yet gave me many hours of quiet leisure, that I contented myself with it. I feared that if I then pushed really into the battle of life these speculations would be likely to dim before me, and probably at last fade in the distance. I now think I was wrong in this—events at least would seem to prove my having been so. At any rate, had I to run the same course over again, I would act differently. I think I ought to have studied law, for which through Judge Maclean[1] the way would have been open to me, and secured to myself a certain social position that would have enabled me in no long time to have given myself to pursuits more congenial to my feelings. I do not believe that either great success or comparative failure in a legal career would have been able to turn me from the occasional contemplation and ultimate pursuit of the magnificent visions of my youth. Yet who knows? . . .

[1] Archibald McLean (1791–1865) was a distinguished legal figure in Upper Canada. He was educated under John Strachan in Cornwall and subsequently studied law. He was a Member of Parliament for Stormont in the period 1820–1837 and twice Speaker of the Upper Canada legislature. He was appointed a Judge (King's Bench) in 1837 and in 1862 became Chief Justice of the Court of Queen's Bench. He played a leading role in the affairs of the Kirk and this is probably how Rae came to know him.

20

John Rae to Dr. Archibald Hall, on Geology*

c. 1857

MY DEAR SIR

About two months since I wrote you and sent you a packet containing the balance of my medical experiences. It was hastily penned and I believe I therefore made several omissions. Probably however it will be found at least long enough. I then informed you that as soon as I could I would send you the conclusion of my geological speculation fancying as I have heard nothing of its reaching you that my packet containing it forwarded about 12 months since must have been lost. Unfortunately my papers when received were in great confusion and several missing. This with the time that has since intervened makes it impossible for me to tell where the first part terminated and the second commenced. Add to this that on reviewing the subject after such a lapse of time its aspect I find changes somewhat in my mind. Nevertheless, taking the opportunity which a little leisure forced on me by indisposition affords I proceed to lay before you as I best can the sum of the results which the question I have started presents to my cogitations. I shall run over the whole de novo but with all possible brevity.

I will first state the chief general conclusions to which I have come; next go over the process of reasoning by which I have arrived at then and lastly give the facts that seem to render them probable or certain.

I conceive that if the interior of our planet be fluid that fluid being subject to the laws regulating the movement of gravid bodies will have certain

---

* Rae mss. The letter itself is undated but in the course of it Rae describes a tidal wave which occurred on Maui "about twenty years since." This appears to be an episode also described by Manley Hopkins (*Hawaii*, 16) which took place on Nov. 7, 1837.

very minute but important motions. The first of these will take their rise from the influence of the sun and moon producing movements somewhat analogous to those by which the tides of the ocean are supposed to be generated and regulated. The next will be produced by the motions generated in a spheroidal liquid mass by the process of cooling, consisting of superficial currents flowing from the equatorial regions to the poles dipping there to the central parts and again rising towards the equator. Two consequences will result from the establishment of such currents. The first that the greatest superficial heat will not be at the equator but at some distance on either side of it in zones where the currents having completely established themselves the hottest particles flow along the surface. 2d The earth's crust will approach to a uniform thickness throughout from equator to poles, its interior surface will be smooth and regular. Any occurring irregularities being gradually melted off and a more uniform temperature will pervade the exterior surface.

If we ever approach to a just understanding of the whole mechanism of the globe it must I conceive be through resources which chemistry does not yet afford. We are comparatively ignorant of the effects of pressure in modifying chemical action. It seems to me more than probable that it has a very extensive operation and, if we adopt the Hypothesis of Leibnitz, very likely that a series of great phenomena have been in succession produced both by the increase of pressure consequent on condensation and by the bringing into close approximation constituents which in the early stage of our planet's history must have been far apart. Earthquakes and volcanoes seem to be the last sequences of these phenomena. In the paper I last sent you I gave you my views on this part of the subject which on reflection I now suppress as probably too vague and at any rate not essentially connected with my theme. I may say however that they pointed to the probability of the same frequent and copious evolutions of gases and consequent upheaving of the crust in former days. It is only necessary for my purpose to assume that gases are and have been continually evolved.

In my first paper I attempted, from the simplest mechanical principles, to deduce the minute motions that would have place in one liquid spheroidal body revolving round another.

It is evident that the centrifugal force of its parts will give to such a body a form more or less oblate towards its equator. But besides this the inequality of the attraction of the parts nearer, and farther removed from the body round which it revolves will produce a farther oblateness somewhat increasing the equatorial diameter in a direction marked at its acme by a line passing through the centre of both the body revolving and that round which it revolves and therefore, in the former, continually shifting place.

The same forces that are conceived to produce the tides on our earth would also operate in the production of these constantly recurring but minute changes of diameter in the equatorial regions of such a mass.

Suppose now that a crust is formed on the surface of such a spheroid. The question arises will that succession of minute oblate movements be continued or will they cease? I answer that will depend altogether on the firmness of the crust. It maybe so unyielding and strong as altogether to resist the efforts of the internal nisus, it may be so pliant as to offer no obstruction to it, so it may partly yield partly resist. It might be impossible in the case supposed from the minuteness of the motion to determine which of the three possible results actually occured.

We may make another supposition. Let the revolving body have spread over its external crust a thin film of water. Suppose its diameter 8,000 miles and the distance therefore from centre to circumference 4,000. Let the depth of water be 2 miles or the 2,000th part. If the constantly recurring equatorial bulging be 20 feet or 240 inches and the crust perfectly yielding then the part in the bulging performed by the exterior fluid would be the 2,000th part of 240 inches or less than the 8th of an inch a quantity which may be altogether neglected. In such a case the bulging being performed almost altogether by the internal fluid the external film of water or ocean would appear to take no part in it so that were a series of rocky pinnacles rising here and there over it, the height of water on these would be uniform, the difference being too small to be measured. But, were the crust altogether immobile, then the part which the internal fluid made an ineffectual nisus to accomplish, would be taken up by the exterior ocean, and partially at least accomplished, by its rushing, in a sort of wave, towards the parts where the bulging should take place. This movement would be indicated on the pinnacles we have supposed, by the different height of water on them, at different hours of the day.

Were the crust partly mobile, and partly immobile, the results would vary accordingly and proportionally. Where it was mobile, there would be no tides, where it was immobile, there would be full tides. Where it was partially mobile, there would be partial tides.

To apply this to our earth. It is obvious, that all the results we have contemplated, though complicated by the combined attractions of the sun and moon, must take place, or must have a tendency to take place. They must however be further complicated by the protrusion of the present continents, breaking and confusing what we may call the natural movements of the ocean, where it has to supply any more or less complete void, which the immobility, more or less perfect, of the crust, may occasion in the operation of the necessarily bulging tendency of the internal fluid.

I shall begin this part of the subject by a sort of priori inquiry as to the mobility, or immobility, of the substances of which the crust consists. I may set out with this proposition. The mobility, whatever it may be, will increase with the depth. For we know, that the mobility of all solids is augmented by the increase of temperature, and that the temperature of the earth's crust increases with the depth we penetrate it.

Allowing that the temperature augments by one degree for every 45 feet, at one mile and a half this would raise the temperature to the boiling point, and if, from our experience of mining operations, we consider the extreme probability of water, or watery vapour, there pervading the rocky masses, would give considerable plasticity to them. The lower strata again, those most contiguous to the central incandescent mass, are, it is most likely, for miles in a viscid or half viscid state, and therefore perfectly and easily flexible. The difficulty of flexure must therefore mainly or altogether subsist in the more exterior parts, in what we call the solid earth. Are these the materials of which this is composed,—the rocks and mountain masses—of a perfectly inflexible nature.

It is a great many years since I studied practical mechanics, but, unless my recollections much deceive me, experiments show that even the most apparently stubborn and unyielding materials have a certain amount of flexibility, and even elasticity. That for instance a long block of granite, such as are used for building purposes, may by sufficient pressure be made to *give* a little, and, on the removal of the pressure will resume its original rectitude of outline.

As I cannot however recollect my authorities, I must let this pass, and view the subject from a point whence the experience of every one may satisfy him of the general correctness of my conclusions.

There is probably no one but will recollect having been at some time or other in a house of stone or brick, by which a heavily loaded cart or waggon passing, has communicated to it a very sensible jar and tremor. It seems to follow that the surface, for some depth, receives a movement, however slight, that pervades all its particles, and which it communicates to the building. This may even reach a great way. I recollect that the astronomical instruments, in the Marischal College Aberdeen, where disturbed by carts passing in the street, although at a distance of about 200 yards. For this reason observatories are built very massive, and in quiet sites.

Now, it is certain, that tremulous motions like these must produce effects, and we accordingly find, that all walls are at length pervaded by slight fissures, these the moisture from rain, and, in certain latitudes, the effects of frost, gradually widen, until, on some sudden shock, the wall gives way, and falls. Whoever has contemplated the gradual decay of ancient castles in Europe may have observed this progress. We are wont indeed to assign it indefinitely to age, and speak of "Times destroying sway" but time alone, obviously, never produces decay. Even the light impression of a rain drop on a muddy beach, may, we know, remain for thousands of ages undefaced and unimpaired, provided it be covered by some protecting medium, and be left undisturbed. Defacement, decay, & the separation of parts, are always the result of mechanical or chemical action, which may indeed be so infinitesmally small, that its effects only become apparent to the senses after a very lengthened series of repetitions, but they nevertheless may have been making a real progress, during every instant of the long lapse of time that series may have occupied.

In most cases the operation of winds, more or less violent, seems to be the cause of those minute and gradually extending fissures, which, at length, bring down the strongest and loftiest towers. I lived for many years in an isolated brick house, and, my dormitory being situated in an upper chamber, in stormy nights, I was sensible of a slight tremor, responding to every violent gust. The walls began to leak at several points, to remedy this the coat of lime and sand with which the building was inverted was stript completely off, when several chinks, running for yards through the body of the wall, became apparent. These were secured by iron clamps, and then a fresh coat of a compound of lime and coarse sand was thrown on. Being then a boy my curiosity was excited by this strife between the force of the wind and human resistance, and I watched carefully the result. In the course of a year or two, small chinks, into which I could put the point of a needle, again became visible in the plaster above the course of the old fissures. The house stood however for thirty years when it was destroyed by fire.

It would appear, then, that the most substantial materials yield in some degree, to apparently slight forces, and that by these, even what we call the solid earth is shaken, and communicates its tremors to remote superstructures.[1] I would now call your attention to the amount of movement that a yielding, to what we may call the internal tides, would tend to generate in the external crust. Suppose that the elevation at its acme at any point is 20 feet, and that a radius of 1,000 miles would sweep round the whole range of movement. This would give a rise of less than $\frac{1}{4}$ of an inch to every mile—a truly minute quantity, requiring no violent dislocation, but only an almost infinitesmal yielding. Many instances might be adduced

[1]Quoniam plaustris concuosa tremis curit
Fecta viam propter non magno pondere tota,
Nec minus exsultant, ubi currus fortis equim vis
Ferratos utrinque rotarum succutit orbeis,

Lucretius L vi 547

of the exterior crust yielding far more than this without dislocation, or permanent displacement.

Some remarkable ones have occurred, and almost every year or so are occurring, in the islands from which I date. Many of them have been recorded by resident missionaries and others; and the recollections and traditions of the natives recall many more. One old woman whom I questioned, recollected three times when great waves from the ocean had invaded the land, sweeping everything before them, and again retiring. The general course of things on these occasions seems to be, first a sudden retiring of the deep, for perhaps a mile, from the shore, leaving the rocks exposed, and the fish struggling on the sand. Then, the as sudden rush of a mighty ocean wave landward not only spreading itself over the old ocean bed, but careering, with headlong fury, over the shore, and burying everything beneath its waters for many hundred yards. This again retires, and after one or two lesser movements of the same sort, the whole shore resumes its exact former condition. There can be no doubt of this latter fact, for the natives along the beach, being fishermen, and constantly on the water, their nice eyes and quick perceptive faculties would unquestionably detect the least perceptible variation, and they uniformly, when questioned, affirm that there is none.

I should mention that the old woman to whom I have referred has resided all her life at Kahului a fishing village on the north shore of the island of Maui. It is to that locality therefore that her recollections relate. The village is on the sea beach and was formerly quite populous. Behind it are a range of sand hills about 30 feet in height, and, behind these, a fresh water pond, gradually diminishing by the inroads of the sand, but which was then probably a mile in diameter. The village of Wailuku lies about two miles inland to the S.W. and Lahaina is a haven on the south west shore. Between the two latter, a volcanic mass of cliffy mountains rises to the height of seven or eight thousand feet. The distance between Kahului and Lahaina, in a direct line, may be somewhat under twenty miles. The last movement occurred in the night about twenty years since, and the first intimation the inhabitants of Kahului had of it was their wakening struggling in the water. Freeing themselves by vigorous efforts from the wreck of houses &c. in which they were involved, with the seemingly instictive energy of their almost amphibious race, each swam about in the place where he was till the commotion subsided. They then almost all found themselves in the middle of the freshwater pond. Their houses, structures framed of poles covered with dry grass, and their nets, calabashes &c. had disappeared, and their wrecks had to be sought for here and there, but they themselves escaped with the loss of one or two old women drowned. Had they been any other race the casualties must have been very much greater, but it is a business of some difficulty to drown a Hawaiian.

On the same night, and probably at the same moment, a similar ocean movement was experienced at Lahaina, and it extended to Hawaii a hundred miles to the S.E. No eruption, or other volcanic phenomena occurred, or were at least noted. A great discharge of gas however might easily have taken place without being perceived.

As concerns our subject two things are particularly deserving of notice in this phenomenon. First that no derangement of the old water line was anywhere remarked. Second that no concussion commotion or disturbance of the earth was felt in the interior parts of the island. At Wailuku, for instance, people knew nothing of what had taken place at Kahului, until next morning. A white friend of mine, then residing in Wailuku, told me, indeed, that he thought he recollected, during the night, some sort of clattering among the dishes in his cupboard, but this was all.

Anyone who reflects on these circumstances must I think come to the conclusion, that, on this occasion, the whole western end of Maui, and a greater or less portion of the surrounding and contiguous crust of the earth, was elevated bodily, for at least twenty feet, again subsided somewhat beneath that depth, and, finally, settled precisely in its former position. Farther, that this movement took place without any perceptible jar or disruption of parts, but was precisely similar to a momentary floating upwards of a body resting on a fluid. Nor is this a solitary instance, numerous similar ones have occurred at no distant date. These all indicate a great facility of movement in the crust of the earth around this region. Now, if such mobility exist, it is reasonable to suppose that here the internal tidal movement would have its effect in diminishing the ocean tide. It cannot be supposed to annul them. The restraining weight of the great mountain masses, rising in the interior of all the Islands, forbid this. We find, accordingly, that the tides here are very small, amounting only to two or three feet. A much greater deviation from the consequences that must follow, if we suppose the crust of the earth everywhere firmly resisting the internal tidal movement, takes place in other parts of the Pacific. Captain Beechy makes the general remark on coral harbours, that they are uninfluenced by tides. If, as I presume, he has reference to islands consisting mainly of coral and coral reefs, and when, consequently, there are no large mountainous masses restraining by their gravity the internal movement, then his evidence strongly corroborates the correctness of my conclusions. In the Society Islands again, where there are mountains, thought not so massive as those of the Sandwich Islands we are informed by the Rev^d Mr. Williams, in his narrative of missionary enterprise, that the rise of water is only eighteen inches or two feet. He also states the very remarkable fact, that these tides always occur at noon and midnight. Now I conceive it is absolutely impossible to explain this phenomenon by the common theory of the tides, or indeed to reconcile it to it. On the contrary there is not much difficulty in reconciling it with my hypothesis. For, the moon from its proximity exercising a greater tidal influence than the sun, it is conceivable, that it may produce an internal tidal bulging or wave, of strength sufficient to elevate the crust, whereas that which the sun tends to generate, being weaker, may be nearly suppressed by the incumbent weight, and the deficiency supplied by the movement of the external ocean. I have somewhere heard, or read, that, at Tahiti, the tide is at its height, not at twelve, but at half past twelve, but cannot now recall my authority. If this be the case, that half hour would probably be fully sufficient to bring up the waters of the deep surrounding Pacific, to the point where the vacancy occurs.

A minute investigation of the actual rise and fall of tides, at all points of the globe, of the set of the current at these points, and of the exact time of flood and ebb, would give results tending greatly either to confirm or invalidate my hypothesis. I had made a short list of some of these from authorities within my reach, but it is lost or mislaid. I shall either recover it, or will make out a fresh, and possibily a fuller one, in time to send with these papers. Meantime I will here make some general observations on the results to be expected from such investigation.

According to the views which I have endeavoured to unfold, it may be laid down as a general principle, that, where the crust of the earth is perfectly firm, there, *caeteris paribus*, will be the greatest ocean tides, and that, when it is most yielding, there these will be minute or will altogether cease.

It is however impossible for us to ascertain exactly where the crust is firm, and where it is yielding. We can only arrive at probable but by no means certain conclusions. It may be said in general, that, in extensive and elevated continents, it must be most firm and resistant. Both its greater absolute thickness there, and the weight of the incumbent mountains, will produce this effect. It is, on the contrary, to be presumed, that it will be most yielding in deep and extensive oceans. The greater thinness of the crust over such extensions of surface, and the absence of any great superincumbent mountain masses, will tend to produce this mobility. Farther, if the hottest, and therefore most yielding portion of the earths crust lie, as I think there is some reason to conclude it does, in two zones considerably north and south of the equator, then along the track of these zones, additional flexibility may be expected.

But though we may be pretty certain that great continents are firm, and the bottoms of great oceans comparatively mobile, yet it is difficult to say precisely where the mobility terminates, and the stability commences. Suppose a great ocean bed capable of being flexed borders an immobile continent. There will then be a tract of greater or less breadth between the two, in which the flexure will cease. This may be termed the line of flexure, for here, it is evident the amount of bending must be greatest. So to express myself, there will be a sort of wide hinge here, the ocean bed forming the door, and the continent the wall. The course which this line takes will regulate the ocean tides. If it be altogether inland, the mobility advancing to its edges, the tide will be small. If its position be outward of the ocean border, the tides will be great. It would seem probable that generally capes would lie without it and deep bays or gulfs within it, and that therefore the tides would usually be small at the former points and large at the latter.

If then there seems a strong probability, or a certainty, that from its first formation for a very protracted period of time the crust of the earth has been affected by these internal tidal movements, to ascertain what may have been the probable or the certain effects of these, becomes an inquiry of some interest.

I think we have some grounds from analogy to conclude, that they must have had a tendency at least to produce slight fissures, not indeed probably discernible by the eye, but nevertheless affecting the body of solid rocks, and as it were marking out, and preparing the way, for those more visible ones, which more energetic movements afterwards completed. These movements themselves being regular in their course, the minute fissures produced by them would also be parallel and regular. They would naturally lie transverse to the line of movement, and, as this was in general from east to west, their general direction should be north and south. It is easy to conceive however that the firmness of continents, and other causes opposing their resistance to the internal tide, might cause it widely to diverge, and proportionally divert the course of the fissures. It is also to be observed that, as almost all stratified rocks however now impacted in solid continents, must, at one time or another of their existence, have been in positions where they would be subjected to the movements we are considering. We may expect to find traces of these in them all. It is farther also to be noted that at the period of the formation of most stratified rocks, the crust of the earth was probably considerably thinner than at present, and consequently of proportionally easier flexure.

Volcanoes, either recent or extinct, are found here and there over the earth in every direction. There can be no reasonable doubt that they are the vents of gases, generated in the interior incandescent mass, and of portions of its superfluous matter. We know that immense volumes of gases often find their vent through them. If these are extricated at a point remote from that of their exit, they must make their way for that distance along the interior of the crust applying an immense force during their whole course to heave it upwards. There can be no reasonable doubt that such movements of great volumes of exceedingly condensed gases are the cause of earthquakes. There is every reason to think that these have been constantly recurring, so that there is no part of the earth's crust that has not been repeatedly subjected to their influence.

Now, in considering the phenomena of earthquakes, there is a circumstance which, to me, and I presume to others, has always seemed remarkable. I allude to that rolling movement of the surface, and doubtless of the depths of the earth, like the waves of the sea, which is generally said to accompany them. It has always seemed wonderful to me how the surface and the parts under could be so affected, without more violent and permanent displacements than actually occur. It appears to me, that the difficulty is to a considerable extent, removed, if we conceive, that the way is, as it were, prepared for these extensive motions, by those more minute and long repeated movements, to which the mass of rock forming the crust have been formerly subjected. There would not be so much breaking, as a stirring, of previously separated parts, generally after the commoving cause had passed, returning to their former positions, and only occasionally slipping by each other, and producing those disruptions of the surface, of which, what are called faults, are the indexes.

When again we examine the structure of deeply exposed rocks, and find them pervaded by what are called fissures, veins, joints &c, we are struck by the general regularity and parallelism of these, and in vain seek to reconcile their production, to the violent and varied agency of earthquakes, to which we nevertheless know they must have been subjected. If however these germs sprang from a more equable and gentle agent, the difficulty, as it seems to me, in a great measure vanishes.

As volcanoes arise from the central fire they ought to be found at points where either the exterior crust is thinnest and weakest, or where it is most exposed to fissure. Accordingly I believe, if you consult a good map in which they are noted, you will find that the great majority of them lie, either in two zones somewhat removed from the equator, or along the course of those hinges I have spoken of, as running along the dividing line of great continents and oceans.

That continental volcanoes usually occur along the course of such a line as the latter has long indeed been noted and was the foundation of the hypothesis first started if I recollect right by Sir Humphrey Davy that these phenomena were to be resolved on the supposition of water finding its way downwards through fissures and being converted into explosive vapours.

I have one or two brief observations to make on this hypothesis. In the first place steam so generated being only a frequent but not an invariable concomitant of volcanic eruptions cannot be held as their true cause. That and that alone which is always present can be held as the cause and this only applied to vapours other than that of steam. Accordingly I believe geologists have not in general adopted the hypothesis in question.

Furthermore I would observe that such an hypothesis even admitting its truth only explains the possible proximate cause of volcanoes. In other words it only shows how if fissures occurred at such points they might produce volcanic phenomena it does not explain why they should there exist. According to my theory on the other hand it is in such localities, that we may reasonably expect them to occur, for through the fissures there likely to be produced the internal gases continually generating beneath would find a passage and in their ascent would incorporate and bear along with them in the form of steam whatever waters they might encounter in their course.

I have said that I was in part led to the conclusions to which I have come by some striking geological phenomena which these islands exhibit. These appearances however are rather suggestive of the opinions I have formed than absolutely going to prove their truth. I will state very briefly the general nature of those characteristics which turned my mind towards this region of speculation [and] have made the deepest impression on my mind.

You are aware that these islands are vast volcanic masses varying in height from four or five to 14 thousand feet. By a very recent barometrical measurement of my friend Remy de Pioria the highest summit in Hawaii is 13,900f. The dimensions of their craters are very great, one on this island measuring probably twelve or fourteen miles in its longer diameter and seven or eight in its shorter. They are also distinguished by the lava flow having in general proceeded from the crater itself and but very seldom from any lateral vent. They are of all ages. Hawaii is now in progress of growth from the over-flowing of the lavas which burst from its summits. Oahu again has been so wrought on by the wasting powers of the ocean waves and of rain as to present only remnants of its former bulk.

Perhaps the most striking of the conclusions, to which the contemplation of these mountain masses leads the mind is the vast lapses of time which must have been occupied by their gradual formation and as gradual greater or less advance towards demolition. I shall take one as an example in which the work of demolition though somewhat advanced may still be considered as but very partial.

There have been two volcanoes on this island each of which has generated its mountain. They lie east and west from each other and are separated by a low isthmus of ten miles across. The one on the east has as yet been but very slightly broken in upon. Its crater of which I have already given the dimensions is as yet complete its sides are only beginning to be furrowed by the descending streams its base to suffer from the wear and tear of the ceaselessly rolling ocean.

It is the one to the westward to which I more particularly wish to refer. Seen at the distance of twelve or twenty miles in almost any direction it presents the appearance of a tolerably regular cone of a very wide base and having its summit smoothed and rounded off. Its height has I believe been ascertained by trigonometrical observations to be about eight thousand feet. It attains this elevation by a very gradual slope the angle being only about seven degrees. At the distance I have specified the deep ravines which penetrate its mass are only faintly discernible. When however one attempts to reach its central parts the scene totally changes and he finds himself involved in the intricacies of very lofty and precipitous mountain chains. The task before him is in fact one of considerable difficulty and even some slight danger.

That you may form an idea of the general aspect which things present to him at almost every point, you must conceive that a series of ravines advance, in irregular waving lines, from all round the base, like radii to a centre, and pierce, through the very bowels of the mountain, to the inner parts, once occupied by the crater. They have dug so deep that the little streams which flow through them are not I think at their summits over fifteen hundred feet above the level of the ocean. At the circumference these ravines are separated by wide stretches of the original mountains slope, but necessarily approaching each other as they proceed towards their common centre, they there leave but fragmentary remnants of this original inclined plain.

Only two modes of advance offer themselves. One must attempt the ascent on the spaces intervening between the vallies, or he may follow the streams, the sides of these vallies or deep ravines being far too precipitous to be passable. If he take the former, his progress, until he attain an elevation of some thousand feet, is easy, but, by and by, the comparatively smooth inclined plain, on which he has been advancing, begins to narrow, so that only a yard or two of unbroken surface remains to him. Beyond this on either hand are enormous precipices. The higher he climbs the path still farther contracts. He finds that the original surface has been so encroached on by the corroding progress of the ravines, that it has given way, and being precipitated into the gulfs below. His farther advance therefore is by the doubtful narrow ridge bounding two precipices. This ridge has a waving outline, often ascending or decending too abruptly to be ventured on, as it is often also only a foot or two wide, and the degree of its stability is hid by the peculiar vegetation of those dizzy tropical heights. Add to this, that the chances, any day of the year, are two to one, that he is involved in dense whirling clouds or perhaps drenching rains.

Should however circumstances be favourable to him, and should he, in clear weather, reach the mountains summit at which he has aimed, the mere sublimity of the scenery all around will richly reward his pains. The necessary brevity of this communication prevents me from entering on such a theme. I confine myself to a single view, explanatory of one of the geological problems these islands suggest.

You have gained, we shall say, one of the more elevated peaks of some of these mountain ridges. Turning on one hand and looking down you see below you a valley more than a mile in perpendicular depth; looking across there faces you, at a like distance, a mighty mountain ridge the counterpart of the one on whose summit you stand. You have of course the fullest and most distinct view of the one opposite. You see that its slope downward is at first very precipitous, often almost, or altogether perpendicular. But casting your eye farther below, you perceive that its base and great part of its heights, are supported by mountainous buttresses of singular regularity, each resembling an Elizabethean roof of extremely steep pitch, tilted up so that its ridge, of many thousand feet in length, makes an angle with the horizon of forty or fifty degrees, its upper end merging in the upper heights, its base commingling with others in the lower depths of the ravine. These are the work of the tiniest collateral rills, some few of which you catch glimpses of in the distance. In the extreme depths below, a stream is just discernible, showing like the finest silvery thread. Though the mild and moist climate of these vast and singular gorges clothes their steep, and often precipitous heights, with a rich vegetation of ferns and other plants suited to these localities, and shade their lower depths with woods of larger growth, the eye is still able, in very many points, to catch the great features of their rocky structures. You detect the course of many successive strata dipping uniformly, in somewhat waving lines, in an angle of about seven degrees corresponding to the general slope of the upper surface of the mountain, and mark in particular the very great length and regularity of their course, more resembling a series of strata formed by deposition than tiers of rocks superimposed on one another by successive volcanic outbursts. You remark also that their continuity is unbroken by fissures or rents or apparent upheavels. Having effected your ascent you next wish to reach the same scenes from below, and seek to penetrate the mountain depths by the course of one of the streams.

In your progress towards the point where this stream comes forth on the plains in which the base of the mountain merges, you probably pass the mouths of several ravines, each giving exit to its little rill. At each of these a separate glen, the entrance to a deep ravine, is seen, and views obtained of the different ranges of rocks exhibited in successive tiers or layers. You remark the same regularity in the dip, and the same extension of surface in the several layers. It would seem, that each successive eruption had spread its thin sheet very far, and very wide. As you pursue your way up the glen you have made choice of as the scene of your farther exploration, you find that a way has been cut for you through layers lying still deeper and deeper, as compared with the upper surface of the mountain, and therefore still more and more ancient. You thus pass several varieties of volcanic rocks, but in general they have a nascent basaltic appearance, and are very commonly separated from each other by thinner layers of conglomerate formed of their own rolled and comminuted fragments. Frequently the only way you can possibly advance is by wading in the bed of the brooks, smooth, and nearly perpendicular rocks rising on each side of it. Should sudden rains then swell the stream your position would not be free from danger. We shall suppose that you have reached a point on which you formerly looked down from the highest summits, and there stop to contemplate the impressive scene. Apart from the feelings of sublimity which mountains rising overhead in seeming perpendicularity for so many thousand feet with all their accessories of foliage, clouds, and mists, naturally excite, the contemplation of these remote vallies, as one deliberately considers them, raises in the mind, from other sources, a sensation of mingled wonderment and awe. It is impossible to assign their formation to any sudden and violent convulsion of nature, for comparing their sides, you see on each the same strata reposing undisturbed in the position in which they had settled on their first flowing forth. You see too the puney looking side rills, and little main valley stream at constant work, and, with laborious chisel, channelling out still deeper the profound trenches, that, diversely wrought by them in ages long past, now give form and linaments to the gigantic masses around. Two things impress the mind. The first of these is the immense time that must have been spent by such tiny agents in the performance of their stupendous task. This feeling of almost painful straining of the mind to compass the apprehension of very long series of ages is produced by many geological phenomena but here it assumes a peculiar character.

In making for instance a geological tour from north to south in Upper Canada though the various strata under your feet are in general covered up you may yet by laborious exploration search out their several outcrops and determine their relative positions. You may then by process of reasoning, from consideration of their structure and organic remains, arrive at some general conclusions as to the immense times that must have elapsed during these Silurian ages. Your reason tells you that it must be so, but your imagination flags in the attempt to reach any just conception of the semblance and duration of the various conditions of being that on this plot of earth have run out their several periods and have only left behind them in record of their existence the chance fragmentary remnants you contemplate. But here on the contrary where the imagination has no room for play where the whole work and the doers of it are at once before you the mind takes a different course—it somehow shrinks back on its own littleness and refuses to admit the conclusions drawn by the reasoning powers. You think it must be some trick of fancy. It is as if one were to talk to you of draining the Pacific with a teacup. Yet nothing can be more certain than that were there a secure reservoir, a cup that wasted not, an arm that wearied not, the Pacific could be drained by a tea cup.

The contemplation becomes still more confounding when one considers that the partial demolition is but a small part of the work, that the progress of growth must have occupied a far longer period, that this is but one of many of these volcanic islands some of which are of far greater antiquity and above all that the term of the duration of the whole body of them is probably but a mere point in the vast series of changes which the broken annals of the globe reveal. When one reflects on these things his thoughts are borne in a sort of dizzy confusion over periods of time the vastness of which has its only correlative in the immensity of the spaces on which modern astronomers speculate.

The second circumstance that arrests the attention of the geological inquirer and leads him to ponder deeply on the scene before him is the undisturbedness of the quiet the rocks he looks on have been suffered to maintain since their first deposition. Wherever the interior structure of any mountain mass is laid open he is accustomed to see strata exhibiting marks of violent displacement—of having been acted on subsequently to their formation by some force that has here penetrated their substance by fresh matter there heaved them up in new positions. He is especially inclined to expect this in the vicinity of volcanoes associated as these are in his mind with violent bursting forth of the central fire and disruption by earthquakes. Whence then the profoundness of that lengthened repose which all here displays and bespeaks. While pondering on this question I was led to pass in review in so far as my recollection served me the various theories which geologists have invented to explain volcanic phenomena. I pass by the speculations in which this involved me and note only two things which it seems to me must be admitted as facts. The first of these is that the massive height of these mountain volcanoes is due in part to very wide lava sheets issuing one after another from a central crater. Their structure gives evidence of this. The second is that it is also in part due to elevation from beneath the surface of the ocean. This the rolled, comminuted, and afterwards cemented structure of a considerable portion of their mass clearly evinces. Now had the elevating force been determined to a small spot its operation must have disturbed the structure of the outpoured layers which it has not done. It must therefore have operated on a large circumference the whole crust under the embrace of which must have been capable of flexure. Nor could this capacity for flexure have been confined to a small interval of time it must have spread over periods, which in our limited comprehension we can only perhaps characterize as very great. From the evidence of the mountain itself therefore a capacity of flexure and some degree of plasticity would seem for a considerable period to have characterized the crust in this region. The question next naturally arises at least to me has the capacity ceased, and what evidence is there on this place for the phenomena here exhibited by volcanoes and earthquakes.

It must be confessed that all which immediately strikes our senses gives us a notion of stability, immoveability and solidity as inseparably connected and thus we speak and think of the firm and solid ground on which we tread than which nothing seems to us more fixed and immoveable. It must also however on the other hand be admitted that the progress of philosophical research has considerably modified and restricted this primary idea and some others connected with it.

Last century the earth was believed to be a solid body the term of whose duration was limited to a few thousand years. That central fires existed was beyond a doubt but their existence was thought to be the great disturbing cause bringing confusion and desolation on the otherwise stable globe. Now we begin to believe that our planet has run through a series of changes occupying periods so great that though our reasoning powers may guess at their calculation our understandings are incapable of grasping the seemingly infinite cycles of ages they embrace. Now also we begin to believe that all but the outer shell is occupied by a central incandescent mass. It seems to me that admitting these conclusions to be correct the prevailing notion of stability as connected with them must undergo a change.

That ancient idea of stability which came down to us from the old times denoted a power to resist all exterior impressions and in this sense a solid

is the stable of bodies. The earth was therefore the most stable of bodies
when it was conceived to be a vast extended solid plain. It was a stable
body when we thought it the dead centre round which the heavens re-
volved. It was even stable in this sense when in our conceptions it constituted a solid mass whose destiny was limited to revolving round the sun
for a few thousand years. But now that that sort of stability begins to
vanish from our view and in so far as we know can only in the whole
universe be predicated with certainty on the thin crust on which we stand.
Our preceding notions of its inseparable connection with solidity are
reduced to a very narrow compass and we begin to apprehend another
sort of stability—a stability founded not on a capacity to resist external
impressions and which is therefore necessarily limited but one of which
on the contrary the essence lies in the capacity of readily and therefore
imperceptibly yielding to them and which consequently is in its very nature
necessarily unlimited. Such it is obvious is the stability of the universe.
It is stable not because it changes not but because all its parts acting
and reacting on each other no one of them is ever in all these changes
thrown from its balance. In this sense the vast central mass of our planet
surrenders itself with mathematical exactitude to the conditions imposed.

This is not a dead but if I may be allowed the expression a living stability. That it has not hitherto lain dormant we gather from various sources.
Astronomy teaches us that it has moulded our planet into the exact form
which its present position in the heavens demands. If we rightly interpret
the teachings of geology we gather from them that the seemingly inter-
minable succession of cycles which preceded the human era changes so vast
have occurred in the condition of the globe as to have necessitated the
extinction of the various tribes of animals and vegetable beings that existed
in each several period. We also learn from the same science that these
revolutions have been brought about—without much violence or great
disturbance, so gradually in fact that the several races of plants and animals
have died out and been extinguished by almost insensible degrees. We look
in vain for any sufficient agent in producing these *adaptations* of things
to their gradually changing condition save the balancing and sustaining
movements of the great central mass. This seems to be the real *res con-
servatrix naturae* enabling our planet without violent convulsion or derangement to play its part self raised in the grand economy of the whole
and gradually to adapt itself and all that it sustains to every change incident to the place in the great harmonious movements of the universe.
If things be so then so far is the hypothesis I have ventured to suggest
from being in reality strange and incredible that it on the contrary seems to
me warranted by analogy and by the course of the general system of the

universe. For if in the grand revolutions of ages the central mass be the great moving and sustaining power it is surely not unreasonable to presume that it may also share in the more frequent and minor revolutions and may have a minute yet distinguishable tidal pulse beating synchronous with its own daily movements in the planetary system.

This the novelty of my views has however something in itself concerning which I wish to add a few words.

What is new is generally contrary to what is old. It very generally therefore has to encounter the opposition of preconceived ideas to which it runs counter. My hypothesis that the great mass of the solid crust of the earth is flexible and hourly constantly bending so that at intervals of a few hours unless where girt down by massive continents it and all that it sustains, towns and great cities rise and fall twenty or thirty feet, is so contrary to all previous conceptions that it will I fear to most appear a doctrine so strange and absurd as to be only fit to raise a smile at the wild fancies of speculative dreamers and from which sober sense may reasonably turn away without other reply than the *"incredulus odi."*

I think however if anyone before passing such hasty judgment will for a moment divest himself of all prejudice and consider things not as they seem to be but as they are known really to exist he will admit that the notion instead of being opposed to the analogies of the creation is quite conformable to them and therefore in truth wears in itself a considerable air of probability.

The views I have ventured to lay before you have I believe so much of novelty in them that I could have wished before doing so to have tested their truth by a much more minute investigation than I have it in my power to give them. Even with regard to the geology of these islands so well deserving as it seems to me of lengthened study I can only say that I have commenced that study [but] other engagements and bad health have confined me to but a few of the laborious explorations necessary for the purposes of completing it. It is but little probable that I shall ever do this in any adequate manner, still I expect to be able to do something towards it. From this cause I have in some measure been obliged and in general have thought it most fitting to state only the great leading points of my hypothesis, leaving it to others who have better opportunity and ability to examine their accordance with nature and reality and if satisfied of this to follow them out to their remote consequences. They would of course modify the whole present theory of the tides which has always seemed to me to fail in explanation of known facts or at least when applied to them to present very many anomalies.

21

R. C. Wyllie to John Rae*
NOVEMBER 20, 1861

Honolulu, 20th November 1861

MY DEAR SIR,

I have to acknowledge and thank you for your letter of 17th July and 15th Inst.

I have not obtained the Seed of the Sea Island Cotton, or of the Carolina Rice, that I wrote for to 3 Several Gentlemen of the South. Owing to the unhappy Civil War, I presume my letters were intercepted in the Northern States. Neither have I any Book—describing the proper cultivation of cotton.

I send to you a small parcel of Georgia Cotton Seed, which I have obtained from H.R.H. Prince Kamehameha.

On the 6th Inst. I received letters from Lady Franklin and Miss Cracroft dated 28th October from San Francisco, informing me that they had taken their passages for England, via Honolulu, Japan, Shanghae &c by the Clipper Eldridge, and that they would again be my guests for 3 or 4 days.

I have no doubt her Ladyship will be as glad to see you, as I will be, and to converse with you on the Polynesian languages, and other matters relating to the Hawaiian people, in whom she takes a most benevolent interest.

I repeat my opinion, formerly expressed, that a man of your fine education, talent and enlarged views on matters of Civil Government and

* Archives of Hawaii, Foreign Office Letter Book, E vol. III, no. 37, Miscellaneous internal correspondence, 66.

political economy, in the approaching Legislature would be a benefit to the Hawaiian Nation.

I shall be very glad to see you here, whenever it may suit your occupations and convenience to come, and I Remain

My dear Sir
Yours truly
R. C. WYLLIE

22

R. C. Wyllie to John Rae*

OCTOBER 27, 1862

Rosebank—27th October 1862.

Private

MY DEAR SIR,

I received on the 20th September, your very interesting letter of the 1st, but have only now time to thank you for it.

In your general political views I fully agree. I shall make them known, as fitting occasions offer, to the King and Prince Kamehameha, who are a century in advance of the Hawaiian people generally and even of the Chiefs.

But, of course, I shall say nothing to them about the *reported blow* which is a vile slander. Nothing of the kind occurred I assure you. In regard to the young Prince, if there was any fault at all, it was in excessive indulgence. He was part of the very life of his Parents and hence wherever they went by land or water, in Coach, waggon or on horseback, he was carried with them—only a boy of great physical strength and courage could have stood such constant and varied excitement.

His disease in the unanimous opinion of his Physicians was *Cerebritis* occasioned probably by exposure to the sun. Unfortunately we have no leeches here. If we had had them, my treatment would have been, almost constant bleeding from the nape of the neck and temples, repeated injections and pediluvia—in that, *the depleting and soothing system, energetically pursued.*

* Archives of Hawaii, Foreign Office Letter Book, E vol. III, no. 37 Miscellaneous internal correspondence, 182–5.

But I am, in faith, a Predestinarian. I believe, if God be a perfect being, He has foreseen the exact hour and minute of the deaths of us all—that we cannot die otherwise, than as he has foreseen. Nevertheless if I find a wild bull running after me on the public road, I would get out of his way as fast as my heels could carry me.

Your letter to me on the Hawaiian Language and your thoughts on Hawaiian Legislation have given great satisfaction in high quarters. If I mistake not, you will find them commented upon, by and bye, in London and perhaps Scotland.

I intend placing a Series of them all complete in the hands of the Right Revd the Lord-Bishop of Honolulu. He and his 2 clergymen, are drawing crowded audiences here. They come to preach *Jesus and him crucified to us*, and not to preach to us *Moses* and the *Prophets*, as I think is too much the case with the disciples of Calvin and John Knox.

The King and Queen are much pleased with them, have fitted up a Royal Pew and attend regularly.

The scandal raised about you and the Pistol is of a peice with that about the "blow". As I have taken under my protection, Miss Atkins of Firville [?], Ireland, a young Lady of 17, of high English Lineage, whose Father is so reduced that he can do nothing for her, I shall be happy, if I escape evil tongues myself—she is now occupying your rooms at Rosebank and is pursuing her education. The King and Queen, Mrs McKibbin and her daughters, Mr & Mrs Synge, Mr & Mrs Allen, Mrs Paty and her 2 young Ladies, Mr and Mrs Damon and Helen Damon, Mrs Judd and her family, have all visited and are very kind to Miss Atkins. It shall be my endeavour to keep her in the best Society of this City, to which by birth and (I am happy to add) by her manners too she is fully entitled.

You say nothing about the box of Tea from Mr Savidge. Did you ever find it?

Hoping that all your agricultural and domestic interests will be so managed as to add to your comfort and independence,

I Remain

My dear Sir

Yours ever truly

R. C. Wyllie

P.S. 28th October—That you may see that what I now write to you, only corresponds, with what I wrote to Mr Eldredge of Lima, I further enclose Press Copy of my letter to him of 15th Inst by the last mail. After perusal, have the kindness to return it to

Yours

R.C.W.

23

John Stuart Mill to R. C. Wyllie*
FEBRUARY 3, 1863

Blackheath Park, Kent
Feb. 3, 1863.

SIR,

I have had the honour of receiving your letter and the printed slips which you have been kind enough to send. These I have read with the attention due to any work of Dr. Rae, and they appear to me quite worthy of his intellect and acquirements. The picture which he draws of the dangers that menace the interesting community of which you are one of the rulers, is most formidable. Of the remedies which he proposes, I cannot be a competent judge, but, as far as my means of judgment extend, he seems to be right in much, perhaps even in all, that he proposes.

The other paper will, I think, place Dr. Rae very high among ethnologists and philologists. After having reached by independent investigation the highest generalization previously made, namely, that all languages have grown by development from a few hundred words, Dr. Rae seems to have supplied the first probable explanation of the manner in which these primitive words may themselves have originated. If his hypothesis is made out, it is the keystone of the science of philology, it is *a priori* extremely probable, and the facts he brings forward establish a strong case of verification *a posteriori*. I hope that Dr. Max Müller has been put in possession of this important speculation.

It must be of great value to your country to have such a man as Dr. Rae settled among you.

* *Sociological Theory of Capital*, xxxiv–xxxv.

It is very gratifying to me that you are disposed to carry the principle of minorities into practical operation. That such should be questions agitated in a country which three-quarters of a century ago was in the savage state is surely one of the most remarkable signs of the very hopeful times in which we live.—I am, Sir, your obedient servant,

J. S. MILL

24

John Rae to John Stuart Mill (draft)*

c. 1866

Sir,

Permit me to render you my thanks for having taken the trouble some two or three years since to write my late friend Mr. Wyllie concerning some papers of mine that had appeared in the Polynesian newspaper of Honolulu, and of which he had sent you copies. You may well suppose I was much gratified by the favourable opinion of one whose judgment deservedly carries so much weight with it as yours in all philosophical questions. I address you at present to request a favour. I desire to dedicate to you a work on the Polynesian language and its connections with the history of speech, and consequently of humanity. You could have formed but a very imperfect idea of my views from my letter to Mr. Wyllie, which was not intended for publication, and in which, from its growing too voluminous on my hands, I often dropped the thread of my argument without pursuing statements I had made to their legitimate consequences. I cannot of course attempt to mend the matter here, or to give even a summary of my argument, but I may state the conclusions at which I have arrived, as well as those at which I might hope to arrive, and thus explain to you the reasons which urge me to make the request I have preferred.

I believe it may be shown that the race from which the Polynesians spring was at the head of civilization of the age of stone, and were settled in Hindustan and along the southern and more fertile shores of Asia. It seems, too, that the facts on which my reasons rest are indisputable, the deduction perfectly logical, and the conclusion therefore irrefragable. This

* *Sociological Theory of Capital,* xxxv–xxxvi.

forms the first part of my book. The second pertains to the language. As to it, there have come into it two sounds, significant of themselves, which have a close analogy to the cries of the higher order of animals, and have somehow been modified by and incorporated into the articulate speech. The one is *a* (the broad Scotch or Italian a) and it may be translated action. The other is *o* which denotes distance and connection. This may seem a contradiction, but in reality if a thing be distant it must be distant from something else, and that something must therefore to the mind have some relation to it or connection with it. The articulate sounds or syllables of the Polynesian language are either simple vowels, or end in vowels. There are about forty of them, and the remarkable fact as to all of them is this: When the organs of speech with the aid of the breath shape an articulate syllable, they also themselves take a shape, form and movement, and in this language, this shape and movement have always an analogy to the thing or action which the sound of the syllable or conjoined syllable denotes.

25

John Rae to an Unknown Cleric*

UNDATED

R<small>EV</small>^D & D<small>EAR</small> S<small>IR</small>

The religious argument connected with Geology thus arranges itself in my mind.

There are two great powers in man distinguishing him from, and raising him superior to the brute. The one Reason the other Conscience or the moral sentiment. I speak of these as innate powers capable of development, not as always and necessarily giving forth distinct manifestations. There are rare individual instances, where one, or others, or both seem to have died away for lack of nourishment in early years or to have been perverted & distorted by opposing forces so as to assume fantastic and monstrous shapes—just as we see seeds sown perishing for lack of moisture and plants twisted hacked and clipt by the hand of the gardener into the forms of bears and centaurs. Should we find a tribe in human form without them they must necessarily be as brutes, making no provision for tomorrow and devoid of the social relations. Should we find such a tribe incapable of having them as it were ingrafted on them by communication we should, despite their human form class them with the brutes. If they had one without the other they would be monsters and miserable.

These powers thus essentially and distinctively human differ in their progress.

The reasoning faculty by means of the intellect is always progressing and extending its sphere of operation from childhood to old age, from generation to generation. Each age has had a store of materials provided for this

* Rae mss.

faculty, which, it in turn has added to, and augmented. In the time of Bacon philosophy and the treasures of Greek, Roman, and Arabic worlds —no inconsiderable store of intellectual wealth—and yet how immense have been the additions which later days have made to it. Nor can we see any limit to its farther increase. At this moment it seems as if achievements that are to open up the kingdom of nature more widely than any that have preceded them were giving us tokens of presently coming within the compass of our ability.

It is not so with the moral sense. There is but a right and wrong in any action and we feel that we are capable of discerning them and discriminating the one from the other. Our appetites and passions often blind this sense or are too powerful for it. Or again the complications of society are so intricate that with the best intentions we are doubtful what is best to be done. I will give you an instance. An American lands in England and is surrounded by a human crowd of wretchedness. Rags, emaciation, filth bespeak the extremity of destitution, hunger, pain, despair. Each individual silently, or with clamour, holds out a meagre hand into which if a cent be put, a gleam of delight shoots over his squalid features and the copper is clutched as a precious treasure. And so probably it is for it will allay for the present the most pressing of his tormentors—hunger. Is this American to give or refuse? He gives, and, on reaching his inn, he finds himself minus a dollar. He relates the circumstance to an English friend. This friend, a Malthusian, rather censures him. He tells him that in old countries, the redundancy of population must be kept down by the check of starvation, that many of those to whom he gave were imposters &c. &c. &c., and concludes with assuring him that if he interferes with the legal charities he is really increasing the evil, or at least if he so interfere he ought to make each beggar conduct him to his home and there examine into the real circumstances and the causes of his distress . . . and so only relieve. How is this American to [act] is a puzzle. In all such cases however it is not the moral sense but the reasoning faculty which is at fault—for here in this instance could that faculty disentangle those intricate relations of social and political existence which perplex us, and show us the consequences immediate and remote of the one or the other course of action the moral sense would have no difficulty in saying this is right positively right, that wrong; or this is the better that the worse.

Now reason and the moral sense differing in this that the one is progressive the other not have one thing in common—the both draw us to God.

It is impossible to contemplate nature, especially with the light which modern science has poured over his inmost recesses, without being struck

—overwhelmed I may say—with the infinite wisdom everywhere displayed. This is more obvious to us in the animal and vegetable kingdoms and what perhaps amazes most is that the minutest forms of both, forms so minute that one of our feet covers a mass of millions of them more numerous than all the aggregated men that have existed from creation to the present hour should be wrought out with what in our darkness we call exquisite skill but which no sane philosopher can doubt contains miracles of art far transcending our limited powers of perception and perhaps of comprehension. We are thus inevitably led to the apprehension of an intelligent power or cause pervading the two infinities of space and time.

Being thus led by our reasoning faculty to have an apprehension of something infinitely wise pervading and governing all things; encompassing us all round extending on and on for ever and ever before and behind us, to which of necessity we [owe] our whole being with all its enjoyments and sufferings its hopes and fears. This apprehension of the intellect awakens our whole soul and [then] it raises itself to see if in any way it can sever its relations with this beautiful but dread Omnipotent who as it were holds it up a while out of the infinite all surrounding ocean and gives it a view of his works.

Our moral being . . .

26

John Rae to an Unknown Correspondent*

UNDATED

From a very early period of my life I had turned my attention and, as occasion presented itself, bent all the powers of my mind to trace out the causes which have given shape and form to humanity, and from whence have come the laws which have hitherto governed and must in future govern its progress ... A train of singularly untoward and to me disastrous circumstances, and of such a character that for the honor of human nature I trust the history of few individuals can present a parallel [have impeded my endeavors] ... Nevertheless wherever I have been, and however situated, the idea of my youth has held possession of me, and has been the central point of all my researches and speculations. Now in my old age I am desirous of recording [as much as possible of the results of my labours] ... I can scarcely hope to tell my fellow-men all that during my life I have gathered together from the recorded past and the actual present, of the paths we have travelled from our first appearance on earth to the present hour, and the ways we have to travel to the end. To me the sun is surely soon to set. Yet while daylight lasts I am desirous of adding what I can to those stores of knowledge and truth which are the only substantial inheritance which age can bequeath to age. I had thought of commencing by giving a sketchy outline of what I may call my system, and had in fact composed a great part of such outlines. Certain circumstances, however, warn me that this plan is imprudent, and that it is better to put forth what

* *Sociological Theory of Capital*, xlii–xliii. Mixter suggests that this letter may have been addressed to Dr. William Beattie. It evidently consists of fragments of different letters assembled by Mixter.

I know and desire to tell in parts, mere fragments of the great whole which is spread out before my view. Each to other men will seem fragmentary; if I live long enough I may form them into a system, or rather the skeleton of a system, which perhaps others may fill up. One of these fragments is the relation which the Polynesian race and language bear to other races and languages, and to the origin of language itself. My investigations as to this last point have, I think, led me to some important discoveries. I am now preparing a work on these subjects which I hope to have published in London. I think it more likely than any other of my speculations to draw some share of public attention. I have not, however, confined myself to this alone, but have drawn out the plan and partly written some essays on subjects having a bearing on what is shadowed out in my mind as a real philosophic history of our race. It was thus that some months since I wrote the essay which I send. I had not, however, thought of publishing it for perhaps a year or two, nor even then until it had been submitted to the judgment of some scientific friend who might be competent to detect any mistake in the mechanical part, if any there were.